Briefs of Leading Cases in Corrections

Briefs of Leading Cases in Corrections, Sixth Edition, offers extensive updates on the leading Supreme Court cases impacting corrections in the United States—prisons and jails, probation, parole, the death penalty, juvenile justice, and sexual assault offender laws. Each chapter contains an introduction to the topic area, making the book more user-friendly and a better source of succinct legal information than before. All cases are briefed in a common format to allow for comparisons among cases and include facts, relevant issues, and the Court's decision and reasoning. The significance of each case is also explained, making clear its impact on prisoners and corrections in general. The book provides students and practitioners with historical and social context for their role in criminal justice and the legal guidelines that should be followed in day-to-day correctional activities. Twenty-one cases have been added, including those in a new section on the Antiterrorism and Effective Death Penalty Act.

Rolando V. del Carmen retired in May 2011 as Distinguished Professor of Criminal Justice (Law) in the College of Criminal Justice, Sam Houston State University. He has authored numerous books and articles in various areas of law related to criminal justice. He has won all three major awards given by the Academy of Criminal Justice Sciences, and has taught numerous graduate and undergraduate classes in law and has been a mentor and friend to many of his students.

Susan E. Ritter is Associate Professor of Criminal Justice at the University of Texas, Brownsville. She specializes in correctional law as well as other corrections and criminal justice issues, many relating to female offending. She holds a Ph.D. in Criminal Justice from Sam Houston State University, an M.A. in Criminal Justice from the University of Texas, Arlington, and a B.S. in Government/Sociology from Texas Woman's University.

Betsy A. Witt is Professor of Criminal Justice at Limestone College. She has been in education for more than 20 years, teaching at various universities. She has co-authored four texts relating to correctional law, juvenile law, jails, and probation, and is a member of the Academy of Criminal Justice Sciences, Juvenile and Corrections Sections. She holds a Ph.D. in Criminal Justice, an M.A. in Criminology, and B.S. in Criminology and Corrections from Sam Houston State University.

RELATED TITLES

Kanovitz, *Constitutional Law for Criminal Justice*, 14th ed.

del Carmen and Walker, *Briefs of Leading Cases in Law Enforcement*, 9th ed.

Latessa and Smith, *Corrections in the Community*, 6th ed.

Latessa, Listwan, and Koetzle, *What Works (and Doesn't) in Reducing Recidivism*.

Whitehead, Dodson, and Edwards, *Corrections: Exploring Crime, Punishment, and Justice in America*, 3rd ed.

Palmer, *Constitutional Rights of Prisoners*, 9th ed.

Briefs of Leading Cases in Corrections

Sixth Edition

Rolando V. del Carmen,

Susan E. Ritter, and

Betsy A. Witt

Routledge
Taylor & Francis Group

NEW YORK AND LONDON

First published 1993
by Routledge

Fifth edition published 2008
by Routledge

Sixth edition published 2017
by Routledge
711 Third Avenue, New York, NY 10017

and by Routledge
2 Park Square, Milton Park, Abingdon, Oxon, OX14 4RN

Routledge is an imprint of the Taylor & Francis Group, an informa business

© 2017 Taylor & Francis

The right of Rolando V. del Carmen, Susan E. Ritter, and Betsy A. Witt
to be identified as authors of this work has been asserted in accordance
with sections 77 and 78 of the Copyright, Designs and Patents Act 1988.

Library of Congress Cataloging in Publication Data
Names: del Carmen, Rolando V., author. | Ritter, Susan E., author. |
Witt, Betsy A., author.
Title: Briefs of leading cases in corrections / Rolando V. del Carmen,
Susan E. Ritter, and Betsy A. Witt
Description: 6th edition. | New York: Routledge, 2016.
Identifiers: LCCN 2016011795| ISBN 9781138692763 (hardback) | ISBN
113869276X (hardback) | ISBN 9781437735086 (pbk.) | ISBN 1437735088
(pbk.) | ISBN 9781315531694 (ebk.)
Subjects: LCSH: Correctional law—United States—Study guides. | LCGFT:
Study guides
Classification: LCC KF9728 .D45 2016 | DDC 344.7303/5—dc23
LC record available at http://lccn.loc.gov/2016011795

ISBN: 978-1-138-69276-3 (hbk)
ISBN: 978-1-4377-3508-6 (pbk)
ISBN: 978-1-315-53169-4 (ebk)

Typeset in Times New Roman
by Florence Production Ltd, Stoodleigh, Devon, UK

Contents

Preface

A case "brief" is a summary of a case decided by a court. It is taken from a lengthier court decision and designed for simplicity and focus. There is no single format prescribed for case briefs. Each author or writer uses a format that suits his or her needs or the needs of the target audience. The format used here is what the authors subjectively consider best for readers' use because of conciseness and clarity.

All cases briefed in this text are decisions by the United States Supreme Court. We have not included cases decided by lower federal or state courts. Only United States Supreme Court cases are briefed because they constitute the most authoritative type of case law and apply throughout the country. There are other legal sources for lower federal and state court decisions. Those need to be identified and studied to supplement United States Supreme Court decisions in order to get the total picture of case law in a particular jurisdiction. State law, state court decisions, and agency policy manuals complete the picture of the governing law in a state or jurisdiction. Some case briefs appear in more than one place in this book in order to aid the reader in finding all the cases relevant to a certain topic at a quick glance.

As in the previous editions, cases briefed in the sixth edition are divided into five sections: Facts, Issue, Holding, Reason, and Case Significance. Each legal brief is preceded by a Capsule, which is usually a shorter version of the Holding, which is the most important part of a court decision.

An introduction precedes each chapter. This provides a source of succinct legal information for students, criminal justice practitioners, and lawyers. The Prisons and Jails and Death Penalty chapters are divided into topics for better understanding of these areas of correctional law.

The fifth edition included cases decided through June 2008. This sixth edition includes United States Supreme Court cases decided through June 2015. The following new cases have been added in this sixth edition:

- On Prisons and Jails, Antiterrorism and Effective Death Penalty Act: *Wall, Director, Rhode Island Dept. of Corrections v. Kholi* and *Gonzalez v. Thaler, Director, Texas Dept. of Criminal Justice, Correctional Institutional Division*
- On Prisons and Jails, Conditions of Confinement—In General: *Barber et al. v. Thomas, Warden* and *Florence v. Board of Chosen Freeholders of County of Burlington et al.*
- On Prisons and Jails, Counsel: *Martinez v. Ryan, Director, Arizona Dept. of Corrections*
- On Prisons and Jails, Damages and Defenses: *Ortiz v. Jordan*
- On Prisons and Jails, Due Process: *Haywood v. Drown et al.*
- On Prisons and Jails, Use of Nondeadly Force in Correctional Facilities: *Wilkins v. Gaddy* and *Kingsley v. Hendrickson et al.*

- On Prisons and Jails, Habeas Corpus: *Wood v. Milyard, Warden, et al.* and *Coleman v. Johnson*
- On Prisons and Jails, Medical Care and Psychological Treatment: *Brown et al. v. Plata et al.*
- On Prisons and Jails, Religion: *Sossamon v. Texas* and *Holt v. Hobbs*
- On Death Penalty, Mentally Impaired Defendants: *Hall v. Florida*
- On Death Penalty, Appeals and Habeas Corpus: *Ryan v. Valencia-Gonzales*
- On Death Penalty, Cruel and Unusual Punishment: *Glossip v. Gross*
- On Juvenile Justice: *Graham v. Florida* and *Miller v. Alabama*
- On Sexual Assault Offender Laws: *Carr v. United States* and *Reynolds v. United States.*

CITATIONS USED

The cases briefed here are taken from several legal sources, each just as reliable as the others, because they all publish decisions in full from the United States Supreme Court. The United States Reports is published by the government and is the official publication outlet of cases decided by the Court. The other sources are published by private companies. The legal citations vary as a result.

The Internet has made legal research speedier and a lot more convenient. The original decisions of the United States Supreme Court in these cases are readily available in various ways, particularly on the Internet. To find these cases, go to the Supreme Court's web site at: www.supremecourtus.gov and click on "Opinions," then the year of the decision. If more research is desired on a case, perform an Internet search, then choose the U.S. Supreme Court decision from the many results. There will likely be many entries on that case, including the decisions of the lower courts that were appealed and commentaries on the case. Make sure the case is the U.S. Supreme Court decision and not that of the trial court, the Court of Appeals, or of a state supreme court.

For readers unfamiliar with legal citation, the following provides guidance to the citations used in this text:

- U.S. means United States Reports. Therefore, the citation: *Turner v. Safley*, 482 U.S. 78 (1987) means that the original of the case of *Turner v. Safley* can be found in Volume 482 of the United States Reports, starting on page 78 (note that the citation never states what page the case ends), and was decided in 1987. The United States Reports is published by the United States government.
- L. Ed. means United States Supreme Court Reports, Lawyer's Edition and is published by a private publisher.
- S. Ct. means Supreme Court Reporter. This source reports United States Supreme Court cases and is published by a private publisher.
- Cr. L. means Criminal Law Reporter. This source reports United States Supreme Court cases and is published by a private publisher.

- USLW means United States Law Week. This source reports United States Supreme Court decisions and is published by a private publisher.

The authors hope these commentaries and case briefs contribute to a better understanding of the many complex topics in corrections law.

Susan E. Ritter
University of Texas at Brownsville/Texas

Betsy A. Witt
Limestone College

Acknowledgments

First and foremost, I would like to thank my mentor, my partner, and friend, Dr. Rolando V. del Carmen, who took a chance on a second-year doctoral student. I would also like to thank my writing partner and friend, Betsy Witt. To my new publishing company, I hope we have a long and fruitful relationship. Finally, to my parents, thank you for encouraging me, no matter what path I was on.

Susan E. Ritter

I would like to thank my co-authors, Dr. Rolando V. del Carmen and Dr. Susan Ritter. Dr. del Carmen has been instrumental in my career in criminal justice. Dr. Ritter has been a friend for many years. I would also like to acknowledge the editors of previous editions of this text, Biz Ebben, Ellen Boyne, and Pam Chester. They were the guiding force in shaping the book and they were excellent in their comments and suggestions. The current editors have been just as helpful. Lastly, I would like to thank my family for their support throughout my career.

Betsy A. Witt

Table of Cases

List of Cases with Principle (Capsule) of Law

Chapter 1: Prisons and Jails

Introductory Cases

Turner v. Safley, 482 U.S. 78 (1987) xxxiv, 4, 10, 11–12, 14, 127–130, 186
A prison regulation that impinges on inmates' constitutional rights is valid if it is reasonably related to legitimate penological interests.

Shaw v. Murphy, 532 U.S. 223 (2001) xxxiv, 4, 10, 13–14, 130–131, 186
The standard established in *Turner v. Safley* applies to all constitutional rights of inmates, including First Amendment rights.

A. Antiterrorism and Effective Death Penalty Act

Wall, Director, Rhode Island Dept. of Corrections v. Kholi, 562 U.S. 545 (2011) 14–16
For purposes of the Antiterrorism and Effective Death Penalty Act's tolling pro-vision, a motion to reduce sentence under state law is an application for collateral review.

Gonzalez v. Thaler, Director, Texas Dept. of Criminal Justice, Correctional Institutions Division, 131 S. Ct. 2989 (2012) 16–18
If a Certificate of Appealability (COA) under the Antiterrorism and Effective Death Penalty Act fails to indicate a constitutional issue, this does not bar the Court of Appeals from reviewing the case. Furthermore, if a petitioner does not seek review in the state's highest court, the judgment becomes final upon the time expiration date for filing the review, under the Antiterrorism and Effective Death Penalty Act (AEDPA).

Burt, Warden v. Titlow, 134 S. Ct. 10 (2013) 19–20
Appellate courts must apply the "doubly differential" standard of review in examining the state court's reasonable fact finding and ineffective assistance of counsel when the record is silent.

B. Clemency and Commutation

Ohio Parole Authority v. Woodard, 523 U.S. 272 (1998) 21–22
Giving an inmate the option of voluntarily participating in a pre-hearing inter-view with members of the parole board, without giving him immunity for his

F. Court Access

Ex Parte Hull, 312 U.S. 546 (1941) 39–40
A state and its officers cannot abridge or impair a prisoner's right, given by federal law, to apply for a federal writ of habeas corpus.

United States v. Muniz, 374 U.S. 150 (1963) 41–42
Federal prisoners are entitled to sue prison officials under the Federal Tort Claims Act for negligent acts resulting in personal injury.

Cooper v. Pate, 378 U.S. 546 (1964) 42–43
An inmate has a cause for relief under 42 U.S.C. § 1983 if he alleges punishment for requesting religious materials.

Johnson v. Avery, 393 U.S. 483 (1969) 43–45
Prison authorities cannot prohibit prisoners from helping other prisoners prepare legal writs unless they provide reasonable alternatives by which inmates can have access to the courts.

G. Counsel

United States v. Gouveia, 467 U.S. 180 (1984) 45–46
Inmates in administrative segregation (as distinguished from those in punitive segregation) are not entitled to counsel prior to the initiation of judicial proceedings.

Murray v. Giarratano, 492 U.S. 1 (1989) 47–48
States are not required by the Constitution to provide inmates with a lawyer in post-conviction (meaning after appeal, as in habeas corpus) proceedings even in death penalty cases.

Bounds v. Smith, 430 U.S. 817 (1977) 48–49
Prison authorities are required to assist inmates by providing meaningful access to the courts.

Lewis v. Casey, 518 U.S. 343 (1996) 50–51
The constitutional right of court access is violated only if a prisoner's attempt to pursue a legal claim is actually hindered by prison officials. Inadequacies in a state's delivery of legal services to inmates are not sufficient as a basis for such a claim. What is needed is showing of widespread actual injury.

McFarland v. Scott, 512 U.S. 849 (1994) 51–53
Federal law requires that an indigent capital offender be given a lawyer even before a habeas petition is filed. Under that law, a federal district court has the authority to stay an execution as soon as the inmate asks for a lawyer to be able to file a habeas petition.

McCleskey v. Zant, 499 U.S. 467 (1991) 105–107
Failure to claim violation of a constitutional right in a first federal habeas corpus petition precludes the same claim from being raised in a second habeas corpus petition.

Wilkinson et al. v. Dotson, 544 U.S. 74 (2005) 107–108
State prisoners challenging parole procedures may file for relief under § 1983 and are not limited exclusively to habeas corpus statutes.

Dodd v. United States, 545 U.S. 353 (2005) 109–110
An inmate's motion under 28 U.S.C. § 2255, must be filed within one year after the date the U.S. Supreme Court initially recognizes the right asserted.

Gonzales v. Crosby, 545 U.S. 524 (2005) 110–112
A prisoner's motion under Federal Rule of Civil Procedure 60(b)(6), which challenges a ruling based on new law, is not considered a successive habeas corpus petition under the Antiterrorism and Effective Death Penalty Act.

Mayle, Warden v. Felix, 545 U.S. 644 (2005) 112–113
Amended habeas corpus petitions under the Antiterrorism and Effective Death Penalty Act's one-year statute of limitations and Federal Rule of Civil Procedure 15(c)(2) must arise out of the same conduct, transaction, or occurrence included in the original petition, not the petitioner's general trial, conviction, or sentence.

Wood v. Milyard, Warden, et al., 132 S. Ct. 1836 (2012) 114–117
Federal appellate courts have the authority to raise the timeliness of a petition in certain habeas corpus cases but should not do so if the state deliberately waived this defense.

Coleman v. Johnson, 132 S. Ct. 2060 (2012) 117–119
In a habeas corpus appeal, the appellate court may overturn the state court's decision only if it was objectively unreasonable.

P. Prison Litigation Reform Act

Miller et al. v. French et al., 530 U.S. 327 (2000) 120–122
The Prison Litigation Reform Act's automatic stay provision does not violate the separation of powers doctrine.

Booth v. Churner, 532 U.S. 731 (2001) 122–123
There is no exception to the exhaustion of administrative remedies requirement of the Prison Litigation Reform Act.

Porter v. Nussle, 534 U.S. 516 (2002) 108, 123–125
The Prison Litigation Reform Act requires all inmate grievances to be exhausted administratively before a lawsuit can be filed. This requirement includes accusations of excessive force and other conditions of confinement issues.

Sell v. United States, 539 U.S. 166 (2003) 141–142
Involuntary administration of antipsychotic drugs to render a mentally ill defendant competent to stand trial on serious criminal charges is constitutional under limited circumstances.

Brown et al. v. Plata et al., 131 S. Ct. 1910 (2011) 6, 142–147
The decision of the three-judge panel in the federal district court in California must be affirmed, and the reduction of the prison population is a necessary remedy, authorized under the Prison Litigation Reform Act.
S. Freedom of the Press

Pell v. Procunier, 417 U.S. 817 (1974) 147–149
A state prison regulation prohibiting media interviews with specific inmates does not violate the constitutional rights of the media or the inmates as long as alternative means of communication are available.

Houchins v. KQED, Inc., 438 U.S. 1 (1978) 149–151
The media have no right of access to inmates and prisons beyond that given to the general public.

T. Protection of Inmates from Injury

DeShaney v. Winnebago County Department of Social Services, 489 U.S. 189 (1989) 151–153
The state has no duty to protect individuals who are not in state custody from harm by private persons. (This implies that the state may be held liable if the individual is under its custody, as when in prison.)

Farmer v. Brennan, 511 U.S. 825 (1994) 153–155
A prison official is not liable under the Eighth Amendment for injury inflicted on an inmate by other inmates "unless the official knows of and disregards an excessive risk of harm to an inmate." It is not enough for liability that "the risk was so obvious that a reasonable person should have noticed it."

U. Religion

Cruz v. Beto, 405 U.S. 319 (1972) 155–156
Inmates must be given reasonable opportunities to exercise their religious beliefs.

O'Lone v. Estate of Shabazz, 482 U.S. 342 (1987) 156–158
Prison policies that in effect prevented inmates from exercising freedom of religion are constitutional because they are reasonably related to legitimate penological interests.

Sossamon v. Texas, et al., 131 S. Ct. 1651 (2011) 158–160
By a state accepting federal funding, it does not consent to waive its sovereign immunity for private suits brought against it for monetary relief under the Religious Land Use and Institutionalized Persons Act of 2000.

Chapter 3: Parole

five months after the parolee's release. The Court did not decide whether state law can be used to defeat a civil liability claim under federal law against the same state officials.

Jago v. Van Curen, 454 U.S. 14 (1981) 212, 223–224

An inmate does not have a due process right in the decision by a parole board to withdraw parole prior to the inmate's release.

Connecticut Board of Pardons v. Dumschat, 452 U.S. 458 (1981) 224–226

Prior actions of the Board of Pardons in granting commutation of life sentences created no right nor entitlement to commutation. Inmates are not constitutionally entitled to reasons from the board for rejecting their application for parole or commutation.

California Department of Corrections v. Morales, 514 U.S. 499 (1995) 213, 226–227, 229, 234

A law decreasing the frequency of parole hearings for certain prisoners does not change the punishment for crimes already committed and, therefore, may be applied retrospectively without violating the ex post facto clause of the Constitution.

Lynce v. Mathis, 519 U.S. 433 (1997) 213, 227–229

A Florida statute canceling an inmate's provisional release is ex post facto if applied to a prisoner who was convicted before the law was in effect.

Young v. Harper, 520 U.S. 143 (1997) 213, 229–231

Oklahoma's pre-parole release program was equivalent to parole, and therefore released prisoners under pre-parole were entitled to due process rights prior to being brought back to prison.

Pennsylvania Bd. of Probation and Parole v. Scott, 524 U.S. 357 (1998) 231–233

The Fourth Amendment does not require the application of the exclusionary rule in parole revocation hearings.

Garner v. Jones, 529 U.S. 244 (2000) 213, 233–235

The Georgia law allowing reconsideration of life-term inmates who have been denied parole at least every eight years is valid. There is no ex post facto violation unless the prisoner can prove that the retroactive application of the new rule will result in longer incarceration.

Samson v. California, 547 U.S. 843 (2006) 235–237

Suspicionless searches of parolees by police officers is allowable under the Fourth Amendment.

Chapter 4: Death Penalty

A. History and Foundation Cases

Louisiana ex rel. Francis v. Resweber, 329 U.S. 459 (1947) 243–245
Carrying out an execution after a failed first attempt does not violate the Constitution.

Furman v. Georgia, 408 U.S. 238 (1972) 241, 245–246
The death penalty violates the equal protection clause of the Fourteenth Amendment and the prohibition against cruel and unusual punishment and is therefore unconstitutional.

Gregg v. Georgia, 428 U.S. 153 (1976) 241, 245, 246–247, 320
Death penalty statutes that contain sufficient safeguards against arbitrary and capricious imposition are constitutional.

B. Discrimination—Racial

McCleskey v. Kemp, 481 U.S. 279 (1987) 247–248
A statistical study suggesting racial discrimination in general in the imposition of death sentences does not make the death penalty unconstitutional.

C. Mentally Impaired Defendants

Ford v. Wainwright, 477 U.S. 399 (1986) 248–249, 250, 267, 316, 361
An insane prisoner cannot be executed because it would constitute cruel and unusual punishment.

Penry v. Lynaugh, 492 U.S. 302 (1989) 249–250, 251
A mentally retarded defendant who has the ability to reason may be given the death penalty.

Atkins v. Virginia, 536 U.S. 304 (2002) 243, 250, 251–252, 253, 254, 321, 365
Executing the mentally retarded violates society's evolving standards of decency and is cruel and unusual punishment prohibited by the Eighth Amendment.

Hall v. Florida, 572 U.S. ___ (2014) 243, 252–254
The measurement of a person's intellectual disability for purposes of inclusion in a death penalty statute cannot be based solely on an IQ of 70.

D. Juveniles

Thompson v. Oklahoma, 487 U.S. 815 (1988) xlvi, 250, 254–255, 256, 257, 329, 331, 360–361
It is cruel and unusual punishment to impose the death penalty on a juvenile who commits their crime at age 15 or younger.

I. Appeals and Habeas Corpus

J. Cruel and Unusual Punishment

Chapter 6: Sexual Assault Offender Laws

Prisons and Jails

INTRODUCTION

The problem of prisoners and prisoners' lawsuits has been endemic in the United States criminal justice system for decades now. That problem will not soon go away. The April 23, 2008, issue of the *New York Times* published the article, "Inmate Count in U.S. Dwarfs other Nations," which stated that "the United States has less than 5 percent of the world's population. But it has almost a quarter of the world's prisoners."[1] It also says the following:

> China, which is four times more populous than the United States, is a distant second, with 1.6 million people in prison.

> [The United States] has 751 people in prison or jail for every 100,000 in population. The only other major industrialized nation that even comes close is Russia, with 627 prisoners for every 100,000 people. The others have much lower rates. England's rate is 151; Germany's is 88; and Japan is 63. The median among all nations is about 125, roughly a sixth of the American rate.

The good news is that the number of prisoners in the United States continued to grow each year until recently. In 2008, the year the above article was published, the prison population in the United States began to decline. This trend continued for four years until the population began to level off. In 2012, the lowest number of prisoners were admitted to state and federal prisons since 1999. California had the most significant decrease, due mainly to a federal mandate to relieve overcrowding in their prisons (refer to the case of *Brown v. Plata* in this text).

Access to court is a highly protected right in the United States. This includes access to court by prisoners and whoever might be in detention. This basic constitutional right and the burgeoning prison population create a perfect storm for prison litigation. This chapter looks at the more important prison law cases, their facts, issues, holdings, and case significance.

"Hands Off" Becomes "Hands On"

There once was a time when courts did not accept, try, or decide cases filed by prisoners. That was the "hands off" era. That era was influenced by the following considerations: (1) that prisoners got the treatment they deserved because they violated the penal code; (2) the courtesy and respect given by judges to decisions made by prison administrators; (3) the concept of the separation of powers between the executive (to which prison administrators belong) and the judicial department; and (4) the lack of visibility of prisons. It was not accidental that during the early years prisons were built in places far from metropolitan centers. The idea was to virtually warehouse prisoners and isolate them from the rest of society.

Starting in the late 1960s and the early 1970s, the "hands off" era gradually gave way to the "hands on" era. A number of factors help explain this 180-degree turn in the attitude of the courts. Some of those factors are: (1) the "equal protection" and "due process" revolution in the courts; (2) the media spotlight being focused on prisons; (3) the change in the attitude of the general public toward prisons; and (4) the realization by the courts that if they did not protect prisoners' rights, no one else would.

The equal protection and due process revolution was initiated by decisions of the United States Supreme Court under then-Chief Justice Earl Warren. "Equal protection" means that everyone should be treated alike, unless there is a justification for treating them differently. For prisoners this meant that they deserved to be treated like the rest of the people in the free world, unless there was justification for treating them differently. "Due process" means "fundamental fairness." The equal protection and due process revolution changed American society, notably in the areas of race, economics, gender, and prisons.

In prisons this meant that prisoners had to be treated fairly, unless a different treatment was justified. Being in prison does not justify unfair treatment. In the early 1970s, the attitude of the public toward prisons started to change, influenced by the mass media coverage of such notable events as the so-called "Attica Rebellion" in the state of New York, where more than 30 prisoners died in the retaking of the prison after a long siege. That event focused media attention for weeks on the plight of prisoners and their keepers. Since then, prisons have become much more than invisible places that nobody cared to write about. Through the years since then, conditions in prisons have been fodder for the mass media and the public has taken notice.

The "Old Philosophy" versus the "New Philosophy" of Prisoners' Rights

The "hands on" era has brought about a change of philosophy in courts regarding prisoners' rights. The "old philosophy" of prisoners' rights was that "lawful incarceration brings about the necessary withdrawal of many privileges and rights, a restriction justified by considerations underlying our prison system." Under this philosophy, prisoners did not have many rights except the basic rights to life and food. Prisoners left their rights in the free world upon entering prison. Under this philosophy, the prisoner, according to an old Virginia Supreme Court decision, was virtually a "slave of the state." That meant the state could do just about anything it wanted to do with the prisoner.

All that has changed, giving way to the "new philosophy" of prisoners' rights. Under this philosophy, "prisoners retain all the rights of free citizens except those on which restriction is necessary to assure their orderly confinement or to provide reasonable protection for the rights and physical safety of all members of the prison community." Three governmental interests, however, justify the curtailment of inmates' rights: (1) maintenance of internal order and discipline; (2) securing the institution against unauthorized access or escape; and (3) rehabilitation of prisoners. Under the new philosophy, prisoners have the same rights as people in the free world, except those that can be denied them based on the above three justifications. Moreover, the burden of establishing those justifications rests with the government.

Under the old philosophy, any regulation issued by the prison system was deemed valid. If challenged by the prisoners, they had the burden of establishing that the regulation was an unjustified violation of their rights. By contrast, under the new philosophy, the presumption is that prisoners have the same rights as people in the free world. Therefore, any regulation issued by the prison system must be justified based on the three considerations mentioned above. The burden of proving that these regulations were justified rests with the prison system. This makes life a bit more difficult for prison officials, but it also minimizes arbitrariness in prison regulations because prison officials have to justify them if challenged. Prison regulations must therefore be justifiable and reasonable, taking into consideration the prison environment.

Habeas Corpus Distinguished from § 1983 Cases

Prisoners file many types of cases, but the most common are habeas corpus and § 1983 cases. A habeas corpus case seeks release from prison, the allegation being that the prisoner is in prison illegally or unconstitutionally. It is filed after the criminal appeal has been exhausted and has no time limit as long as the prisoner is in confinement. Example: Assume that X's appeal of his conviction has expired and therefore X must start serving his sentence. After serving six years of a 10-year sentence, X has proof that there was something terribly wrong with his trial (such as the main witness lied or the jurors were bribed) and therefore he is in prison unconstitutionally. The time for an appeal has expired, but X can file a writ of habeas corpus, asking that he be released and given a new trial. This remedy does not expire and is available to the inmate as long as he or she is in prison.

By contrast, a § 1983 case seeks improvement of conditions of confinement and/or damages from prison officials. It is based on federal law (42 U.S.C. § 1983) and requires the plaintiff to establish two elements in order to succeed: (1) the officer sued must have been acting under color of law; and (2) there must have been a violation of a constitutional right or of a right given by federal law.

These two types of cases may be distinguished as follows:

HABEAS CORPUS CASE

A. Purpose is to seek release from prison or jail
B. Need to exhaust state judicial remedies before going to federal court
C. Starts in state court before it goes to federal court
D. Affects only one prisoner if it succeeds and
E. Filed by one prisoner seeking release

SECTION 1983 CASE

A. Purpose is to improve prison or jail conditions and/or obtain monetary damages from prison or jail officials
B. No need to exhaust state judicial remedies; the case may be filed directly in federal court
C. Starts in federal court
D. Affects all prisoners if it succeeds
E. May be filed as a class action suit, meaning by a group of prisoners

Habeas corpus cases seldom succeed. This is because in most states a habeas corpus case must be filed in the same court that convicted the defendant, after which it goes to the state's highest court, then goes to the federal district court and follows the federal appellate procedure all the way up to the United States Supreme Court, if it ever gets there. Most of the cases briefed in this text are § 1983 cases, meaning that they seek improvement of conditions of confinement. Prisoners across the country file thousands of § 1983 cases each year; only a few get to the United States Supreme Court. Of those that get to the Court, only a few are decided in favor of prisoners. Nonetheless, over the years these cases have gradually carved out the contours of prisoners' rights. The major cases are briefed in this book. Prison law, therefore, is mostly case law. Every state has a penal code and a criminal procedure code; no state has a prison law code.

Effects of Prison Litigation

What have prison litigation and judicial intervention accomplished? In a law journal article (*University of Pennsylvania Law Review*, 1993), Susan P. Sturm identifies the following impact on the organization and management of correctional institutions:

A. It has contributed to a greater understanding and acceptance of constitutional standards governing prisons;
B. It has contributed to the professionalization of corrections leadership and pro-grammatic staff;
C. It has contributed to the bureaucratization of prisons;
D. It has led to short-term demoralization of staff and disruption of institutional order; and
E. It has increased the visibility and accountability of prisons.

In the same article, the author characterizes the future of prison litigation as:

- It will concentrate on gross inadequacies in core conditions of confinement
- It will be more complex and costly to litigate, requiring sophisticated litigation tools and extensive use of experts
- Considerable attention and resources will be devoted to preserving and enforcing existing court orders
- Corrections adjudication will increasingly link up with and come to resemble more informal and systemic forms of advocacy
- Advocates will explore the possibility of bringing successful claims under state law and federal statutes
- The need for effective state and local corrections advocacy is likely to increase over the next decade.

The PLRA and AEDPA

The public has understandably grown weary and tired of prison cases. Their perception is that prisoners are clogging up the courts, getting more rights than victims, and that the courts are "coddling the criminal." To reduce the flood of prisoner petitions in federal courts, Congress passed two laws that became effective in April 1996: the Prison Litigation Reform Act (PLRA) and Title I of the Antiterrorism and Effective Death Penalty Act (AEDPA).

The PLRA seeks to reduce the number of § 1983 cases by limiting what courts can do in prison cases and imposing sanctions on the filing of frivolous cases. Other important provisions of the PLRA include: the exhaustion of administrative remedies before inmates can file a lawsuit in federal court under § 1983; a filing fee of $150 on every case an inmate files, unless the inmate is indigent; limiting attorneys' fees to 150 percent of the hourly rate established for court-appointed attorneys; and the screening of inmate filings and the dismissal of frivolous or malicious lawsuits that fail to state a claim upon which relief can be granted. While inmate lawsuits increased immediately after the PLRA became effective (primarily because lawsuits were filed seeking clarification of the various provisions), the overall effect of the PLRA has been a decrease in inmate lawsuits that are unmeritorious or frivolous.

The AEDPA, on the other hand, seeks to regulate the filing of habeas corpus petitions seeking release from prisons (as opposed to § 1983 cases in which prisoners seek damages, vindication of rights, or improvement of prison conditions), particularly in death penalty cases. Other important provisions of the AEDPA are the following: placing a one-year limit on the period inmates can challenge their convictions through a habeas action; requiring that a prisoner obtain authorization from the federal court of appeals before filing a second or successive action in federal court; and limiting federal court review of state court convictions unless the decision was "contrary to, or involved an unreasonable application of clearly established federal law." Studies indicate that the AEDPA has also brought down the number of cases filed by prisoners seeking release from prison or a review of their conviction.

How the Briefed Cases Are Arranged

The cases under Prisons and Jails in this text are divided into topics and are arranged chronologically within each topic. Despite this arrangement, the case of *Turner v. Safley*, although decided comparatively recently, is the first case briefed in Prisons and Jails because it is arguably the most important case ever decided by the Supreme Court in prison law. It is significant because it sets the legal standard by which prison regulations and state law allegedly infringing on prisoners' rights are judged. It says that prison regulations and state laws are valid as long as they are "reasonably related to legitimate penological interests," such interests being prison security, inmate rehabilitation, and the orderly running of the institution.

The case was decided in 1987 and the standard set has been applied by most courts to prison cases decided since then. It is likely that some cases briefed in this book involving the constitutionality of prison regulations and state law before this case was decided would perhaps be decided differently today using the *Turner* standard.

The case of *Shaw v. Murphy* follows the *Turner* case in this chapter. The *Shaw* case is placed here because it is the case that reiterated that the *Turner* standard is the proper standard in deciding whether inmates' constitutional rights have been violated. This is significant because it affirmed the *Turner* standard when considering the constitutionality of any prison regulation or law 13 years after the original standard was established.

INTRODUCTORY CASES

These are the current standard set by the United States Supreme Court to determine whether prison regulations and laws violate the constitutional rights of inmates and affirmation of this standard as applicable in considering inmates' constitutional rights.

TURNER V. SAFLEY
482 U.S. 78 (1987)

CAPSULE: A prison regulation that impinges on inmates' constitutional rights is valid if it is reasonably related to legitimate penological interests.

FACTS: State prison inmates brought a class action challenging regulations of the Missouri Division of Corrections that (1) permit correspondence between immediate family members who are inmates at different institutions and between inmates concerning legal matters, but allows other inmate correspondence only if each inmate's classification/treatment deems it in the best interest of the parties (this had the effect of prohibiting inmate-to-inmate correspondence); and (2) permit an inmate to marry only with the prison superintendent's permission, which can only be given when there are "compelling" reasons to do so. Testimony indicated that generally only a pregnancy or the birth of an illegitimate child would be considered "compelling."

ISSUES:

1. Does a regulation that permits correspondence between immediate family members who are inmates at different institutions and between inmates concerning legal matters, but allows other correspondence only if it is in the best interests of the parties violate the constitutional rights of inmates? NO.
2. Does a regulation permitting an inmate to marry only when there are compelling reasons violate an inmate's constitutional rights? YES.

HOLDING: A prison regulation that impinges on inmates' constitutional rights is valid if it is reasonably related to legitimate penological interests. The factors to be considered in making the reasonableness determination include:

1. whether there is a valid, rational connection between the regulation and the legitimate government interest put forward to justify it;
2. whether there are alternative means of exercising the right that remain open to prisoners;
3. the impact that accommodation of the asserted right will have on correctional officers and inmates, and on the allocation of prison resources generally; and
4. the existence of ready alternatives to the regulation.

Under the above factors, (1) the inmate-to-inmate correspondence rule is reasonably related to legitimate security concerns of prison officials and (2) the inmate marriage regulation is not reasonably related to any legitimate penological objective and is therefore a denial of inmates' constitutional rights under the First Amendment.

REASON: "The prohibition on correspondence between institutions is logically connected to these legitimate security concerns . . . The rule is content neutral, it logically advances the goals of institutional security and safety identified by Missouri prison officials, and it is not an exaggerated response to these objectives. On that basis, we conclude that the regulation does not unconstitutionally abridge the First Amendment rights of prison inmates.

"The right to marry, like many other rights, is subject to substantial restrictions as a result of incarceration. Many important attributes of marriage remain, however, after taking into account the limitations imposed by prison life. First, inmate marriages, like others, are expressions of emotional support and public commitment ... In addition, many religions recognize marriage as having spiritual significance; ... Third, most inmates eventually will be released by parole or commutation, and therefore most inmate marriages are formed in the expectation that they ultimately will be fully consummated.

"Finally, marital status often is a precondition to the receipt of government benefits, property rights, and other, less tangible benefits ... Taken together, we conclude that these remaining elements are sufficient to form a constitutionally protected marital relationship in the prison context."

CASE SIGNIFICANCE: The effect of this decision is twofold. First, it dispels the confusion as to the proper standard courts should use when balancing inmates' rights and prison authority. In previous cases, the Court used various tests, such as "compelling state interest," "least restrictive means," and "rational relationship" to decide prison cases. No single test was prescribed, thus lower courts adopted the test they wanted to use—depending on the constitutional right invoked. For example, some courts gave better protection to violations of First Amendment rights than to others. This case does not make such a distinction, saying instead that the "reasonably related" test is to be used every time there is an alleged violation of a constitutional right. Second, this decision gives prison authorities more power and authority in prison administration. All they must do is prove that a prison regulation is reasonably related to a legitimate penological interest in order for that regulation to be valid even if a constitutional right is infringed. That standard is easier to establish than the "compelling state interest" or the "least restrictive means" tests. It is therefore a conservative decision that limits constitutional rights and expands state power.

The Court laid out four factors to be considered when determining reasonableness, giving lower courts better guidance when deciding cases. It is obvious from reading these factors, however, that they are far from clear and can be interpreted in various ways. Although precision in standards has yet to be attained, this decision draws a bright line rule by which prison cases alleging violations of constitutional rights are judged. This is an improvement over the unguided past. Note, however, that this standard does not apply to state tort cases filed by prisoners.

SHAW V. MURPHY
532 U.S. 223 (2001)

CAPSULE: The standard established in *Turner v. Safley* applies to all constitutional rights of inmates, including First Amendment rights.

FACTS: Murphy was serving a prison sentence in the Montana State Prison. While incarcerated, he wrote a letter to another inmate who was facing disciplinary charges. In the letter, Murphy offered his assistance in the inmate's case. The letter was intercepted by prison officials and reviewed. Murphy was charged with violating the prison's rules against insolence, interfering with due process hearings, and conduct that disrupted the security and orderly operation of the institution. In a disciplinary hearing, he was found guilty of the first two charges, and given a 10-day suspended sentence along with demerits that could have affected his custody level.

Murphy filed a class-action suit, alleging that the disciplinary action against him violated due process, the rights of inmates to seek access to the courts, and his First Amendment rights. The federal district court rejected Murphy's First Amendment Claim, citing *Turner v. Safley*, which held that a prison regulation impinging on inmates' constitutional rights is valid if it is related to legitimate penological interests. The Ninth Circuit Court of Appeals reversed this decision. It held that inmates have a First Amendment right to assist other inmates with their legal claims, and that the balance of the prisoners' interests against the government's interests was tipped in favor of the inmates in this case.

ISSUE: Does the standard established in *Turner v. Safley* apply to inmates' First Amendment claims? YES.

HOLDING: Inmates do not possess a special First Amendment right to provide legal assistance to fellow inmates that enhances the protections otherwise available under *Turner v. Safley*.

REASON: "Because *Turner* provides the test for evaluating prisoners' First Amendment challenges, the issue before us is whether *Turner* permits an increase in constitutional protection whenever a prisoner's communication includes legal advice. We conclude that it does not. To increase the constitutional protection based upon the content of a communication first requires an assessment of the value of that content. But the *Turner* test, by its terms, simply does not accommodate valuations of content. On the contrary, the *Turner* factors concern only the relationship between the asserted penological interests and the prison regulation. Id., at 89.

"If courts were permitted to enhance constitutional protection based on their assessments of the content of the particular communications, courts would be in a position to assume a greater role in decisions affecting prison administration . . . [W]e reject an alteration of the *Turner* analysis that would entail additional federal-court oversight.

"We thus decline to cloak the provision of legal assistance with any First Amendment protection above and beyond the protection normally accorded prisoners' speech. Instead, the proper constitutional test is the one we set forth in *Turner*. Irrespective of whether the correspondence contains legal advice, the constitutional analysis is the same."

CASE SIGNIFICANCE: As mentioned, *Turner v. Safley* (1987) provides that prison regulations that infringe upon inmates' constitutional rights are valid if they are "reasonably related to legitimate penological interests." In this case, Murphy, the inmate, claimed that this standard should not apply to cases like this one, in which the inmate claims that the communication that was prohibited by the prison system included legal advice. In effect, he claimed that although *Turner v. Safley* applied to infringements of First Amendment rights as well as to other constitutional rights, it did not apply to communications involving legal advice. This was rejected by the Supreme Court.

The significance of this decision is that it reiterates that the standard set in *Turner v. Safley* is the same standard to be used by the courts regardless of the right alleged by the prisoner to have been violated. This decision further strengthens the authority of prison systems to regulate the constitutional rights of inmates.

A. ANTITERRORISM AND EFFECTIVE DEATH PENALTY ACT

WALL, DIRECTOR, RHODE ISLAND DEPARTMENT OF CORRECTIONS V. KHOLI
562 U.S. 545 (2011)

CAPSULE: For purposes of the Antiterrorism and Effective Death Penalty Act's tolling provision, a motion to reduce sentence under state law is an application for collateral review.

FACTS: Kohli was convicted of 10 counts of first-degree sexual assault in a Rhode Island state court. He was sentenced to consecutive life sentences. He first began the appeal process through various challenges on direct appeal, which were denied. His convictions became final when the time expired for filing a writ of *certiorari* in the court (three years after the original convictions). At the same time, Kohli filed two state motions: one to reduce his sentences by having them run concurrently under Rule 35 of the Rhode Island Superior Court Rules of Criminal Procedure, and one for state post-conviction relief. The State Supreme Court affirmed the consecutive sentences as appropriate, denying the Rule 35 motion (six years after sentence was imposed). The trial court denied his motion for post-conviction relief, which was affirmed by the State Supreme Court (thirteen years after sentence was imposed).

Kohli also filed a federal habeas corpus petition 11 years after his conviction was finalized. The Antiterrorism and Effective Death Penalty Act generally requires a habeas corpus petition to be filed within one year of the date that the judgment became final under direct review. However, this limitation is tolled during the time a properly filed application for state post-conviction or other collateral review is made. The federal district court dismissed the habeas corpus petition as untimely, based on the magistrate's recommendation. The magistrate concluded that the Rule 35 motion was not a properly filed application for relief because it was a plea for leniency and did not challenge the legal sufficiency of the sentences. The First Circuit Court of Appeals reversed this decision.

ISSUE: Is a motion to reduce sentence filed in state proceedings an application for collateral review under the Antiterrorism and Effective Death Penalty Act's definition, resulting in a toll of the one-year limitation for filing a habeas corpus petition? YES.

HOLDING:

1. Under the Antiterrorism and Effective Death Penalty Act, collateral review is interpreted as judicial review of a judgment in a proceeding that is not part of a direct review.

2. A motion to reduce sentence based on Rhode Island law is an application for collateral review that triggers the tolling provision of the Antiterrorism and Effective Death Penalty Act.

REASON: "The Courts of Appeals are divided over the question whether a motion to reduce sentence tolls the period of limitation under § 2244(d)(2).2 [of the Antiterrorism and Effective Death Penalty Act]. We granted *certiorari* to answer this question with respect to a motion to reduce sentence under Rhode Island law. The question in this case is whether a motion for reduction of sentence under Rhode Island's Rule 35 is an 'application for State post-conviction or other collateral review.' . . . We agree with respondent's understanding of 'collateral review.' 'Collateral review' is not defined in AEDPA, and we have never provided a comprehensive definition of that term . . . We have previously described a variety of proceedings as 'collateral,' and all of these proceedings share the characteristic that we have identified, i.e., they stand apart from the process of direct review . . . All of the proceedings identified in these prior opinions as 'collateral' are separate from the direct review process, and thus our prior usage of the term 'collateral' buttresses the conclusion that 'collateral review' means a form of review that is not direct . . . We now apply this definition of 'collateral review' to a Rule 35 motion to reduce sentence under Rhode Island law . . . In this case, respondent filed a motion to reduce his sentence, which permits a trial justice to decide 'on reflection or on the basis of changed circumstances that the sentence originally imposed was, for any reason, unduly severe' (quoting *Mendoza, supra,* at 1161)."

"The first—and the critical—question is whether a Rhode Island Rule 35 sentence reduction proceeding is 'collateral.' Respondent and Rhode Island agree that such a motion is not part of the direct review process. Moreover, we have previously referred to a motion to reduce sentence under old Rule 35 of the Federal Rules of Criminal Procedure as invoking a 'collateral' remedy, see Robinson, *supra*, at 230, n. 14, and Rhode Island's Rule 35 motion to reduce sentence is 'substantially similar' to former Federal Rule 35 . . . We thus have little difficulty concluding that a Rhode Island sentence reduction proceeding is 'collateral' . . . Even if we were to assume that a Rhode Island Rule 35 motion is part of direct review, our disposition of this case would not change: Respondent's habeas petition still would be timely, because the limitation period would not have begun to run until after the Rule 35 proceedings concluded . . . We thus hold that a motion to reduce sentence under Rhode Island law is an application for 'collateral review' that triggers AEDPA's tolling provision."

CASE SIGNIFICANCE: This case further defines the meaning of the word "collateral" for purposes of appeal applications. It somewhat broadens the definition based on the Court's interpretation of Rhode Island law. Justice Alito notes that Rule 35 of Rhode Island law allows review of a sentence to "correct an illegal sentence," "correct a sentence imposed in an illegal manner," and "reduce any sentence." The Court states that this is clearly a collateral review that occurred after direct review. Alito also notes that this state law is similar to the Federal Rule of Criminal Procedure 35, which was in effect until 1984. The Court had ruled in the past that Procedure 35 reviews were collateral reviews. The decision by the Court was unanimous.

The impact of this case is that similar cases that exceed the one-year limit to file a habeas corpus petition under the AEDPA invoke the tolling provision of that Act. This allows for a longer period of time before the petition is filed, based on collateral review in the state courts, including a review for a reduction in sentence.

GONZALEZ V. THALER, DIRECTOR, TEXAS DEPT. OF CRIMINAL JUSTICE, CORRECTIONAL INSTITUTIONS DIVISION
131 S. CT. 2989 (2012)

CAPSULE: If a Certificate of Appealability (COA) under the AEDPA fails to indicate a constitutional issue, this does not bar the Court of Appeals from reviewing the case. Furthermore, if a petitioner does not seek review in the state's highest court, the judgment becomes final upon the time expiration date for filing the review, under the AEDPA.

FACTS: Gonzalez was convicted of murder in Texas. He appealed his conviction in the Texas Court of Appeals, which is the state's intermediate appellate court. After his conviction was affirmed, he allowed the time to appeal to the Texas Court of Criminal Appeals, the state's highest appellate court for criminal cases, to expire. Gonzalez then filed a state habeas corpus petition, which was denied, followed by a federal habeas corpus petition. The federal district court ruled that, under the AEDPA provision, his time had expired one month before he filed for federal habeas corpus review. Thus, his COA under the AEDPA was denied.

Petitioner applied to the Fifth Circuit Court of Appeals for a COA based on two issues: (1) his habeas corpus petition was timely and (2) his Sixth Amendment right to a speedy trial was violated because there was a delay of almost 10 years between the time of his indictment and his trial. The Fifth Circuit held that his habeas corpus petition was timely and granted the COA without ruling on the Sixth Amendment issue. However, once the Court heard the appeal, it affirmed the decision of the lower court that the petition was untimely (thus reversing the ruling on the COA), without mentioning the Court's failure to indicate a constitutional issue. When Gonzalez appealed to the U.S. Supreme Court, the State of Texas, for the first time, claimed that the Fifth Circuit did not have jurisdiction to rule on the appeal because it failed to indicate a constitutional issue in the COA.

ISSUES:

1. Does a COA's failure to indicate a constitutional issue bar a Court of Appeals from hearing the case based on jurisdiction? NO.

2. If a state prisoner doesn't seek relief in the state's highest appellate court, does the judgment become final for purposes of review under the AEDPA when the time limit expires? YES.

HOLDING:

1. Under the AEDPA, § 2253(c)(3) is a mandatory rule but not a nonjurisdictional rule. The failure of a COA to indicate a constitutional issue does not deprive a Court of Appeals from reviewing the case.

2. If a state prisoner fails to appeal to the state's highest appellate court, the judgment is final when the time to appeal expires, for purposes of review under the AEDP's § 2244(d)(1)(A).

REASON: "[An] appeals judge granted a COA that identified a debatable procedural ruling, but did not 'indicate' the issue on which Gonzalez had made a substantial showing of the denial of a constitutional right, as required by § 2253(c)(3). The question before us is whether that defect deprived the Court of Appeals of the power to adjudicate Gonzalez's appeal. We hold that it did not. This Court has endeavored in recent years to 'bring some discipline' to the use of the term 'jurisdictional.' . . . We accordingly have applied the following principle: A rule is jurisdictional '[i]f the Legislature clearly states that a threshold limitation on a statute's scope shall count as jurisdictional.' *Arbaugh v. Y & H Corp.*, 546 U.S. 500, 515 (2006). But if 'Congress does not rank a statutory limitation on coverage as jurisdictional, courts should treat the restriction as nonjurisdictional.' Id., at 516.3. That clear-statement principle makes particular sense in this statute. Here, however, even though the requirement of a COA . . . dates back to 1908, Congress did not enact the indication requirement until 1996. There is thus no 'long line of this Court's decisions left undisturbed by Congress' on which to rely . . . Contrary to the dissent's assertions, post, at 8–10 (opinion of SCALIA, J.), that fact does not suggest that the indication requirement is jurisdictional as well. If anything, the inference runs the other way."

"The second provision, 28 U.S.C. § 2244(d)(1)(A), establishes a 1-year limitations period for state prisoners to file federal habeas petitions, running from 'the date on which the judgment became final by the conclusion of direct review or the expiration of the time for seeking such review.' We hold that, for a state prisoner who does not seek review in a State's highest court, the judgment becomes 'final' on the date that the time for seeking such review expires . . . Gonzalez's limitations period elapsed on December 17, 2007—over a month before he filed his federal habeas petition . . . The Circuits have divided over when a judgment becomes final if a petitioner forgoes review in a State's highest court. In *Clay v. United States*, 537 U.S. 522 (2003), we addressed AEDPA's statute of limitations for federal prisoners seeking postconviction relief . . . We held that the federal judgment becomes final 'when this Court affirms a conviction on the merits on direct review or denies a petition for a writ of certiorari,' or, if a petitioner does not seek certiorari, 'when the time for filing a certiorari petition expires.' . . . In so holding, we rejected the argument that, if a petitioner declines to seek certiorari, the limitations period 'starts to run on the date the court of appeals issues its mandate.' . . . A petitioner who has exhausted his or her claims in state court need not await state habeas proceedings to seek federal habeas relief on those claims . . . . Because Gonzalez did not appeal to the Texas CCA, this Court would have lacked jurisdiction over a petition for certiorari from the Texas Court of Appeals' decision affirming Gonzalez's conviction. We therefore decline to incorporate the 90-day period for seeking certiorari in determining when Gonzalez's judgment became final."

CASE SIGNIFICANCE: This case is unusual because judges in the same Circuit Court of Appeals overruled each other on the same issue: the timeliness in filing a federal habeas corpus petition. Although the judges were ruling on different aspects of it, specifically the COA and the appeal review itself, this case indicates the intricacies of the law and how it can be interpreted in a dissimilar manner by federal judges in the same appellate circuit.

In deciding the timeliness of the federal appeal, the Court rejected the petitioner's argument that they should consider this question based on both prongs that correspond to two categories of appeals and begin the one-year limitation at whichever decision date is the latest. The first prong is for those petitioners pursuing direct review all the way to the U.S. Supreme Court. In this situation, the conclusion of direct review occurs when the Court receives the case and either hears it or denies the writ of *certiorari*. In the second prong, the judgment becomes final when the time expires for seeking review, whether it be at the federal level or the state level. The Court recognized that Gonzalez's case fell under the latter category, and that his time did, in fact, expire when the period for seeking review from Texas' highest court ended. This case reaffirmed the Court's interpretation of the categories of appeals and their exclusion from each other, as decided in previous cases. Precedent was followed in this situation.

BURT, WARDEN V. TITLOW
134 S. CT. 10 (2013)

CAPSULE: Appellate courts must apply the "doubly differential" standard of review in examining the state court's reasonable fact finding and the ineffective assistance of counsel when the record is silent, based on past case law and the AEDPA.

FACTS: Titlow and her aunt were arrested and charged with the murder of Titlow's uncle. Her attorney reviewed the evidence with her that indicated she could be convicted of first-degree murder. With his assistance, Titlow agreed to testify against her aunt in exchange for a guilty plea to manslaughter, receiving a 7–15-year sentence. Three days before her aunt's trial began, Titlow hired another attorney. This attorney and Titlow demanded a minimum sentence of three years instead of seven in exchange for her testimony. The prosecutor refused this demand, and Titlow withdrew her plea with the understanding of the consequences of this action. Without her testimony, her aunt was acquitted and she later died.

Titlow stood trial for murder and was subsequently convicted of second-degree murder, receiving a sentence of 20–40 years in prison. On direct appeal, she claimed that she received ineffective assistance of counsel from her second attorney because he advised her to withdraw her guilty plea before he had researched the case thoroughly. The Michigan Court of Appeals held that the attorney acted in a reasonable manner, based on Titlow's protestations of innocence, and citing the case of *Strickland v. Washington*. She then filed a federal writ of habeas corpus. The federal district court denied her petition, holding that the Michigan Court of Appeals' ruling was fully reasonable based on the law and on the facts.

The Sixth Circuit Court of Appeals reversed the lower court's decision, citing ineffective assistance of counsel that resulted in the plea bargain being nullified. The Court remanded the case, ordering the trial court to reoffer the original plea bargain, although there would be no testimony as her aunt was already deceased. At the plea hearing, Titlow refused to provide a factual basis for the plea by admitting her part in the murder. She did, however, eventually admit that she placed the victim in danger by pouring vodka down his throat. The trial court took the plea under advisement while the State of Michigan appealed the Sixth Circuit Court's decision to the Supreme Court.

ISSUE: Did the Sixth Circuit Court of Appeals err in its decision regarding ineffective assistance of counsel by not following guidelines from the AEDPA and the standard established in *Strickland v. Washington*? YES.

HOLDING: The appellate court erred by failing to apply the doubly deferential standard of review in not recognizing the state court's reasonable factual finding and assuming that counsel was ineffective when the record was silent.

REASON: "AEDPA instructs that, when a federal habeas petitioner challenges the factual basis for a prior state-court decision rejecting a claim, the federal court may overturn the state court's decision only if it was 'based on an unreasonable determination of the facts in light of the evidence presented in the State court proceeding.' 28 U.S.C. § 2254(d)(2). The prisoner bears the burden of rebutting the state court's factual findings 'by clear and convincing evidence.' § 2254(e)(1) . . . AEDPA recognizes a foundational principle of our federal system: State courts are adequate forums for the vindication of federal rights . . . The record readily supports the Michigan Court of Appeals' factual finding that Toca advised withdrawal of the guilty plea only after respondent's proclamation of innocence . . . Accepting as true the Michigan Court of Appeals' factual determination that respondent proclaimed innocence to Toca, the Sixth Circuit's Strickland analysis cannot be sustained. Although a defendant's proclamation of innocence does not relieve counsel of his normal responsibilities under *Strickland*, it may affect the advice counsel gives. The Michigan Court of Appeals' conclusion that Toca's advice satisfied *Strickland* fell within the bounds of reasonableness under AEDPA, given that respondent was claiming innocence and only days away from offering self-incriminating testimony in open court pursuant to a plea agreement involving an above-guidelines sentence." "Even more troubling is the Sixth Circuit's conclusion that Toca was ineffective because the 'record in this case contains no evidence that' he gave constitutionally adequate advice on whether to withdraw the guilty plea. 680 F. 3d, at 590. We have said that counsel should be 'strongly presumed to have rendered adequate assistance and made all significant decisions in the exercise of reasonable professional judgment,' *Strickland*, 466 U.S., at 690, and that the burden to 'show that counsel's performance was deficient' rests squarely on the defendant, id., at 687. The Sixth Circuit turned that presumption of effectiveness on its head. It should go without saying that the absence of evidence cannot overcome the 'strong presumption that counsel's conduct [fell] within the wide range of reasonable professional assistance.' Id., at 689."

CASE SIGNIFICANCE: This case confirms the strict standards that make it difficult for a petitioner to succeed in a federal habeas corpus appeal when the state court made a "reasonable factual finding" regarding effective assistance of counsel. AEDPA recognizes that the state courts can adequately address constitutional rights in reviewing cases. The Act requires the prisoner to show that the state courts committed an error "beyond any possibility for fairminded disagreement," *Harrington v. Richter*, 562 U.S. ___ (2011), pp. 4–6, in order to find relief in the habeas corpus petition.

Likewise, the Supreme Court's ruling in *Strickland v. Washington*, 466 U.S. 688 (1984), makes a strong presumption that counsel is effective in the courtroom. The burden to prove otherwise rests with the defendant. In this case, there was no indication in the court record that the attorney did not give adequate advice to the defendant. The Sixth Circuit Court of Appeals found a constitutional violation based on the fact that the court record *didn't* show that the attorney gave adequate advice in telling his client to withdraw her plea. The Supreme Court reiterated the "doubly differential" standard of review that offers state appellate courts and defense attorneys "the benefit of the doubt." *Cullen v. Pinholster*, 563 U.S. ___, ___ (2011).

B. CLEMENCY AND COMMUTATION

OHIO ADULT PAROLE AUTHORITY V. WOODARD
523 U.S. 272 (1998)

CAPSULE: Giving an inmate the option of voluntarily participating in a pre-hearing interview with members of the parole board, without giving him immunity for his statements at the interview, did not compel the inmate to speak and therefore did not violate his Fifth Amendment privilege against self-incrimination.

FACTS: The Ohio Adult Parole Authority is charged with reviewing clemency cases through an interview and hearing process. The Authority then makes a recommendation to the governor, who has the power to grant clemency. In the case of a death sentence, the Authority is required to conduct a clemency hearing within 45 days of the scheduled execution and to grant the inmate, upon request, a pre-hearing interview with one or more parole board members. Legal counsel is not allowed at that interview.

Woodard was sentenced to death for an aggravated murder committed during a carjacking. His conviction and sentence were upheld. When he failed to obtain a stay of execution more than 45 days before his scheduled execution date, a clemency investigation began on his behalf. The Authority informed Woodard that he could have a clemency interview on September 9, 1994, if he wished, and that his clemency hearing would be on September 16, 1994.

ISSUE: Does giving an inmate the option of voluntarily participating in an interview as part of the clemency process, but without giving him immunity for what he would say, violate an inmate's Fifth Amendment rights? NO.

HOLDING: Giving an inmate the option of voluntarily participating in a pre-hearing interview with members of the parole board, without giving him immunity for his statements at the interview, does not compel the inmate to speak and, therefore, does not violate his Fifth Amendment privilege against self-incrimination.

REASON: "Ohio's clemency procedures do not violate due process. Despite the Authority's mandatory procedures, the ultimate decision-maker, the Governor, retains broad discretion. Under any analysis, the Governor's executive discretion need not be fettered by the types of procedural protections sought by respondent. See *Greenholtz, supra*, at 12–16 (recognizing the Nebraska parole statute created a protected liberty interest, yet rejecting a claim that due process necessitated a formal parole hearing and a statement of evidence relied upon by the parole board). There is thus no substantive expectation of clemency. Moreover, under *Conner*, 515 U.S., at 484, the availability of clemency, or the manner in which the State conducts clemency proceedings, does not impose 'atypical and significant hardship on the inmate in relation to the ordinary incidents of prison life.' Ibid.; see 107

F.3d, at 1185–1186. A denial of clemency merely means that the inmate must serve the sentence originally imposed."

CASE SIGNIFICANCE: In this case, the inmate who was sentenced to death claimed that his Fifth Amendment privilege against self-incrimination was violated because his participation in the pre-hearing interview set by the Ohio Parole Authority was not truly voluntary. Moreover, his participation was conditioned on his waiver of the right to remain silent. The procedure he questioned charged the Ohio Adult Parole authority with reviewing clemency cases through an interview and hearing process in which inmates were allowed to participate. That body had the responsibility of making a recommendation to the governor, who has the power to grant clemency.

In a unanimous opinion, the Court disagreed, saying that "giving the inmate the option of voluntarily participating in a re-hearing interview with members of the parole board without giving him immunity for his statements at the interview did not compel the inmate to speak and, therefore, did not violate his Fifth Amendment privilege against self-incrimination." The Court added that although participation did put some pressure on the inmate, it did not create the kind of "compulsion" that is prohibited by the Fifth Amendment. The choice the inmate faced under the procedure "was very similar to the kinds of choices that defendants routinely face through criminal proceedings and which have not been found to violate the privilege."

This brief focuses only on the issue of whether the privilege against self-incrimination was violated by the clemency hearing provisions of the Ohio Adult Parole Authority. The case, however, also raised another important issue: whether the due process clause applies to death penalty inmates who face clemency proceedings. The Court did not reach a decision on that issue.

C. CONDITIONS OF CONFINEMENT—IN GENERAL

BELL V. WOLFISH
441 U.S. 520 (1979)

CAPSULE: "Double bunking," the "publisher only rule," body cavity searches of pretrial detainees after contact visits, and searches of a pretrial detainee's quarters in his absence are constitutional.

FACTS: Pretrial detainees at the New York City Metropolitan Correctional Center (MCC)—a jail—filed a lawsuit alleging violation of their constitutional rights. The Center had opened less than four months before and had been described as "the architectural embodiment of the best and most progressive penological planning" and "unquestionably a top-flight, first-class facility." However, within a short time after opening, the facility became filled above its planned capacity and correctional officials began replacing single bunks in the cells and dormitories with double bunks. The inmates filed a lawsuit alleging violations of statutory and constitutional rights arising from overcrowded conditions, undue length of confinement, improper searches, inadequate recreational facilities, lack of educational and employment opportunities, insufficient staff, and restrictions on the purchase and receipt of personal items and books. The restriction on books and publications prohibited the receipt of all books and magazines mailed from outside the MCC except those sent directly from a publisher or a book club.

ISSUE: Are pretrial detainees' conditions of confinement, which include double bunking, post-contact visit body cavity searches, searches of detainees' quarters, and prohibit the receipt of books and magazines from sources other than the publisher unconstitutional? NO.

HOLDING:

1. "Double bunking" did not deprive the pretrial detainees of liberty without due process of law;
2. The "publisher only" rule did not violate inmates' First Amendment rights;
3. The policy on body cavity searches of pretrial detainees after contact visits did not violate their Fourth Amendment rights; and
4. The rule permitting searches of a pretrial detainee's quarters in his absence did not violate his constitutional rights under the Fourth Amendment.

REASON: "In evaluating the constitutionality of conditions or restrictions of pretrial detention that implicate only the protection against deprivation of liberty without due process of law, we think that the proper inquiry is whether those conditions amount to punishment of the detainee. For under the Due Process Clause, a detainee may not be punished prior to an adjudication of guilt in accordance with the due process of law. Not every disability imposed during pretrial detention amounts to 'punishment' in the constitutional sense, however. Once the Government has exercised its conceded authority to detain a person pending trial, it obviously is entitled to employ devices that are calculated to effectuate this detention. Traditionally, this has meant confinement in a facility which, no matter how modern or how antiquated, results in restricting the movement of a detainee in a manner in which he would not be restricted if he simply were free to walk the streets pending trial.

"Absent a showing of an expressed intent to punish on the part of detention facility officials, the determination generally will turn on '[w]hether an alternative purpose to which [the restriction] may rationally be connected is assignable for it, and whether it appears excessive in relation to the alternative purpose assigned [to it].' Thus, if a particular condition or restriction of pretrial detention is reasonably related to a legitimate governmental objective, it does not, without more, amount to 'punishment.' Judged by this analysis, respondents' claim that double-bunking violated their due process rights fails. Neither the District Court nor the Court of Appeals intimated that it considered double-bunking to constitute punishment: instead, they found that it contravened the compelling necessity test, which today we reject. On this record, we are convinced as a matter of law that double-bunking as practiced at the MCC did not amount to punishment and did not, therefore, violate respondents' rights under the Due Process Clause of the Fifth Amendment.

"A fortiori, pretrial detainees, who have not been convicted of any crimes, retain at least those constitutional rights that we have held are enjoyed by convicted prisoners. But our cases also have insisted on a second proposition: simply because prison inmates retain certain constitutional rights does not mean that these rights are not subject to restrictions and limitations. We conclude that a prohibition against receipt of hardback books unless mailed directly from publishers, book clubs or bookstores does not violate the First Amendment rights of MCC inmates. That limit restriction is a rational response by prison officials to an obvious security problem . . . Corrections officials concluded that permitting the introduction of packages of personal property and food would increase the risk of gambling, theft and inmate fights over that which the institution already experienced by permitting certain items to be purchased from its commissary. It is also all too obvious that such packages are handy devices for the smuggling of contraband. There is simply no basis in this record for concluding that MCC officials have exaggerated their response to these serious problems or that this restriction is irrational. It does not therefore deprive the convicted inmates or pretrial detainees of the MCC of their property without due process of law in contravention of the Fifth Amendment.

"Inmates at all Bureau of Prison facilities, including the MCC, are required to expose their body cavities for visual inspection as a part of a strip search conducted after every contact visit with a person from outside the institution. The searches must be conducted in a reasonable manner. But we deal here with the question whether visual body cavity inspections as contemplated by the MCC rules can ever be conducted on less than probable cause. Balancing the significant and legitimate security interests of the institution against the privacy interest of the inmates, we conclude that they can.

"Judges, after all, are human. They, no less than others in our society, have a natural tendency to believe that their individual solutions to often intractable problems are better and more workable than those of the persons who are actually charged with and trained in the running of the particular institution under examination. But under the Constitution, the first question to be answered is not whose plan is best, but in what branch of the Government is lodged the authority to initially devise the plan. This does not mean that constitutional rights are not to be scrupulously observed. It does mean, however, that the inquiry of federal courts into prison management must be limited to the issue of whether a particular system violates any prohibition of the Constitution, or in the case of a federal prison, a statute."

CASE SIGNIFICANCE: This is one of the few cases decided by the Court on the rights of pretrial detainees who are housed in jails. In essence, the Court rejected the concept of the presumption of innocence for pretrial detainees in favor of the need for jail authorities to run the institution in a secure and orderly manner. The Court said, however, that confinement conditions will constitute a violation of due process if: (1) the detainees are subjected to "genuine privation and hardships over an extended period of time" or (2) if detainees are subjected to conditions that are "not reasonably related to a legitimate goal." These two conditions, however, are not much different from those that would also make unconstitutional the confinement of those already convicted. In effect, the Court gave the go-ahead signal for jail officials to run the institution the way prisons are managed, although jails hold both convicts and pretrial detainees. This case implies that although jails and prisons are different in a number of ways, they are treated by the Court for purposes of inmates' rights as though they are the same. This is because the problems of institutional order and security are similar whether an institution houses pretrial detainees or convicts.

WILSON V. SEITER
501 U.S. 294 (1991)

CAPSULE: "Deliberate indifference" is required for liability in conditions-of-confinement cases. In conditions-of-confinement cases under § 1983, "deliberate indifference" means a "culpable state of mind" on the part of prison officials.

FACTS: Petitioner Pearly Wilson, a felon incarcerated at the Hocking Correctional Facility (HCF) in Nelsonville, Ohio, filed suit under 42 U.S.C. § 1983, alleging that the conditions of his confinement constituted cruel and unusual punishment in violation of the Eighth and Fourteenth Amendments. These conditions of confinement included the following: overcrowding, excessive noise, insufficient locker storage space, inadequate heating and cooling, improper ventilation, unclean and inadequate rest rooms, unsanitary dining facilities and food preparation, and housing with mentally and physically ill inmates. Wilson sought declaratory and injunctive relief in addition to $900,000 in compensatory and punitive damages.

Motions for summary judgment with supporting affidavits were filed by both parties. Wilson's affidavits described the challenged conditions and charged that the authorities failed to take remedial action after notification. Seiter's affidavits denied the existence of some of the alleged conditions and described efforts by prison officials to improve the others.

ISSUE: Does a lawsuit alleging that conditions of confinement constitute cruel and unusual punishment require a showing of "deliberate indifference" on the part of prison officials? YES.

HOLDING:

1. The "deliberate indifference" standard applies generally to inmate challenges to conditions of confinement.
2. An inmate making the claim that conditions of confinement violate the Eighth Amendment must show a "culpable state of mind" (meaning intent) on the part of prison officials.

REASON: "*Estelle v. Gamble, Rhodes v. Chapman, Whitley v. Albers* . . . These cases mandate inquiry into a prison official's state of mind when it is claimed that the official has inflicted cruel and unusual punishment . . . The source of the intent requirement is not the predilections of this Court, but the Eighth Amendment itself, which bans only cruel and unusual punishment. If the pain inflicted is not formally meted out as punishment by the statute or the sentencing judge, some mental element must be attributed to the inflicting officer before it can qualify . . . The long duration of a cruel prison condition may make it easier to establish knowledge and hence some form of intent, cf. *Canton v. Harris*, 489 U.S. 378, 390, n. 10 (1989); but there is no logical reason why it should cause the requirement of intent to evaporate.

"As described above, our cases say that the offending conduct must be wanton . . . Whitley makes clear, however, that in this context wantonness does not have a fixed meaning but must be determined with 'due regard for differences in the kind of conduct against which an Eighth Amendment objection is lodged.' 475 U.S., at 320 . . . The parties agree that the very high state of mind prescribed by *Whitley* does not apply to prison conditions cases. Petitioner argues that, to the extent officials' state of mind is relevant at all, there is no justification for a standard more demanding than *Estelle's* 'deliberate indifference.'

"There is no indication that, as a general matter, the actions of prison officials with respect to these nonmedical conditions are taken under materially different constraints than their actions with respect to medical conditions. Thus, as retired Justice Powell has concluded: 'Whether one characterizes the treatment received by [the prisoner] as inhumane conditions of confinement, failure to attend to his medical needs, or a combination of both, it is appropriate to apply the "deliberate indifference" standard articulated in *Estelle*.'

"The Court of Appeals proceeded to uphold the District Court's dismissal of petitioner's remaining claims on the ground that his affidavits failed to establish the requisite culpable state of mind . . . It appears from this, and from the consistent reference to 'the *Whitley* standard' elsewhere in this opinion, that the court believed that the criterion of liability was whether the respondents acted 'maliciously and sadistically for the very purpose of causing harm,' *Whitley*, 475 U.S., at 320–321. To be sure, mere negligence would satisfy neither that nor the more lenient 'deliberate indifference' standard, so that any error on the point may have been harmless. Conceivably, however, the court would have given further thought to its finding of '[a]t best . . . negligence' if it realized that that was not merely an argument of a fortiori, but a determination almost essential to the judgment. Out of an abundance of caution, we vacate the judgment of the Sixth Circuit and remand the case for reconsideration under the appropriate standard."

CASE SIGNIFICANCE: This case is significant because it makes it difficult for inmates to recover damages from prison officials in conditions-of-confinement cases. The Court in this case said that the "deliberate indifference" standard used in *Estelle v. Gamble*, 429 U.S. 97 (1976) applies to these types of cases. The Court added that "a prisoner claiming that the conditions of his confinement violate the Eighth Amendment must show a culpable state of mind on the part of prison officials," stating further that, "an intent requirement is implicit in that

Amendment's [Eighth] ban on cruel and unusual punishment." It will be difficult for inmates, alleging cruel and unusual punishment stemming from prison conditions, to establish that prison authorities allowed conditions to exist because of a "culpable state of mind," meaning that there was intent on their part that deplorable prison conditions should be allowed to continue. In most cases, poor conditions of confinement are mainly attributable to old facilities or lack of funds, both of which are outside the control of prison administrators. Because prison officials themselves work in the facility, a great majority of them want prison conditions to improve, but they may not have the resources or the authority to do it, thus a "culpable state of mind" is hard to prove.

While this case represents good news for prison administrators, it has the opposite effect for prisoners, who will now find it more difficult to seek improvement in prison conditions by filing cases against prison administrators. Prisoners may now have to seek relief primarily through the political process, an avenue that has traditionally been inhospitable to prisoners.

HELLING V. MCKINNEY
509 U.S. 25 (1993)

CAPSULE: Prison conditions that pose an alleged risk of harm to a prisoner's health, both in the future and in the present, can be actionable under the Eighth Amendment's prohibition against cruel and unusual punishment.

FACTS: McKinney, a Nevada state prisoner, filed a claim under 42 U.S.C. § 1983, stating that he was subjected to environmental tobacco smoke (ETS). The cause of this exposure was a cellmate who smoked five packs of cigarettes a day. The inmate alleged that he experienced health problems as a result of this exposure, which was cruel and unusual punishment, in violation of the Eighth Amendment. Both parties agreed to a jury trial before a magistrate. The magistrate held that the two issues to be considered were whether the inmate had a constitutional right to be housed in a smoke-free environment and whether prison officials showed deliberate indifference to the inmate's serious medical needs. He found that there was no constitutional right to be housed in a smoke-free environment, but that the inmate could state a claim for deliberate indifference if the underlying facts could be proven. However, the magistrate held that the inmate had failed to present evidence that indicated that his medical problems were the result of environmental tobacco smoke or the result of deliberate indifference on the part of prison officials.

ISSUES:
1. Can the health risk posed by a prison inmate's involuntary exposure to environmental tobacco smoke (ETS) form the basis of a claim for relief under the Eighth Amendment? YES.
2. Can a lawsuit be brought even if the prisoner has had no current health problems arising from the environmental tobacco smoke? YES.

HOLDING:

1. The health risk posed by a prison inmate's involuntary exposure to environmental tobacco smoke can form the basis for a cruel and unusual punishment claim.
2. The prisoner does not need to show that the condition he challenges has caused a current health problem; conditions that pose serious threats to his future health are also actionable.

REASON: "We have great difficulty agreeing that prison authorities may not be deliberately indifferent to an inmate's current health problems but may ignore a condition of confinement that is sure or very likely to cause serious illness and needless suffering the next week or month or year. In *Hutto v. Finney*, 437 U.S. 678, 682 (1978), we noted that inmates in punitive isolation were crowded into cells and some of them had infectious maladies such as hepatitis and venereal disease . . . It is 'cruel and unusual punishment to hold convicted criminals in unsafe conditions.' *Youngberg v. Romeo*, 457 U.S. 307, 315–316 (1982). It would be odd to deny an injunction to inmates who plainly proved an unsafe, life-threatening condition in their prison on the ground that nothing yet had happened to them . . . We thus reject petitioner's central thesis that only deliberate indifference to current serious health problems of inmates is actionable under the Eighth Amendment.

"With respect to the objective factor, McKinney must show that he himself is being exposed to unreasonably high levels of ETS. Plainly relevant to this determination is the fact that McKinney has been moved from Carson City to Ely State Prison and is no longer the cellmate of a five-pack-a-day smoker . . . Moreover, the Director of the Nevada State Prisons adopted a formal smoking policy on January 10, 1992 . . . It is possible that the new policy will be administered in a way that will minimize the risk to McKinney and make it impossible for him to prove that he will be exposed to unreasonable risk with respect to his future health or that he is now entitled to an injunction.

"Also with respect to the objective factor, determining whether McKinney's conditions of confinement violate the Eighth Amendment requires more than a scientific and statistical inquiry into the seriousness of the potential harm and the likelihood that such injury to health will actually be caused by exposure to ETS. It also requires a court to assess whether society considers the risk that the prisoner complains of to be so grave that it violates contemporary standards of decency to expose anyone unwillingly to such a risk.

"On remand, the subjective factor, deliberate indifference, should be determined in light of the prison authorities' current attitudes and conduct, which may have changed considerably since the judgment of the Court of Appeals. Indeed, the adoption of the smoking policy mentioned above will bear heavily on the inquiry into deliberate indifference."

CASE SIGNIFICANCE: This case is significant because it: (1) holds that the condition an inmate challenges need not cause a current health problem in order for the condition to be actionable, and (2) gives officials a great deal of authority to control or prohibit smoking in jails and prisons.

In this case, the inmate could not prove a current health damage resulting from excessive smoking by his cellmate. Prison officials therefore said that the allegation of injury to the inmate was "speculative" and "not sufficiently grave" as to be actionable under the cruel and unusual punishment clause. The Court disagreed, saying that "an unreasonable risk of serious damage to his future health states an Eighth Amendment cause of action" against the prison system.

This is the only case decided by the Court thus far on the controversial issue of controlling smoking in prisons. The Court in effect agreed that smoking is a health hazard for inmates and may therefore be curtailed. This decision gives prison officials authority to control or even completely prohibit smoking in prisons, justifying a no-smoking policy on the ground of possible lawsuit emanating from inmates who do not smoke. Many jails and prisons have already banned smoking in their facilities. Challenges in court by inmates who smoke are unlikely to succeed.

HOPE V. PELZER
536 U.S. 730 (2002)

CAPSULE: The use of the hitching post for an extended period unnecessarily and wantonly inflicted pain in violation of the Eighth Amendment. Correctional officers are not entitled to qualified immunity in this case.

FACTS: Hope was an inmate in the Alabama prison system, which engages in the practice of chaining inmates to a hitching post for disciplinary purposes. He was chained to the post for two hours after getting in a fight with another inmate. Hope's arms were chained above shoulder height and he experienced pain whenever he tried to move his arms to improve his circulation because the handcuffs cut into his wrists. One month later, he was again chained to the post for seven hours with his shirt removed after an altercation with a correctional officer. During the seven hours, he was given water only once or twice and he was not allowed to go to the bathroom. A correctional officer taunted him about his thirst. Hope filed suit against the three correctional officers involved in the first incident.

The Magistrate Court concluded that the correctional officers were entitled to qualified immunity without addressing the issue of whether the hitching post punishment violated the Eighth Amendment. The District Court agreed with this decision, as did the Eleventh Circuit Court of Appeals. However, the Circuit Court did decide that use of the hitching post violated the Eighth Amendment's prohibition against cruel and unusual punishment.

ISSUES:
1. Does the use of the hitching post constitute cruel and unusual punishment? YES.
2. Are the officers in this case entitled to qualified immunity? NO.

HOLDING: The use of a hitching post as a form of punishment is a violation of the cruel and unusual punishment clause of the Constitution. Qualified immunity does not apply because the correctional officers violated a clearly established constitutional right of which a reasonable person would have known.

REASON: "The threshold inquiry a court must undertake in a qualified immunity analysis is whether plaintiff's allegations, if true, establish a constitutional violation. *Saucier v. Katz*, 533 U.S. 194, 201 (2001) . . . As the facts are alleged by Hope, the Eighth Amendment violation is obvious. Any safety concerns had long since abated by the time petitioner was handcuffed to the hitching post because Hope has already been subdued, handcuffed, placed in leg irons, and transported back to the prison . . . Despite the clear lack of an emergency situation, the respondents knowingly subjected him to a substantial risk of physical harm, to unnecessary pain caused by the handcuffs and the restricted position of confinement for a 7-hour period, to unnecessary exposure to the heat of the sun, to prolonged thirst and taunting, and to a deprivation of bathroom breaks that created a risk of particular discomfort and humiliation."

"The respondents violated clearly established law. Our conclusion that 'a reasonable person would have known,' *Harlow*, 457 U.S., at 818, of the violation is buttressed by the fact that the DOJ specifically advised the ADOC of the unconstitutionality of its practices before the incidents in this case took place . . . The obvious cruelty inherent in this practice should have provided respondents with some notice that their alleged conduct violated Hope's constitutional protection against cruel and unusual punishment . . . Even if there might once have been a question regarding the constitutionality of this practice, the Eleventh Circuit precedent of *Gates* and *Ort*, as well as the DOJ report condemning the practice, put a reasonable officer on notice that the use of the hitching post under the circumstances alleged by Hope was unlawful. The 'fair and clear warning,' *Lanier*, 520 U.S., at 271, that these cases provided was sufficient to preclude the defense of qualified immunity at the summary judgment stage."

CASE SIGNIFICANCE: This case is significant because it is the latest case to address the type of punishment allowed under the Eighth Amendment. In this case an inmate in Alabama was chained to a hitching post for two hours after getting in a fight with another inmate. His arms were chained above shoulder height and he experienced pain. One month later, he was again chained to the post for several hours with his shirt removed after an altercation with a correctional officer. He was given water only once or twice and was not allowed to go to the bathroom. No clear emergency existed to warrant this treatment. The Court said there was no justification for this type of punishment and that the correctional officers acted with deliberate indifference to the health or safety of inmates. The Court added that "the Eighth Amendment violation here is obvious on the facts alleged."

The officers claimed they were not liable because of qualified immunity. In § 1983 cases (which this was), qualified immunity means that the officer acted in good faith. "Good faith," in turn, means that the "officer did not know he was violating a clearly established constitutional right of which a reasonable person would have known." The Court rejected this defense, saying that "a reasonable officer would have known that using a hitching post . . . was unlawful," and that the "obvious cruelty inherent in the practice should have provided respondents with some notice that their conduct was unconstitutional."

The decision in this case on both issues does not come as a surprise. What is a surprise is that the hitching post is still used as punishment in some prison systems. The thrust of prison law cases on types of punishment and conditions of confinement indicates that courts have long disapproved of the use of this type of punishment and therefore a good faith defense does not succeed.

BARBER ET AL. V. THOMAS, WARDEN
130 S. CT. 2499 (2010)

CAPSULE: The Federal Bureau of Prisons' method for calculating good-time credit to be awarded to prisoners is lawful because it reflects the most natural reading of the statute.

FACTS: Two federal prisoners, Barber and Jihad-Black, challenged the Federal Bureau of Prisons' method for calculating good time for prisoners. The federal statute states that a prisoner who is serving a sentence of more than a year can receive good-time credit at the end of each year up to the amount of 54 days, based on exemplary behavior in that past year. During the last year of imprisonment, the amount of good-time credits are prorated based on the remaining days in the sentence, proportional to the credits awarded in other years.

The prisoners appealed this method of calculation, claiming that § 3624(b)(1) requires a good-time calculation based on the sentence imposed by the judge and not the length of time the prisoner actually serves. The federal district court denied the appeal, and the Ninth Circuit Court of Appeals affirmed the decision.

ISSUE: Is the Federal Bureau of Prisons' method for calculating good time lawful under § 3624(b)(1) of the federal statutes? YES.

HOLDING: The Federal Bureau of Prisons' calculation of good-time credits reflects the most natural reading of the statute and it is the most consistent with its purpose. It is preferable to the prisoners' alternative interpretation.

REASON: "The statute's language and purpose, taken together, support the BOP's method. That method tracks § 3624(b)'s language by providing a prisoner a maximum credit of 54 days for each full year of imprisonment and a proportionally adjusted amount of credit for any additional time served that is less than a full year. As § 3624(b) directs, the BOP awards the credit 'at the end of each year' of imprisonment. Petitioners' approach cannot be reconciled with the statute. Because it awards credit for the sentence imposed, regardless of how much time is actually served, a prisoner could receive credit for a year that he does not spend in prison. Moreover the calculation of credit for such a year would not be made 'at the end of' that year. Nor could the BOP determine whether the prisoner had exemplary behavior 'during that year.' This language did not find its way into the statute by accident. The differences between the prior provision (repealed in 1984)—which granted the prisoner a deduction at the outset of his sentence, subject to forfeiture for breaking prison rules—and the present statute—under which 'credit' is 'earned' 'at the end of' the year based on an evaluation of behavior 'during that year'—show an intent to move from a prospective entitlement to a retrospective award. The BOP's method also furthers the basic purpose of the statute. Section 3624 was part of the comprehensive Sentencing Reform Act of 1984, which sought to achieve both increased sentencing uniformity and greater honesty by 'mak[ing] all sentences basically determinate.' *Mistretta v. United States*, 488 U.S. 361, 367."

"Section 3624(b) states the reason for the exception: to provide an incentive for prisoners to 'compl[y] with institutional disciplinary regulations.' . . . The BOP's approach furthers § 3624's objectives by tying the award directly to good behavior during the preceding year. In contrast, petitioners' approach would allow a prisoner to earn credit for both the portion of his sentence that he served and the portion offset with earned credit, which would loosen the statute's connection between good behavior and the good time award. Pp. 5–8. (b) Arguments to the contrary are unconvincing . . . Petitioners' reliance on legislative history is misplaced. A U.S. Sentencing Commission Supplementary Report is not helpful to them either, because there is no indication that the Commission, in that report or in the Guidelines themselves, considered or referred to the particular question whether to base good time credit on time served or the sentence imposed. Nor, in light of the statute's text, structure, history, and purpose, is this a case in which there is a 'grievous ambiguity or uncertainty in the statute,' *Muscarello v. United States*, 524 U.S. 125, 139, permitting application of the rule of lenity. Because the BOP's calculation system applies the statute as its language is most naturally read, and in accordance with the statute's basic purpose, this Court need not determine the extent to which Congress has granted the BOP authority to interpret the statute more broadly, or differently than it has done here. Cf. *Chevron U.S.A. Inc. v. Natural Resources Defense Council, Inc.*, 467 U.S. 837, 844–845. And because the BOP's approach reflects the statute's most natural reading and is the most consistent with its purpose, it is also preferable to the dissent's alternative interpretation. Pp. 8–17."

CASE SIGNIFICANCE: This case reflects the Court's interpretation of the intent of § 3624(b)(1), mainly that of rewarding good behavior credits so inmates will serve their time without incident while imprisoned. The credits are awarded at the end of the year for exemplary behavior during that year, and the final year of imprisonment is prorated. The Court contends that applying another method of calculation would be too complicated and too confusing for both inmates and administrators.

Conversely, the petitioners believe that the statute should be interpreted to require good-time credits for the sentence imposed by the judge and not actual time served. They state that using the current Bureau of Prisons' method deprives them of seven days of good-time credit per year, which can amount to several months over a lengthy prison sentence. The Court contends that the inmates' proposed method of calculation gives them good-time credits for days they will not actually serve in prison and is in excess of the intent of the statute. However, the dissenting judges in this case (Kennedy, Stevens, and Ginsburg) believe that the Court's interpretation of the statute disadvantages almost 200,000 prisoners in the system, and that the petitioners' proposed alternative calculation is the better interpretation of the statute. Justice Kennedy further notes that the Court's decision "imposes tens of thousands of years of additional prison time . . . according to a mathematical formula they will be unable to understand," not to mention the cost to the taxpayers to house these prisoners for the additional years. It is unlikely, though, that the Court will reexamine this issue anytime soon now that they have made their decision.

FLORENCE V. BOARD OF CHOSEN FREEHOLDERS OF COUNTY OF BURLINGTON ET AL.
132 S. CT. 1510 (2012)

CAPSULE: Extensive body searches of jail detainees arrested for minor offenses do not violate the Fourth and Fourteenth Amendments.

FACTS: The petitioner, Florence, was arrested on a bench warrant after a routine traffic stop. He was originally detained in the Burlington County Detention Center and later moved to another jail, the Essex County Correctional Facility. At that facility, it was determined that the bench warrant was no longer valid. However, the petitioner had been subject to an extensive body search at both jails and he filed a 42 U.S.C., § 1983 action, alleging violations of the Fourth and Fourteenth Amendments had occurred. He stated that any person arrested for a minor offense should not be treated in this manner unless jail officials suspected that the arrestee was concealing weapons, drugs or other contraband. The federal district court granted summary judgment in favor of the petitioner, agreeing that extensive body searches for nonindictable offenses violated the Fourth Amendment. The Third Circuit Court of Appeals reversed the decision.

ISSUE: Are extensive body searches of jail detainees arrested for minor offenses a violation of the Fourth and Fourteenth Amendments? NO.

HOLDING: The search procedures at the jails in question do not violate the Fourth and Fourteenth Amendments because they strike a reasonable balance between the needs of the facilities and the detainee's right to privacy.

REASON: "Maintaining safety and order at detention centers requires the expertise of correctional officials, who must have substantial discretion to devise reasonable solutions to problems. A regulation impinging on an inmate's constitutional rights must be upheld 'if it is reasonably related to legitimate penological interests.' *Turner v. Safley*, 42 U.S. 78, 79."

"Correctional officials have a significant interest in conducting a thorough search as a standard part of the intake process. The admission of new inmates creates risks for staff, the existing detainee population, and the new detainees themselves. Officials therefore must screen for contagious infections and for wounds or injuries requiring immediate medical attention. It may be difficult to identify and treat medical problems until detainees remove their clothes for a visual inspection. Jails and prisons also face potential gang violence, giving them reasonable justification for a visual inspection of detainees for signs of gang affiliation as part of the intake process. Additionally, correctional officials have to detect weapons, drugs, alcohol, and other prohibited items new detainees may possess."

"Petitioner's proposal . . . is unworkable. The seriousness of an offense is a poor predictor of who has contraband, and it would be difficult to determine whether individual detainees fall within the proposed exemption. Even persons arrested for a minor offense may be coerced by others into concealing contraband . . . It may also be difficult to classify inmates by their current and prior offenses before the intake search. Jail officials know little at the outset about an arrestee . . ."

CASE SIGNIFICANCE: This case reinforces standard procedures for individuals who are admitted to a jail, regardless of the offense for which they are charged. Jails and prisons do not make distinctions between misdemeanants and felons when processing them. The overriding concern is institutional safety in preventing injury to both staff and prisoners and preventing contraband from being introduced into the facility. The Court has noted that the search regulations have a legitimate relationship to the institution's needs for facility safety.

The petitioner argued that the extensive search was too severe for someone accused of a minor offense unless officials suspected him of possessing contraband. However, with prisons and jails being overcrowded, correctional officers do not have the time or immediate knowledge to decide whether someone might be a danger to the facility. Uniform procedures are best applied in this situation.

Although distinctions are made between misdemeanants and felons in areas such as amount of bail required, court where the case is heard, in sentencing, and in type of facility to serve the sentence, the Court has ruled that persons can be arrested for even minor offenses (*Atwater v. City of Lago Vista*). Allowing an extensive body search for those accused of a minor offense would be in line with the *Atwater* decision.

D. CONDITIONS OF CONFINEMENT—DOUBLE CELLING

RHODES V. CHAPMAN
452 U.S. 337 (1981)

CAPSULE: Double celling of prisoners does not, in itself, constitute cruel and unusual punishment.

FACTS: State prisoners in the Southern Ohio Correctional Facility brought a class action suit against state officials in federal district court under 42 U.S.C. § 1983, alleging that double celling (the housing of two inmates in a single cell) in itself violated the Constitution, and claiming they were entitled to injunctive relief. The prisoners alleged that double celling confined cellmates too closely and was a source of overcrowding. The inmates sought injunctive relief to bar prison officials from housing more than one inmate in a cell, except as a temporary measure. The District Court decided that double celling was cruel and unusual punishment in violation of the Eighth Amendment. The decision was based on five factors: (1) inmates at the prison were serving long terms of imprisonment; (2) the prison housed 38 percent more inmates than it was designed to hold; (3) several studies recommended that each inmate have at least 50 to 55 feet of living quarters while two double-celled inmates at the institution shared 63 feet; (4) the suggestion that double-celled inmates spend most of their time in their cells with their cellmates; and (5) the fact that the policy of double celling was not a temporary condition.

Prison officials appealed to the Court of Appeals for the Sixth Circuit, which affirmed the decision. The Court of Appeals viewed the District Court's opinion as holding that double celling was cruel and unusual punishment under the circumstances at the Southern Ohio Correctional Facility, not that double celling was unconstitutional per se. The U.S. Supreme Court granted certiorari "because of the importance of the question to prison administration."

ISSUE: Is the housing of two inmates in a single cell cruel and unusual punishment, prohibited by the Eighth and Fourteenth Amendments? NO.

HOLDING: "Double celling" of inmates in prison is not, in and of itself, cruel and unusual punishment. There may be some instances, however, when because of deprivation of food, medical care, crowding, sanitation, and other factors, the conditions may be so poor as to constitute a violation of the Eighth Amendment's cruel and unusual punishment clause. The conditions at the Southern Ohio Correctional Facility did not constitute cruel and unusual punishment.

REASON: "Conditions that cannot be said to be cruel and unusual under contemporary standards are not unconstitutional. To the extent that such conditions are restrictive and even harsh, they are part of the penalty that criminal offenders pay for their offenses against society . . . The double celling made necessary by the unanticipated increase in prison population did not lead to deprivations of essential food, medical care, or sanitation. Nor did it increase violence among inmates or create other conditions intolerable for prison confinement. Although job and educational opportunities diminished marginally as a result of double celling, limited work hours and delay before receiving education do not inflict pain, much less unnecessary and wanton pain; deprivations of this kind simply are not punishments.

"The five considerations on which the District Court relied also are insufficient to support its constitutional conclusion . . . These general considerations fall far short in themselves of proving cruel and unusual punishment, for there is no evidence that double celling under these circumstances either inflicts unnecessary or wanton pain or is grossly disproportionate to the severity of crimes warranting imprisonment."

CASE SIGNIFICANCE: Although this case said that double celling in itself is not cruel and unusual punishment, there are instances when it can be. The key to understanding how the Court ruled in this case is to realize that, as the District Court said, the physical plant at the Southern Ohio Correctional Facility was "unquestionably a top-flight, first-class facility." Among other things, the court found that each cell measures approximately 63 square feet, each contains a bed measuring 36 by 80 inches, has a cabinet-type nightstand, a wall-mounted sink with hot and cold running water, and every cell has a heating and air circulation vent near the ceiling, and 960 of the cells have a window that inmates can open and close. The day rooms are located adjacent to the cell blocks and are open to the inmates between 6:30 a.m. and 9:30 p.m. Each day room contains a wall-mounted television, card tables, and chairs. The facility was built in the early 1970s and is therefore relatively modern.

Given the "top-flight, first-class" nature of the facility, this was not a difficult case for the Court to decide. The decision would have been different had conditions in the particular facility been bad. The Court said: "Courts certainly have a responsibility to scrutinize claims of cruel and unusual confinement, and conditions in a number of prisons, especially older ones, have justly been described as 'deplorable' and 'sordid.'" Double celling, therefore, becomes cruel and unusual punishment if the conditions are bad. How bad must the conditions be? That is a question of fact that must be decided by the courts on a case-by-case basis.

E. CONSENT DECREE—MODIFICATION

RUFO V. INMATES OF SUFFOLK COUNTY JAIL
502 U.S. 367 (1992)

CAPSULE: Modification of a consent decree is allowed by federal law under certain circumstances.

FACTS: After conditions in the Suffolk County Jail were held unconstitutional, the inmates and county officials entered into a consent decree that provided for the construction of a new jail that was to have single-occupancy cells for pretrial detainees. There was a delay in the construction, during which time the inmate population increased beyond projections. While construction was still under way, the sheriff moved to modify the consent decree to allow double bunking so the jail's capacity could be increased. The sheriff relied on Federal Rule of Civil Procedure 60(b), which provides that "upon such terms as are just, the court may relieve a party (from compliance with a consent decree) for the following reasons: . . . (5) . . . it is no longer equitable that the judgment should have prospective operation." The District Court denied relief, saying that "nothing less than a clear showing of grievous wrong evoked by new and unforeseen conditions should lead . . . to change in what was decreed after years of litigation with the consent of all concerned." This decision was affirmed by the Court of Appeals; the sheriff and the county appealed.

ISSUE: Did the District Court apply the correct standard in denying the sheriff's motion for relief from the provisions of the consent decree? NO.

HOLDING: Modification of a consent decree is allowed by federal law "when changed factual conditions make compliance with the decree substantially more onerous, when the decree proves to be unworkable because of unforeseen obstacles, or when enforcement of the decree without modification would be detrimental to the public interest." The stricter "grievous wrong" standard used by the District Court does not apply to requests to modify consent decrees stemming from institutional reform litigation.

REASON: "Although we hold that a district court should exercise flexibility in considering requests for modification of an institutional reform consent decree, it does not follow that a modification will be warranted in all circumstances. Rule 60(b)(5) provides that a party may obtain relief from a court order when 'it is no longer equitable that the judgment should have prospective application,' not when it is no longer convenient to live with the terms of a consent decree. Accordingly, a party seeking modification of a consent decree bears the burden of establishing that a significant change in circumstances warrants revision of the decree. If the moving party meets this standard, the court should consider whether the proposed modification is suitably tailored to the changed circumstances.

"A party seeking modification of a consent decree may meet its initial burden by showing either a significant change in factual conditions or in law.

"Modification of a consent decree may be warranted when changed factual conditions make compliance with the decree substantially more onerous. Such a modification was approved by the District Court in this litigation in 1985 when it became apparent that plans for the new jail did not provide sufficient cell space. Modification is also appropriate when a decree proves to be unworkable because of unforeseen obstacles, *New York State Assn. for Retarded Children, Inc. v. Carey*, 706 F.2d at 969 (modification allowed where State could not find appropriate housing facilities for transfer patients); *Philadelphia Welfare Rights Organization v. Shapp*, 602 F.2d at 1120–1121 (modification allowed where State could not find sufficient clients to meet decree targets); or when enforcement of the decree without modification would be detrimental to the public interest, *Duran v. Elrod*, 760 F.2d 756, 759–761 (modification allowed to avoid pretrial release of accused violent felons).

"Respondents urge that modification should be allowed only when a change in facts is both 'unforeseen and unforeseeable.' Such a standard would provide even less flexibility than the exacting Swift test; we decline to adopt it. Litigants are not required to anticipate every exigency that could conceivably arise during the life of a consent decree.

"Ordinarily, however, modification should not be granted where a party relies upon events that actually were anticipated at the time it entered into a decree . . . If it is clear that a party anticipated changing conditions that would make performance of the decree more onerous but nevertheless agreed to the decree, that party would have to satisfy a heavy burden to convince a court that it agreed to the decree in good faith, made a reasonable effort to comply with the decree and should be relieved of the undertaking under Rule 60(b)."

CASE SIGNIFICANCE: This is a significant case in prison litigation because it addresses an issue that faces many jurisdictions: May a consent decree (a consent decree is an agreement arrived at by the two sides in a case and presented to the judge for approval), once entered, be modified by the parties and, if so, under what conditions?

A consent decree is an approach used by numerous courts to settle disputes in litigation involving prisons and jails. It allows the parties to come together and agree among themselves on conditions for settlement, after which the agreement is presented as a document to the court for approval. Consent decrees have the advantage of arriving at the solution after negotiation by both parties, instead of the solution being imposed on one or both parties by the judge. As the term implies, a consent decree is an agreement acceptable to both parties.

There are instances, however, in which one of the parties desires changes for various reasons. In this case, the sheriff sought modification of the consent decree while construction was still under way to allow double bunking in order to increase the jail's capacity. His reason was that the inmate population had outpaced population projections, and the single-occupancy cell requirement for pretrial detainees under the consent decree had become difficult for the county to meet. The District Court denied modification, saying that the county failed to demonstrate a "grievous wrong evoked by new or unforeseen conditions." This standard was enunciated by the Court in *United States v. Swift & Co.*, 286 U.S. 106 (1932) and, according to the Court, was codified by Rule 60(b)(5) of the Federal Rules of Civil Procedure, the section of law relied upon by the sheriff. The Court disagreed with this strict standard set by the District Court, holding that the "grievous wrong" test does not apply to consent decrees involving institutional reform litigation, such as prison cases. The Court opted for a less stringent and more flexible standard (easier for the government to establish), which states that modification may be allowed under the following conditions: (1) when changed factual conditions make compliance with the decree substantially more onerous; (2) when the decree proves to be unworkable because of unforeseen obstacles; or (3) when enforcement of the decree without modification would be detrimental to the public interest. Under this standard, "the party seeking modification of the consent decree (in this case the sheriff of Suffolk County) bears the burden of establishing that a significant change in facts or law warrants revision of the decree and that the proposed modification is suitably tailored to the changed circumstances."

The new standard set by the Court in this case makes it easier for prison and jail authorities to modify consent decrees as long as any of the three conditions set by the Court above are present. The effect of this decision on prison cases may be two-edged. On the one hand, prison authorities may be more willing to settle cases through consent decrees, knowing that the agreement entered into may be modified later. Conversely, however, they may be tempted to enter into a consent decree without giving much serious thought to the consequences, knowing that the institution can later go back to the court for modification. It makes the provisions of a consent decree more flexible, but less certain.

F. COURT ACCESS

EX PARTE HULL
312 U.S. 546 (1941)

CAPSULE: A state and its officers cannot abridge or impair a prisoner's right, given by federal law, to apply for a federal writ of habeas corpus.

FACTS: Hull was convicted of a sex offense and incarcerated in the Michigan State Prison in Jackson, Michigan. He was later paroled, but then returned to prison because he was convicted of a new sex offense. He prepared a petition for a writ of habeas corpus and exhibits to file before the U.S. Supreme Court. He took the papers to a prison official and asked him to notarize them. Instead, the official advised the inmate that the papers and a registered letter to the clerk of the court would not be accepted for mailing. Hull attempted to mail them by giving them to his father, but the correctional officers confiscated them. Several days later Hull again attempted to mail a letter concerning his case to the clerk of the U.S. Supreme Court but the letter was intercepted and sent to the investigator for the state parole board.

Hull prepared another document that his father filed with the clerk of the U.S. Supreme Court. The document detailed his efforts to file the confiscated papers. He contended that he was unlawfully restrained and requested release from the prison. Prison officials cited a regulation that stated that all legal documents had to be submitted to the institutional welfare office and then to a legal investigator for the parole board before they could be forwarded to the court.

ISSUE: Is a prison regulation that requires a petition for a writ of habeas corpus to be submitted to the institutional welfare office and then to a legal investigator for the parole board valid? NO.

HOLDING: A state and its officers cannot abridge or impair a prisoner's right, given by federal law, to apply for a writ of habeas corpus.

REASON: "The regulation is invalid. The considerations that prompted its formulations are not without merit, but the state and its officers may not abridge or impair petitioner's right to apply to a federal court for a writ of habeas corpus. Whether a petition for writ of habeas corpus addressed to a federal court is properly drawn and what allegations it must contain are questions for that court alone to determine.

"However, the invalidity of the prison regulation does not compel petitioner's release. For that reason it is necessary to examine the petition annexed to the response . . . the next question, therefore, is whether the petition is premature. The petition is not premature . . . There is no reason to suppose that he can compel the parole board to review the record of the second conviction, or to make a declaratory ruling that if that conviction is void his parole will be reinstated."

CASE SIGNIFICANCE: Most writers consider this case as the first major case decided by the United States Supreme Court on prison law. This case is significant as a trail-blazer of prisoners' rights. Decided in 1941, there is no other case of significance preceding it in the United States Supreme Court, although there were other cases involving prisoners in lower courts. This decision indicates that even in the 1940s, when the American public was unconcerned about rights of prisoners, the Court established a principle giving prisoners right of access to the court.

A writ of habeas corpus is a post-conviction proceeding that gives an offender access to court even after the appeals process has been exhausted and the offender has started serving his or her sentence. It is a way in which prisoners gain access to court despite a final conviction. In this case, the State of Michigan imposed a limitation on a prisoner's habeas corpus access by requiring that all legal documents be submitted to the institutional welfare office and then to a legal investigator for the parole board before they could be forwarded to the court. This regulation was declared unconstitutional because it impaired a prisoner's access to courts through the use of this remedy.

UNITED STATES V. MUNIZ
374 U.S. 150 (1963)

CAPSULE: Federal prisoners are entitled to sue prison officials under the Federal Tort Claims Act for negligent acts resulting in personal injury.

FACTS: Winston, a prisoner in a U.S. Penitentiary, suffered loss of balance, dizziness, and vision problems. Treatment by the medical staff at the penitentiary was inadequate or nonexistent and the inmate eventually was diagnosed with a benign brain tumor. Surgery removed the tumor but Winston went blind. He sued prison officials under the Federal Tort Claims Act.

Muniz was a prisoner in a federal correctional institution when he was attacked by 12 other inmates. A correctional officer, witnessing the beginning of the attack, locked the dormitory door to confine the altercation. Muniz suffered a fractured skull and the loss of vision in his right eye as a result of the attack. He sued under the Federal Tort Claims Act, alleging that prison officials were negligent due to inadequate correctional officer numbers to prevent attacks, and by allowing mentally ill inmates to associate with other inmates without adequate supervision.

The two cases were combined into a single case. The district court granted the U.S. government's motion to dismiss on the ground that these suits were not permitted under the Federal Tort Claims Act. The Second Circuit Court of Appeals reversed the decision of the lower court. The Supreme Court granted certiorari due to the importance of the issue and disagreement among the circuit courts concerning this issue.

ISSUE: Can an inmate sue prison officials under the Federal Tort Claims Act for personal injuries due to employee negligence? YES.

HOLDING: Federal inmates who sustain injuries while imprisoned may sue under the Federal Tort Claims Act.

REASON: "An examination of the legislative history of the Act reinforces our conclusion that Congress intended to permit such suits. For a number of reasons, it appears that Congress was well aware of claims by federal prisoners and that its failure to exclude them from the provisions of the Act in 28 U.S.C. § 2680 was deliberate . . . Private claim bills introduced in the Sixty-eighth through the Seventy-eighth Congresses averaged 2,000 or more per Congress . . . Among the private claim bills were a number submitted on behalf of federal prisoners . . . In these circumstances it cannot be assumed that Congress was unaware of their presence."

"A second indication that Congress was conscious of claims by federal prisoners is found in the prior versions of the Act . . . Six of the 31 bills introduced in Congress between 1925 and 1946 either barred prisoners from suing while in federal prison or precluded suit upon any claim for injury to or death of a prisoner. That such an exception was absent from the Act itself is significant in view of the consistent course of development of the bills proposed over the years and the marked reliance by each succeeding Congress upon the language of the earlier bills. We therefore feel that the want of an exception for prisoners' claims reflects a deliberate choice, rather than an inadvertent omission."

CASE SIGNIFICANCE: This is one of the earliest cases on prison law and is important only to prisoners in federal prisons. The issue was whether federal prisoners who suffer injuries may sue under the Federal Tort Claims Act. The FTCA allows private individuals injured by federal agents to sue and recover monetary damages from the federal government. The prison officials in this case argued that the FTCA excluded inmates from suing. The Court disagreed, saying that there were strong indications that Congress, when it passed the law, considered this issue and decided to allow prisoners to sue. The Court noted that the fact that prisoners were not among those specifically excluded by the law from suing meant that Congress allowed prisoners to sue. Note, however, that this case involved federal, not state, prisoners. Most states, however, also have tort claims laws that allow prisoners to sue.

COOPER V. PATE
378 U.S. 546 (1964)

CAPSULE: An inmate can sue for relief under 42 U.S.C. § 1983 if he alleges punishment for requesting religious materials.

FACTS: Cooper was incarcerated in the State Penitentiary in Illinois. He brought suit under 28 U.S.C. § 1343 and 42 U.S.C. §§ 1983 and 1979 against prison officials for placing him in solitary confinement when he requested a copy of the Koran and Arabic and Swahili language books to translate it. Prison officials denied this request because they considered the Black Muslim Movement to be a source of problems in the prison. They stated that the Movement had a history of inciting riots and violence.

Cooper's suit was dismissed in District Court on the ground that he failed to state a claim upon which relief could be granted. He appealed to the Seventh Circuit Court of Appeals, which upheld the decision of the lower court, stating that it was the proper ruling. Cooper then appealed to the U.S. Supreme Court.

ISSUE: Did the prisoner have a valid claim for relief in his allegation that he was punished for requesting religious material? YES.

HOLDING: The allegations of the complaint must be taken as true on a motion to dismiss and therefore the prisoner had a cause of action.

REASON: "We reverse the judgment below. Taking as true the allegations of the complaint, as they must be on a motion to dismiss, the complaint stated a cause of action and it was error to dismiss it."

CASE SIGNIFICANCE: This is one of the earliest prison cases decided by the Court. It recognized the use of the provision of 42 U.S.C. § 1983, a federal law, as a legal remedy for violations of prisoners' rights. A § 1983 lawsuit is filed in federal court by anyone seeking damages because a public officer violated his or her constitutional rights while acting under state law. § 1983 actions have been available since 1871, but this is the first known case in which the Court approved its use by prisoners alleging violation of a constitutional right. In this case the prisoner claimed that his constitutional right to freedom of religion was violated when he was placed in solitary confinement after requesting a copy of the Koran and Arabic and Swahili language books he wanted to translate. Prison officials denied his request because they considered the Black Muslim Movement a source of problems in prison. The Court held that, assuming the allegation to be true, the prisoner was entitled to relief and could use § 1983.

JOHNSON V. AVERY
393 U.S. 483 (1969)

CAPSULE: Prison authorities cannot prohibit prisoners from helping other prisoners prepare legal writs unless they provide reasonable alternatives by which inmates can have access to the courts.

FACTS: Johnson, a Tennessee state prisoner, was transferred to the maximum-security building in the state prison because he assisted other prisoners in preparing writs, in violation of a prison regulation that provided: "no inmate will advise, assist or otherwise contract to aid another, either with or without a fee, to prepare writs or other legal matters." He filed a motion for relief from confinement in the maximum-security building. The District Court held the prison regulation void because it effectively barred illiterate prisoners from access to federal habeas corpus. The prisoner was released from maximum security but was not given regular prison privileges or restored to normal prison conditions until he promised to refrain from assisting other inmates. Another hearing was held before the District Court concerning compliance with the conditions of the original order and this same order was reaffirmed. The Court of Appeals reversed, holding that the State's interest in preserving discipline and limiting the practice of law to attorneys justified any burden the regulation could place on access to federal habeas corpus.

ISSUE: May the state validly enforce a regulation that prohibits prisoners from assisting other prisoners in preparing writs? NO, but with exception.

HOLDING: The State of Tennessee cannot enforce a regulation that absolutely bars inmates from furnishing assistance to other prisoners in the preparation of petitions for post-conviction relief in the absence of a provision by the state for a reasonable alternative to assist illiterate or poorly educated inmates in such preparation.

REASON: "It is indisputable that prison 'writ writers' like petitioner are sometimes a menace to prison discipline and that their petitions are often so unskillful as to be a burden on the courts which receive them. But, as this Court held in *Ex parte Hull*, in declaring invalid a state prison regulation which required that prisoners' legal pleadings be screened by state officials:

The considerations that prompted [the regulation's] formulation are not without merit, but the state and its officers may not abridge or impair petitioner's right to apply to a federal court for a writ of habeas corpus. 312 U.S., at 549.

"Tennessee does not provide an available alternative to the assistance provided by other inmates. The warden of the prison in which petitioner was confined stated that the prison provided free notarization of prisoners' petitions. That obviously meets only a formal requirement. He also indicated that he sometimes allowed prisoners to examine the listing of attorneys in the Nashville telephone directory so they could select one to write to in an effort to interest him in taking the case, and that 'on several occasions' he had contacted the public defender on the request of an inmate. There is no contention, however, that there is any regular system of assistance by public defenders. In its brief the State contends that '[t]here is absolutely no reason to believe that prison officials would fail to notify the court should an inmate advise them of a complete inability, either mental or physical, to prepare a habeas application on his own behalf,' but there is no contention that they have in fact ever done so.

"This is obviously far short of the showing required to demonstrate that, in depriving prisoners of the assistance of fellow inmates, Tennessee has not, in substance, deprived those unable themselves, with reasonable adequacy, to prepare their petitions, of access to the constitutionally and statutorily protected availability of the writ of habeas corpus."

CASE SIGNIFICANCE: This was one of the first major prison cases to be decided by the Court involving an alleged violation of a constitutional right—the right of access to the courts. The State of Tennessee prohibited inmates from helping other inmates in legal matters for fear that doing so would jeopardize prison security and order. Because the offending inmate was placed in solitary confinement as a result of rule violation, the trial court treated the case as a petition for a writ of habeas corpus instead of a § 1983 case.

The Court agreed that prison "writ writers" sometimes constitute a menace to prison discipline and impose a burden on the courts because of their unlawyerly petitions. The Court declared the regulation invalid anyway because Tennessee did not provide an alternative to the assistance provided by prison "writ writers." Stated conversely, prison authorities may prohibit inmates from helping other inmates on legal matters as long as the prison authorities provide reasonable alternative assistance. The question then arises: what types of assistance are reasonable to the Court so as to justify the prohibition against inmate writ writers?

In this decision, the Court enumerated several systems used in other states, including: (1) a public defender system supplying trained attorneys, paid from public funds, who are available to consult with prisoners regarding their habeas corpus petitions; (2) employing senior law students to interview and advise inmates in state prisons; and (3) voluntary programs whereby members of the local bar association make periodic visits to the prison to consult with prisoners concerning their cases. Significantly, however, the Court then added that:

"We express no judgment concerning these plans, but their existence indicates that techniques are available to provide alternatives if the State elects to prohibit mutual assistance among inmates." The Court made clear, however, that Tennessee's system of free notarization of prisoners' petitions, allowing prisoners to examine the listing of attorneys in the Nashville telephone directory so they could select one to write to in an effort to interest him to take the case, and occasionally contacting the public defender at the request of the inmate did not constitute a reasonable alternative.

Subsequent lower court cases have shown that courts have not done a good job of defining what a "reasonable alternative" means. In reality, it is difficult for prison systems to prohibit writ writers from helping other inmates in prison because no court has stated clearly when that "reasonable alternative" requirement is satisfied. Therefore, most prisons in the United States today allow inmates to assist other inmates on legal matters even if the prison system itself provides a law library, access to lawyers, or has full-time lawyers in its staff assisting inmates on legal matters.

G. COUNSEL

UNITED STATES V. GOUVEIA
467 U.S. 180 (1984)

CAPSULE: Inmates in administrative segregation (as distinguished from those in punitive segregation) are not entitled to counsel prior to the initiation of judicial proceedings.

FACTS: Four inmates, including Gouveia, were suspected of murdering a fellow inmate at a federal prison in Lompoc, California. They were placed in the Administrative Detention Unit (ADU) in early December 1978. Later that month, prison officials held disciplinary hearings and determined that all four of the inmates had participated in the murder. Officials ordered their continued confinement in ADU, where the inmates were separated from the general prison population and confined to individual cells. However, they were allowed regular visitation rights, exercise periods, unmonitored phone calls, and access to legal materials.

The inmates remained in the ADU without appointed counsel for approximately 19 months. In June 1980, a federal grand jury returned indictments against them on charges of first-degree murder and conspiracy to commit murder. They were arraigned in federal court in July 1980, at which time counsel was appointed for them. All four of the inmates were subsequently convicted of both counts and were sentenced to consecutive life and 99-year terms of imprisonment.

Before the trial began, the inmates filed a motion to have their indictments dismissed, claiming that their confinement in the ADU without appointed counsel violated their Sixth Amendment right to counsel.

ISSUE: Does the Sixth Amendment require the appointment of counsel before indictment for indigent inmates confined in administrative detention while being investigated for criminal activities? NO.

HOLDING: Inmates are not constitutionally entitled to the appointment of counsel while in administrative segregation and before any adversary judicial proceedings have been initiated against them. The right to counsel attaches only at or after the initiation of judicial proceedings against the defendant.

REASON: "The Court of Appeals majority held that each respondent had been denied his Sixth Amendment right to counsel . . . Five judges dissented from the en banc majority's Sixth Amendment holding. Relying on *Kirby v. Illinois*, *supra*, the dissent concluded that the Sixth Amendment right to counsel is triggered by the initiation of formal criminal proceedings even in the prison context, and that the majority's conclusion to the contrary shows a misunderstanding of the purpose of the counsel guarantee. We agree with the dissenting judges' application of our precedents to this situation, and, accordingly, we reverse the en banc majority's holding that respondents had a Sixth Amendment right to the appointment of counsel during their pre-indictment segregation.

"The view that the right to counsel does not attach until the initiation of adversary judicial proceedings has been confirmed by this court in cases subsequent to *Kirby* . . . that interpretation of the Sixth Amendment right to counsel is consistent not only with the literal language of the Amendment, which requires the existence of both a 'criminal prosecutio[n]' and an 'accused,' but also with the purposes which we have recognized that the right to counsel serves. We have recognized that the 'core purpose' of the counsel guarantee is to assure aid at trial, 'when the accused [is] confronted with both the intricacies of the law and the advocacy of the public prosecutor.'

"Thus, the majority's [Court of Appeal's] attempt to draw an analogy between an arrest and an inmate's administrative detention pending investigation may have some relevance in analyzing when the speedy trial right attaches in this context, but it is not relevant to a proper determination of when the right to counsel attaches."

CASE SIGNIFICANCE: In this case, the Court clarified the limits of the right to counsel for incarcerated prisoners. The Court interpreted the Sixth Amendment to mean that the right to counsel should be invoked only after an indictment and not while a criminal investigation is being conducted, even if the inmate is in administrative segregation at that time. This decision was expected; in fact, a different decision would have been surprising. This is because in an earlier case, *Kirby v. Illinois*, 406 U.S. 682 (1972), the Court held that a suspect has no right to counsel at police lineups or identification procedures prior to the time the suspect is formally charged with a crime. Certainly, inmates do not have more rights than people in the free world, including the right to counsel.

MURRAY V. GIARRATANO
492 U.S. 1 (1989)

CAPSULE: States are not required by the Constitution to provide inmates with a lawyer in post-conviction (meaning after appeal, as in habeas corpus) proceedings even in death penalty cases.

FACTS: Giarratano was a Virginia prisoner under sentence of death. He brought suit under 42 U.S.C. § 1983 against various state officials, including Edward W. Murray, the Director of the Virginia Department of Corrections. Inmate Giarratano claimed that the Constitution required that he be provided with counsel, at state expense, to pursue collateral proceedings (meaning proceedings taken after the appeal on the conviction has been exhausted, such as a habeas corpus) related to his conviction and death sentence.

ISSUE: Does the Eighth Amendment or the due process clause of the Fourteenth Amendment require states to appoint counsel for indigent death row inmates seeking post-conviction relief? NO.

HOLDING: The rule in *Pennsylvania v. Finley*, 481 U.S. 551 (1987), which states that the Constitution does not require states to provide counsel in post-conviction proceedings, applies to capital as well as non-capital cases.

REASON: "In *Finley* we ruled that neither the due process clause of the Fourteenth Amendment nor the equal protection guarantee of 'meaningful access' required the State to appoint counsel for indigent prisoners seeking state post-conviction relief. The Sixth and Fourteenth Amendments to the Constitution assure the right of an indigent defendant to counsel at the trial stage of a criminal proceeding, *Gideon v. Wainwright*, 372 U.S. 335, 83 S. Ct. 792, 9 L. Ed. 2d 799 (1963), and an indigent defendant is similarly entitled as a matter of right to counsel for an initial appeal from the judgment and sentence of the trial court. But we held in *Ross v. Moffitt, supra*, 417 U.S., at 610, 94 S. Ct., at 2443, that the right to counsel at these earlier stages of a criminal procedure did not carry over to a discretionary appeal provided by North Carolina law from the intermediate appellate court to the Supreme Court of North Carolina.

"We think that these cases require the conclusion that the rule of *Pennsylvania v. Finley* should apply no differently in capital cases than noncapital cases. State collateral proceedings are not constitutionally required as an adjunct to the state criminal proceedings and serve a different and more limited purpose than either the trial or appeal. The additional safeguards imposed by the Eighth Amendment at the trial stage of a capital case are, we think, sufficient to assure the reliability of the process by which the death penalty is imposed. We therefore decline to read either the Eighth Amendment or the due process clause to require yet another distinction between the rights of capital case defendants and those in non-capital cases."

CASE SIGNIFICANCE: The significance of this case lies in the Court's holding that an indigent death-row inmate is not entitled to appointed counsel when seeking post-conviction relief even in death penalty cases. The decision is in accordance with the *Finley* decision of 1987, which held that neither the due process clause nor the equal protection clause of the Fourteenth Amendment requires the state to appoint counsel for indigent prisoners seeking post-conviction relief. The Supreme Court noted, however, that death row inmates are entitled to adequate and timely access to a law library during the final weeks before their execution dates. Note that while a death row inmate is not entitled under the Constitution to a court-appointed lawyer in post-conviction proceedings, a lawyer is in fact often provided in these cases by state or federal law. It must also be noted that defendants in death penalty cases are constitutionally entitled to a lawyer during trial and during the appeal of a conviction.

BOUNDS V. SMITH
430 U.S. 817 (1977)

CAPSULE: Prison authorities are required to assist inmates by providing meaningful access to the courts.

FACTS: State prison inmates brought actions in federal court alleging that the state of North Carolina denied them reasonable access to the courts and equal protection as guaranteed by the First and Fourteenth Amendments, by failing to provide them with adequate law library facilities. The actions were consolidated and the District Court granted the inmates' motion for summary judgment, which was modified and affirmed by the Court of Appeals. The court found that the sole prison library in the state was inadequate, especially in view of the decentralized prison system in which 13,000 inmates were housed in 77 prison units in 67 counties. The state proposed a plan to establish seven libraries in the institutions to which the inmates could request appointments where they would be given transportation and housing for a full day's library work. The inmates sought establishment of a library at every prison.

ISSUE: Does the constitutional right of access to the courts require prison authorities to assist inmates in the preparation and filing of meaningful legal papers by providing prisoners with adequate law libraries or adequate assistance from persons trained in the law? YES.

HOLDING: The constitutional right of access to the courts requires prison authorities to assist inmates in the preparation and filing of meaningful legal papers by providing prisoners with adequate law libraries or adequate assistance from persons trained in the law. Adequate law libraries in prisons are one constitutionally acceptable method of assuring meaningful access to the courts, but they are not the only acceptable alternative for providing such access. Any alternatives used, however, must comply with constitutional standards.

REASON: "It is now established beyond doubt that prisoners have a constitutional right of access to the courts . . . While applications for discretionary review need only apprise an appellate court of a case's possible relevance to the development of the law, the prisoner petitions here are the first line of defense against constitutional violations. The need for new legal research or advice to make a meaningful initial presentation to a trial court in such a case is far greater than is required to file an adequate petition for discretionary review. We hold, therefore, that the fundamental constitutional right of access to the courts requires prison authorities to assist inmates in the preparation and filing of meaningful legal papers by providing prisoners with adequate law libraries or adequate assistance from persons trained in law.

"It should be noted that while adequate law libraries are one constitutionally acceptable method to assure meaningful access to the courts, our decision here, as in *Gilmore*, does not foreclose alternative means to achieve that goal . . . Among the alternatives are the training of inmates as paralegal assistants to work under lawyers' supervision, the use of paraprofessionals and law students, either as volunteers or in formal clinical programs, the organization of volunteer attorneys through bar associations or other groups, the hiring of lawyers on a part-time basis, and the use of full-time staff attorneys, working either in new prison legal assistance organizations or as part of public defender or legal services offices."

CASE SIGNIFICANCE: This case is important because it reaffirms the constitutional right of prisoners to meaningful access to the courts. This is in accordance with the previous cases of prisoners' access to the courts, including *Johnson v. Avery* (393 U.S. 483 [1969]) and *Younger v. Gilmore* (404 U.S. 15 [1971]). The *Avery* case concerned access to the courts through legal assistance from other inmates. The *Gilmore* case also dealt with the state's responsibility to furnish inmates with extensive law libraries or to provide them with professional or quasi-professional legal assistance.

The Bounds case lists possible alternatives that prisons can use for complying with the duty to provide access to the courts. These are: (1) training inmates as paralegal assistants to work under lawyers' supervision; (2) using paraprofessionals and law students as volunteers or in formal clinical programs; (3) organizing volunteer attorneys through bar associations or in other groups; (4) hiring lawyers on a part-time consultant basis; and (5) using full-time staff attorneys in new prison legal assistance organizations or as part of the public defender or legal services offices. Moreover, the Court said that indigent inmates must be provided, at state expense, with writing materials (paper and pen) to draft legal documents, with notarial services to authenticate them, and with stamps to mail them. This case expands the list of possible alternatives to court access mentioned in *Johnson v. Avery*, but goes beyond that by requiring prisons to provide items, such as paper and pen, to ensure that inmates can have access to the courts.

It must be noted by the reader, however, that the *Bounds* case, decided in 1977, was reinterpreted by the Court in the case of *Lewis v. Casey*, 518 U.S. 343 (1996), the next case.

LEWIS V. CASEY
518 U.S. 343 (1996)

CAPSULE: The constitutional right of court access is violated only if a prisoner's attempt to pursue a legal claim is actually hindered by prison officials. Inadequacies in a state's delivery of legal services to inmates is not sufficient as a basis for such a claim. What is needed is showing of widespread actual injury.

FACTS: Casey and other inmates of various prisons operated by the Arizona Department of Corrections (ADOC) brought a class action suit against prison officials in Arizona. The lawsuit alleged violation of the First, Sixth, and Fourteenth Amendments by the officials, depriving the inmates of their rights of access to the courts and counsel through inadequate legal research facilities. The inmates alleged that this deprivation violated the ruling in *Bounds v. Smith*, which was decided 19 years before this case. The Bounds case held that the right of access to the courts requires that prison authorities assist inmates in the preparation and filing of meaningful legal papers by providing them with adequate law libraries or adequate assistance from persons trained in the law.

ISSUE: Did the inadequacies in the legal research facilities and the legal services provided by Arizona violate the constitutional rights of inmates in the absence of proof of actual injury? NO.

HOLDING:

1. Theoretical deficiencies in the prison's law library or legal assistance programs are not sufficient to establish a violation of the right of access to court. What is needed is a showing of widespread actual injury.

2. *Bounds v. Smith* did not create a right to a law library or legal assistance; instead, it merely acknowledged a right to court access.

REASON: "Because *Bounds* did not create an abstract, free-standing right to a law library or legal assistance, an inmate cannot establish relevant actual injury simply by establishing that his prison's law library or legal assistance program is sub-par in some theoretical sense . . . the inmate therefore must go one step further and demonstrate that the alleged shortcomings in the library or legal assistance program hindered his efforts to pursue a legal claim . . . Although *Bounds* itself made no mention of an actual-injury requirement, it can hardly be thought to have eliminated that constitutional prerequisite.

"After the trial in this case, the court found actual injury on the part of only one named plaintiff, Bartholic; and the cause of that injury—the inadequacy which the suit empowered the court to remedy—was failure of the prison to provide the special services that Bartholic would have needed, in light of his illiteracy, to avoid dismissal of his case. At the outset, therefore, we can eliminate from the proper scope of this injunction provisions directed at special services or special facilities required by non-English-speakers, by prisoners in lockdown, and by the inmate population at large.

"The District Court here failed to accord adequate deference to the judgment of the prison authorities in at least three significant respects. First, in concluding that ADOC's restrictions on lockdown prisoners' access to law libraries was unjustified ... Second, the injunction imposed by the District Court was inordinately—indeed, wildly—intrusive ... Finally, the order was developed through a process that failed to give adequate consideration to the views of state prison authorities."

CASE SIGNIFICANCE: This is a significant case because it clarifies the extent of an inmate's right of access to court. The inmates in this case alleged constitutional violations because the Arizona system of providing legal help to inmates disadvantaged some inmates, particularly non-English-speaking inmates or those confined in segregation units. The trial court agreed with the inmates and issued an order, applicable throughout the Arizona prison system, mandating that segregated inmates be allowed library access and that legal assistance be provided to inmates lacking reading or English language skills. This order was made despite the absence of a finding by the trial court that the plaintiffs suffered actual injury.

The Court overturned the trial court's system-wide order for relief, saying that there must be proof that the prison officials actually hindered a prisoner's access to court, thus actually injuring that inmate, before relief can be granted. General inadequacies in a state's system of delivery of legal services are insufficient for such claim and cannot be the basis for system-wide relief. Neither are they a violation of constitutional rights.

The Court made clear that *Bounds v. Smith*, decided 19 years earlier, "did not create an abstract, free-standing right to a law library or legal assistance; rather the right that *Bounds* acknowledged was the right of access to the courts." This is significant because prior to *Lewis*, courts throughout the country interpreted *Bounds* to mean that prisons were constitutionally obliged to have law libraries as part of their prisoners' right of access to court. This involved huge expenses for the acquisition and maintenance of law libraries in jails and prisons. This case rejects that interpretation and plainly states that what *Bounds* created was merely the right of access to the courts, which is a much broader right that can include the right to a law library. Whether prison systems will now discontinue the practice of having prison libraries remains to be seen. What is clear is that in this decision the Court has held that access to court is a constitutional right in prisons, but that the right to a law library is not.

MCFARLAND V. SCOTT
512 U.S. 849 (1994)

CAPSULE: Federal law requires that an indigent capital offender be given a lawyer even before a habeas petition is filed. Under that law, a federal district court has the authority to stay an execution as soon as the inmate asks for a lawyer to be able to file a habeas petition.

FACTS: McFarland was convicted of capital murder and sentenced to death. His conviction and sentence were affirmed by the Texas Court of Criminal Appeals.

The inmate filed a pro se (on his own) motion requesting the trial court stay or withdraw his execution date to allow the Texas Resource Center an opportunity to recruit volunteer counsel for his state habeas corpus proceeding. The trial court declined to appoint counsel but did change the inmate's execution date to a later date. Upon learning that the Resource Center could not find volunteer counsel, the court concluded that Texas law did not authorize the appointment of counsel for state habeas corpus proceedings and it did not do so. McFarland then filed a pro se motion in the Texas Court of Criminal Appeals requesting a stay of execution and a remand for counsel. The motion was denied. The inmate then filed a pro se motion in the U.S. District Court challenging his conviction and sentence under federal law and requesting appointment of counsel, also under federal law.

ISSUE: Does federal law authorize the federal court to appoint counsel and stay state execution proceedings as soon as the inmate seeks appointment of counsel and even before a formal application for federal habeas corpus relief has been filed? YES.

HOLDING: Federal law provides that an indigent death row inmate be given counsel before a habeas corpus petition is filed and as soon as the inmate seeks appointment of counsel. This should be done even before a formal application for federal habeas corpus relief has been filed. Moreover, a federal district court has the authority to stay an execution date as soon as the inmate asks for counsel to be able to file a habeas corpus petition.

REASON: "Construing Section 848(q)(4)(B) in light of its related provisions, however, indicates that the right to appointed counsel adheres prior to the filing of a formal, legally sufficient habeas corpus petition. Section 848(q)(4)(B) expressly incorporates 21 U.S.C. Section 848(q)(9), which entitles capital defendants to a variety of expert and investigative services upon a showing of necessity . . . Section 848(q)(9) clearly anticipates that capital defense counsel will have been appointed under Section 848(q)(4)(B) before the need for such technical assistance arises, since the statute requires 'the defendant's attorneys to obtain such services' from the court . . . Congress thus established a right to preapplication legal assistance for capital defendants in federal habeas corpus proceedings . . . This interpretation is the only one that gives meaning to the statute as a practical matter.

"We thus conclude that the two statutes [federal statutes] must be read in pari materia to provide that once a capital defendant invokes his right to appointed counsel, a federal court also has jurisdiction under Section 2251 to enter a stay of execution. Because Section 2251 expressly authorizes federal courts to stay state court proceedings 'for any matter involved in the habeas corpus proceeding,' the exercise of this authority is not barred by the Anti-Injunction Act.

"We conclude that a capital defendant may invoke this right to counseled federal habeas corpus proceeding by filing a motion requesting the appointment of habeas counsel, and that a district court has jurisdiction to enter a stay of execution where necessary to give effect to the statutory right. McFarland filed a motion for appointment of counsel and for stay of execution in this case, and the District Court had authority to grant the relief he sought."

CASE SIGNIFICANCE: This decision is based on the provisions of federal law rather than on the Constitution. Relying on federal law, the inmate sought the appointment of counsel to help him file a habeas corpus petition. Such filing, the Court said, qualifies as the initiation of a habeas corpus proceeding and therefore entitled the inmate to counsel. Moreover, the filing of such a request authorized the court to stay the prisoner's execution.

Inmates do not have a constitutional right to a lawyer in post-conviction (such as habeas corpus) proceedings. Title 21 U.S.C. § 848(q)(4)(B), however, entitles capital defendants to "qualified legal representation in any post-conviction proceeding." This was the law used by the inmate in this case.

Although inmates do not have a constitutional right to counsel in post-conviction proceedings, such right has been given by federal law and, in some cases, also by state law. The realization is that a lawyer is necessary not only during appeal, but also during the filing of a post-conviction case after an appeal has been exhausted. This is particularly true in death penalty cases such as this.

MARTINEZ V. RYAN, DIRECTOR, ARIZONA DEPT. OF CORRECTIONS
132 S. CT. 1309 (2012)

CAPSULE: A procedural default does not bar a federal habeas corpus court from hearing ineffective assistance of trial counsel claims if there was no counsel or ineffective assistance of counsel in the initial review collateral proceeding. Whether ineffective assistance of counsel occurred in the trial or the initial collateral proceeding in this case will be decided on remand.

FACTS: Martinez was convicted of two counts of sexual conduct with a minor under the age of 15. The court appointed him an attorney for the trial and another attorney for his appeal. His appellate attorney began a direct appeal based on insufficient evidence to convict and newly discovered evidence that warranted a new trial. Arizona does not allow an appeal claiming ineffective assistance of counsel to be made on direct appeal, but instead it can be made in state collateral proceedings. Martinez's appellate attorney filed a collateral appeal but did not assert ineffective assistance of counsel at trial. She later filed a statement that she could not find any colorable claims in the case. The appellate court allowed Martinez 45 days to file an appeal himself, seeking collateral relief. He later claimed that he was not aware of this option and that his attorney didn't communicate this to him. The Arizona intermediate court of appeals affirmed his conviction, and the Arizona Supreme Court denied review of his case.

Approximately a year and a half later, Martinez filed another appeal for post-conviction relief with a third attorney. He claimed that he had ineffective assistance of counsel at trial, citing several instances where this occurred. The appellate court denied his appeal, partly because Arizona had a rule that barred relief on an issue that could have been raised in a previous collateral appeal. The intermediate court of appeals (the Arizona Court of Appeals) agreed, and the Arizona Supreme Court denied review. Martinez then filed a writ of habeas corpus with the federal district court, raising the issue of ineffective assistance of counsel during his trial. He acknowledged the error with the state courts, which would have prevented an appeal in federal court under the doctrine of procedural default. However, the petitioner argued that his post-conviction attorney was also ineffective in not raising any claims in the collateral appeal and not notifying him of her actions. The federal district court denied his appeal, citing the Arizona rule and the Ninth Circuit Court of Appeals affirmed.

ISSUE: Does inadequate counsel at an initial review collateral proceeding establish a cause for an inmate's procedural default of a claim of ineffective trial counsel? YES.

HOLDING: A procedural default will not bar a federal habeas corpus court from hearing a claim of ineffective assistance of counsel at trial if there was no counsel or counsel was ineffective in the initial collateral proceeding at the state level, which required the issue to be properly presented at that time.

REASON: "To protect prisoners with a potentially legitimate claim of ineffective assistance of trial counsel, it is necessary to modify the unqualified statement in *Coleman* that an attorney's ignorance or inadvertence in a postconviction proceeding does not qualify as cause to excuse a procedural default. This opinion qualifies *Coleman* by recognizing a narrow exception: Inadequate assistance of counsel at initial-review collateral proceedings may establish cause for a prisoner's procedural default of a claim of ineffective assistance at trial . . . Federal habeas courts reviewing the constitutionality of a state prisoner's conviction and sentence are guided by rules designed to ensure that state-court judgments are accorded the finality and respect necessary to preserve the integrity of legal proceedings within our system of federalism. These rules include the doctrine of procedural default, under which a federal court will not review the merits of claims, including constitutional claims, that a state court declined to hear because the prisoner failed to abide by a state procedural rule . . . The doctrine barring procedurally defaulted claims from being heard is not without exceptions. A prisoner may obtain federal review of a defaulted claim by showing cause for the default and prejudice from a violation of federal law. See *Coleman*, 501 U.S., at 750. There is no dispute that Arizona's procedural bar on successive petitions is an independent and adequate state ground. Thus, a federal court can hear Martinez's ineffective-assistance claim only if he can establish cause to excuse the procedural default."

"Allowing a federal habeas court to hear a claim of ineffective assistance of trial counsel when an attorney's errors (or the absence of an attorney) caused a procedural default in an initial-review collateral proceeding acknowledges, as an equitable matter, that the initial-review collateral proceeding, if undertaken without counsel or with ineffective counsel, may not have been sufficient to ensure that proper consideration was given to a substantial claim. From this it follows that, when a State requires a prisoner to raise an ineffective-assistance-of-trial-counsel claim in a collateral proceeding, a prisoner may establish cause for a default of an ineffective-assistance claim in two circumstances. The first is where the state courts did not appoint counsel in the initial-review collateral proceeding for a claim of ineffective assistance at trial. The second is where appointed counsel in the initial-review collateral proceeding, where the claim should have been raised, was ineffective under the standards of *Strickland v. Washington*, 466 U.S. 668 (1984). To overcome the default, a prisoner must also demonstrate that the underlying ineffective-assistance-of-trial-counsel claim is a substantial one, which is to say that the prisoner must demonstrate that the claim has some merit. Cf. *Miller-El v. Cockrell*, 537 U.S. 322 (2003) . . . The rule of *Coleman* governs in all but the limited circumstances recognized here. The holding in this case does not concern attorney errors in other kinds of proceedings, including appeals from initial-review collateral proceedings, second or successive collateral proceedings, and petitions for discretionary review in a State's appellate courts. See 501 U.S., at 754; *Carrier*, 477 U.S., at 488. It does not extend to attorney errors in any proceeding beyond the first occasion the State allows a prisoner to raise a claim of ineffective assistance at trial, even though that initial-review collateral proceeding may be deficient for other reasons. In addition, the limited nature of the qualification to *Coleman* adopted here reflects the importance of the right to the effective assistance of trial counsel and Arizona's decision to bar defendants from raising ineffective-assistance claims on direct appeal. Our holding here addresses only the constitutional claims presented in this case, where the State barred the defendant from raising the claims on direct appeal."

CASE SIGNIFICANCE: This case establishes an exception to the procedural default rule barring federal habeas corpus courts from hearing a case when the state denied relief under a procedural rule. The Court has emphasized that this is a very narrow exception involving ineffective assistance of counsel at trial when the state appellate court bars this claim on direct appeal. Because of this, the case appears to have limited application in other situations.

However, in his dissent, Justice Scalia proposed that other issues in initial state habeas corpus proceedings will be raised because of this decision. He offers three examples: newly discovered exculpatory evidence, newly discovered prosecutorial misconduct, and newly discovered impeachment of prosecutorial witnesses. He believes this decision has opened the way for such types of appeal. Justice Scalia further noted that this decision would constitutionally require counsel in state collateral review because it could be raised as an appeal issue if the appellant isn't provided counsel. Whether these concerns are valid remains to be seen in future cases.

H. DAMAGES AND DEFENSES

HARLOW V. FITZGERALD
457 U.S. 800 (1982)

CAPSULE: Government officials performing discretionary functions are civilly liable only if their conduct violates a clearly established statutory or constitutional right of which a reasonable person would have known.

FACTS: Harlow and Butterfield, senior aides of President Nixon, were accused of violating Fitzgerald's constitutional rights by conspiring to have Fitzgerald dismissed as an Air Force official. Fitzgerald's allegations against Harlow stemmed from several conversations in which Harlow discussed Fitzgerald's dismissal with the Air Force Secretary. Allegations against Butterfield were based on a memorandum circulated by Butterfield in which he claimed that Fitzgerald planned to "blow the whistle" on Air Force purchasing practices. Fitzgerald alleged that his dismissal was in retaliation for these actions. Fitzgerald filed a lawsuit for unlawful discharge.

ISSUE: Do government officials have absolute immunity when performing discretionary official functions, such as dismissing a subordinate? NO.

HOLDING: Government officials performing discretionary functions are civilly liable only if their conduct violates clearly established statutory or constitutional rights of which a reasonable person would have known.

REASON: "Reliance on the objective reasonableness of an official's conduct, as measured by reference to clearly established law, should avoid excessive disruption of government . . . On summary judgment, the judge appropriately may determine, not only the applicable law, but whether that law was clearly established at the time an action occurred. If the law at that time was not clearly established, an official could not reasonably be expected to anticipate subsequent legal developments, nor could he fairly be said to 'know' that the law forbade conduct not previously identified as unlawful . . . If the law was clearly established, the immunity defense ordinarily should fail, since a reasonably competent public official should know the law governing his conduct. Nevertheless, if the official pleading the defense claims extraordinary circumstances and can prove that he neither knew nor should have known the relevant legal standard, the defense should be sustained . . ."

CASE SIGNIFICANCE: This case involved officials in the office of the United States President, not prison officials. The principle of the case, however, applies to all public officials. The *Fitzgerald* case is important because it set a new test for the "good faith" defense available to public officials, including prison officers. The old test (enunciated by the Court in *Wood v. Strickland*, 420 U.S. 308 [1975]) was that a government official asserting the defense "took action with malicious intention to cause deprivation of constitutional rights or other injury." The new test, under *Fitzgerald*, is that public officials are not civilly liable "if their conduct does not violate clearly established statutory or constitutional rights of which a reasonable person would have known." This new test has "good news and bad news" sides to it. The "good news" is that not every violation of a constitutional right by a prison official leads to civil liability. There is civil liability only if the official violated a "clearly established statutory or constitutional right of which a reasonable person would have known." This means that the "good faith" defense requires that, in order for an official to be held liable, the following must be established by the plaintiff: (1) there must be a violation of a clearly established constitutional right (2) of which a reasonable person would have known. The "bad news" is that prison officials have an obligation to know the clearly established rights of prisoners and detainees. After a period of time, they cannot plead ignorance of a new court decision giving rights to inmates.

SMITH V. WADE
461 U.S. 30 (1983)

CAPSULE: Punitive damages may be awarded in addition to compensatory damages if a correctional officer acts with reckless or callous disregard of, or indifference to, the rights and safety of inmates.

FACTS: Daniel Wade voluntarily checked into a protective custody unit in a reformatory for youthful first offenders because of prior incidents of violence against him. Due to disciplinary violations, he received a short term in punitive segregation before being transferred to administrative segregation. On the first day that he was in administrative segregation, he was placed in a cell with another inmate. Later, William Smith, a correctional officer in the reformatory, placed another inmate in the cell. This third inmate was in administrative segregation for fighting, and Smith made no effort to determine whether another cell was available. Wade was harassed, beaten, and sexually assaulted. He brought suit under 42 U.S.C. § 1983 in federal district court against Smith, four other correctional officers, and correctional officials, alleging that his Eighth Amendment rights had been violated. The prisoner was awarded compensatory damages in the amount of $25,000, and $5,000 in punitive damages.

Smith appealed the award of punitive damages, but not the compensatory damage award, claiming that the trial court judge erred in giving instructions to the jury as to when punitive damages can be awarded to a plaintiff.

ISSUE: Did the federal district court apply the correct legal standard in instructing the jury that it may award punitive damages if the defendant acted with reckless or callous disregard of, or indifference to, the rights and safety of others? YES.

HOLDING: A jury may be permitted to assess punitive damages in a civil rights case if the defendant's conduct: (1) is motivated by actual or malicious intent, and also (2) if the defendant acted with reckless or callous disregard of, or indifference to, the rights and safety of others.

REASON: "The large majority of state and lower federal courts were in agreement that punitive damage awards did not require a showing of actual malicious intent; they permitted punitive awards on variously stated standards of negligence, recklessness, or other culpable conduct short of actual malicious intent.

"The same rule applies today. The *Restatement (Second) of Torts* (1977), for example, states: 'Punitive damages may be awarded for conduct that is outrageous, because of the defendant's evil motive or his reckless indifference to the rights of others.' Most cases under common law, although varying in their precise terminology, have adopted more or less the same rule, recognizing that punitive damages in tort cases may be awarded not only for actual intent to injure or evil motive, but also for recklessness, serious indifference to or disregard for the rights of others, or even gross negligence."

CASE SIGNIFICANCE: There are generally three kinds of negligence for which a person may be held liable: (1) simple; (2) reckless; or (3) callous disregard of, or indifference to, the rights and safety of others, and actual or malicious intent. There are also three kinds of damages: (1) nominal, (2) compensatory, and (3) punitive. Nominal damages are acknowledgments by the court that plaintiff proved his or her allegations but suffered no actual injury, thus the amount awarded is small. Compensatory damages are those given for actual injuries or loss suffered, such as medical bills or lost wages. Punitive damages are those awarded to punish the wrongdoer and are typically awarded when the conduct is reckless, gross, or malicious. The issue in this case involved the award of punitive damages by the jury in accordance with the judge's instructions.

The jury awarded the prisoner, Daniel Wade, $25,000 in compensatory damages. Smith, the correctional officer, did not appeal the award. The compensatory damage award was based on the jury's finding that Smith acted with "reckless or callous disregard of or indifference to the rights and safety of others." Smith, however, objected to the punitive damage award of $5,000, saying that the judge erred in telling the jury that it could also impose a punitive damage award using the same standard as that for the compensatory award, namely: if Smith acted with "reckless or callous disregard of or indifference to the rights and safety of others." Smith maintained that punitive damages could be awarded only if the jury found that he (Smith) acted with "actual or malicious intent." Under this standard, Smith could not have been liable for punitive damages because there was no proof that he acted with actual or malicious intent.

The Court rejected Smith's appeal, saying that the judge could instruct the jury to assess punitive damages in a civil rights case if the defendant's conduct: (1) is motivated by actual or malicious intent, and also (2) if the defendant acted with reckless or callous disregard of, or indifference to, the rights and safety of others. In sum, actual or malicious intent is not needed for punitive damages to be imposed; acting with reckless or callous disregard of, or indifference to, the rights and safety of others (as Smith did here) suffices. This makes it easier for plaintiffs in civil rights cases to recover punitive damages. This is important because many jury awards are high because of punitive damages. Compensatory damages are quantifiable and easy to determine (hospital expenses, lost wages, etc.), but punitive damages are difficult to quantify and thus are often excessive.

CLEAVINGER V. SAXNER
474 U.S. 193 (1985)

CAPSULE: Prison disciplinary board members are entitled to qualified immunity, not absolute immunity.

FACTS: David Saxner and Alfred Cain, Jr., inmates at the Federal Correctional Institution in Terre Haute, Indiana, were found guilty by a prison disciplinary committee of encouraging other inmates to engage in a work stoppage and of other charges. They were ordered to be placed in administrative detention and to forfeit some "good-time" days. On appeal, ultimately to the Regional Director of the Bureau of Prisons, the inmates were ordered released from administrative detention and all materials relevant to the incident in question were ordered expunged from their records. They were later paroled and released.

They brought suit in federal court, alleging violation of various constitutional rights. After a jury trial, the members of the prison disciplinary committee were held to have violated the due process rights of inmates Saxner and Cain; the inmates were awarded damages.

ISSUE: Are members of a federal prison's Institution Discipline Committee, who hear cases in which inmates are charged with rule infractions, entitled to absolute immunity from personal damages for actions that violate inmates' constitutional rights? NO.

HOLDING: Members of prison disciplinary committees are entitled to qualified immunity, not absolute immunity, in the performance of their responsibilities.

REASON: "We conclude, nonetheless, that these concerns, to the extent they are well grounded, are overstated in the context of constitutional violations. We do not perceive the discipline committee's function as a 'classic' adjudicatory one, as petitioners would describe it. Surely, the members of the committee, unlike a federal or state judge, are not 'independent'; to say that they are is to ignore reality. They are not professional hearing officers, as are administrative law judges. They are, instead, prison officials, albeit no longer of the rank and file, temporarily diverted from their usual duties. They are employees of the Bureau of Prisons and they are the direct subordinates of the warden who reviews their decision. They work with the fellow employee who lodges the charge against the inmate upon whom they sit in judgment. The credibility determination they make often is one between a co-worker and an inmate. They thus are under obvious pressure to resolve a disciplinary dispute in favor of the institution and their fellow employee. See *Ponte v. Real*, 471 U.S. 491, ___ (1985) (dissenting opinion). It is the old situational problem of the relationship between the keeper and the kept, a relationship that hardly is conducive to a truly adjudicatory performance.

"Neither do we equate this discipline committee membership to service upon a traditional parole board. The board is a 'neutral and detached' hearing body. *Morrissey v. Brewer*, 408 U.S. 471, 489 (1972). The parole board member has been described as an impartial professional serving essentially 'as an arm of the sentencing judge.' *Sellars v. Procunier*, 641 F.2d, at 1302, n. 15, quoting *Bricker v. Michigan Parole Board*, 405 F. Supp. 1340, 1345 (E.D. Mich. 1975). And in the penalty context, the parole board is constitutionally required to provide greater due process protection than is the institution discipline committee. *Wolff v. McDonnell*, 418 U.S., at 561."

CASE SIGNIFICANCE: This case is significant because it tells us what type of immunity members of a prison disciplinary board are entitled to when deciding prison disciplinary cases. The committee in this case (composed of the associate warden, a correctional supervisor, and the chief of case management) claimed that, like judges, they enjoyed absolute immunity, meaning that they could not be held liable for anything they did in carrying out their duties. The Court conceded that members of a prison disciplinary board do, in a sense, perform "an adjudicatory function in that they hear testimony and receive documentary evidence; and in that they render a decision." Nonetheless, the Court concluded that they are not in the same category as judges and therefore should not be given absolute immunity. Said the Court:

Surely the members of the committee, unlike a federal or state judge, are not 'independent'; to say that they are is to ignore reality. They are not professional hearing officers, as are administrative judges. They are, instead, prison officials, albeit no longer of the rank and file, temporarily diverted from their usual duties. They are employees of the Bureau of Prisons and they are the direct subordinates of the warden who reviews their decision.

The Court then decided that prison disciplinary board members enjoy only qualified immunity, which means that they are immune from civil liability only if they act in good faith. This is the same type of immunity given to prison correctional officers and most other officials in the criminal justice system. Although this case involved the federal prison system, the decision applies equally to state prison disciplinary boards.

RICHARDSON ET AL. V. MCKNIGHT
521 U.S. 399 (1997)

CAPSULE: Prison guards employed by private prisons are not entitled to qualified immunity in civil rights cases.

FACTS: McKnight, a prisoner at a Tennessee correctional facility that had been privatized, brought a § 1983 action against two prison guards for injuring him by placing him in extremely tight physical restraints. The two guards asserted they were entitled to qualified immunity from § 1983 lawsuits and moved to dismiss the action.

The district court noted that a private firm, and not the state, employed the guards; therefore they had no qualified immunity. The guards appealed to the Sixth Circuit, which also ruled against them. The case was then appealed to the U.S. Supreme Court.

ISSUE: Are prison guards employed by a private firm entitled to qualified immunity from suit by prisoners charging a § 1983 violation? NO.

HOLDING: Private prison guards do not have qualified immunity. Only public prison guards enjoy qualified immunity.

REASON: "History does not reveal a 'firmly rooted' tradition of immunity applicable to privately employed prison guards. Correctional services in the United States have undergone various transformations . . . Government employed prison guards may have enjoyed a kind of immunity defense arising out of their status as public employees at common law. But correctional functions have never exclusively been public . . .

"The immunity doctrine's purposes also do not warrant immunity for private prison guards. Mere performance of a governmental function does not support immunity for a private person, especially one who performs a job without government supervision or direction . . . Tennessee, which has not decided to extend sovereign immunity to private prison operators, can, moreover, be understood to have anticipated a certain amount of distraction."

CASE SIGNIFICANCE: This case settles the issue of whether prison guards working in private prisons enjoy qualified immunity. They do not. The qualified immunity doctrine in § 1983 cases holds that public officers (prison guards included) are not liable if they act in "good faith." Good faith, in turn, means that public officers are civilly liable only if they violated a clearly established statutory or constitutional right of which a reasonable person would have known. This is an important defense for public officers sued under § 1983.

In this case, employees of a private prison claimed that they also enjoyed qualified immunity because they performed the same work done by guards in state prisons. The Supreme Court disagreed, saying that neither history nor policy considerations provide a basis for giving qualified immunity to private prison guards: this is bad news, indeed, for the growing number of people working in private prisons.

PENNSYLVANIA DEPARTMENT OF CORRECTIONS ET AL. V. YESKEY

524 U.S. 206 (1998)

CAPSULE: The Americans with Disabilities Act of 1990 applies to state prisons.

FACTS: Yeskey was sentenced to 18 to 36 months in a Pennsylvania correctional facility, but it was recommended that he be placed in a motivational boot camp for first-time offenders. If he successfully completed this camp, he would be eligible for parole in six months. However, Yeskey was refused admission to the boot camp because of his medical history of hypertension.

Yeskey sued, alleging that his exclusion violated the Americans with Disabilities Act of 1990, Title II of which prohibits a public entity from discriminating against a qualified individual with a disability on account of that disability. The district court held that the ADA did not apply to state prison inmates. The Third Circuit Court of Appeals reversed this decision, which was then appealed to the U.S. Supreme Court.

ISSUE: Does the Americans with Disabilities Act apply to state prisons? YES.

HOLDING: State prisons fall squarely within the statutory definition of public entity under the Act and are therefore subject to the provisions of the Act.

REASON: "Assuming, without deciding, that the plain-statement rule does govern application of the ADA to the administration of state prisons, we think the requirement of the rule is amply met: the statute's language unmistakably includes State prisons and prisoners within its coverage. The situation here is not comparable to that in *Gregory*. There, although the ADEA plainly covered state employees, it contained an exception for 'appointee[s] on the policymaking level' which made it impossible for us to 'conclude that the statute plainly cover [ed] appointed state judges.' 501 U.S., at 467. Here, the ADA plainly covers state institutions without any exception that could cast coverage of prisons into doubt.

"Our conclusion that the text of the ADA is not ambiguous causes us also to reject petitioners' appeal to the doctrine of constitutional doubt, which requires that we interpret statutes to avoid 'grave and doubtful constitutional questions,' *United States ex rel. Attorney General v. Delaware and Hudson Co.*, 213 U.S. 366, 408 (1909). That doctrine enters in only 'where a statute is susceptible of two constructions,' ibid. And for that same reason we disregard petitioners' invocation of the statute's title, 'Public Services,' 104 Stat. 337. '[T]he title of a statute . . . cannot limit the plain meaning of the text. For interpretive purposes, [it is] of use only when [it] shed[s] light on some ambiguous word or phrase.' *Trainmen v. Baltimore and Ohio R. Co.*, 331 U.S. 519, 528–529 (1947)."

CASE SIGNIFICANCE: The Americans with Disabilities Act (ADA) of 1990 was passed "to integrate persons with disabilities into the mainstream of society." It is arguably the most significant civil rights legislation since the passage of the Civil Rights Act of 1964, which prohibits discrimination based on race, color, religion, sex, and national origin. The purpose of the ADA is "to provide a clear and comprehensive national mandate for the elimination of discrimination against individuals with disabilities." The goal of the law is "to provide the estimated 43 million persons with disabilities access to employment, to governmental programs, services and activities, and to public accommodations such as restaurants, hotels, theaters, and shopping centers." Predictably, such a comprehensive law raised the issue of whether it applies to prisons. Prison administrators argued that the law was not meant to benefit offenders serving time in prisons. The Court disagreed, saying that their reading of the "statute's language unmistakably includes the State prisons and prisoners within its coverage."

CORRECTIONAL SERVICES CORPORATION V. MALESKO
534 U.S. 61 (2001)

CAPSULE: The *Bivens* cause of action does not extend to inmates suing private corporations that are under contract with federal prisons to house prisoners.

FACTS: Malesko was serving time in a private correctional facility operated by Correctional Services Corporation, under contract with the Federal Bureau of Prisons. He had a diagnosed heart condition that limited his physical activity, including climbing stairs. The private correctional facility had a policy that inmates living below the sixth floor had to use the stairs instead of the elevator. Malesko was assigned a room on the fifth floor, but he was allowed to use the elevator due to his medical condition. However, an employee of the facility insisted one day that Malesko could not use the elevator. Malesko then climbed the stairs and subsequently suffered a heart attack. He fell, injuring his left ear. Malesko filed suit against Correctional Services Corporation and unnamed employees of the corporation. He later amended the complaint to include the name of the correctional employee who would not let him use the elevator among the 10 John Doe defendants.

The federal district court dismissed the suit on the ground that this case did not fall under a *Bivens* action because *Bivens* applies only to an individual, not a corporate entity. The Second Circuit Court of Appeals affirmed in part, reversed in part, and remanded. The Court affirmed the dismissal against the individual defendants based on the statute of limitations. However, the Court ruled that private entities, such as Correctional Services Corporation, should be held liable under *Bivens* to accomplish the goal outlined in *Bivens* of providing a remedy for constitutional violations.

ISSUE: Does the *Bivens* cause of action extend to private entities housing federal prisoners? NO.

HOLDING: Federal prisoners cannot use federal law (§ 1983) to sue private corporations housing federal prisoners under contract.

REASON: ". . . From this discussion, it is clear that the claim urged by respondent is fundamentally different from anything recognized in *Bivens* or subsequent cases. In 30 years of *Bivens* jurisprudence we have extended its holding only twice, to provide an otherwise nonexistent cause of action against individual officers alleged to have acted unconstitutionally, or to provide a cause of action for a plaintiff who lacked any alternative remedy for harms caused by an individual officer's unconstitutional conduct. Where such circumstances are not present, we have consistently rejected invitations to extend *Bivens*, often for reasons that foreclose its extension here.

"There is no reason for us to consider extending *Bivens* beyond this core premise here. To begin with, no federal prisoners enjoy respondent's contemplated remedy. If a federal prisoner in a BOP facility alleges a constitutional deprivation, he may bring a *Bivens* claim against the offending individual officer, subject to the defense of qualified immunity. The prisoner may not bring a *Bivens* claim against the officer's employer, the United States or the BOP. With respect to the alleged constitutional deprivation, his only remedy lies with the individual; a remedy Meyer found sufficient, and which respondent did not timely pursue. Whether it makes sense to impose asymmetrical liability costs on private prison facilities alone is a question for Congress, not us, to decide."

CASE SIGNIFICANCE: The issue in this case was whether prisoners could use 42 U.S.C. § 1983 to sue private agencies housing prisoners. The defendant was a private correctional facility under contract with the Federal Bureau of Prisons to house inmates. In *Bivens v. Six Unknown Federal Narcotics Agents* (1971), the Court held that private individuals could sue federal officials under § 1983. The issue arose because § 1983, a federal law, was originally passed to allow lawsuits against state officials. *Bivens* held that § 1983 could be used by private persons to hold federal officials liable for violating constitutional rights.

The prisoner in this case wanted to extend *Bivens* to cases in which officials of a private corporation allegedly violated an inmate's constitutional rights. The Court held that § 1983 could not be used to sue private agencies housing federal inmates. This decision therefore refused to extend *Bivens*. Its significance is that prisoners in private prisons that are under contract with the state cannot use § 1983 to sue corporations whose officers violated their rights. The federal government and many states are under contract to private agencies to house prisoners (privatization of prisons). This case limits inmates' opportunities to sue under § 1983. Inmates can sue private corporations for damages using state law, but lawsuits under state law are generally more difficult to win.

UNITED STATES V. GEORGIA ET AL.
546 U.S. 151 (2006)

CAPSULE: A disabled state prisoner may sue a state for monetary damages under Title II of the Americans with Disabilities Act. State sovereign immunity in these types of cases does not apply.

FACTS: Goodman, a paraplegic incarcerated in a Georgia state prison, filed a § 1983 case in court, stating that his confinement was unconstitutional and violated the Eighth Amendment. He alleged numerous violations related to his paraplegic condition, and sought relief under § 1983, Title II of the Americans with Disabilities Act (ADA), and other provisions. His suit against the state of Georgia, the Georgia Department of Corrections, and several prison individuals requested injunctive relief and monetary damages.

The district court dismissed Goodman's § 1983 claims and granted summary judgment to the state defendants for the monetary damages claim under Title II of the ADA. The court ruled that state sovereign immunity barred this action. When the case was appealed to the Eleventh Circuit Court of Appeals, the United States became a petitioner, claiming that Title II's abrogation of state sovereign immunity was constitutional. The Eleventh Circuit Court of Appeals ruled that Goodman should be allowed to amend his § 1983 claims, focusing on three areas concerning conditions of confinement. The Court also upheld the decision of the District Court regarding relief under Title II of the ADA.

ISSUE: May a disabled state prison inmate sue a state for monetary damages under Title II of the Americans with Disabilities Act? YES.

HOLDING: Title II of the Americans with Disabilities Act creates a private cause of action to sue for damages against state conduct that actually violates the Fourteenth Amendment. This law abrogates the defense of state sovereign immunity in these types of cases.

REASON: "Goodman's claims for money damages against the State under Title II were evidently based, at least in large part, on conduct that independently violated the provisions of § 1 of the Fourteenth Amendment. See *Louisiana ex rel. Francis v. Resweber*, 329 U.S. 459, 463 (1947) (the Due Process Clause of the Fourteenth Amendment incorporates the Eighth Amendment's guarantee against cruel and unusual punishment). In this respect, Goodman differs from the claimants in our other cases addressing Congress's ability to abrogate sovereign immunity pursuant to its § 5 powers. "While the Members of this Court have disagreed regarding the scope of Congress's 'prophylactic' enforcement powers under § 5 of the Fourteenth Amendment, see, e.g., *Lane*, 541 U.S., at 513 (majority opinion of Stevens, J.); id., at 538 (Rehnquist, C.J., dissenting); id., at 554 (Scalia, J., dissenting), no one doubts that § 5 grants Congress the power to 'enforce . . . the provisions' of the Amendment by creating private remedies against the States for actual violations of those provisions . . . This enforcement power includes the power to abrogate state sovereign immunity by authorizing private suits for damages against the States. See *Fitzpatrick, supra*, at 456. Thus, insofar as Title II creates a private cause of action for damages against the States for conduct that actually violates the Fourteenth Amendment, Title II validly abrogates state sovereign immunity. The Eleventh Circuit erred in dismissing those of Goodman's Title II claims that were based on such unconstitutional conduct."

CASE SIGNIFICANCE: This is an interesting case because it raises the issue of whether an act passed by Congress to protect persons with disabilities also waives sovereign immunity. The ADA is a law enacted by Congress that prohibits discrimination against persons with disabilities and specifying their rights. The issue of whether prisoners can file cases under the ADA was not addressed. The Court simply proceeded on the assumption that they can.

The prisoner alleged that prison conditions in his case constituted a violation of his Fourteenth Amendment right and his right under the ADA. His lawsuit included claims that "the lack of accessible facilities render him unable to use the toilet and shower without assistance, which was often denied." He further alleged that "on multiple occasions, he had injured himself in attempting to transfer from his wheelchair to the shower or toilet on his own and, on several occasions, he had been forced to sit in his own feces and urine while prison officials refused to assist him in cleaning up the waste."

He filed a § 1983 case, a federal remedy against violations of constitutional rights where the plaintiff can seek monetary damages. The issue was whether the government could be sued for damages under Title II although the government enjoys sovereign immunity, a doctrine that states that the government cannot be held liable because it is sovereign. Title II of the ADA provides that "no qualified individual with a disability shall, by reason of such disability, be excluded from participation in or be denied the benefits of the services, programs, or activities of a public entity, or be subjected to discrimination by any entity."

The issues are complex, but ultimately the Court held that Title II of the ADA waives sovereign immunity in these types of law violations that also involve a violation of constitutional rights. Sovereign immunity can be waived by Congress. The Court interpreted Title II as Congress waiving sovereign immunity and authorizing plaintiffs to file a lawsuit for damages.

ORTIZ V. JORDAN, ET AL.
131 S. CT. 884 (2011)

CAPSULE: A party in a lawsuit may not appeal an order denying summary judgment after a full trial has been conducted on its merits.

FACTS: Ortiz was convicted of aggravated assault against her husband and was serving her sentence in an Ohio reformatory. She stated that she was sexually assaulted on two consecutive nights by a male corrections officer in the facility. Ortiz maintained that she reported the first assault to Jordan, a case manager in her unit, and that Jordan did nothing to protect her from further assault. The petitioner also claimed that Bright, a prison investigator, retaliated against her for reporting the assaults. Ortiz was sent to solitary confinement, where, she stated, she was subject to inadequate conditions in her cell. She filed suit, alleging violations of the Eighth and Fourteenth Amendments, because the two named prison officials failed to protect her from violence while she was in custody.

Both Jordan and Bright claimed qualified immunity, requesting summary judgment from the district court. The Court denied the motion, noting factual disputes in Ortiz's claim. The case proceeded to trial, where the jury ruled in favor of Ortiz, awarding her $625,000 in damages. Neither of the officers appealed the denial of their motion for summary judgment, nor did they contest the jury's liability finding. They also did not request a new trial. Instead, they appealed the ruling against them after trial on the basis that the district court erred in denying their motion for summary judgment because they were entitled to qualified immunity. The Sixth Circuit Court of Appeals ruled in the officials' favor, reversing the judgment entered on the jury's verdict and holding that the defendants were entitled to qualified immunity.

ISSUE: May a party appeal an order denying summary judgment after a full trial has been conducted on its merits? NO.

HOLDING: A party may not appeal a denial of a motion for summary judgment after a full trial has been conducted on the merits of the case. Because the defendants did not raise a legal claim of qualified immunity during the trial or when judgment was made, the Sixth Circuit Court of Appeals had no warrant to overrule the jury's verdict regarding the officials' liability.

REASONS: "We granted review, 559 U.S. ___ (2010), to decide a threshold question on which the Circuits are split: May a party, as the Sixth Circuit believed, appeal an order denying summary judgment after a full trial on the merits? Our answer is no . . . Once the case proceeds to trial, the full record developed in court supersedes the record existing at the time of the summary judgment motion. A qualified immunity defense, of course, does not vanish when a district court declines to rule on the plea summarily. The plea remains available to the defending officials at trial; but at that stage, the defense must be evaluated in light of the character and quality of the evidence received in court. When summary judgment is sought on a qualified immunity defense, the court inquires whether the party opposing the motion has raised any triable issue barring summary adjudication. '[O]nce trial has been had,' however, 'the availability of official immunity should be determined by the trial record, not the pleadings nor the summary judgment record.' 15A C. Wright, A. Miller, & E. Cooper, Federal Practice & Procedure § 3914.10, p. 684 (2d ed. 1992 and Supp. 2010)."

"After trial, if defendants continue to urge qualified immunity, the decisive question, ordinarily, is whether the evidence favoring the party seeking relief is legally sufficient to overcome the defense. See Fed. Rule Civ. Proc. 50(a), (b) (stating conditions on which judgment may be granted as a matter of law). In the case before us, the Court of Appeals, although purporting to review the District Court's denial of the prison officials' pretrial summary-judgment motion, 316 Fed. Appx., at 453, several times pointed to evidence presented only at the trial stage of the proceedings, see *id.*, at 453–454. The appeals court erred, but not fatally, by incorrectly placing its ruling under a summary judgment headline. Its judgment was infirm, however, because Jordan's and Bright's failure to renew their motion for judgment as a matter of law under Federal Rule of Civil Procedure 50(b) left the appellate forum with no warrant to reject the appraisal of the evidence by 'the judge who saw and heard the witnesses and ha[d] the feel of the case which no appellate printed transcript can impart.' *Cone v. West Virginia Pulp & Paper Co.*, 330 U.S. 212, 216 (1947)."

CASE SIGNIFICANCE: This case is noteworthy because it sets legal precedent for the Courts of Appeals in determining if they can rule on an appeal after the case has already been adjudicated in a trial court. The answer is that they may not, due to the failure of the defendants to appeal the issue of qualified immunity when the motion was denied and their failure to present other motions properly once the trial proceeded. The Court notes that when a qualified immunity defense is raised in a summary judgment and the motion is denied, this is appealable. Normally it is not, but the Court established this exception in the case of *Mitchell v. Forsyth*.

However, the defendants did not take advantage of this exception and appeal the denial of the motion.

Under Rule 50(b) of the Federal Rule of Civil Procedure, the defendants could have made a post-verdict motion for judgment as a matter of law based on the sufficiency of the evidence. They could have claimed that Ortiz had not proved her case. However, they failed to do so, as well as failing to request a new trial under Rule 59(a). Owing to this lack of action at the proper time during the proceedings, the Court ruled that the appellate court did not have the power to review the jury's decision. Had the defendants made their motions in a timely manner, the Court of Appeals would have been correct in ruling on the issue of qualified immunity.

I. DISCIPLINARY HEARINGS

WOLFF V. MCDONNELL
418 U.S. 539 (1974)

CAPSULE: Inmates are entitled to due process in prison disciplinary proceedings that can result in the loss of good-time credits or in punitive segregation.

FACTS: Inmates at a Nebraska prison filed a complaint for damages and an injunction under 42 U.S.C. § 1983 in which they alleged, among other complaints, that the Nebraska prison disciplinary proceedings violated their constitutional right to due process.

Under Nebraska's disciplinary procedure, forfeiture or withholding of good-time credits or confinement in a disciplinary cell is the penalty imposed for serious misconduct. To establish misconduct: (1) a preliminary conference is held with the chief corrections supervisor and the charging party, in which the prisoner is orally informed of the charge and the merits are preliminarily discussed; (2) a conduct report is prepared and a hearing held before the prison's disciplinary body, which is composed of three prison officials; and (3) the inmate may ask questions of the charging party.

ISSUE: Is due process required in prison disciplinary proceedings? YES.

HOLDING: In prison disciplinary proceedings involving serious misconduct that can result in loss of good-time credits or punitive segregation, the inmate must be given the following due process rights:

1. Advance written notice of the charges must be given to the inmate no less than 24 hours prior to his or her appearance before the committee;
2. There must be a written statement by the fact finders as to the evidence relied on and reasons for the disciplinary action;

3. The inmate should be allowed to call witnesses and present documentary evidence in his or her defense, if permitting him or her to do so will not jeopardize institutional safety or correctional goals;
4. Counsel substitute (either a fellow inmate or staff member) will be permitted when the inmate is illiterate or when the complexity of the issues makes it unlikely that the inmate will be able to collect and present the evidence for an adequate comprehension of the case; and
5. The prison disciplinary board must be impartial.

The state may constitutionally require that mail from an attorney to a prisoner be identified as such, and that his or her name and address appear on the communication, and—as a protection against contraband—that the authorities may open such mail in the inmate's presence. A lawyer desiring to correspond with a prisoner may also be required first to identify him- or herself and his or her client to the prison officials to ensure that letters marked "privileged" are actually from a member of the bar.

REASON: "We hold that written notice of the charges must be given to the disciplinary-action defendant in order to inform him of the charges and to enable him to marshal the facts and prepare a defense. At least a brief period of time after the notice, no less than 24 hours, should be allowed the inmate to prepare for the appearance before the Adjustment Committee . . . Written records of proceedings will thus protect the inmate against collateral consequences based on a misunderstanding of the nature of the original proceeding. Further, as to the disciplinary action itself, the provision for a written record helps to insure that administrators, faced with possible scrutiny by state officials and the public, and perhaps even the courts, where fundamental constitutional rights may have been abridged, will act fairly.

"Many prison officials, on the spot and with the responsibility for the safety of inmates and staff, are reluctant to extend the unqualified right to call witnesses; and in our view, they must have the necessary discretion without being subject to unduly crippling constitutional impediments. There is much play in the joints of the Due Process Clause, and we stop short of imposing a more demanding rule with respect to witnesses and documents . . . As the nature of the prison disciplinary process changes in future years, circumstances may then exist which will require further considerations and reflection of this Court. It is our view, however, that the procedures we have now required in prison disciplinary proceedings represent a reasonable accommodation between the interests of the inmates and the needs of the institution."

CASE SIGNIFICANCE: This is an important case because, for the first time, the Supreme Court acknowledged that inmates are entitled to certain due process rights during prison disciplinary proceedings. Due process can mean many things to many people, but it basically means: "fundamental fairness." Therefore, if something is fundamentally unfair, a claim of a due process right violation can be raised.

These due process rights are not the same as those enjoyed by people in the free world, but they provide a measure of protection against arbitrariness. The Court said that a prisoner "is not wholly stripped of constitutional protections" and that disciplinary proceedings must "be governed by a mutual accommodation between institutional needs and generally applicable constitutional requirements." The Court did not give the inmates all the rights they sought. Specifically, the Court said that an inmate has no constitutional right to: (1) confrontation and cross-examination, although such is discretionary with the prison officials, and (2) retained or appointed counsel.

The rights given in this case do not apply to all disciplinary cases, but only to situations involving serious misconduct, meaning misconduct that can result in forfeiture of good-time credits or punitive segregation. They do not apply to minor offenses, although jail and prison administrators are likely to give the above rights in all disciplinary cases anyway, either because of agency rules or court mandate.

It is important to realize that the term "due process" does not have a fixed meaning in law. Although it basically means "fundamental fairness," what is fundamentally fair varies from one case to another even in a prison setting. The question asked is: What process is due in a particular proceeding? For example, due process in prison disciplinary proceedings, where prisoners have diminished constitutional rights, is different from due process in criminal trials in which the right to due process is at its fullest. Even in prison, the concept of due process varies. The kind of due process needed in prison disciplinary proceedings is different from that required to place an inmate in administrative segregation. Many of the prison due process cases decided after *Wolff* deal with the question of what rights should be given an inmate in a particular prison proceeding, be it an issue of transfer to other facilities, classification, or transfer from prison to a mental institution. Due process rights in these cases are not always the same as those given in *Wolff.*

Although the inmates raised two other issues in this case, *Wolff* is best known as a prison disciplinary proceeding case in which due process rights were given to inmates. The two other issues raised were whether the regulations governing inmates' mail and the inmate legal assistance programs were constitutional. The Court upheld the mail regulation, but remanded the legal assistance issue to the lower court.

BAXTER V. PALMIGIANO
425 U.S. 308 (1976)

CAPSULE: Inmates are not entitled to counsel or cross-examination in prison disciplinary hearings. In addition, silence by the inmate in a disciplinary proceeding may be given adverse evidentiary significance.

FACTS: Palmigiano, an inmate serving a life sentence for murder at the Rhode Island Adult Correctional Institution, was charged by correctional officers with inciting a disturbance and disruption of prison operations, which may have resulted in a riot. Summoned before the prison disciplinary board, he was informed that there was a possibility that he would be prosecuted for a violation of state law but that no charges were pending. He was advised that he should consult his attorney, although the board had not permitted his attorney to be present at the hearing. He was also advised that he had the right to remain silent during the hearing, but that if he did so it would be held against him. Prison rules provided for a counsel-substitute; the prisoner availed himself of these services and remained silent during the hearing. The board decided that Palmigiano should be placed in punitive segregation for 30 days and that his classification status should be downgraded thereafter.

The prisoner filed an action under 42 U.S.C. § 1983 for damages and injunctive relief, claiming that the disciplinary hearing violated the due process clause of the Fourteenth Amendment.

ISSUE: Did the prison disciplinary proceedings in the Rhode Island Adult Correctional Institution violate the equal protection or due process clauses of the Fourteenth Amendment? NO.

HOLDING: Prison inmates do not have the right to either retained or appointed counsel in disciplinary hearings that are not part of a criminal prosecution, nor are they entitled to confront and cross-examine witnesses at all times. Further, an inmate's decision to assert his Fifth Amendment rights and remain silent at a disciplinary proceeding can be given adverse evidentiary significance by the prison board.

REASON: "We see no reason to alter our conclusion so recently made in *Wolff* that inmates do not 'have a right to either retained or appointed counsel in disciplinary hearings.' 418 U.S., at 570. Plainly, therefore, state authorities were not in error in failing to advise Palmigiano to the contrary, i.e., that he was entitled to counsel at the hearing and that the State would furnish counsel if he did not have one of his own.

"No criminal proceedings are or were pending against Palmigiano. The State has not, contrary to *Griffin*, sought to make evidentiary use of his silence at the disciplinary hearing in any criminal proceeding. Rhode Island neither insisted nor asked that Palmigiano waive his Fifth Amendment privilege. He was notified that he was privileged to remain silent if he chose. He was also advised that his silence could be used against him, but a prison inmate in Rhode Island electing to remain silent during his disciplinary hearing, as respondent Palmigiano did here, is not in consequence of his silence automatically found guilty of the infraction with which he has been charged. Under Rhode Island law, disciplinary decisions 'must be based on substantial evidence manifested in the record of the disciplinary proceeding.' *Morris v. Travisono*, 310 F. Supp. 857, 873 (D.R.I. 1970). It is thus undisputed that an inmate's silence in and of itself is insufficient to support an adverse decision by the Disciplinary Board.

"In criminal cases, where the stakes are higher and the State's sole interest is to convict, Griffin prohibits the judge and prosecutor from suggesting to the jury that it may treat the defendant's silence as substantive evidence of guilt. Disciplinary proceedings in state prisons, however, involve the correctional process and important state interests other than conviction for crime. We decline to extend the *Griffin* rule to this context.

"We said in *Wolff v. McDonnell*: 'As the nature of the prison disciplinary process changes in future years, circumstances may then exist which will require further consideration and reflection of this Court. It is our view, however, that the procedures we have now required in prison disciplinary proceedings represent a reasonable accommodation between the interests of the inmates and the needs of the institution.' 418 U.S., at 572. We do not retreat from that view. However, the procedures required by the Courts of Appeals in Nos. 74–1187 and 74–1194 are either inconsistent with the 'reasonable accommodation' reached in *Wolff*, or premature on the bases of the records before us."

CASE SIGNIFICANCE: The Court in this case refused to give inmates more due process rights than those already given to them in *Wolff v. McDonnell*. The significance of this case lies in the statement of the Court that "permitting an adverse inference to be drawn from an inmate's silence at his disciplinary proceedings is not, on its face, an invalid practice . . ." This is different from a criminal trial in which silence on the part of the accused cannot in any way be taken as an indication of guilt, nor can it be commented on by the prosecutor. The Court justified this decision by saying that there must be a "reasonable accommodation" between the interests of the inmates and the needs of the institution. This decision strengthens the hand of prison administrators in running prisons and reiterates the principle that prisoners have diminished constitutional rights.

SUPERINTENDENT, WALPOLE V. HILL
472 U.S. 445 (1985)

CAPSULE: Disciplinary board findings that result in loss of good-time credits must be supported by a "modicum" of evidence to satisfy due process requirements.

FACTS: Gerald Hill and Joseph Crawford, inmates at the Massachusetts State Prison in Walpole, each received a prison disciplinary report charging them with assaulting another inmate. At separate hearings, a prison disciplinary board heard testimony and had a written report from a correctional officer stating that while working at the prison on the day in question the officer heard an inmate ask "What's going on?" twice. The officer opened the door to the walkway and found an inmate bleeding from the mouth and suffering from a swollen eye. There was also dirt scattered about the area, which the officer viewed as further evidence of a fight. He saw three inmates, including Hill and Crawford, leaving the walkway. The correctional officer observed that there were no other inmates in the area, which was enclosed by a chain-link fence. He concluded that one or more of the three inmates leaving had assaulted the fourth inmate. Testimony at the disciplinary hearing from the officer indicated that a prison medic also told him that the injured inmate had been beaten. Both Hill and Crawford declared their innocence before the prison disciplinary board. The injured inmate gave written statements that the three other inmates had not caused his injuries.

The prison disciplinary board found both Hill and Crawford guilty of violating prison regulations because of their involvement in the assault. The board decided that each inmate would lose 100 days of good-time credits and would be confined in isolation for 15 days. The inmates appealed the board's decision to the Superintendent of the prison, but this appeal was denied. Hill and Crawford then filed a complaint in the Massachusetts Superior Court, alleging that their constitutional rights had been violated because there was no evidence to confirm that the assault took place and there was no evidence to show that the inmates were involved in the assault if it did take place.

ISSUE: Must findings of a prison disciplinary board that result in the loss of good-time credits be supported by a certain amount of evidence in order to satisfy the due process clause of the Fourteenth Amendment? YES.

HOLDING: According to Massachusetts law, good-time credits constitute a protected liberty interest and the revocation of such credits must be supported by a modicum of evidence to satisfy the minimum requirements of procedural due process. In this case, however, the evidence before the disciplinary board was sufficient to meet the requirements imposed by the due process clause of the Fourteenth Amendment.

REASON: "Where a prisoner has a liberty interest in good time credits, the loss of such credits threatens his prospective freedom from confinement by extending the length of imprisonment. Thus the inmate has a strong interest in assuring that the loss of good time credits is not imposed arbitrarily. This interest, however, must be accommodated in the distinctive setting of a prison, where disciplinary proceedings 'take place in a closed, tightly controlled environment peopled by those who have chosen to violate the criminal law and who have been lawfully incarcerated for doing so.' *Wolff v. McDonnell*, 418 U.S., at 561. Consequently, in identifying the safeguards required by due process, the Court has recognized the legitimate institutional needs of assuring the safety of inmates and prisoners, avoiding burdensome administrative requirements that might be susceptible to manipulation, and preserving the disciplinary process as a means of rehabilitation.

"Requiring a modicum of evidence to support a decision to revoke good time credits will help to prevent arbitrary deprivations without threatening institutional interests or imposing undue administrative burdens . . . Because the written statement mandated by *Wolff* requires a disciplinary board to explain the evidence relied upon, recognizing that due process requires some evidentiary basis for a decision to revoke good time credits will not impose significant new burdens on proceedings within the prison. Nor does it imply that a disciplinary board's factual findings or decisions with respect to appropriate punishment are subject to second-guessing upon review.

"We hold that the requirements of due process are satisfied if some evidence supports the decision by the prison disciplinary board to revoke good time credits. This standard is met if 'there was some evidence from which the conclusion of the administrative tribunal could be deduced . . .' *United States ex rel. Vajtauer v. Commissioner of Immigration*, 273 U.S., at 106. Ascertaining whether this standard is satisfied does not require examination of the entire record, independent assessment of the credibility of the witnesses, or weighing of the evidence. Instead, the relevant question is whether there is any evidence in the record that could support the conclusion reached by the disciplinary board. We decline to adopt a more stringent evidentiary standard as a constitutional requirement. Prison disciplinary proceedings take place in a highly charged atmosphere, and prison administrators must often act swiftly on the basis of evidence that might be insufficient in less exigent circumstances.

"Instead, due process in this context requires only that there be some evidence to support the findings made in the disciplinary hearing. Although the evidence in this case might be characterized as meager, and there was no direct evidence identifying any one of three inmates as the assailant, the record is not so devoid of evidence that the findings of the disciplinary board were without support or otherwise arbitrary."

CASE SIGNIFICANCE: An earlier case, *Wolff v. McDonnell* (1974), held that inmates are entitled to due process rights in prison disciplinary hearings. *Wolff* was followed by *Baxter v. Palmigiano* (1976), which examined the question of the right to an attorney at such a hearing, and the implications of a prisoner's silence at a disciplinary hearing. The Court in this case held that due process requires that some evidence is necessary for a decision that involves a liberty interest, but that the amount of evidence need not be as much as that required in a trial court. The Supreme Court describes the amount necessary as a "modicum," meaning less or limited.

In this decision, the Court underscores the unique atmosphere that exists in a prison and the competing interests of the inmates and the prison administrators. The Court struck a balance, saying that a "modicum" of evidence is required in prison disciplinary hearings. "Modicum" is defined in *Webster's* dictionary as "a small portion," or a "limited quantity." This is less evidence than that required in criminal trials or civil proceedings. This decision reaffirms the fact that the Court considers prisoners as having diminished constitutional rights.

SANDIN V. CONNER
515 U.S. 472 (1995)

CAPSULE: Hawaii's prison regulation on prison disciplinary hearings does not establish a liberty interest and, therefore, did not entitle the prisoner to the rights given in *Wolff v. McDonnell*.

FACTS: Conner was an inmate at a correctional facility in Hawaii. He was sentenced to 30 days in segregation for violating a prison regulation after he appeared before an adjustment committee. Conner wanted to present witnesses during the disciplinary hearing, but the committee denied this request. He filed suit against prison officials; the state requested summary judgment, which was granted.

The Court of Appeals reversed the District Court decision based on two grounds: (1) Connor had a liberty interest in remaining free of disciplinary segregation; and (2) following the standard established in *Wolff v. McDonnell*, he may not have received due process. The Court reasoned that a liberty interest had been established by a prison regulation that instructed the committee to find guilt when there was substantial evidence that misconduct had occurred.

ISSUES:

1. Was a liberty interest established by the Hawaiian prison regulation, thereby invoking the rights established in *Wolff v. McDonnell?* NO.
2. Was the inmate entitled to the protection of the due process clause in the prison disciplinary hearing by the language of the prison regulation? NO.

HOLDING: Neither the Hawaiian prison regulation nor the due process clause of the Fourteenth Amendment establish a protected liberty interest; therefore, the prisoner is not entitled to *Wolff*'s procedural protections.

REASON: "Under *Wolff*, States may in certain circumstances create liberty interests which are protected by the Due Process Clause . . . The methodology used in *Hewitt v. Helms*, 459 U.S. 460, and later cases has impermissibly shifted the focus of the liberty interest inquiry from one based on the nature of the deprivation to one based on language of a particular regulation. Under *Hewitt*'s methodology, prison regulations, such as the one in this case, have been examined to see whether mandatory language and substantive predicates create an enforceable expectation that the State would produce a particular outcome with respect to the prisoner's confinement condition . . . The time has come to return to those due process principles that were correctly established and applied in *Wolff and Meachum*."

CASE SIGNIFICANCE: The prisoner in this case sued, claiming that he was denied the rights given in *Wolff v. McDonnell* in a prison disciplinary proceeding. He wanted to present witnesses during the disciplinary hearing against him, but the committee denied his request and sent him to segregation for the misconduct. He charged that Hawaii's prison regulation instructed the committee to "find guilt when a misconduct charge is supported by substantial evidence." He said that this wording implied that segregation could not be imposed if the committee did not find substantial evidence of misconduct.

The Court disagreed, saying that neither the due process clause of the Fourteenth Amendment (which was the basis for the decision in *Wolff*) nor the wording of the prison regulation entitled the prisoner to the rights given in *Wolff*. No liberty interest under the Fourteenth Amendment was created by the way the Hawaii prison regulation was worded (saying that the committee could "find guilt when a misconduct charge is supported by substantial evidence") and therefore the amount of evidence used by the committee to send the prisoner to segregation was sufficient. In short, the wording of the prison regulation did not give the prisoner any "liberty interest" that then elevated it to the level of a constitutional right.

J. DISCRIMINATION BASED ON MONEY

SMITH V. BENNETT
365 U.S. 708 (1961)

CAPSULE: A $4 filing fee violates the constitutional rights of indigent inmates.

FACTS: Neal Merle Smith was sentenced to 10 years in the Iowa State Penitentiary for breaking and entering. He was released on parole but his parole was later revoked for violations of conditions. He was arrested and returned to the state penitentiary. Smith then forwarded a petition for a writ of habeas corpus (seeking release from confinement) to the local district clerk. Accompanying the petition was a motion to proceed *in forma pauperis* (which means "in the manner of a pauper") and an affidavit of poverty. The clerk refused to docket the petition without a $4 filing fee. Smith then filed a motion in the Iowa Supreme Court for leave to appeal in forma pauperis, accompanied by a pauper's oath. That court denied the motion without opinion. The United States Supreme Court granted certiorari.

ISSUE: Does the Iowa law that requires the payment of statutory filing fees by an indigent prisoner before an application for a writ of habeas corpus or the allowance of an appeal violate the equal protection clause of the Fourteenth Amendment? YES.

HOLDING: The State of Iowa violates the equal protection clause of the Fourteenth Amendment by failing to extend the privilege of the writ of habeas corpus to its indigent prisoners.

REASON: "It has long been available in the federal courts to indigent prisoners of both the State and Federal Governments to test the validity of their detention . . . When an equivalent right is granted by a State, financial hurdles must not be permitted to condition its exercise.

"Throughout the centuries the Great Writ has been the shield of personal freedom, insuring liberty to persons illegally detained. Respecting the State's grant of a right to test their detention, the Fourteenth Amendment weighs the interest of rich and poor criminals in equal scale, and its hand extends as far to each. In failing to extend the privilege of the Great Writ to its indigent prisoners, Iowa denies them equal protection of the laws."

CASE SIGNIFICANCE: This case is significant because the Supreme Court ruled that a prisoner cannot be denied access to court if he or she is too poor to pay a filing fee. The amount involved was small ($4), but that did not matter to the Court, because the prisoner involved was indigent and could not possibly have paid the fee.

In an earlier case, *Griffin v. Illinois*, 351 U.S. 12 (1956), the Court said that "there can be no equal justice where the kind of trial a man gets depends on the amount of money he has." This principle has since been applied to situations other than trials. For example, in *Douglas v. California*, 372 U.S. 353 (1963), the Court applied the "equal justice" principle to an indigent who sought the help of counsel on first direct appeal. In *Roberts v. LaVallee*, 389 U.S. 40 (1967), the Court held that an indigent person is entitled to a free transcript of his preliminary hearing for use at trial. And in *Williams v. Illinois*, 399 U.S. 235 (1970), the Court ruled that "a State cannot subject a certain class of convicted defendants to a period of imprisonment beyond the statutory maximum solely because they are too poor to pay the fine."

This case is also significant because it implies that the equal protection clause of the Fourteenth Amendment applies equally to prisoners in cases involving money. The fact that prisoners have been convicted and are serving time for crimes committed does not make them a different class for purposes of the equal protection clause. Indigents enjoy the protection of the Constitution whether they are in prison or are free.

K. DISCRIMINATION BASED ON RACE

LEE V. WASHINGTON
390 U.S. 333 (1968)

CAPSULE: Racial segregation in prisons is unconstitutional, except when a compelling state interest justifies it.

FACTS: Inmates in the Alabama prison system filed an action for declaratory and injunctive relief (an order from the court to force public officials to do something) concerning racial segregation in the Alabama state penal system and in county and local jails. The inmates contended that racial segregation was a violation of the Fourteenth Amendment. The Commissioner of Corrections of Alabama argued that racial segregation was necessary to maintain security and order.

ISSUE: Are the Alabama statutes requiring segregation of the races in prisons and jails unconstitutional in violation of the Fourteenth Amendment? YES.

HOLDING: The Alabama statutes requiring racial segregation in prisons and jails are unconstitutional under the equal protection clause of the Fourteenth Amendment.

REASON: "This appeal challenges a decree of a three-judge District Court declaring that certain Alabama statutes violate the Fourteenth Amendment to the extent that they require segregation of the races in prisons and jails, and establishing a schedule for desegregation of these institutions. The State's contentions that Rule 23 of the Federal Rules of Civil Procedure, which relates to class actions, was violated in this case and that the challenged statutes are not unconstitutional, are without merit. The remaining contention of the State is that the specific orders directing desegregation of prisons and jails make no allowance for the necessities of prison security and discipline, but we do not so read the 'Order, Judgment, and Decree' of the District Court, which when read as a whole we find unexceptionable."

CASE SIGNIFICANCE: This case was the first to address racial segregation in prisons. Earlier cases had addressed racial segregation in schools, restaurants, and retail stores. As expected, the U.S. Supreme Court ruled that racial segregation violates the Fourteenth Amendment. In a concurring opinion, Justice Black said that "prison authorities have the right, acting in good faith and in particularized circumstance, to take into account racial tensions in maintaining security, discipline, and good order in prisons and jails." Written in 1968, this statement allows prison authorities to take race into account when trying to ease tension, maintain security, discipline, and good order in prisons. This should be done, however, only with extreme caution and when a compelling state interest is involved, such as in an emergency situation when there is a prison riot. At present, any prison administrator who takes race into consideration when making decisions flirts with a civil rights lawsuit, except in extreme circumstances, such as a racial riot.

JOHNSON V. CALIFORNIA
543 U.S. 499 (2005)

CAPSULE: The "strict scrutiny" standard, not the standard of "reasonably related to a legitimate penological interest," is the proper standard for courts to use when determining the constitutionality of prison racial segregation cases, even if the segregation is temporary.

FACTS: The California Department of Corrections (CDC) had an unwritten policy of segregating prisoners in double cells for up to 60 days when they were first admitted to prison. The justification for the policy was to prevent violence caused by racial gangs. Johnson, an African-American prisoner, challenged this policy, claiming it violated his Fourteenth Amendment right to equal protection.

ISSUE: What standard should be used by the courts when determining the constitutionality of a prison policy that segregates prisoners in double cells for up to 60 days each time they enter a new correctional facility?

HOLDING: "Strict scrutiny" and not "reasonably related to a legitimate penological interest" (which was the standard used by the Court in *Turner v. Safley*, where prison regulations infringed an inmate's constitutional right), is the standard courts should use when determining the constitutionality of prison racial segregation cases.

REASON: "The right not to be discriminated against based on one's race is not susceptible to the logic of *Turner*. It is not a right that need necessarily be compromised for the sake of proper prison administration. On the contrary, compliance with the Fourteenth Amendment's ban on racial discrimination is not only consistent with proper prison administration, but also bolsters the legitimacy of the entire criminal justice system. . . . When government officials are permitted to use race as a proxy for gang membership and violence without demonstrating a compelling government interest and proving that their means are narrowly tailored, society as a whole suffers. . . .

"In the prison context, when the government's power is at its apex, we think that searching judicial review of racial classifications is necessary to guard against invidious discrimination. Granting the CDC (California Department of Corrections) an exemption from the rule that strict scrutiny applies to all racial classifications would undermine our 'unceasing efforts to eradicate racial prejudice from our criminal justice system.'"

CASE SIGNIFICANCE: There have been only two cases decided by the United States Supreme Court on the issue of racial segregation in prisons. The first was *Lee v. Washington* (1968), in which the Court held that racial segregation in prisons is unconstitutional, except when a compelling state interest justifies it. This is known as the "strict scrutiny" standard.

Nineteen years later, in *Turner v. Safley* (1987), the Court held that a prison regulation that impinges on inmates' constitutional rights is valid if "reasonably related to a legitimate penological interest." This is a lower legal standard than "strict scrutiny" and easier for prison administrators to establish. The issue in *Johnson* is which standard courts should use when faced with cases involving racial segregation.

In *Johnson*, the CDC had an unwritten policy where prisoners were segregated in double cells temporarily (up to 60 days each time) when they enter a new prison facility. The justification for this policy was the prevention of violence caused by racial gangs. After a maximum of 60 days, prison officials usually allowed inmates to choose their own cellmates, unless there were security reasons for denying the choice made. CDC presented witnesses in court who testified that "housing inmates in double cells without regard to race threatens not only prison discipline, but also the physical safety of inmates and staff." The majority opinion rejected this, saying there was no evidence to establish that more violence resulted when inmates were not segregated when they first entered prison. They pointed to a study that said that "the rate of violence between inmates segregated by race in double cells surpassed the rate among those racially integrated." The majority then concluded that CDC's justification for its policy was "unsubstantiated and we are unable to confirm or deny its accuracy."

Although the constitutionality of racial segregation in prisons was the broader issue in this case, the immediate and narrow issue was the standard to be used by the courts when determining the constitutionality of racial segregation cases in prisons. California maintained that their policy of temporary segregation to prevent racial violence was constitutional based on the deferential (meaning respect given to decisions made by prison authorities) standard of the policy being "reasonably related to a legitimate penological interest," articulated in *Turner v. Safley*. The Court held that the *Turner* standard did not apply to racial segregation in prisons and therefore racial segregation policies constituted an exception to that rule. In prison cases, the *Lee* standard of "strict scrutiny" applied, meaning that segregation cases in prisons should undergo strict scrutiny and be held constitutional only if there was a "compelling state interest" that justified the policy. In *Johnson*, no compelling state interest justified the policy because California could not establish that violence resulted from racial integration during the first 60 days.

This decision is significant for two reasons. First, it states that any type of racial segregation in prisons (where inmates, unlike people in the free world, enjoyed "diminished" constitutional rights) must nonetheless be scrutinized by the courts strictly and declared constitutional only if a "compelling state interest" justified it. Prisoners, therefore, have the same rights as people in the free world on issues of racial segregation. Second, this decision does not mean that prison authorities can never segregate prisoners. They may do so, but only if: (1) they can present proof that a compelling state interest justifies it, and (2) that the means used are narrowly tailored to meet those needs. This decision makes it difficult for prison authorities to segregate prisoners by race, temporarily (as was the case of the 60-day CDC segregation policy challenged here) or permanently. An instance in which racial segregation in prison will likely be upheld by the courts as constitutional might be if there is an actual prison riot based on race or if prison authorities have proof that racial violence is about to take place. Even at that, prison authorities must prove that racial segregation is the only way the riot can be controlled and that racial segregation is temporary.

L. DUE PROCESS

ESTELLE V. WILLIAMS
425 U.S. 501 (1976)

CAPSULE: An accused cannot be compelled to stand trial before a jury while dressed in identifiable prison clothes.

FACTS: Williams was charged with assault with intent to commit murder after he severely wounded his landlord by stabbing him in the neck, chest, and abdomen with a knife. He was unable to post bail and subsequently was jailed until his trial.

On the day of trial, he requested his civilian clothes from an officer at the jail. The request was denied and he appeared at trial with clothes that were distinctly marked as prison issue. During voir dire, his counsel expressly referred to his jail attire. At no time during the trial, however, did the defendant or his attorney raise an objection to this prison attire. Williams was convicted of the offense, and the conviction was affirmed by the Texas Court of Criminal Appeals.

While in prison, Williams filed a writ of habeas corpus, alleging that requiring a defendant to stand trial in his prison clothing was in violation of the due process and equal protection clauses of the Fourteenth Amendment.

ISSUE: Is an accused who is compelled to wear identifiable prison clothing at his trial by jury denied due process or equal protection of the laws under the Fourteenth Amendment? YES.

HOLDING: The state cannot compel an accused to stand trial before a jury while dressed in identifiable prison clothes. In this case, however, the failure to object to the court about being tried in such clothes negates the presence of the compulsion necessary to establish a constitutional violation.

REASON: "Courts have therefore required an accused to object to being tried in jail garments, just as he must invoke or abandon other rights . . . The record is clear that no objection was made to the trial judge concerning the jail attire either before or at any time during the trial. This omission plainly did not result from any lack of appreciation of the issue, for respondent had raised the question with the jail attendant prior to trial. At trial, defense counsel expressly referred to respondent's attire during voir dire. The trial judge was thus informed that respondent's counsel was fully conscious of the situation.

"Significantly, at the evidentiary hearing respondent's trial counsel did not intimate that he feared any adverse consequences attending an objection to the procedure. There is nothing to suggest that there would have been any prejudicial effect on defense counsel had he made objection, given the decisions on this point in that jurisdiction . . . Nothing in this record, therefore, warrants a conclusion that respondent was compelled to stand trial in jail garb or that there was sufficient reason to excuse the failure to raise the issue before trial. Nor can the trial judge be faulted for not asking the respondent or his counsel whether he was deliberately going to trial in jail clothes.

"Accordingly, although the State cannot, consistently with the Fourteenth Amendment, compel an accused to stand trial before a jury while dressed in identifiable prison clothes, the failure to make an objection to the court as being tried in such clothes, for whatever reason, is sufficient to negate the presence of compulsion necessary to establish a constitutional violation."

CASE SIGNIFICANCE: This case holds that the state cannot compel an accused to stand trial before a jury while dressed in identifiable prison clothes, because that would be fundamentally unfair and therefore a violation of the Fourteenth Amendment due process clause. The problem in this case, however, was the lack of evidence to support the inmate's allegation that he was compelled to stand trial in jail clothes, or that the failure to raise the issue before trial was excusable.

The significance of this case for defendants and lawyers is clear: proper objection must be made before or during trial if the defendant is compelled to wear jail clothes that would predispose the jury to associate the defendant's clothing with guilt. Failure to object means that there may be no sufficient proof later on which to raise an appeal. Note, however, that in this case the defendant did ask to change to his civilian clothes, but the request was denied by the jailer. The defendant must have thought that the jailer spoke for the court when the denial was made. The principle the case establishes is quite simple: objections to violations of constitutional rights must be made before or during trial, regardless of how obvious that violation might be, or there may be no basis on which to raise them on appeal.

HUGHES V. ROWE
449 U.S. 5 (1980)

CAPSULE: Placing a prisoner in segregation without a hearing is unconstitutional, unless justified by emergency conditions. The award of attorney's fees against the prisoner in this case was improper.

FACTS: Hughes, a state prisoner in Illinois, was charged with violation of prison regulations and placed in segregation without a prior hearing. Two days later, Hughes was given a disciplinary hearing and at that time he admitted that he and two other inmates had consumed a homemade alcoholic beverage. Hughes was punished with segregation for 10 days, demotion to C-grade status, and loss of 30 days of statutory good time. He filed a § 1983 case, alleging that the decision to place him in a segregation cell (for the first two days) without a hearing was unconstitutional because it was not justified by any emergency conditions. He also alleged that the order of the district court directing him to pay counsel fees of $400 for services rendered by the Attorney General of Illinois in representing the prison officials in the case was improper.

ISSUES:

1. Did the inmate's segregation in this case without a hearing violate his constitutional right to due process? YES.
2. Was the award of attorney's fees against the prisoner proper? NO.

HOLDING:

1. Segregation without a prior hearing may violate due process if the hearing postponement is not justified by emergency conditions; such conditions must be related to concern for institutional security and safety.
2. The award of attorney's fees against the inmate was not proper because such award could be made only if the district court had found "that the plaintiff's action was frivolous, unreasonable, or without foundation." No such finding supported the fee award in this case.

REASON: "Segregation of a prisoner without a prior hearing may violate due process if the postponement of procedural protections is not justified by apprehended emergency conditions. The amended complaint alleged that segregation was unnecessary in petitioner's case because his offense did not involve violence and he did not present a 'clear and present danger.' There is no suggestion in the record that immediate segregation was necessitated by emergency conditions. Defendants did make the unsworn assertion that petitioner was placed in segregation on 'temporary investigative status,' but the significance of this designation is unclear and it does not, without more, dispose of petitioner's procedural due process claim. The District Court, in dismissing the amended complaint, merely concluded that temporary segregation pending investigation was not actionable. The court cited an Illinois Department of Corrections Administrative Regulation, which authorized segregation of prisoners pending investigation of disciplinary matters, where required 'in the interest of institutional security and safety.' In the absence of any showing that concern for institutional security and safety was the basis for immediate segregation of petitioner without a prior hearing, this regulation does not justify dismissal of petitioner's suit for failure to state a claim.

"In *Christiansburg Garment Co. v. EEOC*, 434 U.S. 412 (1978), we held that the defendant in an action brought under Title VII of the Civil Rights Act of 1964 may recover attorney's fees from the plaintiff only if the District Court finds 'that the plaintiff's action was frivolous, unreasonable, or without foundation, even though not brought in subjective bad faith.' Although arguably a different standard might be applied in a civil rights action under 42 U.S.C. Section 1983, we can perceive no reason for applying a less stringent standard. The plaintiff's action must be meritless in the sense that it is groundless or without foundation. The fact that a plaintiff may ultimately lose his case is not in itself a sufficient justification for the assessment of fees. As we said in *Christiansburg*:

To take the further step of assessing attorney's fees against plaintiffs simply because they do not finally prevail would substantially add to the risks inhering in most litigation and would undercut the efforts of Congress to promote the vigorous enforcement of the provisions of Title VII. Hence, a plaintiff should not be assessed his opponent's attorney's fees unless a court finds that his claim was frivolous, unreasonable, or groundless, or that the plaintiff continued to litigate after it clearly became so."

CASE SIGNIFICANCE: In an earlier case *(Wolff v. McDonnell*, 418 U.S. 539, [1974]), the Court said that a hearing is required before an inmate can be placed in punitive segregation. This case presents a slightly different issue. May an inmate ever be placed in solitary confinement without being given a hearing? The Court replied yes, but only if immediate segregation is necessitated by emergency conditions that would make a hearing impractical. The Court then said, however, that "here, the record did not show that petitioner's immediate segregation was necessitated by emergency conditions, and an administrative regulation authorizing segregation pending investigation of disciplinary matters, where required 'in the interest of institutional security and safety,' did not justify dismissal of the suit in the absence of any showing that concern for institutional security and safety was the basis for petitioner's immediate segregation without a prior hearing." In short, the Court said that inmates may be placed in punitive segregation without a hearing, but only if necessitated by emergency conditions, such emergency conditions being interpreted to mean "concern for institutional security and safety." The placement of inmates in segregation without a hearing has therefore been strictly limited by the Court.

This case is also significant for what it says about when an inmate may be made to pay attorney's fees. The Attorney's Fees Act of 1976 provides that the trial judge may require a party in a § 1983 lawsuit to pay attorney's fees "if the opposing party [the inmate] prevails in at least one of the allegations." In this case, the district court judge imposed a $400 counsel fee not for, but against the inmate for services rendered by the Attorney General of Illinois in representing state prison officials in this action. The Court rejected the fee as improper, saying that such fee is proper only if the district court finds the plaintiff's action to be "frivolous, unreasonable, or without foundation." The Court concluded that there was no such finding in this case, thus the fee could not be awarded. Clearly, this sets two different standards for the recovery of attorney's fees. The Attorney's Fees Act of 1976 makes it easier for inmates to file cases because if they prevail in at least one allegation the judge can then order prison officials and the state to pay the inmate's lawyer's fees. This case reaffirms the Court's ruling in the *Christiansburg* case, mentioned above, and refuses to open the door wider for prison officials to recover attorney's fees from inmates.

PARRATT V. TAYLOR
451 U.S. 527 (1981)

CAPSULE: Loss of inmate hobby materials because a correctional officer failed to follow prison regulations does not amount to a violation of an inmate's due process rights under the Constitution.

FACTS: Taylor, an inmate at the Nebraska Penal and Correctional Complex, ordered hobby materials through the mail at an estimated cost of $23.50. When these materials arrived at the prison hobby center, two employees signed for them. At the time, Taylor was in segregation and was not permitted to have these materials. Prison procedure for the handling of packages provided that the package be delivered to the inmate and a receipt signed or that the prisoner be notified to pick up a package and a receipt be signed. Prison policy allowed only the inmate to whom the package was addressed to sign a receipt for it.

When Taylor was released from segregation he contacted several prison officials to locate his package. These officials could not find his package nor could they determine what caused the package to disappear. Taylor brought an action in federal district court under 42 U.S.C. § 1983 against prison officials, to recover the value of his hobby materials. He claimed that officials were negligent in losing the materials by not following prison regulations and thereby deprived him of property without due process of law in violation of the Fourteenth Amendment.

ISSUE: Did inmate Taylor suffer deprivation of property without due process of law in violation of the Fourteenth Amendment? NO.

HOLDING: To succeed in a § 1983 case, the plaintiff must prove the following: (1) that the conduct complained of was committed by a person acting under color of state law; and (2) that the conduct deprived a person of rights, privileges, or immunities secured by the Constitution or laws of the United States. In this case, the plaintiff established that the prison authorities acted under color of state law, but could not prove that the loss of hobby materials, due to prison officials not strictly following prison procedure, violated the prisoner's right to due process.

REASON: "Unquestionably, respondent's claim satisfies three prerequisites of a valid due process claim: the petitioners acted under color of state law; the hobby kit falls within the definition of property; and the alleged loss, even though negligently caused, amounted to a deprivation. Standing alone, however, these three elements do not establish a violation of the Fourteenth Amendment. Nothing in that Amendment protects against all deprivations of life, liberty, or property by the State. The Fourteenth Amendment protects only against deprivations 'without due process of law.' *Baker v. McCollan*, 443 U.S., at 145. Our inquiry therefore must focus on whether the respondent has suffered a deprivation of property without due process of law. In particular, we must decide whether the tort remedies which the State of Nebraska provides as a means of redress for property deprivations satisfy the requirements of procedural due process.

"Our decision today is fully consistent with our prior cases. To accept respondent's argument that the conduct of the state officials in this case constituted a violation of the Fourteenth Amendment would almost necessarily result in turning every alleged injury which may have been inflicted by a state official acting under 'color of law' into a violation of the Fourteenth Amendment cognizable under Section 1983. It is hard to perceive any logical stopping place to such a line of reasoning . . . Such reasoning 'would make of the Fourteenth Amendment a font of tort law to be superimposed upon whatever systems may already be administered by the States.' *Paul v. Davis*, 424 U.S. 693, 701 (1976). We do not think that the drafters of the Fourteenth Amendment intended the Amendment to play such a role in our society."

CASE SIGNIFICANCE: The Court in this case said that the loss suffered by the inmate as a result of the negligence of prison officials in not following proper procedures did not constitute a violation of a constitutional right. This case says in effect that not every instance of misconduct or negligence on the part of a prison official constitutes a violation of a prisoner's constitutional right. To prove a violation of the constitutional right to due process, the inmate must establish something more than the type of negligence involved in this case. Moreover, the inmate had a remedy available to him under Nebraska tort law that he did not use. Such procedure could have fully compensated the inmate for the loss of property. In a subsequent case, however (*Daniels v. Williams*, 474 U.S. 327 [1986]), the

Court held that federal law (42 U.S.C. § 1983) would not be available to an inmate in these types of cases even if the inmate had no effective remedy under state tort law, therefore overturning this part of the *Taylor* decision.

DANIELS V. WILLIAMS
474 U.S. 327 (1986)

CAPSULE: A negligent act of a prison official (such as leaving a pillow on the stairs) does not violate the due process rights of inmates.

FACTS: Daniels, an inmate at the city jail in Richmond, Virginia, slipped on a pillow left on a stairway. He sustained back and ankle injuries as a result of his fall. Daniels brought suit under 42 U.S.C. § 1983 against Williams, a correctional deputy stationed at the jail who had left the pillow on the stairs. Daniels claimed that Williams' negligence deprived him of his "liberty" interest "without due process of law" within the meaning of the due process clause of the Fourteenth Amendment. Daniels also claimed that he was without an "adequate" state remedy because Williams maintained that he was entitled to sovereign immunity.

ISSUE: Is the due process clause of the Fourteenth Amendment violated by a state official's negligent act that causes unintended loss of, or injury to, an inmate's life, liberty, or property? NO.

HOLDING: The due process clause is not violated by a state official's negligent act that causes unintended loss of, or injury to, life, liberty, or property. To hold that injury caused by such conduct is a deprivation within the meaning of the due process clause would trivialize the centuries-old principle of due process of law.

REASON: "No decision of this Court before *Parratt* supported the view that negligent conduct by a state official, even though causing injury, constitutes a deprivation under the Due Process Clause. This history reflects the traditional and common-sense notion that the Due Process Clause, like its forebear in the Magna Carta, . . . was 'intended to secure the individual from the arbitrary exercise of the powers of government,' *Hurtado v. California*, 110 U.S. 516, 527 (1884).

"Far from an abuse of power, lack of due care suggests no more than a failure to measure up to the conduct of a reasonable person. To hold that injury caused by such conduct is a deprivation within the meaning of the Fourteenth Amendment would trivialize the centuries-old principle of due process of law.

"Jailers may owe a special duty of care to those in their custody under state tort law, see Restatement (Second) of Torts § 314A(4) (1965), but for the reasons previously stated we reject the contention that the Due Process Clause of the Fourteenth Amendment embraces such a tort law concept. Petitioner alleges that he was injured by the negligence of respondent, a custodial official at the city jail. Whatever other provisions of state law or general jurisprudence he may rightly invoke, the Fourteenth Amendment to the United States Constitution does not afford him a remedy."

CASE SIGNIFICANCE: By ruling that a negligent act of a prison officer of the kind involved here (leaving a pillow on the stairs, which caused the inmate to slip) does not fall under the due process clause, the Court severely restricted the scope of the Fourteenth Amendment prisoners' claims in negligence cases. Note, however, that this case dealt with "mere" negligence. What if the act by a prison official constitutes "gross" negligence? Some lower courts have decided that § 1983 can be used as remedy for prisoners in cases of gross negligence, but other lower courts disagree. Scholars also disagree on this issue, which the Court will have to resolve in the future. This case says, however, that "mere" negligence is not a violation of constitutional rights under the Fourteenth Amendment.

The Court in this case also said that even if state tort law does not provide an effective remedy for these types of negligence, it is not actionable anyway under federal law. This overturns a section of the decision in *Parratt v. Taylor* (451 U.S. 527 [1981]), discussed above, which implied that the Supreme Court might allow federal courts to be used if state law did not afford the inmate an effective remedy.

In sum, the types of negligence involved in the *Daniels* and *Taylor* cases did not amount to a violation of a constitutional right that could be the basis for a lawsuit under § 1983. On a scale of 1 to 10 (10 being the most serious type of violation), the negligence involved in these cases is probably a 2 or a 3, very low-level negligence. Other remedies, however, might be available (under state tort law or administratively), but not under § 1983.

WILKINSON V. AUSTIN
545 U.S. 209 (2005)

CAPSULE: Ohio's New Policy for assignment in its supermax prison satisfies due process requirements under the Fourteenth Amendment.

FACTS: Austin and other inmates at Ohio's supermax prison (generally highly secure and tightly restrictive), the Ohio State Penitentiary (OSP), brought suit under § 1983, alleging that the Old Policy procedures in placing prisoners in the institution violated the due process clause of the Fourteenth Amendment. On the eve of trial, Ohio announced a New Policy that included revised procedures in placing inmates in a supermax facility. The district court based its ruling on the New Policy. The court found that the inmates did have a liberty interest in avoiding being sent to the OSP. Further, the Court determined that the new procedures did not provide adequate due process protection, and ordered extensive modification to the policy.

The state of Ohio appealed, saying that the inmates did not have a constitutionally protected liberty interest that entitled them to the relief sought. The State also argued that, if a liberty interest did exist, the New Policy's procedures were constitutionally adequate. The Sixth Circuit Court of Appeals ruled that the inmates had a liberty interest in not being placed in the OSP.

ISSUES:

1. Do inmates have a constitutional right (in the form of a protected liberty interest) in avoiding assignment to the Ohio State Penitentiary? YES.
2. Do the assignment procedures in the New Policy satisfy the due process clause of the Fourteenth Amendment? YES.

HOLDING: Inmates have a constitutional right to avoid assignment to the supermax prison because placement there imposes a hardship much greater than those in other prisons in the system. But the New Policy has sufficient procedural safeguards for placement in the Ohio State Penitentiary, including multiple levels of review, that offer prisoners constitutional protection under the Fourteenth Amendment.

REASON: "We have held that the Constitution itself does not give rise to a liberty interest in avoiding transfer to more adverse conditions of confinement. *Meachum v. Fano*, 427 U.S. 215, 225 (1976) . . . We have also held, however, that a liberty interest in avoiding particular conditions of confinement may arise from state policies or regulations, subject to the important limitations set forth in *Sandin v. Conner*, 515 U.S. 472 (1995) . . . The *Sandin* standard requires us to determine if assignment to OSP 'imposes atypical and significant hardship on the inmate in relation to the ordinary incidents of prison life.' Id., at 484 . . . For an inmate placed in OSP, almost all human contact is prohibited, even to the point that conversation is not permitted from cell to cell; the light, though it may be dimmed, is on for 24 hours; exercise is for 1 hour per day, but only in a small indoor room. Save perhaps for the especially severe limitations on all human contact, these conditions likely would apply to most solitary confinement facilities, but here there are two added components. First is the duration. Unlike the 30-day placement in *Sandin*, placement at OSP is indefinite and, after an initial 30-day review, is reviewed just annually. Second is that placement disqualifies an otherwise eligible inmate for parole consideration. *Austin* I, 189 F. Supp. 2d, at 728. While any of these conditions standing alone might not be sufficient to create a liberty interest, taken together they impose an atypical and significant hardship within the correctional context. It follows that respondents have a liberty interest in avoiding assignment to OSP. *Sandin, supra*, at 483.

"A liberty interest having been established, we turn to the question of what process is due an inmate whom Ohio seeks to place in OSP. Because the requirements of due process are 'flexible and cal[l] for such procedural protections as the particular situation demands,' *Morrissey v. Brewer*, 408 U.S. 471, 481 (1972), we generally have declined to establish rigid rules and instead have embraced a framework to evaluate the sufficiency of particular procedures. The framework, established in *Mathews v. Eldridge*, 424 U.S. 319 (1976), requires consideration of three distinct factors . . . We now hold that the New Policy as described in this opinion strikes a constitutionally permissible balance between the factors of the *Mathews* framework. If an inmate were to demonstrate that the New Policy did not in practice operate in this fashion, resulting in a cognizable injury, that could be the subject of an appropriate future challenge."

CASE SIGNIFICANCE: This case brings added dimension to the concept of the due process rights of prisoners. Inmates brought a lawsuit alleging that assignment to Ohio's supermax prison violated their constitutional right because of the procedures involved, which involved erroneous and haphazard assignments. Ohio correctional officials, however, announced a New Policy that revised that procedure. Under this New Policy, "a prison official conducts a classification review either (1) upon entry into the prison system if the inmate was convicted of certain offenses, e.g. organized crime, or (2) during the incarceration if the inmate engages in specified conduct, e.g., leads a prison gang." The New Policy also provides for a three-tier review process after a recommendation that an inmate be placed in OSP. There were other requirements for review and an opportunity for the inmate to submit objects prior to the final level of review. On appeal, the Court held that inmates do have a right to due process before being assigned to the supermax, but also held that the New Policy complied with the requirements of due process and therefore did not violate constitutional rights.

This decision reaffirms the Court's previous decisions (such as in disciplinary cases in *Morrissey v. Brewer*) that prisoners do have a constitutional right to due process, but that such right is limited. Because conditions in the supermax facility were much harsher than those in the other Ohio prisons, the inmate had a constitutional right to due process before being assigned there. However, the New Policy used by the Ohio prison officials provided enough guarantees that these assignments were made fairly and equitably, including provisions for appeals, review, and a hearing. Taken together, these guidelines gave due process to the inmates. States that have supermax prisons can virtually copy the New Policy of the Ohio prison system if they want to be sure their policy is constitutional.

HAYWOOD V. DROWN ET AL.
556 U.S. 729 (2009)

CAPSULE: A New York state law that divests courts of general jurisdiction from hearing 42 U.S.C., § 1983 cases brought by state prisoners is in violation of the Supremacy Clause of the U.S. Constitution.

FACTS: Haywood, a prisoner at Attica Correctional Facility in New York, brought suit under 42 U.S.C., § 1983, alleging that his civil rights were violated in three prison disciplinary hearings and in an altercation. At the time, New York State had passed Correction Law § 24, based on what it judged to be "frivolous and vexatious" lawsuits by inmates. Under this law, these claims could not be heard in the courts of general jurisdiction but instead were referred to the Court of Claims. In this court, inmates could not receive the same relief and were not afforded the same procedural protections. Plaintiffs have a 90-day notice requirement, are not entitled to a jury trial, cannot receive attorney fees if the judgment is in their favor, and are not entitled to punitive damages or injunctive relief.

When Haywood filed his § 1983 claims in state court, the court dismissed the action because it lacked jurisdiction under Correction Law § 24. The State Court of Appeals affirmed, rejecting the prisoner's claim that the Correction Law violated the Supremacy Clause of the Constitution.

ISSUE: Does New York State Correction Law § 24 violate the Supremacy Clause of the U.S. Constitution? YES.

HOLDING:

1. As applied to § 1983 claims, Correction Law § 24 of New York violates the Supremacy Clause of the Constitution. States may not nullify a federal right or cause of action they believe is inconsistent with their local policies.

2. The law is not a neutral law simply because it treats federal and state claims equally. By divesting state courts of general jurisdiction from hearing state claims and federal claims, including § 1983 claims, the law is in violation of federal law, thus violating the Supremacy Clause.

REASONS: "In our federal system of government, state as well as federal courts have jurisdiction over suits brought pursuant to 42 U.S.C. § 1983, the statute that creates a remedy for violations of federal rights committed by persons acting under color of state law . . . New York's Correction Law § 24 divests those courts of jurisdiction over § 1983 suits that seek money damages from correction officers. New York thus prohibits the trial courts that generally exercise jurisdiction over § 1983 suits brought against other state officials from hearing virtually all such suits . . . The Supremacy Clause, Art. VI, cl. 2, provides: 'This Constitution, and the Laws of the United States which shall be made in Pursuance thereof; and all Treaties made, or which shall be made, under the Authority of the United States, shall be the supreme Law of the Land; and the Judges in every State shall be bound thereby, any Thing in the Constitution or Laws of any State to the Contrary notwithstanding.' . . . The New York Attorney General described Correction Law § 24 as 'further[ing] New York's legitimate interest in minimizing the disruptive effect of prisoner damages claims against correction employees, its courts of jurisdiction over such damages claims and to replace those claims with the State's preferred alternative' . . . under this scheme, a prisoner seeking damages from a correction officer will have his claim dismissed for want of jurisdiction and will be left, instead, to pursue a claim for damages against an entirely different party (the State) in the Court of Claims—a court of limited jurisdiction . . . Although the State has waived its sovereign immunity from liability by allowing itself to be sued in the Court of Claims, a plaintiff seeking damages against the State in that court cannot use § 1983 as a vehicle for redress because a State is not a 'person' under § 1983 . . . This Court has long made clear that federal law is as much the law of the several States as are the laws passed by their legislatures. Federal and state law 'together form one system of jurisprudence, which constitutes the law of the land for the State; and the courts of the two jurisdictions are not foreign to each other, nor to be treated by each other as such, but as courts of the same country, having jurisdiction partly different and partly concurrent.' *Claflin v. Houseman*, 93 U.S. 130, 136–137 (1876); see *Minneapolis & St. Louis R. Co. v.*

Bombolis, 241 U.S. 211, 222 (1916); The Federalist No. 82, p. 132 (E. Bourne ed. 1947) . . . state courts as well as federal courts are entrusted with providing a forum for the vindication of federal rights violated by state or local officials acting under color of state law. See *Patsy v. Board of Regents of Fla.*, 457 U.S. 496, 506–507 (1982) (canvassing the legislative debates of the 1871 Congress and noting that 'many legislators interpreted [§ 1983] to provide dual or concurrent forums in the state and federal system, enabling the plaintiff to choose the forum in which to seek relief'); *Maine v. Thiboutot*, 448 U.S. 1, 3, n. 1 (1980)."

"So strong is the presumption of concurrency that it is defeated only in two narrowly defined circumstances: first, when Congress expressly ousts state courts of jurisdiction, see *Bombolis*, 241 U.S., at 221; *Claflin*, 93 U.S., at 136; and second, '[w]hen a state court refuses jurisdiction because of a neutral state rule regarding the administration of the courts,' *Howlett*, 496 U.S., at 372. Focusing on the latter circumstance, we have emphasized that only a neutral jurisdictional rule will be deemed a 'valid excuse' for departing from the default assumption that 'state courts have inherent authority, and are thus presumptively competent, to adjudicate claims arising under the laws of the United States.' *Tafflin v. Levitt*, 493 U.S. 455, 458 (1990). In determining whether a state law qualifies as a neutral rule of judicial administration, our cases have established that a State cannot employ a jurisdictional rule 'to dissociate [itself] from federal law because of disagreement with its content or a refusal to recognize the superior authority of its source.' *Howlett*, 496 U.S., at 371. In other words, although States retain substantial leeway to establish the contours of their judicial systems, they lack authority to nullify a federal right or cause of action they believe is inconsistent with their local policies . . . It is principally on this basis that Correction Law § 24 violates the Supremacy Clause. In passing Correction Law § 24, New York made the judgment that correction officers should not be burdened with suits for damages arising out of conduct performed in the scope of their employment. Because it regards these suits as too numerous or too frivolous (or both), the State's longstanding policy has been to shield this narrow class of defendants from liability when sued for damages. The State's policy, whatever its merits, is contrary to Congress' judgment that all persons who violate federal rights while acting under color of state law shall be held liable for damages . . . if Correction Law § 24 were understood as offering an immunity defense, *Howlett* would compel the conclusion that it violates the Supremacy Clause . . . Until it has been proved that the claim has no merit, that judgment is not up to the States to make.' *Howlett*, 496 U.S., at 380 . . . That New York strongly favors a rule shielding correction officers from personal damages liability and substituting the State as the party responsible for compensating individual victims is irrelevant. The State cannot condition its enforcement of federal law on the demand that those individuals whose conduct federal law seeks to regulate must nevertheless escape liability."

"Although the absence of discrimination is necessary to our finding a state law neutral, it is not sufficient. A jurisdictional rule cannot be used as a device to undermine federal law, no matter how evenhanded it may appear. As we made clear in

Howlett, '[t]he fact that a rule is denominated jurisdictional does not provide a court an excuse to avoid the obligation to enforce federal law if the rule does not reflect the concerns of power over the person and competence over the subject matter that jurisdictional rules are designed to protect.' 496 U.S., at 381. Ensuring equality of treatment is thus the beginning, not the end, of the Supremacy Clause analysis . . . Because New York's supreme courts generally have personal jurisdiction over the parties in § 1983 suits brought by prisoners against correction officers and because they hear the lion's share of all other § 1983 actions, we find little concerning 'power over the person and competence over the subject matter' in Correction Law § 24. *Id.*, at 381; see *id.*, at 378 (conducting a similar analysis and concluding that the Florida courts of general jurisdiction were 'fully competent to provide the remedies [§ 1983] requires' . . . Our holding addresses only the unique scheme adopted by the State of New York—a law designed to shield a particular class of defendants (correction officers) from a particular type of liability (damages) brought by a particular class of plaintiffs (prisoners). Based on the belief that damages suits against correction officers are frivolous and vexatious, see *supra*, at 3–4, n. 3, Correction Law § 24 is effectively an immunity statute cloaked in jurisdictional garb. . . . The judgment of the New York Court of Appeals is reversed, and the case is remanded to that court for further proceedings not inconsistent with this opinion."

CASE SIGNIFICANCE: This case strikes down a New York law that is ruled to violate the Supremacy Clause of the U.S. Constitution. In previous Supreme Court decisions, the Court has held that both state and federal courts have concurrent jurisdiction on federal issues. The New York law doesn't allow the courts of general jurisdiction to hear § 1983 cases, instead referring them to an alternative court that has restricted relief and limited procedural protections. The Court finds this alternative court to be unacceptable under federal protections offered to state inmates.

The Court also finds unconvincing New York's argument that the law is neutral because it does not allow state or federal claims to be heard in courts of general jurisdiction. This nondiscrimination is not sufficient to show that the law is neutral because it restricts lawsuits of both kinds. The Court states that New York should allow § 1983 claims to be heard in their courts of general jurisdiction because this is the appropriate forum.

New York ranks fifth in the United States in prison population, with 54,100 inmates in 2012. It is understandable that officials don't want prisoners clogging up the state courts with frivolous lawsuits. However, as the Supreme Court notes, barring an entire class of lawsuits (§ 1983 cases) from being heard in the state's courts of general jurisdiction without reviewing the merit of each case is unconstitutional.

M. FORCE—USE OF DEADLY FORCE IN CORRECTIONAL FACILITIES

WHITLEY V. ALBERS
475 U.S. 312 (1986)

CAPSULE: The shooting of a prisoner, without prior verbal warning, to suppress a prison riot did not violate the prisoner's right against cruel and unusual punishment. Liability arises only if such deadly force was used with "obduracy and wantonness."

FACTS: A corrections officer was taken hostage and held in a cell on the upper tier of a cellblock during a riot in an Oregon penitentiary. The prison security manager consulted with two other prison officials and it was agreed that forceful intervention was necessary to protect both the hostage and the non-participating inmates. A squad of officers armed with shotguns entered the cellblock in order to rescue the hostage. One officer was ordered to fire a warning shot and to shoot low at any prisoner climbing the stairs toward the hostage cell. After the rescue squad began moving up the stairs, a warning shot was fired, followed by another shot. A third shot hit the respondent in the left knee as he was climbing up the stairs. As a result, the inmate sustained severe damage to his left leg as well as mental and emotional distress. He brought suit under 42 U.S.C. § 1983 against the prison officials, alleging violation of his Eighth and Fourteenth Amendment rights.

ISSUE: Is the infliction of pain in the course of prison security measures a violation of the right to be free from cruel and unusual punishment under the Eighth Amendment? NO.

HOLDING: The infliction of pain in the course of prison security measures is a violation of the Eighth Amendment only if inflicted unnecessarily and wantonly. The shooting of a prisoner without prior verbal warning, in an effort to suppress a prison riot, did not violate his right to be free from cruel and unusual punishment. There is liability in these cases only if the deadly force was used with obduracy and wantonness.

REASON: "It is obduracy and wantonness, not inadvertence or error in good faith, that characterize the conduct prohibited by the Cruel and Unusual Punishment Clause, whether that conduct occurs in connection with establishing conditions of confinement, supplying medical needs, or restoring control over a tumultuous cell block. The infliction of pain in the course of a prison security measure, therefore, does not amount to cruel and unusual punishment simply because it may appear in retrospect that the degree of force authorized or applied for security purposes was unreasonable, and hence unnecessary in the strict sense.

"Viewing the evidence in the light most favorable to respondent, as must be done in reviewing the decision reversing the trial court's directed verdict for petitioners, it does not appear that the evidence supports a reliable inference of wantonness in the infliction of pain under the above standard. Evidence arguably showing that the prison officials erred in judgment when they decided on a plan that employed potentially deadly force, falls far short of a showing that there was no plausible basis for their belief that this degree of force was necessary."

CASE SIGNIFICANCE: This case is consistent with the trend that gives prison administrators and personnel more discretion in dealing with inmates, particularly in an emergency situation. The Court said that there is liability in these cases, but only if the use of deadly force was obdurate and wanton. One dictionary defines "obdurate" as "hardened in feelings"; it defines "wanton" as "merciless, inhumane, and malicious." What the officers did in this case did not amount to obduracy or wantonness.

Does the standard apply to all use-of-force cases or only cases involving use of deadly force? The decision itself is unclear on that issue. The Court said: "It is obduracy and wantonness, not inadvertence or error in good faith, that characterize the conduct prohibited by the Eighth Amendment, whether that conduct occurs in connection with establishing conditions of confinement, supplying medical needs, or restoring control over a tumultuous cell block." In another part of the decision, however, the Court says: "Where a prison security measure is undertaken to resolve a disturbance that poses significant risks to safety of inmates and prison staff, the question whether the measure taken inflicted wanton pain in violation of the Eighth Amendment ultimately turns on whether the force applied was applied in a good faith effort to maintain or restore discipline or maliciously and sadistically for the purpose of causing harm . . ." A subsequent case (*Hudson v. McMillian*, 60 L.W. 4151 [1992]), however, implies that the standard set in *Whitley v. Albers* is limited only to use of deadly force cases. The Supreme Court set a different standard for liability in non-deadly force cases, as the next case indicates.

N. FORCE—USE OF NONDEADLY FORCE IN CORRECTIONAL FACILITIES

HUDSON V. MCMILLIAN
503 U.S. 1 (1992)

CAPSULE: Use of excessive physical force against a prisoner may constitute cruel and unusual punishment, even though no serious injury results, if that force was used "maliciously and sadistically" to cause harm.

FACTS: Keith Hudson, a prison inmate in Louisiana, brought a 42 U.S.C. § 1983 lawsuit against correctional officers McMillian and Woods as a result of the beating Hudson received from the two officers when they took Hudson out of his cell one morning and walked him toward the prison's administrative lockdown area. Hudson testified that McMillian punched him in the mouth, eyes, chest, and stomach, while Woods held him in place and kicked and punched him from behind. The prisoner also alleged that Mezo, the supervisor on duty, watched the beating but merely told the officers "not to have too much fun." As a result of the beating, the prisoner suffered minor bruises and swelling of the face, mouth, and lip. The beating also loosened Hudson's teeth and cracked his partial dental plate, making it unusable for months. The federal magistrate found excessive use of force by the officers and condonation of their actions by the supervisor. The prisoner was awarded $800 in damages. The Fifth Circuit Court of Appeals reversed, holding that there was no violation of the Eighth Amendment prohibition against cruel and unusual punishment because there was no "significant injury," and that whatever injuries were inflicted were "minor," and required no medical treatment.

ISSUE: Is the use of excessive force against a prisoner cruel and unusual punishment and therefore unconstitutional even if the inmate does not suffer serious injury? YES.

HOLDING: The use of excessive physical force by prison officials against a prisoner may constitute cruel and unusual punishment, and is therefore unconstitutional, even if the inmate does not suffer serious injury if such force was used "maliciously and sadistically" to cause harm.

REASON: "In *Whitley v. Albers*, 475 U.S. 312 (1986), the principal question before us was what legal standard should govern the Eighth Amendment claim of an inmate shot by a guard during a prison riot. We based our answer on the settled rule that 'the unnecessary and wanton infliction of pain . . . constitutes cruel and unusual punishment forbidden by the Eighth Amendment.'

"What is necessary to establish an 'unnecessary and wanton infliction of pain,' we said, varies according to the nature of the alleged constitutional violation. 475 U.S., at 320. For example, the appropriate inquiry when an inmate alleges that prison officials failed to attend to serious medical needs is whether the officials exhibited 'deliberate indifference.' See *Estelle v. Gamble*, 429 U.S. 97, 104 (1976). This standard is appropriate because the State's responsibility to provide inmates with medical care ordinarily does not conflict with competing administrative concerns. *Whitley, supra*, at 320.

"Many of the concerns underlying our holding in *Whitley* arise whenever guards use force to keep order. Whether the prison disturbance is a riot or a lesser disruption, corrections officers must balance the need 'to maintain or restore discipline' through force against the risk of injury to inmates. Both situations may require prison officials to act quickly and decisively. Likewise, both implicate the principle that '[p]rison administrators . . . should be accorded wide-ranging deference in the adoption and execution of policies and practices that in their judgment are needed to preserve internal order and discipline and to maintain institutional security.' In recognition of these similarities, we hold that whenever prison officials stand accused of using excessive physical force in violation of the Cruel and Unusual Punishments Clause, the core judicial inquiry is that set out in *Whitley*: whether force was applied in a good-faith effort to maintain or restore discipline, or maliciously and sadistically to cause harm."

CASE SIGNIFICANCE: This case is significant because it defines when the use of non-deadly force by correctional officers becomes a violation of the constitutional rights of inmates. The Court said that the injury to the prisoner does not have to be "serious" or "significant" in order for it to become a constitutional violation. Instead, the Court used this standard: whether the force was applied in a good faith effort to maintain or restore discipline, or maliciously and sadistically to cause harm. In this case, the majority of the Court concluded that Hudson's constitutional right against cruel and unusual punishment was violated because the correctional officers used force "maliciously and sadistically to cause harm."

The standard used by the court to impose damages in this case is easier for the prisoner to meet than the standard used in previous cases. The cruel and unusual punishment clause of the Eighth Amendment has been the subject of several Court decisions. In one of the earliest cases (*Estelle v. Gamble*, 429 U.S. 97 [1976]), the Court held that "deliberate indifference" to an inmate's medical needs constitutes a violation of the Eighth Amendment. In a subsequent case (*Whitley v. Albers*, 475 U.S. 312 [1986]), the Court applied a different standard in the use of deadly force by prison officials to put down a prison riot. In the present case, the majority of the Court concluded that Hudson's constitutional right against cruel and unusual punishment was violated because the correctional officers used force maliciously and sadistically to cause harm.

This decision does not imply that any injury caused by correctional officers in the performance of responsibilities is per se a violation of the Eighth Amendment and therefore leads to civil liability. The Court specifically rejected such a view, holding instead that this decision does not "say that every malevolent touch by a prison guard gives rise to a federal cause of action." The Court quoted, with approval, a decision by the Second Circuit Court of Appeals (*Johnson v. Glick*, 481 F.2d, at 1033) that says that "not every push or shove, even if it may later seem unnecessary in the peace of a judge's chambers, violates a prisoner's constitutional rights." The question to be asked in each case is: "Was the use of force by the prison guard repugnant to the conscience of mankind?" using contemporary standards. The Court found that what the officers did to Hudson violated this standard, and thus held them civilly liable for the injuries inflicted, even though the injuries were considered "minor" by the lower court.

This case was decided by a seven-to-two vote, the two dissenters being Justices Thomas and Scalia. In his dissent, Justice Thomas wrote: "In my view, a show of force that causes only insignificant harm to a prisoner may be immoral, it may be tortious, it may be criminal, and it may even be remediable under other provisions of the Federal Constitution, but it is not 'cruel and unusual punishment.'" Thomas and Scalia believed that because the lower court found the injuries to the prisoner to be "minor," no damages ought to have been imposed. The dissent also charged that the majority opinion expanded the interpretation of the cruel and unusual punishment clause "beyond all bounds of history and precedent." It must be pointed out, however, that the dissent did not approve of or condone what the officers in this case did to the prisoner. Said the dissent: "Abusive behavior by prison guards is deplorable conduct that properly evokes outrage and contempt. But that does not mean that it is invariably unconstitutional. The Eighth Amendment is not, and should not be turned into a National Code of Prison Regulation." They differed with the majority in that they believed that this type of injury does not constitute cruel and unusual punishment in violation of the Eighth Amendment.

WILKINS V. GADDY
559 U.S. 34 (2010)

CAPSULE: In deciding excessive force claims in a correctional institution, the judgment should be based on the nature of the force rather than the extent of injury.

FACTS: Wilkins was a prisoner in a North Carolina state prison. He filed a 42 U.S.C. § 1983 lawsuit claiming that he was attacked by a correctional officer because he requested a grievance form. The prisoner stated that he sustained multiple physical injuries and also experienced psychological trauma as a result of the attack. His physical injuries included lower back pain, headaches, and dizziness. His psychological trauma included nightmares of the assault. His § 1983 case claimed that Officer Gaddy violated his civil rights under the Eighth Amendment's prohibition against cruel and unusual punishment.

The District Court, without a response from the correctional officer, denied Wilkins' claim. The Court stated that he had to establish that he had received more than a *de minimis* injury in order to claim an Eighth Amendment violation. The Court noted that he had not done so, and that he had failed to even assert that he required medical attention as a result of his injuries. Respondent filed a motion for reconsideration, submitting medical records to indicate that he had been treated by a physician for physical as well as mental issues. The Court did not allow Wilkins to amend his claim, and the Fourth Circuit Court of Appeals affirmed.

ISSUE: Should courts follow the standard established in *Hudson v. McMillian* in determining excessive force in correctional institutions claims? YES.

HOLDING: The *Hudson* standard, which examines whether force was used to maintain order or whether it was maliciously and sadistically applied, is the proper standard to employ in deciding excessive force cases in correctional institutions.

REASONS: "In requiring what amounts to a showing of significant injury in order to state an excessive force claim, the Fourth Circuit has strayed from the clear holding of this Court in *Hudson*. Like Wilkins, the prisoner in *Hudson* filed suit under § 1983 alleging that corrections officers had used excessive force in violation of the Eighth Amendment . . . [T]his Court rejected the notion that 'significant injury' is a threshold requirement for stating an excessive force claim. The 'core judicial inquiry,' we held, was not whether a certain quantum of injury was sustained, but rather 'whether force was applied in a good-faith effort to maintain or restore discipline, or maliciously and sadistically to cause harm.' 503 U.S., at 7; see also *Whitley v. Albers*, 475 U.S. 312, 319–321 (1986). 'When prison officials maliciously and sadistically use force to cause harm,' the Court recognized, 'contemporary standards of decency always are violated . . . whether or not significant injury is evident. Otherwise, the Eighth Amendment would permit any physical punishment, no matter how diabolic or inhuman, inflicting less than some arbitrary quantity of injury.' *Hudson*, 503 U.S., at 9; see also *id.*, at 13–14 . . . The extent of injury may also provide some indication of the amount of force applied . . . An inmate who complains of a 'push or shove' that causes no discernible injury almost certainly fails to state a valid excessive force claim . . . Injury and force, however, are only imperfectly correlated, and it is the latter that ultimately counts. An inmate who is gratuitously beaten by guards does not lose his ability to pursue an excessive force claim merely because he has the good fortune to escape without serious injury . . . The allegations made by Wilkins in this case are quite similar to the facts in *Hudson*, and the District Court's analysis closely resembles the approach Hudson disavowed . . . Dismissing Wilkins' action sua sponte, the District Court did not hold that this purported assault, which allegedly left Wilkins with a bruised heel, back pain, and other injuries requiring medical treatment, involved *de minimis* force. Instead, the court concluded that Wilkins had failed to state a claim because 'he simply has not alleged that he suffered anything more than de minimus [sic] injury.'"

"The Fourth Circuit's strained reading of *Hudson* is not defensible. This Court's decision did not, as the Fourth Circuit would have it, merely serve to lower the injury threshold for excessive force claims from 'significant' to 'non-de minimis'—whatever those ill-defined terms might mean. Instead, the Court aimed to shift the 'core judicial inquiry' from the extent of the injury to the nature of the force—specifically, whether it was nontrivial and 'was applied . . . maliciously and sadistically to cause harm.' 503 U.S., at 7. To conclude, as the District Court did here, that the absence of 'some arbitrary quantity of injury' requires automatic dismissal of an excessive force claim improperly bypasses this core inquiry . . . In holding that the District Court erred in dismissing Wilkins' complaint based on the supposedly de minimis nature of his injuries, we express no view on the underlying merits of his excessive force claim. In order to prevail, Wilkins will ultimately have to prove not only that the assault actually occurred but also that it was carried out 'maliciously and sadistically' rather than as part of 'a good-faith effort to maintain or restore discipline.' *Ibid*. Moreover, even if Wilkins succeeds, the relatively modest nature of his alleged injuries will no doubt limit the damages he may recover. The judgment of the Court of Appeals is reversed, and the case is remanded for further proceedings consistent with this opinion."

CASE SIGNIFICANCE: This case is important because it reinforces the Court's ruling in *Hudson v. McMillian*, which was decided 18 years earlier. The Court notes that some of the Courts of Appeals are misinterpreting their decision in that case, focusing on a level of injury and not the intent behind the correctional officer's actions. If the officer intends to use excessive force for a malicious and sadistic purpose and does so, then the action rises to an Eighth Amendment violation. Conversely, if the officer is using excessive force to maintain order, then there is no constitutional violation. The Court also notes that claims of this nature may not result in a great amount of monetary damages being awarded to the inmate because the injuries may actually be minimal.

Justice Thomas concurred with the judgment that the Fourth Circuit Court of Appeals misinterpreted the *Hudson* decision. However, he again asserts that the *Hudson* case was decided incorrectly. He states that the Eighth Amendment does require that the injury be serious in addition to examining the officer's intentions. By writing the concurring opinion, Justice Thomas is able to reiterate his arguments in the original case.

KINGSLEY V. HENDRICKSON ET AL.
135 S. CT. ___ (2015)

CAPSULE: To prevail in an excessive force claim, a pretrial detainee must only prove that the force purposely or knowingly used against him was objectively unreasonable.

FACTS: Kingsley was a pretrial detainee in a county jail in Wisconsin. When he refused to comply with an order given by correctional officers, he was forcefully removed from his cell. He claimed that two officers used excessive force on him during that time in violation of the Due Process Clause of the Fourteenth Amendment, filing a § 1983 claim. The case went to trial in federal district court. When the jury was preparing to deliberate, the judge instructed them that the claimant was required to prove, *inter alia*, that the officers recklessly disregarded his safety and acted with reckless disregard for his rights. The jury found that this did not occur.

In his appeal, the petitioner claimed that the jury instructions were improper. He argued that the standard of objective unreasonableness should have been applied in making the decision. The Seventh Circuit Court of Appeals instead held that the law required the jury to apply a subjective standard in examining the officers' state of mind. This standard required the jury to determine whether the officers actually intended to violate the petitioner's rights or recklessly disregarded them.

ISSUES:
1. Is a pretrial detainee required to show that correctional officers were subjectively aware that their use of force was unreasonable in an excessive force claim? NO.
2. Were the instructions to the jury in error based on the above standard? YES.

HOLDING: Under 42 U.S.C., § 1983, a pretrial detainee is required only to show that the excessive force purposely or knowingly used against him was objectively unreasonable. The jury instructions were improper, but whether they resulted in harmless error is left to the Seventh Circuit Court of Appeals to decide on remand. **REASON:** "Several considerations have led us to conclude that the appropriate standard for a pretrial detainee's excessive force claim is solely an objective one. For one thing, it is consistent with our precedent. We have said that 'the Due Process Clause protects a pretrial detainee from the use of excessive force that amounts to punishment.' *Graham, supra*, at 395, n. 10. And in *Bell*, we explained that such 'punishment' can consist of actions taken with an 'expressed intent to punish.' 441 U.S., at 538. But the Court went on to explain that, in the absence of an expressed intent to punish, a pretrial detainee can nevertheless prevail by showing that the actions are not 'rationally related to a legitimate nonpunitive governmental purpose' or that the actions 'appear excessive in relation to that purpose.' *Id.*, at 561."

"For another thing, experience suggests that an objective standard is workable. It is consistent with the pattern jury instructions used in several Circuits. We are also told that many facilities, including the facility at issue here, train officers to interact with all detainees as if the officers' conduct is subject to an objective reasonableness standard . . . For these reasons, we have stressed that a court must judge the reasonableness of the force used from the perspective and with the knowledge of the defendant officer. We have also explained that a court must take account of the legitimate interests in managing a jail . . . Additionally, an officer enjoys qualified immunity and is not liable for excessive force unless he has violated a 'clearly established' right, such that 'it would [have been] clear to a reasonable officer that his conduct was unlawful in the situation he confronted.' *Saucier v. Katz*, 533 U.S. 194, 202 (2001); see also Brief for United States as Amicus Curiae 27–28. It is unlikely (though theoretically possible) that a plaintiff could overcome these hurdles where an officer acted in good faith."

"We now consider the lawfulness of the jury instruction given in this case in light of our adoption of an objective standard for pretrial detainees' excessive force claims . . . It required Kingsley to show that the officers 'recklessly disregarded [Kingsley's] safety.' *Id.*, at 278. And it suggested that Kingsley must show the defendants 'acted with reckless disregard of [Kingsley's] rights,' while telling the jury that it could consider several objective factors in making this determination. Ibid. . . . We agree with Kingsley that the instructions were erroneous. '[R]eckles[s] disregar[d] [of Kingsley's] safety' was listed as an additional requirement, beyond the need to find that '[respondents'] use of force was unreasonable in light of the facts and circumstances at the time.' App. 278. See also *ibid.* . . . And in determining whether respondents 'acted with reckless disregard of [Kingsley's] rights,' the jury was instructed to 'consider . . . [w]hether [respondents] reasonably *believed* there was a threat to the safety of staff or prisoners.' *Ibid.* (emphasis added). Together, these features suggested the jury should weigh respondents' subjective reasons for using force and subjective views about the excessiveness of the force. As we have just held, that was error. But because the question whether that error was harmless may depend in part on the detailed specifics of this case, we leave that question for the Court of Appeals to resolve in the first instance. The decision of the Court of Appeals is vacated, and the case is remanded for proceedings consistent with this."

CASE SIGNIFICANCE: This is an important case because it applies a new standard in determining whether excessive force was used in pretrial detainees' claims. The standard is one of objective unreasonableness, as opposed to proving that the officers were *subjectively* aware that their force was unreasonable. This standard does not seek to determine the officers' intent; rather, it examines whether the force was excessive based on the facts of the case, with consideration for the need of the facility to maintain order. Whether it was excessive in this case was in dispute during the trial, before the jury was given its instructions.

The Court also makes the distinction between pretrial detainees who are filing claims under the Fourteenth Amendment's Due Process Clause and convicted offenders who are filing claims under the Eighth Amendment's prohibition against cruel and unusual punishment. The Court notes, "pretrial detainees . . . cannot be punished at all, much less 'maliciously and sadistically.' . . . Thus, there is no need here, as there might be in an Eighth Amendment case, to determine when punishment is unconstitutional. *Whitley* and *Hudson* [the prison cases the respondents cited] are relevant here only insofar as they address the practical importance of taking into account the legitimate safety-related concerns of those who run jails."

In this case, the Court appears to be limiting their ruling to pretrial detainees, excluding those who have been convicted and are housed in jails or prisons. This distinction between those who are "innocent until proven guilty" and those who plead guilty or are found guilty is a fundamental difference recognized by the Court in numerous cases. A convicted prisoner who brings a claim of excessive force under the Fourteenth Amendment's Due Process Clause and the objective unreasonableness standard would most likely be unsuccessful.

Whether the instructions to the jury were harmless error and thus the judgment in favor of the correctional officers will stand remains to be seen. The Seventh Circuit Court of Appeals will make that determination in the future.

O. HABEAS CORPUS

ROSE V. LUNDY
455 U.S. 509 (1982)

CAPSULE: Under federal law, state prisoners must exhaust state court remedies before filing for a writ of habeas corpus in federal court.

FACTS: Noah Lundy was convicted in Tennessee of rape and crimes against nature and was sent to state prison. The Tennessee Court of Criminal Appeals affirmed his convictions and the Tennessee Supreme Court denied review. Lundy filed a petition for post-conviction relief in state court, which was denied. He then filed a petition for a writ of habeas corpus in federal district court under 28 U.S.C. § 2254, alleging the following: "(1) that he had been denied the right to confrontation because the trial court limited the defense counsel's questioning of the victim; (2) that he had been denied the right to a fair trial because the prosecuting attorney stated that the respondent had a violent character; (3) that he had been denied the right to a fair trial because the prosecutor improperly remarked in his closing argument that the State's evidence was uncontradicted; and (4) that the trial judge improperly instructed the jury that every witness is presumed to swear the truth." The federal district court granted the writ of habeas corpus despite claims (3) and (4) not having been litigated in state court. The Court of Appeals affirmed the decision of the federal district court; the government appealed.

ISSUE: Does federal law (28 U.S.C. § 2254 [b] and [c]) require a federal district court to dismiss a state prisoner's petition for a writ of habeas corpus that contains claims that have not been exhausted in the state court? YES.

HOLDING: A district court must dismiss "mixed petitions" (meaning petitions that contain claims that have been exhausted and others that have not been exhausted in state court) because such dismissal furthers the purposes underlying the federal habeas corpus statute.

REASON: "The exhaustion doctrine is principally designed to protect the state courts' role in the enforcement of federal law and prevent disruption of state judicial proceedings. Under our federal system, the federal and state 'courts [are] equally bound to guard and protect rights secured by the Constitution.' Because 'it would be unseemly in our dual system of government for a federal district court to upset a state court conviction without an opportunity for the state courts to correct a constitutional violation,' federal courts apply the doctrine of comity, which 'teaches that one court should defer action on causes properly within its jurisdiction until the courts of another sovereignty with concurrent powers, and already cognizant of the litigation, have had an opportunity to pass upon the matter.'

"The facts of the present case underscore the need for a rule encouraging exhaustion of all federal claims. In his opinion, the District Court Judge wrote that 'there is such mixture of violations that one cannot be separated from and considered independently of the others.' Because the two unexhausted claims for relief were intertwined with the exhausted one, the judge apparently considered all of the claims in ruling on the petition. Requiring dismissal of petitions containing both exhausted and unexhausted claims will relieve the district courts of the difficult if not impossible task of deciding when claims are related, and will reduce the temptation to consider unexhausted claims."

CASE SIGNIFICANCE: Despite the absence of a constitutional issue, this case is significant because it clarifies when state prisoners can file habeas corpus petitions in federal courts. Habeas corpus petitions are filed by inmates to gain release, alleging that something was wrong with their conviction and therefore they are in prison unconstitutionally. This is the prisoner's last hope of freedom after conviction has been affirmed by the courts. Although habeas corpus cases seldom succeed, they give prisoners another judicial avenue to pursue when they believe they have been wrongly convicted.

The "exhaustion of state court remedies" doctrine provides that remedies in state courts must be exhausted before a case can be heard in federal court. As this case states, "the exhaustion doctrine existed long before its codification by Congress in 1948." Although now codified, the "mixed petition" issue was not addressed in the codification, thus the need to clarify it in this case. The purpose of the exhaustion doctrine is to avoid piecemeal litigation. Its benefits are obvious. In the words of the Supreme Court: "To the extent that the exhaustion requirement reduces piecemeal litigation, both the courts and the prisoners should benefit, for as a result the district court will be more likely to review all of the prisoner's claims in a single proceeding, thus providing for a more focused and thorough review."

There are two kinds of habeas corpus proceedings: state habeas corpus and federal habeas corpus. Both are available to prisoners, but this case states that issues brought to federal courts on habeas corpus grounds must first be litigated in state courts. In this case, the prisoner alleged four grounds for relief; two grounds were litigated in state court, and the other two grounds were not litigated in state court. The issue was whether such a "mixed petition" ought to be entertained by the federal court. The Court decided that 28 U.S.C. § 2254 "requires a federal district court to dismiss a petition for a writ of habeas corpus containing any claims that have not been exhausted in the state courts." This is significant because it lengthens the time of potential relief for state prisoners in habeas corpus proceedings. It usually takes a number of years for prisoner habeas corpus cases to be decided in state court. Only after that will the federal forum be available to a state prisoner. This therefore further delays the availability of the federal habeas corpus remedy because state prisoners must first go through state process before taking their case to a federal court, even when some of the allegations have been litigated in state court. It is to be noted, however, that federal prisoners do not have to exhaust state proceedings because they have been tried and convicted under federal law in federal court.

TEAGUE V. LANE
489 U.S. 288 (1989)

CAPSULE: New constitutional rules of criminal procedure are not applicable to other cases in which a conviction was final when the new rule was announced.

FACTS: Teague was convicted by a petit jury in Illinois of attempted murder and other offenses. The jury that convicted him was all white. The prosecutor in the case used all 10 of his peremptory challenges to exclude potential black jurors, stating that he was attempting to balance the jury with equal numbers of men and women. Teague filed an appeal in the district court, saying that the prosecutor's peremptory challenges denied him the right to a representative jury from the community. This appeal was denied and he filed a habeas petition with the federal district court.

In the habeas petition, he again repeated his claim of a fair cross section of the community. Additionally, Teague asserted that a reexamination of a portion of *Swain v. Alabama* was established based on several Justices' opinions in *McCray v. New York*. The *Swain* case decided what a defendant must show in order to establish a case of prima facie discrimination in a peremptory challenge system. Conversely, Teague argued that Swain set a standard allowing a prosecutor to be questioned concerning his peremptory challenges when the prosecutor offered an explanation for them. The federal district court denied relief and Teague filed a petition in the Seventh Circuit Court of Appeals.

The Court of Appeals ruled in favor of Teague's fair cross section assertion but postponed rehearing the case in its entirety until the Supreme Court ruled in *Batson v. Kentucky*. In that case, the Court established a new standard for a prima facie case of discrimination, but Teague was prevented from applying this standard because the Court had ruled in *Allen v. Hardy* that *Batson* could not be applied retroactively to cases that were being reviewed collaterally. The Court of Appeals also ruled that Teague's *Swain* claim was procedurally barred and meritless. The Court held that the fair cross section requirement was limited to jury venire.

ISSUES:

1. Does the ruling in *Batson v. Kentucky* apply retroactively to a case on collateral review? NO.
2. Can the petitioner claim rights under *Swain v. Alabama*? NO.

HOLDING: A retroactive claim will not succeed based on the ruling in *Batson v. Kentucky*. The petitioner is also procedurally barred from raising a claim under *Swain v. Alabama* because he did not raise this claim at trial or on direct appeal.

REASON: "Petitioner's conviction became final two and one half years prior to *Batson*, thus depriving petitioner of any benefit from the rule announced in that case. Petitioner argues, however, that *Batson* should be applied retroactively to all cases pending on direct review at the time certiorari was denied in *McCray* because the opinions filed in *McCray* destroyed the precedential effect of *Swain* . . . We reject the basic premise of petitioner's argument. As we have often stated, the 'denial of a writ of certiorari imports no expression of opinion upon the merits of the case.'

"Under *Wainwright v. Sykes*, petitioner is barred from raising the *Swain* claim in a federal habeas corpus proceeding unless he can show cause for the default and prejudice resulting therefrom . . . Petitioner does not attempt to show cause for his default. Instead, he argues that the claim is not barred because it was addressed by the Illinois Appellate Court. We cannot agree with the petitioner's argument . . . Our application of the procedural default rule here is consistent with *Harris v. Reed* . . . The rule announced in *Harris v. Reed* assumes that a state court has had the opportunity to address a claim that is later raised in a federal habeas proceeding. It is simply inapplicable in a case such as this one, where the claim was never presented to the state courts."

CASE SIGNIFICANCE: This is a habeas case in which the prisoner claimed that he was entitled to release because of a violation of his constitutional right to a fair and impartial jury. His claim was based on the case of *Batson v. Kentucky*, in which the Supreme Court established a new standard for establishing a prima facie case of discrimination in jury selection. Teague claimed that under this new standard, his rights were violated. The problem, however, was that Teague's conviction became final two and one-half years before the *Batson* decision. Moreover, the *Batson* holding was not held to be retroactive to cases on collateral review, such as habeas petitions. Despite this, Teague claimed that the decision applied to him. The Court rejected his claim, saying that a new constitutional rule of criminal procedure (such as that set in *Batson*) did not apply to cases in which the conviction was final when the new rule was announced.

Teague also claimed he should be freed because of the ruling in *Swain v. Alabama*, in which the Court specified what a defendant must show in order to establish prima facie discrimination in peremptory challenges (challenges in jury selection when no reason is stated). He also asserted that *Swain* allowed a prosecutor to be questioned concerning his peremptory challenge and that Teague was denied this right. The Court likewise rejected this claim, saying that this should have been raised during trial or on direct appeal. It could not be raised in a collateral (indirect) proceeding, as in this habeas case.

MCCLESKEY V. ZANT
499 U.S. 467 (1991)

CAPSULE: Failure to claim violation of a constitutional right in a first federal habeas corpus petition precludes the same claim from being raised in a second habeas corpus petition.

FACTS: McCleskey was charged with murder and armed robbery. At his 1978 trial, the State of Georgia called Offie Evans, the occupant of the jail cell next to McCleskey, to rebut the petitioner's alibi defense. Evans testified that McCleskey had admitted to and boasted about the killing. Due to this testimony and other supporting evidence, the jury convicted McCleskey and sentenced him to death. After the Georgia Supreme Court affirmed the trial decision, McCleskey initiated post-conviction proceedings by filing a state habeas corpus petition. McCleskey alleged that his statements to Evans were acquired by the state creating a situation that induced him to make incriminating statements without the assistance of counsel, in violation of the Sixth Amendment. He was denied relief and filed his first federal habeas corpus and second state habeas corpus petitions, which did not contain the Sixth Amendment claim. Both petitions were also denied. He filed a second federal habeas petition in 1987, challenging on Sixth Amendment grounds a 21-page statement that Evans had made to the police. The statement was made available to McCleskey just weeks before he filed his second federal petition. The document not only contained conversations that were consistent with Evans' trial testimony, but also recounted the tactics used by Evans to engage McCleskey in conversation. At the petition hearing, a jailer who was present during McCleskey's pretrial incarceration gave testimony that indicated that Evans' cell assignment had been made at the state's behest.

ISSUE: Does the failure to include a claim of a violation of the Sixth Amendment in his first petition for a federal writ of habeas corpus preclude the same claim from being raised in a second habeas corpus? YES.

HOLDING: The failure to include a claim of a violation of a constitutional right in the first federal habeas corpus petition precludes a similar claim in a second federal habeas petition. Allowing a prisoner to do so constitutes an abuse of the writ.

REASON: "Much confusion exists as to the proper standard for applying the abuse of the writ doctrine, which refers to a complex and evolving body of equitable principles informed and controlled by historical usage, statutory developments, and judicial decisions. This Court has heretofore defined such abuse in an oblique way, through dicta and denials of certiorari petitions or stay applications and, because of historical changes and the complexity of the subject, has not always followed an unwavering line in its conclusions as to the writ's availability.

"Although this Court's federal habeas decisions do not admit of ready synthesis, a review of these precedents demonstrates that a claim need not have been deliberately abandoned in an earlier petition in order to establish that its inclusion in a subsequent petition constitutes abuse of the writ, see, e.g., *Sanders v. United States*, 373 U.S. 1, 18: that such inclusion constitutes abuse if the claim could have been raised in the first petition, but was omitted through inexcusable neglect, see, e.g., *Delo v. Stokes*, 495 U.S. ___, ___, and that, because the doctrines of procedural default and abuse of the writ implicate nearly identical concerns, the determination of inexcusable neglect in the abuse context should be governed by the same standard used to determine whether to excuse a habeas petitioner's state procedural defaults, see, e.g., *Wainwright v. Sykes*, 433 U.S. 72. Thus, when a prisoner files a second or subsequent habeas petition, the government bears the burden of pleading abuse of the writ. This burden is satisfied if the government, with clarity and particularity, notes petitioner's prior writ history, identifies the claims that appear for the first time, and alleges that petitioner has abused the writ. The burden to disprove abuse then shifts to petitioner. To excuse his failure to raise the claim earlier, he must show cause—e.g., that he was impeded by some objective factor external to the defense, such as governmental interference or the reasonable unavailability of the factual basis for the claim—as well as actual prejudice resulting from the errors of which he complains."

CASE SIGNIFICANCE: This case was decided on procedural grounds, but its implication is far-reaching. Habeas corpus petitions by prisoners seek release on the ground of unconstitutional confinement. Such petitions are first heard in state courts and, if denied, may be filed again in a federal court under the Federal Habeas Corpus Act. The prisoner in this case went twice to his state court and then filed a federal habeas corpus proceeding. In his first federal habeas corpus case, however, he failed to allege a violation of his Sixth Amendment rights. Having been turned down, he filed a second federal habeas corpus case but this time he raised a violation of his Sixth Amendment rights as the basis of his release. The Court considered this an abuse of the writ and prohibited him from raising it in the second federal habeas corpus case. The Court said that "such inclusion constitutes abuse if the claim could have been raised in the first petition, but was omitted through inexcusable neglect." The Court added that "to excuse his failure to raise the claim earlier, he must show cause—e.g., that he was impeded by some objective factor external to the defense, such as government interference or the reasonable availability of the factual basis for the claim—as well as actual prejudice resulting from the errors of which he complains." The prisoner failed to establish this in his second petition, thus the issue could no longer be raised.

The effect of this decision is to minimize successive filings of habeas corpus cases in federal court by state prisoners. In effect, the Supreme Court is saying that petitioners must include all constitutional claims in their first petition and not "serialize" them. Any claim not raised in the first petition cannot be raised in a subsequent petition. The only exception is if a prisoner can show that "a fundamental miscarriage of justice—the conviction of an innocent person—would result from such a failure to entertain the claim."

WILKINSON ET AL. V. DOTSON
544 U.S. 74 (2005)

CAPSULE: State prisoners challenging parole procedures may file for relief under § 1983 and are not limited exclusively to habeas corpus statutes.

FACTS: Dotson and Johnson were serving state prison sentences in Ohio. Parole officials decided that Dotson was ineligible for parole and Johnson was not suitable for parole. Dotson's parole eligibility review date was determined based on harsher parole guidelines that were established after he began serving his sentence. He sought declaratory and injunctive relief under § 1983, claiming that applying the new guidelines to him violated the ex post facto and due process clauses of the Constitution.

Johnson was denied parole applying the same harsher parole guidelines. These guidelines were established after he began serving his sentence. Johnson also sought relief under § 1983, saying there were not enough parole board members present at his hearing and he was not allowed to speak, in violation of the due process clause. The federal district court ruled that the prisoners could not proceed under § 1983 but, instead, would have to file a habeas corpus petition. The Sixth Circuit Court of Appeals reversed, stating that § 1983 was an appropriate legal avenue.

ISSUE: Can state prisoners who are challenging the constitutionality of parole procedures file for relief under § 1983? YES.

HOLDING: Prisoners who seek declaratory and injunctive relief against the state's parole procedures can proceed under § 1983. Federal habeas corpus is not the only remedy available to them.

REASON: "Applying these principles to the present case, we conclude that respondents' claims are cognizable under § 1983, i.e., they do not fall within the implicit habeas exception. Dotson and Johnson seek relief that will render invalid the state procedures used to deny parole eligibility (Dotson) and parole suitability (Johnson). See *Wolff*, *supra*, at 554–555. Neither respondent seeks an injunction ordering his immediate or speedier release into the community . . . Success for Dotson does not mean immediate release from confinement or a shorter stay in prison; it means at most new eligibility review, which at most will speed consideration of a new parole application. Success for Johnson means at most a new parole hearing at which Ohio parole authorities may, in their discretion, decline to shorten his prison term . . . Because neither prisoner's claim would necessarily spell speedier release, neither lies at "the core of habeas corpus." *Preiser*, 411 U.S., at 489. Finally, the prisoners' claims for future relief (which, if successful, will not necessarily imply the invalidity of confinement or shorten its duration) are yet more distant from that core. See *Balisok*, *supra*, at 648.

"Ohio says that a decision in favor of respondents would break faith with principles of federal/state comity by opening the door to federal court without prior exhaustion of state-court remedies. Our earlier cases, however, have already placed the States' important comity considerations in the balance, weighed them against the competing need to vindicate federal rights without exhaustion, and concluded that prisoners may bring their claims without fully exhausting state-court remedies so long as their suits, if established, would not necessarily invalidate state-imposed confinement. See Part II, *supra*. Thus, we see no reason for moving the line these cases draw—particularly since Congress has already strengthened the requirement that prisoners exhaust state administrative remedies as a precondition to any § 1983 action. See 42 U.S.C. § 1997e(a); *Porter v. Nussle*, 534 U.S. 516, 524 (2002)."

CASE SIGNIFICANCE: Section 1983 and habeas corpus cases are two entirely different remedies for violations of rights. Section 1983 cases usually seek monetary damages from government officials who violate a person's constitutional rights. In contrast, habeas corpus seeks the release of a person from detention. The prisoners in this case sought both remedies because of the nature of their claims. Prison officials responded by saying that § 1983 relief was improper because they did not violate any constitutional right and that this should be treated as a solely habeas corpus case where the prisoner seeks release from confinement after being denied parole.

The Court disagreed with the government's claim, saying that both types of relief can be used in these types of cases where violations of constitutional rights (ex post facto and due process) and illegal confinement (because of unconstitutional denial of parole) are involved. This decision broadens the remedies available to inmates in cases when continued confinement (the usual trigger for habeas relief) also allegedly violates constitutional rights (the usual trigger for § 1983 cases).

DODD V. UNITED STATES
545 U.S. 353 (2005)

CAPSULE: An inmate's motion under 28 U.S.C. § 2255 must be filed within one year after the date the U.S. Supreme Court initially recognizes the right asserted.

FACTS: Dodd was convicted on several charges involving drugs, including the charge of knowingly and intentionally engaging in a continuing criminal enterprise. He was sentenced to 10 years in federal prison, to be followed by five years of supervised release. Dodd filed an appeal to set aside his conviction of knowingly and intentionally engaging in a continuing criminal enterprise, based on the Supreme Court's decision in *Richardson v. United States*.

Title 28 U.S.C. § 2255 provides that a federal prisoner may file a motion to vacate, set aside, or correct his sentence within a one-year period of the date the Supreme Court initially recognizes the right asserted and makes it retroactively applicable to cases on collateral review. The District Court dismissed Dodd's motion because *Richardson* had been decided more than a year before Dodd filed his motion. Dodd appealed to the Eleventh Circuit Court of Appeals on the basis that the one-year time limit did not begin until the Supreme Court ruled that *Richardson* applied retroactively to cases on collateral appeal. This decision was made in the case of *Ross v. United States*. The Circuit Court held that the correct period began when the Supreme Court initially recognized the right in the *Richardson* case. Dodd's motion was again denied as time-barred.

ISSUE: Does the time limitation of one year under Title 28 U.S.C. § 2255 begin when the Supreme Court initially recognizes the right asserted by the petitioner? YES.

HOLDING: Petitioner's motion was untimely because he did not file it within one year of the Supreme Court's decision in the *Richardson* case, where the right he asserts was initially recognized.

REASON: "Dodd contends that under subparagraph (3), the limitation period runs from the date on which the right asserted was made retroactively applicable. The United States, on the other hand, argues that it runs from the date on which this Court initially recognized the right asserted . . . We believe that the text of ¶6(3) settles this dispute. It unequivocally identifies one, and only one, date from which the 1-year limitation period is measured: 'the date on which the right asserted was initially recognized by the Supreme Court.' We 'must presume that [the] legislature says in a statute what it means and means in a statute what it says there.' *Connecticut Nat. Bank v. Germain*, 503 U.S. 249, 253–254 (1992). What Congress has said in ¶6(3) is clear: an applicant has one year from the date on which the right he asserts was initially recognized by this Court.

"Dodd's interpretation does not square with the only natural reading of the text. Paragraph 6(3) identifies one date and one date only as the date from which the 1-year limitation period runs: 'the date on which the right asserted was initially recognized by the Supreme Court' . . . We recognize that the statute of limitations in ¶6(3) makes it difficult for applicants filing second or successive § 2255 motions to obtain relief . . . Dodd points out that this Court rarely decides that a new rule is retroactively applicable within one year of initially recognizing that right. Thus, because of the interplay between ¶¶8(2) and 6(3), an applicant who files a second or successive motion seeking to take advantage of a new rule of constitutional law will be time barred except in the rare case in which this Court announces a new rule of constitutional law and makes it retroactive within one year . . . Although we recognize the potential for harsh results in some cases, we are not free to rewrite the statute that Congress has enacted. '[W]hen the statute's language is plain, the sole function of the courts—at least where the disposition required by the text is not absurd—is to enforce it according to its terms.' *Hartford Underwriters Ins. Co. v. Union Planters Bank, N.A.*, 530 U.S. 1, 6 (2000) (internal quotation marks omitted)."

CASE SIGNIFICANCE: This case involved an interpretation of federal law and did not raise any constitutional issue. The issue presented was narrow: was the defendant's appeal to set aside his conviction filed on time? Federal law provides that a federal prisoner may file a motion to vacate, set aside, or correct his sentence "within a one-year period" of the date the Supreme Court initially recognizes the right asserted and makes it retroactively applicable to cases on collateral review. The prisoner based his claim on the *Richardson* case, which was decided more than a year before the prisoner filed his motion. He claimed, however, that the one-year limit did not begin until the Court applied the case retroactively and not at the time the right was recognized. The Court disagreed, saying the time limit applied to when the right was recognized and therefore the one-year period in his case had lapsed.

GONZALES V. CROSBY
545 U.S. 524 (2005)

CAPSULE: A prisoner's motion under Federal Rule of Civil Procedure 60(b)(6), which challenges a ruling based on new law, is not considered a successive habeas corpus petition under the Antiterrorism and Effective Death Penalty Act.

FACTS: Gonzales, a Florida state inmate, filed two motions in state court for habeas corpus relief. These motions were denied. Subsequently, he filed a federal habeas corpus petition that the District Court denied on the grounds that the petition was two months late under the Antiterrorism and Effective Death Penalty Act's Statute of Limitations.

Following a U.S. Supreme Court ruling that a state post-conviction relief action can be properly filed even if the state courts dismiss it as procedurally barred, Gonzales filed a motion in federal district court under Federal Rule of Civil Procedure 60(b)(6). This Rule allows a court to relieve a party from the effect of a final judgment. The inmate's motion was denied and he appealed to the Eleventh Circuit Court of Appeals. That court affirmed the District Court's ruling, holding that Gonzales's petition was, in effect, a second habeas corpus petition. Under the Antiterrorism and Effective Death Penalty Act, a habeas corpus petition must be pre-certified by the Court of Appeals before a motion is filed.

ISSUES:

1. Is a Federal Rule of Civil Procedure 60(b)(6) motion that challenges a District Court's ruling on the basis of a new law considered a successive habeas corpus petition that must be pre-certified by a Court of Appeals? NO.
2. Did the inmate's motion, based on a new law, meet the extraordinary circumstances that justify relief under Federal Rule of Civil Procedure 60(b)(6)? NO.

HOLDING: The inmate's Rule 60(b)(6) motion cannot be considered a successive habeas corpus petition because it challenged only the District Court's ruling on the Antiterrorism and Effective Death Penalty Act's statute of limitations and, therefore, does not require precertification by the Court of Appeals. However, relief under Rule 60(b)(6) must be based on a "limited set of circumstances and challenging federal habeas corpus proceedings" does not meet this requirement. The Court of Appeals judgment is affirmed.

REASON: "Several characteristics of a Rule 60(b) motion limit the friction between the Rule and the successive-petition prohibitions of AEDPA, ensuring that our harmonization of the two will not expose federal courts to an avalanche of frivolous postjudgment motions. First, Rule 60(b) contains its own limitations, such as the requirement that the motion 'be made within a reasonable time' and the more specific one-year deadline for asserting three of the most open-ended grounds of relief (excusable neglect, newly discovered evidence, and fraud). Second, our cases have required a movant seeking relief under Rule 60(b)(6) to show 'extraordinary circumstances' justifying the reopening of a final judgment . . . Many Courts of Appeals have construed 28 U.S.C. § 2253 to impose an additional limitation on appellate review by requiring a habeas petitioner to obtain a COA as a prerequisite to appealing the denial of a Rule 60(b) motion. Because petitioner's Rule 60(b) motion challenges only the District Court's previous ruling on the AEDPA statute of limitations, it is not the equivalent of a successive habeas petition. The Eleventh Circuit therefore erred in holding that petitioner did not qualify even to seek Rule 60(b) relief.

"Petitioner's only ground for reopening the judgment denying his first federal habeas petition is that our decision in *Artuz* showed the error of the District Court's statute-of-limitations ruling. We assume for present purposes that the District Court's ruling was incorrect. As we noted above, however, relief under Rule 60(b)(6)—the only subsection petitioner invokes—requires a showing of 'extraordinary circumstances.' Petitioner contends that *Artuz*'s change in the interpretation of the AEDPA statute of limitations meets this description. We do not agree. The District Court's interpretation was by all appearances correct under the Eleventh Circuit's then-prevailing interpretation of 28 U.S.C. § 2244(d)(2). It is hardly extraordinary that subsequently, after petitioner's case was no longer pending, this Court arrived at a different interpretation.

"Although the District Court relied on Eleventh Circuit precedent holding that a state postconviction application is not 'properly filed' if it is procedurally defaulted, and although that precedent was at odds with the rule in several other Circuits, petitioner neither raised that issue in his application for a COA, nor filed a petition for rehearing of the Eleventh Circuit's denial of a COA, nor sought certiorari review of that denial. This lack of diligence confirms that *Artuz* is not an extraordinary circumstance justifying relief from the judgment in petitioner's case . . . Under the Rule 60(b) standards that properly govern petitioner's motion, the District Court was correct to deny relief."

CASE SIGNIFICANCE: The Antiterrorism and Effective Death Penalty Act (AEDPA) was passed by the U.S. Congress to limit the number of federal habeas cases prisoners can file. It was a reaction to what was deemed an abuse of the process by inmates who filed successive habeas cases to, in effect, postpone their execution. A provision of the act requires the prisoner to obtain a pre-certification from the Court of Appeals from that jurisdiction in cases where a second habeas corpus petition is filed. The issue in this case was narrow: Did the motion filed by Gonzales constitute a second habeas petition that needed precertification from the Eleventh Circuit Court of Appeals? The Court said it did not constitute a second habeas petition and therefore did not need precertification.

That said, the Court then went on to say that Gonzales's motion did not meet the extraordinary circumstances that justify relief under the Federal Rule of Civil Procedure. In sum, the Court said to the inmate: You do not need a precertification to file your motion, but that motion fails anyway because the strict requirements for the motion to succeed are not present.

MAYLE, WARDEN V. FELIX
545 U.S. 644 (2005)

CAPSULE: Amended habeas corpus petitions under the Antiterrorism and Effective Death Penalty Act's one-year statute of limitations and Federal Rule of Civil Procedure 15(c)(2) must arise out of the same conduct, transaction, or occurrence included in the original petition, not the petitioner's general trial, conviction, or sentence.

FACTS: Felix, a California state prisoner, was convicted of murder and robbery. He was sentenced to life imprisonment. Felix first appealed his conviction on the grounds that videotaped testimony from the prosecution's witness should not have been allowed at trial. This appeal was made within the Antiterrorism and Effective Death Penalty Act's one-year time limit on habeas petitions. Five months after the time limit expired, he filed an amended appeal based on a Fifth Amendment violation where alleged coercion occurred during the police interrogation. Felix made inculpatory statements at the time. He argued that the amended appeal related back to the date of his original petition and was within the time limit.

The district court dismissed his coerced statements claim, stating that the videotaped witness statements and the pretrial statements by Felix did not come from the same conduct, transaction, or occurrence. The Ninth Circuit Court of Appeals reversed this dismissal.

ISSUE: Does Federal Rule of Civil Procedure 15(c)(2)'s provision of relating back within the Antiterrorism and Effective Death Penalty Act's one-year time limit mean that an amended appeal is allowed if the new claim relates to the petitioner's trial, conviction, or sentence? NO

HOLDING: Under Federal Rule of Civil Procedure 15(c)(2)'s provision of relating back, the amended pleas must arise out of the same conduct, transaction, or occurrence set forth in the original pleading. The facts in these appeals differ in both time and type.

REASON: "This case turns on the meaning of Federal Rule of Civil Procedure 15(c)(2)'s relation-back provision in the context of federal habeas proceedings and AEDPA's one-year statute of limitations. Rule 15(c)(2), as earlier stated, provides that pleading amendments relate back to the date of the original pleading when the claim asserted in the amended plea 'arose out of the conduct, transaction, or occurrence set forth or attempted to be set forth in the original pleading.'

"The majority of Circuits, mindful of 'Congress' decision to expedite collateral attacks by placing stringent time restrictions on [them],' id., at 388, define 'conduct, transaction, or occurrence' in federal habeas cases less broadly . . . They allow relation back only when the claims added by amendment arise from the same core facts as the timely filed claims, and not when the new claims depend upon events separate in 'both time and type' from the originally raised episodes. *Craycraft*, 167 F.3d, at 457. Because Felix's own pretrial statements, newly raised in his amended petition, were separated in time and type from witness Williams' videotaped statements, raised in Felix's original petition, the former would not relate back under the definition of 'conduct, transaction, or occurrence' to which most Circuits adhere. We are not aware, in the run-of-the-mine civil proceedings Rule 15 governs, of any reading of 'conduct, transaction, or occurrence' as capacious as the construction the Ninth and Seventh Circuits have adopted for habeas cases."

CASE SIGNIFICANCE: A number of cases seeking interpretation of the provisions of the AEDPA have been decided by the Supreme Court. This is one of them, but not a highly significant one. The issue in this case was whether the AEDPA Statute of Limitations (providing that inmate cases for habeas corpus must be filed within one year) applied to the prisoner's second petition where he alleged that coercion occurred when the police interrogated him. He claimed that the amended appeal, which contained this claim, related back to the date of his original petition and therefore was within the one-year limitation set by AEDPA. The Court rejected his claim, saying that the law provides that the inmate's claim must arise out of the "same conduct, transaction or occurrence included in the original petition." It does not apply to claims, such as this one, arising from the inmate's trial, conviction, or sentence.

WOOD V. MILYARD, WARDEN, ET AL.
132 S. CT. 1836 (2012)

CAPSULE: Federal appellate courts have the authority to raise the timeliness of a petition in certain habeas corpus cases but should not do so if the state deliberately waived this defense.

FACTS: Wood was serving a life sentence in a Colorado prison after being convicted of murder and other crimes in connection with the murder. He filed petitions in state court for post-conviction relief after failing in his direct appeals regarding his convictions and sentencing. He was unsuccessful in both of his state motions, although he was appointed counsel to assist in filing his second motion. Wood then petitioned the federal district court under a writ of habeas corpus. The Court originally denied the motion due to its untimeliness.

The Court eventually reconsidered the motion, asking the state if it would raise the defense of untimeliness. The state decided not to challenge Wood's appeals on this basis. However, Wood still lost his appeal. The Court dismissed some of the issues because Wood had failed to exhaust state remedies first, and it found there was no merit in his two remaining claims. In one of these, Wood asserted a double jeopardy violation, and in the other one he claimed that his waiver of a jury trial under the Sixth Amendment was invalid. Wood then appealed to the Tenth Circuit Court of Appeals. This Court denied Wood's claims on the basis that his petition was time barred. The Court did so on its own motion, stating that it had the authority to proceed in this manner.

ISSUES:
1. Does the federal appellate court have the authority to raise a timeliness defense on its own in certain cases? YES.
2. Did the appellate court err in this case in dismissing the petitioner's appeal as untimely? YES.

HOLDING:
1. In certain cases, the federal appellate court may raise a timeliness defense on its own in instances such as the state inadvertently overlooking this defense in the lower court, or the state miscalculating the time span in the lower court. There is no absolute rule barring the federal appellate court from raising this defense.
2. The Tenth Circuit Court overstepped its discretionary powers in dismissing the petitioner's appeal as untimely when the state deliberately waived this defense.

REASONS: "Our precedent establishes that a court may consider a statute of limitations or other threshold bar the State failed to raise in answering a habeas petition. *Granberry v. Greer*, 481 U.S. 129, 134 (1987) (exhaustion defense); *Day v. McDonough*, 547 U.S. 198, 202 (2006) (statute of limitations defense). Does court discretion to take up timeliness hold when a State is aware of a limitations defense, and intelligently chooses not to rely on it in the court of first instance? The answer Day instructs is 'no': A court is not at liberty, we have cautioned, to bypass, override, or excuse a State's deliberate waiver of a limitations defense. *Id.*, at 202, 210, n. 11. The Tenth Circuit, we accordingly hold, abused its discretion by resurrecting the limitations issue instead of reviewing the District Court's disposition on the merits of Wood's claims . . . We granted review, 564 U.S. ___ (2011), to resolve two issues: first, whether a court of appeals has the authority to address the timeliness of a habeas petition on the court's own initiative; second, assuming a court of appeals has such authority, whether the State's representations to the District Court in this case nonetheless precluded the Tenth Circuit from considering the timeliness of Wood's petition. Under the Antiterrorism and Effective Death Penalty Act of 1996 (AEDPA), 110 Stat. 1214, a state prisoner has one year to file a federal petition for habeas corpus relief, starting from 'the date on which the judgment became final by the conclusion of direct review or the expiration of the time for seeking such review.' 28 U.S.C. § 2244(d)(1)(A) . . . The state judgment against Wood became final on direct review in early 1990. See *supra*, at 2. Wood's time for filing a federal petition therefore began to run on the date of AEDPA's enactment, April 24, 1996, and expired on April 24, 1997, unless Wood had a 'properly filed' application for state postconviction relief 'pending' in Colorado state court during that period. Wood maintains he had such an application pending on April 24, 1996: the Rule 35(c) motion he filed in 1995. That motion, Wood asserts, remained pending (thus continuing to suspend the one year clock) until at least August 2004, when he filed his second motion for postconviction relief in state court. The 2004 motion, the State does not contest, was 'properly filed.' Wood argues that this second motion further tolled the limitations period until February 5, 2007, exactly one year before he filed the federal petition at issue here. If Wood is correct that his 1995 motion remained 'pending' in state court from April 1996 until August 2004, his federal petition would be timely. In its preanswer response to Wood's petition, the State set forth its comprehension of the statute of limitations issue . . . But rather than inviting a decision on the statute of limitations question, the State informed the District Court it would 'not challenge' Wood's petition on timeliness grounds; instead, the State simply defended against Wood's double jeopardy and Sixth Amendment claims on the merits."

"In *Granberry v. Greer*, we recognized a modest exception to the rule that a federal court will not consider a forfeited affirmative defense. 481 U.S., at 134. The District Court in *Granberry* denied a federal habeas petition on the merits. *Id.*, at 130. On appeal, the State argued for the first time that the petition should be dismissed because the petitioner had failed to exhaust relief available in state court. *Ibid.* We note here the distinction between defenses that are 'waived' and those that are 'forfeited.' A waived claim or defense is one that a party has knowingly and intelligently relinquished; a forfeited plea is one that a party has merely failed to preserve. *Kontrick v. Ryan*, 540 U.S. 443, 458, n. 13 (2004); *United States v. Olano*, 507 U.S. 725, 733 (1993). That distinction is key to our decision in Wood's case . . . the petitioner had failed to exhaust relief available in state court. *Ibid.* Despite the State's failure to raise the nonexhaustion argument in the District Court, the Seventh Circuit accepted the argument and ruled for the State on that ground. We granted certiorari to decide whether a court of appeals has discretion to address a nonexhaustion defense that the State failed to raise in the district court. *Id.*, at 130 . . . we nonetheless concluded that the bar to court of appeals' consideration of a forfeited habeas defense is not absolute. *Id.*, at 133. The exhaustion doctrine, we noted, is founded on concerns broader than those of the parties; in particular, the doctrine fosters respectful, harmonious relations between the state and federal judiciaries. *Id.*, at 133–135 . . . In *Day*, we affirmed a federal district court's authority to consider a forfeited habeas defense when extraordinary circumstances so warrant. 547 U.S., at 201. There, the State miscalculated a time span, specifically, the number of days running between the finality of Day's state-court conviction and the filing of his federal habeas petition. *Id.*, at 203. As a result, the State erroneously informed the District Court that Day's petition was timely. *Ibid.* Although our decision in *Granberry v. Greer*, 481 U.S. 129 (1987), did not expressly distinguish between forfeited and waived defenses, we made clear in *Day v. McDonough*, 547 U.S. 198 (2006), that a federal court has the authority to resurrect only forfeited defenses. See infra, at 8–9. 8 . . . [The] Magistrate Judge caught the State's computation error and recommended that the petition be dismissed as untimely, notwithstanding the State's timeliness concession. *Id.*, at 204 . . . Affording federal courts leeway to consider a forfeited timeliness defense was appropriate, we again reasoned, because AEDPA's statute of limitations, like the exhaustion doctrine, 'implicat[es] values beyond the concerns of the parties.' *Day*, 547 U.S., at 205 (quoting *Acosta v. Artuz*, 221 F. 3d 117, 123 (CA2 2000)); 547 U.S., at 205–206."

"We turn now to the second, case-specific, inquiry. See *Ibid.* Although a court of appeals has discretion to address, sua sponte, the timeliness of a habeas petition, appellate courts should reserve that authority for use in exceptional cases . . . It typically takes a district court more time to decide a habeas case on the merits, than it does to resolve a petition on threshold procedural grounds . . . When a court of appeals raises a procedural impediment to disposition on the merits, and disposes of the case on that ground, the district court's labor is discounted and the appellate court acts not as a court of review but as one of first view. In light of the foregoing discussion of the relevant considerations, we hold that the Tenth Circuit abused its discretion when it dismissed Wood's petition as untimely. In the District Court, the State was well aware of the statute of limitations defense available to it and of the arguments that could be made in support of the defense. See *supra*, at 5–6. Yet the State twice informed the District Court that it 'will not challenge, but [is] not conceding' the timeliness of Wood's petition. See *supra*, at 3. Essentially, the District Court asked the State: Will you oppose the petition on statute of limitations grounds? The State answered: Such a challenge would be supportable, but we won't make the challenge here . . . Its decision not to contest the timeliness of Wood's petition did not stem from an 'inadvertent error,' as did the State's concession in *Day*. See 547 U.S., at 211. Rather, the State, after expressing its clear and accurate understanding of the timeliness issue, see *supra*, at 5–6, deliberately steered the District Court away from the question and towards the merits of Wood's petition. In short, the State knew it had an 'arguable' statute of limitations defense, see *supra*, at 5, yet it chose, in no uncertain terms, to refrain from interposing a timeliness 'challenge' to Wood's petition. The District Court therefore reached and decided the merits of the petition. The Tenth Circuit should have done so as well."

CASE SIGNIFICANCE: This case confirms that exceptions are allowed when a Federal Appellate Court wishes to raise a timeliness defense on its own. Two exceptions noted in the case are when the state inadvertently overlooked this defense in the lower court (the *Granberry* case) or the state miscalculated the time span in the lower court, advising the court that the petition was timely (the *Day* case). In both of these instances, the state made an error that was not planned or deliberate. The Supreme Court ruled that the courts of appeals were acting appropriately in raising the timeliness defense in each case.

However, in this case, the state decided not to challenge the timeliness of the petitioner's appeals when the case was on review in the federal district court. There appeared to be some confusion as to the disposition of the first post-conviction appeal, which the petitioner asserted was still "running," thus allowing him to eventually petition the federal court of appeals. Accordingly, the state decided not to raise the timeliness defense in the habeas corpus review before the federal district court, while at the same time still not conceding that the appeal was timely. The district court then proceeded to assess the case on its merits, which was a lengthy process owing to the many issues the petitioner raised in his appeal. When the Court denied the claims, Wood began his habeas corpus petition to the Tenth Circuit Court of Appeals. This Court requested that both sides present briefs on the merits of the case and the timeliness issue. The petitioner's appeal was denied based on the timeliness issue, which was raised by the Court on its own. The Court stated that it had the authority to do so. The Supreme Court agreed that it did have this power but only in certain instances. However, based on the state's actions in the federal district court concerning the timeliness issue, the Supreme Court held that the federal court of appeals "abused its discretion when it dismissed Wood's petition as untimely." In making the distinction between inadvertent error and deliberate actions on the part of the state, the Supreme Court has further clarified the issue of an appellate court's authority to raise the timeliness issue on its own and whether it should do so under these circumstances.

COLEMAN V. JOHNSON
132 S. CT. 2060 (2012)

CAPSULE: In a habeas corpus appeal, the appellate court may overturn the state court's decision only if it was objectively unreasonable.

FACTS: Johnson was tried jointly with another man in a murder case. Although his co-defendant was found guilty in the murder, Johnson was convicted of being an accomplice and co-conspirator. At the trial, evidence was presented that both men forced the deceased into an alley, but no one testified that he or she actually witnessed the murder. Johnson filed a post-trial motion claiming insufficient evidence to support his conviction. This motion was denied, and Johnson made direct appeal to the Pennsylvania superior court. The Court affirmed his conviction. Johnson then appealed for state post-conviction relief, which was unsuccessful, followed by a habeas corpus petition in federal district court.

When the district court denied his petition, Johnson appealed to the Third Circuit Court of Appeals. This Court reversed the district court's ruling and overturned Johnson's conviction. The Court reasoned that the trial evidence was insufficient to support a conviction under the standard established in *Jackson v. Virginia*.

ISSUE: Did the court of appeals err in its interpretation of the *Jackson* decision? YES.

HOLDING: In deciding a federal habeas corpus appeal, the appellate court must adhere to the standard of the AEDPA, upheld in the *Jackson v. Virginia* decision. The appellate court failed to afford due respect to the jury's decision in the case and didn't establish that the appellate state court decision was objectively unreasonable.

REASONS: "We have made clear that *Jackson* claims face a high bar in federal habeas proceedings because they are subject to two layers of judicial deference. First, on direct appeal, 'it is the responsibility of the jury—not the court—to decide what conclusions should be drawn from evidence admitted at trial. A reviewing court may set aside the jury's verdict on the ground of insufficient evidence only if no rational trier of fact could have agreed with the jury.' *Cavazos v. Smith*, 565 U.S. 1, ___ (2011) (per curiam) (slip op., at 1). And second, on habeas review, 'a federal court may not overturn a state court decision rejecting a sufficiency of the evidence challenge simply because the federal court disagrees with the state court. The federal court instead may do so only if the state court decision was 'objectively unreasonable.' Ibid. (quoting *Renico v. Lett*, 559 U.S. ___, ___ (2010) (slip op., at 5)) . . . Under *Jackson*, evidence is sufficient to support a conviction if, 'after viewing the evidence in the light most favorable to the prosecution, any rational trier of fact could have found the essential elements of the crime beyond a reasonable doubt.' 443 U.S., at 319. In light of the testimony at Johnson's trial, the Court of Appeals acknowledged that '[a] trier of fact could reasonably infer . . . that Johnson and Walker shared a common intent to confront, threaten or harass Williams.' *Johnson v. Mechling*, 446 Fed. Appx. 531, 540 (CA3 2011). As for the notion that 'Johnson shared Walker's intent to kill Williams,' however, the court concluded that was 'mere speculation' that no rational fact-finder could accept as true. Ibid . . . At the outset, we note that it was error for the Court of Appeals to look to Pennsylvania law in determining what distinguishes a reasoned inference from 'mere speculation.' Under *Jackson*, federal courts must look to state law for 'the substantive elements of the criminal offense,' 443 U.S., at 324, n. 16, but the minimum amount of evidence that the Due Process Clause requires to prove the offense is purely a matter of federal law. Under the deferential federal standard, the approach taken by the Court of Appeals was flawed because it unduly impinged on the jury's role as factfinder. Jackson leaves juries broad discretion in deciding what inferences to draw from the evidence presented at trial, requiring only that jurors 'draw reasonable inferences from basic facts to ultimate facts.' Id., at 319. This deferential standard does not permit the type of fine-grained factual parsing in which the Court of Appeals engaged . . . On the basis of these facts, a rational jury could infer that Johnson knew that Walker was armed with a shotgun; knew that he intended to kill Williams; and helped usher Williams into the alleyway to meet his fate. The jury in this case was convinced, and the only question under Jackson is whether that finding was so insupportable as to fall below the threshold of bare rationality. The state court of last review did not think so, and that determination in turn is entitled to considerable deference under AEDPA, 28 U.S.C. § 2254(d)."

"Affording due respect to the role of the jury and the state courts, we conclude that the evidence at Johnson's trial was not nearly sparse enough to sustain a due process challenge under *Jackson*. The evidence was sufficient to convict Johnson as an accomplice and a co-conspirator in the murder of Taraja Williams . . . [T]he judgment of the Court of Appeals for the Third Circuit is reversed, and the case is remanded for further proceedings consistent with this opinion."

CASE SIGNIFICANCE: This case established the standard of "objectively unreasonable" as the proper standard in reviewing state courts' decisions in federal habeas corpus petitions. The Supreme Court found that the *Jackson* decision dictated two considerations. The first consideration is review in direct appeal, involving the state court. Basically, the appellate court cannot decide to reverse the jury's verdict owing to insufficient evidence unless a rational trier of fact would not agree with the trial jury. The second consideration involves habeas corpus appeals at the federal level. This is the most important part of the Court's decision because it applied the objectively unreasonable standard found in the *Jackson* decision to federal appellate court review in accordance with the AEDPA.

The Court states that the federal appellate court must defer to the state appellate court's ruling unless this decision is objectively unreasonable, meaning that the state court did not appear to make a rational decision based on the evidence. In this case, the Supreme Court ruled that the Third Circuit Court of Appeals failed to offer the proper deference to the state appellate court in making its ruling. This Supreme Court decision was based on the provisions of the AEDPA, which were enumerated in *Jackson v. Virginia*. Following the Supreme Court's guidelines, the circuit court of appeals would have ruled in favor of the State of Pennsylvania, not Johnson.

P. PRISON LITIGATION REFORM ACT

The Prison Litigation Reform Act (PLRA) took effect in 1996. It is a major piece of legislation on prisons and was passed as Congress's solution to burgeoning inmate litigation. The number of cases filed by inmates had grown from 6,600 in 1975 to 39,000 in 1994, and increased every year. This understandably drew the concern and ire of Congress.

Much of the testimony in support of the law centered on the theme that prisons "had gotten too comfortable at the hands of federal judges." Senator Kay Bailey Hutchison of Texas noted that "prisons exist for the protection of society, not for the comfort and convenience of criminals," adding that "interference by the federal courts has put the interest of criminals ahead of the interest of victims and law-abiding citizens." Former Senator Robert Dole also spoke in support of the bill, saying that it "will act to restrain liberal federal judges who see violations of constitutional rights in every prisoner complaint and who have used these complaints to micromanage state and local prison systems."

The PLRA is a complex law and has many provisions, all of which seek to limit the power of federal judges over prisons. For example, § 802 of the PLRA reads: "The court shall not grant or approve any prospective relief unless the court finds that such relief is narrowly drawn, extends no further than necessary to correct the violation of the Federal right, and is the least intrusive means necessary to correct the violation of the Federal right." The PLRA also provides that if the federal court orders some form of relief, such relief shall be terminated two years after the date the court granted such relief. Other provisions are that lawsuits by prisoners regarding prison conditions cannot be brought until administrative remedies are exhausted and that failure of a state to adopt or adhere to an administrative grievance procedure does not constitute a basis for legal action by prisoners. The law further requires the payment by prisoners of filing fees and specifies that the court may order the revocation of any earned release credit or good time credit of a prisoner in a federal facility if that prisoner files a malicious or false civil action claim.

MILLER ET AL. V. FRENCH ET AL.
530 U.S. 327 (2000)

CAPSULE: The Prison Litigation Reform Act's automatic stay provision does not violate the separation of powers doctrine.

FACTS: In 1975, conditions in an Indiana prison were found to be in violation of the Eighth Amendment's prohibition against cruel and unusual punishment. The district court ordered injunctive relief that remained in force with periodic modifications. In 1997, the state filed a motion to terminate the injunctive relief under the Prison Litigation Reform Act of 1995. This law provides for an automatic stay during consideration of the motion.

The prisoners filed a motion seeking to prevent the application of the automatic stay provision. The prisoners' motion was granted by the district court. The Seventh Circuit Court of Appeals affirmed this decision, holding that the PLRA's provision violated the separation of powers doctrine. Both the federal government and the state appealed this ruling.

ISSUE: Does the automatic stay provision of the Prison Litigation Reform Act violate the separation of powers doctrine?

HOLDING: The automatic stay provision of the Prison Litigation Reform Act does not violate the separation of powers doctrine. It does not deprive courts of their adjudicatory role; instead, it merely provides a new legal standard for relief and encourages courts to apply that standard.

REASON: "Viewing the automatic stay provision in the context of Section 3626 [of the PLRA] as a whole further confirms that Congress intended to prohibit federal courts from exercising their equitable authority to suspend operation of the automatic stay. The specific appeal provision contained in Section 3626(e) states that '[a]ny order staying, suspending, delaying, or barring the operation of the automatic stay' of Section 3626(e)(2) 'shall be appealable' pursuant to 28 U.S.C. Section 1292(a)(1). Section 3626(e)(4). At first blush, this provision might be read as supporting the view that Congress expressly recognized the possibility that a district court could exercise its equitable discretion to enjoin the stay . . . If the rationale for the provision were that in some situations equity demands that the automatic stay be suspended, then presumably the denial of a motion to enjoin the stay should also be appealable. The one-way nature of the appeal provision only makes sense if the automatic stay is required to operate during a specific time period, such that any attempt by a district court to circumvent the mandatory stay is immediately reviewable.

"In contrast to due process, which principally serves to protect the personal rights of litigants to a full and fair hearing, separation of powers principles are primarily addressed to the structural concerns of protecting the role of the independent Judiciary within the constitutional design. In this action, we have no occasion to decide whether there could be no time constraint on judicial action that was so severe that it implicated these structural separation of powers concerns. The PLRA does not deprive courts of their adjudicatory role, but merely provides a new legal standard for relief and encourages courts to apply that standard promptly.

"Through the PRLA, Congress clearly intended to make operation of the automatic stay mandatory, precluding courts from exercising their equitable powers to enjoin the stay. And we conclude that this provision does not violate separation of powers principles."

CASE SIGNIFICANCE: It is not surprising that the many and complex provisions of the PLRA have led to inmates challenging just about every provision of this complex law. *Miller v. French* is just one such case that reached the United States Supreme Court. It challenged a specific provision of the PLRA— the automatic stay provision. The prisoners maintained that the automatic stay provision violated the separation of powers doctrine in American government. The separation of powers doctrine provides that the three departments of government are co-equal, independent, and separate from each other. The prisoners maintained that limiting the power of the courts, by providing for an automatic stay of a judicial order of relief in favor of prisoners, violated that doctrine. The Court disagreed, saying that the automatic stay provision of the PLRA merely provides for a new legal standard in prison cases for the courts to apply.

The various provisions of the PLRA continue to generate many inmate lawsuits. Some challenges have succeeded, but most have failed. It is ironic, though, that a law passed to limit inmate limitation in fact initially led to many cases being filed against prison systems challenging various provisions. Has the PLRA reduced the number of cases filed by prisoners during the last few years? The answer is yes. A 1999 study by the Office of Human Resources and Statistics of the Administrative Office of the U.S. Courts concludes as follows: "The PLRA appears to have led to a reduction in filings of civil rights prison petition appeals. Therefore, the PLRA seems to have been effective in diminishing the number of prisoner petitions in the U.S. courts of appeals despite the existence of a rapidly growing prison population."

BOOTH V. CHURNER
532 U.S. 731 (2001)

CAPSULE: There is no exception to the exhaustion of administrative remedies requirement of the Prison Litigation Reform Act (PLRA).

FACTS: Booth was serving a prison sentence in Pennsylvania when he alleged that he was physically assaulted by correctional officers and then denied medical attention to treat his injuries. He filed a complaint against the officers, which was denied. Booth then had the option of appealing to an intermediate reviewing authority, followed by an appeal to a central review committee if he was not satisfied. This grievance system could address his complaints of abuse but it could not provide for recovery of monetary damages, which Booth also sought. He did not go beyond the first step in the grievance system before filing a petition in federal district court under 42 U.S.C. § 1983.

The District Court dismissed his petition on the grounds that he did not exhaust all administrative remedies as required by 42 U.S.C. § 1997, in the aftermath of the Prison Litigation Reform Act of 1995. The Third Circuit Court of Appeals affirmed the District Court's decision, and noted that other courts of appeals had found an exception when monetary relief could not be provided, but it did not.

ISSUE: Does the lack of monetary relief in a prison grievance system create an exception to the requirement under the Prison Litigation Reform Act that all administrative remedies be exhausted before a § 1983 petition is filed? NO.

HOLDING: Under the Prison Litigation Reform Act, a prisoner must exhaust all administrative remedies even if no specific provision for monetary relief is provided by the prison system.

REASON: ". . . statutory history confirms the suggestion that Congress meant to require procedural exhaustion regardless of the fit between a prisoner's prayer for relief and the administrative remedies possible. Before Section 1997e(a) was amended by the Act in 1995, a court had discretion (though no obligation) to require a state inmate to exhaust 'such . . . remedies as are available,' but only if those remedies were 'plain, speedy, and effective.' 42 U.S.C. § 1997 e(a) (1994 ed.). That scheme, however, is not a thing of the past, for the amendments eliminated both the discretion to dispense with administrative exhaustion and the condition that the remedy be 'plain, speedy, and effective' before the exhaustion could be required."

CASE SIGNIFICANCE: The Prison Litigation Reform Act (PLRA) of 1995 requires that a prisoner exhaust all administrative remedies within the prison system before going to the federal court to sue prison officials under 42 U.S.C. § 1983. This provision ensures that all possible grievances are heard by the prison system before federal courts are asked by prisoners to intervene. In this case, the prisoner argued that an exception to this requirement should be made because the prison grievance system does not provide for monetary relief, which the prisoner wanted. The Supreme Court disagreed, saying that the PLRA does not allow any exceptions to the requirement of exhaustion of administrative remedies even in instances in which the prison grievance system does not provide for monetary relief. The Court therefore made the exhaustion of administrative remedies an absolute requirement before prisoners could access federal courts.

PORTER V. NUSSLE
534 U.S. 516 (2002)

CAPSULE: The Prison Litigation Reform Act (PLRA) requires all inmate grievances to be exhausted administratively before a lawsuit can be filed. This requirement includes accusations of excessive force and other conditions of confinement issues.

FACTS: Nussle was an inmate in the Connecticut prison system. He alleged that he was the victim of harassment and intimidation by correctional officers at the Cheshire Correctional Institution. Nussle also alleged that he was the victim of a beating by correctional officers, in violation of the Eighth Amendment's prohibition against cruel and unusual punishment. He filed a federal lawsuit without first utilizing the prison's grievance procedure. According to the Prison Litigation Reform Act of 1995, all prisoners must first exhaust the administrative procedure within a prison before resorting to federal court relief.

The District Court dismissed Nussle's lawsuit on the basis of the Prison Litigation Reform Act's requirement of having to exhaust administrative remedies before filing. The Second Circuit Court of Appeals reversed this decision, concluding that the exhaustion of administrative remedies is not required under the Act in this particular case. It reasoned that cases involving assault or excessive force and brought under § 1983 are exempt from the exhaustion requirement because they are individual incidents and not general "prison conditions," as stipulated in the Act.

ISSUE: Does the Prison Litigation Reform Act's requirement of exhausting administrative remedies before filing a lawsuit include individual incidents? YES.

HOLDING: The Prison Litigation Reform Act's exhaustion requirement applies to all inmate suits concerning prison life, whether they involve individual incidents or general prison conditions, including use of excessive force or some other wrong.

REASON: "[T]he pathmarking opinion is *McCarthy v. Bronson*, 500 U.S. 136 (1991) . . . the complaint in *McCarthy* targeted no ongoing prison conditions'; it homed in on 'an isolated incident' of excessive force. 500 U.S., at 138 . . . 'our opinion in *Preiser v. Rodriguez*, 411 U.S. 475 (1973), had described [the] two broad categories of prisoner petitions: (1) those challenging the fact or duration of confinement itself; and (2) those challenging the conditions of confinement.' Ibid.

"The PLRA exhaustion provision is captioned 'Suits by prisoners,' see Section 1997e; this unqualified heading scarcely aids the argument that Congress meant to bi-sect the universe of prisoner suits. See ibid; see also *Almendarez-Torres v. United States*, 523 U.S. 224 (1998) . . . This Court generally 'presume[s] that Congress expects its statutes to be read in conformity with th[e] Court's precedents.' *United States v. Wells*, 519 U.S. 482, 495 (1997). That presumption, and the PLRA's dominant concern to promote administrative redress, filter out groundless claims, and foster better prepared litigation of claims aired in the court, see *Booth*, 532 U.S., at 737, persuade us that Section 1997e(a)'s keywords 'prison conditions' are properly read through the lens of *McCarthy* and *Preiser*. Those decisions tug strongly away from classifying suits about prison guards' use of excessive force, one or many times, as anything other than actions 'with respect to prison conditions.'"

CASE SIGNIFICANCE: This is another case interpreting the provisions of the Prison Litigation Reform Act (PLRA). As noted elsewhere, the PLRA was passed by the United States Congress in 1995 in an effort to limit the filing of cases by prisoners. The issue in this case was more specific: Does the PLRA requirement of exhausting administrative remedies before filing a lawsuit include individual incidents? The prisoner alleged that the PLRA provision only covered general prison conditions (such as overcrowding, lack of medical facilities, lack of access to court, etc.), but not individual incidents such as harassment and intimidation, or prisoner beatings by correctional officers.

The Court held that the PLRA applies to all inmate suits involving all aspects of prison life. The effect of the decision is to force inmates to use administrative remedies (meaning bringing their grievances to the attention of prison officials first) before suing in federal court. This reduces the number of lawsuits filed in federal courts and allows prison officials to address inmate grievances. It also enables them to correct errors, if any, of prison officials before the case is filed in federal court.

WOODFORD ET AL. V. NGO
548 U.S. 81 (2006)

CAPSULE: Under the Prison Litigation Reform Act, prisoners must first exhaust all administrative remedies, following proper procedure, before they can sue concerning prison conditions in federal court.

FACTS: Ngo, a California state prisoner, was convicted of murder and sentenced to life in prison. He filed a grievance with prison officials, alleging that he was not allowed to participate in special religious activities. After informal review, his grievance was denied. He then filed for formal review. However, his petition for formal review was denied on the grounds that he did not file it on time (within 15 working days after the initial denial). He then filed suit seeking damages against prison officials under § 1983.

The District Court granted California prison officials' motion to dismiss, based on Ngo's failure to exhaust his administrative remedies, as required under the Prison Litigation Reform Act of 1995 (PLRA). Inmates cannot challenge prison conditions in federal court until this requirement is satisfied. The Ninth Circuit Court of Appeals reversed on the grounds that Ngo had exhausted his administrative remedies because none remained available to him, under 42 U.S.C. § 1997.

ISSUE: Is the Prison Litigation Reform Act's exhaustion of administrative remedies requirement satisfied by what the inmate did in this case? NO.

HOLDING: Under 42 U.S.C. § 1997, the Prison Litigation Reform Act's exhaustion requirement mandates that administrative remedies be exhausted through proper procedure. This exhaustion requirement is not satisfied when the remedies are no longer available due to the inmate's decision not to follow proper procedure.

REASON: "A centerpiece of the PLRA's effort 'to reduce the quantity . . . of prisoner suits' is an 'invigorated' exhaustion provision, § 1997e(a). *Porter v. Nussle*, 534 U.S. 516, 524 (2002) . . . Exhaustion is no longer left to the discretion of the district court, but is mandatory. See *Booth v. Churner*, 532 U.S. 731, 739 (2001). Prisoners must now exhaust all 'available' remedies, not just those that meet federal standards. Indeed, as we held in *Booth*, a prisoner must now exhaust administrative remedies even where the relief sought—monetary damages—cannot be granted by the administrative process. Id., at 734. Finally, exhaustion of available administrative remedies is required for any suit challenging prison conditions, not just for suits under § 1983. *Nussle, supra*, at 524 . . . There is no dispute that this language requires a prisoner to "exhaust" administrative remedies, but the parties differ sharply in their understanding of the meaning of this requirement . . . Statutes requiring exhaustion serve a purpose when a significant number of aggrieved parties, if given the choice, would not voluntarily exhaust. Aggrieved parties may prefer not to exhaust administrative remedies for a variety of reasons. Although exhaustion promotes overall efficiency, a party may conclude—correctly or incorrectly—that exhaustion is not efficient in that party's particular case. In addition, some aggrieved parties may prefer to proceed directly to federal court for other reasons, including bad faith . . . Because exhaustion requirements are designed to deal with parties who do not want to exhaust, administrative law creates an incentive for these parties to do what they would otherwise prefer not to do, namely, to give the agency a fair and full opportunity to adjudicate their claims. Administrative law does this by requiring proper exhaustion of administrative remedies, which 'means using all steps that the agency holds out, and doing so properly (so that the agency addresses the issues on the merits).'

"While requiring proper exhaustion serves the purposes of the PLRA, respondent's interpretation of § 1997e(a) would make the PLRA exhaustion scheme wholly ineffective. The benefits of exhaustion can be realized only if the prison grievance system is given a fair opportunity to consider the grievance. The prison grievance system will not have such an opportunity unless the grievant complies with the system's critical procedural rules . . . For example, a prisoner wishing to bypass available administrative remedies could simply file a late grievance without providing any reason for failing to file on time. If the prison then rejects the grievance as untimely, the prisoner could proceed directly to federal court. And acceptance of the late grievance would not thwart the prisoner's wish to bypass the administrative process; the prisoner could easily achieve this by violating other procedural rules until the prison administration has no alternative but to dismiss the grievance on procedural grounds. We are confident that the PLRA did not create such a toothless scheme . . . Respondent argues that requiring proper exhaustion is harsh for prisoners, who generally are untrained in the law and are often poorly educated. This argument overlooks the informality and relative simplicity of prison grievance systems like California's, as well as the fact that prisoners who litigate in federal court generally proceed pro se and are forced to comply with numerous unforgiving deadlines and other procedural requirements. For these reasons, we reverse the judgment of the Court of Appeals for the Ninth Circuit and remand the case for proceedings consistent with this opinion."

CASE SIGNIFICANCE: In this case, the Court explains what the Prison Litigation Reform Act means by "exhaustion of administrative remedies." The PLRA was passed in 1995 in an effort to lessen the amount of prison litigation filed in various courts. One of its important provisions requires that lawsuits can be filed in court only after the inmate has exhausted available administrative remedies. It says: "No action shall be brought with respect to prison conditions under Section 1983 of this title, or any other Federal law, by a prisoner confined in any jail, prison, or other correctional facility until such administrative remedies as are available are exhausted."

California prison authorities interpreted this provision to mean that "a prisoner must complete the administrative review process in accordance with the applicable procedural rules, including deadlines, as a precondition to bring suit in federal court." The prisoner had a different interpretation. He said that the PLRA provision "simply means that a prisoner may not bring suit in federal court until administrative remedies are no longer available." He claimed that this meant that administrative remedies are no longer available and that the reason for non-availability is irrelevant. In his case, he maintained that "bare unavailability suffices even if this results from a prisoner's deliberate strategy (as was his strategy in this case) of refraining from filing a timely grievance so that the litigation of the prisoner's claim can begin in federal court." The Court rejected the prisoner's interpretation, saying that the interpretation by the Ohio prison administrators was correct. Therefore, the prisoner's petition for formal review was denied under the PLRA because he did not file it within 15 days, as required by the rules. In short, inmates must strictly follow procedural rules set by the prison system if they are to have exhausted available administrative remedies as required by the PLRA.

Q. MAIL AND THE FIRST AMENDMENT

TURNER V. SAFLEY
482 U.S. 78 (1987)

CAPSULE: A prison regulation that impinges on inmates' constitutional rights (in this case the freedom to send and receive mail) is valid if it is reasonably related to legitimate penological interests.

(Read the Facts, Issue, Decision, and Reasons for this case at the beginning of Chapter 1.)

CASE SIGNIFICANCE: *Turner v. Safley* is discussed more extensively at the beginning of this book because it sets the standard for courts to determine whether prison regulations that allegedly impinge on prisoners' constitutional rights are valid. The rights involved in the challenge were the First Amendment right to communication and the right to marry. On the issue of whether the prison regulation on sending and receiving mail by inmates was valid, the Court said that this prison regulation was reasonably related to legitimate penological interests in that "mail between prisons could be used to communicate escape plans, to arrange violent acts, and to foster prison gang activity." It added that "the prison regulation does not deprive prisoners of all means of expression, but simply bars communication with a limited class of people—other inmates—with whom authorities have particular cause to be concerned." Given these, the Court concluded that the four tests to determine whether a prison regulation was "reasonably related to legitimate penological interests" were complied with, thus the regulation was constitutional.

This case is significant because it sets the current standard to be used by the courts for determining the validity of prison regulations infringing on inmates' constitutional rights. Prison mail regulation has been the subject of numerous court battles between prisoners and prisons. The current standard holds that prison mail regulations are valid as long as they are "reasonably related to a legitimate penological interest." What that means is ultimately decided by the courts on a case-by-case basis.

THORNBURGH V. ABBOTT
490 U.S. 401 (1989)

CAPSULE: Prison regulations regarding receipt of publications by inmates are valid if reasonably related to a legitimate penological interest.

FACTS: Inmates and certain publishers filed suit in district court against the Federal Bureau of Prisons, claiming that the regulations allowing prisoners to receive publications from the outside world, but restricting these publications on the basis of their detriment to the "security, good order, or discipline of the institution" or on the basis of their facilitating criminal activity, violated their First Amendment rights according to the standards set forth in *Procunier v. Martinez*, 416 U.S. 396. These regulations provide procedural safeguards for the prisoner and for the publisher or sender. The warden is the sole authority for rejecting a publication although he may designate a staff member to screen and, where appropriate, to approve incoming publications. If the publication is rejected, the warden must advise the inmate promptly in writing of the reasons for rejection and provide the publisher or sender with a copy of the rejection letter. This notice must refer to "the specific article(s) or material(s) considered objectionable," § 540.71(d), with the option that the publisher or sender may request an independent review of the decision to reject by a timely writing to the Regional Director of the Bureau. Additionally, an inmate may appeal through the Bureau's Administrative Remedy Procedure. The warden must permit the prisoner to review the rejected material for the purpose of filing an appeal. However, the regulations allow the warden to deny review of the material if this review "may provide the inmate with information of a nature which is deemed to pose a threat or detriment to the security, good order or discipline of the institution or to encourage or instruct criminal activity." § 540.71(d).

ISSUE: Are restrictions on receipt of publications from the outside world that are based on the publication's detriment to the security, good order, or discipline of the institution, or on the basis of the publication's facilitation of criminal activity, such determination to be made by the warden, unconstitutional? NO.

HOLDING: Using the test prescribed in *Turner v. Safley*, the Federal Bureau of Prisons regulations are valid because they are reasonably related to a legitimate penological interest.

REASON: "In this case, there is no question that publishers who wish to communicate with those who, through subscription, willingly seek their point of view have a legitimate First Amendment interest in access to prisoners. The question here, as it has been in our previous First Amendment cases in this area, is what standard of review this Court should apply to prison regulations limiting that access.

"The Court set forth in *Turner* the development of this reasonableness standard in the respective decisions in *Pell* and *Jones* and in *Block v. Rutherford*, 468 U.S. 576 (1984), and we need not repeat that discussion here.

"The Court's decision to apply a reasonableness standard in these cases rather than *Martinez'* less deferential approach stemmed from its concern that language in *Martinez* might be too readily understood as establishing a standard of 'strict' or 'heightened' scrutiny, and that such a strict standard simply was not appropriate for consideration of regulations that are centrally concerned with the maintenance of order and security within prisons. See *Turner v. Safley*, 482 U.S., at 81, 87, 89. Specifically, the Court declined to apply the *Martinez* standard in 'prisoners' rights' cases because, as we noted in *Turner*, *Martinez* could be (and had been) read to require a strict 'least restrictive alternative' analysis, without sufficient sensitivity to the need for discretion in meeting legitimate prison needs. 482 U.S., at 89–90. The Court expressed concern that 'every administrative judgment would be subject to the possibility that some court somewhere would conclude that it had a less restrictive way of solving the problem at hand,' id., at 9, and rejected the costs of a 'least restrictive alternative' rule as too high. See also *O'Lone v. Estate of Shabazz*, 482 U.S. 342, 350 (1987) (refusing to apply a least restrictive alternative standard for regulation of prisoner work rules having an impact on religious observance).

"The legitimacy of the Government's purpose in promulgating these regulations is beyond question. The regulations are expressly aimed at protecting prison security, a purpose this Court has said is 'central to all other corrections goals.' *Pell v. Procunier*, 417 U.S., at 823.

"Where the regulations at issue concern the entry of materials into the prison, we agree with the District Court that a regulation which gives prison authorities broad discretion is appropriate . . . A second factor the Court in *Turner* held to be 'relevant in determining the reasonableness of a prison restriction . . . is whether there are alternatives of exercising the right that remain open to prison inmates.' 482 U.S., at 90 . . . As the regulations at issue in the present case permit a broad range of publications to be sent, received, and read, this factor is clearly satisfied.

"In our view, when prison officials are able to demonstrate that they have rejected a less restrictive alternative because of reasonably founded fears that it will lead to greater harm, they succeed in demonstrating that the alternative they in fact selected was not an 'exaggerated response' under Turner."

CASE SIGNIFICANCE: This decision applies the standard set by the Court two years earlier in *Turner v. Safley*, 482 U.S. 78 (1987) to prison "receipt of publications" cases. In the *Turner* case, the Court held that prison regulations that impinge on inmates' constitutional rights are valid if they are "reasonably related to legitimate penological interests." The Court then enumerated four factors to be considered when making the reasonableness determination:

(1) whether there is a valid, rational connection between the regulation and the legitimate government interest put forward to justify it;

(2) whether there are alternative means of exercising the rights that remain open to prisoners;

(3) the impact that accommodation of the asserted right will have on correctional officers and other inmates and on the allocation of prison resources generally; and

(4) the existence of ready alternatives to the regulation. The Court applied these four tests to the federal prison regulation involved in this case and concluded that the regulation was constitutional.

This case is significant because it extends the *Turner* test to "receipt of publication" cases and also illustrates how those tests are applied to actual prison regulations. The *Turner* test makes it difficult for prisoners to overturn prison regulations even if they infringe on First Amendment rights, such as the regulations in question here did. The Court has certainly taken the side of prison administration in the balancing of interests between prison authorities and inmates, even when the constitutional right involved is as important as the First Amendment. This case involved the Federal Bureau of Prisons, but should apply to state prisons as well.

SHAW V. MURPHY
532 U.S. 223 (2001)

CAPSULE: The standard established in *Turner v. Safley* applies to all constitutional rights of inmates, including First Amendment rights.

(Read the Facts, Issue, Decision, and Reasons for this case on page 11.)

CASE SIGNIFICANCE: As mentioned at the beginning of this chapter, *Turner v. Safley* (1987) provides that prison regulations that infringe upon inmates' constitutional rights are valid if they are "reasonably related to legitimate penological interests." In this case, Murphy, the inmate, claimed that this standard should not apply to cases like this one, in which the inmate claims that the communication that was prohibited by the prison system included legal advice. In effect, he claimed that although *Turner v. Safley* applied to infringements of First Amendment rights as well as to other constitutional rights, it did not apply to communications involving legal advice. This was rejected by the Supreme Court.

The significance of this decision is that it reiterates that the standard set in *Turner v. Safley* is the same standard to be used by the courts regardless of the right alleged by the prisoner to have been violated. This decision further strengthens the authority of prison systems to regulate the constitutional rights of inmates.

BEARD V. BANKS
542 U.S. 40 (2006)

CAPSULE: A Pennsylvania prison policy that denies dangerous inmates access to newspapers, magazines, and photographs does not violate the First Amendment because it is adequately justified by prison officials.

FACTS: Banks was an inmate in a Long-Term Segregation Unit in a Pennsylvania prison. He was at the highest level of restrictions within the unit. This included no access to newspapers, magazines, and photographs. Banks filed a lawsuit against the Secretary of the Pennsylvania Department of Corrections under § 1983, alleging that this policy had no reasonable relationship to a legitimate penological interest and that it violated the First Amendment.

The District Court granted a summary judgment motion filed by the Department of Corrections. The Third Circuit Court of Appeals reversed the summary judgment on the ground that the regulation could not be supported as a matter of law by the case's record.

ISSUE: Does the Pennsylvania prison policy that denies access to newspapers, magazines, and photographs to dangerous inmates violate the First Amendment? NO.

HOLDING: The Pennsylvania Department of Corrections adequately justified the prison policy and the inmate failed to present specific facts that would result in a ruling in his favor.

REASON: "The case arises on a motion for summary judgment. While we do not deny the constitutional importance of the interests in question, we find, on the basis of the record now before us, that prison officials have set forth adequate legal support for the policy. And the plaintiff, a prisoner who attacks the policy, has failed to set forth 'specific facts' that, in light of the deference that courts must show to the prison officials, could warrant a determination in his favor. Fed. Rule Civ. Proc. 56(e); *Overton v. Bazzetta*, 539 U.S. 126, 132 (2003) (need for 'substantial deference to the professional judgment of prison administrators') . . . *Turner v. Safley*, 482 U.S. 78 (1987), and *Overton v. Bazzetta*, 539 U.S. 126 (2003), contain the basic substantive legal standards governing this case . . . The Secretary in his motion set forth several justifications for the prison's policy, including the need to motivate better behavior on the part of particularly difficult prisoners, the need to minimize the amount of property they control in their cells, and the need to assure prison safety, by, for example, diminishing the amount of material a prisoner might use to start a cell fire. We need go no further than the first justification, that of providing increased incentives for better prison behavior. Applying the well-established substantive and procedural standards set forth in Part II, we find, on the basis of the record before us, that the Secretary's justification is adequate. And that finding here warrants summary judgment in the Secretary's favor.

"Although summary judgment rules provided Banks with an opportunity to respond to the Secretary's materials, he did not offer any fact-based or expert-based refutation in the manner the rules provide. Fed. Rule Civ. Proc. 56(e) (requiring plaintiff through, e.g., affidavits, etc., to 'set forth specific facts showing that there is a genuine issue for trial'). Instead, Banks filed his own cross-motion for summary judgment in which he claimed that the Policy fell of its own weight, i.e., that the Policy was 'unreasonable as a matter of law' . . . We recognize that the Court of Appeals reached a contrary conclusion. But in doing so, it placed too high an evidentiary burden upon the Secretary."

CASE SIGNIFICANCE: This case involves an alleged violation of an inmate's constitutional right to First Amendment freedoms, including access to newspapers, magazines, and photographs. In an earlier case, *Turner v. Safley* (482 U.S. 78 [1987]), the Court held that a "prison regulation that impinges on inmates' constitutional rights is valid if it is reasonably related to legitimate penological interests." It added that four factors must be considered when determining the reasonableness of the regulation:

1. When there is a valid, rational connection between the regulation and the legitimate government interest used to justify it;
2. Whether there are alternative means of exercising that right that remain open to prisoners;
3. The impact that accommodation of the asserted right will have on correctional officers and inmates, and on the allocation of prison resources generally; and
4. The existence of ready alternatives to the regulation.

Using these factors, the Court held that the prison regulation that denied Long-Term Segregation Unit inmates access to newspapers, magazines, and photographs was reasonable. Such denial could be challenged by inmates, but the Court added that the inmate failed to present specific facts that could support his claim that such denial of access was unreasonable and unrelated to legitimate penological interests.

This case gives substance to the general principle that inmates have constitutional rights, but those rights are limited or diminished. The task of the courts is to determine what rights inmates retain and what rights they lose because of conviction. First Amendment rights, such as were claimed by the inmate in this case, are preferred rights and are therefore highly protected by the courts. Nonetheless, they are subject to the *Turner v. Safley* analysis of reasonable relatedness to legitimate penological concerns. Using this standard, the Court concluded that prison officials were justified in imposing the regulation.

R. MEDICAL CARE AND PSYCHOLOGICAL TREATMENT

ESTELLE V. GAMBLE
429 U.S. 97 (1976)

CAPSULE: "Deliberate indifference" to inmate medical needs constitutes cruel and unusual punishment and is therefore unconstitutional.

FACTS: J.W. Gamble, an inmate of the Texas Department of Corrections, was injured while performing a work assignment. He was granted a pass to the hospital, where he was diagnosed with back strain, treated with medicine, and relieved of prison duty. The pain continued and the inmate was placed on a cell pass for three weeks. After three weeks, he was ordered back to work with continued medication. Gamble refused to work, claiming that he was in too much pain. He was placed in administrative segregation and directed to be seen by another doctor. The medical director treated him with medication for back pain and high blood pressure. However, the prescription took four days to fill because it was temporarily misplaced. Medication was continued for one month while Gamble remained in administrative segregation.

At his next discipline committee hearing, testimony was given that Gamble was in "first-class" medical condition. He was ordered to work; he refused again, and was placed in solitary confinement. Gamble requested medical attention four days later for black-outs and chest pains. He was examined, treated, and placed in administrative segregation. A few days later, he again asked to see a doctor and was denied access for two days. Shortly thereafter, he brought a civil rights action under 42 U.S.C. § 1983 against W.J. Estelle, Jr., Director of the Department of Corrections; H.H. Husbands, warden of the prison; and Dr. Ralph Gray, medical director. Gamble claimed that he was subjected to cruel and unusual punishment in violation of the Eighth Amendment because he received inadequate treatment for a back injury sustained while working in the prison. The District Court dismissed the complaint based on failure to state a claim upon which relief could be granted. The Court of Appeals ordered reinstatement of the complaint, holding that the alleged insufficiency of the medical treatment required it.

ISSUE: Did the action of the state constitute deliberate indifference to the prisoner's injury, thus violating the cruel and unusual punishment clause of the Eighth Amendment? NO.

HOLDING: Deliberate indifference by prison personnel to a prisoner's serious illness or injury constitutes cruel and unusual punishment, in violation of the Eighth Amendment. In this case, however, the claims by the inmate do not constitute deliberate indifference. The facts show that the medical director and other prison medical personnel saw the inmate on 17 occasions during a three-month period and treated his injury and other problems. The failure to perform an X-ray or to use additional diagnostic techniques does not constitute cruel and unusual punishment, but is at most medical malpractice that can be redressed in state courts. **REASON:** "We therefore conclude that deliberate indifference to serious medical needs of prisoners constitutes the 'unnecessary and wanton infliction of pain,' *Gregg v. Georgia*, *supra*, at 173 (joint opinion), proscribed by the Eighth Amendment . . . This conclusion does not mean, however, that every claim by a prisoner that he has not received adequate medical treatment states a violation of the Eighth Amendment . . . Medical malpractice does not become a constitutional violation merely because the victim is a prisoner. In order to state a cognizable claim, a prisoner must allege acts or omissions sufficiently harmful to evidence deliberate indifference to serious medical needs. It is only such indifference that can offend 'evolving standards of decency' in violation of the Eighth Amendment . . . Even applying these liberal standards, however, Gamble's claims against Dr. Gray, both in his capacity as treating physician and as medical director of the Corrections Department, are not cognizable under Section 1983 . . . A medical decision not to order an X-ray, or like measures, does not represent cruel and unusual punishment. At most, it is medical malpractice, and as such the proper forum is the state court under the Texas Tort Claims Act."

CASE SIGNIFICANCE: This case, decided in 1976, was the first major prison medical treatment case decided by the Supreme Court. It is important because it sets the standard by which violations of an inmate's constitutional rights in medical treatment cases are determined. The Court said that "deliberate indifference by prison personnel to a prisoner's serious illness or injury" constitutes cruel and unusual punishment. Having said that, the Supreme Court concluded that there was no violation in this case because the medical personnel saw the inmate on 17 occasions during a three-month span, adding that the failure to perform an X-ray or to use additional diagnostic techniques does not constitute cruel and unusual punishment. The remedy for malpractice in prisons lies in state courts, not in a civil rights (§ 1983) case.

What is "deliberate indifference" by which prison systems are judged in medical treatment cases? Quoting an earlier case, the Court said that "deliberate indifference to serious medical needs of prisoners constitutes the 'unnecessary and wanton infliction of pain . . .'" The Court then added: "This is true whether the indifference is manifested by prison doctors in their response to the prisoner's needs or by prison guards in intentionally denying or delaying access to medical care or intentionally interfering with the treatment, once prescribed." In a footnote, the Court gave examples of deliberate indifference by prison doctors: (1) "doctors choosing the 'easier and less efficacious treatment' of throwing away the prisoner's ear and stitching the stump;" (2) "injection of penicillin with knowledge that the prisoner was allergic, and refusal of the doctor to treat the allergic reaction;" and (3) "prison physician refusing to administer the prescribed painkiller and renders leg surgery unsuccessful by requiring the prisoner to stand despite contrary instructions of the surgeon." These examples, taken by the Supreme Court from lower court cases, are much more severe than what the Texas Department of Corrections did to inmate Gamble, thus there was no violation of Gamble's constitutional right against cruel and unusual punishment.

The phrase "deliberate indifference," popularized by this case, has since been applied to other cases not involving medical care. However, its meaning varies depending upon the prison issue involved. For example, "deliberate indifference" in general prison conditions cases has been construed by the Court to mean a "culpable state of mind," while in use of deadly force cases the Court says it means "obduracy and wantonness." And in use of nondeadly force cases in prisons, the Court says that "deliberate indifference" means "using force maliciously and sadistically to cause pain." Despite its shifting meaning, the term "deliberate indifference" is a convenient phrase by which cruel and unusual punishment is determined in prison cases.

WEST V. ATKINS
487 U.S. 42 (1988)

CAPSULE: Private physicians under contract to the state are "acting under color of state law" when treating prisoners.

FACTS: Inmate West tore his left Achilles tendon while playing volleyball at a state prison in North Carolina. A physician at the prison transferred West to the Central Prison Hospital in Raleigh for orthopedic consultation. Samuel Atkins, M.D., a private physician, provided orthopedic services at the prison hospital through a contract for professional services. He treated West's injury by placing his leg in a series of casts over several months.

West brought an action against Atkins under 42 U.S.C. § 1983, alleging that his Eighth Amendment right to be free from cruel and unusual punishment had been violated. West claimed that Atkins knew that he needed surgery but refused to schedule it and eventually discharged him when his ankle was still swollen and painful. West alleged that Atkins was deliberately indifferent to his serious medical needs by failing to provide adequate treatment.

ISSUE: Is a physician who is under contract to the state to provide medical services to inmates at a state prison hospital on a part-time basis acting "under color of state law" within the meaning of 42 U.S.C. § 1983 when treating an inmate? YES.

HOLDING: A physician who is under contract to the state to provide medical services to inmates in a state prison hospital on a part-time basis acts "under color of state law" when treating an inmate. Therefore, although a private person, the physician can be sued under § 1983.

REASON: "The traditional definition of acting under color of state law requires that the defendant in a Section 1983 action have exercised power 'possessed by virtue of state law and made possible only because the wrongdoer is clothed with the authority of state law.'

"We now make explicit what was implicit in our holding in *Estelle:* Respondent, as a physician employed by North Carolina to provide medical services to state prison inmates, acted under color of state law for purposes of Section 1983 when undertaking his duties in treating petitioner's injury. Such conduct is fairly attributable to the State.

"Under state law, the only medical care West could receive for his injury was that provided by the State. If Doctor Atkins misused his power by demonstrating deliberate indifference to West's serious medical needs, the resultant deprivation was caused, in the sense relevant for state-action inquiry, by the State's exercise of its right to punish West by incarceration and to deny him a venue independent of the State to obtain medical care.

"The State bore an affirmative obligation to provide adequate medical care to West; the State delegated that function to respondent Atkins; and respondent voluntarily assumed that obligation by contract . . . In the State's employ, respondent worked as a physician at the prison hospital fully vested with state authority to fulfill essential aspects of the duty, placed on the State by the Eighth Amendment and state law, to provide essential medical care to those the State had incarcerated. Doctor Atkins must be considered to be a state actor."

CASE SIGNIFICANCE: This case addresses the question of whether private persons under contract to the state can be sued under § 1983, or whether only public employees can be sued under this federal law. By deciding that private persons can be held liable and are acting under "color of law" when performing services, the Supreme Court expanded the number and categories of individuals who may be sued under § 1983. This decision allows prisoners to bring actions under federal statutes against people working in prisons who may not be public employees, but who are under contract to the state to provide services to prisoners. The reason for this is that the state, by contracting with a private provider to perform an essential service, in fact delegated its power to that private person—thus, he or she acts under color of state law.

WASHINGTON V. HARPER
494 U.S. 210 (1990)

CAPSULE: A prisoner with a serious mental illness may be treated with antipsychotic drugs against his will. There must be a hearing prior to such treatment, but the hearing does not have to be before a judge; a hearing before a special committee (in this case composed of a psychiatrist, a psychologist, and a correctional official) is sufficient.

FACTS: Inmate Harper was sentenced to prison in 1976 for robbery. From 1976 to 1980, he was incarcerated at the Washington State Penitentiary, primarily in the mental health unit. Harper was paroled in 1980, one of the conditions being that he participate in psychiatric treatment. In December 1981, his parole was revoked after he assaulted two nurses at a hospital in Seattle.

Upon being returned to prison, Harper was sent to the Special Offender Center (SOC or the Center). The initial diagnosis of Harper indicated that he was suffering from a manic-depressive disorder. He gave voluntary consent to treatment, including the administration of antipsychotic drugs, until November 1982, when he refused to continue taking his prescribed medication. His physician sought to continue his medication despite his objections, pursuant to SOC Policy 600.30.

Policy 600.30 states that if a psychiatrist orders antipsychotic medication, an inmate may be involuntarily treated only if he: (1) suffers from a "mental disorder" and (2) is "gravely disabled" or poses a "likelihood of serious harm" to himself or others. After a hearing in which the above conditions are judged to have been met, a special committee consisting of a psychiatrist, a psychologist, and a Center official, none of whom may be currently involved in the inmate's diagnosis or treatment, can order involuntary medication if the psychiatrist is in the majority. The inmate has a right to notice of the hearing, the right to attend, present evidence, and cross-examine witnesses. He or she has a right to a disinterested lay advisor versed in psychological issues, the right to appeal to the Center's Superintendent, and the right to periodic review of any involuntary medication ordered. The inmate also has a right to judicial review of a committee decision in state court by means of a personal restraint petition or extraordinary writ.

Harper was found to be a danger to others as a result of a mental disease or disorder and consequently the committee approved the involuntary administration of antipsychotic drugs. This decision was appealed to and upheld by the Superintendent. Harper was involuntarily medicated for one year, during which periodic reviews were conducted.

Following this year, Harper was transferred to another facility for one month. During this time, he was not taking medication. He was then transferred back to the Center where another committee meeting was held in accordance with policy. The committee approved involuntary medication and Harper was given antipsychotic drugs. He filed suit in state court under 42 U.S.C. § 1983, claiming that failure to provide a judicial hearing before the involuntary administration of antipsychotic drugs violated the due process, equal protection, and free speech clauses of both the federal and state constitutions, as well as state tort law.

ISSUE: Does the treatment of a mentally ill prisoner with antipsychotic drugs against his will and without a judicial hearing violate the due process clause of the Fourteenth Amendment? NO.

HOLDING:

1. The due process clause permits the state to treat a prisoner who has a serious mental illness with antipsychotic drugs against his will if he is a danger to himself or others and the treatment is in his medical interest. The state has a legitimate interest in medically treating a prisoner, when appropriate, for the purpose of reducing the danger the prisoner poses.

2. A judicial hearing is not required under the due process clause and the Policy's procedures satisfy due process requirements in other respects.

The Special Offender Center's Policy concerning administrative hearing procedures satisfies procedural due process.

REASON: "In *Turner*, we considered various factors to determine the reasonableness of a challenged prison regulation. Three are relevant here. 'First, there must be a "valid, rational connection" between the prison regulation and the legitimate governmental interest put forward to justify it.' 482 U.S. at 89 (quoting *Block v. Rutherford*, 468 U.S. 576, 586 [1984]). Second, a court must consider 'the impact accommodation of the asserted constitutional right will have on guards and other inmates, and on the allocation of prison resources generally.' 482 U.S., at 90. Third, 'the absence of ready alternatives is evidence of the reasonableness of a prison regulation,' but this does not mean that prison officials 'have set up and then shot down every conceivable alternative method of accommodating the claimant's constitutional complaint.' Id., at 90–91; see also *Estate of Shabazz*, *supra*, at 350.

"Applying these factors to the regulation before us, we conclude that the Policy comports with constitutional requirements. There can be little doubt as to both the legitimacy and the importance of the governmental interest presented here . . . Special Offender Center Policy 600.30 is a rational means of furthering the State's legitimate objectives . . . There is considerable debate over the potential side effects of antipsychotic medications, but there is little dispute in the psychiatric profession that proper use of the drugs is one of the most effective means of treating and controlling a mental illness likely to cause violent behavior.

"We hold that, given the requirements of the prison environment, the Due Process Clause permits the State to treat a prison inmate who has a serious mental illness with antipsychotic drugs against his will, if the inmate is dangerous to himself or others and the treatment is in the inmate's medical interest. Policy 600.30 comports with these requirements; we therefore reject respondent's contention that its substantive standards are deficient under the Constitution.

"We address next what procedural protections are necessary to ensure that the decision to medicate an inmate against his will is neither arbitrary nor erroneous under the standards we have discussed above . . . We hold that the administrative hearing procedures set by the SOC Policy do comport with procedural due process, and conclude that the Washington Supreme Court erred in requiring a judicial hearing as a prerequisite for the involuntary treatment of prison inmates . . .

"In sum, we hold that the regulation before us is permissible under the Constitution. It is an accommodation between an inmate's liberty interest in avoiding the forced administration of antipsychotic drugs and the State's interests in providing appropriate medical treatment to reduce the danger that an inmate suffering from a serious mental disorder represents to himself or others. The Due Process Clause does require certain essential procedural protections, all of which are provided by the regulation before us."

CASE SIGNIFICANCE: This case answers the question of whether a state may treat a prisoner with antipsychotic drugs against his or her will and without a judicial hearing. The Supreme Court said yes, holding that the state has a legitimate interest in such treatment, where appropriate, for the purpose of reducing the danger the prisoner poses. The prisoner in this case argued that because of the liberty interest involved (being treated against his will), a hearing before a judge was necessary—in essence saying that the procedure followed by the state of Washington was unconstitutional because the decision was made not by a judge but by a special committee consisting of a psychiatrist, a psychologist, and a Center official. The Court disagreed, saying that the liberty interest of the inmate in this case was adequately protected by such procedure and "perhaps better served, by allowing the decision to medicate to be made by the medical professionals rather than a judge."

The Court's decision did not say that forced treatment of a prisoner who has a serious mental illness by prison authorities could be made arbitrarily. On the contrary, the Court said that due process was required prior to such treatment. In this case, however, the procedure provided by the state of Washington (which included a hearing before a committee, the right to notice, attend the hearing, present evidence, cross-examine witnesses, and the right to appeal to administrators as well as the right to a judicial review of a committee decision in a state court) satisfied the due process requirement of the Constitution. While the Court did not enumerate the due process rights that an inmate is entitled to in forced treatment situations, the Court made clear that there was nothing wrong with the procedure used by the state of Washington. In sum, inmates are entitled to some due process rights prior to forced treatment, but these rights do not include a judicial hearing, nor do they include all the rights to which an inmate is entitled in a judicial hearing. The procedure used by the state of Washington complied with due process requirements.

RIGGINS V. NEVADA
504 U.S. 127 (1992)

CAPSULE: Forced administration of an antipsychotic drug during trial violated a defendant's rights guaranteed by the Sixth and Fourteenth Amendments.

FACTS: After being arrested for homicide, Riggins was treated with an antipsychotic medication when he complained of hearing voices in his head and having difficulty sleeping. The district court found him competent to stand trial. His attorney moved for an order suspending administration of the antipsychotic drug until the completion of his trial, based on three factors: (1) continued use of the drug infringed upon Riggins' freedom; (2) the effect of the drug on his demeanor and mental state during the trial would deny him due process; and (3) an insanity defense would be offered at trial and Riggins had a right to show jurors his true mental state. After hearing testimony from psychiatrists, the court denied this motion without offering a rationale for the decision.

Riggins presented the insanity defense at his trial, testifying on his own behalf. He was convicted of murder and robbery and received a death sentence. Riggins appealed to the Nevada Supreme Court on the ground that the lower court ordered the continued administration of the antipsychotic drug without considering less intrusive options. The Nevada Supreme Court upheld his conviction and sentence, stating that the expert testimony offered at trial was sufficient to inform the jury about the effects of the antipsychotic drug on his demeanor and testimony. The Nevada Supreme Court also held that the lower court's denial of the motion to terminate the medication was neither an abuse of discretion nor a violation of Riggins' rights at trial.

ISSUE: Is forced administration of antipsychotic medication during trial a violation of rights guaranteed by the Sixth and Fourteenth Amendments? YES.

HOLDING: The Fourteenth Amendment requires that the state establish the need for the antipsychotic medication and the medical appropriateness of the drug.

REASON: "Under *Harper*, forcing antipsychotic drugs on a convicted prisoner is impermissible absent a finding of overriding justification and a determination of medical appropriateness. The Fourteenth Amendment affords at least as much protection to persons the State detains for trial . . . Thus, once Riggins moved to terminate administration of antipsychotic medication, the State became obligated to establish the need for Mellaril and the medical appropriateness of the drug.

"The [District] court did not acknowledge the defendant's liberty interest in freedom from unwanted antipsychotic drugs. This error may well have impaired the constitutionally protected trial right Riggins invokes . . . What the testimony of doctors who examined Riggins establishes, and what we will not ignore, is a strong possibility that Riggins' defense was impaired due to the administration of Mellaril . . . We are also persuaded that allowing Riggins to present expert testimony about the effect of Mellaril on his demeanor did nothing to cure the possibility that the substance of his own testimony, his interaction with counsel, or his comprehension at trial were compromised by forced administration of Mellaril. Even if . . . the Nevada Supreme Court was right that expert testimony allowed jurors to assess Riggins' demeanor fairly, an unacceptable risk of prejudice remained."

CASE SIGNIFICANCE: In an earlier case (*Washington v. Harper* [1990]), the Court had held that the prison system could not administer antipsychotic drugs on a prisoner "without overriding justification and determination of medical appropriateness." This case also involved the administration of antipsychotic drugs by prison officials while the detainee was undergoing trial. The detainee argued that it violated his constitutional rights and interfered with his ability to establish an insanity defense in that the antipsychotic drugs might mask his insanity. The Court agreed, saying that there was no overriding justification for the treatment and its medical appropriateness for this particular inmate was not established. Once the inmate raised the issue, the burden shifted to the prison authorities to establish its need and appropriateness—which they failed to do. Everything considered, the Court concluded that there was an "unacceptable risk" that the administration of the drug during trial prejudiced the detainee's right to put up a defense.

SELL V. UNITED STATES
539 U.S. 166 (2003)

CAPSULE: Involuntary administration of antipsychotic drugs to render a mentally ill defendant competent to stand trial on serious criminal charges is constitutional under limited circumstances.

FACTS: Sell was originally charged with submitting fictitious insurance claims for payment in his dentistry practice. Although he had a history of mental illness, he was found competent to stand trial and released on bail. After the court was notified that Sell had sought to intimidate a witness in his case, a bail revocation hearing was held and his bail was revoked. Following this, Sell was charged with attempting to murder the FBI agent who arrested him and a former employee who would testify against him.

Sell requested that a magistrate reconsider his competency to stand trial and subsequently he was found incompetent to stand trial and ordered to be hospitalized for treatment to determine whether he could possibly become competent in the future. The staff at the medical center recommended that he take an antipsychotic medication, which he refused. They then sought to administer the medication involuntarily, which he challenged in court. The District Court upheld this involuntary administration and the Eighth Circuit Court of Appeals affirmed.

ISSUE: Is it constitutional to allow the government to involuntarily administer antipsychotic drugs to a mentally ill defendant in order to render him competent to stand trial on serious criminal charges? YES, under certain circumstances.

HOLDING: The government may administer antipsychotic drugs to a mentally ill defendant against his or her will in order to render the defendant competent to stand trial on serious criminal charges under the following conditions: (1) if the treatment is medically appropriate, (2) if it is substantially unlikely to have side effects that may undermine the trial's fairness; and (3) if less intrusive alternatives have been considered; and (4) if it is necessary to significantly further important governmental trial-related issues.

REASON: "This standard [noted above] will permit involuntary administration of drugs solely for trial competence purposes in certain instances. But those instances may be rare. That is because the standard says or fairly implies the following: First, a court must find that important governmental interests are at stake. The Government's interest in bringing to trial an individual accused of a serious crime is important . . . Second, the courts must conclude that involuntary medication will significantly further those concomitant state interests. It must find that administration of the drugs is substantially likely to render the defendant competent to stand trial. At the same time, it must find that administration of the drugs is substantially unlikely to have side effects that will interfere significantly with the defendant's ability to assist counsel in conducting a trial defense, thereby rendering the trial unfair . . . Third, the court must conclude that involuntary medication is necessary to further those interests. The court must find that any alternative, less intrusive treatments are unlikely to achieve substantially the same results . . . Fourth, as we have said, the court must conclude that administration of the drugs is medically appropriate, i.e., in the patient's best medical interest in light of his medical condition. The specific kinds of drugs at issue may matter here as elsewhere. Different kinds of antipsychotic drugs may produce different side effects and enjoy different levels of success.

"Every State provides avenues through which, for example, a doctor or institution can seek appointment of a guardian with the power to make a decision authorizing medication—when it is in the best interests of a patient who lacks the mental competence to make such a decision . . . We consequently believe that a court, asked to approve forced administration of drugs for purposes of rendering a defendant competent to stand trial, should ordinarily determine whether the Government seeks, or has first sought, permission for forced administration of drugs on these other *Harper-type* grounds; and if not, why not."

CASE SIGNIFICANCE: This case deals with the same issue addressed earlier in *Washington v. Harper* (1990) and *Riggins v. Nevada* (1992)—the use of antipsychotic drugs by prison officials. This time, however, the issue was whether antipsychotic drugs could be administered to a mentally ill defendant so as to render him competent to stand trial. The Court reaffirmed its previous rulings on antipsychotic drugs—that they could be administered provided their justification and appropriateness are established by prison officials. The Court went further, however, and specified four conditions that must be established by prison officials if they are to use antipsychotic drugs so as to render defendant competent to stand trial. After setting the four conditions (see Holding, above), the Court then sent the case back to the lower court to determine whether these conditions could be met by the prison system. Failure to comply with them, as determined by the lower court, would mean that the antipsychotic drugs could not be administered.

BROWN ET AL. V. PLATA ET AL.
131 S. CT. 1910 (2011)

CAPSULE: The decision of the three-judge panel in the federal district court in California must be affirmed and the reduction of the prison population is a necessary remedy, authorized under the Prison Litigation Reform Act.

FACTS: In the original case of *Coleman v. Brown* (1990), the District Court held that seriously mentally ill prisoners did not receive minimal adequate care. A special master was appointed to oversee remedial efforts in the California prison system. A report 12 years later noted that mentally ill prisoners' health care was deteriorating owing to an increase in overcrowding. In the second class-action lawsuit filed in 2001, *Plata v. Brown*, the state conceded that the overall health care offered to its inmates was deficient and in violation of the Eighth Amendment's prohibition against cruel and unusual punishment. At that time, the state agreed to a remedial injunction to improve care for the inmates.

Four years later, the state had still not complied with the injunction, and a receiver was appointed to oversee improvements. Three years after that, the receiver reported continuing deficiencies in mental and physical health care due, again, to overcrowding. The plaintiffs in both suits moved to have a three-judge panel, from the two district courts involved, convened to order a reduction in the prison population. This was allowed under the provisions of the PLRA. The panel ordered the California prison system to reduce its population to 137.5 percent capacity within two years. The panel reached this conclusion after determining that capacity could not be increased significantly through new construction. The State of California appealed the panel's decision to the Supreme Court, asserting that the three-judge court erred in finding that overcrowding was the primary cause of inadequate medical care and thus could not order a reduction in the prison population, among other issues.

ISSUES:

1. Is the court-mandated reduction in the prison population necessary to remedy the violation of prisoners' constitutional rights to adequate medical and mental health care? YES.

2. Is the court-mandated reduction authorized by the Prison Litigation Reform Act? YES.

3. Did the three-judge court err in finding that overcrowding was the primary cause of the violation? NO.

4. Did the three-judge court err in imposing a 137.5 percent capacity cap on the California prison population to be achieved in two years? NO.

HOLDINGS:

1. If a prison deprives inmates of basic sustenance, which includes adequate medical and mental health care, the courts have a responsibility to remedy the Eighth Amendment violation. The district courts acted reasonably in convening the three-judge panel.

2. The three-judge court mandate to reduce the prison population is authorized by the PLRA because the Act stipulates that only a three-judge court may limit a prison population.

3. The three-judge court did not err in finding that overcrowding was the primary cause of the violation because it was permissible to do so. The court examined reports documenting overcrowding and heard testimony from numerous experts that overcrowding was the primary cause of inadequate physical and mental health care.

4. The court did not err in imposing a 137.5 percent capacity cap on the prison population to be achieved in two years. The state did not contest the issue at trial, and the court has made provisions to exercise its discretion to modify this order, considering the state's needs to devise mechanisms and plans for the order to become reality.

REASONS: "This case arises from serious constitutional violations in California's prison system. The violations have persisted for years. They remain uncorrected . . . After years of litigation, it became apparent that a remedy for the constitutional violations would not be effective absent a reduction in the prison system population. The authority to order release of prisoners as a remedy to cure a systemic violation of the Eighth Amendment is a power reserved to a three-judge district court, not a single-judge district court. 18 U.S.C. § 3626(a). . . . The State in this Court has not objected to consolidation [of the two cases], although the State does argue that the three-judge court was prematurely convened. The State also objects to the substance of the three-judge court order, which requires the State to reduce overcrowding in its prisons. The appeal presents the question whether the remedial order issued by the three-judge court is consistent with requirements and procedures set forth in a congressional statute, the Prison Litigation Reform Act of 1995 (PLRA). 18 U.S.C. § 3626; see Appendix A, infra. The order leaves the choice of means to reduce overcrowding to the discretion of state officials. But absent compliance through new construction, out-of-state transfers, or other means—or modification of the order upon a further showing by the State—the State will be required to release some number of prisoners before their full sentences have been served. High recidivism rates must serve as a warning that mistaken or premature release of even one prisoner can cause injury and harm. The release of prisoners in large numbers—assuming the State finds no other way to comply with the order—is a matter of undoubted, grave concern . . . The State may employ measures, including good-time credits and diversion of low-risk offenders and technical parole violators to community-based programs, that will mitigate the order's impact. The population reduction potentially required is nevertheless of unprecedented sweep and extent. Yet so too is the continuing injury and harm resulting from these serious constitutional violations. For years the medical and mental health care provided by California's prisons has fallen short of minimum constitutional requirements and has failed to meet prisoners' basic health needs. Needless suffering and death have been the well documented result. Over the whole course of years during which this litigation has been pending, no other remedies have been found to be sufficient . . . This Court now holds that the PLRA does authorize the relief afforded in this case and that the court-mandated population limit is necessary to remedy the violation of prisoners' constitutional rights. The order of the three-judge court, subject to the right of the State to seek its modification in appropriate circumstances, must be affirmed. The degree of overcrowding in California's prisons is exceptional. . . . The State's prisons had operated at around 200 percent of design capacity for at least 11 years . . . The Corrections Independent Review Panel, a body appointed by the Governor and composed of correctional consultants and representatives from state agencies, concluded that California's prisons are 'severely overcrowded, imperiling the safety of both correctional employees and inmates.' 1 Juris. Statement App., O. T. 2009 . . . Prisoners in California with serious mental illness do not receive minimal, adequate care . . . In 2006, the suicide rate in California's prisons was nearly 80 percent higher than the national average for prison populations; and a court-appointed Special Master found that 72.1 percent of suicides involved 'some measure of inadequate assessment, treatment, or intervention, and were therefore most probably foreseeable and/or preventable.' *Id.*, at 1781. Prisoners suffering from physical illness also receive severely deficient care."

"The three-judge court properly admitted evidence of current conditions as relevant to the issues before it . . . The court relied extensively on the expert witness reports. See generally Juris. App. 85a–143a. The court cited the most current data available on suicides and preventable deaths in the California prisons. *Id.*, at 123a, 125a. The court relied on statistics on staff vacancies that dated to three months before trial, *id.*, at 105a, 108a, and statistics on shortages of treatment beds for the same period, *id.*, at 97a. These are just examples of the extensive evidence of current conditions that informed every aspect of the judgment of the three-judge court. The three-judge court did not abuse its discretion when it also cited findings made in earlier decisions of the *Plata* and *Coleman* District Courts. Those findings remained relevant to establish the nature of these longstanding, continuing constitutional violations . . . The evidence at trial, however, supports the three-judge court's conclusion that an order limited to other remedies would not provide effective relief . . . In light of the State's longstanding failure to remedy these serious constitutional violations, the three-judge court was under no obligation to consider voluntary population-reduction measures by the State as a workable alternative to injunctive relief. . . . The common thread connecting the State's proposed remedial efforts is that they would require the State to expend large amounts of money absent a reduction in overcrowding. The Court cannot ignore the political and fiscal reality behind this case. California's Legislature has not been willing or able to allocate the resources necessary to meet this crisis absent a reduction in overcrowding. There is no reason to believe it will begin to do so now, when the State of California is facing an unprecedented budgetary shortfall. As noted above, the legislature recently failed to allocate funds for planned new construction. *Supra*, at 30–31. Without a reduction in overcrowding, there will be no efficacious remedy for the unconstitutional care of the sick and mentally ill in California's prisons . . . [T]he prison population can be reduced in a manner calculated to avoid an undue negative effect on public safety . . . The State has already made significant progress toward reducing its prison population, including reforms that will result in shifting 'thousands' of prisoners to county jails. See Supp. Brief for Appellants at 1. As the State makes further progress, the three-judge court should evaluate whether its order remains appropriate. If significant progress is made toward remedying the underlying constitutional violations, that progress may demonstrate that further population reductions are not necessary or are less urgent than previously believed. Were the State to make this showing, the three-judge court in the exercise of its discretion could consider whether it is appropriate to extend or modify this timeline . . . These observations reflect the fact that the three-judge court's order, like all continuing equitable decrees, must remain open to appropriate modification. They are not intended to cast doubt on the validity of the basic premise of the existing order. The medical and mental health care provided by California's prisons falls below the standard of decency that inheres in the Eighth Amendment. This extensive and ongoing constitutional violation requires a remedy, and a remedy will not be achieved without a reduction in overcrowding. The relief ordered by the three-judge court is required by the Constitution and was authorized by Congress in the PLRA. The State shall implement the order without further delay. The judgment of the three-judge court is affirmed."

CASE SIGNIFICANCE: This case is a landmark case that affected what was at the time the largest state prison system in the United States, housing more than 156,000 inmates in 2011. The initial case was first filed in 1990 and, 21 years later, was still being litigated. It began as a claim on behalf of seriously mentally ill inmates, asserting that they were not receiving adequate mental health services, in violation of the Eighth Amendment's prohibition against cruel and unusual punishment. Twelve years later, the special master appointed to oversee the proposed remedies reported that medical services were also in violation of the Eighth Amendment. By 2008, a receiver, whose job it was to monitor remedial efforts, noted that overcrowding was a major cause of the system's failure to comply with the remedies. So, the case went from addressing mentally ill inmates' needs to the overall medical needs of inmates to the overcrowding problem in the California prison system in 2011. As overcrowding was the major cause of the inadequate services, it was inevitable that it would be addressed in the case eventually. The vote from the Court was a narrow 5–4 in favor of the prisoners.

Treatment for mentally ill prisoners in both jails and prisons has been an issue for decades, with most systems indicating a steady increase in the percentage of prisoners diagnosed with some form of mental illness entering their facilities. When systems become overcrowded, basic services are sometimes inadequate, as the system's focus is on preventing violence directed toward fellow inmates and staff, preventing escapes, and the logistics of where to place those incarcerated. However, an increase in public awareness of the mentally ill in general and prisoners in particular has spurred efforts to treat them. Mental health courts, which have been developed to address the needs of clients and keep them from cycling in and out of the criminal justice system, have reported success in various parts of the country.

When overcrowding is reduced, there are also more resources available to treat those suffering from mental or physical problems. Following the ruling in this case, California made a concentrated effort to reduce its prison population, despite the dire prediction that it would have to release thousands of criminals out into the streets to prey on innocent victims, increasing the crime rate in the state. In 2012, California reduced its prison population by 10 percent, the largest decrease of any state system that year. The population went from approximately 160,000 inmates to 134,200 inmates, dropping the state into third place behind the Bureau of Prisons and Texas for the greatest number of inmates. This was accomplished in part, not due to the back-end solution of releasing large numbers of prisoners at once, but instead employing a front-end solution of increasing the use of community corrections and housing felons in county jails. However, the latter may increase overcrowding in those facilities. One promising program was the voters' passage of Proposition 47 in 2014, which reclassified some nonviolent offenses as misdemeanors instead of felonies. The cost savings to the public are to be directed toward other needs, including mental health treatment.

In 2013, Governor Brown convinced state legislators to allocate $400 million to address the mental health needs of state prisoners. That same year, he appealed the case to the Supreme Court, requesting a stay in order for the state to continue improvements, aware that the state would not meet the January 31, 2014, deadline to remove 9,600 inmates from the system. The Supreme Court denied his appeal, noting that it lacked jurisdiction in the case, without further comment. It appears that the proper court to hear the appeal was the Ninth Circuit Court of Appeals, not the U.S. Supreme Court. The state continues to negotiate proposed remedies with the district court.

S. FREEDOM OF THE PRESS

PELL V. PROCUNIER
417 U.S. 817 (1974)

CAPSULE: A state prison regulation prohibiting media interviews with specific inmates does not violate the constitutional rights of the media or the inmates as long as alternative means of communication are available.

FACTS: Three professional journalists and four California prison inmates brought suit against California prison authorities under 42 U.S.C. § 1983, challenging the constitutionality of a regulation in the California Department of Corrections Manual stating that the press and other media interviews with "specific individual inmates will not be permitted." The policy was implemented following a violent prison disturbance that was partially attributed to a former rule allowing face-to-face, prisoner-press interviews. Correctional authorities saw these interviews as a way for a relatively small number of inmates to gain disproportionate notoriety and influence among their fellow inmates.

The new regulation was challenged as an infringement on the inmates' and journalists' First Amendment rights to freedom of speech and the journalists' right to a free press.

ISSUE: Does a prison regulation prohibiting media interviews with specific inmates violate the constitutional rights of the media and the inmates? NO.

HOLDING:

1. Because alternative channels of communication are open to the inmates, the interview regulation does not violate freedom of speech. This right must be balanced against the state's legitimate interest in confining prisoners, deterring crime, and protecting society.

2. Because the press is not denied access to information available to the general public, the rights of the media are not infringed by the interview regulation. Reporters are free to visit both maximum- and minimum-security sections of California penal institutions and to speak with inmates whom they may encounter; they are also free to select inmates at random.

REASON: "Challenges to prison restrictions that are asserted to inhibit First Amendment interests must be analyzed in terms of the legitimate policies and goals of the corrections system, to whose custody and care the prisoner has been committed in accordance with due process of law. In order to evaluate the constitutionality of Section 415.071 [the prison regulation] we think that the regulation cannot be considered in isolation but must be viewed in the light of the alternative means of communication permitted under the regulations with persons outside the prison . . . One such alternative available to California prison inmates is communication by mail . . . Thus, it is clear that the medium of written correspondence affords inmates an open and substantially unimpeded channel for communication with persons outside the prison, including representatives of the news media.

"Moreover, the visitation policy of the California Corrections Department does not seal the inmate off from personal contact with those outside the prison. Inmates are permitted to receive limited visits from members of their families, the clergy, their attorneys, and friends of prior acquaintance. This is not a case in which the selection is based on the anticipated content of the communication between the inmate and the prospective visitor. If a member of the press fell within any of these categories, there is no suggestion that he would not be permitted to visit with the inmate. More importantly, however, inmates have an unrestricted opportunity to communicate with the press or any other member of the public through their families, friends, clergy, or attorneys who are permitted to visit them at the prison. Thus, this provides another alternative avenue of communication between prison inmates and persons outside the prison.

"The First and Fourteenth Amendments bar government from interfering in any way with a free press. The Constitution does not, however, require government to accord the press special access to information not shared by members of the public generally. It is one thing to say that a journalist is free to seek out sources of information not available to members of the general public, that he is entitled to some constitutional protection of the confidentiality of sources, cf. *Branzburg v. Hayes*, *supra*, and that government cannot restrain the publication of news emanating from such sources. Cf. *New York Times Co. v. United States*, *supra*. It is quite another thing to suggest that the Constitution imposes upon government the affirmative duty to make available to journalists sources of information not available to members of the public generally . . . Accordingly, since Section 415.071 does not deny the press access to sources of information available to members of the general public, we hold that it does not abridge the protections that the First and Fourteenth Amendments guarantee."

CASE SIGNIFICANCE: This case is significant because it was the first case decided by the Court on the issue of prisoner access to the media and vice versa. In this case, the media sought to declare as unconstitutional a rule prohibiting media interviews with specific inmates, a rule promulgated by prison authorities following a violent prison disturbance that authorities attributed, in part, to their former policy of free, face-to-face, prisoner-press interviews. The Court said that the First Amendment rights of inmates were not violated because there were alternative means of communication available to them, such as correspondence by mail with persons on the outside, including media representatives. They also had visitation rights with family, the clergy, attorneys, and friends, and had unrestricted opportunity to communicate with the press or public through their prison visitors. As for the freedom of the press, the court reiterated an earlier statement in *Branzburg v. Hayes*, 408 U.S. 665, in which the Court said "the First Amendment does not guarantee the press a constitutional right of special access to information not available to the public generally." This decision curtails the First Amendment rights of inmates and press; such curtailment is constitutional as long as other avenues are open. What prison authorities cannot do is completely cut off communication between inmates and the press, and vice versa.

The holding in this case was later extended to federal prisons in the case of *Saxbe v. Washington Post Company*, 417 U.S. 843 (1974).

HOUCHINS V. KQED, INC.
438 U.S. 1 (1978)

CAPSULE: The media have no right of access to inmates and prisons beyond that given to the general public.

FACTS: KQED, a television station, reported the suicide of a prisoner in the Greystone area of the Santa Rita Jail on March 31, 1975. The report included two statements, one from a psychiatrist who said that the conditions at the Greystone facility caused the illnesses of his patient-prisoners there. The other statement was from Sheriff Houchins, who denied that prison conditions were responsible for the prisoners' illnesses. KQED then asked to inspect and take pictures in the Greystone facility. Permission was refused and KQED and the Alameda and Oakland branches of the NAACP filed suit under 42 U.S.C. § 1983. They alleged that Houchins had violated the First Amendment by denying media access to his jail and by failing to provide an effective means by which the public could be informed of conditions in the Greystone facility or learn of prisoners' grievances.

At the time of the suit, there was no formal policy regarding public access to the jail. On July 8, 1975, Sheriff Houchins announced a program of regular monthly tours and invited all interested persons to make arrangements for the tours. The news media were given notice in advance of the public. On July 14, 1975, the first tour was conducted, which included a KQED reporter. Each tour allowed a maximum of 25 persons and access to the jail was limited.

KQED and the NAACP contended that these tours failed to provide adequate access to the jail for two reasons: (1) once the scheduled tours had been filled, media representatives who had not signed up were excluded and therefore unable to cover newsworthy events at the jail; and (2) the prohibition on photography and tape recordings, the exclusion of portions of the jail from the tours, and the practice of keeping inmates generally removed from view substantially reduced the usefulness of such tours to the media. Houchins asserted that unregulated access to the jail by the media would infringe on the inmates' right to privacy and that it would create jail celebrities who would undermine jail security. The sheriff also contended that unscheduled media tours would cause jail operations to be disrupted. He asserted that information concerning the jail could reach the public through current mail, visitation, and phone call regulations.

ISSUE: Does the Alameda County Jail policy regarding public access to the jail violate constitutional rights under the First Amendment? NO.

HOLDING: The Constitution does not guarantee the media a right of access to prisons or inmates beyond that given to the general public. Whether the government should open penal institutions in the way asserted by KQED and the NAACP is a matter for legislative, not judicial, resolution.

REASON: "The public importance of conditions in penal facilities and the media's role of providing information afford no basis for reading into the Constitution a right of the public or the media to enter these institutions, with camera equipment, and take moving and still pictures of inmates for broadcast purposes. This Court has never intimated a First Amendment guarantee of a right of access to all sources of information within governmental control. Nor does the rationale of the decisions upon which respondents rely lead to the implication of such a right.

"Petitioner cannot prevent respondents from learning about jail conditions in a variety of ways, albeit not as conveniently as they might prefer. Respondents have a First Amendment right to receive letters from inmates criticizing jail officials and reporting on conditions. Respondents are free to interview those who render the legal assistance to which inmates are entitled. They are also free to seek out former inmates, visitors to the prison, public officials, and institutional personnel, as they sought out complaining psychiatrists here.

"Neither the First Amendment nor the Fourteenth Amendment mandates a right of access to government information or sources of information with the government's control. Under our holdings in *Pell v. Procunier, supra,* and *Saxbe v. Washington Post Co., supra,* until the political branches decree otherwise, as they are free to do, the media has no special right of access to the Alameda County Jail different from or greater than that accorded the public generally."

CASE SIGNIFICANCE: This case followed two 1974 cases, *Pell v. Procunier* and *Saxbe v. Washington Post Co.*, which also stated that there is no constitutional right of access to prisons or their inmates on the part of the media beyond that afforded the general public. In both cases, prison regulations that prevented media interviews with inmates were challenged, as was part of the basis of this challenge.

In this case, the U.S. Supreme Court again reiterated that there is no "right" guaranteed under the First Amendment for the press to be able to interview prisoners under all circumstances. In deciding that a sheriff can restrict press access to physical parts of a jail, the Court further restricted freedom of the press. An important reason the Court decided this case the way it did was the presence of "access alternatives" made available by Sheriff Houchins to the press. As long as these alternatives were available, freedom of the press was not violated, although the degree of access given by the sheriff was not as extensive as that sought by the press. What prison authorities cannot do is deny access completely; such would be viewed differently by the Court.

T. PROTECTION OF INMATES FROM INJURY

DESHANEY V. WINNEBAGO COUNTY DEPARTMENT OF SOCIAL SERVICES
489 U.S. 189 (1989)

CAPSULE: The state has no duty to protect individuals who are not in state custody from harm by private persons. (This implies that the state may be held liable if the individual is under its custody, as when in prison.)

FACTS: Four-year-old Joshua DeShaney was beaten and permanently injured by his father, to whose custody he had been awarded after a divorce. The county department of social services and social workers received several complaints that the child was being abused by his father. Over a period of time, they took various steps to protect the boy, but they did not remove him from his father's custody. Subsequently, the child was beaten by the father so severely that he suffered permanent brain damage and was rendered severely mentally retarded. He is expected to spend the rest of his life confined to an institution. His father was tried and convicted of child abuse. The mother, acting for and as guardian of the child, later sued the officials of the County Department of Social Services under 42 U.S.C. § 1983, charging that county officials violated the child's constitutional right to due process by failing to intervene to protect him against his father's violence. The District Court decided in favor of the county; the Court of Appeals affirmed.

ISSUE: Does the state have the duty to protect individuals who are not in state custody from harm by a private person? NO, with some exceptions.

HOLDING: The Fourteenth Amendment due process clause does not impose an affirmative duty on the state to protect individuals who are not in state custody from harm by private persons. The county social services agency and the officers who failed to protect the child from severe beatings by the father did not violate the child's due process rights and could not be held civilly liable even though they had knowledge of such abuse and had continuing contact with the family.

REASON: "The Due Process Clause of the Fourteenth Amendment provides that '[n]o State shall . . . deprive any person of life, liberty, or property, without due process of law.' Petitioners contend that the State deprived Joshua of his liberty interest in 'free[dom] from . . . unjustified intrusions on personal security,' by failing to provide him with adequate protection against his father's violence. The claim is one invoking the substantive rather than procedural component of the Due Process Clause; petitioners do not claim that the State denied Joshua protection without according him appropriate procedural safeguards, but that it was categorically obligated to protect him in these circumstances.

"But nothing in the language of the Due Process Clause itself requires the State to protect the life, liberty, and property of its citizens against invasion by private actors. The Clause is phrased as a limitation on the State's power to act, not as a guarantee of certain minimal levels of safety and security. It forbids the State itself to deprive individuals of life, liberty, or property without 'due process of law,' but its language cannot fairly be extended to impose an affirmative obligation on the State to ensure that those interests do not come to harm through other means . . . Its purpose was to protect the people from the State, not to ensure that the State protected them from each other. The Framers were content to leave the extent of governmental obligation in the latter area to the democratic political processes.

"Consistent with these principles, our cases have recognized that the Due Process Clauses generally confer no affirmative right to governmental aid, even where such aid may be necessary to secure life, liberty, or property interests of which the government itself may not deprive the individual.

"If the Due Process Clause does not require the State to provide its citizens with particular protective services, it follows that the State cannot be held liable under the Clause for injuries that could have been averted had it chosen to provide them. As a general matter, then, we conclude that a State's failure to protect an individual against private violence simply does not constitute a violation of the Due Process Clause.

"That the State once took temporary custody of Joshua does not alter the analysis, for when it returned him to his father's custody, it placed him in no worse position than that in which he would have been had it not acted at all; the State does not become the permanent guarantor of an individual's safety by having once offered him shelter. Under these circumstances, the State has no constitutional duty to protect Joshua."

CASE SIGNIFICANCE: This is an important case because for the first time the Court addressed the issue of the civil liability of public officials for failure to protect a member of the public from harm or injury inflicted by a third person (not a government official). The Court decided that there is no constitutional right on the part of the public to be protected from such harm, and therefore failure to protect does not result in civil damages against the state and its officers.

Although not a prison law case, this case is important and is briefed here because of what the Court said about the responsibility of the state to protect prisoners and detainees from harm. After discussing previously decided cases, the Court concluded: "Taken together, they stand only for the proposition that when the State takes a person into its custody and holds him there against his will, the Constitution imposes upon it a corresponding duty to assume some responsibility for his safety and well-being."

Quoting *Youngberg v. Romeo* (457 U.S. 307 [1982]), the Court said: "When a person is institutionalized—and wholly dependent on the State . . . a duty to provide certain services and care does exist." The Court then added: "The rationale for this principle is simple enough: when the State by the affirmative exercise of its power so restrains an individual's liberty that it renders him unable to care for himself, and at the same time fails to provide for his basic human needs—e.g., food, clothing, shelter, medical care, and reasonable safety—it transgresses the substantive limits on state action set by the Eighth Amendment and the Due Process Clause." Clearly, therefore, the state has a responsibility to protect prisoners from injury or harm while in state custody. A breach of that duty constitutes a violation of the ban against cruel and unusual punishment and the right of due process, and subjects the state and its officers to liability.

FARMER V. BRENNAN
511 U.S. 825 (1994)

CAPSULE: A prison official is not liable under the Eighth Amendment for injury inflicted on an inmate by other inmates "unless the official knows of and disregards an excessive risk of harm to an inmate." It is not enough for liability that "the risk was so obvious that a reasonable person should have noticed it."

FACTS: Farmer, a preoperative transsexual, was transferred from a federal correctional institution to a state penitentiary, where he was placed in the general population. Farmer has the appearance and demeanor of a woman, enhanced by silicone breast implants and female hormones, but he had male sex organs. He was serving a 20-year term for credit card fraud in a federal prison for men.

Farmer was beaten and raped by another inmate after transfer to the state penitentiary. He filed an action seeking damages and an injunction barring future confinement in any penitentiary. The inmate alleged that prison officials had acted with deliberate indifference to his safety, in violation of the Eighth Amendment, by placing him in a penitentiary that they knew had a violent environment and a history of inmate assaults, and that they knew that he would be vulnerable to sexual attack.

ISSUE: May prison officials be held liable under the Eighth Amendment for unsafe conditions of confinement if they know that inmates face a substantial risk of serious harm and disregard that risk by failing to take reasonable measures to abate it? YES.

HOLDING: Prison officials are not liable under the Eighth Amendment for injury inflicted on an inmate by other inmates unless the official was aware of and disregarded an excessive risk of harm to the inmate. However, it is not enough for liability that the risk was so obvious that a reasonable person should have noticed.

REASON: "Our cases have held that a prison official violates the Eighth Amendment only when two requirements are met. First, the deprivation alleged must be, objectively, 'sufficiently serious,' *Wilson, supra*, at 298 . . . The second requirement follows from the principle that 'only unnecessary and wanton infliction of pain implicates the Eighth Amendment.' *Wilson*, 501 U.S. at 297 . . . In prison condition cases that state of mind is one of 'deliberate indifference' to inmate health or safety, *Wilson, supra*, at 302–303 . . .

"We reject petitioner's invitation to adopt an objective test for deliberate indifference. We hold instead that a prison official cannot be found liable under the Eighth Amendment for denying an inmate humane conditions of confinement unless the official knows of and disregards an excessive risk to inmate health or safety; the official must both be aware of facts from which the inference could be drawn that a substantial risk of serious harm exists, and he must also draw the inference. This approach comports best with the text of the Amendment as our cases have interpreted it.

"Under the test we adopt today, an Eighth Amendment claimant need not show that a prison official acted or failed to act believing that harm would befall an inmate: it is enough that the official acted or failed to act despite his knowledge of a substantial risk of serious harm. . . . Nor may a prison official escape liability for deliberate indifference by showing that, while he was aware of an obvious, substantial risk to inmate safety, he did not know that the complainant was especially likely to be assaulted by the specific prisoner who eventually committed the assault . . . and it does not matter whether the risk comes from a single source or multiple sources, any more than it matters whether a prisoner faces an excessive risk of an attack for reasons personal to him or because all prisoners in his situation face such risk."

CASE SIGNIFICANCE: This case defines the standard for liability of prison officials under the Eighth Amendment in inmate-on-inmate assault cases. The facts indicate that Farmer was a transsexual who was transferred from a federal prison to a state prison. Given his demeanor and appearance, it was predictable that he would be sexually assaulted in prison—and he was. He then filed a § 1983 case alleging violation of his constitutional right against cruel and unusual punishment. The Court held that in order for prison officials to be liable, the official must have "knowingly disregarded an excessive risk of harm." It is not enough that the official "should have known that harm was inevitable because the risk was so obvious that a reasonable person should have noticed it." Under the standard proposed by the inmate, prison officials would have been held liable because the facts of the case indicated that risk to the inmate was obvious.

This decision makes it difficult for inmates to hold prison officials liable in inmate-on-inmate assault cases. The standard of "knowingly disregarded an excessive risk of harm" is a high standard for inmates to establish. The word "knowingly" indicates that prison officials who are unaware of the risk cannot be held liable. It is difficult for inmates to establish in court that prison officials knew harm was imminent and yet disregarded it. Whether this standard applies to assaults on inmates by correctional officers remains to be seen.

This case sets the standard of liability for injuries inflicted by other inmates, but not for injuries inflicted by prison personnel. That standard was set by the Court in *Hudson v. McMillian*.

U. RELIGION

CRUZ V. BETO
405 U.S. 319 (1972)

CAPSULE: Inmates must be given reasonable opportunities to exercise their religious beliefs.

FACTS: Cruz, a member of the Buddhist faith and a prisoner in the Texas Department of Corrections, was not allowed to use the prison chapel, nor to correspond with his religious advisor in the Buddhist sect. He was placed in solitary confinement on a diet of bread and water for two weeks because he shared his Buddhist religious materials with other inmates. While he was in solitary confinement, he was not allowed access to newspapers, magazines, or other sources of news.

Cruz filed suit under 42 U.S.C. § 1983, alleging that he was denied his First Amendment right to freedom of religion, claiming that Texas encouraged participation in other faiths by providing chaplains for those of the Catholic, Jewish, and Protestant faiths. Texas also provided copies of the Jewish and Christian Bibles and conducted weekly Sunday school classes and services. Cruz alleged that points of good merit were given to inmates as a reward for participation in the Protestant, Jewish, and Catholic faiths and that these points enhanced an inmate's eligibility for promotions in class, job assignments, and early parole consideration.

ISSUE: Must inmates with unconventional religious beliefs be given a reasonable opportunity to exercise those beliefs, comparable to the opportunities offered to those with conventional religious beliefs? YES.

HOLDING: The Texas Department of Corrections discriminated against inmate Cruz by denying him reasonable opportunity to pursue his Buddhist faith comparable to opportunities offered to other inmates of conventional religious beliefs.

REASON: "Federal courts sit not to supervise prisons but to enforce the constitutional rights of all 'persons,' including prisoners. We are not unmindful that prison officials must be accorded latitude in the administration of prison affairs, and that prisoners necessarily are subject to appropriate rules and regulations. But persons in prison, like other individuals, have a right to petition the Government for redress of grievances which, of course, includes 'access of prisoners to the courts for the purpose of presenting their complaints.' *Johnson v. Avery*, 393 U.S. 483, 485; *Ex parte Hull*, 312 U.S. 546, 549 . . . Even more closely in point is *Cooper v. Pate*, 378 U.S. 546, where we reversed a dismissal of a complaint brought under 42 U.S.C. Section 1983.

"If Cruz was a Buddhist and if he was denied a reasonable opportunity of pursuing his faith comparable to the opportunity afforded fellow prisoners who adhere to conventional religious precepts, then there was palpable discrimination by the State against the Buddhist religion, established 600 B.C., long before the Christian era. The First Amendment, applicable to the States by reason of the Fourteenth Amendment, *Torcaso v. Watkins*, 367 U.S. 488, 492–493, prohibits government from making a law 'prohibiting the free exercise' of religion. If the allegations of this complaint are assumed to be true, as they must be on the motion to dismiss, Texas has violated the First and Fourteenth Amendments."

CASE SIGNIFICANCE: This case is considered a landmark case because it clarified the right of an inmate to practice religious beliefs even if those beliefs were not considered a part of mainstream or "traditional" religions. The Supreme Court rejected the federal district court's decision that a complaint involving freedom of religion should be left "to the sound discretion of prison administration." In essence, the Court said that freedom of religion in prisons applies to all religions and not just to those with many adherents in American society. What is important, however, is access to worship and religious observance rather than equal treatment for all religions. A prison does not have to build a chapel for every religious faith; instead, what is required is that the chapel be available for use by various religious groups or individuals in prison.

O'LONE V. ESTATE OF SHABAZZ
482 U.S. 342 (1987)

CAPSULE: Prison policies that in effect prevented inmates from exercising freedom of religion are constitutional because they are reasonably related to legitimate penological interests.

FACTS: Inmates in a New Jersey state prison brought suit under 42 U.S.C. § 1983, claiming that two prison policies violated their free exercise rights under the First Amendment. The inmates were of the Islamic faith and were prevented from attending Jumu'ah, a religious service held on Friday afternoons. The first policy required that inmates who were classified as "gang minimum" work outside the buildings where they were housed and where Jumu'ah was held. The second policy prohibited inmates who worked outside from returning to these buildings during the day, for security reasons. The federal district court held that no constitutional violations had occurred. The Court of Appeals vacated and remanded. It ruled that the prison policies could be sustained only if the State showed that the challenged regulations were intended to and did serve the penological goal of security, and that no reasonable method existed by which prisoners' religious rights could be accommodated without creating bona fide security problems.

ISSUE: Do the prison policies requiring inmates to work outside and preventing them from returning to the building during the day violate the inmates' freedom of religion? NO.

HOLDING: The prison policies do not violate inmate constitutional rights because they are reasonably related to legitimate penological interests.

REASON: "By placing the burden on prison officials to disprove the availability of alternatives, the approach articulated by the Court of Appeals fails to reflect the respect and deference that the United States Constitution allows for the judgment of prison administrators . . . the findings of the District Court establish clearly that prison officials acted in a reasonable manner. *Turner v. Safley, supra,* drew upon our previous decisions to identify several factors relevant to this reasonableness determination. First, a regulation must have a logical connection to legitimate governmental interests invoked to justify it. The policies at issue here clearly meet that standard. The requirement that full minimum and gang minimum prisoners work outside the main facility was justified by concerns of institutional order and security . . . The subsequent policy prohibiting returns to the institution during the day also passes muster under this standard.

"While we in no way minimize the central importance of Jumu'ah to respondents, we are unwilling to hold that prison officials are required by the Constitution to sacrifice legitimate penological objectives to that end . . . These concerns of prison administrators [the effect this would have on other inmates, on prison personnel, and on allocation of prison resources generally] provide adequate support for the conclusion that the accommodations of respondents' request to attend Jumu'ah would have undesirable results in the institution."

CASE SIGNIFICANCE: In *Turner v. Safley* (482 U.S. 78 [1987]), decided one week earlier, the Court held that "a prison regulation that impinges on inmates' constitutional rights is valid if it is reasonably related to legitimate penological interests." In this case, the Court applied that test to freedom of religion cases.

Freedom of religion is a preferred constitutional right, meaning it enjoys greater protection from the courts than other constitutional rights. In this case, the inmates alleged that the two prison regulations violated the free exercise clause of the First Amendment because the regulations prohibited them from doing what their religion allows them to do—attend a congregational service held on Friday afternoons. In previous cases, the Supreme Court used the "compelling state interest" test to determine the constitutionality of prison rules impinging on inmates' freedom of religion. Under that test, the Court determined whether there was any compelling state interest that justified either regulating or prohibiting the exercise of such right. The compelling state interest test was difficult for prison administrators to establish, thus affording inmates more religious freedom. The Turner test gives prison administrators greater authority because all they have to do is prove that the prison regulation that impinges on religious freedom is "reasonably related to legitimate penological interests." The Turner test limited inmates' rights to religious freedom by giving prison authorities more power to issue regulations in the name of a legitimate penological interest, such as prison order and security.

SOSSAMON V. TEXAS, ET AL.
131 S. CT. 1651 (2011)

CAPSULE: By a state accepting federal funding, it does not consent to waive its sovereign immunity for private suits brought against it for monetary relief under the Religious Land Use and Institutionalized Persons Act of 2000.

FACTS: After the Supreme Court declared the Religious Freedom Restoration Act to be unconstitutional because it exceeded Congress' power under the Fourteenth Amendment, Congress passed the Religious Land Use and Institutionalized Persons Act of 2000. One part of this Act concerns restrictions on the religious exercise of institutionalized persons as well as providing for a private cause of action against a state, its instrumentalities and officers, and persons acting under color of state law.

Sossoman, an inmate, brought suit against the State of Texas and prison officials regarding prison policies that barred the use of the prison chapel for religious worship and would not allow prisoners to attend services if they were on cell restriction for disciplinary reasons. The inmate sought injunctive and monetary relief. The district court ruled that sovereign immunity prevented the claimant from receiving monetary relief. The Fifth Circuit Court of Appeals agreed, stating that the wording of the Religious Land Use and Institutionalized Persons Act of 2000 did not "unambiguously" notify the state that it waived sovereign immunity for monetary relief claims by accepting federal funding.

ISSUE: Does accepting federal funding cause a state to waive its sovereign immunity for private suits seeking monetary damages under the Religious Land Use and Institutionalized Persons Act of 2000? NO.

HOLDING: The Religious Land Use and Institutionalized Persons Act's authorization of "appropriate relief against a government" is not an unequivocal expression of a state's consent to waive sovereign immunity when accepting federal funding.

REASONS: "Dual sovereignty is a defining feature of our Nation's constitutional blueprint . . . Immunity from private suits has long been considered 'central to sovereign dignity.' *Alden v. Maine*, 527 U.S. 706, 715, 119 S. Ct. 2240, 144 L.Ed.2d 636 (1999) . . . Sovereign immunity principles enforce an important constitutional limitation on the power of the federal courts. See *Pennhurst State School and Hospital v. Halderman*, 465 U.S. 89, 98, 104 S. Ct. 900, 79 L.Ed.2d 67 (1984). For over a century now, this Court has consistently made clear that 'federal jurisdiction over suits against unconsenting States was not contemplated by the Constitution when establishing the judicial power of the United States.' *Seminole Tribe of Fla. v. Florida*, 517 U.S. 44, 54, 116 S. Ct. 1114, 134 L.Ed.2d 252 (1996) . . . Accordingly, 'our test for determining whether a State has waived its immunity from federal-court jurisdiction is a stringent one.' *College Savings Bank v. Florida Prepaid Postsecondary Ed. Expense Bd.*, 527 U.S. 666, 675, 119 S. Ct. 2219, 144 L.Ed.2d 605 (1999) . . . A State's consent to suit must be 'unequivocally expressed' in the text of the relevant statute. *Pennhurst State School and Hospital, supra*, at 99, 104 S. Ct. 900 . . . Only by requiring this 'clear declaration' by the State can we be 'certain that the State in fact consents to suit.' *College Savings Bank*, 527 U.S., at 680, 119 S. Ct. 2219."

"RLUIPA's authorization of 'appropriate relief against a government,' § 2000cc-2(a), is not the unequivocal expression of state consent that our precedents require. 'Appropriate relief' does not so clearly and unambiguously waive sovereign immunity to private suits for damages that we can that we can 'be certain that the State in fact consents' to such a suit. *College Savings Bank*, 527 U.S., at 680, 119 S. Ct. 2219. 'Appropriate relief' is open-ended and ambiguous about what types of relief it includes, as many lower courts have recognized . . . Far from clearly identifying money damages, the word 'appropriate' is inherently context-dependent . . . The context here—where the defendant is a sovereign—suggests, if anything, that monetary damages are not 'suitable' or 'proper.' See *Federal Maritime Comm'n*, 535 U.S., at 765, 122 S. Ct. 1864 . . . Further, where a statute is susceptible of multiple plausible interpretations, including one preserving immunity, we will not consider a State to have waived its sovereign immunity. See *Dellmuth v. Muth*, 491 U.S. 223, 232, 109 S. Ct. 2397, 105 L.Ed.2d 181 (1989)."

"Sossamon contends that, because Congress enacted § 3 of RLUIPA pursuant to the Spending Clause, the States were necessarily on notice that they would be liable for damages. He argues that Spending Clause legislation operates as a contract and damages are always available relief for a breach of contract, whether the contract explicitly includes a damages remedy or not. Relying on *Barnes* and *Franklin*, he asserts that all recipients of federal funding are 'generally on notice that [they are] subject . . . to those remedies traditionally available in suits for breach of contract,' including compensatory damages . . .We have acknowledged the contract-law analogy, but we have been clear 'not [to] imply . . . that suits under Spending Clause legislation are suits in contract, or that contract-law principles apply to all issues that they raise.' *Barnes, supra*, at 189, n. 2, 122 S. Ct. 2097. We have not relied on the Spending Clause contract analogy to expand liability beyond what would exist under non-spending statutes, much less to extend monetary liability against the States, as Sossamon would have us do. In fact, in *Barnes* and *Franklin*, the Court discussed the Spending Clause context only as a potential *limitation* on liability. See *Barnes, supra*, at 187–188, 122 S. Ct. 2097; *Franklin, supra*, at 74–75, 112 S. Ct. 1028 ... We conclude that States, in accepting federal funding, do not consent to waive their sovereign immunity to private suits for money damages under RLUIPA because no statute expressly and unequivocally includes such a waiver. The judgment of the United States Court of Appeals for the Fifth Circuit is affirmed."

CASE SIGNIFICANCE: This case is noteworthy because it allows states to accept federal funding without waiving their right to sovereign immunity in cases where an institutionalized person would make a monetary claim against them under the Religious Land Use and Institutionalized Persons Act of 2000. If the opposite were true, states would have to be accommodating to all types of inmates' religious demands or face possible lawsuits where monetary damages could possibly be awarded. In addition, unlike the previous cases, the focus of this claim is both that an inmate is being prohibited from practicing his religion and that monetary relief is not available as a remedy for this.

Because this case involves religious practices, several religious organizations submitted amicus briefs in support of the petitioner, including the Christian Legal Society and Prison Fellowship, the National Association of Evangelicals, Americans United for Separation of Church and State, and the Becket Fund for Religious Liberty. The organizations were concerned with the Act lacking teeth (as one brief stated) if monetary damages could not be sought under the Act. The United States also filed a brief in support of the inmate, stating that the US had a significant interest in the question. The United States went on to further note that "[t]he Attorney General may bring actions under the Act for injunctive or declaratory relief but full enforcement of the requirements depends on an effective private judicial remedy. If damages are unavailable in actions against states and their officials the Act's enforcement will be significantly undermined."

Thirty states filed a brief in support of the State of Texas. They reasoned that the sovereign immunity of a state may be universally accepted but it is not universally secure. Furthermore, the brief stated "[r]egardless of the manner by which sovereign immunity is relinquished, the requirement that it be express and via unambiguous language is immutable."

It should be noted that the Supreme Court ruling in this case does not preclude an incarcerated individual from filing suit against the state or its officials for injunctive or declaratory relief. Inmates who feel their religious practices are unduly restricted may also file an administrative grievance within the institution. In the past, correctional institutions have attempted to accommodate inmates' religious rights while at the same time balancing the institution's need for order and security.

HOLT V. HOBBS, DIRECTOR ARKANSAS DOC
574 U.S. ___ (2015)

CAPSULE: The Arkansas Department of Correction's policy regarding beards violates the Religious Land Use and Institutionalized Persons Act of 2000 (RLUIPA).

FACTS: Holt is a devout Muslim incarcerated in the Arkansas Department of Corrections. In accordance with his religious beliefs, he wanted to grow a beard. His faith dictates that he not trim his beard, but he proposed a compromise with prison officials that instead he keep his beard at half-inch length. The Department of Corrections has a policy that, for security reasons, no inmates can have beards, except those with certain medical conditions. The Department notes that inmates can conceal contraband in their beards and can shave them to disguise their identity.

Holt sought an exception to this policy based on his religious beliefs. The Department denied his request, and Holt filed suit in federal district court. The district court dismissed his suit on the basis of security concerns, and the Eighth Circuit Court of Appeals affirmed this decision. The Court cited the provisions of RLUIPA, holding that the Arkansas Department of Correction's policy was "the least restrictive means of furthering its compelling security interests."

ISSUE: Does the Arkansas Department of Correction's policy regarding beards violate the RLUIPA? YES.

HOLDING: The RLUIPA is violated because the Arkansas Department of Correction's policy does not allow a prisoner to grow a half-inch beard according to his religious beliefs.

REASON: "Under RLUIPA, the challenging party bears the initial burden of proving that his religious exercise is grounded in a sincerely held religious belief, see *Burwell v. Hobby Lobby Stores, Inc.*, 573 U.S. ___, ___, n. 28, and that the government's action substantially burdens his religious exercise. Here, petitioner's sincerity is not in dispute, and he easily satisfies the second obligation. The Department's policy forces him to choose between 'engag[ing] in conduct that seriously violates [his] religious belie[f],' id., at ___, or contravening the grooming policy and risking disciplinary action. In reaching the opposite conclusion, the District Court misunderstood the analysis that RLUIPA demands. First, the District Court erred by concluding that the grooming policy did not substantially burden petitioner's religious exercise because he could practice his religion in other ways. Second, the District Court erroneously suggested that the burden on petitioner's religious exercise was slight because petitioner testified that his religion would 'credit' him for attempting to follow his religious beliefs, even if that attempt proved unsuccessful.

"RLUIPA, however, applies to religious exercise regardless of whether it is 'compelled.' § 2000cc–5(7)(A). Finally, the District Court improperly relied on petitioner's testimony that not all Muslims believe that men must grow beards.

Even if petitioner's belief were idiosyncratic, RLUIPA's guarantees are 'not limited to beliefs which are shared by all of the members of a religious sect' *Thomas v. Review Bd. of Indiana Employment Security Div.*, 450 U.S. 707, 715–716. Pp. 6–8.

"Once the challenging party satisfies his burden, the burden shifts to the government to show that substantially burdening the religious exercise of the 'particular claimant' is 'the least restrictive means of furthering [a] compelling governmental interest.' *Hobby Lobby, supra*, at ___; § 2000cc–1(a). The Department fails to show that enforcing its beard prohibition against petitioner furthers its compelling interests in preventing prisoners from hiding contraband and disguising their identities. Pp. 8–13 . . . While the Department has a compelling interest in regulating contraband, its argument that this interest is compromised by allowing an inmate to grow a ½-inch beard is unavailing, especially given the difficulty of hiding contraband in such a short beard and the lack of a corresponding policy regulating the length of hair on the head.

"RLUIPA does not permit the unquestioning deference required to accept the Department's assessment. See *Gonzales v. O Centro Espírita Beneficente União do Vegetal*, 546 U.S. 418, 434. Even if the Department could show that denying petitioner a ½-inch beard furthers its interest in rooting out contraband, it would still have to show that its policy is the least restrictive means of furthering that interest, a standard that is 'exceptionally demanding' and requires the government to 'sho[w] that it lacks other means of achieving its desired goal without imposing a substantial burden on the exercise of religion by the objecting part[y].' *Hobby Lobby, supra*, at ___. Here, the Department fails to establish that its security concerns cannot be satisfied by simply searching a ½-inch beard. Pp. 9–11 . . . Even if the Department's grooming policy furthers its compelling interest in prisoner identification, its policy still violates RLUIPA as applied in the present circumstances."

CASE SIGNIFICANCE: This case is one of the few decided by the U.S. Supreme Court regarding a person's exercise of his or her religious beliefs under RLUIPA. Most of the cases heard by the courts regarding this act involve issues of land use by various religious groups.

In the past, the lower courts have ruled on inmates growing beards while incarcerated. These rulings have mixed results in that some of the decisions favored the institution whereas others favored the inmate. There have also been a variety of religious groups besides Muslims asserting their grooming rights in prison based on their beliefs. These include Native Americans, Jews, and Rastafarians. Most of these cases were heard based on the Religious Freedom Restoration Act, which was held to be unconstitutional by the Supreme Court in 1997.

This decision was unanimous (9–0) in favor of the prisoner, indicating the Court's support of prisoners' religious rights while incarcerated. The Court notes that the prisoner satisfied the provision of the RLUIPA requiring that the inmate prove a sincere religious belief before the burden shifts to the state to prove that their policy is the "least restrictive means of furthering a compelling government interest." This belief can be subjectively interpreted by prison officials but does not appear to be an issue in this particular case.

There appear to be two significant areas in this case that are important in the Court's decision. The first is the applicability of the RLUIPA regarding length of the beard, which is relatively short and is a compromise on the part of the prisoner regarding his religious practices. The Arkansas Department of Corrections argued that beards can be used to conceal contraband, but this is improbable owing to the length of the beard. The second issue is that the Department has no policy restricting hair length for its inmates. Prisoners are far more likely to conceal contraband in long hair than in beards if they are allowed to grow their hair any length they choose. This is a policy that Arkansas changed in June 2015, at which time they mandated short hair for male inmates. Even if the Department had a policy restricting hair length, it is doubtful that the state would prevail in this case, owing to the prisoner's right to practice his religious beliefs under the RLUIPA and the short length of the beard.

V. SEARCHES AND SEIZURES

HUDSON V. PALMER
468 U.S. 517 (1984)

CAPSULE: A prison cell may be searched without a warrant or probable cause because a prison cell is not protected by the Fourth Amendment.

FACTS: Palmer was an inmate at the Bland Correctional Center in Virginia, serving sentences for forgery, uttering a forged instrument, grand larceny, and bank robbery convictions. Hudson, an officer at the Correctional Center, conducted a shakedown search of Palmer's prison locker and cell, together with another officer. The officers discovered a ripped pillow case in the trash basket near his bunk. Palmer was charged with destroying state property. He was found guilty at a prison disciplinary hearing, and was ordered to reimburse the state for the cost of the pillow case. Additionally, a reprimand was entered on Palmer's prison record.

Palmer brought a pro se action in United States District Court under 42 U.S.C. § 1983, claiming that Hudson had conducted the shakedown search of his cell and had brought a false charge for the sole purpose of harassing him. Palmer also claimed that Hudson had intentionally destroyed certain items of his noncontraband personal property during the search, in violation of his Fourteenth Amendment right not to be deprived of property without due process of law.

ISSUES:

1. Does a prison inmate have a reasonable expectation of privacy in a prison cell, entitling him or her to the protection of the Fourth Amendment? NO.
2. Does the intentional destruction of an inmate's personal property during a cell search constitute a violation of a prisoner's due process rights? NO.

HOLDING:

1. A prisoner has no reasonable expectation of privacy in his prison cell; therefore, a cell search does not violate an inmate's Fourth Amendment right.
2. Destruction of an inmate's personal property during the search, even if intentional, does not violate the due process clause of the Fourteenth Amendment because the prisoner in this case has remedies under Virginia law for any loss suffered.

REASON: "We have repeatedly held that prisons are not beyond the reach of the Constitution. No 'iron curtain' separates one from the other. *Wolff v. McDonnell*, 418 U.S. 539, 555 (1974). Indeed, we have insisted that prisoners be accorded those rights not fundamentally inconsistent with imprisonment itself or incompatible with the objectives of incarceration.

"However, while persons imprisoned for crime enjoy many protections of the Constitution, it is also clear that imprisonment carries with it the circumscription or loss of many significant rights. See *Bell v. Wolfish*, 441 U.S., at 545. These constraints on inmates, and in some cases the complete withdrawal of certain rights, are 'justified by the considerations underlying our penal system.' *Price v. Johnston*, 334 U.S. 266, 285 (1948).

"Notwithstanding our caution in approaching claims that the Fourth Amendment is inapplicable in a given context, we hold that society is not prepared to recognize as legitimate any subjective expectation of privacy that a prisoner might have in his prison cell and that, accordingly, the Fourth Amendment proscription against unreasonable searches does not apply within the confines of the prison cell. The recognition of privacy rights for prisoners in their individual cells simply cannot be reconciled with the concept of incarceration and the needs and objectives of penal institutions.

"The administration of a prison, we have said, is 'at best an extraordinarily difficult undertaking.' *Wolff v. McDonnell*, 418 U.S., at 566; *Hewitt v. Helms*, 459 U.S. 460, 467 (1983). But it would be literally impossible to accomplish the prison objectives identified above if inmates retained a right of privacy in their cells. Virtually the only place inmates can conceal weapons, drugs, and other contraband is in their cells. Unfettered access to these cells by prison officials, thus, is imperative if drugs and contraband are to be ferreted out and sanitary surroundings are to be maintained.

"Our holding that respondent does not have a reasonable expectation of privacy enabling him to invoke the protections of the Fourth Amendment does not mean that he is without a remedy for calculated harassment unrelated to prison needs. Nor does it mean that prison attendants can ride roughshod over inmates' property rights with impunity. The Eighth Amendment always stands as a protection against 'cruel and unusual punishments.' By the same token, there are adequate state tort and common law remedies available to respondent to redress the alleged destruction of his personal property. See discussion *infra*, at 534–536.

"If negligent deprivations of property do not violate the due process clause because predeprivation process is impracticable, it follows that intentional deprivations do not violate that Clause provided, of course, that adequate state postdeprivation remedies are available. Accordingly, we hold that an unauthorized intentional deprivation of property by a state employee does not constitute a violation of the procedural requirements of the Due Process Clause of the Four-teenth Amendment if a meaningful postdeprivation remedy for the loss is available. For intentional, as for negligent deprivations of property by state employees, the state's action is not complete until and unless it provides or refuses to provide a suitable postdeprivation remedy."

CASE SIGNIFICANCE: This case followed the precedent set in *Parratt v. Taylor*, 451 U.S. 527 (1981), decided three years earlier. The Supreme Court again ruled that depriving an inmate of personal property is not a violation of the due process clause of the Fourteenth Amendment when state post-deprivation remedies are available (usually a tort action under state law). The Court made clear that an inmate has no reasonable expectation of privacy in his or her cell. This means that prison authorities may search an inmate's cell at any time without a warrant or probable cause as long as the search does not constitute harassment. There is no need for a warrant or probable cause. Once again, the Court balanced institutional needs with an inmate's constitutional rights and decided in favor of the institution, saying that "it would be impossible to accomplish the prison objectives of preventing the introduction of weapons, drugs, and other contraband into the premises if inmates retained the right to privacy in their cells." The Court also rejected the prisoner's claim that the destruction of his personal property constituted an unreasonable seizure, saying that prison officials "must be free to seize from cells any articles which, in their view, disserve legitimate institutional interests." Furthermore, the intentional destruction of that personal property did not violate the due process clause of the Constitution because the inmate had remedies under state law.

W. ADMINISTRATIVE SEGREGATION

HEWITT V. HELMS
459 U.S. 460 (1983)

CAPSULE: A formal hearing is not required to place an inmate in administrative segregation; an informal evidentiary review is sufficient.

FACTS: In December of 1978, a prison riot erupted at the State Correctional Institution in Huntingdon, Pennsylvania. It was quelled with the assistance of state police units, local law enforcement officers, and off-duty correctional officers. Inmate Helms was removed from his cell and the general prison population after the riot ended. He was questioned by the state police and placed in restrictive confinement while the police and prison authorities investigated his role in the riot. The following day, Helms was given a "Misconduct Report" that charged him with assaulting correctional officers and "conspiracy to disrupt normal institution routine by forcefully taking over the control center." Four days later, a hearing committee considered his case and decided that Helms' restricted confinement would be continued although the committee did not find him guilty, due to insufficient evidence.

A second misconduct report charged Helms with assaulting a second officer during the riot. Helms and one correctional officer testified at the subsequent hearing. The Hearing Committee found Helms guilty of the second misconduct charge and ordered him confined in administrative segregation for six months. The Committee also decided to drop the first misconduct charge without determining guilt. Helms sued in the United States District Court, alleging that his confinement in administrative segregation violated his rights under the due process clause of the Fourteenth Amendment.

ISSUE: Is a formal hearing required in order to place an inmate in administrative segregation? NO.

HOLDING: Formal hearings like those used in prison disciplinary cases (*Wolff v. McDonnell*, 418 U.S. 539 [1974]) are not required for placing inmates in administrative segregation. An informal, non-adversary evidentiary review is sufficient both for the decision that the inmate represents a security risk and the decision to confine the inmate to administrative segregation pending completion of the investigation of the alleged misconduct. An inmate must merely receive notice of the charges against him and be given an opportunity to present his views to the prison official who will decide whether to transfer him to administrative segregation.

REASON: "We have repeatedly said both that prison officials have broad administrative and discretionary authority over the institutions they manage and that lawfully incarcerated persons retain only a narrow range of protected liberty interests . . . Accordingly, administrative segregation is the sort of confinement that inmates would reasonably anticipate receiving at some point in their incarceration. This conclusion finds ample support in our decisions regarding parole and good-time credits. Both of these subjects involve release from institutional life altogether, which is a far more significant change in a prisoner's freedoms than that at issue here, yet in *Greenholtz* and *Wolff* we held that neither situation involved an interest independently protected by the Due Process Clause. These decisions compel an identical result here.

"But on balance we are persuaded that the repeated use of explicitly mandatory language in connection with requiring specific substantive predicates demands a conclusion that the State has created a protected liberty interest. That being the case, we must then decide whether the process afforded respondent satisfied the minimum requirements of the Due Process Clause. We think that it did. The requirements imposed by the Clause are, of course, flexible and variable dependent upon the particular situation being examined. E.g., *Greenholtz v. Nebraska Penal Inmates*, 442 U.S., at 12, *Morrissey v. Brewer*, 408 U.S. 471, 481 (1972). In determining what is 'due process' in the prison context, we are reminded that 'one cannot automatically apply procedural rules designed for free citizens in an open society . . . to the very different situation presented by a disciplinary proceeding in a state prison.' *Wolff v. McDonnell*, 418 U.S., at 560. 'Prison administrators . . . should be accorded wide-ranging deference in the adoption and execution of policies and practices that in their judgment are needed to preserve internal order and discipline and to maintain institutional security.' *Bell v. Wolfish*, 441 U.S. 520, 547 (1979). These conditions convince us that petitioners were obligated to engage only in an informal, nonadversary review of the information supporting respondent's administrative confinement, including whatever statement respondent wished to submit, within a reasonable time after confining him to administrative segregation."

CASE SIGNIFICANCE: This case addresses the issue of what rights inmates are entitled to, if any, prior to being placed in administrative segregation. There is a difference between administrative segregation and punitive segregation, in that administrative segregation is primarily for prisoner protection, and punitive segregation is imposed to punish the inmate. While both actions involve isolation from the general inmate population, the Court in this case said that a formal process such as that prescribed for inmates facing punitive segregation (as required in *Wolff v. McDonnell*, 418 U.S. 539 [1974]) is not required for administrative segregation. All that is required is that the inmate receive notice of the charges and an opportunity to present his or her views to the prison officials who are to decide whether to transfer the inmate to administrative segregation. Justifications for the decision are: (1) prison officials have broad administrative and discretionary authority over the institutions they manage, and (2) administrative segregation is the sort of confinement that inmates should reasonably anticipate receiving at some point during their incarceration.

X. PUNITIVE SEGREGATION

HUTTO V. FINNEY
437 U.S. 678 (1978)

CAPSULE: Courts can set time limitations on solitary confinement (punitive segregation); they can also order that plaintiff's attorney's fees be paid from Department of Correction funds.

FACTS: In 1970, a District Court found that conditions in the Arkansas penal system constituted cruel and unusual punishment in violation of the Eighth Amendment. In 1976, after several hearings to check on the progress of prison administrators' improvements to the system, the court concluded that the constitutional violations it identified had not been remedied. The court issued an order placing limits on the number of inmates that could be confined in one cell. It also required that each inmate have a bunk, discontinued the "gruel" diet, which was a poor nutritional mixture, and set 30 days as the maximum isolation sentence. The District Court also considered the matter of fees and expenses. It found that prison officials had acted in bad faith and awarded a counsel fee of $20,000 to the plaintiffs, to be paid by funds from the Arkansas Department of Correction.

Hutto, the Commissioner of Correction, and members of the Arkansas Board of Correction appealed the following: (1) the order placing a limit of 30 days on confinement in punitive isolation; and (2) the award of attorney's fees based on the finding that they had acted in bad faith in failing to cure the previously identified problems in the prison system. Hutto and members of the Board argued that indeterminate sentences of punitive isolation do not always constitute cruel and unusual punishment in violation of the Eighth Amendment. They also alleged that the District Court's award of attorney's fees violated the Eleventh Amendment's prohibition against such.

ISSUES:
1. Was the District Court's imposition of a 30-day limit on punitive isolation in the Arkansas Department of Correction constitutional? YES.
2. Was the District Court's award of attorney's fees to be paid out of Department of Correction funds constitutional? YES.

HOLDING:
1. The District Court did not err in including the 30-day limit on sentences of isolation as part of its comprehensive remedy to correct violations of constitutional rights.
2. The District Court's award of attorney's fees to be paid out of Department of Correction funds is adequately supported by its finding that petitioners had acted in bad faith, and does not violate the Eleventh Amendment.

REASON: "Confinement in a prison or in an isolation cell is a form of punishment subject to scrutiny under Eighth Amendment standards . . . [P]etitioners single out the portion of the District Court's most recent order that forbids the Department to sentence inmates to more than 30 days in punitive isolation. Petitioners assume that the District Court held that indeterminate sentences to punitive isolation always constitute cruel and unusual punishment. This assumption misreads the District Court's holding. Read in its entirety, the District Court's opinion made it abundantly clear that the length of isolation sentences was not considered in a vacuum. In the court's words, punitive isolation 'is not necessarily unconstitutional, but it may be, depending on the duration of the confinement and the conditions thereof.' 410 F. Supp., at 275.

"In fashioning a remedy, the District Court had ample authority to go beyond earlier orders and to address each element contributing to the violation. The District Court had given the Department repeated opportunities to remedy the cruel and unusual conditions in the isolation cells. If petitioners had fully complied with the court's earlier orders, the present time limit might well have been unnecessary. But taking the long and unhappy history of the litigation into account, the court was justified in entering a comprehensive order to insure against the risk of inadequate compliance.

"The order is supported by the interdependence of the conditions producing the violation. The vandalized cells and the atmosphere of violence were attributable, in part, to overcrowding and to deep-seated enmities growing out of months of constant daily friction. The 30-day limit will help to correct these conditions. Moreover, the limit presents little danger of interference with prison administration, for the Commissioner of Correction himself stated that prisoners should not ordinarily be held in punitive isolation for more than 14 days. Id. at 278.

"Like the Court of Appeals, we find no error in the inclusion of a 30-day limitation on sentences to punitive isolation as a part of the District Court's comprehensive remedy.

"In exercising their prospective powers under *Ex parte Young* and *Edelman v. Jordan*, federal courts are not reduced to issuing injunctions against state officers and hoping for compliance. Once issued, an injunction may be enforced. Many of the court's most effective enforcement weapons involve financial penalties.

"In this case, the award of attorney's fees for bad faith served the same purpose as a remedial fine imposed for civil contempt. It vindicated the District Court's authority over a recalcitrant litigant . . . We see no reason to distinguish this award from any other penalty imposed to enforce a prospective injunction. Hence the substantive protections of the Eleventh Amendment do not prevent an award of attorney's fees against the Department's officers in their official capacities.

"Petitioners, as the losing litigants in the Court of Appeals, were ordered to pay an additional $2,500 to counsel for the prevailing parties 'for their services on this appeal.' 548 F.2d, at 743. The order does not expressly direct the Department of Correction to pay the award, but since petitioners are sued in their official capacities, and since they are represented by the Attorney General, it is obvious that the award will be paid by state funds. It is also clear that this order is not supported by any finding of bad faith. It is founded instead on the provisions of the Civil Rights Attorney's Fees Awards Act of 1976. Pub. L. No. 94–559, 90 Stat. 2641, 42 U.S.C. § 1988 (1976 ed.). The Act declares that, in suits under 42 U.S.C. § 1983 and certain other statutes, federal courts may award prevailing parties reasonable attorney's fees 'as part of the costs.'

"There is no indication in this case that the named defendants litigated in bad faith before the Court of Appeals. Consequently, the Department of Correction is the entity intended by Congress to bear the burden of the counsel-fees award."

CASE SIGNIFICANCE: This was one of the first cases appealed to the Supreme Court in which an entire state prison system was declared unconstitutional by a state district court and ordered to institute massive reform. The prison authorities in this case tested the limits of the power of a district court judge to order reforms. The power of the judge to set a limit on the length of punitive isolation of inmates was questioned; so was his power to award attorney's fees. The Court upheld the power of the judge in both instances, implying that the discretion of a trial court judge in prison cases is not narrowly circumscribed.

The 30-day limitation on punitive segregation was deemed valid because of the past record of the Department of Correction in failing to correct constitutional violations. Said the Court: "Where the question before the court was whether past constitutional violations had been remedied, it was entitled to consider the severity of the violations in assessing the constitutionality of conditions in the isolation cells, the length of time each inmate spent in isolation being simply one consideration among many."

The award of $20,000 to inmates' counsel from the Department of Correction funds was also held valid in accordance with the Civil Rights Attorney's Fees Award Act of 1976. This act states that in civil rights cases the federal courts may award prevailing parties reasonable attorney's fees. Corrections officials had argued that such an award was unconstitutional because under the Eleventh Amendment Arkansas enjoys immunity. The Court replied that "costs have traditionally been awarded against States without regard for the States' Eleventh Amendment immunity, and it is much too late to single out attorney's fees as the one kind of litigation cost whose recovery may not be authorized by Congress without an express statutory waiver of States' immunity."

Y. SELF-INCRIMINATION

MCKUNE V. LILE
536 U.S. 24 (2002)

CAPSULE: Requiring an inmate to participate in a sexual abuse treatment program where he or she must take responsibility for the present offense and detail past sexual offenses does not violate the inmate's privilege against self-incrimination under the Fifth Amendment.

FACTS: Lile was a convicted sex offender, confined in a Kansas prison. He was ordered to participate in the Sexual Abuse Treatment Program before his release. Part of the program requires inmates to sign an "Admission of Responsibility" form, where the inmate discusses and accepts responsibility for the present crime. Inmates must also complete a sexual history form in which they detail prior sexual offenses, whether they were charged for these offenses or not. This information is not privileged and Kansas retains the option of using this information in further criminal proceedings. Kansas law also requires that the staff in the program report any uncharged sexual offenses with minors to law enforcement. Prison officials advised Lile that his prison privileges would be reduced if he refused to participate in the program. This would automatically curtail his visitation rights, earnings, work opportunities, ability to send money to his family, canteen expenditures, access to a personal television, and transfer to a potentially more dangerous maximum-security institution. Lile refused to participate in the program, stating that his Fifth Amendment privilege against self-incrimination would be violated.

The District Court agreed with Lile's contention. The Tenth Circuit Court of Appeals affirmed, stating that the resulting sanctions for refusal to participate in the program established the compulsion element of the Fifth Amendment.

ISSUE: Do the requirements of the Kansas Sexual Abuse Treatment Program (SATP) violate the Fifth Amendment prohibition against self-incrimination? NO.

HOLDING: The Kansas Sexual Abuse Treatment Program serves a vital penological purpose and does not amount to compelled self-incrimination prohibited by the Fifth Amendment.

REASON: "The SATP does not compel prisoners to incriminate themselves in violation of the Constitution. The Fifth Amendment Self-Incrimination Clause, which applies to the States via the Fourteenth Amendment, *Malloy v. Hogan*, 378 U.S. 1 (1964), provides that no person 'shall be compelled in any criminal case to be a witness against himself.' The 'Amendment speaks of compulsion,' *United States v. Monia*, 317 U.S. 424, 427 (1943), and the Court has insisted that the 'constitutional guarantee is only that the witness not be compelled to give self-incriminating testimony.' *United States v. Washington*, 431 U.S. 181, 188 (1977). The consequences in question here—a transfer to another prison where television sets are not placed in each inmate's cell, where exercise facilities are not readily available, and where work and wage opportunities are more limited—are not ones that compel a prisoner to speak about his past crimes despite a desire to remain silent. The fact that these consequences are imposed on prisoners, rather than ordinary citizens, moreover, is important in weighing respondent's constitutional claim.

"The Court has instructed that rehabilitation is a legitimate penological interest that must be weighed against the exercise of an inmate's liberty. See, e.g., *O'Lone v. Estate of Shabazz*, 482 U.S. 342, 348, 351 (1987). Since 'most offenders will eventually return to society, [a] paramount objective of the corrections system is the rehabilitation of those committed to its custody.' *Pell v. Procunier*, 417 U.S. 817, 823 (1974). Acceptance of responsibility in turn demonstrates that an offender 'is ready and willing to admit his crime and to enter the correctional system in a frame of mind that affords hope for success in rehabilitation over a shorter period of time than might otherwise be necessary.' *Brady v. United States*, 397 U.S. 742, 753 (1970)."

CASE SIGNIFICANCE: This case is important because it addresses an issue to which correctional officials had no authoritative answer. That question is: Is a treatment program that requires inmates (or probationers or parolees) to admit guilt prior to participation a violation of the Fifth Amendment privilege against self-incrimination? The Supreme Court said no.

Many prison, probation, and parole treatment programs require admission of guilt as a condition of participation. The justification for the requirement is that "admission of responsibility" is deemed the first step toward treatment and rehabilitation. In Kansas, the staff involved in the program may report any uncharged sexual offenses with minors to law enforcement officers who may then investigate further and file criminal charges. Under Kansas law, non-participation in the program because the inmate refuses to sign the "Admission of Responsibility" form could limit prison privileges. Refusal to participate, therefore, had some serious consequences.

The Court held that the Kansas Sexual Abuse Treatment Program (similar programs are used in many states to treat sexual offenders) did not violate the Fifth Amendment, saying that "a prison clinical rehabilitation program, which is acknowledged to bear a rational relation to a legitimate penological objective, does not violate the privilege against self-incrimination if the adverse consequence an inmate faces for not participating are related to the program objectives and do not constitute atypical and significant hardships in relation to the ordinary incidents of prison life." Under Kansas law, the consequences of non-participation are those that do not impose atypical and undue hardship on the inmate and are similar to the "ordinary incidents of prison life." It would have been different if the consequences included "extension of prison term" or "affect inmate's eligibility for good-time credits or parole." If these were the penalties involved for refusal to participate, the regulation would have violated the Fifth Amendment.

This decision legitimizes correctional programs, usually aimed at sexual offenders, that require guilt admission as a requirement for participation. It further indicates that the concept that "prisoners have diminished constitutional rights" is alive and well.

Z. TRANSFER

MEACHUM V. FANO
427 U.S. 215 (1976)

CAPSULE: Inmates are not entitled to due process when transferred intrastate (meaning from one prison to another within the state), even if conditions in one prison are less favorable than in another.

FACTS: There were nine serious fires during a two-and-one-half month period at the Massachusetts Correctional Institution at Norfolk, a medium-security institution. After a hearing, the Classification Board recommended that inmate Royce be placed in administrative segregation for 30 days because of his involvement with the fires. Inmates Fano, Dussault, and McPhearson were to be transferred to Walpole, a maximum-security institution with living conditions that were substantially less favorable than those at Norfolk. Inmates DeBrosky and Hathaway were to be transferred to Bridgewater, which had both maximum- and medium-security facilities.

The recommendations of the Board were reviewed by the Acting Deputy Commissioner for Classification and Treatment and by the Commissioner of Corrections. They accepted the recommendations with respect to Fano, Dussault, Hathaway, and McPhearson, and ordered DeBrosky and Royce to be transferred to Walpole.

The inmates brought an action under 42 U.S.C. § 1983, alleging that they were being deprived of liberty without due process of law because the petitioners had ordered them transferred to an institution where conditions were less favorable, without an adequate fact-finding hearing.

ISSUE: Does the due process clause of the Fourteenth Amendment entitle a state prisoner to a hearing when he or she is transferred to a prison where conditions are less favorable? NO.

HOLDING: The due process clause of the Fourteenth Amendment does not protect a prisoner against transfer from one prison to another. The fact that conditions in one prison are less favorable than in another also does not mean that a Fourteenth Amendment liberty interest is violated if a prisoner is transferred there.

REASON: "The initial inquiry is whether the transfer of the inmates from Norfolk to Walpole and Bridgewater infringed or implicated a 'liberty' interest of the respondents within the meaning of the Due Process Clause. Contrary to the Court of Appeals, we hold that it did not. We reject at the outset the notion that any grievous loss visited upon a person by the State is sufficient to invoke the procedural protections of the Due Process Clause.

"Similarly, we cannot agree that any change in the conditions of confinement having a substantial adverse impact on the prisoner involved is sufficient to invoke the protections of the Due Process Clause. The Due Process Clause by its own force forbids the State from convicting any person of crime and depriving him of his liberty without complying fully with the requirements of the Clause. But given a valid conviction, the criminal defendant has been constitutionally deprived of his liberty to the extent that the State may confine him and subject him to the rules of its prison system so long as the conditions of confinement do not otherwise violate the Constitution. The Constitution does not require that the State have more than one prison for convicted felons; nor does it guarantee that the convicted prisoner will be placed in any particular prison if, as is likely, the State has more than one correctional institution.

"Neither, in our view, does the Due Process Clause in and of itself protect a duly convicted prisoner against transfer from one institution to another within the state prison system. Confinement in any of the State's institutions is within the normal limits or range of custody which the conviction has authorized the State to impose. That life in one prison is much more disagreeable than in another does not in itself signify that a Fourteenth Amendment liberty interest is implicated when a prisoner is transferred to the institution with the more severe rules.

"Here, Massachusetts law conferred no right on the prisoner to remain in the prison to which he was initially assigned, defeasible only upon proof of specific acts of misconduct. Insofar as we are advised, transfers between Massachusetts prisons are not conditioned upon the occurrence of specified events. On the contrary, transfer in a wide variety of circumstances is vested in prison officials. The predicate for invoking the protection of the Fourteenth Amendment as construed and applied in *Wolff v. McDonnell* is totally nonexistent in this case.

"A prisoner's behavior may precipitate a transfer; and absent such behavior, perhaps transfer would not take place at all. But, as we have said, Massachusetts prison officials have the discretion to transfer prisoners for any number of reasons. Their discretion is not limited to instances of serious misconduct. As we understand it no legal interest or right of these respondents under Massachusetts law would have been violated by their transfer whether or not their misconduct had been proved in accordance with procedures that might be required by the Due Process Clause in other circumstances.

"Holding that arrangements like this are within reach of the procedural protections of the Due Process Clause would place the Clause astride the day-to-day functioning of state prisons and involve the judiciary in issues and discretionary decisions that are not the business of federal judges. We decline to so interpret and apply the Due Process Clause. The federal courts do not sit to supervise state prisons, the administration of which is of acute interest to the States.

Preiser v. Rodriguez, 411 U.S. 475, 491–492 (1973); *Cruz v. Beto*, 405 U.S. 319, 321 (1972); *Johnson v. Avery*, 393 U.S. 483, 486 (1969)."

CASE SIGNIFICANCE: In this case, the Court refused to extend due process protection to the transfer of an inmate from one prison to another within the state. The inmates here alleged that their transfer to a less favorable institution (from a medium-security institution to a maximum-security institution where the living conditions were not as good), without an adequate fact-finding hearing, violated their right to due process. They maintained that such a transfer could be made only if they were given due process rights. The Court disagreed, saying that "would subject to judicial review a wide spectrum of discretionary actions that traditionally have been the business of prison administrators rather than of the federal courts." The Court added that "whatever expectation the prisoner may have in remaining at a particular prison so long as he behaves himself, it is too ephemeral and insubstantial to trigger procedural due process protections as long as prison officials have discretion to transfer him for any reasons whatsoever or for no reason at all." In sum, the Court decided that as long as the transfer of such prisoners is discretionary under state law or agency policy, there was no need to give inmates a hearing or other due process rights.

MONTANYE V. HAYMES
427 U.S. 236 (1976)

CAPSULE: A prisoner is not entitled to a hearing before being transferred to another prison facility within the state even if the reason for the transfer was disciplinary or punitive.

FACTS: Haymes, an inmate at the Attica Correctional Facility in New York, was removed from his assignment as a clerk in the law library. That afternoon he was observed circulating a petition signed by 82 other inmates, complaining that each of them had been deprived of legal assistance as a result of the removal of Haymes and another inmate from the prison law library. The following day, Haymes was advised that he would be transferred to the Clinton Correctional Facility which, like Attica, was a maximum-security facility. He was transferred the next day with no loss of good time, segregated confinement, loss of privileges, or any other disciplinary measures.

Haymes filed a petition with the United States District Court seeking relief against Montanye, who was then the Superintendent of Attica. Haymes complained that the seizure and retention of his petition not only violated Administrative Bulletin No. 20, which allegedly made any communication to a court privileged and confidential, but also infringed on his federally guaranteed right to petition the court for redress of grievances. He further alleged that his removal to Clinton was to prevent him from continuing his legal remedies and in reprisal for his legal assistance to various prisoners, as well as for seeking to petition the court.

ISSUE: Does the due process clause of the Fourteenth Amendment require that a hearing be held if a state prisoner is to be transferred to another institution in the state, whether or not this is a disciplinary or punitive transfer? NO.

HOLDING: The due process clause of the Fourteenth Amendment does not require a hearing if a prisoner is to be transferred to another facility in the state, whether or not such transfer resulted from the prisoner's misbehavior or was disciplinary or punitive.

REASON: "As long as the conditions or degree of confinement to which the prisoner is subjected is within the sentence imposed upon him and is not otherwise violative of the Constitution, the Due Process Clause does not in itself subject an inmate's treatment by prison authorities to judicial oversight. The Clause does not require hearings in connection with transfers whether or not they are the result of the inmate's misbehavior or may be labeled as disciplinary or punitive.

"We also agree with the State of New York that under the law of that State Haymes had no right to remain at any particular prison facility and no justifiable expectation that he would not be transferred unless found guilty of misconduct. Under New York law, adult persons sentenced to imprisonment are not sentenced to particular institutions, but are committed to the custody of the Commissioner of Corrections . . . [T]he Commissioner is empowered by statute to 'transfer inmates from one correctional facility to another.' N.Y. Correc. Law, Section 23(1) (McKinney Supp. 1975–1976)."

CASE SIGNIFICANCE: This case is significant in light of *Meachum v. Fano*, 427 U.S. 215 (1976), which was heard at the same time. Because the Court decided in the *Meachum* case that a prisoner was not entitled to have a hearing if he was being transferred from one prison to another within the state, even if to a less desirable prison, it would make sense that the Court would also rule that a transfer to the same type of prison would not require a hearing even if such transfer was for purposes of punishment. In essence, the Court ruled that, in the absence of prohibition under state law, prison officials can transfer prisoners from one prison to another without giving them due process—thus affording prison officials discretion in the transfer of prisoners intrastate.

VITEK V. JONES
445 U.S. 480 (1980)

CAPSULE: Inmates are entitled to due process in involuntary transfers from prison to a mental hospital.

FACTS: Jones, a Nebraska prison inmate convicted of robbery, was transferred to the penitentiary hospital seven months after he was sentenced to prison. After two days in the hospital he was placed in solitary confinement. While there, he set his mattress on fire, severely burning himself. The burn unit of a private hospital treated him and he was then transferred to the security unit of the Lincoln Regional Center, a state mental hospital that was run by the Department of Public

Institutions. Jones was transferred to the mental hospital under Nebraska statute § 831–180, which stated that when a designated physician or psychologist finds that a prisoner "suffers from a mental disease or defect" and "cannot be given proper treatment in that facility," the Director of Corrections may transfer him for examination, study, and treatment to another institution, whether it is within the Department of Correctional Services or not. Jones was found to be suffering from a mental illness or defect and he could not receive proper treatment in the penal complex; thus the transfer was ordered.

Jones then intervened in this case, which was brought by other prisoners against the appropriate state officials, including Vitek, the Director of Corrections. The case challenged the Nebraska statutes that permitted transfers of prisoners from the prison complex to a mental hospital without procedural due process as a violation of the Fourteenth Amendment. Jones was subsequently paroled, violated his parole, and returned to prison before the U.S. Supreme Court heard the case.

ISSUE: Are inmates entitled to due process rights when being involuntarily transferred from prison to a mental hospital? YES.

HOLDING: The involuntary transfer of a prisoner to a mental hospital implicates a liberty interest that is protected by the due process clause of the Fourteenth Amendment. Although a conviction and sentence extinguish an individual's right to freedom for the term of his sentence, they do not authorize the state to classify him as mentally ill and subject him to involuntary psychiatric treatment without affording him additional due process protections. These protections include:

1. written notice to the prisoner that such a transfer is being considered;
2. a full hearing held after a reasonable period has passed to allow the prisoner to prepare for it;
3. an opportunity for the prisoner to present witnesses at his hearing and, when feasible, the opportunity to cross-examine witnesses called by the state;
4. an independent decision maker to preside over the hearing;
5. a written statement to the prisoner citing the evidence and reasons for the transfer; and
6. prisoners must be advised of all their procedural rights.

REASON: "We have repeatedly held that state statutes may create liberty interests that are entitled to the procedural protections of the Due Process Clause of the Fourteenth Amendment . . . We think the District Court properly understood and applied these decisions. Section 83–180(1) provides that if a designated physician finds that a prisoner 'suffers from a mental disease or defect' that 'cannot be given proper treatment' in prison, the Director of Correctional Services may transfer a prisoner to a mental hospital . . . This 'objective expectation, firmly fixed in state law and official Penal Complex practice,' that a prisoner would not be transferred unless he suffered from a mental disease or defect that could not be adequately treated in the prison, gave Jones a liberty interest that entitled him to the benefits of appropriate procedures in connection with determining the conditions that warranted his transfer to a mental hospital.

"In *Morrissey*, *Gagnon*, and *Wolff*, the States had adopted their own procedures for determining whether conditions warranting revocation of parole, probation, or good-time credits had occurred; yet we held that those procedures were constitutionally inadequate. In like manner, Nebraska's reliance on the opinion of a designated physician or psychologist for determining whether the conditions warranting a transfer exist neither removes the prisoner's interest from due process procedures nor answers the question of what process is due under the Constitution.

"Were an ordinary citizen to be subjected involuntarily to these consequences, it is undeniable that protected liberty interests would be unconstitutionally infringed absent compliance with the procedures required by the Due Process Clause. We conclude that a convicted felon also is entitled to the benefit of procedures appropriate in the circumstances before he is found to have a mental disease and transferred to a mental hospital.

"A criminal conviction and sentence of imprisonment extinguish an individual's right to freedom from confinement for the term of his sentence, but they do not authorize the State to classify him as mentally ill and to subject him to involuntary psychiatric treatment without affording him additional due process protections.

"In light of the findings made by the District Court, Jones' involuntary transfer to the Lincoln Regional Center pursuant to Section 83–180, for the purpose of psychiatric treatment, implicated a liberty interest protected by the Due Process Clause . . . Because prisoners facing involuntary transfer to a mental hospital are threatened with immediate deprivation of liberty interests they are currently enjoying and because of the inherent risk of a mistaken transfer, the District Court properly determined that procedures similar to those required by the Court in *Morrissey v. Brewer*, 408 U.S. 471 (1972), were appropriate in the circumstances present here."

CASE SIGNIFICANCE: This case gives procedural due process rights to prisoners being transferred from a penal institution to a state mental hospital. The case follows the trend toward recognizing due process rights for the convicted. The first case was *Morrissey v. Brewer* in 1972, which extended due process rights to parole revocation hearings. This was followed by *Gagnon v. Scarpelli* in 1973, giving due process rights in probation revocation hearings; and *Wolff v. McDonnell* in 1974, which required due process in prison disciplinary hearings. The Court noted in this case that due process procedures are necessary for two reasons: (1) although conviction and sentencing mean that a person's freedom can be extinguished, they do not authorize the prison authorities to classify the inmate as mentally ill and subject to psychiatric treatment, and (2) the subjection of inmates to mandatory behavior modification as treatment for mental illness constitutes the kind of action that requires due process protection. The court said that the severity of the effects of such transfer and the stigma it carries require protection under the due process clause.

It is important to realize that the term "due process," used in this case as well as in other prison cases throughout this text, has different meanings depending upon the kind of proceeding involved. Therefore, "due process" is "variable."

Although it basically means "fundamental fairness," what is fundamentally fair varies from one situation to another. For example, what is fundamentally fair in a prison disciplinary proceeding that results in solitary confinement is different from what is fundamentally fair in a disciplinary proceeding that results in administrative segregation. What is fundamentally fair in prison transfer of inmates is different from what is fundamentally fair in involuntary transfers of inmates from prison to a mental hospital. Because of the differences in the specifics of due process, the rights given in each situation vary depending upon the type of proceeding involved. For example, prison disciplinary proceedings that result in solitary confinement require the giving of seven rights, as required in *Wolff v. McDonnell*, 418 U.S. 539 (1974). By contrast, prison proceedings that result in administrative segregation do not even require a formal hearing. Instead, an informal evidentiary review suffices (*Hewitt v. Helm*, 459 U.S. 460 (1983)).

OLIM V. WAKINEKONA
461 U.S. 238 (1983)

CAPSULE: A prisoner transferred from one prison system to another within the same state is not entitled to due process rights under the Fourteenth Amendment.

FACTS: Delbert Kaahanui Wakinekona is serving a sentence of life imprisonment without the possibility of parole due to his conviction for murder in a Hawaii state court. He was also serving time for various other crimes including rape, robbery, and escape. Due to his convictions and the seriousness of his crimes, he was classified as a maximum-security risk and placed in a maximum control unit. A program committee made up of various Hawaii State Prison officials held hearings on August 2, 1976, to determine why there was a breakdown in discipline and the failure of certain programs within the prison's maximum control unit. Unit inmates appeared at these hearings. It was determined that Wakinekona and another inmate were troublemakers. On August 5, Wakinekona received notice that the committee, at a hearing to be held on August 10, would review his correctional program to determine whether his classification within the system should be changed and whether he should be transferred to another Hawaii facility or to a mainland institution.

The August 10 hearing was conducted by the same persons involved in the hearings held on August 2. Wakinekona was represented by counsel. The committee recommended that his classification as a maximum risk be continued and that he be transferred to a prison on the mainland. The recommendation was accepted by Administrator Olim of the Hawaii State Prison and Wakinekona was transferred to Folsom State Prison in California.

Contained in the Supplementary Rules and Regulations of the Corrections Division, Department of Social Services and Housing of the State of Hawaii were the procedures for inmate classification. The rule requires a hearing prior to a prison transfer involving "a grievous loss to the inmate," which the Rule defines as "a serious loss to a reasonable man." An impartial program committee is established by the Administrator to conduct such a hearing. The committee is to be "composed of at least three members who were not actively involved in the process by which the inmate . . . was brought before the committee." The rules also stipulate that the committee must give the inmate written notice of the hearing, permit the confrontation and cross-examination of witnesses, afford him the opportunity to be heard, and apprise him of the committee's findings. The committee makes a recommendation to the administrator, who then decides what action to take. The rules contain no standards governing the administrator's exercise of discretion.

ISSUE: Does the transfer of a prisoner from one state prison system to another state prison system (an interstate instead of an intrastate transfer) involve a liberty interest that is protected by the due process clause of the Fourteenth Amendment? NO.

HOLDING: An intrastate prison transfer does not deprive an inmate of any liberty interest protected by the due process clause of the Fourteenth Amendment. Therefore, the inmate is not entitled to due process protections (such as those given in *Wolff v. McDonnell*) when such transfer is made.

REASON: "In short, it is neither unreasonable nor unusual for an inmate to serve practically his entire sentence in a State other than the one in which he was convicted and sentenced, or to be transferred to an out-of-state prison after serving a portion of his sentence in his home State. Confinement in another State, unlike confinement in a mental institution, is 'within the normal limits or range of custody which the conviction has authorized the State to impose.' *Meachum*, 427 U.S., at 225. Even when, as here, the transfer involves long distances and an ocean crossing, the confinement remains within constitutional limits. The difference between such a transfer and an intrastate or interstate transfer of shorter distance is a matter of degree, not of kind, and *Meachum* instructs that 'the determining factor is the nature of the interest involved rather than its weight.' 427 U.S., at 224. The reasoning of *Meachum* and *Montanye* compels the conclusion that an interstate prison transfer, including one from Hawaii to California, does not deprive an inmate of any liberty interest protected by the Due Process Clause in and of itself."

"Hawaii's prison regulations place no substantive limitations on official discretion and thus create no liberty interest entitled to protection under the Due Process Clause. As Rule IV itself makes clear, and as the Supreme Court of Hawaii has held in *Lono v. Ariyoshi*, 63 Haw., at 144–145, 621 P.2d, at 980–981, the prison Administrator's discretion to transfer an inmate is completely unfettered. No standards govern or restrict the Administrator's determination. Because the Administrator is the only decisionmaker under Rule IV, we need not decide whether the introductory paragraph of Rule IV, see n. 1, *supra*, places any substantive limitations on the purely advisory Program Committee."

CASE SIGNIFICANCE: In previous cases, the Court had held that the state does not have to give due process rights (such as a hearing, presentation of witnesses, right to cross-examination, and right to notice of charges) when transferring prisoners from one prison unit to another prison unit within the state itself (intrastate prison transfer). This case extends that holding to transfers from the prison system of one state to the prison system of another state (interstate prison transfers). Here the inmate was transferred from the Hawaii prison system to the California prison system. He alleged his constitutional right was violated because he was not given due process prior to such transfer. Saying that "just as an inmate has no justifiable expectation that he will be incarcerated in any particular prison system within a State, he has no justifiable expectation that he will be incarcerated in a particular State."

The inmate in this case also alleged that Hawaii prison rules themselves, as worded, created a "liberty interest" that entitled him to due process rights. The Court disagreed, holding that although a state may have created a liberty interest by placing self-imposed substantive limitations on its official discretion to transfer prisoners, the wording of Hawaii prison regulations placed no such substantive limitation on the prison administrator's discretion to transfer an inmate.

Taken together, the cases on inmate transfers say that inmates are not entitled to due process rights on transfers from one prison to another, whether that transfer be intrastate (within the state) or interstate (outside the state).

AA. UNION MEMBERSHIP AND ACTIVITIES

JONES V. NORTH CAROLINA PRISONERS' LABOR UNION, INC.
433 U.S. 119 (1977)

CAPSULE: A ban on prison union membership and activities is valid. Prisoners do not retain First Amendment rights that are inconsistent with their prison status or with the legitimate objectives of the corrections system.

FACTS: The North Carolina Prisoners' Labor Union was incorporated in 1974 with several goals, including: (1) to promote charitable labor union purposes; (2) to form a prisoners' labor union at every prison and jail in North Carolina to improve working conditions through collective bargaining; (3) to work toward the alteration or elimination of practices and policies of the Department of Correction of which it did not approve; and (4) to serve as a vehicle for the presentation and resolution of inmates' grievances. In 1975, there were approximately 2,000 members of this union in 40 prison units throughout the state. The State of North Carolina decided to prevent inmates from effectively forming or operating a union. The state allowed individual membership or belief in the union but prohibited the following: inmate solicitation of other inmates, meetings between union members, and bulk mailings concerning the union from outside sources.

The North Carolina Prisoners' Labor Union, Inc., brought suit under 42 U.S.C. § 1983, alleging that its First Amendment and equal protection rights under the Fourteenth Amendment were violated by the Department of Correction's regulations, which had not yet gone into effect. The First Amendment claim was based on the no-meeting and no-solicitation rules. The Fourteenth Amendment claim was based on deprivation of equal protection of the laws, because Alcoholics Anonymous and the Jaycees were permitted to have meetings and other organizational rights, which included distribution of bulk mailing materials. The union sought a declaratory judgment and injunction against the state's policies, as well as substantial damages.

ISSUE: Do regulations that prohibit inmate solicitation of other inmates, meetings of union members, and bulk mailings concerning the union, violate the First or Fourteenth Amendment? NO.

HOLDING:

1. Prisoners' First Amendment rights are not violated by the ban on membership, solicitation, and group meetings, because inmates do not retain First Amendment rights that are inconsistent with their prison status or with legitimate objectives of the corrections system. Restrictions imposed on union activities are reasonable and consistent with the legitimate operational considerations of the institution.

2. The prohibition against the receipt by and distribution to the inmates of bulk mail from the union as well as the prohibition of union meetings among inmates do not violate the equal protection clause. Prison officials are entitled to conclude that organizations such as Alcoholics Anonymous and the Jaycees serve a rehabilitative purpose and, as such, their activities are desirable, unlike the prisoners' union, which not only pursues an adversary relationship with prison officials, but also has an illegal purpose under North Carolina law.

REASON: "The fact of confinement and the needs of the penal institution impose limitations on constitutional rights, including those derived from the First Amendment, which are implicit in incarceration . . . Because the realities of running a penal institution are complex and difficult, we have also recognized the wide-ranging deference to be accorded the decisions of prison administrators . . . It is in this context that the claims of the Union must be examined.

"The case of a prisoners' union, where the focus is on the presentation of grievances to, and encouragement of adversary relations with, institution officials surely would rank high on anyone's list of potential trouble spots. If the appellants' views as to the possible detrimental effects of the organizational activities of the Union are reasonable, as we conclude they are, then the regulations are drafted no more broadly than they need to be to meet the perceived threat—which stems directly from group meetings and group organizational activities of the Union. When weighed against the First Amendment rights asserted, these institutional reasons are sufficiently weighty to prevail.

"Prison administrators may surely conclude that the Jaycees and Alcoholics Anonymous differ in fundamental respects from appellee Union, a group with no past to speak of, and with the avowed intent to pursue an adversary relationship with prison officials. Indeed, it would be enough to distinguish the Union from Alcoholics Anonymous to note that the chartered purpose of the Union, apparently pursued in the prison, was illegal under North Carolina law.

"It is precisely in matters such as this, the decision as to which of many groups should be allowed to operate within the prison walls, where, confronted with claims based on the Equal Protection Clause, the courts should allow the prison administrators full latitude of discretion, unless it can be firmly stated that the two groups are so similar that discretion has been abused. That is surely not the case here."

CASE SIGNIFICANCE: This is the only case decided by the Supreme Court involving prisoners' unions. In this case, the prisoners alleged violations of First Amendment and Fourteenth Amendment equal protection rights. The Court rejected both contentions, saying that prison officials enjoy a great deal of discretion in regulating the conduct of inmates. The Court concluded that First Amendment rights were not "unduly abridged," stating that the finding by prison authorities that "the presence of a prisoners' union would be detrimental to prison order and security has not been conclusively shown to be wrong." As for the equal protection challenge, the Court said that prison officials do not have to treat all organizations equally, adding that they have the power to determine which organizations are desirable or undesirable.

Although this case involved a ban on prison union membership and activities, it should follow that prison unions themselves can be banned in prisons. States may allow prisoners to form unions, but they are not constitutionally required to allow it.

Decided in 1977, this case did not prescribe clear guidelines as to how alleged First Amendment violations are to be resolved. If this case were decided today, the standard used would be whether the regulations questioned are "reasonably related to legitimate penological interests," as prescribed in *Turner v. Safley*, 482 U.S. 78 (1987).

BB. VISITATION

BLOCK V. RUTHERFORD
468 U.S. 576 (1984)

CAPSULE: Prisoners have no constitutional right to contact visits or to observe shakedown searches of their cells.

FACTS: Pretrial detainees at the Los Angeles County Central Jail brought a class action under 42 U.S.C. § 1983 against the county sheriff, certain administrators of the Central Jail, and the county Board of Supervisors. This jail, with a capacity of more than 5,000, had a policy of denying pretrial detainees contact visits with their spouses, relatives, children, and friends. The jail also had a practice of conducting random "shakedown" searches of cells while the detainees were away at meals, recreation, or other activities. The detainees challenged these two policies, claiming that the policies deprived them of liberty without due process in violation of the Fourteenth Amendment.

ISSUE: Do pretrial detainees have a constitutional right to contact visits and to observe shakedown searches of their cells by jail officials? NO.

HOLDING:

1. The jail's blanket prohibition on contact visits is an entirely reasonable, nonpunitive response to legitimate security concerns, consistent with the Fourteenth Amendment.

2. The jail's practice of conducting random, irregular "shakedown" searches of cells in the absence of the cell occupants is also a reasonable response by jail officials to legitimate security concerns.

REASON: "The question before us, therefore, is narrow: whether the prohibition of contact visits is reasonably related to legitimate governmental objectives. More particularly, because there is no dispute that internal security of detention facilities is a legitimate governmental interest, our inquiry is simply whether petitioners' blanket prohibition on contact visits at Central Jail is reasonably related to the security of that facility.

"That there is a valid, rational connection between a ban on contact visits and internal security of a detention facility is too obvious to warrant extended discussion. The District Court acknowledged as much. Contact visits invite a host of security problems. They open the institution to the introduction of drugs, weapons, and other contraband. Visitors can easily conceal guns, knives, drugs, or other contraband in countless ways and pass them to an inmate unnoticed by even the most vigilant observers. And these items can readily be slipped from the clothing of an innocent child, or transferred by other visitors permitted close contact with inmates.

"Contact visitation poses other dangers for a detention facility, as well. Detainees—by definition persons unable to meet bail—often are awaiting trial for serious, violent offenses, and many have prior criminal convictions. Exposure of this type of person to others, whether family, friends, or jail administrators, necessarily carries with it risks that the safety of innocent individuals will be jeopardized in various ways.

"[C]ontrary to respondents' suggestion, we have previously considered not only a Fourth Amendment challenge but also a due process challenge to a room search procedure almost identical to that used at Central Jail, and we sustained the practice on both scores. We have no reason to reconsider that issue; the identical arguments made by respondents here were advanced by the respondents in *Wolfish*. The security concerns that we held justified the same restriction in *Wolfish*, see id., at 555, n. 36, are no less compelling here. Moreover, we could not have been clearer in our holding in *Wolfish* that this is a matter lodged in the sound discretion of the institutional officials. We reaffirm that 'proper deference to the informed discretion of prison authorities demands that they, and not the courts, make the difficult judgments which reconcile conflicting claims affecting the security of the institution, the welfare of the prison staff, and the property rights of the detainees.' Id., at 557, n. 38."

CASE SIGNIFICANCE: This case was the second Supreme Court case to address the rights of pretrial detainees, the first being *Bell v. Wolfish*, 441 U.S. 520 (1979). The Supreme Court continued the legacy of *Wolfish* in this decision. Relying heavily on *Wolfish*, the Court once again came up with a conservative decision that favors penal administrators. It found that denying contact visits and not allowing detainees to observe cell searches was reasonably related to a legitimate governmental interest.

The Court quoted the *Wolfish* case, saying: "[P]rison administrators [are to be] accorded wide-ranging deference in the adoption and execution of policies and practices that in their judgment are needed to preserve internal order and discipline and to maintain institutional security." 441 U.S. at 547. What this case also says is that there is no difference in the standard used for the constitutionality of regulations involving pretrial detainees and convicts—despite the presumption of innocence for pretrial detainees.

OVERTON V. BAZETTA
539 U.S. 126 (2003)

CAPSULE: Restrictions on prison visitations are reasonable if they bear a rational relationship to legitimate penological interests.

FACTS: The Michigan Department of Corrections modified its prison visitation regulations in response to an increased number of visitors to prisons in the state and concern for increased substance abuse among inmates. A part of the new regulations stated that prisoners who committed two substance abuse violations could receive only clergy and attorneys as visitors, not family members, for a minimum of two years. After that time, inmates would be allowed to apply for reinstatement of visitation privileges.

Inmates, their friends, and family members filed a § 1983 lawsuit, alleging that the visitation regulations violated the First, Eighth, and Fourteenth Amendments. The District Court agreed with the respondents and the Sixth Circuit Court of Appeals affirmed this decision.

ISSUE: Are the Michigan Department of Corrections visitation regulations constitutional? YES.

HOLDING: The visitation regulations bear a rational relation to legitimate penological interests and are therefore constitutional under the *Turner v. Safley* standard.

REASON: "The very object of imprisonment is confinement. Many of the liberties and privileges enjoyed by other citizens must be surrendered by the prisoner. An inmate does not retain rights inconsistent with proper incarceration. See *Jones v. North Carolina Prisoners' Labor Union, Inc.*, 433 U.S. 119, 125 (1977); *Shaw v. Murphy*, 532 U.S. 223, 229 (2001). And, as our cases have established, freedom of association is among the rights least compatible with incarceration. See *Jones, supra*, at 125–126; *Hewitt v. Helms*, 459 U.S. 460 (1983). Some curtailment of that freedom must be expected in the prison context.

"In *Turner* we held that four factors are relevant in deciding whether a prison regulation affecting a constitutional right that survives incarceration withstands constitutional challenge: whether the regulation has a 'valid, rational connection' to a legitimate governmental interest; whether alternative means are open to inmates to exercise the asserted right; what impact an accommodation of the right would have on guards and inmates and prison resources; and whether there are 'ready alternatives' to the regulation. 482 U.S., at 89–91 . . . Having determined that each of the challenged regulations bears a rational relationship to a legitimate penological interest, we consider whether inmates have alternative means of exercising the constitutional right they seek to assert. *Turner, supra*, at 90. Were it shown that no alternative means of communication existed, though it would not be conclusive, it would be some evidence that the regulations were unreasonable. That showing, however, cannot be made . . . Accommodating respondents' demands would cause a significant reallocation of the prison system's financial resources and would impair the ability of correctional officers to protect all who are inside a prison's walls. When such consequences are present, we are 'particularly deferential' to prison administrators' regulatory judgments. *Turner, supra*, at 90 . . . *Turner* does not impose a least-restrictive-alternative test, but asks instead whether the prisoner has pointed to some obvious regulatory alternative that fully accommodates the asserted right while not imposing more than a de minimis cost to the valid penological goal. 482 U.S. at 90–91. Respondents have not suggested alternatives meeting this high standard for any of the regulations at issue."

CASE SIGNIFICANCE: This case applies the *Turner v. Safley* standard to prison cases involving prison visitation. The inmates alleged that the new Michigan prison regulations (which provided in part that prisoners who committed two substance abuse violations could receive only clergy and attorneys as visitors for a minimum of two years) violated their constitutional rights. The Supreme Court rejected these allegations, saying that the prison visitation regulations are governed by the same standard set in *Turner v. Safley*. That standard holds that prison regulations that infringe upon inmates' constitutional rights are valid if they are reasonably related to legitimate penological interests. The Court declared the Michigan prison regulations valid.

The *Turner* standard has been applied by the Court to other cases alleging violations of constitutional rights. This is the first case, however, in which the standard was applied to visitation regulations. In fact, this is the first case ever decided by the Court that directly or indirectly upholds prison regulations on visitation rights. The assumption has been that visitation is not a constitutional right and therefore could be regulated by prison systems. This case addresses for the first time the issue of visitation regulations and sets the same *Turner v. Safley* standard to determine whether prison regulations are valid. Again, the Court is saying to the lower courts: when inmates allege a violation of constitutional rights, use the same standard—that set in *Turner v. Safley*—to determine which side wins.

NOTE

1   *The New York Times*, April 23, 2008.

Probation

INTRODUCTION

Probation is a type of sentence in which an offender is allowed to remain free in the community subject to court-imposed conditions and under the supervision of a probation officer. If the imposed conditions are violated, the probation may be revoked and the probationer is sent to jail or prison. Probation is a privilege, not a right. This means it is given at the discretion of the judge or jury as a matter of grace. A defendant cannot demand that the judge or jury grant probation, unless it is the penalty specifically imposed by law for his or her particular offense. Once given, however, probation becomes an entitlement, meaning it cannot be taken away without giving the probationer basic due process rights.

Probation is given for a specified number of years, which usually coincides with the prison term imposed. Judges have a great deal of authority in setting the terms and conditions of probation, limited only by what protects society or rehabilitates the offender, and as long as the conditions are clear, reasonable, and constitutional.

The usual conditions are: the probationer must not violate any law; must report to the probation officer regularly; must refrain from using drugs or alcoholic beverages and submit to drug testing; must have a job and support his or her family; and must obtain permission from the probation officer before going to another county. In addition to regular conditions, the judge may also impose special conditions. These are conditions tailored specifically to meet the needs of the offender. Example: A shoplifter can be required by the judge to carry a sign near a store saying, "I stole from this store," or have a sign posted near his home that reads, "I am a convicted sex offender." Conditions imposed on an offender can be as imaginative as the judge wants. "Creative" special conditions are usually upheld by the courts as long as they are reasonably related to the offense committed.

Only a few probation cases have been decided by the Supreme Court over the years. Those cases are briefed in this section. The first case (*Ex parte United States*, otherwise known as the *Killits* case) involving probation was decided in 1916. It settled the issue of whether a federal district court, based on common law, could suspend a sentence imposed by the legislature. The Supreme Court said no, in effect saying that if a sentence is to be suspended it should have authorization from the legislature. The effect has been that in just about every state, probation is authorized by the legislature instead of being initiated on his or her own by the judge.

The cases briefed here address the rights probationers have while on probation. *Mempa v. Rhay* (1967) held that a defendant has a constitutional right to a lawyer during probation revocation that is followed by sentencing. *Gagnon v. Scarpelli* (1973) is the most important case ever decided on probation law. It holds that probationers are entitled to due process rights before probation can be revoked. This is because revocation represents a loss of liberty and is therefore a "grievous loss." *Bearden v. Georgia* (1983) holds that an indigent probationer cannot be revoked if he or she cannot pay fine or court costs. To do so would be to discriminate against the offender based on finances. *Fare v. Michael C.* (1979) is a juvenile probation case, but its holding applies to adult probation cases as well. The Court said that asking for a probation officer during an interview with the police is not equivalent to asking for a lawyer, and therefore any admission or confession obtained by the police is admissible in court without *Miranda* warnings. The other important principle from this case is that the loyalty of a probation officer belongs to the court, not to the probationer. *Minnesota v. Murphy* (1984) holds that statements made by a probationer to a probation officer during interrogation and while not in custody are admissible in a subsequent criminal trial unless the probationer specifically asks for a lawyer during the interrogation. *Griffin v. Wisconsin* (1987) is an important case because it helps define the Fourth Amendment rights of probationers. The Court said that the search of a probationer's home without a warrant or probable cause is constitutional as long as it is based on reasonable grounds. This is significant because the term "reasonable grounds" denotes a lower degree of certainty than "probable cause." This decision says that probationers do have Fourth Amendment rights, but they are "diminished" because of being on probation.

Three of the cases briefed here involve probation officers rather than probationers. These cases are not important for probationers, but they are of interest to current or potential probation officers because they affect their employment. In *Cabell v. Chavez-Salido* (1982), the Supreme Court ruled that requiring probation officers to be American citizens is constitutional because of the nature of the job they perform. In *Forrester v. White* (1988), the Court said that judges are not protected by absolute immunity when dismissing a probation officer from a job. Judges have absolute immunity only when performing judicial or adjudicative acts, not when they are performing administrative duties, such as dismissing a probation officer. And in *Alden v. Maine* (1999), the Court held that Congress has no authority to allow states to be sued by public officers or private individuals. States enjoy sovereign immunity under the Eleventh Amendment. That immunity holds unless waived by the states themselves. Congress cannot force states to waive sovereign immunity by passing laws that allow them to be sued under the Federal Labor Standards Act (FLSA).

EX PARTE UNITED STATES (KILLITS)
242 U.S. 27 (1916)

CAPSULE: The common law does not give a federal court discretion to permanently decline to enforce a law by suspending its application. That power belongs to the legislature, not to the courts.

FACTS: Killits pleaded guilty to an indictment charging him with several counts of embezzling the money of a national bank of which he was an officer, and making false entries in its books. He was sentenced to five years' imprisonment. The federal district court ordered that the execution of his sentence be suspended for five years, dependent upon his good behavior. The United States District Attorney moved to set aside this order on the ground that it was not a temporary suspension to enable legal proceedings pending or contemplated to be revised, or an application for pardon to be made, or any other legal relief against the sentence. Instead, it was a permanent suspension based upon considerations extraneous to the legality of the conviction and it was equivalent to a refusal to carry out the statute governing sentencing in such cases.

ISSUE: Does the common law allow the courts to suspend a sentence permanently? NO.

HOLDING: Common law does not give a federal court discretion to permanently decline to enforce a law by suspending its application. That power belongs to the legislature, not to the courts.

REASON: "While it may not be doubted under the common law as thus stated that courts possessed and asserted the right to exert judicial discretion in the enforcement of the law to temporarily suspend either the imposition of sentence or its execution when imposed to the end that pardon might be procured, or that a violation of law in other respects might be prevented, we are unable to perceive any ground for sustaining the proposition that, at common law, the courts possessed or claimed the right which is here insisted upon. No elaboration could make this plainer than does the text of the passages quoted.

"Nor from the fact that common-law courts possessed the power by recognizance to secure good behavior, that is, to enforce the law, do we think any support is afforded for the proposition that those courts possessed the arbitrary discretion to permanently decline to enforce the law . . . So far as the courts of the United States are concerned it suffices to say that we have been referred to no opinion maintaining the asserted power, and, on the contrary, in the opinion in the only case in which the subject was considered, it was expressly decided the power was wanting. *United States v. Wilson*, 46 F. 748 (1891).

". . . [S]o far as the future is concerned, that is, the causing of the imposition of penalties as fixed to be subject, by probation legislation or such other means as the legislative mind may devise, to such judicial discretion as may be adequate to enable courts to meet, by the exercise of an enlarged but wise discretion, the infinite variations which may be presented to them for judgment, recourse must be had to Congress, whose legislative power on the subject is, in the very nature of things, adequately complete."

CASE SIGNIFICANCE: This case holds that courts do not have the authority under common law to suspend a sentence for five years, which was the same imprisonment time imposed by law on the offender. Such act in effect negates the penalty imposed by the legislature and is unauthorized.

The power to impose punishment is derived by the courts from the legislature, which imposes punishment categories through the penal code. In this case, the court in effect suspended the sentence permanently. Authority for this act was not given by statute, but the judge sought to justify it under common law. The Supreme Court concluded that even under common law no such authority for the judge's action existed.

This case was decided in 1916 and was arguably the first case ever to be brought to the Supreme Court involving suspension of sentence (the equivalent at that time of probation). The Court did not say that probation could not be granted; what it said was that this type of sentence could not be granted under common law and without any legislative authorization. The implication is that probation is a valid punishment, but it must be granted by law. Without statutory authorization, the granting of probation is questionable, particularly if the law specifies that judges do not possess discretion in imposing sentences. Probation in just about every state in the United States today is authorized by law, thus judicial authority to grant probation is no longer an issue.

MEMPA V. RHAY
389 U.S. 128 (1967)

CAPSULE: A defendant has a constitutional right to a lawyer during probation revocation that is followed by the imposition of a deferred sentence.

FACTS: Mempa pleaded guilty, on the advice of his attorney, to the offense of "joyriding," and was placed on probation for 10 years. The imposition of sentence was deferred under Washington law and the defendant was placed on probation. About four months later, the prosecutor moved to have Mempa's probation revoked due to his apparent involvement in a burglary. At the revocation hearing, Mempa was not represented by counsel, nor asked if he wanted counsel. He admitted to being involved in the burglary. Without further questioning, the court revoked Mempa's probation and, in accordance with state law, imposed the maximum sentence of 10 years. The court stated that it would recommend to the parole board that Mempa serve only one year. While serving his sentence, Mempa filed a writ of habeas corpus, seeking release from an unconstitutional confinement, claiming that he had been denied his right to counsel at a hearing in which his probation was revoked and sentence imposed.

ISSUE: Does a defendant have a constitutional right to counsel during a probation revocation hearing that is followed by the imposition of a deferred sentence? YES.

HOLDING: The Sixth Amendment requires that counsel be provided to a defendant in a probation revocation proceeding that is followed by the imposition of a deferred sentence.

REASON: "It is true that sentencing in Washington offers fewer opportunities for the exercise of judicial discretion than in many other jurisdictions. The applicable statute requires the trial judge in all cases to sentence the convicted person to the maximum term provided by law for the offense of which he was convicted. The actual determination of the length of time to be served is to be made by the Board of Prison Terms and Paroles within six months after the convicted person is admitted to prison.

"Even more important in a case such as this is the fact that certain legal rights may be lost if not exercised at this stage. For one, Washington law provides that an appeal in a case involving a plea of guilty followed by probation can only be taken after sentence is imposed following revocation of probation. Therefore in a case where an accused agreed to plead guilty, although he had a valid defense, because he was offered probation, absence of counsel at the imposition of the deferred sentence might well result in loss of the right to appeal. While ordinary appeals from a plea of guilty are less frequent than those following a trial on the merits, the incidence of improperly obtained guilty pleas is not so slight as to be capable of being characterized as de minimis."

CASE SIGNIFICANCE: This case was the first of several cases that give procedural safeguards in revocation hearings. The Supreme Court ruled that a probationer is entitled to counsel in a probation revocation hearing in cases in which a sentence has been deferred (meaning that probation was first revoked and then a sentence to prison imposed). The Court said that defendant had a constitutional right to a lawyer. By contrast, the Court in *Gagnon v. Scarpelli*, 411 U.S. 778 (1973), held that whether a probationer is entitled to a lawyer during probation revocation must be decided on a case-by-case basis, implying that there is no constitutional right to a lawyer in every probation revocation proceeding.

The difference in these two decisions is explained by the fact that *Mempa* involved the revocation of a suspended sentence followed by being sentenced to a prison term, while *Gagnon* involved regular probation in which the defendant was found guilty and then placed on probation. In *Mempa*, the prison sentence was not imposed, whereas in *Gagnon* the prison sentence was imposed, but its enforcement was suspended and the offender was placed on probation. *Mempa* says that a lawyer must be provided during sentencing, but that the right to counsel during probation revocation is not a constitutional right. It may, however, be given by state law. In sum, a defendant is entitled to a lawyer during sentencing, but not during probation revocation. *Mempa* must therefore be considered a sentencing case (although preceded by a suspended sentence, which is a form of probation), while *Gagnon* is a probation revocation case.

GAGNON V. SCARPELLI
411 U.S. 778 (1973)

CAPSULE: Probationers are entitled to due process rights before probation can be revoked. The right to counsel, however, should be decided on a case-by-case basis.

FACTS: Scarpelli, a felony probationer, was arrested after committing a burglary. At first he admitted involvement in the crime, but later claimed that his admission was made under duress and thus was invalid. His probation was revoked without a hearing and without a lawyer being present. After serving three years of his sentence, Scarpelli filed for a writ of habeas corpus, claiming denial of due process because his probation was revoked without a hearing or counsel.

ISSUES:
1. Is a probationer entitled to due process rights in a revocation proceeding? YES.
2. Is a probationer constitutionally entitled to be represented by counsel in a probation revocation hearing? NO.

HOLDING:
1. Probationers, like parolees, are entitled to the following due process rights prior to probation revocation:
    a. Preliminary and final revocation hearings;
    b. Written notice of the alleged probation violation;
    c. Disclosure to the probationer of the evidence of violation;

  d. Opportunity to be heard in person and to present evidence as well as witnesses;

  e. Right to confront and cross-examine adverse witnesses, unless good cause can be shown for not allowing this confrontation;

  f. Right to judgment by a detached and neutral hearing body;

  g. Written statement of reasons for revoking probation, as well as of the evidence used in arriving at that decision.

2. The right to counsel during probation revocation should be decided on a case-by-case basis. Although the state is not constitutionally obliged to provide counsel in all cases, it should do so when the indigent probationer or parolee may have difficulty presenting his or her version of disputed facts without the examination or cross-examination of witnesses or the presentation of complicated documentary evidence. The grounds for refusal to provide counsel must be stated in the record.

REASON: "Of greater relevance is our decision last Term in *Morrissey v. Brewer*, 408 U.S. 471 (1972). There we held that the revocation of parole is not a part of a criminal prosecution. Parole arises after the end of the criminal prosecution, including imposition of sentence. Revocation deprives an individual, not of the absolute liberty to which every citizen is entitled, but only of the conditional liberty properly dependent on observance of special parole restrictions.

"Even though the revocation of parole is not part of the criminal prosecution, we held that the loss of liberty entailed is a serious deprivation requiring that the parolee be accorded due process. Specifically, we held that a parolee is entitled to two hearings, one a preliminary hearing at the time of his arrest and detention to determine whether there is probable cause to believe he has committed a violation of his parole, and the other a somewhat more comprehensive hearing prior to the making of the final revocation decision.

"Petitioner does not contend that there is any difference relevant to the guarantee of due process between the revocation of parole and the revocation of probation, nor do we perceive one. Probation revocation, like parole revocation, is not a stage of a criminal prosecution, but does result in a loss of liberty. Accordingly, we hold that a probationer, like a parolee, is entitled to a preliminary and a final revocation hearing, under the conditions specified in *Morrissey v. Brewer*."

CASE SIGNIFICANCE: This is the most significant case thus far decided by the Supreme Court in probation law. *Gagnon* was decided one year after *Morrissey v. Brewer*, 408 U.S. 471 (1972), a parole revocation case in which the Supreme Court held that parolees were entitled to the same seven due process rights, enumerated here, prior to parole revocation. The Court in *Gagnon* extended the due process rights given to parolees in *Morrissey v. Brewer* to probationers, reasoning that, in both parole and probation, revocation resulted in loss of liberty, which is a "grievous loss." The common element, therefore, between *Gagnon* and *Morrissey* is that both represent a "grievous loss" and therefore require due process.

On the issue of the right to counsel, the Court refused to require the presence of counsel in every probation revocation proceeding, holding that, as in parole, the right to counsel must be decided by the hearing judge or body on a case-by-case basis. The Court added, however, that counsel should be provided where the indigent probationer may have difficulty presenting his or her version of disputed facts without the examination or cross-examination of witnesses or the presentation of complicated documentary evidence. This is determined by the trial court, but the grounds for refusal to provide counsel must be stated in the record.

In both *Morrissey v. Brewer* (parole revocation) and *Gagnon v. Scarpelli* (probation revocation), the Court prescribed a two-step procedure for revocation, consisting of: (1) the preliminary hearing, and (2) the final hearing. In subsequent cases, however, the Supreme Court and lower courts relaxed these requirements, holding instead that there need not be two separate proceedings as long as some type of hearing is afforded. In a number of jurisdictions, there is only one hearing given to a parolee or probationer prior to revocation. This hearing should, however, feature all the rights given to probationers and parolees in the *Gagnon* and *Morrissey* cases.

FARE V. MICHAEL C.[1]
442 U.S. 707 (1979)

CAPSULE: A request by a juvenile to see his probation officer is not equivalent to asking for a lawyer.

FACTS: Michael C., a juvenile, was taken into police custody under suspicion of murder. Prior to questioning by two police officers, Michael C. was advised of his *Miranda* rights. When asked if he wanted to waive his right to have an attorney present during questioning, he responded by asking for his probation officer. He was informed by the police that the probation officer would be contacted later, but that he could talk to the police if he wanted to. Michael C. agreed to talk and during questioning made statements and drew sketches that incriminated him. He was charged with murder in juvenile court. Michael C. moved to suppress the incriminating statements and sketches, alleging that they were obtained in violation of his *Miranda* rights and that his request to see his probation officer was, in effect, an assertion of his right to remain silent and that this was equivalent to his having requested an attorney.

ISSUE: Is the request by a probationer to see his probation officer during police questioning the same as the request for an attorney, thus invoking the Fifth Amendment right to remain silent, pursuant to *Miranda*? NO.

HOLDING: The request by a juvenile probationer during police questioning to see his probation officer, after having been given the *Miranda* warnings by the police, is not equivalent to asking for a lawyer and therefore is not considered an assertion of the right to remain silent. Evidence voluntarily given by the juvenile probationer is therefore admissible in court in a subsequent criminal trial.

REASON: "A probation officer is not in the same posture [as is a lawyer] with regard to either the accused or the system of justice as a whole. Often he is not trained in the law, and so is not in a position to advise the accused as to his legal rights. Neither is he a trained advocate, skilled in the representation of the interests of his client before police and courts. He does not assume the power to act on behalf of his client by virtue of his status as advisor, nor are the communications of the accused to the probation officer shielded by the lawyer-client privilege.

"Moreover, the probation officer is the employee of the State which seeks to prosecute the alleged offender. He is a peace officer, and as such is allied, to a greater or lesser extent, with his fellow peace officers. He owes an obligation to the State notwithstanding the obligation he may also owe the juvenile under his supervision. In most cases, the probation officer is duty bound to report wrongdoing by the juvenile when it comes to his attention, even if by communication from the juvenile himself."

CASE SIGNIFICANCE: Although this case involved a juvenile probationer, the Supreme Court's decision should apply to adult probationers and parolees as well. In essence, the Court said that a probation officer does not perform the same function as a lawyer; therefore a request by a probationer to see his probation officer is not equivalent to a request to see a lawyer. The Court then proceeded to distinguish between a probation officer and a lawyer. First, the Court stated that the communications of the accused to the probation officer are not shielded by the lawyer-client privilege. This means that information given by a client to the probation officer may be disclosed in court, unlike information shared by a client with a lawyer. Second, the Court makes clear that a probation officer's loyalty and obligation is to the state, despite any obligation he or she may also have to the probationer. This means that despite an officer's feelings for or rapport with a client, there should be no question of where his or her loyalties lie. Professionalism requires that these two obligations not be confused and that it be made clear to the probationer and the officer, particularly in situations in which confidences are shared, that the officer's loyalty is ultimately with the state, not with the probationer.

CABELL V. CHAVEZ-SALIDO
454 U.S. 432 (1982)

CAPSULE: Requiring American citizenship in order to become a probation officer is constitutional.

FACTS: A California statute requires that public employees declared by law to be peace officers must be United States citizens. In the state of California, probation officers are "peace officers" and therefore must be American citizens. This requirement was challenged by a class of lawfully admitted permanent resident aliens after having been denied positions as deputy probation officers in Los Angeles County because they were not American citizens.

ISSUE: Is a state law requiring U.S. citizenship for probation officer positions constitutional? YES.

HOLDING: A state law requiring U.S. citizenship for public officers or employees, including probation officers, declared by law to be peace officers, is valid and constitutional. Because probation officers take part in the exercise of coercive power by the sovereign over the individual, the citizenship requirement is justified.

REASON: "The exclusion of aliens from basic governmental processes is not a deficiency in the democratic system but a necessary consequence of the community's process of political self-definition. Self-government, whether direct or through representatives, begins by defining the scope of the community of the governed and thus of the governors as well: Aliens are by definition those outside of this community. Judicial incursions in this area may interfere with those aspects of democratic self-government that are most essential to it. This distinction between the economic and political functions of government has, therefore, replaced the old public/private distinction. Although this distinction rests on firmer foundations than the old public/private distinction, it may be difficult to apply in particular cases.

"Looking at the functions of California probation officers, we conclude that they, like the state troopers involved in *Foley*, sufficiently partake of the sovereign's power to exercise coercive force over the individual that they may be limited to citizens. Although the range of individuals over whom probation officers exercise supervisory authority is limited, the powers of the probation officer are broad with respect to those over whom they exercise that authority. The probation officer has the power both to arrest and to release those over whom he has jurisdiction. He has the power and the responsibility to supervise probationers and insure that all the conditions of probation are met and that the probationer accomplishes a successful reintegration into the community. With respect to juveniles, the probation officer has the responsibility to determine whether to release or detain offenders, and whether to institute judicial proceedings or take other supervisory steps over the minor.

"From the perspective of the probationer, his probation officer may personify the State's sovereign powers; from the perspective of the larger community, the probation officer may symbolize the political community's control over, and thus responsibility for, those who have been found to have violated the norms of social order. From both of these perspectives, a citizenship requirement may seem an appropriate limitation on those who would exercise and, therefore, symbolize this power of the political community over those who fall within its jurisdiction."

CASE SIGNIFICANCE: This case addresses the question of whether resident aliens can be disqualified from certain public positions through a state law that requires U.S. citizenship. The Supreme Court answered yes, saying that "a citizenship requirement is an appropriate limitation on those who exercise and, therefore, symbolize this power of the political community over those who fall within its jurisdiction." Said the Court:

The exclusion of aliens from basic governmental processes is not a deficiency in the democratic system, but a necessary consequence of the community's process of political self-definition. Self-government, whether direct or through representatives, begins by defining the scope of the community of the governed and thus of the governors as well: Aliens are by definition those outside of this community.

This decision does not mean that resident aliens may, by law, be disqualified from any and all public positions by requiring U.S. citizenship as a condition for employment. Such a law would be unconstitutional as overinclusive, meaning that it would disqualify individuals without justification. Citizenship can be required only in certain public positions. "Looking at the functions of California probation officers," the Court said, "we conclude that they, like state troopers . . . sufficiently partake of the sovereign's power to exercise coercive force over the individual that they may be limited to citizens." The implication is that public positions that do not "sufficiently partake of the sovereign's power to exercise coercive force over the individual" cannot be limited to American citizens.

BEARDEN V. GEORGIA
461 U.S. 660 (1983)

CAPSULE: It is unconstitutional to revoke probation based on failure to pay a fine or restitution if the probationer is indigent.

FACTS: Bearden pleaded guilty in state court to burglary and theft by receiving stolen goods. He was a first-time offender and under Georgia statute was given probation on the condition that he pay a $500 fine and $250 in restitution, with $100 payable that day, $100 the next day, and the balance within four months. Bearden borrowed money and paid off the first $200 but was laid off from his job about one month later. He tried to find other work but was unsuccessful. Shortly before the $550 balance became due, he notified the probation office that his payment was going to be late. Bearden's probation was revoked because of nonpayment and he was sent to prison.

ISSUE: Can probation be revoked based on the failure to pay a fine and restitution if the probationer does not have the resources to pay? NO.

HOLDING: A judge cannot constitutionally revoke probation because of failure to pay a fine or restitution in the absence of evidence and a finding that the probationer was somehow responsible for the failure or that alternative forms of punishment were inadequate to meet the state's interest in punishment and deterrence.

REASON: "This Court has long been sensitive to the treatment of indigents in our criminal justice system. Over a quarter-century ago, Justice Black declared that 'there can be no equal justice where the kind of trial a man gets depends on the amount of money he has.' (*Griffin v. Illinois*, 351 U.S. 12, [1956]). *Griffin*'s principle of 'equal justice,' which the Court applied there to strike down a state practice of granting appellate review only to persons able to afford a trial transcript, has been applied in numerous other contexts. See e.g., *Douglas v. California*, 372 U.S. 353 (1963) (indigent entitled to counsel on first direct appeal); *Roberts v. LaVallee*, 389 U.S. 40 (1967) (indigent entitled to free transcript of preliminary hearing for use at trial); *Mayer v. Chicago*, 404 U.S. 189 (1971) (indigent cannot be denied an adequate record to appeal a conviction under a fine-only statute). Most relevant to the issue here is the holding in *Williams v. Illinois*, 399 U.S. 235 (1970), that a State cannot subject a certain class of convicted defendants to a period of imprisonment beyond the statutory maximum solely because they are too poor to pay a fine."

CASE SIGNIFICANCE: This case reiterates the principle enunciated in previous Supreme Court cases, that "there can be no equal justice where the kind of trial a man gets depends on the amount of money he has." To revoke the probation of an indigent probationer would be to violate the equal protection clause of the Constitution because the only reason the probationer would then be sent to prison is that he or she is too poor to pay. Note the following points, however, in connection with this case:

1. The decision states that "a sentencing court cannot properly revoke a defendant's probation for failure to pay a fine and make restitution, absent evidence and findings that he was somehow responsible for the failure . . ." A distinction must be made between inability to pay because of indigence and refusal to pay even if resources are available. Failure to pay because of indigence cannot lead to revocation because such revocation would violate the equal protection clause of the Constitution; refusal to pay, however, can result in a valid revocation because there is no equal protection issue.

2. The decision also states that "a sentencing court cannot properly revoke a defendant's probation without ascertaining that alternative forms of punishment were inadequate to meet the State's interest in punishment and deterrence . . ." The Court rules out an automatic probation revocation without first determining whether other, alternative forms of punishment are in fact adequate to satisfy the state's purpose of punishment and deterrence. Bearden does not categorically say that failure to pay because of indigence can never lead to revocation under any circumstance. Revocation can be resorted to even in cases of indigence as long as the judge first determines that "alternative forms of punishment were inadequate to meet the State's interest in punishment and deterrence . . ." In reality, however, it is difficult to imagine instances in which alternative forms of punishment (such as community service) would not suffice as an alternative form of punishment to fine or restitution, thus effectively ruling out imprisonment resulting from revocation in indigence cases.

MINNESOTA V. MURPHY
465 U.S. 420 (1984)

CAPSULE: Statements made by a probationer to a probation officer during interrogation while not in custody are admissible in a subsequent criminal trial. The exception is if the probationer specifically asks for a lawyer during such interrogation and a lawyer was not provided.

FACTS: Murphy was prosecuted for criminal sexual conduct and pleaded guilty to the lesser charge of false imprisonment. He received a suspended prison sentence and was placed on probation for three years. The terms of Murphy's probation provided that he participate in a treatment program for sexual offenders, report to his probation officer as directed, and be truthful with the probation officer "in all matters." Murphy was told that failure to comply with the conditions of his probation could result in probation revocation.

Murphy's probation officer learned from one of the counselors at the treatment facility that Murphy had confessed to a rape and murder in 1974. Armed with this information, the probation officer met with Murphy and confronted him with the information from the counselor. After further questioning by the probation officer, Murphy admitted his involvement in the 1974 rape and murder.

Murphy was charged with first-degree murder. During the trial he attempted to suppress the confession made to the probation officer on the ground that it was obtained in violation of the Fifth and Fourteenth Amendments. The trial court admitted the evidence, ruling that Murphy was not "in custody" when he confessed to the probation officer and that the confession was neither compelled nor involuntary despite the absence of *Miranda* warnings.

ISSUE: Is a statement made by a probationer to his probation officer without *Miranda* warnings admissible in a subsequent criminal trial? YES.

HOLDING: Statements made by a probationer to a probation officer during interrogation while not in custody are admissible in a subsequent criminal trial. The exception is if the probationer specifically asks for a lawyer during such interrogation and a lawyer was not provided.

REASON: "The general obligation to appear before his probation officer and answer questions truthfully did not in itself convert respondent's otherwise voluntary statements into compelled ones.

"A witness confronted with questions that the government should reasonably expect to elicit incriminating evidence ordinarily must assert the Fifth Amendment privilege rather than answer if he desires not to incriminate himself. If he chooses to answer rather than assert the privilege, his choice is considered to be voluntary since he was free to claim the privilege and would suffer no penalty as a result of his decision to do so.

"Respondent cannot claim the benefit of the 'in custody' exception to the general rule that the Fifth Amendment privilege is not self-executing. It is clear that respondent was not 'in custody' for purposes of receiving *Miranda* protection since there was no formal arrest or restraint on freedom of movement of the degree associated with formal arrest. The fact that the probation officer could compel respondent's attendance and truthful answers and consciously sought incriminating evidence, that respondent did not expect questions about prior criminal conduct and could not seek counsel before attending the meeting, and that there were no observers to guard against abuse or trickery, neither alone nor in combination, are sufficient to excuse respondent's failure to claim the privilege in a timely manner."

CASE SIGNIFICANCE: This case answers a question that probation officers face whenever they ask questions of or are interviewing probationers. The question is: Should *Miranda* warnings be given by the probation officer when asking questions of a probationer? The answer is complex and may be presented in a chart as follows:

	A. Evidence To Be Used In a Revocation Proceeding	*B. Evidence To Be Used In a Criminal Trial*
I. If Probationer Is Not In Custody	No	No, unless the probationer asserts his or her right (this situation is the *Murphy* case).
II. If Probationer Is In Custody	Some states say no; others, yes. It depends on statutory or case law.	Yes

As the above chart shows, it is important to know whether the evidence obtained is to be used in a revocation proceeding or in a criminal trial, and whether the probationer is in custody or not in custody. Evidence obtained by probation officers is usually used in probation revocation proceedings, which are administrative proceedings. There are instances, however, when the evidence obtained by the probation officer might be needed by the prosecutor in a subsequent criminal trial of that offender. In these cases, *Miranda* warnings must be given if the evidence is to be used in a criminal trial and if the probationer is in custody.

The important question is: When is a probationer in custody or not in custody? Jurisdictions differ, but the general rule is: If the probation officer will allow the probationer to leave after the interrogation, then the probationer is not in custody. Conversely, if the probation officer knows he or she will not allow the probationer to leave after the interrogation, that probationer is in custody. Under this test, asking routine questions during a routine visit with a probationer is considered non-custodial; however, asking the probationer to come to the office after the officer receives information from the police, as well as the officer asking the police to take the probationer into custody after the interrogation, imply that the probationer is in custody. Although this case involves a probationer, there is every reason to believe that the same rules outlined above also apply to parolees who, like probationers, are under supervision but are not in custody.

BLACK V. ROMANO
471 U.S. 606 (1985)

CAPSULE: A sentencing judge does not have to indicate that he or she considered alternatives to incarceration before revoking probation.

FACTS: Black, after pleading guilty to two counts of transferring and selling controlled substances, was placed on probation for five years and given suspended prison sentences. Two months later he was arrested and charged with leaving the scene of an automobile accident. At Black's probation revocation hearing, he offered no explanation of his involvement in the accident. The judge found that Black had violated the conditions of his probation by committing a felony; Black's probation was revoked.

ISSUE: Does the due process clause of the Constitution require that a sentencing court indicate that it considered alternatives to incarceration before revoking probation? NO.

HOLDING: The due process clause of the Fourteenth Amendment does not require that the sentencing judge indicate consideration of alternatives to incarceration before probation can be revoked.

REASON: "The Due Process Clause of the Fourteenth Amendment does not generally require a sentencing court to indicate that it has considered alternatives to incarceration before revoking probation. The procedures for revocation of probation—written notice to the probationer of the claimed probation violations, disclosure of the evidence against him, an opportunity for the probationer to be heard in person and to present witnesses and documentary evidence, a neutral hearing body, a written statement by the factfinder as to the evidence relied on and the reasons for revoking probation, the right to cross-examine adverse witnesses unless the hearing body finds good cause for not allowing confrontation, and the right to assistance of counsel—do not include an express statement by the factfinder that alternatives to incarceration were considered and rejected. The specified procedures adequately protect the probationer against revocation of probation in a constitutionally unfair manner."

CASE SIGNIFICANCE: This case further explores the limits of due process guarantees available to probationers during the revocation hearing. In *Gagnon v. Scarpelli*, 411 U.S. 778 (1973), the Court said that probationers are entitled to the following due process rights prior to revocation: (1) Preliminary and final revocation hearings; (2) written notice of the alleged probation violation; (3) opportunity to be heard in person and to present evidence as well as witnesses; (5) right to confront and cross-examine adverse witnesses; (6) right to judgment by a detached and neutral hearing body; and (7) written statement of reasons for revoking probation, as well as of the evidence used in arriving at that decision.

In this case, the probationer sought to add to these rights, saying that the due process clause requires a sentencing court to indicate that alternatives to incarceration were considered by the judge before revoking probation. The Supreme Court disagreed, saying that the rights guaranteed in *Gagnon* ensured fairness in the revocation proceedings. Aside from refusing to add to a probationer's due process rights beyond those given in *Gagnon v. Scarpelli*, the Court in this case reiterated the accepted legal principle that probation is a privilege and not a right. This means that probation may be given or withheld by the court and the court may refuse to extend probation to a defendant even if other non-incarceration alternatives are available.

GRIFFIN V. WISCONSIN
483 U.S. 868 (1987)

CAPSULE: The search of a probationer's home by probation officers based on reasonable grounds is constitutional. No warrant or probable cause is needed.

FACTS: In 1980, Griffin, who had a prior criminal record, was convicted in state court of resisting arrest, disorderly conduct, and obstructing an officer. He was placed on probation.

Probationers in Wisconsin are subject to conditions set by the court as well as by rules and regulations established by the State Department of Health and Social Services. One of the Department's regulations permits any probation officer to search a probationer's home without a warrant upon supervisory approval, and as long as there are "reasonable grounds" to believe the probationer is in possession of contraband.

The supervisor of Griffin's probation officer received information from a detective that there were or might be guns in Griffin's apartment. Probation officers searched the apartment and discovered a handgun. Griffin was tried and convicted of the charge of possession of a firearm by a convicted felon and was sentenced to two years' imprisonment.

ISSUE: Is the warrantless search based on "reasonable grounds" (which is a lower standard than probable cause) of a probationer's home by probation officers constitutional? YES.

HOLDING: The search of a probationer's home based on reasonable grounds is constitutional. No warrant or probable cause is needed.

REASON: "A state's operation of a probation system, like its operation of a school, government office or prison, or its supervision of a regulated industry, likewise presents 'special needs' beyond normal law enforcement that may justify departures from the usual warrant and probable cause requirements.

"We think it clear that the special needs of Wisconsin's probation system make the warrant requirement impracticable and justify replacement of the standard of probable cause by 'reasonable grounds' as defined by the Wisconsin Supreme Court."

CASE SIGNIFICANCE: The Fourth Amendment requires that searches and seizures by the police be made with probable cause and a warrant. This case is significant because it holds that searches and seizures of probationers by probation officers may be made based on "reasonable grounds" (less than probable cause) and without a warrant. This lower standard is justified by the "special needs" of probation supervision and because probationers, having been convicted of a crime, have diminished constitutional rights. Such warrantless searches, based on reasonable grounds, however, must be authorized either by state law, agency policy, or the conditions of probation.

It must be noted that the police cannot, on their own, search the homes or dwellings of probationers without a warrant (subject to exceptions) or probable cause. They may, however, be asked by the probation officer to help in the search, as long as such request is legitimate and not an excuse for the police officer to search without probable cause. A combined probation officer-police search of a probationer's home must not be at the instigation of the police to accomplish what the police otherwise cannot do. In sum, a probation officer can "use" the police to help in a search, but a probation officer should not be "used" by the police to conduct what otherwise would be a prohibited search because of the absence of a warrant and probable cause.

FORRESTER V. WHITE
484 U.S. 219 (1988)

CAPSULE: Judges enjoy absolute immunity in § 1983 cases only when performing judicial or adjudicate acts, not when performing administrative acts.

FACTS: Forrester, a former probation officer, filed a lawsuit seeking damages from White, a state court judge. Under Illinois law, a judge had the authority to appoint and discharge probation officers. Forrester alleged that White demoted and later discharged her from her duties on account of her sex, in violation of the equal protection clause of the Fourteenth Amendment. The jury decided in Forrester's favor. However, the district court ruled that the judge had absolute immunity from a civil damages suit.

ISSUE: Does a state court judge have absolute immunity from damages in a § 1983 (civil rights) suit for a decision to demote and dismiss a subordinate? NO.

HOLDING: Judges enjoy absolute immunity in § 1983 cases only when performing judicial or adjudicative acts, not when performing administrative acts. The demotion and dismissal of a probation officer are administrative acts.

REASON: "Respondent's decisions to demote and discharge petitioner were administrative rather than judicial or adjudicative in nature. Such decisions are indistinguishable from those of an executive branch official responsible for making similar personnel decisions, which, no matter how crucial to the efficient operation of public institutions, are not entitled to absolute immunity from liability in damages under Section 1983. The Court of Appeals reasoned that the threat of vexatious lawsuits by disgruntled ex-employees could interfere with the quality of the judge's decisions. However true this may be, it does not serve to distinguish judges from other public officials who hire and fire subordinates. In neither case is the danger that officials will be deflected from the effective performance of their duties great enough to justify absolute immunity."

CASE SIGNIFICANCE: Judges enjoy absolute immunity when performing judicial or adjudicative (something to do with adjudication) acts. This means that, if sued, the lawsuit will be dismissed because of absolute immunity. That form of immunity for judges, however, is limited to instances in which judges perform "judicial or adjudicative" acts. This case is significant because the Court said that the demotion and dismissal of a probation officer (who, in many states, is "hired and fired" by a judge) is not a judicial act, but is instead an administrative act for which the judge does not enjoy absolute immunity. Probation officers are thus afforded better protection under this case against capricious and arbitrary administrative decisions of a judge.

Although the Supreme Court is aware that government officials must have some protection in order to fulfill their duties, the Court also recognizes that these officials should not be totally exempt from accountability. The Court examines the functions with which a particular official or class of officials has been lawfully entrusted and "evaluates the effect that exposure to particular forms of liability would likely have on the appropriate exercise of those duties."

Immunity for judicial acts is justified and defined by the functions it protects, but there is a significant distinction between judicial acts and the administrative, legislative, or executive functions that judges often perform. In this case, the judge was acting in an administrative capacity, thus his actions did not enjoy absolute immunity from liability under § 1983.

ALDEN V. MAINE
527 U.S. 706 (1999)

CAPSULE: Article I of the Constitution does not empower Congress to subject non-consenting states to private suits in state courts; therefore, the state of Maine could not be held liable for overtime pay and liquidated damages under the Fair Labor Standards Act (FLSA) because it did not consent to such lawsuit.

FACTS: In 1992, a group of probation officers filed suit against their employer, the state of Maine. The officers alleged that the state had violated the overtime provisions of the Fair Labor Standards Act of 1938 (FLSA) and sought compensation and liquidated damages. While the suit was pending, the U.S. Supreme Court decided *Seminole Tribe of Florida v. Florida*, 517 U.S. 44 (1996). In that case the Court ruled that Congress does not have the power under Article

I of the U.S. Constitution to do away with the state's sovereign immunity from suits begun or prosecuted in the federal courts.

ISSUE: Does Congress have authority under Article I of the U.S. Constitution to subject non-consenting states to private suits for damages in state courts? NO.

HOLDING: Article I of the Constitution does not empower Congress to subject non-consenting states to private suits for damages in state courts; therefore the state of Maine could not be held liable for overtime pay and liquidated damages under the FLSA because it did not consent to such lawsuit.

REASON: "The Constitution, by delegating to Congress the power to establish the supreme law of the land when acting within its enumerated powers, does not foreclose a State from asserting immunity to claims arising under federal law merely because the law derived not from the State itself but from the national power. A contrary view could not be reconciled with *Hans v. Louisiana, supra,* which sustained Louisiana's immunity in a private suit arising under the Constitution itself; with *Employees of Dept. of Public Health and Welfare of Mo. v. Department of Public Health and Welfare of Mo.,* 411 U.S. 279, 283 (1973), which recognized that the FLSA was binding upon Missouri but nevertheless upheld the State's immunity to a private suit to recover under that Act; or with numerous other decisions to the same effect. We reject any contention that substantive federal law by its own force necessarily overrides the sovereign immunity of the States. When a State asserts its immunity to suit, the question is not the primacy of federal law but the implementation of the law in a manner consistent with the constitutional sovereignty of the States.

In light of the language of the Constitution and the historical context, it is quite apparent why neither the ratification debates nor the language of the Eleventh Amendment addressed the State's immunity from suit in their own courts. The concerns voiced at the ratifying conventions, the furor raised by *Chisholm,* and the speed and unanimity with which the Amendment was adopted, moreover, underscore the jealous care with which the founding generation sought to preserve the sovereign immunity of the States. To read this history as permitting the interference that the Constitution stripped the States of immunity in their own courts and allowed Congress to subject them to suit there would turn on its head the concern of the founding generation—that Article III might be used to circumvent state-court immunity. In light of the historical record it is difficult to conceive that the Constitution would have been adopted if it had been understood to strip the States of immunity from suit in their own courts and cede to the Federal Government a power to subject non-consenting States to private suits in these fora."

CASE SIGNIFICANCE: This case does not address an issue involving probationers; instead, it settles an issue arising from the filing of a lawsuit by probation officers against a state for overtime pay under a law passed by the Congress of the United States. The Fair Labor Standards Act (FLSA), passed in 1938, is a comprehensive piece of legislation aimed at guaranteeing that workers in the private ands public sectors are paid fairly. It was enacted after the Great

Depression to prevent employers from "taking advantage of the tight labor market to subject workers to horrible conditions and impossible working hours."

Probation officers in Maine sued under the law, claiming that the state owed them overtime pay. The Court rejected their claim, holding that Congress did not have any constitutional authority under Article I of the Constitution to terminate the sovereignty of states, given under the Eleventh Amendment, and subject states to lawsuits without their consent. The Eleventh Amendment provides that states have sovereign immunity and cannot be sued without the state's consent. Some states waive sovereign immunity and allow the state to be sued. Maine has not done that, thus it cannot be sued even by its own employees.

This was an easy case for the Court to decide because after the lawsuit was filed, the Court decided *Seminole Tribe of Florida v. Florida* (1996) which held that Congress could not strip states of sovereign immunity from cases filed in federal court. Alden therefore extends that ruling to cases filed in state courts. In sum, state sovereign immunity cannot be terminated by Congress by legislation. Only the state itself can waive sovereign immunity.

UNITED STATES V. KNIGHTS
534 U.S. 112 (2001)

CAPSULE: The warrantless search of a probationer's apartment is not in violation of the Fourth Amendment.

FACTS: Knights was sentenced to probation in California for a drug offense. A condition of his probation allowed various types of searches by a probation officer or law enforcement officer with or without a search warrant. These searches included searches of his residence. A detective searched Knights' apartment based on reasonable suspicion and without a search warrant. The items that the detective found resulted in Knights' arrest and indictment by a federal grand jury for conspiracy to commit arson, possession of an unregistered destructive device, and being a felon in possession of ammunition. Knights moved to suppress the evidence obtained during the search, and the District Court granted this motion. The Court ruled that the search was 'investigatory' rather than 'probationary' in nature. The Ninth Circuit Court of Appeals affirmed this decision, noting that the probation order limited the searches to probation searches and not investigation searches.

ISSUE: Is the warrantless search of a probationer's apartment, based on reasonable suspicion and authorized by a probation condition, a violation of the Fourth Amendment? NO.

HOLDING: Warrantless searches involving probationers, supported by reasonable suspicion and authorized by a condition of probation, are allowed as reasonable under the Fourth Amendment.

REASON: "Just as other punishments for criminal convictions curtail an offender's freedoms, a court granting probation may impose reasonable conditions that deprive the offender of some freedoms enjoyed by law-abiding citizens. The judge who sentenced Knights to probation determined that it was necessary to condition the probation on Knights' acceptance of the search provision . . . The probation order clearly expressed the search condition and Knights was unambiguously informed of it."

"In assessing the governmental interest side of the balance, it must be remembered that 'the very assumption of the institution of probation' is that the probationer 'is more likely than the ordinary citizen to violate the law.' *Griffin*, 483 U.S., at 880 . . . We hold that the balance of these considerations requires no more than reasonable suspicion to conduct a search of this probationer's house . . . The same circumstances that lead us to conclude that reasonable suspicion is constitutionally sufficient also render a warrant requirement unnecessary . . . Because our holding rests on ordinary Fourth Amendment analysis that considers all the circumstances of a search, there is no basis for examining official purpose. With the limited exception of some special needs and administrative search cases, see *Indianapolis v. Edmond*, 531 U.S. 32, 45 (2000), 'we have been unwilling to entertain Fourth Amendment challenges based on the actual motivations of individual officers.' *Whren v. United States*, 517 U.S. 806, 813 (1996) . . . We therefore hold that the warrantless search of Knights' apartment, supported by reasonable suspicion and authorized by a condition of probation, was reasonable within the meaning of the Fourth Amendment."

CASE SIGNIFICANCE: This is an important case because it clarifies further the extent of probationers' rights under the Fourth Amendment. The general rule is that all searches and seizures must be with a warrant and based on probable cause. But in *Griffin v. Wisconsin* (1987) the Court held that searches involving probationers without a warrant and based on reasonable grounds are valid. The *Knights* case goes further and holds that searches involving probationers without a warrant and based on reasonable suspicion (a lower degree of certainty than probable cause or reasonable grounds) are valid.

Offenders on probation are subject to conditions of probation. In most cases, these conditions provide that the probationer can be searched or seized based on less than probable cause and without a warrant. This was one of the conditions imposed by the judge in this case. The probationer argued that the condition violated his Fourth Amendment right, particularly because this was an investigatory search (meaning the search was for a possible crime violation) rather than a probationary search (meaning a search to enforce the conditions of probation). The Court disagreed, saying that the type of search did not matter and that the search was valid. One interesting aspect of this case is that the search was done by a detective instead of by a probation officer. It raises the following question: can a judge authorize police officers (not only probation officers) to enforce conditions of probation? Although the issue was not directly raised or answered, the

Court in essence indicated yes, saying that whether the search was investigatory (done by a police officer) or probationary (done by a probation officer) did not matter. Both searches of probationers are reasonable under the Fourth Amendment. This decision re-emphasizes the general principle that like prisoners and parolees, probationers have diminished constitutional rights.

NOTE

1   This case is also briefed in Chapter 5, Juvenile Justice.

Parole

3

INTRODUCTION

Parole is defined as release from jail, prison, or other confinement after actually serving part of the sentence. Like probation, parole is a privilege and not a right. This means that parole may be given or denied by the state. Parole and probation have much in common. They both are forms of offender community supervision, both involve conditions for release, release conditions are usually similar, and both can be revoked if the conditions imposed are violated. Their differences may be summarized as follows:

1. Parole is given after the offender has served time in jail or prison for the offense, whereas probation is given before the offender serves time for that offense. Therefore, parole denotes that the offender is "halfway out," whereas probation denotes that the offender is "halfway in."

2. Parolees are usually supervised by the executive department of the state, usually under a state Board of Pardons and Paroles, whereas probationers are supervised by the courts through probation officers.
3. Parole revocation hearings are conducted by the Parole Board or its representatives, whereas probation revocation hearings are held by the judge.

Parole has been used in the United States for a long time and is based on the philosophy that some prisoners are sufficiently rehabilitated so they can safely be released to the community. While that is an ideal, parole in many states is, in reality, used as a form of prison population management. Many inmates are released not because they have been rehabilitated, but because of limited prison space. The practice has led to such a level of concern that in some states parole has been completely abolished, in some cases under the guise of "truth in sentencing." Many aspects of parole have drawn criticism. Among them are the criteria for release and insufficient supervision.

Parolees, like probationers, have diminished constitutional rights. The cases decided by the Supreme Court and briefed in this chapter address the issue of the rights that parolees retain while under supervision. The issues addressed by the Court over the years are varied. The best known and arguably the most significant case ever decided in parole law is *Morrissey v. Brewer*, the first case briefed in this chapter. In that case, the Supreme Court said that a parolee is entitled to due process rights prior to parole revocation because revocation constitutes a "grievous loss" of freedom. This decision is significant because it establishes the principle that although parole is a privilege, once given, it becomes an entitlement—meaning that it cannot be taken away without giving the parolee due process.

Perhaps of greater legal significance than *Morrissey* is *Greenholtz v. Nebraska Penal Inmates* (1979). In this case, the Court held that inmates are not entitled to due process rights under the Constitution in discretionary parole release determinations. The greater significance of *Greenholtz*, however, is in the Court's holding that "there is no constitutional or inherent right of a convicted person to be conditionally released before the expiration of a valid sentence." That statement reaffirms the principle that parole is a privilege and not a right and thus may be given or withheld by the state. Taken together with *Morrissey*, the Court has therefore ruled that no due process rights need to be given to inmates when being considered for parole, but once parole is given it cannot be taken away without giving the parolee due process. What starts off as a privilege becomes an entitlement once given.

The Court has not been sympathetic to parolees in most of the cases it has decided. For example, in *Moody v. Daggett* (1976), the Court held that an incarcerated (after revocation) parolee has no constitutional right to a prompt judicial hearing after a detainer is used against him. In *Jago v. Van Curen* (1981), the Court ruled that an inmate does not have a right to due process if the parole board decides to withdraw parole prior to the inmate's release. Most recently, in the case of *Samson v. California* (2006), the Court held that police officers may search parolees even if they do not have reasonable suspicion for the search.

The hot issue in parole during the last few years concerns the prohibition against ex post facto laws, referring to laws passed after the fact or after the act was committed. Four of the most recent cases have addressed this issue. In *California Department of Corrections v. Morales* (1995), the Court decided in favor of the government, saying that a law decreasing the frequency of parole hearings for certain prisoners does not change the punishment for crimes already committed and therefore may be applied retrospectively. But in *Lynce v. Mathis* (1997) and *Young v. Harper* (1997), the Court decided in favor of the inmates. In *Lynce*, the Court held that a statute canceling an inmate's provisional release is ex post facto if applied to a prisoner who was convicted before the law was in effect. In *Harper*, the Court said that the state's pre-parole release program was equivalent to parole and therefore released prisoners under pre-parole were entitled to due process rights before being brought back to prison. And in *Garner v. Jones* (2000), the Court concluded that there is no ex post facto violation unless the prisoner can prove that the retroactive application of the new parole rule will result in longer incarceration.

As in probation, the Court has not decided many cases on parole. Unlike prison law, in which the legal landscape is littered with Supreme Court cases seeking to define the extent of prisoners' rights during incarceration, parole has generated only a few cases, the most important of which are briefed here.

MORRISSEY V. BREWER
408 U.S. 471 (1972)

CAPSULE: A parolee must be given due process rights prior to parole revocation because revocation constitutes a "grievous loss" of freedom.

FACTS: Morrissey pleaded guilty to, and was convicted in 1967 of false drawing or uttering of checks. He was paroled from the Iowa State Penitentiary in 1988. Seven months later, Morrissey's parole was revoked for violating the conditions of his parole by buying a car under an assumed name and operating it without permission, giving false statements to the police concerning his address and insurance company after a minor accident, obtaining credit under an assumed name, and failing to report his residence to his parole officer. The parole officer's report also showed that Morrissey had been interviewed, had admitted to the violations, and could not explain why he had not contacted his parole officer.

ISSUE: Does the due process clause of the Fourteenth Amendment give a parolee due process rights prior to parole revocation? YES.

HOLDING: A parolee is entitled to the following due process rights if parole is to be revoked:
1. Preliminary and final revocation hearings;
2. Written notice of the claimed violations of parole;
3. Disclosure to the parolee of evidence against him;
4. Opportunity to be heard in person and to present witnesses and documentary evidence;

5. The right to confront and cross-examine adverse witnesses, unless the hearing officer specifically finds good cause for not allowing confrontation;
6. A neutral and detached hearing body such as a traditional parole board, members of which need not be judicial officers or lawyers; and
7. Written statement by the fact finders as to the evidence relied on and reason for revoking parole.

REASON: "We begin with the proposition that the revocation of parole is not part of a criminal prosecution and thus the full panoply of rights due a defendant in such a proceeding does not apply to parole revocations. Cf. *Mempa v. Rhay*, 389 U.S. 128 (1967). Parole arises after the end of the criminal prosecution, including imposition of sentence. Supervision is not directly by the court but by an administrative agency, which is sometimes the arm of the court and sometimes of the executive. Revocation deprives an individual, not of absolute liberty to which every citizen is entitled, but only of the conditional liberty properly dependent on observance of special parole restrictions.

"The liberty of a parolee, although indeterminate, includes many of the core values of unqualified liberty and its termination inflicts a 'grievous loss' on the parolee and often on others. It is hardly useful any longer to try to deal with this problem in terms of whether a parolee's liberty is a 'right' or a 'privilege.' By whatever name, the liberty is valuable and must be seen as within the protection of the Fourteenth Amendment. Its termination requires some orderly process.

". . . [M]ost States have recognized that there is no interest on the part of the State in revoking parole without any procedural guarantees at all. What is needed is an informal hearing structured to assure that the finding of a parole violation will be based on verified facts and that the exercise of discretion will be informed by an accurate knowledge of the parolee's behavior."

CASE SIGNIFICANCE: This case is the "mother" of most corrections cases (parole, probation, prisons, or juvenile proceedings) that have sought due process rights for offenders who are under state supervision. It is significant because, for the first time, the Supreme Court said that parolees are entitled to some form of due process in the parole revocation process. Prior to this, offenders under supervision of the state hardly had any due process rights. Relying on previous non-parole cases, the Court said that "whether any procedural protections are due depends on the extent to which an individual will be 'condemned to suffer grievous loss.'" Parole revocation constitutes a "grievous loss" of freedom and therefore due process rights must be given.

Morrissey is also significant because it has been used as precedent by offenders who claim similar due process rights in such proceedings as the decision to release an inmate on parole (*Greenholtz v. Nebraska Penal Inmates*, 442 U.S. 1 (1979); probation revocation (*Gagnon v. Scarpelli*, 411 U.S. 778 (1973); and prison disciplinary proceedings (*Wolff v. McDonnell*, 418 U.S. 539 (1974). The Court has decided that offenders are entitled to *Morrissey* due process rights in probation revocation and prison disciplinary proceedings, but not in the decision to release an inmate on parole. The standard used in these cases by the Court has been whether the offender will "suffer grievous loss" from such proceedings.

Morrissey said that there are two important stages in parole revocation: (1) the arrest and preliminary hearing of the parolee, and (2) the final revocation hearing. In both stages, the parolee is entitled to the due process rights enumerated above. Some writers interpret *Morrissey* to mean that parolees are also constitutionally entitled to a two-stage hearing process (a preliminary hearing and a final hearing) prior to revocation. There is nothing in *Morrissey* to indicate that a two-stage hearing process is constitutionally required. Many jurisdictions have in effect only one hearing, with the seven due process rights enumerated above being given. Although not decided by the U.S. Supreme Court, most lower courts have held that a two-stage hearing (a preliminary hearing and a final revocation that are separate) is not constitutionally required and that one proceeding in which the above due process rights are given suffices.

MOODY V. DAGGETT
429 U.S. 78 (1976)

CAPSULE: An incarcerated parolee has no constitutional right to a prompt judicial hearing after a detainer is issued against him.

FACTS: Moody was convicted in 1962 of rape on an Indian reservation. He received a 10-year sentence, but was paroled in 1966. While on parole, Moody shot and killed two people on the Fort Apache Indian Reservation. He was found guilty of one count of manslaughter and one count of second-degree murder. He received concurrent 10-year sentences for these two offenses. Commission of these offenses violated Moody's 1966 parole. The United States Board of Parole issued, but did not execute, a parole violator warrant soon after Moody was incarcerated for the two homicides. The warrant was lodged with prison officials as a "detainer" (defined as "an instrument issued by a competent officer, authorizing the keeper of a prison to keep in custody a person therein named"). Moody asked that the warrant be executed immediately so that any imprisonment imposed for violating his earlier parole could run at the same time as the homicide sentences. The Board rejected the request, saying that the warrant would be executed only upon Moody's release from his second sentence. Moody brought suit against the Board, asking for dismissal of the parole violator warrant, alleging that he had been denied a prompt hearing at which the pending parole revocation issues could be examined.

ISSUE: Is a federal parolee, imprisoned for a crime committed while on parole, constitutionally entitled to a prompt revocation hearing when a detainer is issued and lodged with the institution where he is serving time? NO.

HOLDING: An incarcerated parolee is deprived of no constitutionally protected rights simply by the issuance of a parole violator warrant. An adversary parole hearing need not take place until such time as the individual is taken into custody as a parole violator by execution of the warrant.

REASON: "Petitioner's present confinement and consequent liberty loss derive not in any sense from the outstanding parole violator warrant, but from his two 1971 homicide convictions. Issuance of the warrant and notice of that fact to the institution of confinement did no more than express the Board's intent to defer consideration of parole revocation to a later time. Though the gravity of petitioner's subsequent crimes places him under a cloud, issuance of the warrant was not a determination that petitioner's parole under his 1962 rape conviction will be revoked; the time at which the Commission must make that decision has not yet arrived. With only a prospect of future incarceration which is far from certain, we cannot say that the parole violator warrant has any present or inevitable effect upon the liberty interests which Morrissey sought to protect.

"The other injuries petitioner claims to suffer either do not involve a loss of protected liberty or have not occurred by reason of the warrant and detainer. His real complaint is that he desires to serve his sentence for the 1982 rape conviction concurrently with his sentences for two 1971 homicides. But, as we have noted, even after completion of the homicide sentences the Commission retains full discretion to dismiss the warrant or decide, after hearing, that petitioner's parole need not be revoked. If revocation is chosen, the Commission has power to grant, retroactively, the equivalent of concurrent sentences and to provide for unconditional or conditional release upon completion of the subsequent sentence.

"The statutory hearing to which petitioner will be entitled upon his application for release on parole will give him the same full opportunities to persuade the Commission that he should be released from federal custody as would an immediate hearing on the parole violator warrant. Whether different issues would be presented by the prospect of adverse action by different and autonomous parole authorities, we need not consider."

CASE SIGNIFICANCE: The *Moody* case answers the following question: Is an incarcerated parolee entitled to a prompt hearing after a detainer is issued against him? The Supreme Court said no. It found no liberty loss simply because the parole board wished to defer revocation consideration, stating that the parolee's present confinement was for crimes committed while on parole and not due to the detainer.

The federal parolee in this case argued that he was constitutionally entitled to an immediate parole revocation hearing when the parole violator warrant was issued and lodged with the institution as a detainer, but which the institution did not execute. The parolee was hoping that, if the warrant was issued, he could serve his new homicide sentences and his parole revocation simultaneously. The Court added that "as a practical matter, in cases such as this, in which the parolee has been convicted of an offense plainly constituting a parole violation, a decision to revoke parole would often be foreordained, so that given the predictive nature of parole revocation hearings, it is appropriate that such a hearing be held at the time at which prediction as to the parolee's ability to live in society without committing anti-social acts is both relevant and most accurate—at the expiration of the parolee's intervening sentence."

The Court did not wish to interfere with the parole board's powers and stated that the parolee would be given a statutory hearing at the parole board's discretion, at which time he would be given an opportunity to persuade the board that any sentence he received if parole was revoked should be retroactive.

What if the parolee is in confinement not because of the conviction for a new offense (as in this case), but solely because of a detainer? The Court has not addressed this, but chances are that a prompt hearing would be required because the detainer alone would have caused the parolee to suffer loss of liberty.

GREENHOLTZ V. NEBRASKA PENAL INMATES
442 U.S. 1 (1979)

CAPSULE: Inmates are not entitled to due process rights under the Constitution in discretionary parole release determinations.

FACTS: Inmates at the Nebraska Penal and Correctional Complex who had been denied parole brought a class action against the Nebraska Parole Board, claiming that they had been denied procedural due process. Under Nebraska law, a prison inmate becomes eligible for discretionary parole when his minimum term, minus good-time credits, has been served. Each case is decided through a two-stage hearing in the form of: (1) an initial review hearing and (2) a final parole hearing. Each inmate receives an initial review at least once a year. During the review the Parole Board does the following: (1) examines the inmate's pre-confinement and post-confinement record, (2) interviews the inmate, and (3) considers any documentation presented in support of a claim for release. If it is determined that the inmate is not yet a good risk for release, the Board denies parole, stating why release was not granted. If it is determined that the inmate is a good risk, a final hearing is scheduled, at which time the following rights are given. The inmate may: (1) present evidence; (2) call witnesses; (3) be represented by counsel; and (4) be given a written statement of the reasons if parole is denied. The State of Nebraska, therefore, gave inmates statutory rights prior to parole revocation. Despite these rights, inmates filed suit, claiming more rights than those provided by Nebraska statute and claiming that their due process rights were being denied. They wanted the same rights given to parolees prior to parole revocation, as given in the case of *Morrissey v. Brewer*.

ISSUES:
1. Does the due process clause of the Fourteenth Amendment apply to discretionary parole release determinations made by the Nebraska Parole Board? NO.
2. If Nebraska inmates are not entitled to due process under the Constitution prior to discretionary parole release determinations, are they nonetheless entitled to due process because of the way the Nebraska law is worded? YES.
3. If the answer to (2) is yes, did the Nebraska law provide for sufficient due process rights? YES.

HOLDINGS:

1. The mere possibility of discretionary parole release does not carry with it due process rights under the Constitution, therefore inmates are not entitled to due process rights.

2. In the case of the Nebraska inmates, however, they are entitled to due process rights not because of the U.S. Constitution, but because the Nebraska statute is worded so as to create a "liberty interest" that entitles inmates to due process.

3. The rights given to inmates by the Nebraska statute, however, satisfy the due process requirements of the Constitution, thus inmates were afforded proper due process under Nebraska law.

REASONS:

1. There is no constitutional or inherent right of a convicted person to be conditionally released before the expiration of a valid sentence. The natural desire of an individual to be released is indistinguishable from the initial resistance to being confined. But the conviction, with all its procedural safeguards, has extinguished the liberty right: '[G]iven a valid conviction, the criminal defendant has been constitutionally deprived of his liberty.' *Meachum v. Fano*, 427 U.S. 215, 224 (1976).

   "A state may, as Nebraska has, establish a parole system, but it has no duty to do so. Moreover, to insure that the state-created parole system serves the public interest purposes of rehabilitation and deterrence, the state may be specific or general in defining the conditions for release and the factors that should be considered by the parole authority. It is thus not surprising that there is no prescribed or defined combination of facts which, if shown, would mandate release on parole. Indeed, the very institution of parole is still in an experimental stage . . .

   "The fallacy in respondent's position is that parole release and parole revocation are quite different. There is a crucial distinction between being deprived of a liberty one has, as in parole, and being denied a conditional liberty that one desires.

   "Respondents emphasize that the structure of the [Nebraska] provision together with the use of the word 'shall' binds the Board of Parole to release an inmate unless one of the four specifically designated reasons is found. In their view, the statute creates a presumption that parole release will be granted, and that this in turn creates a legitimate expectation of release absent the requisite finding that one of the justifications for deferral exists.

   "We can accept respondents' view that the expectancy of release provided in this statute is entitled to some measure of constitutional protection.

2. "Here, as we noted previously, the Parole Board's decision is subjective in part and predictive in part. Like most parole statutes, it vests very broad discretion in the Board. No ideal, error-free way to make parole-release decisions has been developed; the whole question has been and will continue to be the subject of experimentation involving analysis of psychological

factors combined with fact evaluation guided by the practical experience of the actual parole decisionmakers in predicting future behavior. Our system of federalism encourages this state experimentation. If parole determinations are encumbered by procedures that states regard as burdensome and unwarranted, they may abandon or curtail parole.

"At the Board's initial interview hearing, the inmate is permitted to appear before the Board and present letters and statements on his own behalf. He is thereby provided with an effective opportunity first, to insure that the records before the Board are in fact the records relating to his case; and second, to present any special considerations that demonstrate why he is an appropriate candidate for parole. Since the decision is one that must be made largely on the basis of the inmates' files, this procedure adequately safeguards against serious risks of error and thus satisfies due process.

"Next, we find nothing in the due process concepts as they have thus far evolved that requires the Parole Board to specify the particular 'evidence' in the inmate's file or at his interview on which it rests the discretionary determination that an inmate is not ready for conditional release. The Board communicates the reason for its denial as a guide to the inmate for his future behavior.

3. "The Nebraska procedure affords an opportunity to be heard, and when parole is denied it informs the inmate in what respects he falls short of qualifying for parole; this affords the process that is due under these circumstances. The Constitution does not require more."

CASE SIGNIFICANCE: This case is perhaps the most significant parole case decided thus far by the Supreme Court. The inmates argued that they were entitled to due process rights in the determination of whether to release an inmate on parole. In the absence of such a constitutional right, they alternatively argued that the provisions of the Nebraska law created such a right.

The Court held that they were not entitled under the Constitution to due process in the decision of whether to release on parole. However, they were nonetheless entitled to some type of due process because of the wording of the Nebraska law. The wording of the Nebraska statute established a right (a state-created liberty interest protected by the Fourteenth Amendment) to due process where otherwise none was given by the Constitution. Having said that, however, the Court then held that the rights given under Nebraska law (see the facts above) were sufficient to comply with the due process requirement. In short, the inmates won the battle but lost the war.

The Court in this case laid down three important constitutional principles on the granting or non-granting of parole:

1. "There is no constitutional or inherent right of a convicted person to be conditionally released before the expiration of a valid sentence." Simply stated, parole is a privilege and not a right, and thus may be granted or withheld by the state.

2. "A state may, as Nebraska has, establish a parole system, but it has no duty to do so." This means that parole is optional with the state. If a state wants to abolish parole it may do so without violating the constitutional rights of inmates. Again, parole is a privilege and not a right.

3. "There is a crucial distinction between being deprived of a liberty one has, as in parole, and being denied a conditional liberty one desires." The Court said this in response to inmate claims that parole release should be protected by the same due process rights given to parole revocation in *Morrissey v. Brewer*, 408 U.S. 471 (1972). The Court rejected such claim by articulating the distinction between parole revocation ("being deprived of a liberty one has") and parole release ("being denied a conditional liberty that one desires").

This case also illustrates the concept of the "state-created liberty interest." This is an often-misunderstood concept that means that the constitutional right to due process may be given because of the way a state words its law or policy. The concept of the "state-created liberty interest" is best stated this way: "Where the government theoretically has complete discretion in a matter, but chooses, through statute, administrative rule, policy or similar sort of document, to limit its discretion in some way, then the state must follow some sort of procedural steps (due process) to assure that it is making the decision consistent with the limitations it has imposed on itself" (*Legal Responsibility and Authority of Correctional Officers*. American Correctional Association, 1987, at 40).

Greenholtz is a good illustration of the "state-created liberty interest" concept because the inmates argued that even if they were not entitled to due process under the Constitution, the way the Nebraska statute was worded created a "protectible expectation of parole." The section of the Nebraska law on which the inmates relied was worded as follows:

Whenever the Board of Parole considers the release of a committed offender who is eligible for release on parole, it shall order his release unless it is of the opinion that his release should be deferred because:

(a) There is a substantial risk that he will not conform to the conditions of parole;

(b) His release would depreciate the seriousness of his crime or promote disrespect for law;

(c) His release would have a substantially adverse effect on institutional discipline; or

(d) His continued correctional treatment, medical care, or vocational or other training in the facility will substantially enhance his capacity to lead a law-abiding life when released at a later date. (Nebraska Revised Statutes, § 88–1, 114 (1).)

The Supreme Court agreed that the above provision, as worded, created a due process right for the inmates, but the Court quickly added that the provisions of the Nebraska law (which gave inmates certain rights at the initial review hearing and the final hearing) complied with due process requirements, therefore the inmates did not have any legal basis on which to base their claim of a denial of due process.

MARTINEZ V. CALIFORNIA
444 U.S. 277 (1980)

CAPSULE: A California law exempting parole officers from civil liability under California law is valid. Parole board members are not liable for the death of a person killed five months after the parolee's release. The Court did not decide whether state law can be used to defeat a civil liability claim under federal law against the same state officials.

FACTS: A parolee, Thomas, was convicted of rape in 1969 and sentenced to a term of one to 20 years, with a recommendation that he not be paroled. Prior to being sentenced to prison, Thomas had been committed to a state mental hospital as a "Mentally Disordered Sex Offender not amenable to treatment." After having served only five years, Thomas was paroled to the care of his mother. The California parole authorities were aware of Thomas's history and the likelihood that he would commit another violent crime. Five months after his release, Thomas tortured and killed a 15-year-old girl. The girl's survivors brought suit against state officials seeking damages under state law and 42 U.S.C. § 1983, claiming that the state's action in releasing Thomas subjected the deceased to a deprivation of her life without due process of law.

ISSUES:

1. Are parole board officials liable under California law for the death of a person killed by a parolee five months after the parolee's release? NO.
2. Are parole board officials liable under federal law (42 U.S.C. § 1983) for the death of a person killed by a parolee five months after parolee's release? NO.

HOLDINGS:

1. Parole officials are not liable under California law for the death because state statute provides that "neither a public entity nor a public employee is liable for any injury resulting from determining whether to parole or release a prisoner or from determining the terms or conditions of his parole or release or from determining whether to revoke his parole or release." Such statute is constitutional and did not deprive the deceased of her right to due process.
2. Parole officials are not liable under federal law (42 U.S.C. § 1983) because the action of the parolee, which took place five months after his release, could not be characterized as "state action," which is a requirement for liability under federal law.

REASON: "Like the California courts, we cannot accept the contention that this statute deprived Thomas's victim of her life without due process of law because it condoned a parole decision that led indirectly to her death. The statute neither authorized nor immunized the deliberate killing of any human being. It is not the equivalent of a death penalty statute which expressly authorizes state agents to take a person's life after prescribed procedures have been observed. This statute merely provides a defense to potential state tort-law liability. At most, the availability of such a defense may have encouraged members of the parole board to take somewhat greater risks of recidivism in exercising their authority to release prisoners than they otherwise might. But the basic risk that repeat offenses may occur is always present in any parole system. A legislative decision that has an incremental impact on the probability that death will result in any given situation—such as setting the speed limit at 55 miles per hour instead of 45—cannot be characterized as state action depriving a person of life just because it may set in motion a chain of events that ultimately leads to the random death of an innocent bystander. "Her life was taken by the parolee five months after his release. He was in no sense an agent of the parole board. Cf. *Scheuer v. Rhodes*, 416 U.S. 232. Further, the parole board was not aware that appellants' decedent, as distinguished from the public at large, faced any special danger. We need not and do not decide that a parole officer could never be deemed to 'deprive' someone of life by action taken in connection with the release of a prisoner on parole. But we do hold that at least under the particular circumstances of this parole decision, appellants' decedent's death is too remote a consequence of the parole officers' action to hold them responsible under the federal civil rights law."

CASE SIGNIFICANCE: This is a civil liability case in which the family members of a murder victim sought monetary damages from state officials for their decision to parole a prisoner, alleging that the state officials were aware of the inmate's violent nature prior to release and were directly responsible for the parolee's act.

The Court addressed two issues. The first issue concerned the constitutionality of a state statute that exempts parole officials from liability in job-related decisions. The family members argued that such a law was unconstitutional when applied to defeat a tort claim arising under state law. The Court disagreed, saying that the law, which merely provides a defense to potential state tort law liability, did not deprive the 15-year-old girl of her life without due process of law. The Court said that the statute was rational and justified "because the California Legislature could reasonably conclude that judicial review of parole decisions 'would inevitably inhibit the exercise of discretion' and that this inhibiting effect could impair the state's ability to implement a parole program designed to promote rehabilitation of inmates as well as security within prisons by holding out a promise of potential rewards."

As to the second issue of possible liability under federal law (42 U.S.C. § 1983), the Court did not address that issue head-on, stating instead that "although the decision to release Thomas from prison was action by the State, the action of Thomas five months later cannot be fairly characterized as state action." In view of this, the Court refused to decide whether the victim was deprived of a right secured by the Constitution and laws of the United States (a requirement for recovery under federal law). There are two requirements for a § 1983 lawsuit to succeed: (1) the officer must have been acting under color of law (referring to some type of state action or state involvement), and (2) there must have been a violation of a constitutional right or of a right given by federal (not state) law. In this case the action of the parolee five months after release could not be attributed to the state and thus precluded recovery of damages.

The Court did not decide the issue of whether state officials can be protected from liability under federal law by a state law, such as the above, exempting state officials from liability both under state and federal law. Had the Court decided this issue, it would likely have held that such a state law would not protect state officials from liability under federal law because an established principle of law states that in case of a conflict between state law (providing exemption from liability) and federal law (holding officials liable), federal law prevails. Federal law creating civil liability supersedes state law granting immunity to state officials.

JAGO V. VAN CUREN
454 U.S. 14 (1981)

CAPSULE: An inmate does not have a due process right in the decision by a parole board to withdraw parole prior to the inmate's release.

FACTS: Van Curen pleaded guilty to a charge of embezzlement and was sentenced to not less than six nor more than 100 years in prison. Under Ohio law, he would have been eligible for parole in March 1976. In 1974, however, Ohio enacted a "shock parole" statute that provided for the early parole of first-time offenders who had served more than six months in prison for nonviolent offenses. Under this program, Van Curen was interviewed in 1974 by a panel representing the Ohio Adult Parole Authority. This panel recommended that Van Curen be paroled "on or after April 23, 1974." The parole authority approved the recommendation and the inmate was notified of its decision. Several days after Van Curen was interviewed, the Ohio Adult Parole Authority was informed that he had not been truthful during his interview nor in the parole plan that he submitted to his parole officers. Van Curen had told the panel that he had embezzled $1 million when in fact he had embezzled $6 million. In his parole plan, Van Curen stated that he would be living with his half-brother if paroled; it was discovered that Van Curen actually intended to live with his homosexual lover. The parole authorities rescinded the early parole decision as a result of these revelations and, at a later meeting, formally denied Van Curen parole. At no time was Van Curen granted a hearing to explain the false statements he had given the parole authorities. He brought suit against the Ohio Adult Parole Authority, claiming that the rescission of parole without a hearing violated his constitutional right to due process.

ISSUE: Does a parolee have the right to be heard in a parole rescission (withdrawal of parole prior to inmate release) proceeding? NO.

HOLDING: The due process clause of the Fourteenth Amendment does not guarantee a hearing on the rescission of parole, nor did the Ohio statute create any protected "liberty" interest in early parole.

REASON: "We do not doubt that respondent suffered 'grievous loss' upon OAPA's rescission of his parole. But we have previously '[rejected] . . . the notion that any grievous loss visited upon a person by the State is sufficient to invoke the procedural protections of the Due Process Clause.' In this case, as in our previous cases, '[t]he question is not merely the weight of the individual's interest, but whether the nature of the interest is one within the contemplation of the liberty or property language of the Fourteenth Amendment.' *Morrissey v. Brewer*, 408 U.S. 471, 481 (1972).

"We would severely restrict the necessary flexibility of prison administrators and parole authorities were we to hold that any one of their myriad decisions with respect to individual inmates may, as under the general law of contracts, give rise to protected 'liberty' interests which could not thereafter be impaired without a constitutionally mandated hearing under the Due Process Clause."

CASE SIGNIFICANCE: In *Morrissey v. Brewer*, 408 U.S. 471 (1972), the Court ruled that state parole statutes would have to be examined individually on the question of whether they created a protected "liberty" interest. The Court held that the Ohio statute created no such liberty interest, thus no process was required prior to parole rescission.

Parole decisions in Ohio are solely at the discretion of the state's parole authorities. Van Curen lied to the board during his interview and in the parole plan submitted to his parole officer. The Court ruled that the parole board was within its authority to rescind its earlier decision to parole Van Curen on the basis of his false statements and there were no due process violations in not providing Van Curen a hearing in which he could explain his actions. He was not entitled to a hearing, either under the Constitution or Ohio law, prior to being released on parole. The fact that he was scheduled for parole, but prior to actual release the board's decision was rescinded because of Van Curen's false statements, did not give Van Curen any constitutional right to a hearing. In effect, the Court said that parole rescission prior to release is not equivalent to parole revocation, in which due process rights must be given because of consequent "grievous loss" of liberty.

It is evident from this decision that the Court considers parole rescission to be in the same legal category as the decision to grant parole or not to grant parole, rather than the decision to revoke parole.

CONNECTICUT BOARD OF PARDONS V. DUMSCHAT
452 U.S. 458 (1981)

CAPSULE: Prior actions of the Board of Pardons in granting commutation of life sentences created no right or entitlement to commutation. Inmates are not constitutionally entitled to reasons from the Board for rejecting their application for parole or commutation.

FACTS: Dumschat was sentenced to life imprisonment for murder in 1964. Under Connecticut law, he was not eligible for parole until December 1983. In Connecticut, the Board of Pardons had the authority to commute the sentences of life inmates by reducing the minimum prison term, thus accelerating eligibility for parole. Dumschat applied several times for a commutation of his sentence.

The Board rejected each application without explanation. Dumschat sued the Board of Pardons under 42 U.S.C. § 1983, alleging that the Board's failure to provide him with a written statement of reasons for denying commutation violated his rights guaranteed by the due process clause of the Fourteenth Amendment. Relying mainly on the fact that in the past the board had granted approximately three-fourths of all applications for commutation of life sentences, the federal district court held that all prisoners serving life sentences in Connecticut state prisons have a constitutionally protected "entitlement" to a statement of reasons why commutation is not granted if their applications are denied.

ISSUE: Did the fact that the Connecticut Board of Pardons had, in the past, granted approximately three-fourths of the applications for commutation of life sentences create a constitutional "liberty interest" or "entitlement" in life-term inmates so as to require the board to explain its reasons for denying an application for commutation? NO.

HOLDING: The mere existence of a power vested in the Connecticut Board of Pardons to commute sentences under state statute and the granting of commutation to many inmates confers no right or "entitlement" to inmates beyond the right to seek commutation. The Board did not have to give reasons for denying the applications.

REASON: "In terms of the Due Process Clause, a Connecticut felon's expectation that a lawfully imposed sentence will be commuted or that he will be pardoned is no more substantial than an inmate's expectation, for example, that he will be transferred to another prison; it is simply a unilateral hope.

"The Court of Appeals correctly recognized that Connecticut has conferred 'unfettered discretion' on its Board of Pardons, but—paradoxically—then proceeded to fetter the Board with a halter of constitutional 'entitlement.' The statute imposes no limit on what procedure is to be followed, what evidence may be considered, or what criteria are to be applied by the Board. Respondents challenge the Board's procedure precisely because of 'the absence of any apparent standards.' Brief for Respondents 28. We agree that there are no explicit standards by way of statute, regulation, or otherwise.

"This contrasts dramatically with the Nebraska statutory procedures in Greenholtz, which expressly mandated that the Nebraska Board of Parole 'shall' order an inmate's release 'unless' it decided that one of four specified reasons for denial was applicable. 442 U.S., at 11. The Connecticut statute, having no definitions, no criteria, and no mandated "shalls," creates no analogous duty or constitutional entitlement."

CASE SIGNIFICANCE: In this case, the inmate argued that the fact that in the past the board had granted approximately three-fourths of all applications for commutation of life sentences meant that a constitutional "entitlement" had been created by such practice so that inmates were now entitled to know the reasons for the rejection of their applications for commutation. The Court disagreed, saying that "no matter how frequently a particular form of clemency has been granted, the statistical probabilities generate no constitutional protections." This means that board or agency practice never rises to the level of a constitutional right and therefore parole boards may engage in release practices without having to be concerned that what they do may create a constitutional right that will limit their actions in the future.

Inmates are not constitutionally entitled to reasons from the board for rejecting their application for parole or commutation of sentence. This is because the decision to grant parole or commutation is discretionary with the board. Parole is not a right, but a privilege that may be given or withheld by the state.

CALIFORNIA DEPARTMENT OF CORRECTIONS V. MORALES
514 U.S. 499 (1995)

CAPSULE: A law decreasing the frequency of parole hearings for certain prisoners does not change the punishment for crimes already committed and, therefore, may be applied retrospectively without violating the ex post facto clause of the Constitution.

FACTS: Morales was twice convicted of murder, once in 1971 and once in 1980. In 1980 he was sentenced to a term of 15 years to life, but became eligible for parole beginning in 1990. In 1989 he had a hearing before the California Board of Prison Terms to determine his suitability for parole, in accordance with state law. At that time he was found to be unsuitable for parole for numerous reasons.

Under state law at the time Morales committed his second murder, he would have been entitled to subsequent suitability hearings on an annual basis. However, in 1981, the California legislature authorized the Board to defer subsequent suitability hearings for up to three years if the prisoner had been convicted of more than one offense that involved the taking of a life and the Board found that it was not reasonable to expect that parole would be granted at a hearing during the following years and it stated the bases for the finding. The Board determined the above conditions in Morales' case and scheduled his next hearing for 1992. Morales filed a federal habeas corpus petition in U.S. District Court alleging that he was being held in custody in violation of the ex post facto clause of the Constitution.

ISSUE: Does the 1981 amendment to the California statutes in effect increase the punishment attached to Morales' crime, in violation of the ex post facto clause of the Constitution? NO.

HOLDING: Application of the new California parole law to prisoners who committed their crimes before it was enacted does not violate the ex post facto clause of the Constitution.

REASON: "The amendment did not increase the 'punishment' attached to the respondent's crime. It left untouched his indeterminate sentence and the substantive formula for securing any reductions to the sentencing range. By introducing the possibility that the Board would not have to hold another parole hearing in the year or two after the initial hearing, the amendment simply alters the method to be followed in fixing a parole release date under identical substantive standards.

"Under respondent's expansive view, the Clause would forbid any legislative change that has any conceivable risk of affecting a prisoner's punishment. In contrast, this Court has long held that the question of what legislative adjustments are of sufficient moment to transgress the constitutional prohibition must be a matter of degree, and has declined to articulate a single 'formula' for making this determination. There is no need to do so here, either, since the amendment creates only the most speculative and attenuated possibility of increasing the measure of punishment for covered crimes, and such conjectural effects are insufficient under any threshold that might be established under the Clause. This amendment applies only to those who have taken more than one life, a class of prisoners for whom the likelihood of release on parole is quite remote. In addition, it affects the timing only of subsequent hearings, and does so only when the Board makes specific findings in the first hearing. Moreover, the Board has the authority to tailor the frequency of subsequent hearings."

CASE SIGNIFICANCE: This case decided that the then-new California parole law did not violate the ex post facto clause of the Constitution and therefore could be applied retrospectively. The new law merely altered the former system of mandatory annual parole hearings by providing the following: It "allowed the parole board, after it finds a prisoner unsuitable for parole at his initial hearing, to defer subsequent hearings for up to three years if the prisoner has been convicted of more than one offense involving the taking of life and the board determines that it is not reasonable to expect that the prisoner would be granted parole at a hearing within the intervening period, and the board states its reasons for that determination."

The Court held that this was not an ex post facto law because it merely decreased the frequency of parole hearings for certain prisoners. It did not change the punishment for crimes already committed, which in this case was 15 years to life. The purpose of the law was merely "to relieve the board of the need to conduct futile hearings for prisoners it determined had no reasonable chance for parole." As such, it may be applied retrospectively without running afoul of the ex post facto provision of the Constitution.

LYNCE V. MATHIS
519 U.S. 433 (1997)

CAPSULE: A Florida statute canceling an inmate's provisional release is ex post facto if applied to a prisoner who was convicted before the law was in effect.

FACTS: Lynce was convicted of attempted murder in 1986 and sentenced to 22 years in a Florida prison. He was released in 1992 based on the Department of Corrections' determination that he had accumulated five different types of early release credits totaling 5,668 days, 1,860 of which were provisional credits given as a result of prison overcrowding.

After the prisoner was released, the Florida State Attorney General issued an opinion that a 1992 statute retroactively canceled all provisional credits awarded to inmates convicted of murder or attempted murder. Lynce was rearrested and returned to custody. He filed a petition for a writ of habeas corpus, alleging that the retroactive cancellation of provisional credits violated the ex post facto clause of the Constitution.

ISSUE: Does the 1992 Florida statute canceling provisional credits for certain classes of offenders after they have been awarded violate the ex post facto clause of the Constitution? YES.

HOLDING: The 1992 Florida statute canceling provisional release credits for certain classes of offenders after they have been awarded violates the ex post facto clause of the Constitution.

REASON: "To fall within the ex post facto prohibition, a law must be retrospective—that is, 'it must apply to events occurring before its enactment'— and it 'must disadvantage the offender affected by it' . . . by altering the definition of criminal conduct or increasing the punishment for the crime, see *Collins v. Youngblood*, 497 U.S. 37, 50 (1990). In this case, the operation of the 1992 statute to effect the cancellation of overcrowding credits and the consequent reincarceration of petitioner was clearly retrospective. The narrow issue that we must decide upon is thus whether those consequences disadvantaged petitioner by increasing his punishment.

"Respondents also argue that the retroactive cancellation of overcrowding credits is permissible because overcrowding gain-time—unlike the incentive gain-time at issue in *Weaver*, which is used to encourage good prison behavior and prison rehabilitation—'b[ears] no relationship to the original penalty assigned the crime or the actual penalty calculated under the sentencing guidelines' . . . As we recognized in *Weaver*, retroactive alteration of parole or early release provisions, like the retroactive application of provisions that govern initial sentencing, implicates the ex post facto clause because such credits are 'one determinant of petitioner's prison term . . . and . . . [the petitioner's] effective sentence is altered once this determinant is changed.' Ibid. We explained in *Weaver* that the removal of such provisions can constitute an increase in punishment . . .

"In this case, unlike in *Morales*, the actual course of events makes it unnecessary to speculate about what might have happened. The 1992 statute has unquestionably disadvantaged the petitioner because it resulted in his rearrest and prolonged his imprisonment. Unlike the California amendment at issue in *Morales*, the 1992 Florida statute did more than simply remove a mechanism that created an opportunity for early release for a class of prisoners whose release was unlikely; rather, it made ineligible for early release a class of prisoners who were previously eligible—including some, like petitioner, who had actually been released."

CASE SIGNIFICANCE: This case prohibits the retroactive application of laws that disadvantage an inmate when obtaining parole. Parole is a privilege, thus it may be granted or withheld by the state. Once granted, however, it becomes an entitlement, meaning it cannot be taken away without giving the inmate certain basic due process guarantees.

This case addresses a slightly different issue: may a state take away early-release credits through a statute that cancels provisional credits awarded to inmates convicted of and already serving time? The Court said no, saying that such a statute violates the ex post facto clause when applied to an inmate who had already earned the credits before the law was passed. The law could be applied to inmates who had not yet earned the credits, but not to inmates who had already earned them.

The Constitution prohibits the enactment of ex post facto laws. An ex post facto law is a law passed after the occurrence of a fact or commission of an act, which retrospectively changes the legal consequences or relations of such fact or deed.

This case is significant because it limits the impact of newly enacted restrictive parole laws on inmates. The public has become suspicious of parole and wants to limit it. That can be done, but any new restrictive law would apply only to inmates who have not as yet earned parole credits. It cannot apply to inmates who have already earned such credits under an earlier and more liberal law.

This case differs from *California Department of Corrections v. Morales*, 514 U.S. 499 (1995), in that the *Morales* case merely involved a procedure whereby an inmate was considered for parole by providing that the parole hearing could be deferred for up to three years instead of a mandatory annual parole hearing. *Morales* did not affect the length of the punishment being served. In contrast, in *Lynce*, prison time was in effect extended by the statute that retroactively canceled all provisional credits the inmate had already earned.

YOUNG V. HARPER
520 U.S. 143 (1997)

CAPSULE: Oklahoma's pre-parole release program was equivalent to parole and therefore released prisoners under pre-parole were entitled to due process rights prior to being brought back to prison.

FACTS: The State of Oklahoma has a Pre-parole Conditional Supervision Program. That is, when Oklahoma's prisons become overcrowded, the Pardon and Parole Board is authorized to conditionally release prisoners before the expiration of their sentences. Upon the determination of the Board, an inmate could be placed on pre-parole after serving 15 percent of his or her sentence. An inmate became eligible for parole only after one-third of his sentence had elapsed. The Governor granted parole on the Board's recommendation. Both Program participants and parolees were released subject to similar constraints. The Board reviewed Harper's criminal record and prison conduct and simultaneously recommended him for parole and released him under the pre-parole program. At the time, he had served 15 years of a life sentence. After five months of Pre-parole Program release, the

Governor denied Harper's parole. On March 14, 1991, he was ordered by his parole officer to report back to prison, which he did.

ISSUE: Is Oklahoma's Pre-parole Conditional Supervision Program sufficiently like parole as to be protected under the Fourteenth Amendment? YES.

HOLDING: The Oklahoma Pre-Parole Program in existence when respondent was released was equivalent to parole; therefore, the offender on pre-parole must be given the rights granted in *Morrissey v. Brewer* prior to revocation.

REASON: "The essence of parole is release from prison, before the completion of sentence, on the condition that the prisoner abide by certain rules during the balance of the sentence." *Morrissey*, 408 U.S., at 477. In *Morrissey*, we described the 'nature of the interest of the parolee in his continued liberty: [H]e can be gainfully employed and is free to be with family and friends and to form the other enduring attachments of normal life. Though the State properly subjects him to many restrictions not applicable to other citizens, his condition is very different from that of confinement in a prison. . . . The parolee has relied on at least an implicit promise that parole will be revoked only if he fails to live up to the parole conditions.'

"This passage could just as easily have applied to respondent while he was on pre-parole. In compliance with state procedures, he was released from prison before the expiration of his sentence. He kept his own residence; he sought, obtained, and maintained a job; and he lived a life generally free from the incidents of imprisonment. To be sure, respondent's liberty was not unlimited. He was not permitted to use alcohol, to incur other than educational debt, or to travel outside the county without permission. And he was required to report regularly to a parole officer. The liberty of a parolee is similarly limited, but that did not in *Morrissey*, 408 U.S., at 478, render such liberty beyond procedural protection."

"Petitioners do not ask us to revisit *Morrissey*; they merely dispute that pre-parole falls within its compass. Our inquiry, they argue, should be controlled instead by *Meachum v. Fano*, 427 U.S. 215 (1976). There, we determined that the interest of a prisoner in avoiding an intrastate prison transfer was 'too ephemeral and insubstantial to trigger procedural due process protections as long as prison officials have discretion to transfer him for whatever reason or for no reason at all.' Petitioners contend that reincarceration of a pre-parolee was nothing more than a transfe[r] to a higher degree of confinement' or a 'classification to a more supervised prison environment,' Brief for Petitioners 18, which, like transfers within a prison setting, involved a liberty interest."

CASE SIGNIFICANCE: This case dealt with the issue of whether the pre-parole release program used in the State of Oklahoma to relieve prison overcrowding was equivalent to parole. If so, then inmates who were released under the program were entitled to the procedural protections mandated by the Court in *Morrissey v. Brewer*, 408 U.S. 471 (1972). The Court said yes, holding that due process protections were needed prior to the inmate's being brought back to prison.

In this case, an inmate was released by the Oklahoma Pardon and Parole Board, but was denied parole by the Governor five "uneventful months later." He was ordered back to prison without being given due process rights, the assumption being he was still a prisoner and, technically, was not on parole.

Morrissey v. Brewer, 408 U.S. 471 (1972), provides that the following due process rights be given a parolee before parole is revoked:

1. Preliminary and final revocation hearings;
2. Written notice of the alleged parole violation;
3. Disclosure to the parolee of the evidence of violation;
4. Opportunity to be heard in person and to present evidence as well as witnesses;
5. Right to confront and cross-examine adverse witnesses, unless good cause can be shown for not allowing this confrontation;
6. Right to judgment by a detached and neutral hearing body; and
7. Written statement of reasons for revoking parole, as well as of the evidence used in arriving at that decision.

The Court concluded that there was no significant difference between pre-parole and parole under Oklahoma procedures, therefore the *Morrissey* due process requirements are needed when revoking parolees who are on pre-parole.

PENNSYLVANIA BOARD OF PROBATION AND PAROLE V. SCOTT

524 U.S. 357 (1998)

CAPSULE: The Fourth Amendment does not require the application of the exclusionary rule in parole revocation hearings.

FACTS: Scott pleaded nolo contendere to a charge of third-degree murder and was sentenced to 10 to 20 years in prison. Ten years later, Scott was released on parole. One of his parole conditions was that he would not own or possess any firearm or weapon. The parole agreement he signed included consent to search his person, property, and residence without a warrant by agents of the Pennsylvania Board of Probation and Parole. Any items ever found in Scott's possession that constituted a violation of parole were subject to seizure and could be used as evidence in the parole revocation process. About five months later, an arrest warrant was obtained and Scott was arrested based on evidence that he possessed firearms, had consumed alcohol, and had assaulted a co-worker. After the arrest, the parole officers, without a warrant, searched the home he shared with his mother where they found five firearms, a compound bow, and three arrows.

At his parole violation hearing, Scott objected to the introduction of the evidence found during the search of his home on the ground that the search by the parole officers, which led to the discovery of the five firearms, bow, and arrows, was unreasonable because they did not have a warrant and lacked probable cause. The objection was rejected and Scott was recommitted to prison to serve 36 months back time.

ISSUE: Does the Fourth Amendment require the application of the exclusionary rule in parole revocation hearings? NO.

HOLDING: The Fourth Amendment does not require the application of the exclusionary rule in parole revocation hearings. The rule would apply, however, in a subsequent criminal trial for offenses committed while on parole, if police officers conduct an illegal search of a parolee's person or premises.

REASON: "We have emphasized repeatedly that the State's use of evidence obtained in violation of the Fourth Amendment does not itself violate the Constitution. See, e.g., *United States v. Leon*, 468 U.S. 897, 906 (1984); *Stone v. Powell*, 428 U.S. 465, 482, 486 (1976). Rather, a Fourth Amendment violation is "fully accomplished" by the illegal search or seizure, and no exclusion of evidence from a judicial or administrative proceeding can "cure the invasion of the defendant's rights which he has already suffered." *United States v. Leon*, *supra*, at 906 (quoting *Stone v. Powell*, *supra*, at 540 (White, J., dissenting)). The exclusionary rule is instead a judicially created means of deterring illegal searches and seizures. *United States v. Calandra*, 414 U.S. 338 (1974). As such, the rule does not 'proscribe the introduction of illegally seized evidence in all proceedings or against all persons, *Stone v. Powell*, *supra* at 486, but applies only in contexts 'where its remedial objectives are thought most efficaciously served,' *United States v. Calandra*, *supra*, at 348; see also *United States v. Janis*, 428 U.S. 433, 454 (1976) ('If . . . the exclusionary rule does not result in appreciable deterrence, then, clearly, its use in the instant situation is unwarranted'). Moreover, because the rule is prudential rather than constitutionally mandated, we have held it to be applicable only where its deterrence benefits outweigh its 'substantial social costs.' *United States v. Leon*, 468 U.S., at 907.

"Recognizing these costs, we have repeatedly declined to extend the exclusionary rule to proceedings other than criminal trials. Id., at 909; *United States v. Janis*, *supra*, at 447. For example, in *United States v. Calandra*, we held that the exclusionary rule does not apply to grand jury proceedings; in so doing, we emphasized that such proceedings play a special role in the law enforcement process and that the traditionally flexible, nonadversarial nature of those proceedings would be jeopardized by application of the rule. 414 U.S., at 343–346, 349–350. Likewise, in *United States v. Janis*, we held that the exclusionary rule did not bar the introduction of unconstitutionally obtained evidence in a civil tax proceeding because the costs of excluding relevant and reliable evidence would outweigh the marginal deterrence benefits, which, we noted, would be minimal because the use of the exclusionary rule in criminal trials already deterred illegal searches. 428 U.S., at 448, 454. Finally, in *INS v. Lopez-Mendoza*, 468 U.S. 1032 (1984), we refused to extend the exclusionary rule to civil deportation proceedings, citing the high social costs of allowing an immigrant to remain illegally in this country and noting the incompatibility of the rule with the civil, administrative nature of those proceedings. Id., at 1050.

"As in *Calandra*, *Janis*, and *Lopez-Mendoza*, we are asked to extend the operation of the exclusionary rule beyond the criminal trial context. We again decline to do so. Application of the exclusionary rule would both hinder the functioning of state parole systems and alter the traditionally flexible, administrative nature of parole revocation proceedings. The rule would provide only minimal deterrence benefits in this context, because application of the rule in the criminal trial context already provides significant deterrence of unconstitutional searches. We therefore hold that the federal exclusionary rule does not bar the introduction at parole revocation hearings of evidence seized in violation of a parolee's Fourth Amendment rights."

CASE SIGNIFICANCE: The exclusionary rule provides that evidence obtained by the police in violation of the Fourth Amendment prohibition against unreasonable searches and seizures is not admissible in a criminal proceeding.

In this case, the parolee claimed that the evidence used against him in the parole revocation proceeding was obtained by the parole officers illegally and therefore could not be used against him. The parolee alleged that the Fourth Amendment required that the evidence be excluded from the revocation hearing. The Court disagreed, saying that the exclusionary rule does not apply to proceedings other than criminal trials. Applying the rule to parole revocation proceedings "would both hinder the functioning of state parole systems and alter the traditionally flexible, administrative nature of parole revocation proceedings."

The Court did not say that the exclusionary rule cannot apply in any parole revocation proceeding. What it said instead was that the Fourth Amendment does not require its application in revocation cases. Therefore, illegally obtained evidence can be admitted if state law or parole board policy allows its admission. What the Court simply held is that if the state wants to admit illegally seized evidence during parole revocation proceedings, it may constitutionally do so; the Fourth Amendment does not require its exclusion.

GARNER V. JONES
529 U.S. 244 (2000)

CAPSULE: The Georgia law allowing reconsideration of life-term inmates who have been denied parole at least every eight years is valid. There is no ex post facto violation unless the prisoner can prove that the retroactive application of the new rule will result in longer incarceration.

FACTS: Jones began serving a life sentence for murder in 1974. He escaped from prison five years later and, after being a fugitive for more than two years, committed another murder. He was apprehended, convicted, and in 1982 was sentenced to a second life term in prison.

Under Georgia law, the State Board of Pardons and Parole (the Board) is required to consider inmates serving life sentences for parole after seven years. At the time Jones committed his second murder, the Board's rules required that they reconsider parole denials every three years. In 1985, after Jones began serving his second life term, the Board, acting under its authority, amended the rule to review reconsideration of life term inmates who have been denied parole at least every eight years. Jones was denied parole in 1989 and reconsideration was set for 1997, eight years later. The U.S. Court of Appeals held that retroactive application of the amended rule violated the ex post facto clause and Georgia, in order to comply with that decision, reconsidered Jones' case in 1992 and 1995. The Board denied parole in both instances, citing Jones' "multiple offenses" and the "circumstances and nature" of the second offense. In 1995, Georgia determined that the U.S. Court of Appeals erred based on a U.S. Supreme Court decision and resumed scheduling parole reconsiderations at least every eight years. At Jones' 1995 hearing, the Board set its next review for 2003.

ISSUE: Does the retroactive application of a Georgia law permitting the extension of intervals between parole considerations violate the ex post facto clause? NO.

HOLDING: The Georgia law is valid. There is no ex post facto violation unless the prisoner can prove that the retroactive application of the new rule will result in longer incarceration.

REASON: "Our recent decision in *Morales* is an appropriate beginning point. There a California statute changed the frequency of reconsideration for parole every year to up to every three years for prisoners convicted of more than one homicide. *Morales*, 514 U.S., at 503. We found no ex post facto violation, emphasizing that not every retroactive procedural change creating a risk of affecting an inmate's terms or conditions of confinement is prohibited. Id., at 508–509. The question is 'a matter of "degree."' Id., at 509 (quoting *Beazell*, *supra*, at 171). The controlling inquiry, we determined, was whether retroactive application of the change in California law created 'a significant risk of increasing the measure of punishment attached to the covered crimes.' 514 U.S., at 509.

"Our decision in *Morales* did not suggest all States must model their procedures governing consideration for parole after those of California to avoid offending the ex post facto clause. The analysis undertaken in *Morales* did identify factors which convinced us the amendment to California law created an insignificant risk of increased punishment for covered inmates. Our opinion was careful, however, not to adopt a single formula for identifying which legislative adjustments, in matters bearing on parole, would survive an ex post facto challenge. Id., at 509. We also observed that the ex post facto clause should not be employed for 'the micro-management of an endless array of legislative adjustments to parole and sentencing procedures.' Id., at 508. These remain important concerns. The States must have due flexibility in formulating parole procedures and addressing problems associated with confinement and release."

CASE SIGNIFICANCE: The prisoner in this case alleged that the new rule providing for parole consideration violated the ex post facto clause because it extended the period until he could again be considered for parole. When he was convicted, the rule required parole consideration every three years, but the rule was later changed to every eight years. Jones started serving his second life term in 1985. He was denied parole in 1989 and reconsideration was set for 1997— eight years later, in accordance with the new rule. He alleged that this new rule adversely affected him, therefore violating the prohibition against ex post facto laws.

An ex post facto law is a law "passed after the occurrence of a fact or commission of an act, which retrospectively changes the legal consequences or relations of such fact or deed." It is prohibited by Article I, sections 9 and 10, of the U.S. Constitution. The Supreme Court held that there was no ex post facto violation in this case, because there was no proof that the policy change was "certain" to result in increased punishment, which is the reason for the ex post facto prohibition. The question to be asked in ex post facto cases is: Does the new rule create a significant risk of increasing the measure of punishment attached to the crime? The Court answered no in this case and therefore the law was constitutional. In essence, the Court said that the change in the rule was merely procedural, not substantive, in that it did not result in "certain" increased punishment.

SAMSON V. CALIFORNIA
547 U.S. 843 (2006)

CAPSULE: Suspicionless searches of parolees by police officers is allowable under the Fourth Amendment.

FACTS: Samson was on parole in the State of California. A condition of parole in that state was the parolee's agreement, in writing, to allow searches and seizures by a parole officer or any other peace office, at any time, with or without a search warrant and with or without cause. A San Bruno police officer stopped Samson on the street, knowing that Samson was on parole. The officer also believed that Samson had an outstanding parole warrant, which he denied existed. The officer confirmed, via the radio, that Samson was on parole and that he had no outstanding warrants. However, the officer searched Samson based on his parole status. The officer found a box in Samson's breast pocket that contained methamphetamine.

Samson's motion to suppress this evidence was denied by the trial court, saying it was justified by the California law allowing searches and the determination that the search was neither arbitrary nor capricious. Samson was convicted and sentenced to seven years imprisonment. The California Court of Appeal affirmed the conviction, stating that the search was reasonable because it was not arbitrary, capricious, or harassing.

ISSUE: Does a suspicionless search of a parolee by a police officer violate the Fourth Amendment? NO.

HOLDING: A parolee has a diminished reasonable expectation of privacy under the Fourth Amendment. This allows suspicionless searches by police officers.

REASON: "'[U]nder our general Fourth Amendment approach' we 'examin[e] the totality of the circumstances' to determine whether a search is reasonable within the meaning of the Fourth Amendment . . . Whether a search is reasonable 'is determined by assessing, on the one hand, the degree to which it intrudes upon an individual's privacy and, on the other, the degree to which it is needed for the promotion of legitimate governmental interests' . . . We recently applied this approach in *United States v. Knights* . . . Because the search at issue in *Knights* was predicated on both the probation search condition and reasonable suspicion, we did not reach the question whether the search would have been reasonable under the Fourth Amendment had it been solely predicated upon the condition of probation. Id., at 120, n. 6. Our attention is directed to that question today, albeit in the context of a parolee search.

"Examining the totality of the circumstances pertaining to petitioner's status as a parolee, 'an established variation on imprisonment,' *Morrissey*, 408 U.S., at 477, including the plain terms of the parole search condition, we conclude that petitioner did not have an expectation of privacy that society would recognize as legitimate. The State's interests, by contrast, are substantial. This Court has repeatedly acknowledged that a State has an overwhelming interest in supervising parolees because 'parolees . . . are more likely to commit future criminal offenses.' *Pennsylvania Bd. of Probation and Parole*, 524 U.S., at 365 (explaining that the interest in combating recidivism 'is the very premise behind the system of close parole supervision'). Similarly, this Court has repeatedly acknowledged that a State's interests in reducing recidivism and thereby promoting reintegration and positive citizenship among probationers and parolees warrant privacy intrusions that would not otherwise be tolerated under the Fourth Amendment. See *Griffin*, 483 U.S., at 879; *Knights*, *supra*, at 121 . . . The concern that California's suspicionless search system gives officers unbridled discretion to conduct searches, thereby inflicting dignitary harms that arouse strong resentment in parolees and undermine their ability to reintegrate into productive society, is belied by California's prohibition on 'arbitrary, capricious or harassing' searches."

CASE SIGNIFICANCE: This case is interesting because it virtually says that parolees have no rights under the Fourth Amendment. The general rule is that police searches and seizures require probable cause and a warrant. Neither was present in this case. The officer admitted it was a suspicionless search and that the only reason he conducted the search was because he knew Samson was on parole. Samson claimed that a suspicionless search was unconstitutional even if he was a parolee. The Court decided in favor of the officer and held that the seizure of the methamphetamine found in Samson was valid and could be used as evidence in court.

The Court said that the suspicionless search was valid because "parolees, who are on the 'continuum' of state-imposed punishments, have fewer expectations of privacy than probationers, because parole is more akin to imprisonment than probation is." It added that an "inmate electing to complete his sentence out of physical custody remains in the Department of Corrections legal custody for the remainder of his term and must comply with the terms and conditions of his parole." In short, parolees are considered prisoners for purposes of the Fourth Amendment. Moreover, parolee Samson signed the parole order that allowed submission to a suspicionless search and was fully aware of that condition. Everything considered, Samson did not enjoy any expectation of privacy. By contrast, the State had reasons to supervise parolees properly because they commit a disproportionate number of crimes. Moreover, the need to reduce recidivism and to promote reintegration into society justified close supervision of parolees even if that means a limitation of their right against unreasonable searches and seizures.

Death Penalty

4

INTRODUCTION

The death penalty, although used for a long time in the United States, has generated a lot of cases in the United States Supreme Court only in the last four decades. In the early years, it was assumed that there was nothing constitutionally wrong with it and therefore executions took place without intervention from the courts. It was not until the early 1970s that the constitutionality of the death penalty drew attention from the Court. Prior to that time, the death penalty cases that reached the United States Supreme Court dealt more with the procedure for execution than with the constitutionality of the penalty itself. For example, in 1878, the Court found that execution by firing squad was not cruel and unusual (*Wilkerson v. Utah*, 99 U.S. 130 [1878]). And in 1890, death by electrocution was found not to be cruel and unusual punishment (*In re Kemmler*, 136 U.S. 436 [1890]).

Of the death penalty cases briefed here, the most important are *Furman v. Georgia* (1972) and *Gregg v. Georgia* (1976). In *Furman*, the Court said that the death penalty was unconstitutional because it violated two provisions of the Constitution: the equal protection clause and the prohibition against cruel and unusual punishment. After the *Furman* decision, 35 states and the federal government revised their capital punishment statutes to eliminate equal protection problems. Four years later, the Court in *Gregg* declared the death penalty constitutional.

The *Gregg* decision settled, by a seven-to-two vote, the issue of constitutionality of the death penalty. Since then, however, the Supreme Court continues to address death penalty issues. The Court is in the process of refining death penalty issues. Since *Gregg*, hardly a year passed without the Court addressing issues involving the death penalty. Death is different as a form of punishment because it is final and irreversible. It is not surprising, therefore, that the Court has given it a great deal of attention.

The more significant cases over the years are briefed in this chapter. Some issues address the constitutionality of statutes; others involve statutory interpretation. It is conceivable that the Court might at some future time change its mind and ban the death penalty altogether. The chances of that happening in the next decade, however, are remote, even if more liberal justices are appointed to the Court.

In the latter part of the twentieth century and the early years of the new millennium, the controversy over the death penalty shifted from the courts to state legislatures. As of the year 2014, 36 states and the federal government had death penalty laws. Lobby groups have intensified efforts to abolish the death penalty through repeal of death penalty laws in the various states. These efforts are fueled by humanitarian concerns, but have also received boosts from well-publicized releases of death row inmates whose innocence has been established by DNA findings.

In 2005, the United States Supreme Court decided *Roper v. Simmons*. That case revisited the issue of whether the death penalty for juveniles is constitutional. The Court, by a split vote, decided that executing offenders who are 16 or 17 years of age at the time the offense was committed is unconstitutional. Thus, the execution of offenders who commit crimes before reaching age 18 is now unconstitutional in the United States.

In 1996, the United States Congress passed the Anti-Terrorism and Effective Death Penalty Act, which limits the review through habeas proceedings of state convictions. The AEDPA has greatly curtailed the number of cases reaching federal courts, including death penalty cases. Prior to 1996, death row prisoners had ample access to federal courts, which had the effect of almost indefinitely postponing executions for as long as legal issues could be raised. This law hastens executions by limiting the number of habeas filings by a prisoner and providing a time limit for filing habeas cases.

The American public recoils at the prospect of executing an innocent person. There has been a slowdown in executions, doubtless a product of evolving times and the realization that some inmates on death row may, in fact, be innocent. This is fueled by the release in the last few years of death row inmates who were found innocent because of DNA evidence that disproved guilt. Interestingly, though, there has not been a single documented case of an innocent person who has been executed. There is simply the presumption that because DNA has led to the release of individuals on death row, innocent persons may have been executed in the history of the United States prior to the development of DNA technology.

Two of the most significant cases to have reached the United States Supreme Court are *Kennedy v. Louisiana* (554 U.S. 407 [2008]), and *Baze v. Rees* (553 U.S. 35 [2008]), both briefed in this chapter.

The *Kennedy* case is significant because the Court ruled that the death penalty as a sentence for the rape of a child violates the Eighth and Fourteenth Amendments. At the time, six states had laws allowing the death penalty as an option for this offense, and several states were considering enacting laws with this option. In this ruling, the Court confirmed that the death penalty should be a sentence given only when a death results, not any other action, including a child being raped.

Baze is the case that raised the issue of whether Kentucky's lethal injection procedure violated the Eighth Amendment prohibition against cruel and unusual punishment. Proponents and opponents of the death penalty either looked forward to or feared the decision in that case. Proponents hoped the Court would keep the penalty in place, perhaps constitutionally stronger; opponents hoped the Court would administer a final blow to the death penalty. The opinion turned out to be a disappointment to both sides, although in varying degrees. It held that Kentucky's lethal injection procedure did not constitute cruel and unusual punishment because it did not present a substantial or objectively intolerable risk of serious harm. Nonetheless, the Court left a small window for opponents of the death penalty when it said that "a State's refusal to adopt proffered alternative procedures may violate the Eighth Amendment only where the alternative procedure is feasible, readily implemented, and . . . significantly reduces a substantial risk of severe pain." Thus, the constitutionality of the death penalty is still a controversial issue in the United States and will likely remain so in the years to come.

More recently, there have been three important cases examined by the Court on the death penalty. In *Ryan v. Valencia-Gonzales*, 568 U.S. ___ (2013), it was ruled that, if an offender becomes incompetent during habeas corpus proceedings, it is constitutional to continue those proceedings without his or her input. Habeas corpus proceedings are based totally on the record, and actual assistance by the offender is not necessary. In 2014, the U.S. Supreme Court expanded on the *Atkins v. Virginia* (2002) ruling that held it was unconstitutional to execute a mentally retarded person. One of the significant discoveries in *Hall v. Florida*, 572 U.S. ___, is the Court's adoption of the medical field's designation of the "intellectually disabled" for this category of people. The Court also recognized that there is a margin of error that must be acknowledged when computing a person's IQ, and therefore a state cannot base a sentence of death for an offender solely on an IQ test. Additionally, in 2015, the Court examined Oklahoma's use of the drug midazolam in its execution protocol in the case of *Glossip v. Gross*, 576 U.S. ___. Relying on its decision in *Baze v. Rees* (2008), the Court ruled that the drug's use did not violate the cruel and unusual punishment clause of the Eighth Amendment.

A. HISTORY AND FOUNDATION CASES

LOUISIANA EX REL. FRANCIS V. RESWEBER
329 U.S. 459 (1947)

> **CAPSULE:** Carrying out an execution after a failed first attempt does not violate the Constitution.
>
> **FACTS:** Francis was convicted of murder and in 1945 was sentenced to death. Pursuant to a proper death warrant, Francis was placed in the official electric chair

of the state of Louisiana and received through his body a current of electricity intended to cause death. The execution attempt failed due to a mechanical defect in the electric chair. Francis was removed from the chair and returned to prison. A new death warrant was issued.

ISSUE: Is carrying out the execution of a criminal after a failed first attempt a violation of the Constitution? NO.

HOLDING: Carrying out the execution of a convicted murderer after the first execution attempt failed because of a mechanical defect in the electric chair does not constitute "double jeopardy," nor does it constitute "cruel and unusual punishment," and therefore it is not forbidden by the Constitution.

REASON: "Petitioner's suggestion is that because he once underwent the psychological strain of preparation for electrocution, now to require him to undergo this preparation again subjects him to a lingering or cruel and unusual punishment. Even the fact that petitioner has already been subjected to a current of electricity does not make his subsequent execution any more cruel in the constitutional sense than any other execution. The cruelty against which the Constitution protects a convicted man is cruelty inherent in the method of punishment, not the necessary suffering involved in any method employed to extinguish life humanely. The fact that an unforeseeable accident prevented the prompt consummation of the sentence cannot, it seems to us, add an element of cruelty to a subsequent execution."

CASE SIGNIFICANCE: This was the first case decided by the Supreme Court on the death penalty and it involved bizarre circumstances. The defendant was placed in the electric chair, received a current of electricity intended to cause death, but death did not occur due to a mechanical defect in the electric chair. He was returned to prison and given a new execution date. The defendant objected, claiming that the carrying out of a second execution attempt after a failed first attempt violated his protection from double jeopardy and cruel and unusual punishment.

The Court rejected both objections, holding that "when an accident, with no suggestion of malevolence, prevents the consummation of a sentence, the state's subsequent course in the administration of its criminal law is not affected on that account by any requirement of due process . . ." The Court added that it saw "no difference from a constitutional point of view between a new trial or error of law at the instance of the state that results in a death sentence instead of imprisonment for life and an execution that follows a failure of equipment." This statement refers to a case decided 10 years before (*Palko v. Connecticut*, 302 U.S. 319 [1937]), which held that the double jeopardy provision of the Fifth Amendment did not (at that time) apply to the states, thus Francis (a defendant in state court) was not protected by the due process guarantee.

As for the allegation of cruel and unusual punishment, the Court did not find the second attempt at execution as constituting a violation of this constitutional protection, saying that "even the fact that the petitioner has already been subjected to a current of electricity does not make his subsequent execution any more cruel in the constitutional sense than any other execution." The Court added that "the cruelty against which the Constitution protects a convicted man is cruelty inherent in the method of punishment, not the necessary suffering involved in any method employed to extinguish life humanely." In sum, the Court said that the taking of life does not itself constitute cruel and unusual punishment; what is prohibited instead is the method of punishment that may be cruel and unusual. It is ironic that the imposition of corporal punishment (such as public whipping) is considered cruel and unusual punishment, while the death penalty is not.

FURMAN V. GEORGIA
408 U.S. 238 (1972)

CAPSULE: The death penalty violates the equal protection clause of the Fourteenth Amendment and the prohibition against cruel and unusual punishment and is therefore unconstitutional.

FACTS: Furman attempted to enter a private home at night. He shot and killed the homeowner through a closed door. He was 26 years old and had a sixth-grade education. Prior to trial, Furman was committed to the Georgia Central State Hospital for a psychiatric examination on his plea of insanity. The hospital superintendent reported that the staff diagnosis concluded that "this patient should retain his present diagnosis of Mental Deficiency, Mild to Moderate, with Psychotic Episodes associated with Convulsive Disorder." The physicians added that although Furman was not psychotic at present, he was not capable of cooperating with his counsel in the preparation of his criminal defense and they believed he needed further treatment. The superintendent later amended the report by stating that Furman knew right from wrong and was capable of cooperating with counsel. Furman was tried and found guilty of the murder of the homeowner. A jury sentenced him to death.

ISSUE: Is the death penalty constitutional? NO.

HOLDING: The death penalty violates provisions of the Constitution, particularly the "equal protection" clause and the prohibition against "cruel and unusual punishment." (Note: This was overruled in 1976 by *Gregg v. Georgia*.)

REASON: "In a Nation committed to equal protection of the laws there is no permissible 'caste' aspect of law enforcement. Yet we know that the discretion of judges and juries in imposing the death penalty enables the penalty to be selectively applied, feeding prejudices against the accused if he is poor and despised, lacking political clout, or if he is a member of a suspect or unpopular minority, and saving those who by social position may be in a more protected position. In ancient Hindu law a Brahman was exempt from capital punishment, and in those days, '[g]enerally, in the law books, punishment increased in severity as social status diminished.' We have, I fear, taken in practice the same position, partially as a result of making the death penalty discretionary and partially as a result of the ability of the rich to purchase the services of the most respected and resourceful legal talent in the Nation."

CASE SIGNIFICANCE: For the first time, the Supreme Court in *Furman v. Georgia* declared the death penalty unconstitutional, based on two constitutional provisions: the equal protection clause and the prohibition against cruel and unusual punishment. Had the five justices based their decision solely on a violation of the cruel and unusual punishment clause, the death penalty could never have been imposed. Only two justices, however (Brennan and Marshall), used this provision, while the three others based their decision on the manner in which death penalties were being carried out. Their objection was not to the death penalty itself, but to the way it was being selectively enforced against the poor and the powerless, thus violating the equal protection clause.

GREGG V. GEORGIA
428 U.S. 153 (1976)

CAPSULE: Death penalty statutes that contain sufficient safeguards against arbitrary and capricious imposition are constitutional.

FACTS: While hitchhiking in Florida, Gregg and a companion were picked up by two motorists. The bodies of the two motorists were later found beside a road near Atlanta, Georgia. The next day Gregg and his companion were arrested. A .25 caliber pistol was found in Gregg's possession and subsequently identified as the murder weapon. Gregg confessed to the robberies and murders but claimed self-defense. He was found guilty of all four counts and was sentenced to death.

ISSUES:
1. Is the death penalty constitutional as a form of punishment? YES.
2. If the death penalty is constitutional, does the Georgia statute contain sufficient safeguards against arbitrary and capricious imposition? YES.

HOLDING:
1. The death penalty is constitutional as a form of punishment.
2. The Georgia law is constitutional because it contains sufficient safeguards against arbitrary and capricious imposition. (This case overrules *Furman v. Georgia*.)

REASON: "Four years ago, the petitioners in *Furman* and its companion cases predicated their argument primarily upon the asserted proposition that standards of decency had evolved to the point where capital punishment no longer could be tolerated. The petitioners in those cases said, in effect, that the evolutionary process had come to an end, and that standards of decency required that the Eighth Amendment be construed finally as prohibiting capital punishment for any crime regardless of its depravity and impact on society. This view was accepted by two Justices. Three other Justices were unwilling to go so far; focusing on the procedures by which convicted defendants were selected for the death penalty rather than on the actual punishment inflicted, they joined in the conclusion that the statutes before the Court were constitutionally invalid."

CASE SIGNIFICANCE: *Gregg v. Georgia* is the most important case ever to be decided by the Supreme Court on the death penalty. For the first time, a majority of the Court said that the death penalty is not in itself unconstitutional and may therefore be imposed. *Gregg v. Georgia* therefore overrules *Furman v. Georgia*. This did not mean, however, that the statutes in the various states were automatically declared constitutional and that executions could commence. What it meant was that the Court could now examine each statute in an appropriate case to determine whether its provisions contained guarantees against arbitrary and capricious imposition.

B. DISCRIMINATION—RACIAL

MCCLESKEY V. KEMP
481 U.S. 279 (1987)

CAPSULE: A statistical study suggesting racial discrimination in general in the imposition of death sentences does not make the death penalty unconstitutional.

FACTS: In 1978, McCleskey, a black man, was found guilty of the robbery of a store and the murder of a white police officer. After considering mitigating and aggravating circumstances, the jury imposed the death penalty.

ISSUE: Does a statistical study suggesting that racial considerations enter into capital sentencing determinations prove that Georgia's capital sentencing procedures are arbitrary, capricious, and in violation of the equal protection clause? NO.

HOLDING: A statistical study suggesting that racial considerations enter into capital sentencing in Georgia does not establish racial discrimination or that the death sentence is applied in an arbitrary or capricious manner.

REASON: "To prevail under that Clause, petitioner must prove that the decisionmakers in his case acted with discriminatory purpose. Petitioner offered no evidence specific to his own case that would support an inference that racial considerations played a part in his sentence, and the Baldus study is insufficient to support an inference that any of the decisionmakers in his case acted with discriminatory purpose. This Court has accepted statistics as proof of intent to discriminate in the context of a State's selection of the jury venire and in the context of statutory violations under Title VII of the Civil Rights Act of 1964. However, the nature of the capital sentencing decision and the relationship of the statistics to that decision are fundamentally different from the corresponding elements in the venire-selection or Title VII cases. Petitioner's statistical proffer must be viewed in the context of his challenge to decisions at the heart of the State's criminal justice system. Because discretion is essential to the criminal justice process, exceptionally clear proof is required before this Court will infer that the discretion has been abused."

CASE SIGNIFICANCE: This case declares that in death penalty cases, statistical studies showing discrimination in the imposition of the penalty do not in themselves prove that the state has violated the equal protection clause of the Constitution. In order for a claim of discrimination to succeed, "petitioner must prove that decisionmakers in his case acted with discriminatory purpose." It is not enough to allege and prove through statistical study that a particular race has been discriminated against (as established by the Baldus Study); the person alleging discrimination must prove that there was discrimination in his or her particular case.

C. MENTALLY IMPAIRED DEFENDANTS

FORD V. WAINWRIGHT
477 U.S. 399 (1986)

CAPSULE: An insane prisoner cannot be executed because it would constitute cruel and unusual punishment.

FACTS: In 1974, Ford was found guilty of murder and sentenced to death. At no time during the commission of the offense, at his trial, or at sentencing, did Ford show signs of incompetence. Beginning in 1982, however, Ford exhibited incompetent behavior that rendered him incapable of communication.

ISSUES:
1. Does the Eighth Amendment prohibit the execution of a prisoner who is insane at the time of the scheduled execution? YES.
2. Are the procedures used by the State of Florida to determine the sanity of a person who is to be executed adequate? NO.

HOLDING:
1. The Eighth Amendment prohibits a state from carrying out a sentence of death on a prisoner who is insane.
2. Florida's procedures for determining the sanity of a person who has been sentenced to death are not "adequate to afford a full and fair hearing"; therefore, an evidentiary hearing to determine competency must be granted.

REASONS: "The reasons at common law for not condoning the execution of the insane—that such an execution has questionable retributive value, presents no example to others and thus has no deterrence value, and simply offends humanity—have no less logical, moral, and practical force at present. Whether the aim is to protect the condemned from fear and pain without comfort of understanding, or to protect the dignity of society itself from the barbarity of exacting mindless vengeance, the restriction finds enforcement in the Eighth Amendment.

"The first defect in Florida's procedure is the failure to include the prisoner in the truth-seeking process. Any procedure that precludes the prisoner or his counsel from presenting material relevant to his sanity or bars consideration of that material by the factfinder is necessarily inadequate. A related flaw in the procedures is the denial of any opportunity to challenge or impeach the state-appointed psychiatrist's opinions, thus creating a significant possibility that the ultimate decision made in reliance on those experts will be distorted. And perhaps the most striking defect in the procedures is the placement of the ultimate decision wholly within the Executive Branch. The Governor, who appoints the experts and ultimately decides whether the State will be able to carry out the death sentence and whose subordinates have been responsible for initiating every stage of the prosecution, cannot be said to have the neutrality that is necessary for reliability in the fact-finding proceedings."

CASE SIGNIFICANCE: In this case, the defendant was sane at the time of the commission of the offense, but later became insane. It therefore raises a different issue from that of insanity at the time of the commission of the crime. The rule is that a defendant is not guilty if he or she was insane at the time the crime was committed. What if the person is insane at the time of the trial? Courts have said that competence to stand trial is necessary before a defendant can be tried. This case goes a step beyond that, raising the issue of whether a defendant who was sane when the crime was committed can be executed if he or she later becomes insane after having been found guilty.

PENRY V. LYNAUGH
492 U.S. 302 (1989)

CAPSULE: A mentally retarded defendant who has the ability to reason may be given the death penalty.

FACTS: Penry was charged with capital murder in Texas state court. He raised the insanity defense. Evidence during the trial showed that Penry had an IQ of 54 and the mental age of six and one-half years. He also had the social maturity of a nine- or 10-year-old. He was 22 years old at the time the crime was committed. The jury found Penry competent to stand trial and he was found guilty.

ISSUES:

1. Does the Constitution prohibit the execution of a person who is mentally retarded? NO.
2. Should the jury be instructed, upon request, to consider mental retardation as a mitigating circumstance during the sentencing stage of a death penalty case? YES.

HOLDINGS:

1. A mentally retarded defendant who has the ability to reason may be given the death penalty.
2. When a request is made by the defense to instruct the jury concerning the mitigating evidence of mental retardation and child abuse, the request must be granted. (This was overruled in 2002 in *Atkins v. Virginia*.)

REASON: "The Eighth Amendment's categorical prohibition upon the infliction of cruel and unusual punishment applies to practices condemned by the common law at the time the Bill of Rights was adopted, as well as to punishments which offend our society's evolving standards of decency as expressed in objective evidence of legislative enactments and the conduct of sentencing juries. Since the common law prohibited the punishment of 'idiots'—which term was generally used to describe persons totally lacking in reason, understanding, or the ability to distinguish between good and evil—it may indeed be 'cruel and unusual punishment' to execute persons who are profoundly or severely retarded and wholly lacking in the capacity to appreciate the wrongfulness of their actions. Such persons, however, are not likely to be convicted or face the prospect of punishment today, since the modern insanity defense generally includes 'mental defect' as part of the legal definition of insanity, and since *Ford v. Wainwright*, *supra*, prohibits the execution of persons who are unaware of their punishment and why they must suffer it. Moreover, petitioner is not such a person, since the jury (1) found him competent to stand trial and therefore to have a rational as well as factual understanding of the proceedings; and (2) rejected his insanity defense, thereby reflecting the conclusion that he knew his conduct was wrong and was capable of conforming it to the requirements of the law. Nor is there sufficient objective evidence today of a national consensus against executing mentally retarded capital murderers, since petitioner has cited only one state statute that explicitly bans that practice and has offered no evidence of the general behavior of juries in this regard. Opinion surveys indicating strong public opposition to such executions do not establish a social consensus, absent some legislative reflection of the sentiment expressed therein."

CASE SIGNIFICANCE: In *Thompson v. Oklahoma*, 487 U.S. 815 (1988), the Court held that the execution of a person who was under the age of 16 at the time of the commission of the offense constituted cruel and unusual punishment. In *Stanford v. Kentucky*, 492 U.S. 361 (1989), the Court held that the death penalty was not cruel and unusual punishment for an offender who committed murder at age 16 or 17. The issue in the *Penry* case was different: whether a mentally retarded offender can be sentenced to death. The Court answered in the affirmative, stating that, "The Eighth Amendment does not categorically prohibit the execution of mentally retarded capital murderers of petitioner's reasoning ability."

ATKINS V. VIRGINIA
536 U.S. 304 (2002)

CAPSULE: Executing the mentally retarded violates society's evolving standards of decency and is cruel and unusual punishment prohibited by the Eighth Amendment.

FACTS: On August 16, 1996, Daryl Renard Atkins and William Jones, armed with a semiautomatic handgun, abducted Eric Nesbitt, robbed him, and drove him to an automated teller machine in his pickup truck where cameras recorded their withdrawal of money. They then took him to an isolated location where they shot Nesbitt eight times, killing him. Jones and Atkins both testified in the guilt phase of Atkins' trial. Both provided details that confirmed the other's account of the incident, but both identified the other as the one who shot and killed Nesbitt. Atkins was convicted of abduction, armed robbery, and capital murder. He was sentenced to death.

ISSUE: Is it constitutional to execute a mentally retarded offender? NO.

HOLDING: The execution of mentally retarded criminals constitutes cruel and unusual punishment prohibited by the Eighth Amendment because there now exists a national consensus that executing the mentally retarded violates society's evolving standards of decency. (This case overruled *Penry v. Lynaugh*.)

REASON: "It is not so much the number of these States that is significant, but the consistency of the direction of the change. Given the well-known fact that anti-crime legislation is far more popular than legislation providing protections for persons guilty of violent crime, the large number of States prohibiting the execution of mentally retarded persons (and the complete absence of States passing legislation reinstating the power to conduct such executions) provides powerful evidence that today our society views mentally retarded offenders as categorically less culpable than the average criminal. The evidence carries even greater force when it is noted that the legislatures that have addressed the issue have voted overwhelmingly in favor of the prohibition. Moreover, even in those States that allow the execution of mentally retarded offenders, the practice is uncommon . . ."

CASE SIGNIFICANCE: This is an important case because it categorically declares that the execution of mentally retarded offenders constitutes cruel and unusual punishment and is unconstitutional. This reverses the Court's decision in *Penry v. Lynaugh* (1989), which held that mentally retarded offenders who have the ability to reason may be given the death penalty.

1. "Because of their disabilities in areas of reasoning, judgment, and control of their impulses,. . . they do not act with the level of moral culpability that characterizes the most serious adult criminal conduct;
2. "Their impairments can jeopardize the reliability and fairness of capital proceedings; and
3. "Evolving standards of decency now require that the execution of the mentally retarded be declared unconstitutional."

The Court noted that since the *Penry* decision in 1989, much had changed. Since 1989, many states have enacted laws prohibiting the execution of the mentally retarded. By contrast, no state had passed any law allowing such executions. The Court then declared that "It is not so much the number of these States that is significant, but the consistency of the direction of the change." The Court concluded by saying, "We are not persuaded that the execution of mentally retarded criminals will measurably advance the deterrent or the retributive purpose of the death penalty. Construing and applying the Eighth Amendment in the light of our evolving standards of decency, we therefore conclude that such punishment is excessive and that the Constitution places a substantive restriction on the State's power to take the life of a mentally retarded offender." That certainly settles the issue authoritatively and forever unless the Supreme Court later changes its mind.

HALL V. FLORIDA
572 U.S. ___ (2014)

CAPSULE: The measurement of a person's intellectual disability for purposes of inclusion in a death penalty statute cannot be based solely on an IQ of 70.

FACTS: In 1978, Hall and an accomplice kidnapped, beat, raped, and murdered Karol Hurst, a pregnant, 21-year-old newlywed. That same day, they drove to a convenience store that they planned to rob and killed a sheriff's deputy in the store parking lot. Hall received the death penalty for both murders. Owing to insufficient evidence of premeditation, the sentence for the murder of the deputy was later reduced. After the *Atkins v. Virginia* (2002) decision that declared the execution of intellectually disabled persons unconstitutional, Hall filed a motion declaring parts of the Florida death penalty statute unconstitutional.

ISSUE: Is the Florida law defining intellectual disability for purposes of death penalty sentences in violation of the Eighth and Fourteenth Amendments? YES.

HOLDING: The Florida courts have interpreted the statute too narrowly by relying only on an IQ test score—which itself is not infallible—and by not also considering other evidence regarding the offender's intellectual disability.

REASON: "As the Court noted in *Atkins*, the medical community defines intellectual disability according to three criteria: significantly sub-average intellectual functioning, deficits in adaptive functioning (the inability to learn basic skills and adjust behavior to changing circumstances), and onset of these deficits during the developmental period. See *id.*, at 308, n. 3; DSM–5, at 33; Brief for American Psychological Association et al. as *Amici Curiae* 12–13 (hereinafter APA Brief). This last factor, referred to as 'age of onset,' is not at issue.

"The first and second criteria—deficits in intellectual functioning and deficits in adaptive functioning—are central here. In the context of a formal assessment, '[t]he existence of concurrent deficits in intellectual and adaptive functioning has long been the defining characteristic of intellectual disability.' *Id.*, at 11.

"On its face this statute could be interpreted consistently with *Atkins* and with the conclusions this Court reaches in the instant case. Nothing in the statute precludes Florida from taking into account the IQ test's standard error of measurement, and as discussed below there is evidence that Florida's Legislature intended to include the measurement error in the calculation. But the Florida Supreme Court has interpreted the provisions more narrowly. It has held that a person whose test score is above 70, including a score within the margin for measurement error, does not have an intellectual disability and is barred from presenting other evidence that would show his faculties are limited. See *Cherry v. State*, 959 So. 2d 702, 712–713 (Fla. 2007) (*per curiam*). That strict IQ test score cutoff of 70 is the issue in this case.

"Pursuant to this mandatory cutoff, sentencing courts cannot consider even substantial and weighty evidence of intellectual disability as measured and made manifest by the defendant's failure or inability to adapt to his social and cultural environment, including medical histories, behavioral records, school tests and reports, and testimony regarding past behavior and family circumstances. This is so even though the medical community accepts that all of this evidence can be probative of intellectual disability, including for individuals who have an IQ test score above 70. See APA Brief 15–16 ('[T]he relevant clinical authorities all agree that an individual with an IQ score above 70 may properly be diagnosed with intellectual disability if significant limitations in adaptive functioning also exist'); DSM–5, at 37 ('[A] person with an IQ score above 70 may have such severe adaptive behavior problems . . . that the person's actual functioning is comparable to that of individuals with a lower IQ score')."

"Thus, at most nine States mandate a strict IQ score cutoff at 70. Of these, four States (Delaware, Kansas, North Carolina, and Washington) appear not to have considered the issue in their courts. On the other side of the ledger stand the 18 States that have abolished the death penalty, either in full or for new offenses, and Oregon, which has suspended the death penalty and executed only two individuals in the past 40 years. See *Roper*, 543 U.S., at 574 ('[The] Court should have considered those States that had abandoned the death penalty altogether as part of the consensus against the juvenile death penalty'). In those States, of course, a person in Hall's position could not be executed even without a finding of intellectual disability. Thus in 41 States an individual in Hall's position—an individual with an IQ score of 71—would not be deemed automatically eligible for the death penalty."

"In summary, every state legislature to have considered the issue after *Atkins*—save Virginia's—and whose law has been interpreted by its courts has taken a position contrary to that of Florida. Indeed, the Florida Legislature, which passed the relevant legislation prior to *Atkins*, might well have believed that its law would not create a fixed cutoff at 70. The staff analysis accompanying the 2001 bill states that it 'does not contain a set IQ level. . . . Two standard deviations from these tests is approximately a 70 IQ, although it can be extended up to 75.' Fla. Senate Staff Analysis and Economic Impact Statement, CS/SB 238, p. 11 (Feb. 14, 2001).

But the Florida Supreme Court interpreted the law to require a bright-line cutoff at 70, see *Cherry*, 959 So. 2d, at 712–713, and the Court is bound by that interpretation.

"The rejection of the strict 70 cutoff in the vast majority of States and the 'consistency in the trend,' *Roper*, *supra*, at 567, toward recognizing the SEM provide strong evidence of consensus that our society does not regard this strict cutoff as proper or humane."

CASE SIGNIFICANCE: This case further clarifies the decision in *Atkins v. Virginia* (2002). In *Atkins*, the Court ruled that executing intellectually disabled persons is cruel and unusual punishment and in violation of the Eighth Amendment. Capital punishment states enacted legislation to identify people who would qualify as intellectually disabled for purposes of death penalty sentencing. The Court examined the varied state laws and came to the conclusion that, although most states did recognize an IQ score of 70 as the cutoff between the abled versus the disabled, most of those states also allowed for defendants to show other relative materials that supported their disability. The Florida rule "misconstrues the Court's statements in *Atkins* that intellectual disability is characterized by an IQ of 'approximately 70.' 536 U.S., at 308, n 3." As the Court explained, when working with test scores, there must be acknowledged a margin of error. One person may have a similar history and show the exact same signs of intellectual disability as another, and yet one may have an IQ of 68 and the other an IQ of 75. Both of these scores would fall within the standard margin of error allowed by medical experts, yet only one of them would be excused under Florida law. The Court found Florida's inflexibility in violation of both the spirit and the meaning of the *Atkins* ruling.

D. JUVENILES

THOMPSON V. OKLAHOMA[1]
487 U.S. 815 (1988)

CAPSULE: It is cruel and unusual punishment to impose the death penalty on a juvenile who commits their crime at age 15 or younger.

FACTS: Thompson, at age 15, actively participated in the brutal murder of his brother-in-law. Although considered a child under Oklahoma law, the district attorney sought to have him tried as an adult. Thompson was tried as an adult and was found guilty of the murder. Due to the heinous nature of the crime, Thompson was sentenced to death.

ISSUE: Is the death penalty cruel and unusual punishment for a crime committed by a 15-year-old? YES.

HOLDING: The execution of a person who was under 16 years of age at the time of the offense is cruel and unusual punishment and therefore is prohibited by the Eighth and Fourteenth Amendments.

REASON: "In determining whether the categorical Eighth Amendment prohibition applies, this Court must be guided by the 'evolving standards of decency that mark the progress of a maturing society,' *Trop v. Dulles*, 356 U.S. 86, 101, and in doing so must review relevant legislative enactments and jury determinations and consider the reasons why a civilized society may accept or reject the death penalty for a person less than 16 years old at the time of the crime."

CASE SIGNIFICANCE: Under this ruling, any offender who was 15 years old or younger at the time the crime was committed could not be given the death penalty, regardless of the nature or heinousness of the offense. The Court took into account the fact that the statutes of approximately 18 states require that the defendant be at least 16 years old at the time of the commission of the offense in order for the death penalty to be imposed, saying that "it would offend civilized standards of decency to execute a person who was less than 16 years old at the time of his or her offense." In a concurring opinion, however, Justice O'Connor noted that "the Federal Government and 19 States have authorized capital punishment without setting any minimum age, and have also provided for some 15-year-olds to be prosecuted as adults." This indicates, she said, that there was no consensus about whether 15-year-olds should be executed.

STANFORD V. KENTUCKY[2]
492 U.S. 361 (1989)

CAPSULE: It is not cruel and unusual punishment to impose the death penalty on a juvenile who commits the crime at age 16 or older.

FACTS: Stanford was charged with capital murder. He was 17 years old when the crime was committed. He was transferred to adult court after a juvenile hearing under state statute. Stanford was convicted, and because of the heinousness of the crime, was sentenced to death.

ISSUE: Does the imposition of the death penalty for a crime committed at age 16 or 17 constitute cruel and unusual punishment? NO.

HOLDING: It is not cruel and unusual punishment to impose capital punishment on an offender who was 16 or 17 years old at the time the crime was committed. (This case was overruled in 2005 in *Roper v. Simmons*.)

REASON: "Whether a particular punishment violates the Eighth Amendment depends on whether it constitutes one of 'those modes or acts of punishment . . . considered cruel and unusual at the time the Bill of Rights was adopted.' *Ford v. Wainwright*, 477 U.S. 399, 405, or is contrary to the 'evolving standards of decency that mark the progress of a maturing society,' *Trop v. Dulles*, 356 U.S. 86, 101. Petitioners have not alleged that their sentences would have been considered cruel and unusual in the eighteenth century, and could not support such a contention, since, at that time, the common law set the rebuttable presumption of incapacity to commit felonies (which were punishable by death) at the age of 14."

CASE SIGNIFICANCE: This case resolves an issue that the Court refused to address the previous year in *Thompson v. Oklahoma*, 487 U.S. 815 (1988). That issue is whether a defendant who was of juvenile age (either 16 or 17) at the time the offense was committed could be given the death penalty. The Court's ruling here is clear, stating that "the imposition of capital punishment on an individual for a crime committed at 16 or 17 years of age does not constitute cruel and unusual punishment under the Eighth Amendment." Thus the Court set the minimum age at 16 if the state is to impose the death penalty. Juveniles who are age 15 or younger during the commission of the offense cannot be given the death penalty.

In reaching that conclusion, the Court relied on "evolving standards of decency that mark the progress of a maturing society." It then concluded that there was no consensus against the execution of 16- and 17-year-olds, stating that "of the 37 States that permit capital punishment, 15 states decline to impose it on 16-year-olds and 12 on 17-year-olds." The Court said that "this does not establish the degree of national agreement this Court has previously thought sufficient to label a punishment cruel and unusual."

Thus the issue was settled, at least until 2005: executing 15-year-olds is cruel and unusual punishment, thus unconstitutional; executing juveniles who are 16 years old or older was constitutional. This case was overruled, however, in 2005 in *Roper v. Simmons*. The crucial time is age at the commission of the offense, not the age of the juvenile at the time of arrest, trial, or conviction. There must be state or federal law, however, authorizing the imposition of the death penalty on juveniles before that form of punishment can be administered in any jurisdiction.

ROPER V. SIMMONS[3]
546 U.S. 551 (2005)

CAPSULE: The Eighth and Fourteenth Amendments prohibit the death penalty for juveniles who committed their crime before the age of 18.

FACTS: When Christopher Simmons was 17 years old he committed a brutal murder. Before committing the crime, Simmons stated that he wanted to kill someone, even going to the extent of discussing his plan to commit the act with his friends. On the night of the crime at about 2:00 A.M., Simmons and his accomplice entered the home of Shirley Crook through an open window and awakened the victim. Simmons later stated that he intended to kill Mrs. Crook because of their mutual involvement in a previous car accident.

ISSUE: Is it cruel and unusual punishment to impose the death penalty on offenders who commit crimes before reaching the age of 18? YES.

HOLDING: The Eighth and Fourteenth Amendments prohibit the imposition of the death penalty on offenders who commit their crimes before reaching the age of 18.

REASON: "Both objective indicia of consensus, as expressed in particular by the enactments of legislatures that have addressed the question, and the Court's own determination in the exercise of its independent judgment, demonstrate that the death penalty is a disproportionate punishment for juveniles."

CASE SIGNIFICANCE: This case is the most important case decided thus far on the issue of the constitutionality of the death penalty for juveniles. It holds that the death penalty constitutes cruel and unusual punishment for offenders who commit their crime before reaching the age of 18. The Court, in *Thompson v. Oklahoma* (1988) held that executing offenders who were 15 years old or younger at the time of the commission of the offense is unconstitutional. *Simmons* extends that rule to include 16- and 17-year-olds, and therefore overturns its earlier decision in *Stanford v. Kentucky*.

E. JURIES AND JURORS

WITHERSPOON V. ILLINOIS
391 U.S. 510 (1968)

CAPSULE: It is unconstitutional for prosecutors in a death penalty case to remove potential jurors "for cause" merely because of conscientious scruples against, or opposition to, capital punishment.

FACTS: Witherspoon was charged with capital murder in Cook County, Illinois. He was found guilty and given the death penalty. At the time of his conviction, Illinois law provided that: "In trials for murder it shall be a cause for challenge of any juror who shall, on being examined, state that he has conscientious scruples against capital punishment, or that he is opposed to the same." This eliminated about half of the potential jurors because they had expressed qualms about the death penalty.

ISSUE: Does the Illinois law that allows the prosecution to challenge for cause any potential juror who "has conscientious scruples against capital punishment, or is opposed to the same" violate the due process right of the defendant? YES.

HOLDING: The Illinois law authorizing prosecutors to challenge "for cause" potential jurors who have conscientious scruples against capital punishment, or are opposed to it, is unconstitutional because it deprives the defendant of a neutral jury and violates the defendant's right to due process.

REASON: "The issue before us is a narrow one. It does not involve the right of the prosecution to challenge for cause those prospective jurors who state that their reservations about capital punishment would prevent them from making an impartial decision as to the defendant's guilt. Nor does it involve the State's assertion of a right to exclude from the jury in a capital case those who say that they could never vote to impose the death penalty or that they would refuse even to consider its imposition in the case before them. For the State of Illinois did not stop there, but authorized the prosecution to exclude as well all who said that they were opposed to capital punishment and all who indicated that they had conscientious scruples against inflicting it."

CASE SIGNIFICANCE: This was one of the early cases decided by the Supreme Court on the selection of jurors in death penalty cases and was the original "hanging jury" case. The case involved the constitutionality of an Illinois law that authorized the prosecutor to challenge "for cause" (meaning disqualifying a juror based on a cause provided by law), and therefore exclude, potential jurors who had conscientious scruples against capital punishment or were opposed to it. Witherspoon claimed that this practice violated his right to due process because it biased the jury in favor of conviction, making it more inclined to impose the death penalty and made it a "hanging jury."

LOCKHART V. MCCREE
476 U.S. 162 (1986)

CAPSULE: Prospective jurors whose opposition to the death penalty is so strong as to prevent or impair the performance of their duties at the sentencing phase of the trial may be disqualified from jury membership.

FACTS: McCree was charged with capital felony murder. He was arrested when found driving a car that matched an eyewitness's description of a vehicle seen driving away from a gift shop/gas station where a robbery and murder of the owner had just taken place. McCree admitted to being in the shop at the time of the murder but claimed that a stranger had done the killing, using McCree's rifle. McCree said that the stranger then rode in McCree's car for a short time, got out, and walked away with the rifle. This story was refuted by eyewitnesses who had seen only one person in the car during the time when McCree claimed he had a passenger. The rifle was located and ballistics tests identified it as the murder weapon.

ISSUE: Does the Constitution allow the removal for cause, during the guilt phase of a capital trial, of prospective jurors whose opposition to the death penalty is so great as to substantially impair their performance as jurors at the sentencing phase of the trial? YES.

HOLDING: Prospective jurors, whose opposition to the death penalty is so strong as to prevent or impair the performance of their duties as jurors at the sentencing phase of a trial, may be removed for cause from jury membership.

REASON: "'Death qualification' of a jury does not violate the fair cross-section requirement of the Sixth Amendment, which applies to jury panels or venires but does not require that petit juries actually chosen reflect the composition of the community at large. Even if the requirement were extended to petit juries, the essence of a fair cross-section claim is the systematic exclusion of a 'distinctive group' in the community—such as blacks, women, and Mexican-Americans—for reasons completely unrelated to the ability of members of the group to serve as jurors in a particular case. Groups defined solely in terms of shared attitudes that would prevent or substantially impair members of the group from performing one of their duties as jurors, such as the 'Witherspoon-excludables' at issue here, are not 'distinctive groups' for fair cross-section purposes. 'Death qualification' is carefully designed to serve the State's legitimate interest in obtaining a single jury that can properly and impartially apply the law to the facts of the case at both the guilt and sentencing phases of a capital trial."

CASE SIGNIFICANCE: In an earlier case, *Witherspoon v. Illinois*, 391 U.S. 510 (1968), the Court said that an Illinois law that allowed prosecutors to exclude potential jurors who had conscientious scruples against capital punishment or were merely opposed to it violated the defendant's right to due process because it stacked the jury in favor of the death penalty. *McCree* goes beyond that kind of a law, because the judge had removed for cause prospective jurors who stated that they could not vote for the imposition of the death penalty under any circumstances. The Court said that such disqualification was constitutional (a practice that led to "death qualified" juries). The difference between *Witherspoon* and *McCree* is this: The law at issue in *Witherspoon* (which allowed the dis-qualification of potential jurors who had conscientious scruples or were merely opposed to the death penalty) violated the defendant's right to a neutral jury, whereas the practice used in *McCree* (which allowed the disqualification of jurors whose opposition to the death penalty was so great as to substantially impair their performance as jurors at the sentencing stage of the trial) nonetheless preserved the defendant's right to a neutral jury in that a jury member could not be neutral if he or she would in essence refuse to vote for a death sentence regardless of circumstances. This principle was first articulated by the Supreme Court in *Adams v. Texas*, 448 U.S. 38 (1980). *McCree* followed the precedent set in that case.

MORGAN V. ILLINOIS
504 U.S. 719 (1992)

CAPSULE: The defendant in a death penalty case must be allowed to ask a juror whether he or she would automatically vote to impose the death penalty upon conviction.

FACTS: In the state of Illinois, a capital trial is conducted in two phases, with the same jury determining both the defendant's guilt and whether the death penalty should be imposed. As required by state law, the trial court, rather than the attorneys, conducted the voir dire (the questioning of prospective jurors) to select the jury for Morgan's capital murder trial was convicted and sentenced to death.

ISSUE: Is it constitutional for a trial court to refuse inquiry into whether a potential juror would automatically impose the death penalty upon conviction in a capital case? NO.

HOLDING: A trial court's refusal to allow defendants to inquire whether potential jurors would automatically impose the death penalty upon conviction in a capital case is inconsistent with the due process clause of the Fourteenth Amendment, and therefore is unconstitutional.

REASON: "Due process demands that a jury provided to a capital defendant at the sentencing phase must stand impartial and indifferent to the extent commanded by the Sixth Amendment."

CASE SIGNIFICANCE: In *Witherspoon v. Illinois*, 391 U.S. 510 (1968), the Supreme Court implied that in choosing juries to sentence defendants in capital cases, prosecutors (or in this case, the judge) may exclude for cause potential jurors who say that they are unwilling to vote for a death sentence under any circumstance. That ruling led to "death-qualified" juries. However, *Witherspoon* held that mere opposition to the death penalty does not constitute sufficient grounds for dismissal; rather, the juror must indicate that he or she would automatically vote against the death penalty regardless of the circumstances surrounding the case.

Part of the guaranty of a defendant's right to an impartial jury is an adequate voir dire to identify unqualified jurors. Morgan could not exercise intelligently his challenge for cause against prospective jurors who would unwaveringly impose death after a finding of guilt unless he was given the opportunity to identify such persons by questioning them at voir dire about their views on the death penalty. Absent that opportunity, his right not to be tried by those who would always impose death would be rendered as nugatory and meaningless as the State's right, in the absence of questioning, to strike those who never do so.

SIMMONS V. SOUTH CAROLINA
512 U.S. 154 (1994)

CAPSULE: Death penalty defendants are entitled to a jury instruction informing the jury that a "life" sentence means life imprisonment without parole.

FACTS: In 1990, Jonathan Simmons beat Josie Lamb to death in her home. Ms. Lamb was an elderly woman. Prior to the start of his capital murder trial, Simmons pleaded guilty to first-degree burglary and two counts of criminal sexual conduct in connection with two prior assaults on elderly women. Simmons was convicted of both violent offenses. The two violent offense convictions made him ineligible for parole if convicted of any other violent crime offense under South Carolina law. Prior to jury selection in the capital murder trial, the prosecutor was granted a motion by the trial judge barring the defense from making any mention of parole. The defense was expressly prohibited from questioning prospective jurors as to whether they understood the meaning of a "life" sentence under the state law. Simmons was convicted of the murder. During the penalty phase of the trial, the state argued that Simmons' future dangerousness was a factor the jury needed to consider when deciding whether to sentence him to death or life imprisonment. The defense pointed out that Simmons' future dangerousness was limited to elderly women and there was no reason to expect violent acts from him in prison. During jury instructions, the judge refused to point out to the jury that Simmons would be ineligible for parole under South Carolina law. At some point during the deliberation, the jury inquired whether life imprisonment carried the possibility of parole. The judge instructed the jury not to consider parole in reaching its verdict and that "the terms life imprisonment and death sentence were to be understood to have their plan [sic] and ordinary meaning." Simmons was given the death penalty.

ISSUE: Does the refusal to provide the jury with information regarding life without parole in a death penalty case violate the due process clause of the Fourteenth Amendment? YES.

HOLDING: Due process requires that the sentencing jury be informed that the defendant is not eligible for parole when the defendant's future dangerousness is at issue, and state law prohibits the defendant's release on parole.

REASON: "In assessing future dangerousness, the actual duration of the defendant's prison sentence is indisputably relevant. Holding all other factors constant, it is entirely reasonable for a sentencing jury to view a defendant who is eligible for parole as a greater threat to society than a defendant who is not. Indeed, there may be no greater assurance of a defendant's future nondangerousness to the public than the fact that he will never be released on parole. The trial court's refusal to apprise the jury of information so crucial to its sentencing determination, particularly when the prosecution alluded to the defendant's future dangerousness in its argument to the jury, cannot be reconciled with our well established precedents interpreting the Due Process Clause."

CASE SIGNIFICANCE: This case deals with an issue raised by an increasing number of state laws that prohibit release on parole for certain heinous offenses. South Carolina law provided that for the type of offense committed by the defendant in this case, imprisonment for life meant that the defendant could not be released on parole. This is important because jurors might not impose the death penalty and opt for life imprisonment if they are informed that life imprisonment for some defendants means that these defendants will never be released from prison. The assumption is that if life imprisonment can mean parole, jurors would rather impose the death penalty so that society may be protected from dangerous parolees. However, if jurors know that life imprisonment means that the defendant will never be released, then future danger to society does not become a consideration in imposing the penalty. The Court said that due process requires that the information on "life without parole" as an alternative to the death penalty in certain states be made known to the jury when determining the sentence to be imposed. It could make the difference whether an accused receives a life sentence or the death penalty.

HARRIS V. ALABAMA
513 U.S. 504 (1995)

CAPSULE: A capital sentencing law that calls for the sentencing judge to consider an advisory jury verdict need not specify the weight the judge must give to the advisory verdicts.

FACTS: Louise Harris was having an affair with Lorenzo McCarter. McCarter was asked by Harris to find someone to kill her husband. Michael Stockwell and Alex Hood were each paid $100 by McCarter, with a vague promise of more money, upon completion of the crime. The victim was shot with a shotgun at point-blank range by Stockwell when he stopped at a stop sign. After Harris was arrested, McCarter agreed to testify against her in exchange for a promise by the prosecutor not to seek the death penalty against him. McCarter testified that Harris had asked him to kill her husband so they could share in his death benefits of $250,000.

ISSUE: Is a capital punishment sentencing scheme that requires a judge to only consider a sentencing jury's advisory verdict, but does not spell out the specific weight to be given to the jury's recommendation, a violation of the Eighth Amendment? NO.

HOLDING: The Eighth Amendment's cruel and unusual punishment clause does not require a state's sentencing law to specify the weight the sentencing judge must give to the advisory verdict.

REASON: "We have rejected the notion that 'a specific method for balancing mitigating and aggravating factors in a capital sentencing proceeding is constitutionally required.' Equally settled is the corollary that the Constitution does not require a State to ascribe any specific weight to particular factors, either in aggravation or mitigation, to be considered by the sentencer. To require that 'great weight' be given to the jury recommendation here, one of the criteria to be considered by the sentencer, would offend these established principles and place within constitutional ambit micromanagement tasks that properly rest within the State's discretion to administer its criminal justice system."

CASE SIGNIFICANCE: The Court in this case was asked to decide whether a capital sentencing scheme that requires a judge to consider a sentencing jury's advisory verdict before imposing sentence but does not specify the weight to be given to that jury's recommendation was in violation of the Eighth Amendment's prohibition against cruel and unusual punishments. The Court held that it was not.

BUCHANAN V. ANGELONE
522 U.S. 269 (1998)

CAPSULE: A death penalty jury does not have to be given specific instructions by the judge on mitigating factors.

FACTS: Buchanan was convicted of murdering four members of his family. A separate sentencing hearing was held in which the prosecution sought the death penalty based on the Virginia aggravating factor that the crime was vile. During the sentencing phase of the trial, the defense presented evidence concerning Buchanan's troubled childhood. Both the prosecution and the defense presented the concept of mitigation to the jury. The prosecution told the jury that it would have to weigh factors favorable to the defendant against the crimes he had committed. The trial court refused to give additional instructions proposed by the defense, listing mitigating factors the jury might consider or should consider in mitigation of the offense. The jury returned a sentence of death.

ISSUE: Is failure to provide the jury with express guidance on the concept of mitigation and instruction on particular statutorily defined mitigating factors a violation of the Eighth and Fourteenth Amendment rights to be free from the arbitrary and capricious imposition of the death penalty? NO.

HOLDING: A jury may return a verdict in favor of the death penalty without being instructed on the concept of mitigating evidence or in the particular statutorily defined mitigating factors the defense claims the evidence shows.

REASON: "The jury instruction here does not violate these constitutional principles. The instruction did not foreclose the jury's consideration of any mitigating evidence. By directing the jury to base its decision on 'all the evidence,' the instruction afforded jurors an opportunity to consider mitigating evidence. The instruction informed the jurors that if they found the aggravating factor proved beyond a reasonable doubt then they 'may fix' the penalty at death, but directed that if they believed that all the evidence justified a lesser sentence then they 'shall' impose a life sentence. The jury was thus allowed to impose a life sentence even if it found the aggravating factor proved. Moreover, in contrast to the Texas special issues scheme in question in *Penry*, *supra*, at 326, the instructions here did not constrain the manner in which the jury was able to give effect to mitigation."

CASE SIGNIFICANCE: The U.S. Supreme Court ruled that the jury instructions in Buchanan's case were sufficient and did not prevent the jury from considering all of the mitigating evidence. The Constitution merely requires that the defendant be allowed to present any mitigating evidence and that the jury be allowed to hear and consider it. In this case, the jury heard two full days of testimony on mitigating evidence and the Court thought it "unlikely" that the jury would not consider it after being instructed to consider "all of the evidence."

PENRY V. JOHNSON
532 U.S. 782 (2001)

CAPSULE: Jury instructions that do not permit the jury to consider and give effect to mitigating evidence violate due process.

FACTS: In 1989, the U.S. Supreme Court, in *Penry v. Lynaugh*, held that Johnny Paul Penry was sentenced to death in violation of the Eighth Amendment. Penry was retried in 1990 and again found guilty of capital murder. The defense, as it did in the first trial, presented extensive evidence during the sentencing hearing regarding Penry's mental retardation and history of being abused. One witness presented by the defense was a clinical neuropsychologist who testified that he believed Penry suffered from organic brain impairment and mental retardation. On cross-examination, the doctor referred to a psychiatric examination prepared by Dr. Felix Peebles in 1977. The report was prepared at the request of Penry's attorney to determine Penry's competency to stand trial on a 1977 rape charge. Dr. Peebles' professional opinion was that if Penry was released from custody he would pose a danger to other people. The prosecutor repeated this conclusion by Dr. Peebles in his closing argument. When the case was submitted to the jury, it was with the instruction from the trial court that the jury was to determine Penry's sentence by answering the same three special issues that were considered in the original *Penry* case. The jury was then given a "supplemental instruction" which said: "[W]hen you deliberate on the . . . special issues, you are to consider mitigating circumstances . . ., you must decide how much weight they deserve, if any and therefore, give effect and consideration to them in assessing the defendant's personal culpability at the time you answer the special issue. If you determine, when giving effect to the mitigating evidence, if any, that a life sentence, as reflected by a negative finding to the issue under consideration, rather than a death sentence, is an appropriate response to [Penry's] personal culpability a negative finding should be given to one of the special issues." The verdict form, however, contained only the text of the three special issues, and gave the jury two choices with respect to each: "Yes" or "No." Because the jury unanimously answered "yes" to each special issue, Penry was sentenced to death again.

ISSUES:
1. Is the admission into evidence of a report referring to future dangerousness a violation of the Fifth Amendment? NO.
2. Are jury instructions constitutionally inadequate if they do not permit the jury to consider and give effect to mitigating evidence? YES.

HOLDINGS:
1. The introduction of psychological evidence did not constitute an unreasonable application of clearly established federal law. Even if it did, the error in this case was harmless and therefore the conviction is affirmed.
2. The modified jury instructions violated due process and the state court's failure to so hold constituted an unreasonable application of clearly established federal law.

REASON: "Even if our precedent were to establish squarely that the prosecution's use of the Peebles report violated Penry's Fifth Amendment privilege against self-incrimination, that error would justify overturning Penry's sentence only if Penry could establish that the error 'had substantial and injurious effect or influence in determining the jury's verdict.' *Brecht v. Abrahamson*, 507 U.S. 619, 637 (1993) (quoting *Kotteakos v. United States*, 328 U.S. 750, 776 (1946)). We think it unlikely that Penry could make such a showing."

CASE SIGNIFICANCE: This is the second case involving a mentally retarded capital offender in Texas. In *Penry* I (*Penry v. Lynaugh*, 1989), the Court held that a mentally retarded defendant who has the ability to reason may be given the death penalty. Having said that, the Court also held, however, that the death penalty in this case could not be carried out because "the judge did not instruct the jury that it could consider and give effect to Penry's mitigating evidence of mental retardation and abuse, hence depriving the jury of a vehicle for expressing its 'reasoned moral response' to these circumstances." Penry was tried again and given the death penalty. This is that case (*Penry* II).

If you find that there are any mitigating circumstances in this case, you must decide how much weight they deserve, if any, and therefore, give effect and consideration to them in assessing the defendant's personal culpability at the time you answer the special issue. If you determine, when giving effect to the mitigating evidence, if any, that a life sentence, as reflected by a negative finding to the issue under consideration, rather than a death sentence, is an appropriate response to the personal culpability of the defendant, a negative finding should be given to one of the special issues.

KELLY V. SOUTH CAROLINA
534 U.S. 246 (2002)

CAPSULE: The jury must be instructed that a defendant would not be eligible for parole if sentenced to life in a capital case, if state law so provides.

FACTS: In 1996, William Kelly was indicted for a brutal murder, kidnapping, and armed robbery, as well as for possession of a knife during the commission of a violent crime.

ISSUE: Is it constitutional for a trial court in a death penalty case to refuse to instruct the jury that the defendant would be ineligible for parole under a life sentence? NO.

HOLDING: A defendant in a death penalty case is entitled to a jury instruction that, by state law, he would not be eligible for parole if sentenced to life in prison. Failure by the judge to give that instruction violates the defendant's due process rights. Raising the issue of character during trial was equivalent to raising the issue of future dangerousness.

REASON: "We take the State Supreme Court's reasons out of order, for the second one can be answered with little more than citation to *Shafer*, in which we reversed a South Carolina judgment last term. The state court said that '*Simmons* is inapplicable under [South Carolina's] new sentencing scheme because life without the possibility of parole is not the only legally available sentence alternative to death.' 343 S.C., at 364, 540 S.E. 2d, at 858. That statement mistakes the relationship of *Simmons* to the state sentencing scheme. It is true that a defendant charged with murder carrying the possibility of a death sentence can, under some circumstances, receive a sentence less than life imprisonment. But, as we explained in *Shafer*, under the South Carolina sentencing scheme a jury now makes a sentencing recommendation only if the jurors find the existence of an aggravating circumstance. When they do make a recommendation, their only alternatives are death or life without parole. 532 U.S., at 49–50. We therefore hold, as we did in *Shafer*, that the state court's reasoning is not to the point."

CASE SIGNIFICANCE: This is another case that focused on the issue of jury instructions in death penalty cases in South Carolina. The two other cases are *Simmons v. South Carolina* (1994) and *Shafer v. South Carolina* (2001). In *Shafer*, the Court said that a jury instruction in a capital case (explaining that life means life without the possibility of parole) is required under due process if state law provides for that kind of a sentence. In *Shafer*, the fact that state law provided that if the jury found one aggravating circumstance, such finding automatically limited the jury choice of a sentence to death or life without parole, required that the jury be instructed that a life sentence in these cases meant life without parole.

RING V. ARIZONA
536 U.S. 584 (2002)

CAPSULE: The finding of a fact that raises the maximum penalty in death penalty cases must be determined by a jury.

FACTS: In 1994, a Wells Fargo armored van pulled up to a department store at the Arrowhead Mall in Glendale, Arizona. Courier Dave Moss entered the store to pick up money. When he returned, the van and its driver, John Magoch, had disappeared. The van was found later that day by sheriff's deputies. The van's doors were locked and its engine was running. Inside the vehicle they found Magoch, dead from a single gunshot to the head. According to Wells Fargo records, more than $833,000 in cash and checks was also missing. Following an informant's tip, the Glendale police sought to determine whether Timothy Ring and James Greenham were involved in the robbery. The police investigation revealed that the two had made several expensive cash purchases in late 1994 and early 1995. Wiretaps were placed on the telephones of Ring, Greenham, and a third suspect, William Ferguson. The wiretaps produced several vague references to the robbery and murder but nothing concrete. The police executed a search warrant at Ring's house, discovering a duffel bag in his garage containing more than $271,000 in cash. They also found a note with the number "575,995" on it, followed by the words "splits" and the letters "F," "Y," and "T." The prosecution asserted that "F" was Ferguson, "Y" was Yoda (Greenham's nickname) and "T" was Timothy Ring.

ISSUE: Is a state's capital sentencing scheme that entrusts to a judge the finding of a fact that raises the defendant's maximum penalty constitutional? NO.

HOLDING: Capital offense defendants are entitled to a jury determination of any fact that results in an increase in the maximum punishment.

REASON: "Apart from the Eighth Amendment provenance of aggravating factors, Arizona presents 'no specific reason for excepting capital defendants from the constitutional protections . . . [extended] to defendants generally, and none is readily apparent.' Id., at 539 (O'Connor, J., dissenting). The notion 'that the Eighth Amendment's restrictions on a state legislature's ability to define capital crimes should be compensated for by permitting States more leeway under the Fifth and Sixth Amendments in proving an aggravating fact necessary to a capital sentence . . . is without precedent in our constitutional jurisprudence.' Ibid."

CASE SIGNIFICANCE: This case is a follow-up to *Apprendi v. New Jersey* (2000). In *Apprendi* (a hate-crime case in which New Jersey law provided that the penalty could be doubled if the judge found that the crime was racially motivated), the Supreme Court said that any fact that increases a defendant's sentence beyond that provided by statute must be submitted to the jury and proved beyond a reasonable doubt. In this case, *Ring v. Arizona*, the issue was whether a state's capital sentencing scheme that left to the judge the finding of a fact that raised the maximum penalty was constitutional. The Court said no and held that capital offense defendants are entitled to a jury determination of any fact that results in an increase in the maximum punishment.

UTTECHT, SUPERINTENDENT, WASHINGTON STATE PENITENTIARY V. BROWN
551 U.S. 1 (2007)

CAPSULE: Reviewing courts must give respect to trial courts in the determination of a potential juror's demeanor and qualifications.

FACTS: Cal Coburn Brown robbed, raped, tortured, and murdered a woman in Washington. Two days later, he robbed, raped, tortured, and attempted to murder another woman in California. Brown was captured and confessed to these crimes. He pleaded guilty to the California offenses and received a sentence of life imprisonment. A trial was held in Washington because the state was seeking the death penalty. During jury selection, three potential jurors were excused due to a concern that they could not be impartial in deciding whether to impose a death sentence. Brown was found guilty and given the death penalty.

ISSUE: Did the U.S. Court of Appeals for the Ninth Circuit fail to give proper respect to a trial judge's dismissal of a juror on the grounds that he could not carry out the duties of a juror in a capital sentencing case? YES.

HOLDING: Courts reviewing claims of error under *Witherspoon* and *Wainwright*, especially federal habeas courts, owe respect to the trial court, which is in a superior position to determine a potential juror's demeanor and qualifications.

REASON: "These precedents establish at least four principles of relevance here. First, a criminal defendant has the right to an impartial jury drawn from a venire that has not been tilted in favor of capital punishment by selective prosecutorial challenges for cause. *Witherspoon*, 391 U.S., at 521. Second, the State has a strong interest in having jurors who are able to apply capital punishment within the framework state law prescribes. *Witt*, 469 U.S., at 416. Third, to balance these interests, a juror who is substantially impaired in his or her ability to impose the death penalty under the state-law framework can be excused for cause; but if the juror is not substantially impaired, removal for cause is impermissible. Id., at 424. Fourth, in determining whether the removal of a potential juror would vindicate the State's interest without violating the defendant's right, the trial court makes a judgment based in part on the demeanor of the juror, a judgment owed deference by reviewing courts. Id., at 424–434.

"Deference to the trial court is appropriate because it is in a position to assess the demeanor of the venire, and of the individuals who compose it, a factor of critical importance in assessing the attitude and qualifications of potential jurors. Id., at 428; *Darden*, *supra*, at 178. Leading treatises in the area make much of non-verbal communication. See, e.g., V. Starr & M. McCormick, *Jury Selection* 389–523 (3rd ed. 2001); J. Frederick, *Mastering Voir Dire and Jury Selection* 39–56 (2d ed. 2005).

"The requirements of the Antiterrorism and Effective Death Penalty Act of 1996 (AEDPA), 110 Stat. 1214, of course, provide additional, and binding, directions to accord deference. The provisions of that statute create an independent, high standard to be met before a federal court may issue a writ of habeas corpus to set aside state-court rulings. See 28 U.S.C. §§ 2254(d)(1)–(2); *Williams v. Taylor*, 529 U.S. 362, 413 (2000)."

CASE SIGNIFICANCE: This case is important because it addresses the issue of whose determination prevails on issues involving the disqualification of jurors in a death penalty case. In this case, the trial court disqualified a potential juror (Juror Z) because it considered this potential juror as lacking the qualifications needed in a death penalty case. The trial transcript revealed that despite proper instructions, "Juror Z had both serious misunderstandings about his responsibility as a juror and an attitude toward capital punishment that could have prevented him from returning a death sentence under the facts of this case." The disqualification was upheld by the state courts. Brown later filed a habeas petition in federal court, which denied the petition. The denial, however, was reversed by the Court of Appeals for the Ninth Circuit, saying that "under *Witherspoon v. Illinois*, 391 U.S. 510, and its progeny, the state trial court had violated Brown's Sixth and Fourteenth Amendment rights by excusing 'Juror Z' for cause on the ground that he could not be impartial in deciding whether to impose a death sentence." This ruling was appealed to the U.S. Supreme Court.

The Court reversed the decision of the Ninth Circuit Court of Appeals, saying that "On this record, the trial court acted well within its discretion in granting the State's motion to excuse Juror Z. His answers, on their face, could have led the trial court to believe that he would be substantially impaired in his ability to impose the death penalty absent the possibility that Brown would be released and would re-offend. The trial court, furthermore, is entitled to deference because it had an opportunity to observe Juror Z's demeanor."

Reviewing its previous decisions on the issue of whether a juror might be disqualified because of some opposition to or reservations about imposing the death penalty, the Court said that previous cases established at least four relevant principles that guide the issue of disqualification. These are:

"First, a criminal defendant has the right to an impartial jury drawn from a venire that has not been tilted in favor of capital punishment by selective prosecutorial challenges for cause.

"Second, the State has a strong interest in having jurors who are able to apply capital punishment within the framework state law prescribes.

"Third, to balance these interests, a juror who is substantially impaired in the ability to impose the death penalty under the state-law framework can be excused for cause, but if the juror is not so impaired, removal for cause is impermissible; and

"Fourth, in determining whether a potential juror's removal would vindicate the State's interest without violating the defendant's right, the trial court based its judgment in part on the juror's demeanor, a judgment owed deference by reviewing courts."

F. COUNSEL

MICKENS V. TAYLOR
535 U.S. 162 (2002)

CAPSULE: A defendant must establish that a conflict of interest adversely affected his counsel's performance in order to establish a Sixth Amendment violation of the right to effective counsel.

FACTS: In 1993, Walter Mickens was convicted in the premeditated murder of Timothy Hall during or following the commission of an attempted forcible sodomy. In the sentencing phase of the trial, the jury found the murder to be "outrageously and wantonly vile" and sentenced Mickens to death. In 1998, Mickens filed a petition for a writ of habeas corpus alleging he was denied effective counsel because one of his court-appointed attorneys, Bryan Saunders, had been representing Hall (the victim) on assault and concealed weapons charges at the time of the murder. The attorney had only once met, briefly, with Hall, 10 days before his body was found. The same judge that had appointed Saunders to the Hall case appointed him to represent Mickens. Saunders did not disclose to the court, his co-counsel, or Mickens that he had previously represented Hall.

ISSUE: Is it unconstitutional when the trial court fails to inquire into a potential conflict of interest about which it knew or reasonably should have known? NO.

HOLDING: In order to demonstrate a Sixth Amendment violation of the right to effective counsel (where the trial court fails to inquire into a potential conflict of interest about which it knew or reasonably should have known), a defendant must establish that a conflict of interest adversely affected his counsel's performance. None was established in this case.

REASON: "Petitioner's proposed rule of automatic reversal when there existed a conflict that did not affect counsel's performance, but the trial judge failed to make the *Sullivan*-mandated inquiry, makes little policy sense. As discussed, the rule applied when the trial judge is not aware of the conflict (and thus not obligated to inquire) is that prejudice will be presumed only if the conflict has significantly affected counsel's performance—thereby rendering the verdict unreliable, even though *Strickland* prejudice cannot be shown. See *Sullivan, supra*, at 348–349. The trial court's awareness of a potential conflict neither renders it more likely that counsel's performance was significantly affected nor in any other way renders the verdict unreliable. Cf. *United States v. Cronic*, 466 U.S., at 662, n. 31. Nor does the trial judge's failure to make the *Sullivan*-mandated inquiry often make it harder for reviewing courts to determine conflict and effect, particularly since those courts may rely on evidence and testimony whose importance only becomes established at the trial."

CASE SIGNIFICANCE: This is an interesting case involving the right to effective counsel. In this case, the lawyer representing a death penalty defendant had previously represented the victim on assault and concealed weapons charges. Moreover, he was appointed to be the lawyer in that case by the same judge who presided over the trial of this death penalty defendant. On appeal, the defendant claimed that the fact that this was not disclosed to the co-counsel or to the defendant during trial and because the issue of a potential conflict of interest was not explored by the judge, these two facts demonstrated that there was ineffective representation.

The Supreme Court disagreed, saying that more than these allegations are needed to reverse a conviction. What is needed is proof by the defendant that a conflict of interest adversely affected the lawyer's performance. The defendant could not establish that in this case, therefore the conviction was affirmed.

This case highlights the difficulty defendants face when alleging ineffective counsel. This is as it should be. Were it otherwise, courts would be flooded with cases alleging ineffective representation, because many defendants could claim that the fact that they were convicted indicated that they had ineffective counsel. The bar has been raised higher for defendants who claim ineffective representation.

BELL, WARDEN V. CONE
535 U.S. 807 (2002)

CAPSULE: Failure by a defense lawyer to introduce mitigating evidence and waiving the closing argument does not necessarily mean that the defendant had ineffective counsel.

FACTS: In 1982, Gary Bradford Cone was convicted of, and sentenced to death for, the murder of an elderly couple. The killings ended a two-day crime spree that began on a Saturday when Cone robbed a jewelry store of $112,000 in merchandise. He later shot a police officer and another person, and demanded, at gunpoint, that another citizen hand over his car keys. He attempted to shoot the fleeing car owner, but his gun was out of ammunition. Cone eluded police throughout the afternoon and the next morning. Meanwhile, police inventoried his car and found illegal and prescription drugs, the stolen merchandise, and a substantial amount of cash. Early Sunday morning, Cone drew a gun on an elderly woman when she refused to let him in to use her phone. That afternoon, Cone broke into the home of Shipley and Cleopatra Todd, aged 93 and 79 years old, and killed them by repeatedly beating them about the head with a blunt instrument. Before leaving, he moved the bodies to make them less visible and then ransacked the first floor of their home. He changed his appearance by shaving his beard and fled to Florida. He was finally arrested there for robbing a drugstore. He admitted killing the Todds and shooting the police officer.

ISSUE: Does the failure to introduce mitigating evidence and the waiving of final arguments by a defense attorney in a capital case mean that defendant had ineffective counsel? NO.

HOLDING: The doctrine of "presumed prejudice" in death penalty cases applies only if a defense attorney completely fails to oppose the prosecution's case. Failing to introduce mitigating evidence and waiving closing argument are specific errors that are subject to the general "performance and prejudice" standard set by the Court in *Strickland*.

REASON: "The aspects of counsel's performance challenged by respondent—the failure to adduce mitigating evidence and the waiver of closing argument—are plainly of the same ilk as other specific attorney errors we have held subject to *Strickland*'s performance and prejudice components. In *Darden v. Wainwright*, 477 U.S. 168, 184 (1986), for example, we evaluated under *Strickland* a claim that counsel was ineffective for failing to put on any mitigating evidence at a capital sentencing hearing. In *Burger v. Kemp*, 483 U.S. 776, 788 (1987), we did the same when presented with a challenge to counsel's decision at a capital sentencing hearing not to offer any mitigating evidence at all."

CASE SIGNIFICANCE: The defendant in this death penalty case claimed that he had ineffective counsel because his defense lawyer waived the closing argument and failed to introduce mitigating evidence during his sentencing. The defense lawyer did not introduce mitigating evidence during sentencing, but presented mitigating evidence during the trial itself. The defense lawyer also waived final argument, but such waiver was a procedural tactic by the defense lawyer to prevent the lead prosecutor, who was an "extremely effective advocate" from arguing in rebuttal.

The Court held that the standard set in *Strickland v. Washington* (1984) in claims of ineffective counsel applied in this case. *Strickland* set the following standard: "The Court assumes that effective assistance of counsel is present unless the adversarial process is so undermined by counsel's conduct that the trial cannot be relied upon to have produced a just result."

To successfully claim ineffective counsel, the defendant must show: "(1) deficient performance by counsel and (2) a reasonable probability that, but for such deficiency, the result of the proceedings would have been different."

The Court then held that the state court's application of the *Strickland* attorney-performance standard, which led the state court to deny defendant's claim of ineffective counsel, was reasonable. The Supreme Court therefore reversed the judgment of the Court of Appeals, which had reversed the judgment of the trial court.

This case reaffirms the *Strickland* standard, which has been in place since 1984, and makes it difficult for defendants in all cases, including death penalty cases, to succeed in reversing a conviction based on claims of ineffective counsel.

WIGGINS V. SMITH
539 U.S. 510 (2003)

CAPSULE: The right to effective counsel is violated when defense attorneys in capital cases fail to conduct a reasonable investigation of defendant's childhood history before deciding not to present a mitigation case during sentencing.

FACTS: In 1989, Kevin Wiggins was convicted of the capital murder of 77-year-old Florence Lacs, who was found drowned in her bathtub. He chose to be sentenced by a jury. One of his defense attorneys told the jury in her opening statement that it would hear, among other things, about Wiggins' difficult life, but the defense never introduced such evidence. In motions to the court, the defense continued to refer to mitigating circumstances but never once mentioned Wiggins' life history or family background. The jury sentenced Wiggins to death. In a habeas petition, Wiggins' new lawyer alleged that Wiggins was denied effective counsel during trial when his lawyer "failed to investigate and present mitigating evidence of his dysfunctional background." The trial court denied Wiggins' habeas petition and the appeals court agreed, saying that the trial counsel made a reasoned choice to go with his best defense.

ISSUE: Does failure to conduct a reasonable investigation of defendant's childhood history before deciding not to present a mitigating case at sentencing in a capital case constitute a violation of the right to effective counsel? YES.

HOLDING: Defense attorneys in capital cases violate the Sixth Amendment right to effective assistance of counsel by failing to conduct a reasonable investigation of defendant's childhood history before deciding not to present a mitigation case at the sentencing phase of the trial.

REASON: "In light of these standards, our principal concern in deciding whether Schlaich and Nethercott exercised '[reasonable professional judgment],' id., at 691, is not whether counsel should have presented a mitigation case. Rather, we focus on whether the investigation supporting counsel's decision not to introduce mitigating evidence of Wiggins' background was itself reasonable. Ibid. Cf. *Williams v. Taylor, supra*, at 415 (O'Connor, J., concurring) (noting counsel's duty to conduct the 'requisite, diligent' investigation into his client's background). In assessing counsel's investigation, we must conduct an objective review of their performance, measured for 'reasonableness under prevailing professional norms,' *Strickland*, 466 U.S., at 688, which includes a context-dependent consideration of the challenged conduct as seen 'from counsel's perspective at the time,' id., at 689 ('[E]very effort [must] be made to eliminate the distorting effects of hindsight')."

CASE SIGNIFICANCE: This is one of several cases decided by the Supreme Court in the last few years on the issue of what constitutes ineffective counsel. In this case, defendant's lawyers failed to conduct a reasonable investigation of the defendant's childhood history and did not present any mitigating circumstances during sentencing. The defendant was sentenced to death. On appeal, and with a new lawyer, Wiggins alleged ineffective counsel. The Court agreed, saying, "Counsel did not conduct a reasonable investigation. Their decision not to expand their investigation beyond a pre-sentence investigation (PSI) report and Baltimore City Department of Social Services (DSS) records fell short of the professional standards prevailing in Maryland in 1989. Standard practice in Maryland capital cases at that time included the preparation of a social history report. Although there were funds to retain a forensic social worker, counsel chose not to commission a report. Their conduct similarly fell short of the American Bar Association's defense work standards. Moreover, in light of the facts counsel discovered in the DSS records concerning Wiggins' alcoholic mother and his problems in foster care, counsel's decision to cease investigating when they did was unreasonable. Any reasonably competent attorney would have realized that pursuing such leads was necessary to making an informed choice among possible defenses, particularly given the apparent absence of aggravating factors from Wiggins' background."

FLORIDA V. NIXON
543 U.S. 175 (2004)

CAPSULE: Counsel's performance is not automatically deficient because counsel fails to obtain defendant's express consent to a strategy of conceding guilt in order to concentrate on the penalty.

FACTS: On August 13, 1984, Jeane Bickner's charred body was discovered near Tallahassee, Florida. She had been tied to a tree and set on fire while she was still alive. The next day, police arrested Joe Elton Nixon, after Nixon's brother informed the sheriff's office that Nixon had confessed to the murder. Nixon described to the police in graphic detail how he had kidnapped and killed Bickner.

The evidence the state gathered establishing that Nixon had committed the murder was irrefutable and Nixon was indicted for first-degree murder, kidnapping, robbery, and arson. Public defender Michael Corin was assigned to represent Nixon and filed a plea of not guilty. After interviewing all the state's witnesses, Corin concluded that the strength of the state's case left no room to dispute his client's guilt. Corin then began plea negotiations, hoping the prosecution would drop the death penalty in exchange for Nixon's guilty plea to all charges. Negotiations ceased when it became evident that the prosecution was unwilling to recommend a sentence other than death.

Corin was an experienced capital defense attorney and believed it was in the best interests of his client to put his energies into the penalty phase of Nixon's trial rather than try to dispute the very damaging evidence that would be presented during the guilt/innocence phase of the trial. He believed that the only way to save Nixon's life would be to present extensive mitigating evidence concerning Nixon's mental instability. Corin feared that if they denied that Nixon had committed the crimes he was accused of, they would lose credibility with the jury and that he would then be unable to convince the jury that Nixon's conduct was the product of his mental illness. This strategy was explained to Nixon at least three times. He never verbally approved or disapproved Corin's proposed strategy. In fact, Nixon was mostly unresponsive during all their discussions. He gave Corin little assistance or direction in preparing the case and even refused to attend hearings on pretrial motions. Corin exercised his professional judgment and pursued his strategy.

When the trial began, Nixon was so unresponsive that he became disruptive and violent. On the second day of jury selection, Nixon pulled off his clothes, demanded a black judge and lawyer, refused to be escorted into the courtroom, and threatened to force the guards to shoot him. Nixon was examined by the judge to determine his fitness and Nixon stated he had no interest in the trial and threatened to misbehave if forced to attend. The judge determined that Nixon had intelligently and voluntarily waived his right to be present at trial. Corin went forward with his pretrial strategy and conceded Nixon's guilt whenever afforded the opportunity. He also continued to stress to the jury the importance of the penalty phase of the trial. During his closing argument he said, "I will hope to . . . argue to you and give you reasons not that Mr. Nixon's life be spared one final and terminal confinement forever, but that he not be sentenced to die." The jury found Nixon guilty on all counts.

During the penalty phase, Corin produced witnesses who testified about Nixon's difficult childhood, his erratic behavior before the murder, his antisocial behavior, his history of emotional instability, his low I.Q., and the possibility he had suffered brain damage. The state presented little new evidence, reminding the jury of its guilt-phase evidence. Corin produced a powerful closing argument and reemphasized to the jury that Nixon would never be released if given a life sentence. The jury recommended death after deliberating for three hours. The trial court imposed the death penalty and commended Corin for his performance during the trial. The court stressed that because of the overwhelming evidence of his client's guilt, to infer that Mr. Nixon was not guilty would have brought question to Corin's credibility during the penalty phase.

ISSUE: Does a strategic decision to concede without express consent from the defendant, during the guilt phase of a trial, the defendant's commission of murder, and to concentrate the defense on establishing, at the penalty phase, cause for sparing the defendant's life automatically rank as prejudicial ineffective counsel? NO.

HOLDING: Counsel's failure to obtain the defendant's express consent to a strategy of conceding guilt in a capital trial does not automatically render counsel's performance deficient.

REASON: "The Florida Supreme Court, as just observed, see *supra*, at 9, required Nixon's 'affirmative, explicit acceptance' of Corin's strategy because it deemed Corin's statements to the jury 'the functional equivalent of a guilty plea.' *Nixon* II, 758 So. 2d, at 624. We disagree with that assessment.

"Despite Corin's concession, Nixon retained the rights accorded a defendant in a criminal trial. Cf. Boykin, at 395 U.S., at 242–243, and n. 4 (a guilty plea is 'more than a confession which admits that the accused did various acts,' it is a stipulation that no proof by the prosecution need be advanced'). The State was obliged to present during the guilt phase competent, admissible evidence establishing the essential elements of the crimes with which Nixon was charged. That aggressive evidence would thus be separated from the penalty phase, enabling the defense to concentrate that portion of the trial on mitigating factors. See *supra*, at 4, 7. Further, the defense reserved the right to cross-examine witnesses for the prosecution and could endeavor, as Corin did, to exclude prejudicial evidence. See supra, at 6. In addition, in the event of errors in the trial or jury instructions, a concession of guilt would not hinder the defendant's right to appeal.

"Corin was obliged to, and in fact several times did, explain his proposed trial strategy to Nixon. See supra, at 4, 9. Given Nixon's constant resistance to answering inquiries put to him by counsel and court, see *Nixon* III, 857 So. 2d, at 187–188 (Wells, J., dissenting), Corin was not additionally required to gain express consent before conceding Nixon's guilt. The two evidentiary hearings conducted by the Florida trial court demonstrate beyond doubt that Corin fulfilled his duty of consultation by informing Nixon of counsel's proposed strategy and its potential benefits. Nixon's characteristic silence each time information was conveyed to him, in sum, did not suffice to render unreasonable Corin's decision to concede guilt and to home in, instead, on the life or death penalty issue."

CASE SIGNIFICANCE: Here we have yet another case questioning the effectiveness of counsel. This case differs from the others in that the evidence showing the culpability of the defendant was so overwhelming that there was very little any defense counsel could have done to avoid a guilty verdict. The question before the Court, however, was if counsel, without the express approval of the defendant, could concede to the state's evidence and target his energies toward producing mitigating evidence at the penalty phase of the trial. By conceding to the state's overwhelming evidence rather than offering a guilty plea at the initial stages of the trial, counsel was able to retain his client's Fifth and Sixth Amendment trial rights. Defense counsel was able to cross-examine witnesses and the state was forced to prove all the essential elements of the crimes against the accused. The Supreme Court acknowledged that Mr. Corin was an experienced capital defense attorney and that his professional judgment on how to proceed with this case was made from a sound analysis of what lay before him. The Court also stressed that Corin was not in error moving forward with his strategy due to the disruptive and uncooperative behavior of his client. Mr. Nixon had ample opportunities to voice his objections to the strategy and did not do so. The Supreme Court ruled that the lack of an expressed approval of a defense strategy does not automatically equate to ineffective counsel.

ROMPILLA V. BEARD, SECRETARY, PENNSYLVANIA DEPT. OF CORRECTIONS
545 U.S. 374 (2005)

CAPSULE: Defense counsel must make reasonable efforts to obtain and review material that counsel knows the prosecution will probably rely on as evidence of aggravation at the sentencing phase of a capital trial.

FACTS: On January 14, 1988, the body of James Scanlon was discovered in a bar he ran in Allentown, Pennsylvania. Scanlon had been stabbed numerous times and his body had been set on fire. Ronald Rompilla was found guilty of the crime in a death penalty-eligible case. During the penalty phase of the trial, the prosecution presented three aggravating factors to justify a death sentence: that the murder was committed in the course of another felony; that the murder was committed by torture; and that Rompilla had a significant history of felony convictions that included the use or threat of violence. The jury found all three aggravating factors had been proven. The defense presented five members of Rompilla's family, who testified to Rompilla's innocence (residual doubt) and beseeched the jury for mercy. The defense did not present evidence to the jury concerning Rompilla's extremely abusive childhood or that he suffered from mental illness and alcoholism. The jury found the aggravating factors outweighed the mitigating factors and sentenced Rompilla to death.

ISSUE: Does a defense attorney in a capital punishment case have to make reasonable efforts to obtain and review material that counsel knows the prosecution will probably rely on as evidence of aggravation at the trial's sentencing phase? YES.

HOLDING: "Even when a capital defendant's family members and the defendant himself have suggested that no mitigating evidence is available, defendant's lawyer is bound to make reasonable efforts to obtain and review material that counsel knows the prosecution will probably rely on as evidence of aggravation at the sentencing phase of trial."

REASON: "Under 28 U.S.C. § 2254, Rompilla's entitlement to federal habeas relief turns on showing that the state court's resolution of his claim of ineffective counsel under *Strickland v. Washington, supra*, 'resulted in a decision that was contrary to, or involved an unreasonable application of, clearly established Federal law, as determined by the Supreme Court of the United States,' § 2254(d)(1). An 'unreasonable application' occurs when a state court 'identifies the correct governing legal principle from this Court's decisions but unreasonably applies that principle to the facts of petitioner's case.' *Wiggins v. Smith, supra*, at 520 (quoting *Williams v. Taylor, supra*, at 409 (internal quotation marks omitted))."

"Ineffective assistance under *Strickland* is deficient performance by counsel resulting in prejudice, 466 U.S., at 687, with performance being measured against an 'objective standard of reasonableness,' id., at 688, 'under prevailing professional norms.' Ibid.; *Wiggins v. Smith, supra*, at 521. This case, like some others recently, looks to norms of adequate investigation in preparing for the sentencing phase of a capital trial, when defense counsel's job is to counter the State's evidence of aggravated culpability with evidence of mitigation. In judging the defense's investigation, as in applying *Strickland* generally, hindsight is discounted by pegging adequacy to 'counsel's perspective at the time' investigative decisions are made. 466 U.S., at 689, and by giving a 'heavy measure of deference to counsel's judgments,' id., at 691."

"The notion that defense counsel must obtain information that the state has and will use against the defendant is not simply a matter of common sense. As the district court points out, the American Bar Association Standards for Criminal Justice in circulation at the time of Rompilla's trial describes the obligation in terms no one could misunderstand in the circumstances of a case like this one:

It is the duty of the lawyer to conduct a prompt investigation of the circumstances of the case and to explore all avenues leading to facts relevant to the merits of the case and the penalty in the event of conviction. The investigation should always include efforts to secure information in the possession of the prosecution and law enforcement authorities. The duty to investigate exists regardless of the accused's admissions or statements to the lawyer of facts constituting guilt or the accused's stated desire to plead guilty. 1 ABA Standards for Criminal Justice 4–4.1 (2d ed. 1982 Supp.).

"The dissent thinks this analysis creates a 'rigid, per se,' rule that requires defense counsel to do a complete review of the file on any prior conviction introduced, post, at 9 (opinion of Kennedy, J.), but that is a mistake. Counsel fell short here because they failed to make reasonable efforts to review the prior conviction file, despite knowing that the prosecution intended to introduce Rompilla's prior conviction not merely by entering a notice of conviction into evidence but by quoting damaging testimony of the rape victim into that case. The unreasonableness of attempting no more than they did was heightened by the easy availability of the file at the trial courthouse, and the great risk that testimony about a similar violent crime would hamstring counsel's chosen defense of residual doubt. It is owing to these circumstances that the state courts were objectionably unreasonable in concluding that counsel could reasonably decline to make any effort to review the file. Other situations, where a defense lawyer is not charged with knowledge that the prosecution intends to use a prior conviction in this way, might well warrant a different assessment."

CASE SIGNIFICANCE: This case addresses the recurring issue in death penalty cases of adequate legal representation. Lawyers for Rompilla failed to examine the file on the defendant's prior record, which included rape and an assault conviction. They failed to do this despite knowledge that the government would seek the death penalty against their client "by proving that Rompilla had a significant history of felony convictions indicating the use or threat of violence, that it would attempt to establish this history by proving the prior conviction, and that it would emphasize his violent character by introducing a transcript of the rape victim's trial testimony." The Court added that, "although the prior conviction was a public record, readily available at the courthouse where Rompilla was to be tried, counsel looked at no part of it until warned by the prosecution a second time, and even then did not examine the entire file." The Court then observed that "it is difficult to see how counsel could have failed to realize that not examining the file would seriously compromise their opportunity to respond to an aggravation case. Their duty to make all reasonable efforts to learn what they could about the offense the prosecution was going to use certainly included obtaining the Commonwealth's own readily available file to learn what it knew about the crime . . ."

Instead of doing their own investigation and probing into Rompilla's troubled background and case history, the lawyers in this case simply relied on the testimony of Rompilla himself and members of his family as to what they recalled about his background. They failed to search for "school reports, juvenile records, and evidence of drinking habits" in an effort to rebut what the prosecutors would present. They knew that such evidence would be presented against their client. The behavior of the lawyers was deemed by the Court as inadequate by any standard. The Court found that had counsel done a better job they would have discovered a great deal of evidence that would likely have led to a different result in the penalty imposed.

G. DUE PROCESS

LANKFORD V. IDAHO
500 U.S. 110 (1991)

CAPSULE: Lack of adequate notice during the sentencing hearing that the defendant might be given the death penalty violates due process if the judge later imposes the death penalty.

FACTS: On December 1, 1983, Bryan Lankford was charged with first-degree murder. Identical charges were also filed against Lankford's older brother, Mark. At the arraignment, the trial judge advised Bryan Lankford that "the maximum punishment that you may receive if you are convicted on either of the two charges is imprisonment for life or death." During plea negotiations, the prosecutor became convinced that Lankford's older brother Mark was primarily responsible for the crimes and was the actual killer of both victims. The parties agreed on an indeterminate sentence with a 10-year minimum in exchange for a guilty plea, subject to a commitment from the trial judge that he would impose the sentence. The trial judge refused to make the commitment and the case went to trial. A jury found Bryan Lankford guilty on both counts of first-degree murder. Prior to the sentencing hearing, the court ordered the state to provide notice of whether it would seek the death penalty, and if so, to file a statement of the aggravating circumstances on which it intended to rely. The state filed a negative response, and there was no discussion of the death penalty as a possible sentence at the sentencing hearing. Rather, both defense counsel and the prosecutor argued the merits of concurrent or consecutive, and fixed or indeterminate sentence terms. At the hearing's conclusion, the trial judge indicated a disbelief in Lankford's testimony, stating that the crime's seriousness warranted more severe punishment than the state had recommended, and mentioned the possibility of death as a sentencing option. The trial judge later sentenced Lankford to death based on five specific aggravating circumstances.

ISSUE: Did the sentencing process in this case satisfy the requirements of the due process clause of the Fourteenth Amendment? NO.

HOLDING: The sentencing process in this case violated the due process clause of the Fourteenth Amendment because at the time of the sentencing hearing, Lankford and his counsel did not have adequate notice that the judge might sentence him to death.

REASON: "At the very least, this is a case in which reasonable judges might differ concerning the appropriateness of the death sentence. It is therefore a case in which some of the reasoning that motivated our decision in *Gardner v. Florida*, 430 U.S. 349 (1977), is applicable. In that case, relying partly on the Due Process Clause of the Fourteenth Amendment and partly on the Eighth Amendment's prohibition against cruel and unusual punishment, the Court held that a procedure for selecting people for the death penalty that permits consideration of secret information about the defendant is unacceptable. The plurality opinion, like the opinion concurring in the judgment, emphasized the special importance of fair procedure in the capital sentencing context. We emphasized that 'death is a different kind of punishment from any other which may be imposed in this country.' We explained:

Although the trial judge in this case did not rely on secret information, his silence following the State's response to the presentencing order had the practical effect of concealing from the parties the principal issue to be decided at the hearing. Notice of issues to be resolved by the adversary process is a fundamental characteristic of fair procedure."

CASE SIGNIFICANCE: This is an important case on the issue of what constitutes "fair notice" in death penalty cases. After the jury found the defendant guilty, the judge ordered the state to provide notice of whether it would seek the death penalty and, if the state wanted to do that, to list the aggravating circumstances it intended to rely upon, in accordance with state law. The state filed a negative response and there was no mention of the death penalty at the sentencing hearing. Nonetheless, the judge imposed the death penalty anyway, saying that he did not believe the defendant's testimony. Moreover, the judge based the death sentence on five specific aggravating circumstances.

On appeal, the Supreme Court declared the procedure unconstitutional, concluding that "if defense counsel had been notified that the trial judge was contemplating a death sentence based on five specific aggravating circumstances, presumably she would have advanced arguments that addressed these circumstances; however, she did not make these arguments because they were entirely inappropriate in a discussion about the length of petitioner's possible incarceration." The Court added: "Although the trial judge in this case did not rely on secret information, his silence following the State's response to the presentencing order had the practical effect of concealing from the parties the principal issue to be decided at the hearing." The Court concluded by saying that "notice of issues to be resolved by the adversary process is a fundamental characteristic of fair procedure," and that "without such notice, the Supreme Court is denied the benefit of the adversary process."

This case points to the importance of giving the defendant in a death penalty case fair notice of anything and everything that happens in the case, including the issues that are to be raised in the sentencing phase. Not to do so is to violate a defendant's right to due process, as this case illustrates. Had there been fair notice that the death penalty might be imposed, counsel for the defendant could have introduced evidence to rebut the five specific aggravating circumstances used by the judge, thus making the death penalty inappropriate. Denial of the opportunity for the defense counsel to do so violates due process.

PAYNE V. TENNESSEE
501 U.S. 808 (1991)

CAPSULE: A victim impact statement is admissible in the sentencing phase of death penalty cases.

FACTS: Payne was convicted of the first-degree murders of Charisse Christopher and her two-year-old daughter, and of the first-degree assault with intent to murder of Charisse's three-year-old son, Nicholas. During the sentencing phase of the trial, Payne called his parents, his girlfriend, and a clinical psychologist on his behalf. They testified to various mitigating aspects of Payne's background and character. The state called Nicholas's grandmother, who testified that the child missed his mother and baby sister. During the prosecutor's plea for the death penalty, the continuing effects upon Nicholas due to the attack and the effects of the crimes upon the victim's family were mentioned. The jury sentenced Payne to death on each of the murder counts. Payne's contention that the admission of the grandmother's testimony and the state's closing argument violated his Eighth Amendment rights was rejected by the Tennessee Supreme Court. Payne based his arguments on *Booth v. Maryland*, 482 U.S. 496 (1987), and *South Carolina v. Gathers*, 490 U.S. 805 (1989), which held that evidence and arguments relating to the victim and the impact of the victim's death on the victim's family are per se inadmissible in death penalty cases.

ISSUE: Does the Eighth Amendment prohibit the admission of victim impact evidence during the penalty phase of a capital trial? NO.

HOLDING: The Eighth Amendment does not per se prohibit a capital sentencing jury from considering "victim impact" evidence relating to the victim's personal characteristics and the emotional impact of the murder on the victim's family, nor does it preclude a prosecutor from arguing such evidence at a capital sentencing hearing.

REASON: "Virtually no limits are placed on the relevant mitigating evidence a capital defendant may introduce concerning his own circumstances. The State has a legitimate interest in counteracting such evidence, but the *Booth* rule prevents it from doing so. Similarly, fairness to the prosecution requires rejection of Gathers' extension of the *Booth* rule to the prosecutor's argument, since, under the Eighth Amendment, this Court has given the capital defendant's attorney broad latitude to argue relevant mitigating evidence reflecting his client's individual personality. Booth also erred in reasoning that it would be difficult, if not impossible, for a capital defendant to rebut victim impact evidence without shifting the focus of the sentencing hearing away from the defendant to the victim. The mere fact that for tactical reasons it might not be prudent for the defense to rebut such evidence makes the case no different from others in which a party is faced with this sort of dilemma. Nor is there merit to the concern voiced in *Booth* that admission of such evidence permits a jury to find that defendants whose victims were assets to their communities are more deserving of punishment than those whose victims are perceived to be less worthy. Such evidence is not generally offered to encourage comparative judgments of this kind, but is designed to show instead each victim's uniqueness as an individual human being. In the event that victim impact evidence is introduced that is so unduly prejudicial that it renders the trial fundamentally unfair, the Fourteenth Amendment's due process clause provides a mechanism for relief. Thus, a State may properly conclude that for a jury to assess meaningfully the defendants' moral culpability and blameworthiness, it should have before it at the sentencing phase victim impact evidence."

CASE SIGNIFICANCE: This case virtually overrules *Booth v. Maryland*, 41 Cr. L. 3282 (1987), which held that victim impact statements (which typically describe a victim's characteristics and the effect of the crime on the victim's family) are not admissible in death penalty cases. The Court said that although the doctrine of stare decisis (adherence to decided cases) is usually the best policy, it is "not an inexorable command," particularly in cases in which the decisions are "unworkable or badly reasoned." Decided only four years earlier, the Court considered the rule in *Booth* to be unworkable and badly reasoned, and overruled that part of the decision. The Court said that the *Booth* decision was based on two premises: "that evidence relating to a particular victim or to the harm caused a victim's family does not in general reflect on the defendant's 'blameworthiness,' and that only evidence of 'blameworthiness' is relevant to the capital sentencing decision." The Court rejected these statements, saying that "assessment of the harm caused by the defendant has long been an important factor in determining the appropriate punishment, and victim impact evidence is simply another method of informing the sentencing authority about such harm."

Decided by a six-to-three vote, this decision reflects the definite imprint of a conservative Court that has shown willingness to allow into the sentencing phase evidence that previously was considered inadmissible. The Court rejected the concept that such evidence must be kept out of death penalty cases because a capital defendant must be treated as a "uniquely individual human being," saying that because there are virtually no limits placed on the relevant mitigating evidence that may be introduced for the defendant in a capital offense, the same should also be true with regard to aggravating circumstances. The Court seeks to place the prosecution and the defense on the same level in the introduction of evidence in the sentencing phase, even in death penalty cases.

SHAFER V. SOUTH CAROLINA
532 U.S. 36 (2001)

CAPSULE: A jury instruction in a capital case explaining that "life" means life without possibility of parole is required under due process, if state law provides for a "life without possibility of parole" sentence.

FACTS: During an attempted robbery in South Carolina, Wesley Aaron Shafer Jr. shot and killed a convenience store cashier. He was charged with murder, attempted armed robbery, and criminal conspiracy. Shafer was informed that the prosecution would seek the death penalty. He was also informed that the prosecution would present evidence of Shafer's "prior bad acts" and his "propensity for [future] violence and unlawful conduct."

ISSUE: Is a jury instruction in a capital case explaining that "life" means life without the possibility of parole required under the due process clause of the Fourteenth Amendment? YES.

HOLDING: Whenever future dangerousness is at issue in a capital sentencing proceeding, due process requires that the jury be informed that a life sentence carries no possibility of parole if such a sentencing option is provided by state law. This is in accordance with the Supreme Court's ruling in *Simmons v. South Carolina* (1994).

REASON: "The South Carolina Supreme Court was no doubt correct to this extent: At the time the trial judge instructed the jury in Shafer's case, it was indeed possible that Shafer would receive a sentence other than death or life without the possibility of parole. That is so because South Carolina, in line with other States, gives capital juries, at the penalty phase, discrete and sequential functions. Initially, capital juries serve as fact-finders in determining whether an alleged aggravating circumstance exists. Once that factual threshold is passed, the jurors exercise discretion in determining the punishment that ought to be imposed."

CASE SIGNIFICANCE: In *Simmons v. South Carolina* (1994), an earlier case referred to as precedent in this case, the Court ruled that death penalty defendants are entitled to a jury instruction that a life sentence means life imprisonment without parole in cases in which the defendant's future dangerousness is at issue and the only sentencing alternative available, other than death, is life without the possibility of parole. *Shafer* is a follow-up of the *Simmons* case. The issue in *Shafer* was whether, in cases in which future dangerousness was at issue in sentencing, due process requires that the jury be informed that a life sentence carries no possibility of parole if there were two alternatives to the death penalty instead of just one—"life without parole." The Court held that in these types of cases the answer is yes, the jury must be informed.

SATTAZAHN V. PENNSYLVANIA
537 U.S. 101 (2003)

CAPSULE: After a reversal of conviction, it is constitutional to seek the death penalty even if the initial sentence imposed was life imprisonment.

FACTS: On April 12, 1987, David Allen Sattazahn and his accomplice, Jeffrey Hammer, hid in a wooded area waiting to rob Richard Boyer, manager of the Heidelberg Family Restaurant. They approached Boyer in the parking lot with guns drawn. They demanded the bank deposit bag containing the day's receipts. Boyer threw the bag toward the roof of the restaurant. Sattazahn ordered Boyer to retrieve the bag but Boyer tried to run away instead. Both Sattazahn and Hammer fired their weapons and Boyer was killed. The two men grabbed the deposit bag and fled. The Commonwealth of Pennsylvania brought Sattazahn to trial and sought the death penalty. He was convicted on first-, second-, and third-degree murder charges.

ISSUE: Is it a violation of the double jeopardy clause to seek the death penalty at a retrial when the sentence at the initial trial was life in prison? NO.

HOLDING: A life sentence imposed by state law when a jury is unable to reach a unanimous verdict at the penalty phase does not constitute an "acquittal" and therefore does not prevent the imposition of the death penalty under the double jeopardy clause of the Fifth Amendment upon retrial, following a reversal of the defendant's conviction as the result of an appeal.

REASON: "Normally, 'a retrial following a "hung jury" does not violate the Double Jeopardy Clause.' *Richardson v. United States*, 468 U.S. 317, 324 (1984). Petitioner contends, however, that given the unique treatment afforded capital-sentencing proceedings under *Bullington*, double-jeopardy protections were triggered when the jury deadlocked at his first sentencing proceeding and the court prescribed a sentence of life imprisonment pursuant to Pennsylvania law."

CASE SIGNIFICANCE: This case is significant because it addresses the issue of the kind of penalty a capital offense defendant can receive after reversal of a conviction on appeal. In this case, Sattazahn was convicted of murder charges and given a life sentence because Pennsylvania law provided that the jury must unanimously find at least one aggravating circumstance and no mitigating circumstances in order for the death penalty to be imposed. The sentencing jury was deadlocked at nine to three for life imprisonment. The judge then sentenced Sattazahn to life imprisonment. Sattazahn appealed his conviction and sentence and won a new trial. On retrial, the defendant was again convicted, but this time the second jury sentenced him to death. The legal question was whether Sattazahn could be sentenced to death after having been given a life sentence during his first trial.

The Court said yes, concluding that the first trial did not constitute an acquittal of the defendant. The judge had to impose a life sentence because the jury was deadlocked on a vote of nine to three. Because Pennsylvania law provided that the death penalty could be imposed only if the jury was unanimous on the type of sentence to be imposed, the judge had to impose a life sentence. This is not equivalent to an acquittal of the defendant; therefore, he could be sentenced to death on retrial if the second jury was unanimous on the penalty to be imposed. There was no violation of the double jeopardy provision of the Constitution, which mandates that "no person shall . . . be subject for the same offence to be twice put in jeopardy of life or limb."

DECK V. MISSOURI
544 U.S. 622 (2005)

CAPSULE: The use of visible shackles during a capital trial's penalty phase is prohibited unless the use is "justified by a state interest" specific to the defendant.

FACTS: In 1998, Carman Deck was tried by the State of Missouri for robbing and murdering an elderly couple. During the trial, Deck was required to wear leg braces that apparently were not visible to the jury. Deck was found guilty and given a death sentence. The state supreme court upheld Deck's conviction but ordered a new sentencing proceeding.

Deck appeared on the first day of the new hearing shackled with leg irons, handcuffs, and a belly chain. Before, during, and after the voir dire, defense counsel objected and moved to have the jury panel stricken "because of the fact that Mr. Deck is shackled in front of the jury and makes them think that he is . . . violent today." All objections were overruled, the court stating that his "being shackled takes any fear out of their minds." Deck was again sentenced to death.

ISSUE: Does the use of visible shackles during the penalty phase of a capital trial violate the federal Constitution? YES.

HOLDING: The Fifth and Fourteenth Amendments prohibit the use of visible shackles during a capital trial's penalty phase unless that use is "justified by an essential state interest" specific to the defendant on trial.

REASON: "We first consider whether, as a general matter, the Constitution permits a State to use visible shackles routinely in the guilt phase of a criminal trial. The answer is clear: The law has long forbidden routine use of visible shackles during the guilt phase; it permits a State to shackle a criminal defendant only in the presence of a special need."

"This rule has deep roots in the common law. In the eighteenth century, Blackstone wrote that 'it is laid down in our ancient books, that, though under an indictment of the highest nature,' a defendant must be brought to the bar without irons, or any manner of shackles or bonds; unless there be evident danger of an escape 4 W. Blackstone, *Commentaries on the Laws of England* 317 (1769) (footnote omitted)."

"More recently, this Court has suggested that a version of this rule forms part of the Fifth and Fourteenth Amendments' due process guarantee. Thirty-five years ago, when considering the trial of an unusually obstreperous criminal defendant, the court held that the Constitution sometimes permitted special measures, including physical restraints. *Allen*, 397 U.S., at 343–344. The court wrote that 'binding and gagging might possibly be the fairest and most reasonable way to handle' such a defendant. Id., at 344. But the court immediately added that 'even to contemplate such a technique . . . arouses a feeling that no person should be tried shackled and gagged except as a last resort.' Ibid."

"The considerations that militate against the routine use of visible shackles during the guilt phase of a criminal trial apply with like force to penalty proceedings in capital cases. This is obviously so in respect to the latter two considerations mentioned, securing a meaningful defense and maintaining dignified proceedings. It is less obviously so in respect to the first consideration mentioned, for the defendant's conviction means that the presumption of innocence no longer applies. Hence shackles do not undermine the jury's effort to apply that presumption."

"Nonetheless, shackles at the penalty phase threaten related concerns. Although the jury is no longer deciding between guilt and innocence, it is deciding between life and death. That decision, given the 'severity' and 'finality' of the sanction, is no less important than the decision about guilt. *Monge v. California*, 524 U.S. 721, 732 (1998) (quoting *Gardner v. Florida*, 430 U.S. 349, 357 (1977)."

CASE SIGNIFICANCE: The Court has held in a number of cases that the use of shackles during trial is unconstitutional because it might bias the judge or jury against the defendant and makes a trial less dignified. The implication when shackles are used is that the defendant is violent and needs to be restrained. Moreover, it jeopardizes the presumption that a defendant is innocent unless proved otherwise. This case, however, presented a different issue: Can a death penalty defendant be shackled during the penalty phase of a trial? The Court said no, thus prohibiting the use of this form of restraint during either the guilt-innocence stage or the penalty stage of the trial.

The only time shackles can be used during trial is if such restraint is "justified by a state interest specific to the particular defendant on trial." What does this mean? The Court replies: "In the judge's discretion, account may be taken of special circumstances in the case at hand, including security concerns that may call for shackling in order to accommodate the important need to protect the courtroom and its occupants." In sum, routinely putting the defendant in shackles during any part of the trial is unconstitutional unless the judge determines that such is necessary in that particular case to meet an important need. It cannot be based on the general assumption that defendants in a death penalty case are dangerous and need to be restrained.

BELL, WARDEN V. THOMPSON
545 U.S. 794 (2005)

CAPSULE: Withholding a mandate for five months after the U.S. Supreme Court denied review was an abuse of discretion by the Sixth Circuit Court of Appeals.

FACTS: In 1985, Gregory Thompson abducted and murdered Brenda Blanton Lane by stabbing her repeatedly. Prior to trial, the judge referred Thompson to a 30-day stay in a state-run mental facility to explore his mental condition. Thompson was deemed competent to stand trial. He offered no evidence during the guilt phase of his trial and was convicted by a jury of first-degree murder. During the sentencing phase of trial, defense attorneys presented Thompson's positive qualities and his capacity to adjust to prison life as mitigating factors. A former girlfriend also claimed that Thompson's behavior became erratic after he suffered head injuries during an attack by three fellow servicemen while he was in the Navy. In rebuttal, the State called the clinical psychologist who led the pretrial evaluation of Thompson's competence. He testified that his examination of Thompson revealed no significant mental illness. Thompson was sentenced to death.

Thompson's claims that his counsel had failed to adequately investigate his mental health were unsuccessful in the state courts. His claims were also rejected by the federal district court. Thompson's habeas counsel, however, had failed to include in the record the deposition and report of Dr. Faye Sultan, who concluded that, at the time of trial, Thompson's symptoms indicated that he was "suffering serious mental illness at the time of the 1985 offense for which he has been convicted and sentenced. This mental illness would have substantially impaired Mr. Thompson's ability to conform his conduct to the requirements of the law." The documents were included with Thompson's petition to the Sixth Circuit Court of Appeals but that claim was also rejected. Thompson then petitioned the U.S. Supreme Court and the Sixth Circuit stayed its mandate until the Court decided whether to hear the case. The Court denied the petition and the Sixth Circuit stayed its mandate again pending the Supreme Court's decision on Thompson's petition for rehearing, which the Court denied. The Sixth Circuit still did not issue a mandate. Five months later the Sixth Circuit issued an amended opinion on Thompson's habeas petition, overturning the district court's dismissal of his ineffective counsel claim and ordered hearings based on that claim.

ISSUE: Did the Sixth Circuit abuse its discretion by withholding its mandate in the case for more than five months without entering a formal order after the U.S. Supreme Court denied *certiorari* and a petition for rehearing? YES.

HOLDING: Even assuming a court may withhold its mandate after the denial of certiorari in some cases, the Court of Appeals' decision to do so here was an abuse of discretion.

REASON: "We find an abuse of discretion for the following reasons. Prominent among our concerns is the length of time between this Court's denial of certiorari and the Court of Appeals' issuance of its amended opinion. We denied Thompson's petition for certiorari in December 2003 and his petition for rehearing one month later. From this last denial, however, the Court of Appeals delayed issuing its mandate for over five months, releasing its amended opinion in June."

"The parties' assumption that Thompson's habeas proceedings were complete was all the more reasonable because the Court of Appeals' delay in issuing its mandate took place after we had denied certiorari. As a practical matter, a decision by this Court denying discretionary review usually signals the end of litigation. While Rule 41(b) may authorize a court to stay the mandate after certiorari is denied, the circumstances where such a stay would be warranted are rare. See, e.g., *First Gibraltar Bank, FSB v. Morales*, 42 F.3d 895 (CA5 1995); *Alphin v. Henson*, 552 F.2d 1033 (CA4 1977). In the typical case, where the stay of mandate is entered solely to allow this Court time to consider a petition for certiorari, Rule 41(d)(2)(D) provides the default: 'The court of appeals must issue the mandate immediately when a copy of the Supreme Court order denying the petition for writ of *certiorari* is filed.'"

"A court's discretion under Rule 41 must be exercised, however, in a way that is consistent with the 'State's interest in the finality of convictions that have survived direct review within the state court system.' Id., at 555 (quoting *Brecht v. Abrahamson*, 507 U.S. 619, 635 (1993)). Tennessee expended considerable time and resources in seeking to enforce a capital sentence rendered 20 years ago, a sentence that reflects the judgment of the citizens of Tennessee that Thompson's crimes merit the ultimate punishment. By withholding the mandate for months—based on evidence that supports only an arguable constitutional claim—while the State prepared to carry out Thompson's sentence, the Court of Appeals did not accord the appropriate level of respect to that judgment. See *Calderon v. Thompson, supra*, at 554–557."

CASE SIGNIFICANCE: This case loses much significance because of its convoluted facts, which are difficult to understand, as well as the absence of a direct constitutional question, although due process (interpreted as fundamental fairness) is somehow involved. The Court's decision was instead based on the provisions of the Federal Rules of Appellate Procedure and did not rest on a direct constitutional issue, which is usually the path taken in death penalty cases. The Court's holding said: "Assuming that Federal Rule of Appellate Procedure 41 authorizes a stay of a mandate following a denial or *certiorari* and that a court may stay the mandate without entering an order, the Sixth Circuit's decision to do so here was an abuse of discretion." This case involved layer upon layer of technical proceedings best understood by appellate court lawyers and judges, but is not of much interest to laypersons. Its ultimate legal value lies in the message sent to lower courts that decisions must be made public in a timely manner, particularly in death penalty cases where so much is at stake for both the defendant and society.

OREGON V. GUZEK

546 U.S. 517 (2006)

CAPSULE: The Constitution does not prohibit a state from limiting the type of evidence a capital defendant can introduce at a sentencing proceeding.

FACTS: Randy Lee Guzek and two associates robbed and murdered Rod and Lois Houser. During the investigation of the crime, police discovered that Guzek held a special grudge against the Housers. The three suspects were arrested and the associates confessed. They testified at Guzek's murder trial and identified Guzek as the ringleader. The defense presented two alibi witnesses as part of its trial strategy. Guzek's grandfather and mother stated that he was with one or the other at the time of the crime. The jury did not believe the alibi and convicted him of murder. Guzek was sentenced to death. The Oregon Supreme Court vacated his sentence three times.

ISSUE: Do the Eighth and Fourteenth Amendments provide a right to introduce live alibi testimony at a re-sentencing proceeding? NO.

HOLDING: In a death penalty case, the state may limit the introduction of innocence-related evidence during the sentencing proceeding. The defendant has no constitutional right during sentencing to present the kind of evidence (new evidence that shows he was not present at the scene of the crime) he wants to present.

REASON: "As our discussion in Part II, *supra*, makes clear, the federal question before us is a narrow one. Do the Eighth and Fourteenth Amendments grant Guzek a constitutional right to present evidence of the kind he seeks to introduce, namely new evidence that shows he was not present at the scene of the crime? That evidence is inconsistent with Guzek's prior conviction. It sheds no light on the manner in which he committed the crime for which he was convicted. Nor is it evidence that Guzek contends was unavailable to him at the time of the original trial. And, to the extent it is evidence he introduced at that time, he is free to introduce it now, albeit in transcript form. Or. Rev. Stat. § 138.012(2)(b) (2003). We can find nothing in the Eighth or Fourteenth Amendments that provides a capital defendant a right to introduce new evidence of this kind at sentencing."

"Three circumstances, taken together, convince us that the State possesses the authority to regulate, through exclusion, the evidence that Guzek seeks to present. First, sentencing traditionally concerns how, not whether, a defendant committed the crime. See *United States Sentencing Commission Guidelines Manual* § 1A1.1, editorial note, § 4(a), p.4 (Nov. 2004). But the evidence at issue here—alibi evidence—concerns only whether, not how, he did so.

"Second, the parties previously litigated the issue to which evidence is relevant—whether the defendant committed the basic crime. The evidence thereby attacks a previously determined matter in a proceeding at which, in principle, that matter is not at issue. The law typically discourages collateral attacks of this kind. Cf. *Allen v. McCurry*, 449 U.S. 90 (1980) ('As this court and other courts have often recognized, res judicata and collateral estoppel relieve parties of the cost and vexation of multiple lawsuits, conserve judicial resources, and, by preventing inconsistent decisions, encourage reliance on adjudication').

"Third, the negative impact of a rule restricting defendant's ability to introduce new alibi evidence is minimized by the fact that Oregon law gives the defendant the right to present to the sentencing jury all the evidence of innocence from the original trial regardless. The law permits the defendant to introduce at re-sentencing transcripts and exhibits from his prior trial. Ore. Rev. Stat. § 138.012(2)(b) (2003). The defendant here has not claimed that the evidence at issue was unavailable at the time of his original trial. Thus, he need only have introduced it at that time to guarantee its presentation (albeit through transcripts) to a re-sentencing jury as well."

CASE SIGNIFICANCE: This case is interesting because the Court said it is constitutional to set a limit on the type of evidence a defendant in a death penalty case can introduce during the sentencing phase of the trial. Defendant Guzek was convicted of a capital offense. During the sentencing phase, he sought to introduce new evidence he said would show that he was not present at the scene of the crime and was therefore innocent. This evidence was a live testimony from his mother that gave Guzek an alibi and therefore was to establish that he was not at the crime scene at the time the crime was allegedly committed. Oregon rules provide that any evidence presented during the sentencing phase has to be evidence that was introduced at the original trial, not new evidence such as Guzek sought to introduce. The Court upheld the denial to present new evidence, saying that "the Constitution does not prohibit a State from limiting the innocence-related evidence in a capital defendant can introduce at a sentencing proceeding to the evidence introduced at the original trial." Such a rule does not violate a defendant's constitutional right to due process. In essence, the Court ruled that evidence presented during the sentencing stage can be limited to the issue of what penalty should be imposed instead of whether the defendant is guilty or innocent.

HOLMES V. SOUTH CAROLINA
547 U.S. 319 (2006)

CAPSULE: Denying a defendant the opportunity to present evidence of third-party guilt during trial, if forensic evidence of guilt is strong, is unconstitutional.

FACTS: On December 31, 1989, 86-year-old Mary Stewart was beaten, raped, and robbed in her home. She later died of complications stemming from her injuries. During his criminal trial, Bobby Lee Holmes questioned the prosecution's forensic evidence by introducing expert testimony suggesting that the evidence had been contaminated and the police had framed him. Holmes also tried to introduce evidence that another man, Jimmy McCaw White, had been in the victim's neighborhood the morning of the crime and that White had either acknowledged Holmes' innocence or admitted to committing the crimes himself. The trial court excluded Holmes' third-party guilt evidence. Holmes was convicted by jury of murder, first-degree criminal sexual conduct, first-degree burglary, and robbery. He was sentenced to death.

ISSUE: Does a state evidence rule that denies a defendant the opportunity to present proof of third-party guilt, if the government has presented strong forensic evidence that supports a guilty verdict, deprive the defendant of the constitutional right to due process? YES.

HOLDING: A criminal defendant's constitutional right is violated by an evidence rule under which the defendant cannot present evidence of third-party guilt if the prosecution has introduced strong forensic evidence supporting a guilty verdict.

REASON: "'[S]tate and federal rule makers have broad latitude under the Constitution to establish rules excluding evidence from criminal trials.' *United*

States v. Scheffer, 523 U.S. 303, 308 (1998); see also *Crane v. Kentucky*, 476 U.S. 683, 689–690 (1986); *Marshall v. Lonberger*, 459 U.S. 422, 438, n. 6 (1983); *Chambers v. Mississippi*, 410 U.S. 284, 302–303 (1973); *Spencer v. Texas*, 385 U.S. 554, 564 (1967). This latitude, however, has limits. 'Whether rooted directly in the Due Process Clause of the Fourteenth Amendment or in the Compulsory Process or Confrontation clauses of the Sixth Amendment, the Constitution guarantees criminal defendants "a meaningful opportunity to present a complete defense." *Crane, supra*, at 690 (quoting *California v. Trombetta*, 467 U.S. 479, 485 (1984); citations omitted). This right is abridged by evidence rules that 'infring[e] upon a weighty interest of the accused' and are '"arbitrary" or "disproportionate to the purposes they are designed to serve."' *Scheffer, supra*, at 308 (quoting *Rock v. Arkansas*, 483 U.S. 44, 58, 56 (1987)."

"While the Constitution thus prohibits the exclusion of defense evidence under rules that serve no legitimate purpose or that are disproportionate to the ends that they are asserted to promote, well-established rules of evidence permit trial judges to exclude evidence that if its probative value is outweighed by certain other factors such as unfair prejudice, confusion of the issues, or potential to mislead the jury. See. e.g., Fed. Rule Evid. 403; Uniform Rule of Evid. 45 (1953); ALI, Model Code of Evidence Rule 303 (1942); 3 J. Wigmore, *Evidence* (1863, 1904 (1904)). Plainly referring to rules of this type, we have stated that the constitution permits judges 'to exclude evidence that is "repetitive . . ., only marginally relevant" or poses an undue risk of "harassment, prejudice, [or] confusion of the issues." *Crane, supra*, at 689–690 (quoting *Delaware v. Van Arsdall*, 475 U.S. 673, 679 (1986); ellipsis and brackets in original). See also *Montana v. Egelhoff*, 518 U.S. 37, 42 (1996) (plurality opinion) (terming such rules 'familiar and unquestionably constitutional')."

"The rule applied in this case appears to be based on the following logic: Where (1) it is clear that only one person was involved in the commission of a particular crime and (2) there is strong evidence that the defendant was the perpetrator, it follows that the evidence of third-party guilt must be weak. But this logic depends on an accurate evaluation of the prosecution's proof, and the true strength of the prosecution's proof cannot be assessed without considering challenges to the reliability of the prosecution's evidence. Just because the prosecution's evidence, if credited, would provide strong support for a guilty verdict, it does not follow that evidence of third-party guilt has only a weak logical connection to the central issues in the case. And where the credibility of the prosecution's witnesses or the reliability of its evidence is not conceded, the strength of the prosecution's case cannot be assessed without making the sort of factual findings that have traditionally been reserved for the trier of fact and the South Carolina courts did not purport to make in this case."

CASE SIGNIFICANCE: State Supreme Court decisions in South Carolina prior to this case had held that "where there is strong forensic evidence of an appellant's guilt, proffered evidence about a third party's alleged guilt does not raise a reasonable inference as to the appellant's own innocence." In this case, defendant

Holmes sought to introduce evidence during trial that, he claimed, would prove that another man, a certain Jimmy McCaw White, "was in the victim's neighborhood on the morning of the assault and that White had either acknowledged petitioner's innocence or admitted to committing the crimes himself." White, however, had denied in a pretrial testimony that he made such a statement.

The forensic evidence introduced against Holmes during trial was indeed strong. It established, among others, that "his palm print was found just above the door knob on the interior side of the front door of the victim's house; and fiber consistent with a black sweatshirt owned by Holmes were found on the victim's bed sheets; matching blue fibers were found on the pink nightgown and on Holmes' underwear." There was other evidence introduced during trial that also pointed to Holmes' guilt.

The trial court denied Holmes' motion to introduce the evidence, basing its ruling on decisions of the South Carolina Supreme Court. On appeal, the Court held Holmes' constitutional right was violated, saying: "The point is that, by evaluating the strength of only one party's evidence, no logical conclusion can be reached regarding the strength of contrary evidence offered by the other side to rebut or cast doubt. Because the rule applied by the State Supreme Court in this case did not heed this point, the rule is 'arbitrary' . . ."

H. AGGRAVATING AND MITIGATING CIRCUMSTANCES

TISON V. ARIZONA
481 U.S. 137 (1987)

CAPSULE: The death penalty may be imposed on defendants who did not specifically intend to kill their victims but played a major role in the killing.

FACTS: Brothers Ricky and Raymond Tison, along with other family members, planned and effected the escape of their father from a prison where he was serving a life sentence. Ricky and Raymond Tison entered the prison with an ice chest filled with guns, and armed their father and another convicted murderer. They later helped to abduct, detain, and rob a family of four, and watched their father and the other convict murder the members of that family with shotguns. Although the brothers later stated that they were surprised by the killings, neither of them attempted to help the victims. Instead, they drove away in the victim's car along with the rest of the escape party. Ricky and Raymond Tison received the death penalty under Arizona's felony-murder and accomplice liability statutes. They appealed their death sentences, alleging that the Supreme Court decision in *Enmund v. Florida*, 458 U.S. 782 (1982) required reversal of their sentences because they were merely accomplices and not principals.

ISSUE: Is imposition of the death penalty on defendants who did not specifically intend to kill the victims or inflict the fatal wounds constitutional? YES.

HOLDING: Defendants who took part in a felony-murder, but did not themselves intend to kill, or commit the specific act leading to that result, may be sentenced to death as long as their participation in the felony was major and their mental state was one of reckless indifference to the value of human life.

REASON: "The issue raised by this case is whether the Eighth Amendment prohibits the death penalty in the intermediate case of the defendant whose participation is major and whose mental state is one of reckless indifference to the value of human life. *Enmund* does not specifically address this point.

"Like the *Enmund* Court, we find the state legislatures' judgment as to proportionality in these circumstances relevant to this constitutional inquiry. The largest number of States still fall into the intermediate categories discussed in *Enmund*. Four States authorize the death penalty in felony-murder cases upon a showing of culpable mental state such as recklessness or extreme indifference to human life. Two jurisdictions require that the defendant's participation be substantial and the statutes of at least six more, including Arizona, take minor participation in the felony expressly into account in mitigation of the murder. These requirements significantly overlap both in this case and in general, for the greater the defendant's participation in the felony-murder, the more likely that he acted with reckless indifference to human life. At a minimum, however, it can be said that all these jurisdictions, as well as six States which *Enmund* classified along with Florida as permitting capital punishment for felony-murder simpliciter, and the three States which simply require some additional aggravation before imposing the death penalty upon a felony-murderer, specifically authorize the death penalty in a felony-murder case where, though the defendant's mental state fell short of intent to kill, the defendant was a major actor in a felony in which he knew death was highly likely to occur."

CASE SIGNIFICANCE: The *Enmund* Court ruled that accomplices to a crime who participated in a minor role and had no prior knowledge that lethal force might be used in the commission of a felony could not be held responsible for that lethal force. It held that punishment by death in such a case is disproportionate to the crime and thus is prohibited by the Eighth Amendment. The Tison brothers attempted to use that ruling to overturn their death sentences, claiming that the death penalty was disproportionate to their participation in the crime committed. The Court disagreed and concluded that the Tison brothers played a major role in the killing of four family members and that their actions during the commission of the crime also suggested a reckless indifference to life. Based on these findings, the Supreme Court stated that it could not find fault with the sentences handed down by the trial court and that a survey of other state procedures in similar cases showed that society was also in agreement with severe punishments for accomplices who actively participated in violent crimes.

SUMNER V. SHUMAN
483 U.S. 66 (1987)

CAPSULE: A mandatory death penalty for inmates convicted of murder while in prison is unconstitutional.

FACTS: In 1958, Shuman was convicted of first-degree murder. He had been charged in the shooting death of a truck driver during a roadside robbery. Nevada statute provided the jury, in cases of first-degree murder, with sentencing options of the death penalty or life imprisonment with or without the possibility of parole. Shuman was sentenced to life imprisonment without the possibility of parole.

ISSUE: Does a statute that requires the death penalty for a prison inmate who is convicted of murder while serving a life sentence constitute cruel and unusual punishment, in violation of the Eighth Amendment? YES.

HOLDING: A mandatory death sentence for a prison inmate who is convicted of murder while serving a life sentence is unconstitutional. The sentencing authority must consider mitigating factors relating to the defendant and the offense.

REASON: "Under the individualized capital-sentencing doctrine, it is constitutionally required that the sentencing authority consider, as a mitigating factor, any aspect of the defendant's character or record and any circumstances of the particular offense."

CASE SIGNIFICANCE: This case reiterates the Court's decision in *Gregg v. Georgia*, 428 U.S. 153 (1976), which states that mitigating circumstances must be taken into account to determine whether a defendant deserves the death penalty. The Court believes that this requirement minimizes, and in some cases eliminates, arbitrary and capricious imposition of the death penalty. Taken together, *Gregg* and *Shuman* declare unconstitutional any statute that automatically imposes the death penalty. States may impose the death penalty, but must require that surrounding circumstances be considered in imposing the penalty. Regardless of the gravity of the offense, mandatory imposition of the death penalty without consideration of these circumstances will be declared unconstitutional by the Court. Judges must instruct the jury, during the sentencing stage, that mitigating circumstances, if any, must be considered in deciding whether to impose death or life imprisonment on a person convicted of a capital offense.

ARAVE V. CREECH
507 U.S. 463 (1993)

CAPSULE: The capital sentencing provision in the state of Idaho that singles out first-degree murders committed with "utter disregard for human life" satisfies constitutional standards.

FACTS: In 1981, Thomas Creech beat and kicked to death a fellow inmate while both were incarcerated in the Idaho State Penitentiary. Creech pleaded guilty to first-degree murder and the judge sentenced him to death. One of the aggravating circumstances that served as partial basis for the sentence was that "[b]y the murder, or circumstances surrounding its commission, the defendant exhibited utter disregard for human life." In an earlier case, the Idaho Supreme Court identified a limiting construction of "utter disregard" to "be reflective of acts or circumstances surrounding the crime which exhibit the highest, the utmost, callous disregard for human life, i.e., the coldblooded, pitiless slayer."

ISSUE: Does Idaho's "utter disregard" provision in its death penalty law sufficiently limit sentencing discretion as required by the Eighth and Fourteenth Amendments? YES.

HOLDING: Because of the definition given the "utter disregard" provision of the Idaho law in an earlier case by the Idaho Supreme Court, the law meets the constitutional requirements of the Eighth and Fourteenth Amendments.

REASON: "This case is governed by the standards we articulated in *Walton*, *supra*, and *Lewis v. Jeffers*, 497 U.S. 764 (1990). In Jeffers we reaffirmed the fundamental principle that, to satisfy the Eighth and Fourteenth Amendments, a capital sentencing scheme must 'suitably direc[t] and limi[t]' the sentencer's discretion 'so as to minimize the risk of wholly arbitrary and capricious action.' The State must 'channel the sentencer's discretion by clear and objective standards that provide specific and detailed guidance, and that make rationally reviewable the process for imposing a sentence of death.'"

CASE SIGNIFICANCE: This case once again addresses the issue of whether a state's death penalty law was so vague as to be unconstitutional. Idaho law provided that one of the aggravating circumstances that could be considered by the jury when deciding whether to impose the death penalty was that "by the murder, or circumstances surrounding its commission, the defendant exhibited utter disregard for human life." The issue on appeal was whether that phrase was so vague as to violate the due process provision of the Constitution. The Court answered no, saying that the Idaho Supreme Court, in *State v. Osborn*, 102 Idaho 405 (1981), interpreted "utter disregard" to mean "be reflective of acts or circumstances surrounding the crime which exhibit the highest, the utmost, callous disregard for human life . . ." This, said the Court, gave definite meaning to that phrase and therefore saved the Idaho law. This case is significant in that the Supreme Court over the years has continued to monitor state laws to ensure that death penalty statutes do not suffer from vagueness that can lead to an arbitrary application of the law. The Court also says, however, that vague legislation can be saved if given a more restrictive meaning by state court decision.

JOHNSON V. TEXAS
509 U.S. 350 (1993)

CAPSULE: A special instruction advising a death penalty jury that it could consider age as a mitigating factor is not required as long as age itself is not excluded as a mitigating factor.

FACTS: In 1986, Dorsie Johnson, then 19 years of age, and a companion, Amanda Miles, robbed a convenience store and killed the store clerk. They emptied the cash registers of $160 in cash, grabbed a carton of cigarettes, and fled the store.

ISSUE: Is the Texas death penalty special issues provision sufficient to allow a sentencing jury to give adequate mitigating effect to a defendant's youth? YES.

HOLDING: The Texas death penalty special issues provision is consistent with the Eighth and Fourteenth Amendments in that there is room in the future dangerousness assessment of the law for a juror to take account of youth as a mitigating factor.

REASON: "The joint opinion determined that the Texas system satisfied the requirements of the Eighth and Fourteenth Amendments concerning the consideration of mitigating evidence: 'By authorizing the defense to bring before the jury at the separate sentencing hearing whatever mitigating circumstances relating to the individual defendant can be adduced, Texas has ensured that the sentencing jury will have adequate guidance to enable it to perform its sentencing function."

CASE SIGNIFICANCE: This case is a follow-up of an earlier case, *Graham v. Collins*, 506 U.S. 461 (1993), also discussed in this chapter. The difference is that in this case the defendant brought the case to the Supreme Court on direct review instead of through habeas corpus (a collateral proceeding) and so the *Teague* question that limited the decision in *Graham* was not a problem here. The Court said that "[t]here is no dispute that a defendant's youth is a relevant mitigating circumstance that must be within the effective reach of a capital sentencing jury. . . ." It concluded, however, that under the Texas statute, there was plenty of room for jurors to take youth into account as a mitigating factor. The Court stated: "By authorizing the defense to bring before the jury at the separate sentencing hearing whatever mitigating circumstances related to the individual defendant can be adduced," Texas ensured that the state could take into account the defendant's age when determining the death penalty. This case, therefore, holds that age does not have to be mentioned by law as a mitigating factor in death penalty cases as long as the law is worded in such a way that age is not excluded as a mitigating factor and can be considered by the jury in determining whether the death penalty should be imposed.

TUILAEPA V. CALIFORNIA
512 U.S. 967 (1994)

CAPSULE: California law concerning the circumstances of the crime, the defendant's history of violent crimes, and the age of the defendant are sufficiently clear and therefore are constitutional as sentencing factors in death penalty cases.

FACTS: In California, a defendant is eligible for the death penalty when a jury finds him or her guilty of first-degree murder and finds one or more of the special circumstances listed in the California Penal Code Annotated, § 190.2. Once the case is in the penalty phase, the jury is then instructed to consider numerous other factors listed in § 190.3 in deciding whether to impose death.

ISSUE: Are California's death penalty phase factors constitutional? YES.

HOLDING: California's death penalty phase factors are sufficiently clear and therefore do not violate the Eighth Amendment.

REASON: "In our decisions holding a death sentence unconstitutional because of a vague sentencing factor, the State had presented a specific proposition that the sentencer had to find true or false (e.g., whether the crime was especially heinous, atrocious, or cruel). We have held, under certain sentencing schemes, that a vague propositional factor used in the sentencing decision creates an unacceptable risk of randomness, the mark of the arbitrary and capricious sentencing process prohibited by *Furman v. Georgia*, 408 U.S. 238 (1972). Those concerns are mitigated when a factor does not require a yes or a no answer to a specific question, but instead only points the sentencer to a subject matter. Both types of factors (and the distinction between the two is not always clear) have their utility. For purposes of vagueness analysis, however, in examining the propositional content of a factor, our concern is that the factor have some 'common-sense core of meaning . . . that criminal juries should be capable of understanding.'"

CASE SIGNIFICANCE: This case addresses again the issue of whether the factors listed by state law that the jury must consider during the sentencing phase of a death penalty case are so vague as to be unconstitutional. Under California law, the factors to be considered, among others, are: (a) "circumstances of the crime of which the defendant was convicted . . . and the existence of any special circumstances found to be true;" (b) "the presence or absence of criminal activity involving the use or attempted use of force or violence or the express or implied threat to use force or violence;" and (c) defendant's age at the time of the crime. The Court said that these factors are not vague and are constitutional. Once again, the Court made sure that state laws governing the penalty phase of capital offenses are not so vague as to be susceptible to arbitrary application by juries. Whether the specific provisions of a state law are vague or not is ultimately for the Supreme Court to decide in a specific case. This helps explain why, decades after the death penalty was declared to be constitutional in *Gregg v. Georgia* (1976), many death penalty cases continue to reach the Court from the various states on the issue of the constitutionality of a particular state law.

BROWN, WARDEN V. SANDERS
546 U.S. 212 (2006)

CAPSULE: A death sentence remains valid even when a sentencing factor is invalidated if one of the other sentencing factors enables the sentencer to give aggravating weight to the same facts and circumstances.

FACTS: Ronald Sanders and a companion invaded the home of Dale Boender. Boender and his girlfriend, Janice Allen, were bound and blindfolded by the two and then struck on the head with a heavy blunt object. Allen died from the blow to her head. Sanders was convicted of first-degree murder, of attempt to murder Boender, and of robbery, burglary, and attempted robbery. He was sentenced to death by the trial jury after its consideration of four special aggravating circumstances. Two of these circumstances were later invalidated by the state supreme court, but Sanders' sentence was upheld.

ISSUE: Is the Eighth Amendment violated when a death sentence is upheld even though two of the four special aggravating circumstances considered by the jury were found to be invalid? NO.

HOLDING: An invalidated sentencing factor will render the sentence unconstitutional by reason of its adding an improper element to the aggravation scale in the weighing process. The exception is if one of the other sentencing factors enables the sentencer to give aggravating weight to the same facts and circumstances.

REASON: "Since *Furman v. Georgia*, 408 U.S. 238 (1972) (per curiam), we have required States to limit the class of murderers to which the death penalty may be applied. This narrowing requirement is usually met when the trier of fact finds at least one statutorily defined eligibility factor at either the guilt or penalty phase. See *Tuilaepa v. California*, 512 U.S. 967, 971–972 (1994). Once the narrowing requirement has been satisfied, the sentencer is called upon to determine whether a defendant thus found eligible for the death penalty should in fact receive it. Most states channel this function by specifying the aggravating factors (sometimes identical to the eligibility factors) that are to be weighed against mitigating considerations. The issue in the line of cases we confront here is what happens when the sentencer imposes the death penalty after at least one valid eligibility factor has been found, but under a scheme in which an eligibility factor or a specified aggravating factor is later held to be invalid."

"This weighing/non-weighing scheme is accurate as far as it goes, but it now seems to us needlessly complex and incapable of providing for the full range of possible variations. For example, the same problem that gave rise to our weighing-State jurisprudence would arise if it were a sentencing factor, and not an eligibility factor, that was later found to be invalid. The weighing process would just as clearly have been prima facie 'skewed' and skewed for the same basic reason: The sentencer might have given weight to a statutorily or constitutionally invalid aggravator. And the prima facie skewing could in appropriate cases be shown to be illusory for the same reason that separates weighing States from non-weighing States: One of the other aggravating factors, usually an omnibus factor but conceivably another one, made it entirely proper for the jury to consider as aggravating the facts and circumstances underlying the invalidated factor.

"We think it will clarify the analysis and simplify the sentence-invalidating factors we have hitherto applied to non-weighing States, see *supra*, at 5–6, if we are henceforth guided by the following rule: An invalidated sentencing factor (whether an eligibility factor or not) will render the sentence unconstitutional by reason of its adding an improper element to the aggravation scale in the weighing process unless one of the other sentencing factors enables the sentencer to give aggravating weight to the same facts and circumstances.

"This test is not, as Justice Breyer describes it, 'an inquiry based solely on the admissibility of the underlying evidence.' Post, at 15 (dissenting opinion). If the presence of the invalid sentencing factor allowed the sentencer to consider evidence that would not otherwise have been before it, due process would mandate reversal without regard to the rule we apply here. See *supra*, at 6; see also n. 6, this page. The issue we confront is the skewing that could result from the jury's considering as aggravation properly admitted evidence that should not have weighed in favor of the death penalty. See, e.g., *Stringer*, 503 U.S., at 232 ('[W]hen the sentencing body is told to weigh an invalid factor in its decision, a reviewing court may not assume it would have made no difference if the thumb had been removed from death's side of the scale.') As we have explained, such skewing will occur, and give rise to constitutional error, only where the jury could not have given aggravating weight to the same facts and circumstances under the rubric of some other, valid sentencing factor."

CASE SIGNIFICANCE: This is another of the many complex cases involving mitigating and aggravating circumstances and how they are weighed against each other. Earlier cases have held that the death penalty cannot be imposed unless consideration of its imposition in a particular case is individualized. This means that aggravating and mitigating circumstances must be taken into account in determining whether the death penalty or any other type of punishment should be imposed. Mandatory death penalties are not allowed. This narrows the type of cases in which death can be imposed. The Court in this case said that "once this narrowing requirement has been satisfied, the sentencer must determine whether an eligible defendant should receive the death penalty; many States channel this function by specifying aggravating factors that are weighed against mitigating considerations." This balancing of aggravating and mitigating factors can be complex, particularly when some provisions thereof are later invalidated.

This case involves an interpretation of the California death penalty law. Two of the four special circumstances that could lead to the death penalty being imposed were later invalidated, but the remaining two were considered sufficient by the Supreme Court to satisfy the requirement set by the Court in earlier cases. Thus the procedure for the imposition of the death penalty in this case was deemed constitutional.

KANSAS V. MARSH
548 U.S. 163 (2006)

CAPSULE: Imposition of the death penalty is constitutional when mitigating and aggravating factors are in equipoise (meaning they balance each other).

FACTS: Michael Lee Marsh II broke into the home of Marry Ane Pusch. When Pusch entered her home with her 19-month-old daughter, Marsh proceeded to repeatedly shoot Marry Ane, stab her, and slash her throat. The home was then set on fire with Pusch's daughter inside and the child burned to death. Marsh was convicted by a jury of the capital murder of the child, the first-degree premeditated murder of Marry Ane Pusch, aggravated arson, and aggravated burglary. At sentencing the jury found, beyond a reasonable doubt, the existence of three aggravating circumstances, and that those circumstances were not outweighed by any mitigating circumstances. Marsh was sentenced to death for the capital murder.

ISSUE: Is a death penalty statute constitutional if it provides that if a unanimous jury finds that aggravating circumstances are not outweighed by mitigating circumstances, the death penalty shall be imposed? YES.

HOLDING: A death penalty statute is constitutional even if it provides for the imposition of the death penalty if the state finds beyond a reasonable doubt that mitigating circumstances do not outweigh aggravating circumstances.

REASON: "This Court noted that, as a requirement of individualized sentencing, a jury must have the opportunity to consider all evidence relevant to mitigation, and that a state statute that permits a jury to consider any mitigating evidence comports with that requirement. Id., at 652 (citing *Blystone v. Pennsylvania*, 494 U.S. 299, 307 (1990)). The court also pointedly observed that while the Constitution requires that a sentencing jury have discretion, it does not mandate that discretion be unfettered; the States are free to determine the manner in which a jury may consider mitigating evidence. 497 U.S., at 652 (citing *Boyde v. California*, 494 U.S. 370, 374 (1990)). So long as the sentencer is not precluded from considering relevant mitigating evidence, a capital sentencing statute cannot be said to impermissibly, much less automatically, impose death. 497 U.S., at 652 (citing *Woodson v. North Carolina*, 428 U.S. 280 (1976) (plurality opinion), and *Roberts v. Louisiana*, 428 U.S. 325 (1976) (Plurality opinion). Indeed, *Walton* suggested that the only capital sentencing systems that would be impermissibly mandatory were those that would 'automatically impose death upon conviction for certain types of murder.' 494 U.S., at 652."

"Contrary to Marsh's contentions and the Kansas Supreme Court's conclusions, see 278 Kan., at 536–538, 102 P. 3d, at 459, the question presented in the instant case was squarely before this Court in *Walton*. Though, as Marsh notes, the *Walton* Court did not employ the term 'equipoise,' that issue undeniably gave rise to the question this Court sought to resolve, and it was necessarily included in Walton's argument that the Arizona system was unconstitutional because it required the death penalty unless the mitigating circumstances outweighed the aggravating circumstances. See *supra*, at 5 . . .”

“Our conclusion that *Walton* controls here is reinforced by the fact that the Arizona and Kansas statutes are comparable in important respects. Similar to the express language of the Kansas statute, the Arizona statute at issue in *Walton* has been consistently construed to mean that the death penalty will be imposed upon a finding that aggravating circumstances are not outweighed by mitigating circumstances. See *State v. Ysea*, 191 Ariz. 372, 375, 956 P. 2d 499, 502 (1998) (en banc); *State v. Gretzler*, 135 Ariz. 42, 55, 659 P. 2d 1, 14 (1983) (en banc); *Adamson*, 865 F. 2d, at 1041–1043. Like the Kansas statute, the Arizona statute places the burden of proving the existence of aggravating circumstances on the State, and both statutes require the defendant to proffer mitigating evidence.”

“The statutes are distinct in one respect. The Arizona statute, once the State has met its burden, tasks the defendant with the burden of proving sufficient mitigating circumstances to overcome the aggravating circumstances and that a sentence less than death is therefore warranted. In contrast, the Kansas statute requires the State to bear the burden of proving to the jury, beyond a reasonable doubt, that aggravators are not outweighed by mitigators and that a sentence of death is therefore appropriate; it places no additional evidentiary burden on the capital defendant. This distinction operates in favor of Kansas capital defendants. Otherwise the statutes function in substantially the same manner and are analogous for our purposes. Thus, *Walton* is not distinguishable from the instant case.”

CASE SIGNIFICANCE: The constitutional issue raised in this case was whether the Kansas statute, which provided that the death penalty could be imposed in cases where the mitigating and aggravating factors were balanced, is constitutional. The jury found three aggravating circumstances during trial that were not outweighed by mitigating circumstances. They convicted defendant Michael Lee Marsh II and imposed the death sentence. He appealed, saying the provision of the Kansas law “establishes an unconstitutional presumption in favor of death by directing imposition of the death penalty when aggravating and mitigating circumstances are in equipoise.” The Kansas law specifically provides that: “A life sentence must be imposed if the State fails to demonstrate the existence of an aggravating circumstance beyond a reasonable doubt, if the State cannot prove beyond a reasonable doubt that aggravating circumstances are not outweighed by mitigating circumstances, or if the jury is unable to reach a unanimous decision in any respect.” The Supreme Court said this provision is constitutional.

AYERS, ACTING WARDEN V. BELMONTES
549 U.S. 7 (2006)

CAPSULE: A jury may consider forward-looking mitigating circumstances when instructed to consider any other circumstances that lighten the gravity of the crime. This can be done even if the circumstances are not a legal excuse for the crime.

FACTS: In 1982, Fernando Belmontes was found guilty of murder in the first degree by a jury in the State of California. The jury was then directed by the trial court during the sentencing phase, with other instructions, to consider certain specific factors either as aggravating or mitigating. The jury was also instructed to consider "any other circumstance which extenuates the gravity of the crime even though it is not a legal excuse for the crime." This general or catch-all factor in California death penalty statutes is referred to as "factor (k)." Belmontes was sentenced to death.

ISSUE: Does California's "factor (k)" prohibit jurors from considering forward-looking mitigating evidence in violation of his Eighth Amendment right to present all mitigating evidence in death penalty cases? NO.

HOLDING: A jury is not reasonably likely to believe itself barred from considering the defense's evidence as a factor "extenuat[ing] the gravity of the crime." The factor (k) instruction is consistent with the constitutional right to present mitigating evidence in capital sentencing proceedings.

REASON: "The Court of Appeals failed to heed the full import of *Payton*'s holding, a holding that has significance even where AEDPA is inapplicable. *Payton* indicated that reading factor (k) to preclude consideration of post crime evidence would require 'the surprising conclusion that remorse could never serve to lessen or excuse a crime.' 544 U.S., at 142. So, too, would it be counter intuitive if a defendant's capacity to redeem himself through good works could not extenuate his offense and render him less deserving of a death sentence.

"In any event, since respondent sought to extrapolate future behavior from pre-crime conduct, his mitigation theory was more analogous to the good-character evidence examined in *Boyde* and held to fall within factor (k)'s purview. See 494 U.S., at 38 (describing the evidence at issue as including evidence of the defendant's 'strength of character.'). Both types of evidence suggest the crime stemmed more from adverse circumstances than from an irredeemable character. See 414 F.3d, at 1141–1142 (O'Scannlain, J., concurring in part and dissenting in part); cf. *Johnson v. Texas*, 509 U.S. 350, 369 (1993) (noting that the 'forward-looking' future-dangerousness inquiry 'is not independent of an assessment of personal culpability')."

"As the Court of Appeals recognized, future-conduct evidence was central to the mitigation case presented by the defense. See 414 F.3d, at 1134. Indeed, although the defense also adduced evidence of a troubled upbringing, respondent testified that he could not use his difficult life 'as a crutch to say I am in a situation right now, I'm here now because of that.' App. 40. Given this assertion, and considering the extensive, forward-looking evidence presented at sentencing—evidence including testimony from two prison chaplains, respondent's church sponsors, and respondent himself—the jurors could have disregarded respondent's future potential only if they drew the unlikely inference that 'the court's instructions transformed all of this "favorable testimony into a virtual charade,"' *Boyde*, *supra*, at 383 (quoting *Brown*, 479 U.S., at 542). It is improbable the jurors believed that the parties were engaging in an exercise in futility when respondent presented (and both counsel later discussed) his mitigating evidence in open court."

CASE SIGNIFICANCE: The issue of mitigating and aggravating circumstances has raised a lot of issues the Court must address because they are so different in each case. The issue in this case was whether "factor (k) and the trial court's other instructions barred the jury from considering his forward-looking mitigation evidence" in violation of defendant's Eighth Amendment right to present all mitigating evidence in capital sentencing proceedings. Defendant Ayers in this case "introduced mitigating evidence to show . . . that he would lead a constructive life if incarcerated rather than executed. He testified that he had done so during a previous incarceration when he became a Christian. Two prison chaplains and Ayers' Christian sponsor also testified for him.

The trial judge told the jury to consider "any other circumstance which extenuates the gravity of the crime even though it is not a legal excuse for the crime." This instruction was then known in California as "factor (k)", the law at the time of Ayers' conviction. Ayers later argued that "factor (k) and the trial court's other instructions barred the jury from considering his forward-looking (meaning the prospect of his leading a constructive life if incarcerated) mitigation evidence" and therefore violated his constitutional right. The Court disagreed, saying California's "factor (k) provision did not have such an effect on the jury, adding that: "It is improbable that the jury believed that the parties were engaged in an exercise in futility when respondent [defendant] presented extensive forward-looking evidence in open court. Both prosecution and defense arguments assumed the evidence was relevant."

ABDUL-KABIR FKA COLE V. QUARTERMAN
550 U.S. 233 (2007)

CAPSULE: Death penalty juries must be given the opportunity to give meaningful consideration and effect to all mitigating evidence, including a destructive family history and mental defects.

FACTS: In December, 1987, Jalil Abdul-Kabir, formerly known as Ted Calvin Cole, along with his stepbrother Michael Hickey and Michael's wife, Kelly, robbed and killed Kelly's grandfather, Raymond Richardson to obtain some cash. Cole strangled Richardson with a dog leash and the group removed $20 from the house. They bought food and beer with the money. The next day, Michael and Kelly surrendered to police and confessed. Cole was arrested and he also confessed. Cole was tried by a jury and convicted of capital murder. At the conclusion of the sentencing hearing, the jury was instructed to give effect to all mitigating evidence by making yes-or-no determinations on Texas's two "special issues" for capital sentencing: the deliberateness of the crime and the future dangerousness of the criminal.

ISSUE: Do Texas's "special issues" instructions to the jury in a capital sentencing allow jurors to give full consideration and effect to mitigating evidence about a defendant's destructive family history and mental defects, as required by the Eighth Amendment? NO.

HOLDING: The Texas jury instructions are unconstitutional because they conflict with Supreme Court precedents that require jurors be given the opportunity "to give meaningful consideration and effect to all mitigating evidence that might provide a basis for refusing to impose the death penalty."

REASON: "The former special issues (as composed at the time of both Penry's and Cole's sentencing proceedings) provided an adequate vehicle for the evaluation of mitigating evidence offered to disprove deliberateness or future dangerousness. As Judge Reavley noted in his opinion for the Court of Appeals (CCA) in *Penry* I, however, they did not tell the jury as to what 'to do if it decided that Penry, because of retardation, arrested emotional development and a troubled youth, should not be executed.' Id., at 324 (internal quotation marks omitted)."

"In recommending denial of Cole's application for collateral relief, the Texas trial judge did not analyze *Penry* I itself. Under the framework set forth in *Penry* I, the testimony of Cole's mother and aunt, as well as portions of the expert testimony suggesting that his dangerous character may have been the result of his rough childhood and possible neurological damage, were not relevant to either of the special verdict questions, except, possibly, as evidence supporting the State's argument that Cole would be dangerous in the future. This would not satisfy the requirement of *Penry* I, however, that the evidence be permitted its mitigating force beyond the scope of the special issues. Therefore, it would have followed that those questions failed to provide the jury with a vehicle for expressing its 'reasoned moral response' to that evidence."

"Before turning to those more recent cases, it is appropriate to identify the reasons why the CCA's ruling was not a reasonable application of *Penry* I itself. First, the ruling ignored the fact that even though Cole's mitigating evidence may not have been as persuasive as Penry's, it was relevant to the question of Cole's moral culpability for precisely the same reason as Penry's. Like Penry's evidence, Cole's evidence of childhood deprivation and lack of self-control did not rebut either deliberateness or future dangerousness but was intended to provide the jury with an entirely different reason for not imposing a death sentence. Second, the judge's assumption that it would be appropriate to look at 'other testimony in the record' to determine whether the jury could give mitigating effect to the testimony of Cole's mother and aunt is neither reasonable nor supported by the *Penry* opinion. App. 160. Third, the fact that the jury could give mitigating effect to some of the experts' testimony, namely, their predictions that Cole could be expected to become less dangerous as he aged, provides no support for the conclusion that the jury understood it could give such effect to other portions of the experts' testimony or that of other witnesses. In sum, the judge ignored our entire line of cases establishing the importance of allowing juries to give meaningful effect to any mitigating evidence providing a basis for a sentence of life rather than death. His recommendation to the CCA was therefore unsupported by either the text or the reasoning in *Penry* I."

CASE SIGNIFICANCE: This is a Texas case that was decided based on *Penry v. Lynaugh*, 492 U.S. 302 (1989), an earlier Texas death penalty case. In *Penry*, the Court said that a mentally retarded defendant who has the ability to reason may be given the death penalty. (This decision was later overturned in *Atkins v. Virginia*, 536 U.S. 304 (2002), which held that executing a mentally retarded offender violates the Eighth Amendment prohibition against cruel and unusual punishment.) Penry, however, could not be executed because the instructions given to the jury fell far short of proper instructions for the jury to consider mitigating circumstances. *Penry* requires "that juries be given instructions allowing them to give effect to a defendant's mitigating evidence and to express their reasoned moral response to that evidence in determining whether to recommend death." This was interpreted by the trial court in this case to mean that in evaluating *Penry* claims of mental retardation, a defendant is required to show a connection between his "uniquely severe permanent condition and the criminal act attributed to that condition." Since defendant Cole in this case failed to prove that, his claim to mitigating circumstances that would have spared him from the death penalty failed.

On appeal, the Court upheld Cole's claim, saying that "because there is a reasonable likelihood that the state trial court's instructions prevented jurors from giving meaningful consideration to constitutionally relevant mitigating evidence, the Court of Criminal Appeals' merits adjudication 'resulted in a decision that was contrary to, or involved in an unreasonable application of clearly established Federal Law, as determined by this Court.'" Because of the trial court's misinterpretation of the Penry requirements, the Court decided for defendant Cole in this habeas corpus case.

BREWER V. QUARTERMAN, DIRECTOR, TDCJ, CI DIVISION
550 U.S. 286 (2007)

CAPSULE: Capital sentencing statutes must allow the jury to give meaningful consideration to constitutionally relevant mitigating evidence.

FACTS: Brent Ray Brewer was convicted of murder committed during the course of a robbery in 1991. During his sentencing trial he introduced several different types of mitigating evidence that included his suffering from depression three months before the murder; his hospitalization for that depression; that his female co-defendant dominated and manipulated him; that as a child he was abused by his father; that he had witnessed his father abusing his mother; and that he had abused drugs. Brewer submitted instructions for the trial judge to present to the jury designed to give effect to the mitigating evidence he presented. The trial judge rejected the proposed instructions. The jury was instructed to answer only two special issues:

"Do you find from the evidence beyond a reasonable doubt that the conduct of the defendant, BRENT RAY BREWER, that caused the death of the deceased, Robert Doyle Laminack, was committed deliberately and with the reasonable expectation that the death of the deceased would result?"

"Do you find from the evidence beyond a reasonable doubt that there is a probability that the defendant, BRENT RAY BREWER, would commit criminal acts of violence that would constitute a continuing threat to society?"

During the closing argument the prosecutor used Brewer's extensive history of physical abuse and the abuse to his mother as supportive evidence to the claim of Brewer's "Future Dangerousness." He deemphasized any mitigating effect this evidence might have. The prosecutor also told the jury it lacked the power to exercise moral judgment in determining Brewer's sentence. Both special issues were answered by the jury in the affirmative and Brewer was sentenced to death.

ISSUE: Does the former Texas sentencing statute impermissibly prevent the sentencing jury from giving meaningful consideration to constitutionally relevant mitigating evidence? YES.

HOLDING: "Because the Texas capital sentencing statute as interpreted by the Court of Criminal Appeals (CCA) impermissibly prevented the jury from giving meaningful consideration and effect to constitutionally relevant mitigating evidence, the CCA's decision denying relief under *Penry v. Lynaugh*, 492 U.S. 302 (*Penry* I) was both 'contrary to' and 'involved an unreasonable application of clearly established federal law as determined by this Court.'"

REASON: "Like the petitioner in *Abdul-Kabir*, Brewer contends that the same constitutional error that infected Penry's sentencing hearing occurred in his trial. We agree. As did Penry's, Brewer's mitigating evidence served as a 'two-edged sword' because it tended to confirm the State's evidence of future dangerousness as well as lessen his culpability for the crime. *Penry* I, 492 U.S., at 324. It may well be true that Brewer's mitigating evidence was less compelling than Penry's, but, contrary to the view of the CCA, that difference does not provide an acceptable justification for refusing to apply the reasoning in *Penry* I to this case. There is surely a reasonable likelihood that the jurors accepted the prosecutor's argument at the close of the sentencing hearing that all they needed to decide was whether Brewer had acted deliberately and would likely be dangerous in the future, necessarily disregarding any independent concern that, given Brewer's troubled background, he may not be deserving of a death sentence.

"Also unpersuasive in distinguishing the instant case from others to which *Penry* I applies is the Fifth Circuit's explanation regarding the lack of expert evidence in Brewer's case (as compared to that presented by the petitioner in *Abdul-Kabir*) and its distinction between mental illness and mental retardation. In its opinion reversing the District Court's conditional grant of habeas relief, the court of Appeals noted that, under its precedents, '[t]he only instances in which mental illness has given rise to *Penry* I violations involve those where the illness in question is chronic and/or immutable [as in the case of mental retardation].' 442 F.3d, at 280. The court also emphasized the lack of expert psychiatric evidence in this case, contrasting the record below with that in *Abdul-Kabir*, and concluding that Brewer 'came nowhere near to producing evidence sufficient for us to grant relief.' 442 F.3d, at 281. Nowhere in our *Penry* line of cases have we suggested that the question whether mitigating evidence could have been adequately considered by the jury is a matter purely of quantity, degree, or immutability. Rather, we have focused on whether such evidence has mitigating relevance to the special issues and the extent to which it may diminish a defendant's moral culpability for the crime. The transient quality of such mitigating evidence may make it more likely to fall in part within the ambit of the special issues; however, as we explained in *Penry* I, such evidence may still have 'relevance to the defendant's moral culpability beyond the scope of the special verdict questions.' 492 U.S., at 322 (citing and quoting *Franklin v. Lynaugh*, 487 U.S. 164, 185 (1988)."

CASE SIGNIFICANCE: This is another Texas case about whether the jury was given sufficient instructions on mitigating circumstances that could have spared defendant from the death penalty. Convicted of murder, Brewer introduced the following mitigating circumstances during the sentencing phase: "evidence of his mental illness, his father's extensive abuse of him and his mother, and his substance abuse." The trial court judge declined to have the jury consider the mitigating evidence he presented. Instead, the judge instructed the jury to focus on two issues required by Texas law: (1) "whether the act was committed deliberately and with the reasonable expectation that the death of the deceased would result," and (2) whether the jury found "from the evidence beyond a reasonable doubt that there is a probability that the defendant, Brent Ray Brewer, would commit criminal acts of violence that would constitute a continuing threat to society." The jury answered yes to both issues and sentenced Brewer to death.

The Texas Court of Criminal Appeals upheld Brewer's conviction on direct appeal as well as later in an application for a writ of habeas corpus. The case went to the United States Supreme Court, which decided that "jury instructions that merely articulated the Texas special issues, without directing the sentencing jury to 'consider fully Penry's mitigating evidence as it bears on his personal culpability,' did not provide an adequate opportunity for the jury to decide whether that evidence might provide a legitimate basis for imposing a sentence other than death." The Court decided in favor of the inmate because of the inadequacy of the instructions given to the jury.

I. APPEALS AND HABEAS CORPUS

GRAHAM V. COLLINS
506 U.S. 461 (1993)

CAPSULE: The relief sought by the prisoner could not be granted because it would require the announcement of a new rule of constitutional law that could not occur in habeas corpus cases. In addition, the Texas statute is constitutional because it adequately narrowed the class of murder defendants eligible for the death penalty and permitted the sentencing authority to consider the mitigating circumstances raised by the defendant.

FACTS: In 1981, Gary Graham approached Bobby Lambert in a grocery store parking lot and attempted to grab his wallet. Lambert resisted and Graham shot him to death. Graham was convicted of capital murder. During the sentencing phase of his trial, the state offered aggravating evidence that the murder was just the beginning of a week of violent attacks during which the 17-year-old Graham committed a series of robberies and assaults, and one rape. This evidence was not contested by the defense. The defense offered, in mitigation, testimony from Graham's stepfather and grandmother concerning his upbringing and positive character traits. The testimony included the fact that Graham had two children he was trying to support and that he had lived on and off with his grandmother during his childhood because his mother was periodically hospitalized for a "nervous condition." The grandmother also testified she had never known Graham to be violent and that he attended church regularly. In its closing argument to the jury, the defense described Graham's behavior as a moral lapse, an aberration, and urged the jury to consider Graham's youth in deciding his punishment. He was convicted and given the death penalty in accordance with the Texas capital sentencing statute. The statute required the jury to answer three special issues. If the jury responded in the affirmative to all three questions, then the death penalty could be imposed.

ISSUES:

1. Should the habeas corpus relief sought by the prisoner be granted? NO.
2. Did the Texas death penalty law, specifically the three questions asked during the sentencing phase, allow the jury to consider the mitigating factors of youth, family background, and positive character traits of the defendant? YES.

HOLDINGS:

1. The relief sought by the prisoner should not be granted because it would require the announcement of a new rule of constitutional law that could not occur in habeas corpus cases.
2. The Texas statute is constitutional because it adequately narrowed the class of murder defendants eligible for the death penalty and permitted the sentencing authority to consider the mitigating circumstances raised by the defendant.

REASON: "Because this case is before us on Graham's petition for a writ of habeas corpus, 'we must determine, as a threshold matter, whether granting him the relief he seeks would create a "new rule" of constitutional law. Under *Teague*, new rules will not be applied or announced in cases on collateral review unless they fall into one of two exceptions.' This restriction on our review applies to capital cases as it does to those not involving the death penalty."

CASE SIGNIFICANCE: The first issue in this case deals with the so-called *Teague* rule, mandated by the Court in the earlier case of *Teague v. Lane* (1989). In *Teague*, the Court said that new rules will not be applied or announced in cases on collateral review (such as a habeas corpus case) unless they fall into one of two exceptions. This case did not come under either exception and therefore the habeas corpus sought should be denied. The Court further said, however, that the Texas death penalty law was constitutional because it allowed the jury to consider the mitigating circumstances that should be taken into account in a death penalty case. The Supreme Court has consistently ruled that provisions should be made in the law for the jury to be allowed to consider mitigating circumstances when deciding death penalty cases. The specific provisions of the Texas law challenged in *Graham* were the three special issues to which the jury had to answer "yes" before it could impose the death penalty. The Court said that these limiting provisions nonetheless allowed the jury to adequately consider mitigating factors and therefore the statute was constitutional.

MILLER-EL V. COCKRELL
537 U.S. 322 (2003)

CAPSULE: The Antiterrorism and Effective Death Penalty Act (AEDPA) does not require proof that a decision is objectively unreasonable when considering a request for a certificate of appealability.

FACTS: Thomas Joe Miller-El, his wife Dorothy, and Kenneth Flowers robbed a Dallas, Texas, Holiday Inn. They emptied the cash drawers and ordered two employees, Doug Walker and Donald Hall, to lie on the floor. The victims were gagged and their hands and feet were bound. Miller-El asked Flowers if he was going to kill Walker and Hall. When Flowers hesitated, Miller-El shot them both. Walker died from his wounds. Miller-El was indicted for capital murder. During jury selection at his trial, Miller-El moved to strike the jury on the grounds that the prosecution violated the equal protection clause of the Fourteenth Amendment by excluding 10 of the 11 eligible blacks through the use of peremptory challenges. He then presented extensive evidence supporting his motion at a pretrial hearing, but the trial judge denied relief, finding no evidence indicating a systematic exclusion of blacks, as was required by Supreme Court decisions. After trial the jury sentenced Miller-El to death.

ISSUE: Do the standards of the Antiterrorism and Effective Death Penalty Act (AEDPA) for granting habeas relief apply to the granting of a certificate of appealability? NO.

HOLDING: The standards of the AEDPA for granting habeas relief to state prisoners do not apply when a federal court of appeals considers whether to grant an unsuccessful petitioner's request for a certificate of appealability (COA). Moreover, the AEDPA's standard of clear and convincing evidence for rebutting the presumptive correctness of state court factual findings does not apply to decisions on COAs.

REASON: "The COA determination under Section 2253 (c) requires an overview of the claims in the habeas petition and a general assessment of their merits. We look to the District Court's application of AEDPA to petitioner's constitutional claims and ask whether the resolution was debatable among jurists of reason. This threshold inquiry does not require full consideration of the factual or legal bases adduced in support of the claims. In fact, the state forbids it. When a Court of Appeals sidesteps this process by first deciding the merits of an appeal, and then justifying its denial of a COA based on its adjudication of the actual merits, it is in essence deciding an appeal without jurisdiction."

CASE SIGNIFICANCE: This was not really a death penalty case because it involved the applicability of AEDPA law rather than whether a defendant receives the death penalty or not. The issue was narrow: whether the AEDPA standards for granting habeas relief also applied to an application for a certificate of appealability (COA).

The Antiterrorism and Effective Death Penalty Act (AEDPA) was passed by Congress in 1996 to limit the use of habeas petitions by prisoners. The AEDPA provides, among others, that the prisoner has no automatic right to appeal a habeas denial by the federal district court. Instead, the prisoner must first obtain a certificate of appeability (COA) with a Court of Appeals before being allowed to appeal. Another provision of the AEDPA states that the proceedings of the trial court where the defendant was convicted are presumed proper unless it is proved to be otherwise by "clear and convincing evidence." This is a difficult bar for the prisoner to overcome because it is higher than mere "preponderance of the evidence."

The immediate issue in *Miller-El* is therefore quite narrow: Is the standard for granting habeas (that standard being the "petitioner must demonstrate that a state court's finding of the absence of purposeful discrimination was incorrect by clear and convincing evidence, and that the corresponding factual determination was objectively unreasonable in light of the record before the court") the same standard the defendant must establish to obtain a COA? The Court said no, the standards are different. The standard to be used to obtain a COA was lower one—whether the District Court's decision denying habeas was debatable. In this case, the facts showed it was; therefore the defendant was entitled to a COA.

RYAN V. VALENCIA-GONZALES
568 U.S. ___ (2013)

CAPSULE: There is no statutory or constitutional right to competence in habeas corpus proceedings.

FACTS: Valencia-Gonzales was convicted of felony murder, armed robbery, aggravated assault, burglary, and theft. He was sentenced to death on the murder charge and received various prison terms for his other crimes. Valencia-Gonzales filed a petition for a writ of habeas corpus in federal district court after exhausting all state remedies. Before any action was taken on the petition, Valencia-Gonzales' appointed counsel requested to stay the proceedings. His contention was that Gonzales' was no longer capable of assisting in his own case.

ISSUE: Does the incompetence of a death row prisoner require the suspension of the prisoner's federal habeas corpus proceedings? NO.

HOLDING: Neither a statutory nor a constitutional right to competence exists during federal habeas corpus proceedings.

REASON: "We are not persuaded by the Ninth Circuit's assertion that a habeas petitioner's mental incompetency could 'eviscerate the statutory right to counsel' in federal habeas proceedings. Given the backward-looking, record-based nature of most federal habeas proceedings, counsel can generally provide effective representation to a habeas petitioner regardless of the petitioner's competence. Indeed, where a claim is 'adjudicated on the merits in State court proceedings,' 28 U.S.C. § 2254(d) (2006 ed.), counsel should, in most circumstances, be able to identify whether the 'adjudication . . . resulted in a decision that was contrary to, or involved an unreasonable application of, clearly established Federal law, as determined by the Supreme Court of the United States,' § 2254(d)(1), without any evidence outside the record. See *Cullen v. Pinholster*, 563 U.S. ___, ___ (2011) (slip op., at 9) ('[R]eview under [28 U.S.C.] § 2254(d)(1) is limited to the record that was before the state court that adjudicated the claim on the merits. . . . This backward-looking language requires an examination of the state-court decision at the time it was made. It follows that the record under review is limited to the record in existence at that same time—*i.e.*, the record before the state court'). Attorneys are quite capable of reviewing the state-court record, identifying legal errors, and marshaling relevant arguments, even without their clients' assistance."

"Both Gonzales and Carter argued at length in their briefs and at oral argument that district courts have the equitable power to stay proceedings when they determine that habeas petitioners are mentally incompetent. Neither petitioner disputes that; '[d]istrict courts . . . ordinarily have authority to issue stays, where such a stay would be a proper exercise of discretion.' *Rhines v. Weber*, 544 U.S. 269, 276 (2005) (citation omitted); see also *Enelow v. New York Life Ins. Co.*, 293 U.S. 379, 382 (1935) (explaining that a district court may stay a case 'pending before it by virtue of its inherent power to control the progress of the cause so as to maintain the orderly processes of justice'). Similarly, both petitioners agree that

'AEDPA does not deprive district courts of [this] authority.' *Rhines*, *supra*, at 276. Petitioners and respondents disagree, however, about the types of situation in which a stay would be appropriate and about the permissible duration of a competency-based stay. We do not presume that district courts need unsolicited advice from us on how to manage their dockets. Rather, the decision to grant a stay, like the decision to grant an evidentiary hearing, is 'generally left to the sound discretion of district courts.' *Schriro v. Landrigan*, 550 U.S. 465, 473 (2007). For purposes of resolving these cases, it is unnecessary to determine the precise contours of the district court's discretion to issue stays. We address only its outer limits."

"In Gonzales' case, the District Court correctly found that all of Gonzales' properly exhausted claims were record based or resolvable as a matter of law, irrespective of Gonzales' competence. 617 F. Supp. 2d, at 863; see also *State v. Gonzales*, 181 Ariz. 502, 509–515, 892 P. 2d 838, 845–851 (1995) (adjudicating Gonzales' claims on the merits). The court therefore denied Gonzales' motion for a stay. The District Court did not abuse its discretion in so holding, because a stay is not generally warranted when a petitioner raises only record-based claims subject to 28 U.S.C. § 2254(d)."

"The same principle obtains in the context of competency based stays. At some point, the State must be allowed to defend its judgment of conviction. If a district court concludes that the petitioner's claim could substantially benefit from the petitioner's assistance, the district court should take into account the likelihood that the petitioner will regain competence in the foreseeable future. Where there is no reasonable hope of competence, a stay is inappropriate and merely frustrates the State's attempts to defend its presumptively valid judgment."

CASE SIGNIFICANCE: In this case, the Court examines whether or not there is a statutory or constitutional right to competence during federal habeas corpus proceedings. It held there was not. As federal habeas corpus proceedings are totally record-based, it was the Court's position that counsel for the petitioner could provide effective representation. The Court stated that, although the district court has broad discretion to grant a stay on these types of proceeding, a stay was not necessary here because communication between the petitioner and his counsel was unnecessary.

J. CRUEL AND UNUSUAL PUNISHMENT

STEWART V. LAGRAND
526 U.S. 115 (1999)

CAPSULE: Choosing execution by lethal gas over lethal injection waives the defendant's claim to cruel and unusual punishment under that method of execution.

FACTS: In 1984, Walter LaGrand and his brother, Karl LaGrand, were each convicted of first-degree murder, attempted murder in the first degree, attempted armed robbery, and two counts of kidnapping. Both were sentenced to death. At the time, execution in the gas chamber was the only method provided by Arizona law. Walter LaGrand did not challenge the method of execution on direct appeal or in his petition for state post-conviction relief. By the time of his writ of habeas corpus, Arizona had changed its law to provide that death sentences would be carried out by means of lethal injection unless the prisoner chose lethal gas. Walter LaGrand chose gas and then challenged its use as a violation of the Eighth Amendment.

ISSUE: Does lethal gas as a method of execution violate the Eighth Amendment's cruel and unusual punishment clause? NO.

HOLDING: By choosing lethal gas over lethal injection, the defendant waived his claim of cruel and unusual punishment under that method of execution.

REASON: "Walter LaGrand, by his actions, has waived his claim that execution by lethal gas is unconstitutional. At the time Walter LaGrand was sentenced to death, lethal gas was the only method of execution available in Arizona, but the State now provides inmates a choice of execution by lethal gas or lethal injection, see Ariz. Rev. Stat. § 13–704(B) (creating a default rule of execution by lethal injection). Walter LaGrand was afforded this choice and decided to be executed by lethal gas. On March 1, 1999, Governor Hull of Arizona offered Walter LaGrand an opportunity to rescind this decision and select lethal injection as his method of execution. Walter LaGrand again insisted that he desired to be executed by lethal gas. By declaring his method of execution, picking lethal gas over the state's default form of execution—lethal injection—Walter La Grand has waived any objection he might have to it. See, e.g., *Johnson v. Zerbst*, 304 U.S. 458, 464 (1938). To hold otherwise, and to hold that Eighth Amendment protections cannot be waived in the capital context, would create and apply a new procedural rule in violation of *Teague v. Lane*, 489 U.S. 288 (1989)."

CASE SIGNIFICANCE: This is an interesting case that is primarily only significant to the defendant involved. The defendant had a choice of to how he would be executed—by lethal gas or lethal injection. He chose death by lethal gas, then challenged it as a form of cruel and unusual punishment. The Court rejected his claim, saying "[b]y declaring his method of execution, picking lethal gas over the state's default form of execution—lethal injection—Walter LaGrand has waived any objection he might have to it." In sum, choosing a form of execution waives the right to challenge its constitutionality later. Is execution by lethal gas in itself cruel and unusual punishment? Although the Court did not answer this question directly, it indicated that this method of execution has been used in the United States since 1921 and, despite challenges, no court has declared it unconstitutional.

PANETTI V. QUARTERMAN, DIRECTOR, TDCJ, CI DIVISION
551 U.S. 930 (2007)

CAPSULE: The Fifth Circuit Court of Appeals misinterpreted *Ford v. Wainwright* in its clarification of an inmate's rational understanding of his/her impending execution.

FACTS: Scott Louis Panetti awoke before dawn one morning in 1992 and dressed himself in camouflage. He drove to the home of his estranged wife's parents, broke into the house, and shot and killed his wife's mother and father in front of his wife and daughter. He then took his wife and daughter hostage before surrendering to the police the next day. Panetti tried to represent himself in his capital murder trial in 1995. A psychiatric evaluation was ordered by the court, which indicated that Panetti suffered from a fragmented personality, delusions, and hallucinations. It was also noted that he had been hospitalized many times for these disorders. The court found him competent to stand trial and to waive counsel. His behavior during his trial was described by his standby counsel as "bizarre," "scary," and "trancelike." The attorney added that Panetti's behavior both in private and in front of the jury made it evident that he was suffering from "mental incompetence." The jury found Panetti guilty of capital murder and sentenced him to death. Less than two months after receiving his sentence, Panetti was found to be incompetent to waive the appointment of state habeas counsel. He was denied relief on his initial state and federal proceedings. He did not argue that mental illness rendered him incompetent to be executed in any of these proceedings.

ISSUE: Is the execution of an inmate constitutional if the inmate knows why the state is executing him, but because of mental illness, lacks a rational understanding of the justification for such execution? NOT AUTHORITATIVELY ANSWERED.

HOLDING: The Court did not resolve this constitutional issue, holding instead that the Fifth Circuit's interpretation of the leading case on this issue, *Ford v. Wainwright*, was too restrictive because that court considered the defendant's mental condition as irrelevant as long as he had some factual awareness of the state's reason for executing him. The case was remanded to the lower court for further proceedings.

REASON: "Petitioner claims that the Eighth and Fourteenth Amendments of the Constitution, as elaborated by *Ford*, entitled him to certain procedures not provided in the state court; that the failure to provide these procedures constituted an unreasonable application of clearly established Supreme Court law; and that under § 2254(d) this misapplication of *Ford* allows federal-court review of his incompetency claim without deference to the state court's decision.

"We agree with petitioner that no deference is due. The state court's failure to provide the procedures mandated by *Ford* constituted an unreasonable application of clearly established law as determined by this Court. It is uncontested that petitioner made a substantial showing of incompetency. This showing entitled him to, among other things, an adequate means by which to submit expert psychiatric evidence in response to the evidence that had been solicited by the state court. And it is clear from the record that the state court reached its competency determination after failing to provide petitioner with this process, notwithstanding counsel's sustained effort, diligence, and compliance with court orders. As a result of this error, our review of petitioner's underlying incompetency claim is unencumbered by the deference AEDPA normally requires."

"The Court of Appeals stated that the competency is determined by whether a prisoner is aware "'that he [is] going to be executed and why he [is] going to be executed,"' 448 F.3d, at 819 (quoting *Barnard*, 13 F.3d at 877); see also 448 F.3d at 818 (discussing *Ford*, 477 U.S., at 421–422 (Powell, J., concurring in part and concurring in judgment). To this end, the Court of Appeals identified the relevant District court findings as follows: first, petitioner is aware that he committed the murders; second, he is aware that he will be executed; and, third, he is aware that the reason the State has given for the execution is his commission of the crimes in question. 448 F.3d, at 817. Under circuit precedent this ends the analysis as a matter of law; for the Court of Appeals regards these three factual findings as necessarily demonstrating that a prisoner is aware of the reason for his execution.

"The Court of Appeals concluded that its standard foreclosed petitioner from establishing incompetency by the means he now seeks to employ: a showing that his mental illness obstructs a rational understanding of the State's reason for his execution. Id., at 817–818. As the court explained, '[b]ecause we hold that "awareness" as the term is used in *Ford*, is not necessarily synonymous with "rational understanding," as argued by [petitioner,] we conclude that the district court's findings are sufficient to establish that [petitioner] is competent to be executed.' Id., at 821."

"The Court of Appeals' standard treats a prisoner's delusional belief system as irrelevant if the prisoner knows that the State has identified his crimes as the reason for his execution. See 401 F. Supp. 2d, at 712 (indicating that under Circuit precedent 'a petitioner's delusional beliefs—even those which may result in a fundamental failure to appreciate the connection between the petitioner's crime and his execution—do not bear on the question of whether the petitioner "knows the reason for his execution" for the purposes of the Eighth Amendment'); see also id., at 711–712. Yet the *Ford* opinions nowhere indicate that delusions are irrelevant to '[comprehension]' or 'aware[ness]' if they so impair the prisoner's concept of reality that he cannot reach a rational understanding of the reason for the execution. If anything, the *Ford* majority suggests the opposite."

CASE SIGNIFICANCE: In an earlier case, *Ford v. Wainwright*, 477 U.S. 399 (1986), the Court ruled that a prisoner who is insane may not be executed because such would constitute cruel and unusual punishment. The facts in *Panetti v. Quarterman* are interesting and present a variation of *Ford*. Convicted of murder, defendant Panetti was not "insane" in that he knew what was happening. He "had the ability to understand the reason he was to be executed." Panetti, however, believed that "the State actually wants to execute him to stop him from preaching." Based on its own earlier decision, the Fifth Circuit concluded that "such delusions are simply not relevant to whether a prisoner can be executed so long as he is aware that the State has identified the link between his crime and the punishment to be inflicted."

On appeal, the Court held that "this test ignores the possibility that even if such awareness exists, gross delusions stemming from a severe mental disorder may put that awareness in a context so far removed from reality, that the punishment can serve no proper purpose," further saying that "a prisoner's awareness of the State's rationale for an execution is not the same as a rational understanding of it." In sum, the Court considered the Fifth Circuit did not interpret *Ford v. Wainwright* properly and therefore remanded the case to the lower court. Said the Court: "Petitioner's submission is that he suffers from a severe, documented mental illness that is the source of gross delusions preventing him from comprehending the meaning and purpose of the punishment to which he has been sentenced. This argument, we hold, should have been considered."

It is important to realize that although the Court in this case rejected the standard set by the Fifth Circuit, it refused to set its own standard that would govern all competency determinations. Instead, the states are to determine what standard is to be applied.

BAZE V. REES
553 U.S. 35 (2008)

CAPSULE: A lethal injection procedure that does not pose a "substantial" or "objectively intolerable" risk of serious harm is constitutional.

FACTS: Ralph Baze and Thomas C. Bowling were both convicted of two counts of capital murder and sentenced to death in the State of Kentucky. Kentucky's current form of execution is the lethal infection of three drugs: sodium thiopental to render unconsciousness; pancuronium bromide to paralyze the lungs; and potassium chloride, which induces cardiac arrest. As part of Kentucky's lethal injection protocol, those persons responsible for inserting the intravenous (IV) catheters into the prisoner must be qualified personnel with at least one year's professional experience. Kentucky uses a certified phlebotomist and an emergency medical technician (EMT) to perform these functions. The warden and deputy warden stay in the execution chamber with the prisoner and if the prisoner is not unconscious within 60 seconds of administering the first drug, sodium thiopental, a second dose of the drug is administered before injecting the other drugs. Between injections, members of the execution team flush the IV lines with saline to prevent clogging of the lines.

ISSUE: Does Kentucky's lethal injection procedure violate the Eighth Amendment prohibition against cruel and unusual punishment? NO.

HOLDING: Kentucky's lethal injection procedure does not violate the Eighth Amendment because it does not present a substantial or objectively intolerable risk of serious harm. "A State's refusal to adopt proffered alternative procedures may violate the Eighth Amendment only where the alternative procedure is feasible, readily implemented, and . . . significantly reduces a substantial risk of severe pain."

REASON: "Petitioners do not claim that lethal injection or the proper administration of the particular protocol adopted by Kentucky by themselves constitute the cruel or wanton infliction of pain. Quite the contrary, they concede that 'if performed properly,' an execution carried out under Kentucky's procedures would be 'humane and constitutional.' That is because, as counsel for petitioners admitted at oral argument, proper administration of the first drug, sodium thiopental, eliminates any meaningful risk that a prisoner would experience pain from the subsequent injections of pancuronium and potassium chloride.

"Instead, petitioners claim that there is a significant risk that procedures will not be properly followed—in particular, that the sodium thiopental will not be properly administered to achieve its intended effect—resulting in severe pain when the other chemicals are administered. Our cases recognize that subjecting individuals to a risk of future harm—not simply actually inflicting pain—can qualify as cruel and unusual punishment. To establish that such exposure violates the Eighth Amendment, however, the conditions presenting the risk must be 'sure or very likely to cause serious illness and needless suffering,' and give rise to 'sufficiently imminent dangers.' *Helling v. McKinney*, 509 U.S. 25, 33, 34–35 (1993) (emphasis added). We have explained that to prevail on such a claim there must be a 'substantial risk of serious harm,' an 'objectively intolerable risk of harm' that prevents prison officials from pleading that they were 'subjectively blameless for purposes of the Eighth Amendment.' *Farmer v. Brennan*, 511 U.S. 825, 842, 846, and n. 9 (1994)."

"Much of petitioner's case rests on the contention that they have identified a significant risk of harm that can be eliminated by adopting alternative procedures, such as a one-drug protocol that dispenses with the use of pancuronium and potassium chloride, and additional monitoring by trained personnel to ensure that the first dose of sodium thiopental has been adequately delivered. Given what our cases have said about the nature of the risk of harm that is actionable under the

Eighth Amendment, a condemned prisoner cannot successfully challenge a State's method of execution merely by showing a slightly or marginally safer alternative."

"Instead, the proffered alternatives must effectively address a 'substantial risk of serious harm.' *Farmer v. Brennan, supra*, at 842. To qualify, the alternative procedure must be feasible, readily implemented, and in fact significantly reduce a substantial risk of severe pain. If a State refuses to adopt such an alternative in the face of these documented advantages, without a legitimate penological justification for adhering to its current method of execution, then a State's refusal to change its method can be viewed as 'cruel and unusual' under the Eighth Amendment."

CASE SIGNIFICANCE: This April 2008 case on the death penalty was considered one of the most serious challenges to the death penalty since the decision in *Gregg v. Georgia* in 1976. It came at a time when the country entertained strong reservations about the wisdom and constitutionality of the death penalty, particularly because of the possibility of executing innocent defendants. Massive publicity about defendants, including those on death row, who were freed because DNA evidence proved they were innocent caused the public to pause and ask if the country had in fact executed an innocent person or if it will in the future. Executing innocent defendants is understandably something the public will not and cannot tolerate.

Prior to the decision, there was massive media publicity and predictions it would put the issue of the death penalty to its final and deserved rest. To the disappointment of death penalty opponents, the case did not turn out to be that significant after all. The reason is that it focused on a narrow issue: whether Kentucky's method of execution constituted cruel and unusual punishment. The federal government and at least 30 states use the same combination of drugs as are used in Kentucky. The case generated a lot of attention because of the widespread use of the three-drug method of execution. Were Kentucky's procedure declared unconstitutional, it would have forced the other states and the federal government to find new ways to execute defendants by lethal injection. It would also have put a temporary halt to executions (it already had, pending decision by the Court) while the states searched for an acceptable procedure. It would have taken years before executions could resume.

The defendant in this case admitted that the death penalty is constitutional; what he challenged was Kentucky's method of execution which, he claimed, "would cause a significant risk that the procedures will not be properly followed." He said that the "sodium thiopental will not be properly administered to achieve its intended effect—resulting in severe pain when the other chemicals are administered." The Court disagreed, saying there was nothing constitutionally wrong with the three-drug combination that Kentucky used. Key to understanding the Court's decision is the standard used by a plurality (three justices out of the six who voted for constitutionality) of the Court to determine whether procedural issues in death penalty cases violated the Eighth Amendment. The Court set this standard: "To constitute cruel and unusual punishment, an execution method must present a 'substantial' or 'objectively intolerable' risk of serious harm." It is not enough, as the defendant claimed, that other humane methods of execution were available and could have been used. The defendant had identified methods used in some states that supposedly eliminated these risks. Said the Court: "[A]llowing a condemned prisoner to challenge a State's execution method merely by showing a slightly or marginally safer alternative finds no support in this Court's cases, would embroil the courts in ongoing scientific controversies beyond their expertise, and would substantially intrude on the role of state legislatures in implementing execution procedures . . ." The Court concluded by saying that "Petitioners have not carried their burden of showing that the risk of pain from maladministration of a concededly humane lethal injection protocol, and the failure to adopt untried and untested alternatives, constitute cruel and unusual punishment."

With this decision, the Court gave the "go ahead" signal for executions to resume. Three weeks after the case was decided, on April 16, 2008, the state of Georgia conducted the first post-*Baze* execution. Other states soon followed.

KENNEDY V. LOUISIANA
554 U.S. 407 (2008)

CAPSULE: It is unconstitutional to impose the death penalty for the rape of a child.

FACTS: Kennedy raped his eight-year-old stepdaughter at their home. Her injuries were so severe that emergency surgery was necessary. Initially, the victim denied that Kennedy had committed the rape, but she eventually named him as the perpetrator.

Kennedy was convicted of rape of a child under 12 years of age. Louisiana law allowed for the death penalty in these cases and the jury subsequently imposed it. Kennedy appealed to the Supreme Court of Louisiana on the basis that the punishment was disproportionate to the crime and violated the Eighth Amendment's prohibition against excessive punishments. The Louisiana Supreme Court held that the statute allowing the death penalty for this crime was constitutional.

ISSUE: Is the Louisiana statute that allows the death penalty to be imposed for the rape of a child under 12 years of age constitutional? NO.

HOLDING: If an offender rapes a child but did not kill the child or, if the offender did not intend to assist another person in the killing of the child, then the imposition of the death penalty is unconstitutional under the Eighth and Fourteenth Amendments.

REASON: "As we shall discuss, punishment is justified under one or more of three principal rationales: rehabilitation, deterrence, and retribution . . . It is the last of these, retribution, that most often can contradict the law's own ends. This is of particular concern when the Court interprets the meaning of the Eighth

Amendment in capital cases. When the law punishes by death, it risks its own sudden descent into brutality, transgressing the constitutional commitment to decency and restraint."

"Though the death penalty is not invariably unconstitutional, see *Gregg v. Georgia*, 428 U.S. 153 (1976), the Court insists upon confining the instances in which the punishment can be imposed . . . The Court further has held that the death penalty can be disproportionate to the crime itself where the crime did not result, or was not intended to result, in death of the victim . . . Louisiana reintroduced the death penalty for the rape of a child in 1995 . . . Five States have since followed Louisiana's lead . . . By contrast, 44 States have not made child rape a capital offense . . . The evidence of a national consensus with respect to the death penalty for child rapists, as with respect to juveniles, mentally retarded offenders, and vicarious felony murderers, shows divided opinion but, on balance, an opinion against it . . . Statistics about the number of executions may inform the consideration whether capital punishment for the crime of child rape is regarded as unacceptable in our society."

"Rape has a permanent psychological, emotional, and sometimes physical impact on the child . . . It does not follow, though, that capital punishment is a proportionate penalty for the crime. The constitutional prohibition against excessive or cruel and unusual punishments mandates that the State's power to punish 'be exercised within the limits of civilized standards' . . . The goal of retribution, which reflects society's and the victim's interests in seeing that the offender is repaid for the hurt he caused, see *Atkins*, 536 U.S., at 319; *Furman*, *supra*, at 308 (Stewart, J., concurring), does not justify the harshness of the death penalty here . . . With respect to deterrence, if the death penalty adds to the risk of non-reporting, that, too, diminishes the penalty's objectives . . . In addition, by in effect making the punishment for child rape and murder equivalent, a State that punishes child rape by death may remove a strong incentive for the rapist not to kill the victim . . . The rule of evolving standards of decency with specific marks on the way to full progress and mature judgment means that resort to the penalty must be reserved for the worst of crimes and limited in its instances of application. In most cases justice is not better served by terminating the life of the perpetrator rather than confining him and preserving the possibility that he and the system will find ways to allow him to understand the enormity of his offense. Difficulties in administering the penalty to ensure against its arbitrary and capricious application require adherence to a rule reserving its use, at this stage of evolving standards and in cases of crimes against individuals, for crimes that take the life of the victim."

CASE SIGNIFICANCE: This is the first time that the Supreme Court considered whether the death penalty is unconstitutional as punishment for rape of a child. In 1972, in the case of *Coker v. Georgia*, the Court held that this penalty was not appropriate for the rape of an adult. However, six states had statutes allowing the death penalty as a possible sentence for the rape of a child at the time this case (*Kennedy v. Louisiana*) was heard. This ruling means that these states will have to revise their statutes to exclude the death penalty as a possible sentence, and the states that were considering enacting such laws will be unable to do so, according to this ruling.

In two recent cases, the Court has held that a juvenile cannot be sentenced to death (*Roper v. Simmons*), nor can a mentally retarded person receive this punishment (*Atkins v. Virginia*). Both of these cases mention an evolving standard of decency in society. This case also includes this principle. However, the two former cases focus on the culpability of the offender and their lesser degree of responsibility. This case does not focus on the offender's culpability, but, rather, on the act itself. Thus the Court is applying this principle in a different manner than the two previous cases. The Court has decided that the death penalty should only be imposed if a person's life was taken. While acknowledging the long-term consequences of a child being raped, the Court holds that this does not meet the greater loss of a life being taken.

This was a 5–4 decision and Justice Alito, who dissented, believes that Kennedy did not meet the burden of proving the Louisiana statute unconstitutional under the Eighth Amendment. Justice Alito also contends that society indicates a growing concern with sexual offenders who commit crimes against children. Based on this, society's evolving standard of decency would be to punish child rapists to the greatest degree. It is possible that the Court could reach a different conclusion concerning this issue in the future, due to a change in the Court's composition and society's reaction to sexual offenders who prey on children.

GLOSSIP V. GROSS
567 U.S. ___ (2015)

CAPSULE: The use of midazolam in an execution protocol does not violate the Eighth Amendment.

FACTS: Oklahoma death row inmates filed a § 1983 action claiming that the drug midazolam (the first drug used in Oklahoma's three-drug lethal injection protocol) fails to render a person insensate to pain. Oklahoma began using midazolam instead of the more common sodium thiopental or pentobarbital after anti–death penalty advocates pressured both domestic and international pharmaceutical companies to stop selling the drugs to those using them to carry out death sentences.

Following other states' examples, in 2014 Oklahoma substituted midazolam for pentobarbital as part of its three-drug protocol. In April 2014, Clayton Lockett was the first inmate executed under the new protocol. Lockett cut himself twice "at the bend of the elbow" on the morning of his execution. That evening, it was difficult for the execution team to establish intravenous (IV) access to Lockett's cardiovascular system. It took over one dozen attempts at various points on his body, and the team finally believed it had succeeded through Lockett's right femoral vein. The injection's access point was then covered with a sheet. Once a physician had determined that Lockett was unconscious, the second drug (vecuronium bromide) and most of the third drug (potassium chloride) were also administered. Lockett began to move and speak, and it was determined that the IV fluid had not entered Lockett's bloodstream but had "leaked into the tissue surrounding the IV access point." *Warner v. Gross*, 776 F. 3d 721, 725 (CA10, 2015). At this point the execution team stopped administering what was left of the potassium chloride and terminated the execution about 33 minutes after midazolam was first injected. Lockett was pronounced dead about 10 minutes later.

The Lockett execution was investigated, and it was determined that "the viability of the access point was the single greatest factor that contributed to the difficulty in administering the execution drugs." The investigation recommended several changes to Oklahoma's execution protocol, including the use of 500 milligrams of midazolam followed by the other two drugs and the adoption of procedural safeguards to ensure that an inmate remain insensate to any pain caused by those other drugs.

ISSUE: Does the method of execution used in Oklahoma violate the cruel and unusual punishment clause of the Eighth Amendment because it creates an unacceptable risk of severe pain? NO.

HOLDING: Oklahoma's method of execution does not violate the Eighth Amendment. The use of midazolam in a lethal injection protocol does not create an unacceptable risk of severe pain.

REASON: "Our first ground for affirmance is based on petitioners' failure to satisfy their burden of establishing that any risk of harm was substantial when compared to a known and available alternative method of execution. In their amended complaint, petitioners proffered that the State could use sodium thiopental as part of a single-drug protocol. They have since suggested that it might also be constitutional for Oklahoma to use pentobarbital. But the District Court found that both sodium thiopental and pentobarbital are now unavailable to Oklahoma's Department of Corrections. The Court of Appeals affirmed that finding, and it is not clearly erroneous. On the contrary, the record shows that Oklahoma has been unable to procure those drugs despite a good-faith effort to do so.

"Petitioners do not seriously contest this factual finding, and they have not identified any available drug or drugs that could be used in place of those that Oklahoma is now unable to obtain. Nor have they shown a risk of pain so great that other acceptable, available methods must be used. Instead, they argue that they need not identify a known and available method of execution that presents less risk. But this argument is inconsistent with the controlling opinion in *Baze*, 553 U.S., at 61, which imposed a requirement that the Court now follows."

"We also affirm for a second reason: The District Court did not commit clear error when it found that midazolam is highly likely to render a person unable to feel pain during an execution. We emphasize four points at the outset of our analysis.

"First, we review the District Court's factual findings under the deferential 'clear error' standard. This standard does not entitle us to overturn a finding 'simply because [we are] convinced that [we] would have decided the case differently.' *Anderson v. Bessemer City*, 470 U.S. 564, 573 (1985).

"Second, petitioners bear the burden of persuasion on this issue. *Baze, supra*, at 41. Although petitioners expend great effort attacking peripheral aspects of Dr. Evans' testimony, they make little attempt to prove what is critical, *i.e.*, that the evidence they presented to the District Court establishes that the use of midazolam is sure or very likely to result in needless suffering.

"Third, numerous courts have concluded that the use of midazolam as the first drug in a three-drug protocol is likely to render an inmate insensate to pain that might result from administration of the paralytic agent and potassium chloride. See, *e.g.*, 776 F. 3d 721 (case below affirming the District Court); *Chavez v. Florida SP Warden*, 742 F. 3d 1267 (affirming the District Court); *Banks v. State*, 150 So. 3d 797 (Fla. 2014) (affirming the lower court); *Howell v. State*, 133 So. 3d 511 (Fla. 2014) (same); *Muhammad v. State*, 132 So. 3d 176 (Fla. 2013) (same). (It is noteworthy that one or both of the two key witnesses in this case—Dr. Lubarsky for petitioners and Dr. Evans for respondents—were witnesses in the *Chavez*, *Howell*, and *Muhammad* cases.) 'Where an intermediate court reviews, and affirms, a trial court's factual findings, this Court will not "lightly overturn" the concurrent findings of the two lower courts.' *Easley v. Cromartie*, 532 U.S. 234, 242 (2001). Our review is even more deferential where, as here, multiple trial courts have reached the same finding, and multiple appellate courts have affirmed those findings. Cf. *Exxon Co., U.S.A. v. Sofec, Inc.*, 517 U.S. 830, 841 (1996) (explaining that this Court "'cannot undertake to review concurrent findings of fact by two courts below in the absence of a very obvious and exceptional showing of error'", quoting *Graver Tank & Mfg. Co. v. Linde Air Products Co.*, 336 U.S. 271, 275 (1949)).

"Fourth, challenges to lethal injection protocols test the boundaries of the authority and competency of federal courts. Although we must invalidate a lethal injection protocol if it violates the Eighth Amendment, federal courts should not 'embroil [themselves] in ongoing scientific controversies beyond their expertise.' *Baze, supra*, at 51. Accordingly, an inmate challenging a protocol bears the burden to show, based on evidence presented to the court, that there is a substantial risk of severe pain."

CASE SIGNIFICANCE: This case is controlled by the U.S. Supreme Court decision in *Baze v. Rees*, where it was held that for an Eighth Amendment claim concerning the method of execution "a prisoner must show that the method creates a demonstrated risk of severe pain and that the risk is substantial when compared to the known and available alternatives." The plaintiffs in this case were unable to do so.

The State of Oklahoma introduced midazolam into its execution protocol when it could no longer obtain either sodium thiopental or pentobarbital. The unfortunate events of the Lockett execution caused Oklahoma to examine its execution protocol. The state increased the dosage of midazolam from 100 milligrams to 500 milligrams, which virtually puts the prisoner in a coma. The plaintiffs were unable to provide scientific data that would prove otherwise. If the prisoner is in a coma-like state before the other drugs in the execution protocol are administered, the Court ruled that the plaintiffs failed to show that there was a demonstrated and substantial risk of severe pain.

K. OTHER ISSUES

PULLEY V. HARRIS
465 U.S. 37 (1984)

CAPSULE: Proportionality review is not required in death penalty cases.

FACTS: Harris was convicted of capital murder in a California court. In a separate sentencing hearing, the jury found several aggravating factors and sentenced him to death. Harris challenged the sentence, claiming that the California capital punishment statute was unconstitutional because it failed to require the California Supreme Court to compare Harris' sentence to the sentences imposed in similar capital cases to determine whether the sentence was proportionate.

ISSUE: In death penalty cases, does the Eighth Amendment require a state appellate court to compare the sentence in the case before it with the penalties imposed in similar cases? NO.

HOLDING: The Eighth Amendment does not require as an invariable rule in every case that a state appellate court, before it affirms a death sentence, compare the sentence in the case before it with the sentence imposed in similar cases, even if asked to do so by the prisoner.

REASON: "At the outset, we should more clearly identify the issue before us. Traditionally, 'proportionality' has been used with reference to an abstract evaluation of the appropriateness of a sentence for a particular crime. Looking to the gravity of the offense and the severity of the penalty, to sentences imposed for other crimes, and to sentencing practices in other jurisdictions, this Court has occasionally struck down punishments as inherently disproportionate, and there-fore cruel and unusual, when imposed for a particular crime or category of crime. The death penalty is not in all cases a disproportionate penalty in this sense."

CASE SIGNIFICANCE: The Supreme Court ruled in this case that state appellate courts are not constitutionally required to provide, upon request by the defendant, a "proportionality review" of death sentences in which the court would compare the sentence in the case before it to penalties imposed in similar cases in that state. Proportionality reviews are constitutional and are provided for by law or judicial practice in some states, but such reviews are not required by the

Constitution. For example, the Court found the Texas death penalty statute to be constitutional even though neither the law nor judicial practice provide for any form of proportionality review. The Court did not completely close the door to proportionality review, however, in some extreme cases. It said: "assuming that there could be a capital sentencing scheme so lacking in other checks or arbitrariness that it could not pass constitutional muster without comparative proportional review, the California statute involved here is not of that sort."

WHITMORE V. ARKANSAS
495 U.S. 149 (1990)

CAPSULE: A person other than the defendant cannot challenge the validity of a death sentence.

FACTS: Ronald Gene Simmons was convicted of capital murder and sentenced to death on two separate occasions for two separate sets of criminal charges. In both instances, Simmons made a statement under oath that he wanted no action taken on his behalf to appeal or in any way change the sentences. In both cases, the trial court conducted a hearing concerning Simmons' competence to waive further proceedings, and concluded that his decision was knowing and intelligent. Arkansas law does not require a mandatory appeal in all death penalty cases. Whitmore, another death row inmate in Arkansas, however, intervened in the case both individually and as "next friend" of Simmons and sought to appeal the conviction and sentence.

ISSUE: Does a third party have standing to challenge the validity of a death sentence imposed on a defendant who elected to forgo his right of appeal? NO.

HOLDING: A state death row inmate lacks standing, either in a personal capacity or as "next friend," to seek review by the U.S. Supreme Court of a death sentence imposed upon a fellow inmate who has knowingly, intelligently, and voluntarily waived the right to pursue an appeal.

REASON: "Petitioner Whitmore asks this Court to hold that despite Simmons' failure to appeal, the Eighth and Fourteenth Amendments require the State of Arkansas to conduct an appellate review of his conviction and sentence before it can proceed to execute him. It is well established, however, that before a federal court can consider the merits of a legal claim, the person seeking to invoke the jurisdiction of the court must establish the requisite standing to sue. Article III, of course, gives the federal courts jurisdiction over only 'cases and controversies,' and the doctrine of standing serves to identify those disputes which are appropriately resolved through the judicial process."

CASE SIGNIFICANCE: The Supreme Court ruled in this case that Whitmore lacked standing, either in a personal capacity or as "next friend" to appeal the death sentence imposed on inmate Ronald Gene Simmons. This is significant because it means that a third party cannot initiate an appeal for a defendant who refuses to do so. This is bad news for organizations and individuals who espouse anti-death penalty causes. The Court said that to be able to appeal, an individual must clearly demonstrate that he or she suffered "injury in fact" and that such injury "can be fairly traced to the challenged action," and "is likely to be redressed by a favorable decision."

HILL V. MCDONOUGH, INTERIM SECRETARY, FLORIDA DEPT. OF CORRECTIONS ET AL.
546 U.S. 573 (2006)

CAPSULE: How the death penalty is carried out can be challenged in a § 1983 action.

FACTS: In 1983, Clarence E. Hill was convicted of first-degree murder and sentenced to death. Five years later his conviction and sentence became final. The method of execution in Florida at that time was electrocution. On January 14, 2000, just a few days after the conclusion of Hill's first unsuccessful attempts at federal habeas corpus litigation, Florida amended its death penalty statutes and identified lethal injection as the primary method of execution "unless the person sentenced to death affirmatively elects to be executed by electrocution." The statute does not specify a particular lethal injection procedure. The Florida Department of Corrections, the agency responsible for implementing death sentences, had not issued rules establishing a specific lethal injection protocol either.

On November 29, 2005, the Governor of Florida signed Hill's death warrant, which ordered him to be executed on January 24, 2006. Hill requested information about the lethal injection protocol but was provided none. Hill challenged the state's lethal injection procedure based on the Eighth Amendment and requested an evidentiary hearing. He was denied, the state dismissing his claim as procedurally barred. Hill then brought a § 1983 action in District Court alleging that the first drug Florida would inject, sodium pentothal, would not be a sufficient anesthetic to render painless the administration of the second and third drugs, pancuronium bromide and potassium chloride.

ISSUE: Is a prisoner's challenge to a particular form of execution—but not the execution sentence itself—barred if the prisoner has already sought habeas review? NO.

HOLDING: Challenging the form of execution is fundamentally different from challenging the lawfulness of a conviction or sentence and is similar to a § 1983 action, which can be filed even after a habeas review.

REASON: "In *Nelson v. Campbell*, *supra*, we addressed whether a challenge to a lethal injection procedure must proceed as a habeas corpus action. The complainant had severely compromised peripheral veins, and Alabama planned to apply an invasive procedure on his arm or leg to enable the injection. He sought to enjoin the procedure, alleging it would violate the Eighth Amendment. The court observed that the question whether a general challenge to a method of execution must proceed under habeas was a difficult one. The claim was not easily described as a challenge to the fact or duration of a sentence: yet in a state where the legislation has established lethal injection as the method of execution, 'a constitutional challenge seeking to permanently enjoin the use of lethal injection may amount to a challenge to the fact of the sentence itself.' Id., at 644."

"In the case before us we conclude that Hill's § 1983 action is controlled by the holding in *Nelson*. Here, as in *Nelson*, Hill's action if successful would not necessarily prevent the State from executing by lethal injection. The complaint does not challenge the lethal injection sentence as a general matter but seeks instead only to enjoin the respondents 'from executing [Hill] in the manner they currently intend.' App. 22 (Complaint ¶20). The specific objection is that the anticipated protocol allegedly causes 'a foreseeable risk of . . . gratuitous and unnecessary' pain. Id., at 46 (Application for Stay of Execution and for Expedited Appeal). Hill concedes that 'other methods of lethal injection the Department could choose to use would be constitutional,' Brief for Petition 17, and respondents do not contend, at least to this point in the litigation, that granting Hill's injunction would leave the State without any other practicable, legal method of executing Hill by lethal injection. Florida law, moreover, does not require the Department of Corrections to use the challenged procedure. See Fla. Stat. §§ 922.105(1), (7) (prescribing lethal injection and leaving implementation to the Department of Corrections). Hill's challenge appears to leave the State free to use an alternative lethal injection procedure. Under these circumstances a grant of injunctive relief could not be seen as barring the execution of Hill's sentence.

"One difference between the present case and *Nelson*, of course, is that Hill challenges the chemical injection sequence rather than a surgical procedure preliminary to the lethal injection. In *Nelson*, however, the State argued that the invasive procedure was not a medical operation separable from the lethal injection but rather a 'necessary prerequisite to, and thus an indispensable part of, any lethal injection procedure.' 541 U.S., at 645. The court reasoned that although venous access was necessary for lethal injection, it did not follow that the State's chosen means of access were necessary; 'the gravamen of petitioner's entire claim' was that the procedure was 'gratuitous.' Ibid. (emphasis deleted). The same is true here. Although the injection of lethal chemicals is an obvious necessity for the execution, Hill alleges that the challenged procedure presents a risk of pain the State can avoid while still being able to enforce the sentence ordering a lethal injection."

CASE SIGNIFICANCE: Capital punishment cases where death is imposed are automatically appealed directly to the state supreme court in many states. This is known as a direct appeal to determine whether the finding of guilt and the sentence imposed are proper and constitutional. If the sentence is affirmed, the execution date is set and defendant is held in death row. This does not mean, however, that challenges to the conviction end. The defendant may use a post-conviction remedy in the form of a habeas corpus petition. Habeas petitions seek the release of a defendant allegedly because his or her constitutional rights were violated during trial or that subsequent facts have been found that establish the impropriety of the conviction.

Habeas corpus process can be abused, as when inmates file habeas petitions in serial fashion that can take years for each allegation to be resolved. This delays execution and results in defendants staying in death row for years before execution takes place, if it ever does. In 1994, Congress passed the Antiterrorism and Effective Death Penalty Act (AEDPA), which limits the filing of habeas cases. In essence, it provides that, with some exceptions, death row inmates have one shot at habeas corpus and then that right lapses and no further filings are allowed.

This was the issue in this case. The defendant had already used his habeas corpus opportunity when he subsequently filed this action under 42 U.S.C. § 1983. This federal law (§ 1983) allows anyone, inmates included, to seek civil damages from government officials if they can prove a violation of constitutional rights. Inmate Hill claimed that the three-drug lethal injection procedure Florida uses was unconstitutional and therefore sought the prohibition of its use on him. The issue was whether that action was barred under the provisions of AEDPA. The Court said no, saying that such a claim does not have to be alleged in a habeas corpus case. It could proceed under § 1983 and therefore the filing was allowed. This case gives death row inmates an extended opportunity to go to federal courts for vindication of constitutional rights.

NOTES

1   This case is also briefed in Chapter 5, Juvenile Justice.
2   This case is also briefed in Chapter 5, Juvenile Justice.
3   This case is also briefed in Chapter 5, Juvenile Justice.

Juvenile Justice

5

INTRODUCTION

Juvenile justice is heavily influenced by *parens patriae*, a Latin term for "the state as parent." This means that the state serves as sovereign and guardian of persons under legal disability, such as juveniles. *Parens patriae* led to the family model of processing juveniles, which treats juveniles like members of a family. The main concern of the juvenile court is to ensure that legal proceedings are presided over by judges who, acting as wise parents, have the best interests of the child in mind. Constitutional safeguards under *parens patriae* used to be minimal or nonexistent; instead, personal attention, love, and care were to be provided.

Over the years, pure *parens patriae* declined, paving the way for more due process. This means that juveniles now have essentially the same rights as adults, at least during adjudication proceedings. The case that signaled the erosion of *parens patriae* was *In re Gault* (1967), briefed below. In that case, the U.S. Supreme Court said that "neither the Fourteenth Amendment nor the Bill of Rights is for adults alone." Since then, the United States Supreme Court has decided other cases giving rights to juveniles that they previously did not have.

Juvenile proceedings at present are considered by most courts as either civil or administrative in nature, but the only constitutional rights presently denied juveniles are the right to a jury trial, the right to bail, the right to a public trial, and the right to a grand jury indictment. These rights, however, are usually given to juveniles by state law. As one writer aptly says, the juvenile justice process over the years has become "adultified," at least during the adjudication process.

The differences between the juvenile justice and adult justice processes may be summarized as follows:

Adult Proceedings	*Juvenile Proceedings*
1. Arrested	1. Taken into custody by police
2. Charged	2. Prosecutor petitions court
3. Accused of crime under the penal code	3. Violation comes under the juvenile code or family code
4. Trial	4. Adjudication
5. Formal, public trial	5. Usually a private, informal hearing
6. Judge is neutral	6. Judge acts as wise parent
7. Found guilty of a criminal offense by an impartial judge or jury	7. Found to have engaged in delinquent conduct
8. Sentenced if found guilty	8. Disposition
9. Sent to jail or prison	9. Committed to a state facility for juveniles
10. Judge or jury determines length of incarceration	10. Youth detention authorities determine when to release
11. Serves sentence for definite term, subject to parole law	11. Committed for an indeterminate period, but usually released upon reaching age of majority
12. Purpose is punishment	12. Purpose is rehabilitation
13. Released on parole, if eligible	13. Released on aftercare
14. A criminal case	14. A civil or quasi-civil case

As noted above, giving due process rights to juveniles began with *In re Gault*. This case gave juveniles the following rights in proceedings that involved possible institutionalization:

1. counsel in adjudication hearings
2. notice of charges
3. confrontation of adverse witnesses
4. prohibition against self-incrimination

Since then, other cases have been decided by the Court giving more constitutional rights to juveniles. For example, the Court has determined that the standard of guilt beyond a reasonable doubt should be applied during juvenile adjudication, replacing the standard of preponderance of the evidence (*In re Winship*, 1970). The Court has also held that a juvenile could not be tried as a juvenile and then as an adult for the same offense, because this violates the prohibition against double jeopardy (*Breed v. Jones*, 1975). The Court has ruled that the Fourth Amendment prohibition against unreasonable searches and seizures applies to juveniles in schools, although a lower degree of certainty is required—reasonable grounds rather than probable cause (*New Jersey v. T.L.O.*, 1985).

On the important issue of the death penalty for juveniles, the Court held in *Thompson v. Oklahoma* (1988) that juveniles who are 15 years of age at the time of the commission of the offense cannot be given the death penalty because that would violate the Eighth Amendment prohibition against cruel and unusual punishment. A year later, the Court said in *Stanford v. Kentucky* (1989) that it is constitutional to impose the death penalty on a juvenile who commits the crime at age 16 or older. Sixteen years later, in *Roper v. Simmons* (2005), the Court resolved the issue of juvenile executions by holding that executing juveniles who were 16 or 17 years of age at the time their crime was committed is unconstitutional because it violates the Eighth Amendment prohibition on cruel and unusual punishment. *Roper v. Simmons* overruled *Stanford v. Kentucky*. The brief for this decision also appears in Chapter 4, Death Penalty. And, more recently, the Court has dealt with the mandatory sentencing of juveniles to life without parole. Five years ago, the Court ruled, in *Graham v. Florida* (2010), that the Eighth Amendment requires us to treat juveniles individually in non-homicide cases, which makes mandatory life sentences without the possibility of parole unconstitutional. The Court then extended its ruling to juvenile homicide cases in *Miller v. Alabama* (2012).

The first juvenile court in the United States was established in Chicago, Illinois, in 1899. Juvenile courts have therefore been a part of the juvenile justice system in the United States for more than a century. As this collection of juvenile cases shows, however, there have been only a few cases addressing the constitutional rights of juveniles. When one compares the number of cases decided by the Supreme Court in prison law and juvenile law, one might conclude that the Court cares more about prisoners than it does about juveniles. That may be a misperception, because the reality is that conditions in juvenile facilities are generally better monitored through state law and regulations, thus there are more cases filed by prisoners than by juveniles in institutions. Moreover, many rights that juveniles enjoy in various states are given by state law rather than by the Constitution, whereas very few rights are given by state law to adult prisoners beyond those given by court decisions. Finally, although definitely eroded, the *parens patriae* approach to juvenile justice is still a consideration to be reckoned with when anyone challenges what the state does to a juvenile.

HALEY V. OHIO
332 U.S. 596 (1948)

CAPSULE: Coerced confessions are not admissible as evidence in a juvenile proceeding.

FACTS: On October 14, 1945, a confectionery store was robbed; the owner of the store was shot and killed. Five days later, a 15-year-old black juvenile named Haley was arrested for his alleged involvement in the crime. Beginning sometime after midnight, Haley was questioned for five hours by the police. He was questioned in relays by various police officers or teams of police officers. At no time during this questioning was anyone present on Haley's behalf. After being shown alleged confessions of the other participants in the robbery, Haley confessed. At no time was Haley informed of his right to counsel. A statement appeared at the top of the written confession informing Haley that the document could be used against him and that he was giving his statement voluntarily. He was then held incommunicado for three days before being taken before a magistrate and formally charged. An attorney attempted to see him twice but was refused admission. His mother was not allowed to see him until five days after his arrest. At Haley's trial, the defense objected to the admission of the confession on the grounds that it violated Haley's rights under the Fourteenth Amendment. The judge admitted the confession into evidence and instructed the jury to disregard the confession if it believed that the confession was not given voluntarily and of free will. Haley was convicted of murder in the first degree and sentenced to life imprisonment.

ISSUE: Does the Fourteenth Amendment prohibit the use of coerced confessions in juvenile proceedings? YES.

HOLDING: The due process clause of the Fourteenth Amendment prohibits the police from extracting involuntary or coerced confessions from adults and juveniles; any evidence obtained involuntarily cannot be used in court.

REASON: "We do not think the methods used in obtaining this confession can be squared with that due process of law which the Fourteenth Amendment commands.

"What transpired would make us pause for careful inquiry if a mature man was involved. And when, as here, a mere child—an easy victim of the law—is before us, special care in scrutinizing the record must be used. Age 15 is a tender and difficult age for a boy of any race. He cannot be judged by more exacting standards of maturity.

"No friend stood at the side of this 15-year-old boy as the police, working in relays, questioned him hour after hour, from midnight until dawn. No lawyer stood guard to make sure that the police went so far and no farther, to see that they stopped short of the point where he became the victim of coercion . . .

"This disregard of the standards of decency [is] underlined by the fact that he was held incommunicado for over three days during which the lawyer retained to represent him twice tried to see him and twice was refused admission. A photographer was admitted at once, but his closest friend—his mother—was not allowed to see him for over five days after his arrest. It is said that these events are not germane to the present problem because they happened after the confession was made. But they show such a callous attitude of the police towards the safeguards which respect for ordinary standards of human relationships compels that we take with a grain of salt their present apologia that the five-hour grilling of this boy was conducted in a fair and dispassionate manner.

"The age of the petitioner, the hours when he was grilled, the duration of his quizzing, the fact that he had no friend or counsel to advise him, the callous attitude of the police towards his rights combine to convince us that this was a confession wrung from a child by means which the law should not sanction. Neither man nor child can be allowed to stand condemned by methods which flout constitutional requirements of due process of law."

CASE SIGNIFICANCE: In this case, the Supreme Court for the first time suggested that, despite *parens patriae* (the doctrine stating that the state serves as the "parent" of juveniles), there are constitutional requirements that protect all accused persons, whether they are adults or juveniles. The Court was not willing to go so far as to say that juveniles have recognized constitutional rights, but it held that juveniles cannot be held to higher standards than adults. Juveniles stand a lesser chance of protecting themselves against police tactics, thus it is only reasonable that a juvenile be given the same, if not greater, protection against coercion than adults.

This decision is easy to accept today, but was not as easily reached in 1948 under the pure *parens patriae* philosophy. At present, the concept that juveniles deserve better protection than adults against possible police abuses is accepted. This was not the case in 1948, when *parens patriae* insulated police and courts from judicial scrutiny on the ground that these agencies were entitled to greater authority when dealing with juveniles.

KENT V. UNITED STATES
383 U.S. 541 (1966)

CAPSULE: A juvenile must be given due process rights before being transferred from a juvenile court to an adult court.

FACTS: Kent, at age 16, was arrested and charged with housebreaking, robbery, and rape. Because of his age, he came under the jurisdiction of the District of Columbia Juvenile Court. That court, however, could waive jurisdiction after a "full investigation" (in accordance with District of Columbia law) and transferred him to the United States District Court for an adult criminal trial. Kent's attorney filed motions to have a hearing on the waiver. He also recommended that Kent be hospitalized for psychiatric observation and that he be allowed access to the file that the juvenile court had on his client. The juvenile court did not rule on these motions. Instead, the judge ordered that jurisdiction be transferred to the adult criminal court and stated that this finding was made after the required "full investigation." The judge held no hearing before his ruling and gave no reason for the waiver. Kent was convicted in criminal court on six counts of housebreaking and robbery, and was acquitted on two rape counts by reason of insanity.

ISSUE: Do juveniles have any due process rights in cases in which jurisdiction over a juvenile is transferred from a juvenile court to an adult court? YES.

HOLDING: A transfer of jurisdiction in a juvenile hearing is a "critically important" stage in the juvenile process. Therefore, the juvenile is entitled to the following due process rights:

1. a hearing;
2. to be represented by counsel at such hearing;
3. to be given access to records considered by the juvenile court; and
4. to a statement of reasons in support of the waiver order.

REASON: "Because the State is supposed to proceed in respect of the child as *parens patriae* and not as adversary, courts have relied on the premise that the proceedings are 'civil' in nature and not criminal, and have asserted that the child cannot complain of the deprivation of important rights available in criminal cases. It has been asserted that he can claim only the fundamental due process right to fair treatment . . .

"While there can be no doubt of the original laudable purpose of juvenile courts, studies and critiques in recent years raise serious questions as to whether actual performance measures well enough against theoretical purpose to make tolerable the immunity of the process from the reach of constitutional guaranties applicable to adults. There is much evidence that some juvenile courts, including that of the District of Columbia, lack the personnel, facilities and techniques to perform adequately as representatives of the State in a *parens patriae* capacity, at least with respect to children charged with law violation. There is evidence, in fact, that there may be grounds for concern that the child receives the worst of both worlds: that he gets neither the protections accorded to adults nor the solicitous care and regenerative treatment postulated for children.

"The net, therefore, is that petitioner—then a boy of 16—was by statute entitled to certain procedures and benefits as a consequence of his statutory right to the 'exclusive' jurisdiction of the Juvenile Court. In these circumstances, considering particularly that decision as to waiver of jurisdiction and transfer of the matter to the District Court was potentially as important to petitioner as the difference between five years' confinement and a death sentence, we conclude that, as a condition to a valid waiver order, petitioner was entitled to a hearing, including access by his counsel to the social records and probation or similar reports which presumably are considered by the court, and to a statement of reasons for the Juvenile Court's decision. We believe that this result is required by the statute read in the context of constitutional principles relating to due process and the assistance of counsel."

CASE SIGNIFICANCE: Although not as significant as *In re Gault* (see brief on p. 336), this case is important because it marks the first time that basic due process rights were extended to juveniles, thus heralding the demise of the pure *parens patriae* approach. The justification for this departure was stated by the Court when it said:

There is much evidence that some juvenile courts, including that of the District of Columbia, lack the personnel, facilities and techniques to perform adequately as representatives of the State in a parens patriae capacity, at least with respect to children charged with law violation. There is evidence, in fact, that there may be grounds for concern that the child receives the worst of both worlds: that he gets neither the protections accorded to adults nor the solicitous care and regenerative treatment postulated for children.

Though limited in scope, these rights infused juvenile proceedings with due process guarantees. The Court said that the *parens patriae* philosophy "is not an invitation to procedural arbitrariness." It then added that "the waiver of jurisdiction is a 'critically important' action determining vitally important statutory rights of the juvenile."

The rights given in *Kent* are limited to waiver of jurisdiction hearings and are not extended to any other phase of the juvenile proceeding. While these rights, as well as others, were extended one year later to juvenile delinquency proceedings in cases in which the juvenile might be institutionalized (*In re Gault*, 387 U.S. 1 [1967]), they still do not apply constitutionally to all phases of juvenile proceedings. The Supreme Court based its decision in this case on the "critically important" nature of the waiver proceeding. Indeed, a waiver of jurisdiction (other terms used in various states are "transfer of jurisdiction," and "certification") carries far-reaching consequences for the juvenile. For example, instead of being kept in a juvenile institution and automatically released upon reaching adulthood, a juvenile tried in an adult criminal court is treated just like any other criminal and can be subjected to incarceration or a longer period of punishment. The consequences of juvenile proceedings are also vastly different from the effects of an adult conviction. In sum, the Court saw the serious consequences to the juvenile with such a transfer, and provided for due process rights before the transfer of jurisdiction could take place.

IN RE GAULT
387 U.S. 1 (1967)

CAPSULE: Juveniles must be given four basic due process rights in adjudication proceedings that can result in confinement in an institution.

FACTS: On June 8, 1964, a 15-year-old named Gault and a friend were taken into custody as a result of a complaint that they had made lewd telephone calls. Gault's parents were not informed that he was in custody. The parents were never shown the complaint that was filed against their son. The complainant did not appear at any hearing and no written record was made at the hearings. Gault was committed to the State Industrial School as a delinquent until he reached majority, a total of six years from the date of the hearing. The maximum punishment for an adult found guilty of the same offense was a fine from $5 to $50, or imprisonment for a maximum of two months.

ISSUE: Is a juvenile entitled to procedural due process rights during the adjudication stage of a juvenile delinquency proceeding that might result in commitment to an institution? YES.

HOLDING: Juveniles are entitled to procedural due process rights during adjudication that might result in commitment to an institution in which their freedom would be curtailed. These rights are:

1. Right to reasonable notice of the charges;
2. Right to counsel, his or her own, or appointed by the state if indigent;
3. Right to confront and cross-examine witnesses;
4. Privilege against self-incrimination, including the right to remain silent.

REASON: "The right of the state, as *parens patriae* to deny to the child procedural rights available to his elders was elaborated by the assertion that a child, unlike an adult, has a right 'not to liberty but to custody.' If his parents default in effectively performing their custodial functions—that is, if the child is 'delinquent'—the state may intervene. In doing so, it does not deprive the child of any rights, because he has none. It merely provides the 'custody' to which the child is entitled. On this basis, proceedings involving juveniles were described as 'civil' not 'criminal' and therefore not subject to the requirements which restrict the state when it seeks to deprive a person of his liberty.

"Accordingly, the highest motives and enlightened impulses led to a peculiar system for juveniles, unknown to our law in any comparable context. The constitutional and theoretical basis for this peculiar system is—to say the least—debatable. And in practice, as we remarked in the *Kent* case, supra, the results have not been entirely satisfactory. Juvenile court history has again demonstrated that unbridled discretion, however benevolently motivated, is frequently a poor substitute for principle and procedure. . . . The absence of substantive standards has not necessarily meant that children receive careful, compassionate, individualized treatment. The absence of procedural rules based upon constitutional principles has not always produced fair, efficient, and effective procedures.

Departures from established principles of due process have frequently resulted not in enlightened procedures, but in arbitrariness.

"Failure to observe the fundamental requirements of due process has resulted in instances, which might have been avoided, of unfairness to individuals and inadequate or inaccurate findings of fact and unfortunate prescriptions of remedy. Due process of law is the primary and indispensable foundation of individual freedom. It is the basic and essential term in the social compact which defines the rights of the individual and delimits the powers which the state may exercise . . .

". . . We do not mean by this to denigrate the juvenile court process or to suggest that there are not aspects of the juvenile system relating to offenders which are valuable. But the features of the juvenile system which its proponents have asserted are of unique benefit will not be impaired by constitutional domestication. For example, the commendable principles relating to the processing and treatment of juveniles separately from adults are in no way involved or affected by the procedural issues under discussion . . .

"Further, it is urged that the juvenile benefits from informal proceedings in the court. The early conception of the Juvenile Court proceeding was one in which a fatherly judge touched the heart and conscience of the erring youth by talking over his problems, by paternal advice and admonition, and in which, in extreme situations, benevolent and wise institutions of the State provided guidance and help 'to save him from a downward career.' Then, as now, goodwill and compassion were admirably prevalent. But recent studies have, with surprising unanimity, entered sharp dissent as to the validity of this gentle conception. They suggest that the appearance as well as the actuality of fairness, impartiality and orderliness— in short, the essentials of due process—may be a more impressive and more therapeutic attitude as far as the juvenile is concerned. . . . Of course, it is not suggested that juvenile court judges should fail appropriately to take account, in their demeanor and conduct, the emotional and psychological attitude of the juveniles with whom they are confronted. While due process requirements will, in some instances, introduce a degree of order and regularity to Juvenile Court proceedings to determine delinquency, and in contested cases will introduce some elements of the adversary system, nothing will require that the conception of the kindly juvenile judge be replaced by its opposite, nor do we rule upon the question whether ordinary due process requirements must be observed with respect to hearings to determine the disposition of the delinquent child.

". . . it would be extraordinary if our Constitution did not require the procedural regularity and exercise of care implied in the phrase 'due process.' Under our Constitution, the condition of being a boy does not justify a kangaroo court."

CASE SIGNIFICANCE: *In re Gault* is unquestionably the most important case ever to be decided by the Supreme Court on juvenile justice and is the most widely known case on the rights of juveniles. It says that juvenile proceedings, even though deemed civil in nature, require the due process protections that are given to adults in criminal proceedings. Since the *Gault* case, the Court has decided other cases extending most constitutional rights to juvenile proceedings. At present the only constitutional rights not given to juveniles are: (1) the right to a grand jury indictment; (2) the right to bail; (3) the right to a jury trial; and (4) the right to a public hearing.

This case represents a significant erosion in the pure *parens patriae* approach that characterized juvenile proceedings since the founding of the first juvenile court in Chicago in 1899. *Gault* was decided in 1967, indicating that for a long time the Court respected the *parens patriae* approach and adopted a "hands-off" attitude in juvenile proceedings. The major change started with *In re Gault*.

What led to the erosion of *parens patriae*? The answer lies in a footnote in the *Gault* case. Quoting an earlier case (*Kent v. United States*, 383 U.S. 541 [1966]), the Court said: "There is evidence . . . that there may be grounds for concern that the child receives the worst of both worlds: that he gets neither the protections accorded to adults nor the solicitous care and regenerative treatment postulated for children." In the face of this concern, the Court abandoned the pure *parens patriae* approach and injected due process into juvenile proceedings. Once that approach was taken, other constitutional rights for juveniles followed.

Gault must be understood in the proper context, which is that it applies only in proceedings that might result in the commitment of a juvenile to an institution in which freedom will be curtailed. Thus, the rights given in *Gault* do not apply in every juvenile proceeding. *Gault* says that in adjudication proceedings that might result in institutionalization, a juvenile must be given basic due process rights. Conversely, in a proceeding that will not result in institutionalization (in many Conduct In Need of Supervision cases, as opposed to juvenile delinquency cases, the highest form of punishment is probation, not being sent to a juvenile institution), the rights given to juveniles depend on state law. For example: X, a juvenile, is charged with truancy—a CINS case in her state. Assume further that the highest penalty under state law for X is probation. X is not constitutionally entitled to a lawyer during the adjudication proceeding. However, by law, the state may provide a lawyer for X.

IN RE WINSHIP
397 U.S. 358 (1970)

CAPSULE: Proof beyond a reasonable doubt, not simply a preponderance of the evidence, is required in juvenile adjudication hearings in cases in which the act would have been a crime if it had been committed by an adult.

FACTS: During an adjudication hearing, a New York Family Court judge found that the juvenile involved, then a 12-year-old boy, had entered a locker and stolen $112 from a woman's purse. The petition, which charged the juvenile with delinquency, alleged that his act, "if done by an adult, would constitute the crime or crimes of larceny." The judge acknowledged that guilt might not have been established beyond a reasonable doubt but that the New York Family Court Act required that the verdict need only be based on a preponderance of the evidence.

At the dispositional hearing (the equivalent of sentencing), the juvenile was ordered to be placed in training school for an initial period of 18 months, subject to annual extensions of his commitment until his eighteenth birthday.

ISSUE: Does the due process clause of the Fourteenth Amendment require proof beyond a reasonable doubt in a juvenile adjudication hearing? YES.

HOLDING: Proof beyond a reasonable doubt, not simply a preponderance of the evidence, is required during the adjudicatory stage, if a juvenile is charged with an act that would constitute a crime if committed by an adult.

REASON: "The requirement of proof beyond a reasonable doubt has this vital role in our criminal procedure for cogent reasons. The accused during a criminal prosecution has at stake interests of immense importance, both because of the possibility that he may lose his liberty upon conviction and because of the certainty that he would be stigmatized by the conviction . . .

"We turn to the question whether juveniles, like adults, are constitutionally entitled to proof beyond a reasonable doubt when they are charged with a violation of a criminal law. The same considerations that demand extreme caution in factfinding to protect the innocent adult apply as well to the innocent child.

"Nor do we perceive any merit in the argument that to afford juveniles the protection of proof beyond a reasonable doubt would risk destruction of beneficial aspects of the juvenile process. Use of the reasonable doubt standard during the adjudicatory hearing will not disturb New York's policies that a finding that a child has violated a criminal law does not constitute a criminal conviction, that such a finding does not deprive the child of his civil rights, and that the juvenile proceedings are confidential. Nor will there be any effect on the informality, flexibility, or speed of the hearing at which the factfinding takes place. And the opportunity during the post-adjudicatory or dispositional hearing for a wide-ranging review of the child's social history for his individualized treatment will remain unimpaired. Similarly, there is no effect on the procedures distinctive to juvenile proceedings that are employed prior to the adjudicatory hearing.

"Finally, we reject the Court of Appeals' suggestion that there is, in any event, only a 'tenuous difference' between the reasonable doubt and preponderance standards. The suggestion is singularly unpersuasive. In this very case, the trial judge's ability to distinguish between the two standards enabled him to make a finding of guilt that he conceded he might not have made under the standard of proof beyond a reasonable doubt. Indeed, the trial judge's action evidences the accuracy of the observation of commentators that 'the preponderance test is susceptible to the misinterpretation that it calls on the trier of fact merely to perform an abstract weighing of the evidence in order to determine which side has produced the greater quantum, without regard to its effect in convincing his mind of the truth of the proposition asserted.'"

CASE SIGNIFICANCE: Juvenile proceedings are civil proceedings and as such are generally decided by a "preponderance of the evidence" standard. In this case, however, the Supreme Court said that in juvenile cases in which a juvenile is charged with an act that would constitute a crime if committed by an adult, the standard of proof is not a preponderance of the evidence, but proof beyond a reasonable doubt. The implication is that although juvenile proceedings generally are considered civil proceedings, they are in fact treated like criminal proceedings in some instances. This gives credence to the assertion by some writers that juvenile proceedings are civil in name only and that in reality they are criminal proceedings and are considered as such by the United States Supreme Court, at least in delinquency (as opposed to Conduct in Need of Supervision) cases.

This case does not hold that all juvenile proceedings require proof beyond a reasonable doubt. What it says is that all juvenile proceedings in which a juvenile "is charged with an act that would constitute a crime if committed by an adult" are subject to a higher standard of proof—proof beyond a reasonable doubt. Any juvenile proceeding that does not fall under this category is governed by the pre-ponderance of the evidence standard. The reason for this distinction is the serious-ness of the offense and possible punishment. Most cases in which a juvenile is charged with an act that would constitute a crime if committed by an adult constitute juvenile delinquency, which can result in institutionalization and there-fore a deprivation of freedom. On the other hand, CINS, CHINS, MINS, or PINS cases (usually status or relatively minor offenses) result in probation or other forms of non-punitive rehabilitative sanctions and therefore are not subject to the proof beyond a reasonable doubt standard. The exception is if proof beyond a reasonable doubt is required by state law even for minor offenses or violations. In these cases, state law prevails.

MCKEIVER V. PENNSYLVANIA
403 U.S. 528 (1971)

CAPSULE: Juveniles have no constitutional right to trial by jury in a delinquency proceeding.

FACTS: In 1968, 16-year-old McKeiver was charged with robbery, larceny, and receiving stolen goods, all acts of juvenile delinquency. Under Pennsylvania criminal law these offenses were felonies. McKeiver was represented by counsel at his adjudication hearing. He requested but was denied trial by jury. The judge ruled that McKeiver had violated a law of the Commonwealth and was adjudged a delinquent. He was placed on probation.

ISSUE: Do juveniles have a constitutional right to trial by jury in a delinquency proceeding? NO.

HOLDING: Juveniles do not have a constitutional right to trial by jury in a juvenile adjudication hearing.

REASON: "All the litigants agree that the applicable due process standard in juve-nile proceedings, as developed by *Gault* and *Winship*, is fundamental fairness. As that standard was applied in those two cases, we have an emphasis on factfinding procedures. The requirements of notice, counsel, confrontation, cross-examination and standard of proof naturally flowed from this emphasis. But one cannot say that in our legal system the jury is a necessary component of accurate fact-finding.

"There is the possibility, at least, that the jury trial, if required as a matter of constitutional precept, will remake the juvenile proceeding into a fully adversary process and will put an effective end to what has been the idealistic prospect of an intimate, informal protective proceeding.

"The imposition of the jury trial on the juvenile court system would not strengthen greatly, if at all, the fact-finding function, and would, contrarily, provide an attrition of the juvenile court's assumed ability to function in a unique manner. It would not remedy the defects of the system. Meager as has been the hoped-for advance in the juvenile field, the alternative would be regressive, would lose what has been gained, and would tend once again to place the juvenile squarely in the routine of the criminal process.

"If the jury trial were to be injected into the juvenile court system as a matter of right, it would bring with it into that the traditional delay, the formality, and the clamor of the adversary system and, possibly, the public trial . . ."

CASE SIGNIFICANCE: Unlike other leading juvenile cases, this case does not give juveniles any constitutional rights. What it says instead is that juveniles are not entitled to a jury trial in an adjudication hearing (the equivalent of a trial) or at any stage of a juvenile proceeding. The Supreme Court gave a number of reasons for not extending the right to trial by jury to juvenile criminal proceedings. They are:

1. "Compelling a jury trial might remake the proceeding into a fully adversary process and effectively end the idealistic prospect of an intimate, informal protective proceeding;

2. "Imposing a jury trial on the juvenile court system would not remedy the system's defects and would not greatly strengthen the fact-finding function;

3. "Jury trial would entail delay, formality, and clamor of the adversary system, and possibly a public trial; and

4. "Equating the adjudicative phase of the juvenile proceeding with a criminal trial ignores the aspects of fairness, concern, sympathy, and paternal attention inherent in the juvenile court system."

The right to trial by jury is one of the few constitutional rights not enjoyed by juveniles. The other constitutional rights not extended to juveniles are: (1) the right to a public trial; (2) the right to bail; and (3) the right to grand jury indictment. Note, however, that although the right to a jury trial is not constitutionally required, some states by law give juveniles the right to a jury trial either during the adjudication process, the revocation process (if the juvenile is placed on probation), or both.

IVAN V. CITY OF NEW YORK
407 U.S. 203 (1972)

CAPSULE: The decision in *In re Winship*—that juveniles are entitled to proof beyond a reasonable doubt in adjudication hearings—should be applied retroactively to all cases in the appellate process.

FACTS: Petitioner was adjudicated delinquent in the Family Court of Bronx County, New York, for the delinquent act of stealing a bicycle at knifepoint from another youth.

Based on a preponderance of evidence, the court found the child delinquent on the grounds that he committed an act that would be considered robbery in the first degree if he were an adult. This case was heard before the Supreme Court that decided *In re Winship*. On direct appeal, the adjudication was reversed by the Appellate Division, First Department, holding that *Winship* should be applied retroactively to all cases that were still in the appeal process. The New York Court of Appeals reversed. On remand to the Appellate Division, the delinquency adjudication of the appellant was upheld. The case was appealed to the Supreme Court of New York, First Judicial Division.

ISSUE: Did the *Winship* decision (holding that a juvenile is entitled to proof beyond a reasonable doubt in an adjudication hearing when charged with an act that would be a crime if committed by an adult) apply retroactively to all cases on appeal at that time? YES.

HOLDING: The *Winship* decision is retroactive to all cases that were on appeal at the time that it was decided.

REASON: "Where the major purpose of new constitutional doctrine is to overcome an aspect of the criminal trial that substantially impairs its truth-finding function and so raises serious questions about the accuracy of guilty verdicts in past trials, the new rule has been given complete retroactive effect. Neither good-faith reliance by state or federal authorities on prior constitutional law or accepted practice, nor severe impact on the administration of justice has sufficed to require prospective application of these circumstances." *Williams v. United States*, 401 U.S. 646, 653 (1971). See *Adams v. Illinois*, 405 U.S. 278, 280 (1972); *Roberts v. Russell*, 392 U.S. 293, 295 (1968).

"*Winship* expressly held that the reasonable-doubt standard is a prime instrument for reducing the risk of convictions resting on factual error. The standard provides concrete substance for the presumption of innocence—that bedrock 'axiomatic and elementary' principle whose 'enforcement lies at the foundation of the administration of our criminal law.' . . . 'Due process commands that no man shall lose his liberty unless the Government has borne the burden of . . . convincing the fact finder of his guilt.' To this end, the reasonable-doubt standard is indispensable, for it 'impresses on the trier of fact the necessity of reaching a subjective state of certitude of the facts in issue.' 397 U.S. at 363–364.

"Plainly, then, the major purpose of the constitutional standard of proof beyond a reasonable doubt announced in *Winship* was to overcome an aspect of a criminal trial that substantially impairs the truth-finding function, and *Winship* is thus to be given complete retrospective effect. The motion for leave to proceed in forma pauperis and the petition for writ of *certiorari* are granted. The judgment of the Appellate Division of the Supreme Court of New York, First Judicial Department, is reversed and the case is remanded for further proceedings not inconsistent with this opinion."

CASE SIGNIFICANCE: The juvenile in this case had been adjudicated delinquent in Family Court in New York. The judge had applied the preponderance of the evidence standard in adjudicating the child delinquent. At the time of the hearing, the Supreme Court had not yet handed down the decision in *In re Winship*.

The question in this case was whether *In re Winship* was to be applied retroactively to cases that were in the appeals process. *Winship* held that juveniles must be adjudicated beyond a reasonable doubt when the delinquent act is something that would constitute a crime if committed by an adult. In this case, the court held that *Winship* was to be applied retroactively to all cases in the appellate process. Preponderance of the evidence (used in this case) is lower in certainty than guilt beyond a reasonable doubt (required by *Winship*).

This case has lost current significance because it was decided in 1972 and applied only to cases that were pending decisions in courts at that time. It shows, however, another step in the progression of Supreme Court cases that gave due process rights to juveniles.

DAVIS V. ALASKA
415 U.S. 308 (1974)

CAPSULE: Despite state confidentiality laws, the probation status of a juvenile witness may be brought out by the opposing lawyer on cross-examination.

FACTS: Davis was convicted of grand larceny and burglary in an Alaska court. A key prosecution witness during the trial was Richard Green, a juvenile. The trial court, on motion of the prosecuting attorney, issued a protective order prohibiting the defendant's attorney from questioning Green about his having been adjudicated as a juvenile delinquent because of a burglary he had committed and about his probation status at the time of the events about which he was to testify. The court's protective order was based on state law protecting the anonymity of juvenile offenders.

ISSUE: Does the confrontation clause of the Sixth Amendment allow a defendant in a criminal case to bring out the probation status of a juvenile witness on cross-examination even if state law protects the anonymity of juvenile offenders? YES.

HOLDING: The accused in a criminal trial is entitled to confront and cross-examine witnesses under the Sixth and Fourteenth Amendments. This right prevails over a state policy protecting the anonymity of juvenile offenders.

REASON: "Cross-examination is the principal means by which the believability of a witness and the truth of his testimony are tested. Subject always to the broad discretion of a trial judge to preclude repetitive and unduly harassing interrogation, the cross-examiner is not only permitted to delve into the witness' story to test the witness' perceptions and memory, but the cross-examiner has traditionally been allowed to impeach, i.e. discredit, the witness. One way of discrediting the witness is to introduce evidence of a prior criminal conviction of that witness. By doing so the cross-examiner intends to afford the jury a basis to infer that the witness' character is such that he would be less likely than the average trustworthy citizen to be truthful in his testimony. The introduction of evidence of prior crime is thus a general attack on the credibility of the witness.

"The State's policy interest in protecting the confidentiality of a juvenile offender's record cannot require yielding of so vital a constitutional right as the effective cross-examination for bias of an adverse witness. The State could have protected Green from exposure of his juvenile adjudication in these circumstances by refraining from using him to make out its case; the State cannot, consistent with the right of confrontation, require the petitioner to bear the full burden of vindicating the State's interest in the secrecy of juvenile criminal records."

CASE SIGNIFICANCE: The message in this case is clear: the constitutional right of a criminal defendant to confrontation and cross-examination prevails over a right given by state law that affords anonymity to juvenile offenders.

In this case, the lawyer for the petitioner wanted to introduce Green's juvenile record to show that at the time that Green was assisting the police in identifying the accused, Green was on probation for burglary and therefore Green acted out of fear or concern of possible revocation of probation if he did not provide the testimony needed by the police. The lawyer for the petitioner wanted to show that Green might have made a quick and faulty identification of the accused to shift suspicion away from himself as one of the possible perpetrators, and also that Green's identification of the accused may have been made out of fear of possible probation revocation, were Green found to be somehow involved in the crime. This attempt to make public, in court, Green's probation status was denied by the trial judge because of state law providing anonymity to juveniles. The Supreme Court disagreed with the trial judge's ruling and held that because Green was a key witness, his probation status could be disclosed.

What the Court did was balance an accused's right to a fair trial and a juvenile's right, given by state law, to anonymity. The Court concluded that "the right of confrontation is paramount to the State's policy of protecting a juvenile offender," adding that "whatever temporary embarrassment might result to Green or his family by disclosure of his juvenile record . . . is outweighed by petitioner's right to probe into the influence of possible bias in the testimony of a crucial identification witness." In sum, between an accused's constitutional right and a state policy to protect juveniles from disclosure of record, the accused's constitutional right prevails.

GOSS V. LOPEZ
419 U.S. 565 (1975)

CAPSULE: Due process must be given to juveniles even in short-term suspension cases.

FACTS: This class action suit was filed on behalf of all students of the Columbus, Ohio, Public School System (CPSS) who had been suspended for 10 days or less, with little or no due process. The only statutory requirement afforded to students suspended for 10 days or less was parental notification within 24 hours. There was no policy for administrative review or appeal.

The students' appeal asserted that they had been unconstitutionally deprived of their right to an education without a hearing of any kind, a violation of the due process clause of the Fourteenth Amendment.

ISSUES:

1. Are students facing temporary suspension from a public school entitled to protection under the due process clause of the Fourteenth Amendment? YES.
2. If yes, what type of due process should be given?

HOLDING: Students facing temporary suspension from a public school have property and liberty interests and are entitled to due process rights. Due process in these cases requires, at a minimum: (1) oral or written notice of charges supporting the suspension; (2) an explanation of evidence if the student denies involvement; and (3) an opportunity to present the student's version. Such notice and hearing should precede the suspension but, under extenuating circumstances, may follow as soon as possible after the suspension.

REASON: "In holding as we do, we do not believe that we have imposed procedures on school disciplinarians which are inappropriate in a classroom setting. Instead we have imposed requirements which are, if anything, less than a fair-minded school principal would impose upon himself in order to avoid unfair suspensions ... We stop short of construing the due process clause to require, countrywide, that hearings in connection with short suspensions must afford the student the opportunity to secure counsel, to confront and cross-examine witnesses supporting the charge, or to call his own witnesses to verify his version of the incident. Brief disciplinary suspensions are almost countless. To impose in each such case even truncated trial-type proceedings might well overwhelm administrative facilities in many places and, by diverting resources, cost more than it would save in educational effectiveness. Moreover, further formalizing the suspension process and escalating its formality and adversary nature may not only make it too costly as a regular disciplinary tool but also destroy its effectiveness as part of the teaching process.

"On the other hand, requiring effective notice and an informal hearing permitting the student to give his version of the events will provide a meaningful hedge against erroneous action. At least the disciplinarian will be alerted to the existence of disputes about facts and arguments about cause and effect. He may then determine himself to summon the accuser, permit cross-examination, and allow the student to present his own witnesses. In more difficult cases, he may permit counsel. In any event, his discretion will be more informed and we think the risk of error substantially reduced . . . Requiring that there be at least an informal give-and-take between student and disciplinarian, preferably prior to the suspension, will add little to the fact-finding function where the disciplinarian himself has witnessed the conduct forming the basis of the charge. But things are not always as they seem to be, and the student will at least have the opportunity to characterize his conduct and put it in what he deems the proper context."

CASE SIGNIFICANCE: This case dealt with short-term school suspensions that were imposed by school administrators with no initial hearing. The case involved many students whose alleged offenses ranged from involvement in a disturbance to being in the wrong place at the wrong time. The school had no procedures to deal with minor violations of school rules of this nature other than notification of the student's parents.

The Court ruled that regardless of the nature of the disciplinary infraction, schools must provide some due process to ensure that students who received short-term suspensions were actually guilty of the charges against them and that the punishment was appropriate to the rule violation. Anything less than a full review of the circumstances that led to the suspension would be fundamentally unfair to the juvenile regardless of the nature of the rule violation. The Court further indicated that the state itself had partially created the set of circumstances that required that due process be established for school rule violations by asserting that all individuals had a right under state law to avail themselves of an education, thereby creating a right to education and therefore a liberty interest when students are deprived of such education, regardless of the extent of deprivation.

The significance of this case lies in the Court's requirement that a due process hearing is needed for rule violations in school, even if it merely results in a short-term suspension. Note, however, that the due process rights required are minimal and do not even include the right of confrontation and cross examination. In short—an abbreviated version of due process.

BREED V. JONES
421 U.S. 519 (1975)

CAPSULE: Juveniles are entitled to the constitutional right against double jeopardy.

FACTS: On February 9, 1971, a petition was filed in the Los Angeles County Juvenile Court, alleging that a 17-year-old male had committed acts that, if committed by an adult, would constitute the crime of robbery with a deadly weapon. A detention hearing was held the following day and the accused was ordered to be detained pending a hearing on the petition. At the adjudicatory hearing (the equivalent of a trial), the juvenile court found the allegations against the accused to be true and ordered further detention. At the dispositional hearing (the equivalent of sentencing), the juvenile court said that it intended to find the juvenile offender unfit for the programs available through its juvenile facilities. The defense was not prepared for a fitness hearing and the matter was continued for one week. At the conclusion of the court's next hearing, it declared the offender unfit for treatment as a juvenile and ordered that he be prosecuted as an adult. The juvenile was subsequently found guilty of robbery in the first degree by the criminal court and it was ordered that he be committed to the California Youth Authority. The juvenile appealed, claiming a violation of his constitutional right against double jeopardy because he was adjudicated in the juvenile court and then tried by the criminal court.

ISSUE: Does the double jeopardy clause of the Fifth Amendment protect a juvenile from being prosecuted as an adult after undergoing adjudication proceedings in juvenile court? YES.

HOLDING: A juvenile who has undergone adjudication proceedings in juvenile court cannot be tried on the same charge as an adult in a criminal court because it would constitute double jeopardy.

REASON: "Jeopardy denotes risk. In the constitutional sense, jeopardy describes the risk that is traditionally associated with a criminal prosecution . . .

"Although the juvenile-court system has its genesis in the desire to provide a distinctive procedure and setting to deal with the problems of youth, including those manifested by antisocial conduct, our decisions in recent years have recognized that there is a gap between the originally benign conception of the system and its realities. With the exception of *McKeiver v. Pennsylvania*, 403 U.S. 528 (1971), the Court's response to that perception has been to make applicable in juvenile proceedings constitutional guarantees associated with traditional criminal prosecutions. *In re Gault*, 387 U.S. 1 (1967); *In re Winship*, 397 U.S. 358 (1970).

"We believe it is simply too late in the day to conclude, as did the District Court in this case, that a juvenile is not put in jeopardy at a proceeding whose object is to determine whether he has committed acts that violate a criminal law and whose potential consequences include both the stigma inherent in such a determination and the deprivation of liberty for many years.

"In *In re Gault*, this Court concluded that, for purposes of the right to counsel, a 'proceeding where the issue is whether the child will be found to be "delinquent" and subjected to the loss of his liberty for years is comparable in seriousness to a felony prosecution.'

"Thus, in terms of potential consequences, there is little to distinguish an adjudicatory hearing such as was held in this case from a traditional criminal prosecution. For that reason, it engenders elements of 'anxiety and insecurity' in a juvenile, and imposes a 'heavy personal strain.'

"We deal here, not with the 'formalities of the criminal adjudicative process,' *McKeiver v. Pennsylvania*, 403 U.S., at 551, but with an analysis of an aspect of the juvenile-court system in terms of the kind of risk to which jeopardy refers.

Under our decisions we can find no persuasive distinction in that regard between the proceeding conducted in this case and a criminal prosecution, each of which is designed 'to vindicate [the] very vital interest in enforcement of criminal laws.' We therefore conclude that respondent was put in jeopardy at the adjudicatory hearing. Jeopardy attached when respondent was 'put to trial before the trier of the facts,' 400 U.S. at 479, that is, when the Juvenile Court, as the trier of the facts, began to hear evidence."

CASE SIGNIFICANCE: This case is significant for two reasons: (1) it extends double jeopardy protection to juvenile proceedings, and (2) it implies that juvenile proceedings, although considered civil proceedings, in fact have penal consequences and are therefore equivalent to criminal trials. The juvenile in this case had been adjudicated, but the judge transferred jurisdiction to the adult criminal court because he found the juvenile "unfit for the programs available through its juvenile facilities." The juvenile was subsequently tried in an adult court and convicted. The Supreme Court concluded that there was double jeopardy, saying that "the Double Jeopardy Clause . . . is written in terms of potential or risk of trial and conviction, not punishment." The Court added: "Respondent was subjected to the burden of two trials for the same offense; he was twice put to the task of marshaling his resources against those of the State, twice subjected to the 'heavy personal strain' which such an experience represents."

Some scholars maintain that although juvenile proceedings are civil in nature, the Supreme Court considers the substance and effect of the proceedings to be criminal. This case reinforces that assertion. Double jeopardy is generally defined as successive prosecution for the same offense by the same jurisdiction. Double jeopardy applies only to criminal, not civil, cases. Nonetheless, the Court in this case considered juvenile adjudication as equivalent to a trial and thus applied the double jeopardy prohibition. The giving of rights to juveniles in adjudication proceedings, as mandated in the *Gault* case (*In re Gault*, 387 U.S. 1, [1967]) further attests to the "criminalization" of juvenile proceedings and the further erosion of *parens patriae*.

The policy implication of this case is clear: if a juvenile is to be transferred to the adult criminal court for trial in connection with a criminal offense, such transfer (or "waiver" or "certification") must be made prior to the adjudication hearing, otherwise double jeopardy attaches.

SWISHER V. BRADY
438 U.S. 204 (1978)

CAPSULE: Double jeopardy does not attach in juvenile cases when, after a hearing before a master, a juvenile court judge goes ahead and holds a new hearing or makes supplemental findings on the same case.

FACTS: Several minors brought a class action suit against the state of Maryland under § 42 U.S.C. § 1983. The minors sought to prevent the state from filing exceptions with the juvenile court to proposed non-delinquency findings made by masters of that court pursuant to a rule of procedure (Rule 911). The rule permits the state to file such exceptions, but also allows the juvenile court judge, who is empowered to accept, modify, or reject the master's proposals, to act on the exceptions only on the basis of the record made before the master, except that he may receive additional evidence to which the parties do not object.

ISSUE: Does the double jeopardy clause prohibit state officials, acting in accordance with Rule 911, from taking exceptions to a master's proposed findings? NO.

HOLDING: Double jeopardy does not attach in juvenile cases when, after a hearing before a master, a juvenile court judge goes ahead and holds a new hearing or makes supplemental findings on the same case that had already been heard by the master.

REASON: "Importantly, a Rule 911 proceeding does not impinge on the purposes of the Double Jeopardy Clause. A central purpose 'of the prohibition against successive trials' is to bar 'the [438 U.S. 204, 216] prosecution [from] another opportunity to supply evidence which it failed to muster in the first proceeding.' *Burks v. United States*, 437 U.S. 1, 11 (1978). A Rule 911 proceeding does not provide the prosecution that forbidden 'second crack.' The State presents its evidence once before the master. The record is then closed, and additional evidence can be received by the Juvenile Court judge only with the consent of the minor."

"Finally, there is nothing in the record to indicate that the procedure authorized under Rule 911 unfairly subjects the defendant to the embarrassment, expense, and ordeal of a second trial proscribed in *Green v. United States*, 355 U.S. 184 (1957). Indeed, there is nothing to indicate that the juvenile is even brought before the judge while he conducts the 'hearing of record,' or that the juvenile's attorney appears at the 'hearing' and presents oral argument or written briefs. But even if there was such participation or appearance, the burdens are more akin to those resulting from a judge's permissible request for post-trial briefing or argument following a bench trial than to the 'expense' of a full-blown second trial contemplated by the Court in *Green*."

CASE SIGNIFICANCE: This case is significant because it addresses the issue of whether what masters in juvenile proceedings do, as specified by state law, is equivalent to judicial trials that are subject to the prohibition against double jeopardy of the Constitution. Many states use masters in juvenile proceedings. They perform functions assigned to them by law and the juvenile court judge. For the most part, they serve as the "right hand" of the judge because in many states judges have duties other than adjudicating juvenile cases and are therefore busy.

In this case, the juvenile sued "to prevent the State of Maryland from filing exceptions with the Juvenile Court to propose non-delinquency findings made by the masters of the court." Rule 911 permitted the state of Maryland "to file such exceptions but further providing that the Juvenile Court judge . . . can act on the exceptions only on the basis of the record made before the master, except that he may receive additional evidence to which the parties do not object."

The juvenile challenged this procedure as constituting double jeopardy, saying in effect that the proceeding before the master also amounted to a judicial proceeding and therefore to allow the judge to change or modify it constituted double jeopardy. The Court rejected this contention, saying, among others, that:

"(a) The State by filing such exceptions does not require an accused to stand trial a second time, but rather the State has created a system with Rule 911 in which an accused juvenile is subjected to a single proceeding which begins with a master's hearing and culminates with an adjudication by a judge.

"(b) A Rule 911 proceeding does not provide the prosecution the forbidden 'second crack' at the accused, since under the rule the State presents its evidence once before the master, and the record is then closed unless the minor consents to the presentation of additional evidence before the judge.

"(c) Nor does Rule 911, on the alleged ground that it gives the State a chance to persuade two fact finders—the master and the judge—violate the Double Jeopardy Clause's prohibition against the prosecutor's enhancing the risk that an innocent defendant may be convicted, since the Rule confers the role of fact-finder and adjudicator only on the judge, who is empowered to accept, modify, or reject the master's proposal."

The key to understanding the holding in this case is to look at the way the state of Maryland worded Rule 911. The Court said that the authorization given by Rule 911 to the master and the judge's subsequent review of what the master did did not amount to two trials. In sum, authorizations given to a master similar to that provided for by Rule 911 do not constitute a separate trial and therefore a subsequent review and action by a juvenile court judge does not amount to double jeopardy. States must be careful, however, in crafting rules that authorize what juvenile court masters can do. There may be cases in which such rules would constitute double jeopardy, but Maryland's Rule 911 did not.

FARE V. MICHAEL C.[1]
442 U.S. 707 (1979)

CAPSULE: A request by a juvenile to see his probation officer is not equivalent to asking for a lawyer.

FACTS: Michael C., a juvenile, was taken into police custody under suspicion of murder. Prior to questioning by two police officers, Michael C. was advised of his *Miranda* rights. When asked if he wanted to waive his right to have an attorney present during questioning, he responded by asking for his probation officer. He was informed by the police that the probation officer would be contacted later, but that he could talk to the police if he wanted to. Michael C. agreed to talk and during questioning made statements and drew sketches that incriminated him. He was charged with murder in juvenile court. Michael C. moved to suppress the incriminating statements and sketches, alleging that they were obtained in violation of his *Miranda* rights and that his request to see his probation officer was, in effect, an assertion of his right to remain silent and that this was equivalent to his having requested an attorney.

ISSUE: Is the request by a probationer to see his probation officer during police questioning equivalent to asking for an attorney, thus invoking the Fifth Amendment right to remain silent, pursuant to *Miranda*? NO.

HOLDING: The request by a juvenile probationer during police questioning to see his probation officer, after having been given the *Miranda* warnings by the police, is not equivalent to asking for a lawyer and therefore is not considered an assertion of the right to remain silent. Evidence voluntarily given by the juvenile probationer is therefore admissible in court in a subsequent criminal trial.

REASON: "A probation officer is not in the same posture [as is a lawyer] with regard to either the accused or the system of justice as a whole. Often he is not trained in the law, and so is not in a position to advise the accused as to his legal rights. Neither is he a trained advocate, skilled in the representation of the interests of his client before police and courts. He does not assume the power to act on behalf of his client by virtue of his status as advisor, nor are the communications of the accused to the probation officer shielded by the lawyer-client privilege.

"Moreover, the probation officer is the employee of the State which seeks to prosecute the alleged offender. He is a peace officer, and as such is allied, to a greater or lesser extent, with his fellow peace officers. He owes an obligation to the State notwithstanding the obligation he may also owe the juvenile under his supervision. In most cases, the probation officer is duty bound to report wrongdoing by the juvenile when it comes to his attention, even if by communication from the juvenile himself."

CASE SIGNIFICANCE: Although this case involved a juvenile probationer, the Court's decision should apply to adult probationers and parolees as well. In essence, the Court said that a probation officer does not perform the same function as a lawyer; therefore a request by a probationer to see his probation officer is not equivalent to a request to see a lawyer. The Court then proceeded to distinguish between a probation officer and a lawyer. First, the Court stated that the communications of the accused to the probation officer are not shielded by the lawyer-client privilege. This means that information given by a client to the probation officer may be disclosed in court, unlike information shared by a client with a lawyer. Second, the Court makes clear that a probation officer's loyalty and obligation is to the state, despite any obligation he or she may also have to the probationer. This means that despite an officer's feelings for or rapport with a client, there should be no question of where his or her loyalties lie. Professionalism requires that these two obligations not be confused and that should be clear to the probationer and the officer, particularly in situations in which confidences are shared, that the officer's loyalty is ultimately with the state, not with the probationer. This is important in cases in which a probationer wants to share confidential information ("I will tell you something, but please do not tell it to anybody.") with the probation officer with whom the probationer has trust. The probation officer can be forced to disclose that information later in court.

SMITH V. DAILY MAIL PUBLISHING CO.
443 U.S. 97 (1979)

CAPSULE: A state law making it a crime to publish the name of a juvenile charged with a crime is unconstitutional.

FACTS: On February 9, 1978, a 15-year-old student was shot and killed at a junior high school. A 14-year-old classmate was identified by seven eyewitnesses as the assailant and was arrested soon after the incident. The Charleston Daily Mail and the Charleston Gazette routinely monitored the police band radio frequency and, upon learning of the shooting, dispatched reporters and photographers to the scene of the shooting. Both newspapers obtained the name of the alleged assailant from various witnesses, the police, and an assistant prosecuting attorney, who were at the school.

Both newspapers published articles about the incident. The Daily Mail's first article did not mention the juvenile suspect's name because of a Virginia statute prohibiting such publication without prior court approval. The Gazette published both the juvenile's name and picture in its article. The name of the alleged attacker was also broadcast over at least three radio stations on the days the newspaper articles appeared. Because the juvenile's name had become public knowledge, the Daily Mail included the information in a subsequent article it printed. An indictment was brought against both papers alleging that each had knowingly published the name of the juvenile in violation of state statute.

ISSUE: Does a state statute that makes it a crime for a newspaper to publish, without written approval of the juvenile court, the name of any youth charged as a juvenile offender violate the First and Fourteenth Amendments to the Constitution? YES.

HOLDING: The state cannot punish the truthful publication of an alleged juvenile delinquent's name lawfully obtained by a newspaper because to do so would be a violation of the First and Fourteenth Amendments. The state's interest in protecting the anonymity of the juvenile offender cannot justify the statute's imposition of criminal sanctions on the press for the publication of a juvenile's name when lawfully obtained by the press.

REASON: "The sole interest advanced by the State to justify its criminal statute is to protect the anonymity of the juvenile offender. It is asserted that confidentiality will further his rehabilitation because publication of the name may encourage further antisocial conduct and also may cause the juvenile to lose future employment or suffer other consequences for this single offense. In *Davis v. Alaska*, 415 U.S. 308 (1974), similar arguments were advanced by the State to justify not permitting a criminal defendant to impeach a prosecution witness on the basis of his juvenile record. We said there that '[w]e do not and need not challenge the State's interest as a matter of its own policy in the administration of criminal justice to seek to preserve the anonymity of a juvenile offender.' Id., at 319. However, we concluded that the State's policy must be subordinated to the defendant's Sixth Amendment right of confrontation. The important rights created by the First Amendment must be considered along with the rights of defendants guaranteed by the Sixth Amendment. See *Nebraska Press Ass'n v. Stuart*, 427 U.S., at 581. Therefore, the reasoning of Davis that the constitutional right must prevail over the state's interest in protecting juveniles applies with equal force here.

"The magnitude of the State's interest in this statute is not sufficient to justify application of a criminal penalty to respondents. Moreover, the statute's approach does not satisfy constitutional requirements. The statute does not restrict the electronic media or any form of publication, except 'newspapers,' from printing the names of youths charged in a juvenile proceeding. . . . Thus, even assuming the statute served a state interest of the highest order, it does not accomplish its stated purpose."

CASE SIGNIFICANCE: This case represents a classic confrontation between freedom of the press and a juvenile's right to anonymity in the name of rehabilitation. The Court said that freedom of the press prevails over the state's interest in protecting juveniles. Nonetheless, the Court emphasized that its decision in this case is narrow and must be so interpreted. It said: "At issue is simply the power of a state to punish the truthful publication of an alleged juvenile delinquent's name lawfully obtained by a newspaper. The asserted state interest cannot justify the statute's imposition of criminal sanctions on this type of publication."

What about prohibitions by the court, backed up by threats of judicial sanction, against the publication of names in a juvenile proceeding? Most states have such rules, which are strictly enforced by judges. Such rules are constitutional although they infringe on the freedom of the press. This is because these rules are not considered punitive actions taken as a form of prior restraint. What a judge does, instead, is use the judicial contempt power to enforce court-mandated rules in an effort to maintain anonymity. Citation for contempt is not equivalent to a penal sanction for a criminal offense, although both can result in imprisonment. Generally, a court's contempt power is subject to fewer constitutional restraints and is not viewed as punitive. In sum, what the legislature cannot do by statute, the judge can most likely do through the exercise of contempt powers.

EDDINGS V. OKLAHOMA
455 U.S. 104 (1982)

CAPSULE: Mitigating circumstances, including age and relevant social history, must be considered in juvenile capital cases.

FACTS: Eddings, age 16, and several younger minors stole a car and ran away from home in Missouri. Eddings had a shotgun and several rifles in the car, which he had stolen from his father. An Oklahoma Highway Patrol officer pulled Eddings over for a traffic violation, whereupon Eddings shot and killed the officer. Eddings was certified as an adult and charged with murder in the first degree. He pleaded nolo contendere (no contest). During the sentencing phase, Eddings' social history was introduced as a mitigating factor. His parents had divorced when he was five, he stayed with his alcoholic and promiscuous mother until he was 14 when he was sent to his father who, unable to control him, resorted to physical abuse. Likewise, Eddings' age was introduced as indicative of his capacity to be rehabilitated. The state offered the following aggravating circumstances:

1. that the murder was especially heinous, atrocious, or cruel;
2. that the crime was committed for the purpose of avoiding or preventing a lawful arrest;
3. that there was a probability that the defendant would commit criminal acts of violence that would constitute a continuing threat to society.

The judge considered Eddings' age as a mitigating factor, rejected his social history as irrelevant, weighed his age against the aggravating factors, and sentenced Eddings to death.

ISSUE: Must mitigating circumstances, such as social history, be considered in the sentencing phase of a juvenile capital case? YES.

HOLDING: The court must consider any and all mitigating factors in determining the sentence in a juvenile capital case. The weight and relevance of such factors are discretionary, but total exclusion of a mitigating factor is improper.

REASON: "In *Lockett v. Ohio*, 438 U.S 586 (1978), Chief Justice Burger, writing for the plurality, stated the rule that we apply today:

We conclude that the Eighth and Fourteenth Amendments require that the sentencer . . . not be precluded from considering, as a mitigating factor, any aspect of a defendant's character or record and any of the circumstances of the offense that the defendant proffers as a basis for the sentence less than death. Id., at 604. Recognizing 'that the imposition of death by public authority is . . . profoundly different from all other penalties,' the plurality held that the sentencer must be free to give 'independent mitigating weight to aspects of the defendant's character and record and to circumstances of the offense proffered in mitigation . . . Id., at 605.

"The trial judge recognized that youth must be considered a relevant mitigating factor. But youth is more than a chronological fact. It is a time and condition of life when a person may be most susceptible to influence and to psychological damage. Our history is replete with laws and judicial recognition that minors, especially in their earlier years, generally are less mature and responsible than adults.

"Even the normal 16-year-old customarily lacks the maturity of an adult. In this case, Eddings was not a normal 16-year-old; he had been deprived of care, concern, and paternal attention that children deserve. On the contrary, it is not disputed that he was a juvenile with serious emotional problems, and had been raised in a neglectful, sometimes even violent background. In addition, there was testimony that Eddings' mental and emotional development were at a level several years below his chronological age. All of this does not suggest an absence of responsibility for the crime of murder, deliberately committed in this case. Rather, it is to say that just as the chronological age of a minor is itself a relevant mitigating factor of great weight, so must the background and mental and emotional development of a youthful defendant be duly considered in sentencing."

CASE SIGNIFICANCE: In this case, the Supreme Court held that all reasonably relevant mitigating factors must be considered in a juvenile capital offense sentencing determination. This includes social history factors that may or may not have an impact on the behavior that resulted in the charge of murder in the first degree in this case. The Court did not say what weight should be given to specific evidence, choosing instead to leave such decisions up to the judge in whose court the case is tried. It required, however, that there be proof in the record of the case that all relevant mitigating evidence was considered by the court prior to sentencing.

The Court ruled that "age" is a relevant mitigating factor to consider. It also held that, in cases involving juveniles, all social history mitigating factors must be seriously considered by the court prior to sentencing. While a judge usually enjoys discretion in determining which mitigating factors are to be considered during sentencing, that discretion is narrowed in capital cases involving juveniles.

SCHALL V. MARTIN
467 U.S. 253 (1984)

CAPSULE: Preventive detention of juveniles is constitutional.

FACTS: Martin was arrested on December 13, 1977, and was charged with first-degree robbery, second degree assault, and criminal possession of a weapon. Martin was 14 years old at the time of the arrest and therefore came under the jurisdiction of New York's Family Court. Martin's alleged offenses happened late at night and he lied to the police about where and with whom he lived. At the delinquency proceedings, the Family Court judge ordered Martin detained under New York statute, citing the possession of the loaded weapon, the false address given to the police, and the lateness of the hour, as evidence of lack of supervision.

Five days later, a probable cause hearing was held and probable cause was found to exist for all charges against Martin. At the fact-finding hearing, Martin was found guilty of robbery and criminal possession of a weapon. He was adjudicated a delinquent and placed on two years' probation. Martin was detained a total of 15 days.

The New York law challenged by Martin in this case contained the following provisions: it authorized the pretrial detention of an accused juvenile delinquent on the basis of a finding, preceded by notice and a hearing and supported by a statement of reasons and fact, of a "serious risk" that the child "may before the return date commit an act which if committed by an adult would constitute a crime," and provided for a more formal hearing within at least 17 days if detention was ordered.

ISSUE: Does the preventive detention of accused juveniles violate the due process clause of the Fourteenth Amendment? NO.

HOLDING: Preventive detention is constitutional because it serves to protect both the juvenile and society from the hazards of pretrial crime.

REASON: "There is no doubt that the Due Process Clause of the Fourteenth Amendment is applicable to juvenile proceedings. . . . We have held that certain basic constitutional protections enjoyed by adults accused of crimes also apply to juveniles. But the Constitution does not mandate elimination of all differences in the treatment of juveniles. See, e.g., *McKeiver v. Pennsylvania*, 403 U.S. 528 (1971) (no right to a jury trial). The state has a '*parens patriae* interest in preserving and protecting the welfare of the child,' *Santosky v. Kramer*, 455 U.S. 745, 766 (1982) which makes a juvenile proceeding fundamentally different from an adult criminal trial. We have tried to strike a balance—to respect the 'informality' and 'flexibility' that characterize juvenile proceedings and yet to ensure that such proceedings comport with the 'fundamental fairness' demanded by the Due Process Clause.

"In *Bell v. Wolfish* we left open the question whether any governmental objective other than ensuring a detainee's presence at trial may constitutionally justify pretrial detention. As an initial matter, therefore, we must decide whether, in the context of the juvenile system, the combined interest in protecting both the community and the juvenile himself from consequences of future criminal conduct is sufficient to justify such detention.

"The 'legitimate and compelling state interest' in protecting the community from crime cannot be doubted. *De Veau v. Braisted*, 363 U.S. 144 (1960) . . . The harm suffered by the victim of a crime is not dependent upon the age of the perpetrator. And the harm to society generally may even be greater in this context given the high rate of recidivism among juveniles.

"The juvenile's countervailing interest in freedom from institutional restraints, even for a brief time involved here, is undoubtedly substantial as well. But that interest must be qualified by the recognition that juveniles, unlike adults, are always in some form of custody. Children, by definition, are not assumed to have the capacity to take care of themselves. They are assumed to be subject to the control of their parents, and if parental control falters, the State must play its part as *parens patriae*. In this respect, the juvenile's liberty interest may, in appropriate circumstances, be subordinated to the State's '*parens patriae* interest in preserving and promoting the welfare of the child.' *Santosky v. Kramer, supra,* at 766."

CASE SIGNIFICANCE: This case is important because, for the first time, the Supreme Court recognized the constitutionality of preventive detention of juveniles, an issue previously unresolved. Preventive detention is defined as detention for the purpose of preventing the juvenile from committing crimes in the future. It is questionable because of the presumption of innocence and because it punishes a juvenile for crimes he or she has not yet committed.

The Supreme Court held that while a juvenile's constitutional interests must be protected, the interests of the State and society must also be considered. When these interests appear to conflict, it is the court's duty to weigh and balance these interests and rule in favor of the more compelling interest. The type of preventive detention used in New York has the best interests of both the child and the community in mind. Under the New York law, the juvenile is held only as long as necessary to process the case and these proceedings are bound by time requirements. What little harm may be done to the juvenile while being detained does not outweigh the harm that conceivably could be inflicted on community members by an unsupervised juvenile.

This decision does not say that unlimited preventive detention is constitutional. The New York law that was upheld in this case provided for preventive detention on the basis of a finding, preceded by notice and a hearing, and supported by a statement of reasons and facts of a serious risk that the child "may before the return date commit an act which if committed by an adult would constitute a crime." The law also provided for a more formal hearing within at least 17 days if detention was ordered. These provisions of the New York law were deemed constitutional. What this means is that any state statute with provisions for preventive detention similar to New York's would also be upheld as constitutional. Those with different provisions, particularly if they are more arbitrary, might not merit the Court's approval. State juvenile detention laws will be decided by the Court on a case-by-case basis. The closer the provisions of these laws are to the New York statute, the greater their chances of being declared constitutional.

NEW JERSEY V. T.L.O.
469 U.S. 325 (1985)

CAPSULE: "Reasonable grounds" is all that public school officials need to search students; they do not need a warrant or probable cause.

FACTS: A 14-year-old girl was discovered smoking a cigarette in a high school lavatory in violation of school rules. She was taken to the principal's office by a teacher. When the student denied that she had been smoking, the assistant vice principal demanded to see her purse. Inside the purse, a pack of cigarettes and a package of cigarette rolling papers, commonly associated with the use of marijuana, were discovered. The assistant vice principal then proceeded to search the purse thoroughly and found marijuana, a pipe, plastic bags, a substantial amount of money, an index card containing a list of names of students who owed her money, and two letters that implicated her in marijuana dealing. The state brought delinquency charges against the student in juvenile court. She moved to have the evidence found in her purse suppressed, alleging that the search was illegal.

ISSUES:

1. Does the Fourth Amendment prohibition against unreasonable searches and seizures apply to high school officials? YES.
2. Do the warrant and probable cause requirements of the Fourth Amendment apply to searches performed by high school officials? NO.

HOLDINGS:

1. The Fourth Amendment prohibition against unreasonable searches and seizures applies to searches by high school officials, but the school's legitimate need to maintain a learning environment requires some easing of Fourth Amendment restrictions.
2. For a search to be valid, what public school officials need is "reasonable grounds" to suspect that the search will produce evidence that the student has violated or is violating either the law or the rules of the school. They do not need a warrant or probable cause.

REASON: "In determining whether the search at issue in this case violated the Fourth Amendment, we are faced initially with the question whether that Amendment's prohibition on unreasonable searches and seizures applies to searches conducted by public school officials. We hold that it does.

"It is now beyond dispute that 'the Federal Constitution, by virtue of the Fourteenth Amendment, prohibits unreasonable searches and seizures by state officers.' *Elkins v. United States*, 364 U.S. 206, 213 (1960). . . . Equally indisputable is the proposition that the Fourteenth Amendment protects the rights of students against encroachment by public school officials . . .

"These two propositions—that the Fourth Amendment applies to the States through the Fourteenth Amendment, and that the actions of public school officials are subject to the limits placed on state action by the Fourth Amendment—might appear sufficient to answer the suggestion that the Fourth Amendment does not proscribe unreasonable searches by school officials. On reargument, the State of New Jersey has argued that the history of the Fourth Amendment indicates that the Amendment was intended to regulate only searches and seizures carried out by law enforcement officials; accordingly, although public school officials are concededly state agents for purposes of the Fourteenth Amendment, the Fourth Amendment creates no rights enforceable against them.

". . . this Court has never limited the Amendment's prohibition on unreasonable searches and seizures to operations conducted by the police. Rather, the Court has long spoken of the Fourth Amendment's strictures as restraints imposed upon 'governmental action'—that is, 'upon the activities of sovereign authority.' *Burdeau v. McDowell*, 256 U.S. 465, 475 (1921). Accordingly, we have held the Fourth Amendment applicable to the activities of civil as well as criminal authorities: building inspectors . . . and even firemen entering privately owned premises to battle a fire . . . all are subject to the restraints imposed by the Fourth Amendment . . .

"The school setting also requires some modification of the level of suspicion of illicit activity needed to justify a search. Ordinarily, a search–even one that may permissibly be carried out without a warrant—must be based on 'probable cause' to believe that a violation of the law has occurred . . . However, 'probable cause' is not an irreducible requirement of a valid search. The fundamental command of the Fourth Amendment is that searches and seizures be reasonable, and although 'both the concept of probable cause and the requirement of a warrant bear on the reasonableness of a search,. . . in certain limited circumstances neither is required.' *Almeida-Sanchez v. United States* (413 U.S. 266 [1973]) at 277.''

CASE SIGNIFICANCE: This case clarifies the issue of whether public school officials must obtain a warrant before conducting a search, and what degree of certainty is needed for a valid search by public school officials. The Court said that public school officials are representatives of the state and as such are limited by the provisions of the Fourth Amendment. But the Court also recognized that in order to maintain an environment in which learning can take place, some restrictions placed on public authorities by the Fourth Amendment had to be eased. Therefore, the Court ruled that public school officials: (1) need not obtain a warrant before conducting a search, and (2) do not need probable cause to justify a search; they only need reasonable grounds—a lower standard of certainty than probable cause. To illustrate: "reasonable grounds" needs between 30 and 40 percent certainty on the part of school officials that an offense has been committed, whereas "probable cause" needs more than 50 percent certainty for the police to be able to act legally.

Whether the ruling applies to college students or to high school students in private schools was not addressed by the Court. It would be reasonable to assume, however, that this ruling would also apply to public elementary school students. On the other hand, lower court decisions have usually held that college students, regardless of age, are considered adults and therefore this case probably does not apply to college students or campuses.

This case applies only to high school teachers and administrators who are conducting a search. It does not apply to police officers, who are bound by the "probable cause" requirement even in school searches. The only possible exception might be if the officers are to perform the search at the request of public school authorities, as long as they are merely helping school officials conduct the search. In contrast, if they are searching on their own, police officers need probable cause.

THOMPSON V. OKLAHOMA[2]
487 U.S. 815 (1988)

CAPSULE: It is cruel and unusual punishment to impose the death penalty on a juvenile who commits a heinous crime at age 15 or younger.

FACTS: Thompson, at age 15, actively participated in the brutal murder of his brother-in-law. Although considered a child under Oklahoma law, the district attorney sought to have him tried as an adult. Thompson was tried as an adult and was found guilty of the murder. Due to the heinous nature of the crime, Thompson was sentenced to death.

ISSUE: Is the death penalty cruel and unusual punishment for a crime committed by a 15-year-old? YES.

HOLDING: The execution of a person who was under 16 years of age at the time of the offense is cruel and unusual punishment and therefore is prohibited by the Eighth and Fourteenth Amendments.

REASON: "In determining whether the categorical Eighth Amendment prohibition applies, this Court must be guided by the 'evolving standards of decency that mark the progress of a maturing society,' *Trop v. Dulles*, 356 U.S. 86, 101, and in doing so must review relevant legislative enactments and jury determinations and consider the reasons why a civilized society may accept or reject the death penalty for a person less than 16 years old at the time of the crime.

"Relevant state statutes—particularly those of the 18 states that have expressly considered the question of a minimum age for imposition of the death penalty, and have uniformly required that the defendant have attained at least the age of 16 at the time of the capital offense—support the conclusion that it would offend civilized standards of decency to execute a person who was less than 16 years old at the time of his or her offense.

"The juvenile's reduced culpability, and the fact that the application of the death penalty to this class of offenders does not measurably contribute to the essential purposes underlying the penalty, also support the conclusion that the imposition of the penalty on persons under the age of 16 constitutes unconstitutional punishment."

CASE SIGNIFICANCE: Under this ruling, any offender who was 15 years old or younger at the time the crime was committed could not be given the death penalty, regardless of the nature or heinousness of the offense. The Court took into account the fact that the statutes of approximately 18 states require that the defendant be at least 16 years old at the time of the commission of the offense in order for the death penalty to be imposed, saying that "it would offend civilized standards of decency to execute a person who was less than 16 years old at the time of his or her offense." In a concurring opinion, however, Justice O'Connor noted that "the Federal Government and 19 States have authorized capital punishment without setting any minimum age, and have also provided for some 15-year-olds to be prosecuted as adults." This indicates, she said, that there was no consensus about whether 15-year-olds should be executed.

What this decision did not say was whether juveniles could be executed at all. Is 15 the minimum age, or would juvenile status be a better determinant of whether the offender should be executed? Opponents of the Oklahoma law wanted the Court to declare any execution of a juvenile to be unconstitutional. The Court did not go that far; however, the issue of the absolute age when an execution could take place was decided by the Court one year later in the case of *Stanford v. Kentucky*, 492 U.S. 361 (1989).

STANFORD V. KENTUCKY[3]
492 U.S. 361 (1989)

CAPSULE: It is not cruel and unusual punishment to impose the death penalty on a juvenile who commits the crime at age 16 or older.

FACTS: Stanford was charged with capital murder. He was 17 years old when the crime was committed. He was transferred to adult court after a juvenile hearing under state statute. Stanford was convicted, and because of the heinousness of the crime, was sentenced to death.

ISSUE: Does the imposition of the death penalty for a crime committed at age 16 or 17 constitute cruel and unusual punishment? NO.

HOLDING: It is not cruel and unusual punishment to impose capital punishment on an offender who was 16 or 17 years old at the time the crime was committed.

REASON: "Whether a particular punishment violates the Eighth Amendment depends on whether it constitutes one of 'those modes or acts of punishment . . . considered cruel and unusual at the time the Bill of Rights was adopted.' *Ford v. Wainwright*, 477 U.S. 399, 405, or is contrary to the 'evolving standards of decency that mark the progress of a maturing society,' *Trop v. Dulles*, 356 U.S. 86, 101. Petitioners have not alleged that their sentences would have been considered cruel and unusual in the 18th century, and could not support such a contention, since, at that time, the common law set the rebuttable presumption of incapacity to commit felonies (which were punishable by death) at the age of 14.

"In determining whether a punishment violates evolving standards of decency, this Court looks not to its own subjective conceptions, but, rather, to the conceptions of modern American society as reflected by objective evidence. E.g., *Coker v. Georgia*, 433 U.S. 584, 592. The primary and most reliable evidence of national consensus—the pattern of federal and state laws—fails to meet petitioner's heavy burden of proving a settled consensus against the execution of 16- and 17-year-old offenders."

CASE SIGNIFICANCE: This case resolves an issue that the Court refused to address the previous year in *Thompson v. Oklahoma*, 487 U.S. 815 (1988). That issue is whether a defendant who was of juvenile age (either 16 or 17) at the time the offense was committed could be given the death penalty. The Court's ruling here is clear, stating that "the imposition of capital punishment on an individual for a crime committed at 16 or 17 years of age does not constitute cruel and unusual punishment under the Eighth Amendment." Thus the Court set the minimum age at 16 if the state is to impose the death penalty. Juveniles who are age 15 or younger during the commission of the offense cannot be given the death penalty.

In reaching that conclusion, the Court relied on "evolving standards of decency that mark the progress of a maturing society." It then concluded that there was no consensus against the execution of 16- and 17-year-olds, stating that "of the 37 States that permit capital punishment, 15 states decline to impose it on 16-year-olds and 12 on 17-year-olds." The Court said that "this does not establish the degree of national agreement this Court has previously thought sufficient to label a punishment cruel and unusual."

Stanford v. Kentucky, however, has now been overruled by *Roper v. Simmons*, the case briefed below.

ROPER V. SIMMONS[4]
546 U.S. 551 (2005)

CAPSULE: The Eighth and Fourteenth Amendments prohibit the death penalty for juveniles who committed their crime before the age of 18.

FACTS: When Christopher Simmons was 17 years old he committed a brutal murder. Before committing the crime, Simmons stated that he wanted to kill someone, even going to the extent of discussing his plan to commit the act with his friends. On the night of the crime at about 2:00 A.M., Simmons and his accomplice entered the home of Shirley Crook through an open window and awakened the victim. Simmons later stated that he intended to kill Mrs. Crook because of their mutual involvement in a previous car accident.

ISSUE: Is it cruel and unusual punishment to impose the death penalty on offenders who commit crimes before reaching the age of 18? YES.

HOLDING: The Eighth and Fourteenth Amendments prohibit the imposition of the death penalty on offenders who commit their crimes before reaching the age of 18.

REASON: "Both objective indicia of consensus, as expressed in particular by the enactments of legislatures that have addressed the question, and the Court's own determination in the exercise of its independent judgment, demonstrate that the death penalty is a disproportionate punishment for juveniles."

CASE SIGNIFICANCE: This case is arguably the most important case decided thus far on the issue of the constitutionality of the death penalty for juveniles. It holds that the death penalty constitutes cruel and unusual punishment for offenders who commit their crime before reaching the age of 18. The Court, in *Thompson v. Oklahoma* (1988) held that executing offenders who were 15 years old or younger at the time of the commission of the offense is unconstitutional. *Simmons* extends that rule to include 16- and 17-year-olds, and therefore overturns its earlier decision in *Stanford v. Kentucky*.

This case puts an end to the execution of juveniles in the United States—for now. The Court can always change its mind, reverse this decision, and declare the execution of juveniles constitutional again. This case was decided on a five-to-four vote. A change in the composition of the United States Supreme Court can lead to a change of vote in a proper case. For now, however, juveniles in the United States cannot be executed, regardless of the seriousness of their crime. This decision renders unconstitutional all laws (state and federal) that allow juveniles to be executed. Legislatures can repeal those laws or allow them to stay on the books, but they cannot now be enforced.

GRAHAM V. FLORIDA
560 U.S. ___ (2010)

CAPSULE: The Eighth Amendment prohibits the sentencing of a juvenile to life without parole for a non-homicide crime.

FACTS: Defendant Graham was 16 years of age in 2003 when he and three other youths attempted to rob a restaurant. The restaurant manager was struck twice in the back of the head with a metal bar by one of Graham's accomplices during the robbery attempt. The restaurant manager required stitches for his injury. No money was taken. Florida statute permits prosecutors the discretion to try juveniles as adults in particular cases. That discretion was utilized in this case. Graham accepted a plea agreement and was sentenced to probation, and adjudication of guilt was withheld. Graham was arrested again in 2004 for participating in a home invasion robbery. It was found that Graham had violated his probation, and he was sentenced to life in prison for the previous burglary. Because Florida no longer has a parole system, the life sentence meant no possibility of release for Graham except executive clemency.

ISSUE: Does the Eighth Amendment's Cruel and Unusual Clause allow a juvenile offender to be sentenced to life in prison without parole for a non-homicide crime? NO.

HOLDING: The Eighth Amendment prohibits the imposition of a life-without-parole (LWOP) sentence on a juvenile offender who did not commit homicide. A State need not guarantee the offender eventual release, but, if it imposes a sentence of life, it must provide him or her with some realistic opportunity to obtain release before the end of that term.

REASON: "No recent data provide reason to reconsider the Court's observations in *Roper* about the nature of juveniles. As petitioner's *amici* point out, developments in psychology and brain science continue to show fundamental differences between juvenile and adult minds. For example parts of the brain involved in behavior control continue to mature through late adolescence. See Brief for American Medical Association et al. as *Amici Curiae* 16–24; Brief for American Psychological Association et al. as *Amici Curiae* 22–27. Juveniles are more capable of change than are adults, and their actions are less likely to be evidence of 'irretrievably depraved character' than are the actions of adults. *Roper*, 543 U.S., at 570. It remains true that '[f]rom a moral standpoint it would be misguided to equate the failings of a minor with those of an adult, for a greater possibility exists that a minor's character deficiencies will be reformed.' *Ibid.* These matters relate to the status of the offenders in question; and it is relevant to consider next the nature of the offenses to which this harsh penalty might apply.

"The Court has recognized that defendants who do not kill, intend to kill, or foresee that life will be taken are categorically less deserving of the most serious forms of punishment than are murderers. *Kennedy, supra*; *Enmund*, 458 U.S. 782; *Tison v. Arizona*, 481 U.S. 137 (1987); *Coker*, 433 U.S. 584. . . ."

"It follows that, when compared to an adult murderer, a juvenile offender who did not kill or intend to kill has a twice diminished moral culpability. The age of the offender and the nature of the crime each bear on the analysis.

"As for the punishment, life without parole is 'the second most severe penalty permitted by law.' *Harmelin*, 501 U.S., at 1001 (opinion of KENNEDY, J.). It is true that a death sentence is 'unique in its severity and irrevocability,' *Gregg v. Georgia*, 428 U.S. 153, 187 (1976) (joint opinion of Stewart, Powell, and STEVENS, JJ.); yet life without parole sentences share some characteristics with death sentences that are shared by no other sentences. The State does not execute the offender sentenced to life without parole, but the sentence alters the offender's life by a forfeiture that is irrevocable. It deprives the convict of the most basic liberties without giving hope of restoration, except perhaps by executive clemency—the remote possibility of which does not mitigate the harshness of the sentence. *Solem*, 463 U.S., at 300–301. As one court observed in overturning a life without parole sentence for a juvenile defendant, this sentence 'means denial of hope; it means that good behavior and character improvement are immaterial; it means that whatever the future might hold in store for the mind and spirit of [the convict], he will remain in prison for the rest of his days.' *Naovarath v. State*, 105 Nev. 525, 526, 779 P. 2d 944 (1989)."

"The penological justifications for the sentencing practice are also relevant to the analysis. *Kennedy, supra*, at ___ (slip op., at 30–36); *Roper*, 543 U.S., at 571–572; *Atkins, supra*, at 318–320. Criminal punishment can have different goals, and choosing among them is within a legislature's discretion. See *Harmelin, supra*, at 999 (opinion of KENNEDY, J.) ('[T]he Eighth Amendment does not mandate adoption of any one penological theory'). It does not follow, however, that the purposes and effects of penal sanctions are irrelevant to the determination of Eighth Amendment restrictions. A sentence lacking any legitimate penological justification is by its nature disproportionate to the offense. With respect to life without parole for juvenile non-homicide offenders, none of the goals of penal sanctions that have been recognized as legitimate—retribution, deterrence, incapacitation, and rehabilitation, see *Ewing*, 538 U.S., at 25 (plurality opinion)—provides an adequate justification."

CASE SIGNIFICANCE: This case is very significant because this is the first time the U.S. Supreme Court has declared a penalty "like" the death penalty, in that life without possibility of parole is final. The Court argued that, although this may not be cruel and unusual for an adult, it could be for juvenile offenders. That means that the Eighth Amendment concerns in this case would be approached with the same intensity and procedural rules that were recognized in the death penalty cases of *Kennedy v. Louisiana* (2008), *Roper v. Simmons* (2005), and *Atkins v. Virginia* (2002). The Court recognized that a juvenile facing a sentence of life without possibility of parole would be robbed of all hope and would not have the maturity to cope with the finality of the situation. The Court also argued that state criminal sentencing schemes are tailored for adult offenders and not intended for juvenile offenders. Court-produced research showed most states intentionally keep their criminal and juvenile justice systems separate, recognizing that juveniles are a special category of offenders and must be treated differently from adults. "Juveniles are more capable of change than are adults, and their actions are less likely to be evidence of 'irretrievably depraved character' than are the actions of adults," *Roper*, 543 U.S., at 570. Mandatory sentencing does not allow for the individual consideration of change or growth in a youthful offender. The Court also pointed out that offenders who do not kill or intend to kill are less deserving of our most serious penalties. Finally, the Court could find no legitimate penological justification for punishing juvenile non-homicide offenders in the manner presented in this case.

MILLER V. ALABAMA
567 U.S. ___ (2012)
(*JACKSON V. HOBBS*)

CAPSULE: The Eighth Amendment prohibits the mandatory sentence of life without parole for juveniles in homicide cases.

FACTS: In 1999, 14-year-old Jackson and two other boys decided to rob a video store. Jackson discovered on the way to the store that one of the other boys was carrying a sawed-off shotgun under his coat sleeve. Jackson decided to stay outside when the other boys entered the store. The gun was pointed at the store clerk, and there was a demand for money. The store clerk refused. Jackson entered the store soon after and heard further demands for money. The clerk threatened to call the police, at which point she was shot and killed. The boys fled. Arkansas law allows prosecutors the discretion to charge 14-year-olds as adults when facing certain serious offenses. That authority was exercised in the charging of Jackson with capital felony murder and aggravated robbery. Jackson was convicted of both crimes and sentenced to life without parole.

Miller was also 14 years old at the time of his crime. He had been in and out of foster care owing to an alcoholic, drug-addicted mother and an abusive stepfather. Miller was also known to use alcohol and other drugs and had attempted suicide four times, the first time at age six. Miller was at home with a friend on a night in 2003, when a neighbor came by with drugs for his mother. The two boys and the neighbor went back to the neighbor's trailer, and all three smoked marijuana and played drinking games. After the neighbor passed out, Miller stole the neighbor's wallet, removed about $300, and split the money with the other boy. The neighbor woke up when Miller attempted to return the wallet, at which point he grabbed Miller by the throat. Miller's friend picked up a baseball bat and hit the neighbor. After freeing himself, Miller took the bat and repeatedly struck the neighbor with it. At some point the boys left, but they later returned to cover up the evidence of their crime. The trailer was set on fire, and the neighbor eventually died from his injuries and smoke inhalation. Alabama law allows the district attorney to try juveniles as adults in certain circumstances. Miller was charged as an adult with murder in the course of arson. That crime carries a mandatory minimum punishment of life without parole. Miller was found guilty.

ISSUE: Does the Eighth Amendment's Cruel and Unusual Clause allow a juvenile offender to be sentenced to mandatory life in prison without parole for the crime of homicide? NO.

HOLDING: The Eighth Amendment forbids a sentencing scheme in homicide cases that mandates life in prison without a possibility of parole for juvenile offenders.

REASON: ". . . Thus, *Roper* held that the Eighth Amendment bars capital punishment for children, and *Graham* concluded that the Amendment also prohibits a sentence of life without the possibility of parole for a child who committed a non-homicide offense. *Graham* further likened life without parole for juveniles to the death penalty itself, thereby evoking a second line of our precedents. In those cases, we have prohibited mandatory imposition of capital punishment, requiring that sentencing authorities consider the characteristics of a defendant and the details of his offense before sentencing him to death. See *Woodson v. North Carolina*, 428 U.S. 280 (1976) (plurality opinion); *Lockett v. Ohio*, 438 U.S. 586 (1978). Here, the confluence of these two lines of precedent leads to the conclusion that mandatory life-without-parole sentences for juveniles violate the Eighth Amendment.

"To start with the first set of cases: *Roper* and *Graham* establish that children are constitutionally different from adults for purposes of sentencing. Because juveniles have diminished culpability and greater prospects for reform, we explained, 'they are less deserving of the most severe punishments; *Graham*, 560 U.S., at ___ (slip op., at 17). Those cases relied on three significant gaps between juveniles and adults. First, children have a 'lack of maturity and an underdeveloped sense of responsibility,' leading to recklessness, impulsivity, and heedless risk-taking. *Roper*, 543 U.S., at 569. Second, children 'are more vulnerable . . . to negative influences and outside pressures,' including from their family and peers; they have limited 'contro[l] over their own environment' and lack the ability to extricate themselves from horrific, crime-producing settings. *Ibid*. And third, a child's character is not as 'well formed' as an adult's; his traits are 'less fixed' and his actions less likely to be 'evidence of irretrievabl[e] deprav[ity].' *Id.*, at 570."

"Most fundamentally, *Graham* insists that youth matters in determining the appropriateness of a lifetime of incarceration without the possibility of parole. In the circumstances there, juvenile status precluded a life-without-parole sentence, even though an adult could receive it for a similar crime. And in other contexts as well, the characteristics of youth, and the way they weaken rationales for punishment, can render a life-without-parole sentence disproportionate. Cf. *id.*, at ___ (slip op., at 20–23) (generally doubting the penological justifications for imposing life without parole on juveniles). 'An offender's age,' we made clear in *Graham*, 'is relevant to the Eighth Amendment,' and so 'criminal procedure laws that fail to take defendants' youthfulness into account at all would be flawed.' *Id.*, at ___ (slip op., at 25)."

"But the mandatory penalty schemes at issue here prevent the sentencer from taking account of these central considerations. By removing youth from the balance—by subjecting a juvenile to the same life-without-parole sentence applicable to an adult—these laws prohibit a sentencing authority from assessing whether the law's harshest term of imprisonment proportionately punishes a juvenile offender. That contravenes *Graham*'s (and also *Roper*'s) foundational principle: that imposition of a State's most severe penalties on juvenile offenders cannot proceed as though they were not children."

"In light of *Graham*'s reasoning, these decisions too show the flaws of imposing mandatory life-without-parole sentences on juvenile homicide offenders. Such mandatory penalties, by their nature, preclude a sentencer from taking account of an offender's age and the wealth of characteristics and circumstances attendant to it. Under these schemes, every juvenile will receive the same sentence as every other—the 17-year-old and the 14-year-old, the shooter and the accomplice, the child from a stable household and the child from a chaotic and abusive one. And still worse, each juvenile (including these two 14-year-olds) will receive the same sentence as the vast majority of adults committing similar homicide offenses— but really, as *Graham* noted, a *greater* sentence than those adults will serve. In meting out the death penalty, the elision of all these differences would be strictly forbidden. And once again, *Graham* indicates that a similar rule should apply when a juvenile confronts a sentence of life (and death) in prison."

CASE SIGNIFICANCE: The *Miller* and *Jackson* cases deal with two 14-year-old boys who were convicted of murder and sentenced to mandatory life imprisonment without a possibility of parole. There was no discretion in the state laws to impose any other sentence. The individual characteristics of these boys and their cases were not considered as mitigating evidence before sentences were imposed. The differences between juveniles and adults were also not considered. These factors run counter to the U.S. Supreme Court holdings requiring individualized sentencing for defendants facing our most serious penalties. The Court first ruled in *Graham v. Florida* (2010) that mandatory life without parole was unconstitutional for juveniles involved in non-homicide cases. That Eighth Amendment holding was extended to juvenile homicide cases here.

NOTES

1   This case is also briefed in Chapter 2, Probation.
2   This case is also briefed in Chapter 4, Death Penalty.
3   This case is also briefed in Chapter 4, Death Penalty.
4   This case is also briefed in Chapter 4, Death Penalty.

Sexual Assault Offender Laws

6

INTRODUCTION

The area of sexual offenders in corrections law has generated a great deal of interest among states and has already produced interesting court decisions. The impetus for these cases started with the passage of the so-called Megan's laws in the early 1990s. Megan Kanka was a seven-year-old New Jersey girl who was killed in 1994 by a juvenile, the son of neighbors who were friends of her family. The juvenile killer had a previous record of sexual assault, but that was not known to Megan's parents because at that time the laws of New Jersey and other states prohibited the disclosure of such records to anyone, including neighbors or law enforcement officers. Megan's killing caused a national outcry because the parents claimed that had they been informed or known of the killer's sexual assault record the killing would not have taken place. It resonated with the public that had long felt that confidentiality of juvenile records protected the offender more than the public. By 1996, every state in the United States and the federal government had enacted a variation of Megan's law.

These laws generally call for eliminating or restricting the reach of strict confidentiality laws of juvenile sexual offenders. Many states go beyond that, however, and require the registration of sexual offenders, regardless of age. There are five cases in this chapter, but more cases are sure to follow. The issues in these cases revolve around the retroactive application of the law and whether the law constitutes cruel and unusual punishment because it usually extends beyond the time served by the offender. The issue of fairness is also raised, defendants saying that they no longer constitute a danger to society and therefore continued monitoring of their conduct by the state is unwarranted. Determining continued dangerousness after treatment is a challenge that states are often asked to prove if regulation or punishment of sexual offenders is to continue beyond the period of confinement. Extending the period of confinement beyond that usually provided for by the state's criminal law is also challenged as violative of the prohibition against double jeopardy or cruel and unusual punishment.

Kansas v. Hendricks (1997) was one of the early cases that reached the Court. In that case, the Court held that the Kansas law that provided for virtually indefinite confinement of sexually violent predators was constitutional and did not violate either the double jeopardy prohibition or the constitutional ban on ex post facto legislation. *Kansas v. Crane* (1997) also dealt with the Kansas Sexually Violent Predator Act. The Court held that the commitment of a dangerous sex offender is constitutional, but there must be proof that there is serious difficulty in controlling such behavior. Connecticut's version of Megan's law was challenged in *Connecticut Department of Public Safety et al. v. Doe* (2003). The Court held that the public posting of a sex offender registry does not violate the due process clause of the Fourteenth Amendment. In *Smith v. Doe* (2003), the Court said that Alaska's Sex Offender Registration Act is regulatory rather than punitive; therefore, it could be applied retroactively without violating the ex post facto clause. Part of this upsurge of sexual offender cases is the case of *Stogner v. California* (2003), in which the Supreme Court held that a California law that allowed the prosecution of a sexual offense that had expired under the statute of limitations violated the ex post facto clause of the U.S. Constitution. Finally, *Carr v. United States* (2010) and *Reynolds v. United States* (2012) examine the issues of travel and registration of people who were identified as sex offenders before the passage by Congress in 2006 of the Sexual Offender and Registration and Notification Act (SORNA). In the *Carr* case, the Court ruled that SORNA did not apply to sex offenders' interstate travel if it occurred before the Act's enactment. The *Reynolds* case makes it clear that pre-enactment sex offenders are not required to register under the federal Act until that action is specified by the Attorney General. The Court pointed out that, if it had been Congress's intent to require all sex offenders to register, then SORNA would specifically state that. It does not.

Supreme Court decisions in these cases are mixed, but are mostly protective of the public's desire to limit exposure to sexual offenders. In the future, the Court will continue to be asked to judge the constitutionality of state and federal laws that seek to protect the public from sexual offenders. How to balance individual rights and public safety in these cases is an issue that will require the Court's attention in years to come. However, as these cases show, the Supreme Court has already made a strong start.

KANSAS V. HENDRICKS
521 U.S. 346 (1997)

CAPSULE: A Kansas statute that permits the potentially indefinite confinement of sexually violent predators is constitutional.

FACTS: Kansas established a Sexually Violent Predator Act that allows for the civil commitment of persons who are likely to engage in predatory acts of sexual violence due to a mental or personality disorder. Hendricks had an extensive history of sexually molesting children. He was scheduled for release from prison. The state filed a petition to commit Hendricks under this Act. Hendricks filed a challenge to the Act's constitutionality. The court reserved ruling on this, but granted his request for a jury trial.

During the trial, Hendricks testified that he agreed with the state physician's diagnosis that he suffers from pedophilia and is not cured and that he continues to harbor sexual desires for children that he cannot control when he gets stressed out. The jury in the trial determined that he was a sexually violent predator and subsequently the court ordered him committed on the ground that pedophilia qualifies as a mental abnormality under the Act. Hendricks appealed to the State Supreme Court, which invalidated the Act, saying that the pre-commitment condition of mental abnormality did not satisfy the substantive due process requirement that involuntary civil commitments be based on a mental illness finding.

ISSUES:

1. Does the Sexually Violent Predator Act's definition of mental abnormality satisfy the substantive due process requirements of an involuntary civil commitment? YES.

2. Does the Act violate the Constitution's double jeopardy prohibition or its ban on ex post facto lawmaking? NO.

HOLDING: The Kansas Sexually Violent Predator Act is constitutional. It complies with due process requirements and does not violate the prohibition against double jeopardy. Neither does it violate the prohibition against ex post facto lawmaking.

REASON: "Indeed, we have never required State legislatures to adopt any particular nomenclature in drafting civil commitment statutes. Rather, we have traditionally left to legislators the task of defining terms of a medical nature that have legal significance. Cf. *Jones v. United States*, 463 U.S. 354, 365, n. 13 (1983). As a consequence, the States have, over the years, developed numerous specialized terms to define mental health concepts. Often, these definitions do not fit precisely with the definitions employed by the medical community . . . To the extent that the civil commitment statutes we have considered set forth criteria relating to an individual's inability to control his dangerousness, the Kansas Act set forth comparable criteria and Hendricks' condition doubtless satisfies those criteria.

"The Double Jeopardy Clause provides: '[N]or shall any person be subject for the same offence to be twice put in jeopardy of life or limb.' Although generally understood to preclude a second prosecution for the same offense, the Court has also interpreted this prohibition to prevent the State from 'punishing twice, or attempting a second time to punish criminality, for the same offense.' *Witte v. United States*, 515 U.S. 389, 396 (1995) (emphasis and internal quotation marks omitted). Hendricks argues that, as applied to him, the Act violates double jeopardy principles because his confinement under the Act, imposed after a conviction and term of incarceration, amounts to both a second prosecution and a second punishment for the same offense. We disagree ... Because we have determined that the Kansas Act is civil in nature, initiation of its commitment proceedings does not constitute a second prosecution. Cf. *Jones v. United States*, 463 U.S. 354 (1983).

"Hendricks' ex post facto claim is similarly flawed. The Ex Post Facto Clause, which 'forbids the application of any new punitive measures to a crime already consummated,' has been interpreted to pertain exclusively to penal statutes. *California Dept. of Corrections v. Morales*, 514 U.S. 499, 505 (1995) (quoting *Lindsey v. Washington*, 301 U.S. 397, 401 (1987)). As we have previously determined, the Act does not impose punishment; thus, its application does not raise ex post facto concerns. Moreover, the Act clearly does not have retroactive effect. Rather, the Act permits involuntary confinement based upon a determination that the person currently both suffers from a 'mental abnormality' or 'personality disorder' and is likely to pose a future danger to the public. To the extent that past behavior is taken into account, it is used, as noted above, solely for evidentiary purposes. Because the Act does not criminalize conduct legal before its enactment, nor deprive Hendricks of any defense available to him at the time of his crimes, the Act does not violate the Ex Post Facto Clause."

CASE SIGNIFICANCE: This case addresses the constitutionality of laws regarding sexual predators. Kansas passed a law allowing civil commitment after imprisonment of persons likely to engage in predatory acts of sexual violence due to a mental or personality disorder. It also provided its own definition of what mental or personality disorder means, a definition that did not adhere closely to the definitions used in the medical community. The defendant challenged the constitutionality of the Kansas law, saying he was being penalized twice and therefore it violated his due process rights and the ban on ex post facto lawmaking. The Court disagreed, saying that the law was constitutional.

The ruling is important because it addresses a current issue: whether a civil commitment after serving a criminal penalty for the offense constitutes double jeopardy in violation of the Constitution. The Court reasoned that for double jeopardy to attach, both punishments must be criminal in nature. In this case, the civil commitment, after serving the penalty for the criminal offense, was civil in nature, thus double jeopardy did not apply. This ruling legalizes statutes in many states that seek to protect society from violent sexual offenders who have served their time in prison. It presents a constitutional alternative to outright release, thus protecting society and calming public fears.

KANSAS V. CRANE
534 U.S. 407 (2002)

CAPSULE: The civil commitment of a dangerous sex offender is not permitted without proof of serious difficulty in controlling behavior.

FACTS: The state of Kansas sought the civil commitment of Michael Crane, a previously convicted sexual offender. A state psychiatric witness testified that Crane suffered from both exhibitionism and antisocial personality disorder. After a jury trial, the Kansas District Court ordered Crane's civil commitment. The Kansas Supreme Court reversed that order, ruling that the *Hendricks* decision insists upon "a finding that the defendant cannot control his dangerous behavior"— even if (as provided by Kansas law) problems of "emotional capacity" and not "volitional capacity" prove the "source of bad behavior" warranting commitment. The trial court had not made such a finding.

ISSUE: Is a state always required to prove that a dangerous individual is completely unable to control his behavior prior to a civil commitment? NO.

HOLDING: The Constitution does not require that total or complete lack of control be established by the state prior to civil commitment of the type of dangerous sexual offenders considered in *Hendricks*. What is needed instead is proof of serious difficulty in controlling behavior.

REASON: "We do not agree with the State, however, insofar as it seeks to claim that the Constitution permits commitment of the type of dangerous sexual offender considered in Hendricks without any lack-of-control determination. See Brief for Petitioner 17; Tr. Of Oral Arg. 22, 30–31. *Hendricks* underscored the constitutional importance of distinguishing a dangerous sexual offender subject to civil commitment 'from other dangerous persons who are perhaps more properly dealt with exclusively through criminal proceedings.' 521 U.S., at 360. That distinction is necessary lest 'civil commitment' become a 'mechanism for retribution or general deterrence'—functions properly those of criminal law, not civil commitment. Id., at 372–373 (Kennedy, J., concurring; cf. also Moran, 'The Epidemiology of Antisocial Personality Disorder,' 34 *Social Psychiatry & Psychiatric Epidemiology* 231, 234 (1999) (noting that 40–60 percent of the male prison population is diagnosable with Antisocial Personality Disorder). The presence of what the 'psychiatric professions itself [classified] . . . as a serious mental disorder' helped to make that distinction in *Hendricks*. And a critical distinguishing feature of that 'serious . . . disorder' there consisted of a special and serious lack of ability to control behavior.

"In recognizing that fact, we did not give to the phrase 'lack of control' a particularly narrow or technical meaning. And we recognize that in cases where lack of control is at issue 'inability to control behavior' will not be demonstrable with mathematical precision. It is enough to say that there must be proof of serious difficulty in controlling behavior. And this, when viewed in light of such features of the case as the nature of the psychiatric diagnosis, and the severity of the mental abnormality itself, must be sufficient to distinguish the dangerous sexual offender whose serious mental illness, abnormality, or disorder subjects him to civil commitment from the dangerous but typical recidivist convicted in an ordinary criminal case. 521 U.S., at 357–358; see also *Foucha v. Louisiana*, 504 U.S. 71, 82–83 (1992) (rejecting an approach to civil commitment that would permit the indefinite confinement 'of any convicted criminal' after completion of a prison term)."

CASE SIGNIFICANCE: The legal issue in this case was: What level of proof is needed for the civil commitment of sexually dangerous offenders? It is a follow-up of *Kansas v. Hendricks* (1997), which held that a Kansas law that permits the potentially indefinite confinement of sexually violent predators is constitutional. This case sets the type of proof needed for the civil commitment of such offenders. The Kansas Supreme Court had interpreted *Hendricks* as "requiring the State always to prove that a dangerous individual is completely unable to control his behavior" before he or she could be civilly committed.

The Court disagreed with the holding of the Kansas Supreme Court, saying instead that proof of serious difficulty in controlling behavior is sufficient. It stressed, however, that the commitment of the type of dangerous sexual offenders considered in *Hendricks* without any lack-of-control determination is unconstitutional. The Court then added that "*Hendricks* underscored the constitutional importance of distinguishing a dangerous sexual offender subject to civil commitment 'from other dangerous persons who are perhaps more properly dealt with exclusively through criminal proceedings.'" The Court concluded: "That distinction is necessary lest 'civil commitment' become a 'mechanism for retribution or general deterrence'—functions properly those of criminal law, not civil commitment." The Court also noted that the ruling here and in Hendricks was limited to sexually dangerous offenders and not just any person with a mental abnormality.

In sum, the *Hendricks* and *Crane* cases say that the civil commitment of dangerous sex offenders is constitutional, but the state must prove prior to a civil commitment that the offender is unable to control his behavior.

CONNECTICUT DEPARTMENT OF PUBLIC SAFETY ET AL. V. DOE

538 U.S. 1 (2003)

CAPSULE: The public posting of a sex offender registry does not violate the due process clause of the Fourteenth Amendment.

FACTS: Connecticut enacted a statute designed to protect its communities from sex offenders and to help apprehend repeat sex offenders. Connecticut's "Megan's Law" applies to all people convicted of criminal offenses against a minor, violent and non-violent sexual offenses, and felonies committed for a sexual purpose. The targeted offenders must register with the Connecticut Department of Public Safety (DPS) upon their release into the community. The personal information that must be provided to the DPS includes name, address, photograph, and DNA samples, and notification of any change in residence. The offender must also periodically update his or her photograph. Most offenders must register for 10 years, although those convicted of sexually violent offenses must register for life.

The DPS compiles the information and is mandated to publicize it by posting a sex offender registry on a World Wide Web site and to make the registry available to the public in certain state offices. The registry is accompanied by the following warning: "Any person who uses information in this registry to injure, harass, or commit a criminal act against any person included in the registry or any other person is subject to criminal prosecution."

ISSUE: Does the public posting of a sex offender registry deprive registered sex offenders of a "liberty interest" and, therefore, violate the due process clause of the Fourteenth Amendment? NO.

HOLDING: The public posting of a sex offender registry does not violate the due process clause of the Fourteenth Amendment.

REASONS: "In cases such as *Wisconsin v. Constantineau*, 400 U.S. 433 (1971), and *Goss v. Lopez*, 419 U.S. 565 (1975), we held that due process required the government to accord the plaintiff a hearing to prove or disprove a particular fact or set of facts. But in each of these cases, the fact in question was concededly relevant to the inquiry at hand. Here, however, the fact that respondent seeks to prove—that he is currently not dangerous—is of no consequence under Connecticut's Megan's Law. As the DPS Website explains, the law's requirements turn on an offender's conviction alone—a fact that a convicted offender has already had a procedurally safeguarded opportunity to contest. 271 F. 3d. at 44 ("'Individuals included within the registry are included *solely* by virtue of their conviction record and state law'" (emphasis added)). No other fact is relevant to the disclosure of registrants' information. Conn. Gen. Stat. Sections 54–257, 54–258 (2001). Indeed, the disclaimer on the website explicitly states that respondent's alleged non-dangerousness simply does not matter. 271 F.3d, at 44 ("'[DPS] has made no determination that any individual included in the registry is currently dangerous'")."

"In short, even if respondent could prove that he is not likely to be currently dangerous, Connecticut has decided that the registry information of all sex offenders—currently dangerous or not—must be publicly disclosed. Unless respondent can show that that substantive rule of law is defective (by conflicting with a provision of the Constitution), any hearing on current dangerousness is a bootless exercise . . .."

CASE SIGNIFICANCE: This case settles the issue of the constitutionality of registration and publication laws for sex offenders, otherwise known as Megan's Laws. The laws are named for Megan Kanka, a seven-year-old child from New Jersey who was sexually molested and murdered by the teenage son of neighbors who were friends of her parents. The teenage boy had a history of sexual assault, but this was not known to Megan's parents, because at that time juvenile records were held confidential.

These laws typically require the registration of sexual offenders and the posting of their names in neighborhoods where they reside. Many states have passed Megan's laws to protect the public from and help catch sex offenders. Offenders, however, claim that the law is unfair because their debt to society has been paid and some of them are no longer dangerous. In this case, the defendant further claimed that he was not a dangerous sexual offender and that the absence of notice or meaningful opportunity to be heard deprived him of a liberty interest and therefore violated his right to due process.

The Supreme Court disagreed, saying that the Connecticut registry law required that all sex offenders, "currently sexually dangerous or not," must register. Under the law, prior conviction involving a sexual offense was all that was required—not dangerousness. The defendant had to register because he was a sexual offender, not because he continued to be dangerous. Such registration and posting laws are valid and do not violate the defendant's liberty interest and due process rights even if no prior opportunity was given to prove that the defendant is not dangerous.

SMITH V. DOE
538 U.S. 84 (2003)

CAPSULE: A sex offender registration and notification law that is not punitive does not violate the ex post facto clause of the Constitution.

FACTS: John Doe I and John Doe II were convicted of sexual abuse of a minor, an aggravated sex offense. Both were released from prison in 1990 and completed rehabilitation programs for sex offenders. Although convicted before the passage of the Alaska Sex Offender Registration Act (Act), both offenders are covered by it.

The Act contains two components: a registration requirement and a notification system. Both are retroactive. Targeted offenders must register either with the Department of Corrections (if the individual is incarcerated) or with the local law enforcement authorities (if the individual is at liberty). Information that must be provided includes the offender's name, aliases, identifying features, address, place of employment, date of birth, conviction information, driver's license number, information about vehicles to which he has access, and post-conviction treatment history. The offender must also allow authorities to photograph and fingerprint him. Offenders convicted of an aggravated sex offense must register for life and verify the information quarterly. The offender must also notify his local police department if he moves. An offender who knowingly fails to comply with the Act is subject to criminal prosecution. All the information is forwarded to the Alaska Department of Public Safety, which maintains a central registry of sex offenders. Although some of the information is kept confidential, a substantial amount of the registry information is made public via the Internet.

ISSUE: Does the Alaska sex offender registration and notification law violate the ex post facto clause of the Constitution? NO.

HOLDING: Because the Alaska Offender Act regulates rather than punishes, its retroactive application does not violate the ex post facto clause.

REASON: "Respondents seek to cast doubt upon the non-punitive nature of the law's declared objective by pointing out that the Alaska Constitution lists the need for protecting the public as one of the purposes of criminal administration. Brief for Respondent 23 (citing Alaska Const., Art. I, Section 12). As the Court stated in *Flemming v. Nestor*, rejecting an ex post facto challenge to a law terminating benefits to deported aliens, where a legislative restriction 'is an incident of the State's power to protect the health and safety of its citizens,' it will be considered 'as evidencing an intent to exercise that regulatory power, and not a purpose to add to the punishment.' 363 U.S., at 616 (citing *Hawker v. New York*, 170 U.S. 189 (1898)). The court repeated this principle in 89 Firearms, upholding a statute requiring forfeiture of unlicensed firearms against a Double Jeopardy challenge. The Court observed that, in enacting the provision, Congress 'was concerned with the widespread traffic in firearms and with their general availability to those whose possession thereof was contrary to the public interest.' 465 U.S., at 364 (quoting *Huddleston v. United States*, 415 U.S. 814, 824 (1974)). This goal was 'plainly more remedial than punitive.' 465 U.S., at 364. These precedents instruct us that even if the objective of the Act is consistent with the purposes of the Alaska criminal justice system, the State's pursuit of it in a regulatory scheme does not make the objective punitive.

"The Ex Post Facto Clause does not preclude a State from making reasonable categorical judgments that conviction of specified crimes should entail particular regulatory consequences. We have upheld against ex post facto challenges laws imposing regulatory burdens on individuals convicted of crimes without any corresponding risk assessment. See *De Veau*, 363 U.S. at 160; *Hawker*, 170 U.S., at 197. As stated in *Hawker*: 'Doubtless, one who has violated the criminal law may thereafter reform and become in fact possessed of good moral character. But the legislature has no power in cases of this kind to make a rule of universal application . . .' Ibid. The State's determination to legislate with respect to convicted sex offenders as a class, rather than require individual determination of their dangerousness, does not make the statute a punishment under the Ex Post Facto Clause."

CASE SIGNIFICANCE: This case challenged the constitutionality of Alaska's Megan's Law. The sexual offenders in this case had been released from prison and had completed rehabilitation programs for sex offenders. Moreover, they were convicted before the law was passed. They claimed that its application to crimes that were already committed and sentence served violated the ex post facto provision of the Constitution because they were being punished for something that was not yet punishable when the crime was committed. Moreover, they had already served their time.

The Court decided the case in favor of Alaska, saying that the Alaska Sex Offender Registration Act meant to establish a civil proceeding, not a criminal proceeding; therefore the ex post facto prohibition did not apply because it applies only to criminal proceedings. The crucial question is: What determines whether a law is civil or criminal? The Court said that this is judged by what the state legislature wanted to do. If the legislature wanted to regulate conduct when it passed the law, then it is civil, but if the legislature wanted to punish, then it is criminal. If the legislature intended to regulate conduct, the Court may still find the law to be criminal if "the statutory scheme is so punitive either in purpose or effect as to negate the state's intention to deem it civil." In determining whether the law is civil or criminal, the Court ordinarily respects the stated purpose of the legislature, adding that "only the clearest proof will suffice to override that intent and transform what has been denominated a civil remedy into a criminal penalty." The Court held Alaska's law to be civil in nature, saying that the offenders challenging the law "cannot show, much less by clearest proof, that the Act's effects negate Alaska's intention to establish a civil regulatory scheme."

STOGNER V. CALIFORNIA
539 U.S. 607 (2003)

CAPSULE: The prosecution of a crime that is barred by the state's statute of limitations violates the ex post facto clause of the Constitution.

FACTS: California enacted a new criminal statute of limitations for sex-related child abuse crimes in 1993. The new statute allows for prosecution of crimes that were under previous statutes of limitations that have expired, provided that "(1) a victim has reported an allegation of abuse to the police, (2) there is independent evidence that clearly and convincingly corroborates the victim's allegation, and (3) the prosecution is begun within one year of the victim's report." In 1996, California added a provision to the statute that clarifies that a prosecution satisfying the above three conditions "shall revive any cause of action barred by [prior statutes of limitations.]"

In 1998, Marion Stogner was indicted and charged with sex-related child abuse that occurred between 1955 and 1973. Without the revival provision, California would not have been allowed to bring these charges against Stogner because the statute of limitations at the time of the alleged offenses was three years. These charges would have been filed 20 years too late.

ISSUE: Does the ex post facto clause forbid the revival of a prosecution that was previously barred by the statute of limitations? YES.

HOLDING: A law enacted after expiration of a previously applicable statute of limitations violates the ex post facto clause if it is applied to revive a previously time-barred prosecution.

REASON: "First, the new statute threatens the kinds of harm that, in this court's view, the Ex Post Facto Clause seeks to avoid. Long ago the Court pointed out that the Clause protects liberty by preventing governments from enacting statutes with 'manifestly unjust and oppressive' retroactive effects. *Calder v. Bull*, 3 Dall. 386, 391 (1978). Judge Learned Hand later wrote that extending a limitations period after the State has assured 'a man that he has become safe from pursuit . . . seems to most of us unfair and dishonest.' *Falter v. United States*, 23 F. 2d 420, 426 (CA2), *cert. denied*, 277 U.S. 590 (1928). In such a case, the government has refused 'to play by its own rules,' *Carmell v. Texas*, 529 U.S. 513, 533 (2000). It has deprived the defendant of the 'fair warning,' *Weaver v. Graham*, 450 U.S. 24, 28 (1981), that might have led him to preserve exculpatory evidence. F. Wharton, *Criminal Pleading and Practice* Section 316, p. 210 (8th ed. 1880P ('The statute [of limitations] is . . . an amnesty, declaring that after a certain time . . . the offender shall be at liberty to return to his country . . . and . . . may cease to preserve the proofs of his innocence'). And a Constitution that permits such an extension, by allowing legislatures to pick and choose when to act retroactively, risks both 'arbitrary and potentially vindictive legislation,' and erosion of the separation of powers, *Weaver, supra*, at 29, and n. 10. See *Fletcher v. Peck*, 6 Cranch 87, 137–138 (1810) (viewing the Ex Post Facto Clause as a protection against 'violent acts which might grow out of the feelings of the moment')."

". . . we believe that the outcome of this case is determined by the nature of the harms that California's law creates, by the fact that the law falls within Justice Chase's second category as Chase understood that category, and by a long line of authority holding that a law of this type violates the Ex Post Facto Clause."

CASE SIGNIFICANCE: This case involves a California law that authorized the prosecution of a sex-related child abuse crime after the statute of limitations, which was operational when the crime was allegedly committed, had expired. A statute of limitations is a law in most states that provides that crimes must be prosecuted within a specified time after commission, otherwise they can no longer be prosecuted. A new California law, passed in 1993, authorized the prosecution of sex-related child abuse cases if "a victim had reported an allegation of abuse to the police, there is independent evidence that clearly and convincingly corroborates the victim's allegation, and the prosecution is begun within one year of the victim's report."

Stogner allegedly committed sexual child abuse between 1955 and 1973, but was not prosecuted at that time. He was indicted for the offenses in 1998 under the new law. At the time the crimes were allegedly committed, the statute of limitations was three years. Stogner moved to dismiss the charges against him, saying that the statute of limitations had clearly passed.

The Supreme Court agreed with Stogner, saying that California law violates the ex post facto clause "when it is applied to revive a previously time-barred prosecution." Laws that extend the time for prosecution after the previous time limitation has expired are prohibited by the Constitution. This was one of those laws and was therefore unconstitutional.

CARR V. UNITED STATES
560 U.S. ___ (2010)

CAPSULE: The Sexual Offender and Registration and Notification Act does not include the pre-enactment travel of sex offenders.

FACTS: Carr pleaded guilty in an Alabama state court to first-degree sexual abuse in May 2004. He was released on probation on July 3, 2004, and, per Alabama law, registered as a sex offender. Prior to the enactment of the Sexual Offender and Registration and Notification Act (SORNA), Carr moved from Alabama to Indiana. He failed to register as a sex offender under Indiana state law requirements. In July 2007, he was involved in a fight and came to the attention of law enforcement. In August 2007, Carr was indicted in a federal district court and charged with failing to register in violation of § 2250 of SORNA.

ISSUE: Does the Sex Offender and Registration and Notification Act include offenders whose interstate travel occurred before the Act's enactment? NO.

HOLDING: The Sex Offender and Registration and Notification Act does not apply to sex offenders whose interstate travel occurred before the Act's enactment.

REASON: "Carr's interpretation better accords with the statutory text. By its terms, the first element of § 2250(a) can only be satisfied when a person 'is required to register *under the Sex Offender Registration and Notification Act*.' § 2250(a)(1) (emphasis added). In an attempt to reconcile its preferred construction with the words of the statute, the Government insists that this language is merely 'a shorthand way of identifying those persons who have a [sex offense] conviction in the classes identified by SORNA.' Brief for United States 19–20. To reach this conclusion, the Government observes that another provision of SORNA, 42 U.S.C. § 16913(a), states that the Act's registration requirements apply to 'sex offender[s].' A 'sex offender' is elsewhere defined as 'an individual who was convicted of a sex offense.' § 16911(1). Thus, as the Government would have it, Congress used 12 words and two implied cross-references to establish that the first element of § 2250(a) is that a person has been convicted of a sex offense. Such contortions can scarcely be called 'shorthand.' It is far more sensible to conclude that Congress meant the first precondition to § 2250 liability to be the one it listed first: a 'require[ment] to register under [SORNA].' Once a person becomes subject to SORNA's registration requirements, which can occur only after the statute's effective date, that person can be convicted under § 2250 if he thereafter travels and then fails to register.

"That § 2250 sets forth the travel requirement in the present tense ('travels') rather than in the past or present perfect ('traveled' or 'has traveled') reinforces the conclusion that pre-enactment travel falls outside the statute's compass. Consistent with normal usage, we have frequently looked to Congress' choice of verb tense to ascertain a statute's temporal reach. See, *e.g.*, *United States v. Wilson*, 503 U.S. 329, 333 (1992) ('Congress' use of a verb tense is significant in construing statutes'); *Gwaltney of Smithfield, Ltd. v. Chesapeake Bay Foundation*,

Inc., 484 U.S. 49, 57 (1987) ('Congress could have phrased its requirement in language that looked to the past . . ., but it did not choose this readily available option'); *Barrett v. United States*, 423 U.S. 212, 216 (1976) (observing that Congress used the present perfect tense to 'denot[e] an act that has been completed'). The Dictionary Act also ascribes significance to verb tense. It provides that, '[i]n determining the meaning of any Act of Congress, unless the context indicates otherwise [,] . . . words used in the present tense include the future as well as the present.' 1 U.S.C. § 1. By implication, then, the Dictionary Act instructs that the present tense generally does not include the past. Accordingly, a statute that regulates a person who 'travels' is not readily understood to encompass a person whose only travel occurred before the statute took effect. Indeed, neither the Government nor the dissent identifies any instance in which this Court has construed a present-tense verb in a criminal law to reach pre-enactment conduct."

"None of the legislative materials the Government cites as evidence of SORNA's purpose calls this reading into question. To the contrary, the report of the House Judiciary Committee suggests not only that a prohibition on post-enactment travel is consonant with Congress' goals, but also that it is the rule Congress in fact chose to adopt. As the Government acknowledges, the bill under consideration by the Committee contained a version of § 2250 that 'would not have reached pre-enactment interstate travel.' Brief for United States 24, n. 9. This earlier version imposed federal criminal penalties on any person who 'receives a notice from an official that such person is required to register under [SORNA] and . . . thereafter travels in interstate or foreign commerce, or enters or leaves Indian country.' H. R. Rep. No. 109–218, pt. 1, at 9; see also *id.*, at 26 ('[S]ex offenders will now face Federal prosecution . . . if they cross a State line and fail to comply with the sex offender registration and notification requirements contained in the legislation'). Yet this did not stop the Committee from describing its legislation as a solution to the problem of missing sex offenders. See *id.*, at 23–24, 26, 45–46. The Government identifies nothing in the legislative record to suggest that, in modifying this language during the course of the legislative process, Congress intended to alter the statute's temporal sweep. At the very least, the close correspondence between the Committee's discussion of missing sex offenders and its recognition of the travel element's prospective application would seem to confirm that reading § 2250 to reach only post enactment travel does not contravene SORNA's underlying purposes, let alone result in an absurdity that would compel us to disregard the statutory text. Cf. *Arlington Central School Dist. Bd. of Ed.* v. *Murphy*, 548 U.S. 291, 296 (2006) ('We have stated time and again that courts must presume that a legislature says in a statute what it means and means in a statute what it says there. When the statutory language is plain, the sole function of the courts—at least where the disposition required by the text is not absurd—is to enforce it according to its terms' (internal quotation marks and citation omitted))."

CASE SIGNIFICANCE: Since 1994, federal law has required states to have a system in place to register sex offenders and to notify communities of their presence. In 2006, Congress, in an effort to make the state systems more comprehensive and uniform, enacted the Sex Offender and Registration and Notification Act. In this case, the Court examined whether sex offenders who traveled from state to state before the enactment of the Sexual Offender and Registration and Notification Act could be penalized for that travel. The Court pointed out that Congress means exactly what it says in a statute and, if it had meant to include the pre-enactment travel of sex offenders in the Act, then it would have said so.

REYNOLDS V. UNITED STATES
562 U.S. ___ (2012)

CAPSULE: Pre-SORNA offenders do not have to register under the Act until the Attorney General specifies that the Act applies to them.

FACTS: The federal Sex Offender Registration and Notification Act (SORNA) requires convicted sex offenders to provide, and to update state governments with, their personal information for inclusion on state and federal sex offender registries. SORNA includes pre-Act offenders and gives the Attorney General "the authority to specify the applicability of the [registration] requirement . . . to sex offenders convicted before the enactment of this chapter or its implementation in a particular jurisdiction. . . ."

Reynolds is a pre-Act offender. He was convicted in a Missouri court of a sex offense in October 2001. He served his prison term and was released in July 2005. He registered in Missouri as a sex offender but moved to Pennsylvania in September 2007. He did not update his Missouri registration (as Missouri law required) and did not register in Pennsylvania. A federal grand jury charged him with knowingly failing to register and update a registration as required by the Act for the time period of September 16 to October 16, 2007. Reynolds argued against the charge, stating that the Act's registration requirements had not yet become applicable to pre-Act offenders before the time period in question.

ISSUE: Does the Sex Offender Registration and Notification Act require pre-Act offenders to register at a time before the Attorney General validly specified that the Act's registration provisions apply to them? NO.

HOLDING: The Act's registration requirements do not apply to pre-Act offenders until the Attorney General so specifies.

REASON: "The question before us is whether the Act requires pre-Act offenders to register before the Attorney General validly specifies that the Act's registration provisions apply to them. We believe that it does not. For one thing, a natural reading of the textual language supports our conclusion. The text consists of four statements. See supra, at 3. Statement One says that '[a] sex offender shall register, and keep the registration current.' Statement Two says that a sex offender must initially register before completing his 'sentence of imprisonment' (or, if the sentence does not involve imprisonment, within three days of conviction). Statement Three says that the sex offender must update a registration within three business days of any change of 'name, residence, employment, or student status.' Statement Four says that '[t]he Attorney General shall have the authority to specify the applicability of the requirements of this subchapter to sex offenders convicted before the enactment of this chapter.'

"Read naturally, the Fourth Statement modifies the First. It specifically deals with a subset (pre-Act offenders) of a broad general class (all sex offenders) to which the First Statement applies. And it therefore should control the Act's application to that subset. See *Gozlon-Peretz v. United States*, 498 U.S. 395, 407 (1991) (specific statutory provision normally controls over one of more general application); see also *Bloate v. United States*, 559 U.S. ___, ___ (2010) (slip op., at 10) (same).

"At the same time, the Fourth Statement says that the Attorney General has authority to specify the Act's 'applicability,' not its 'nonapplicability.' And it consequently is more naturally read as conferring the authority to apply the Act, not the authority to make exceptions. That is how we normally understand a term such as 'authority to specify' in the context of applying new rules to persons already governed by pre-existing rules. If, for example, the Major League Baseball Players Association and the team owners agreed that the Commissioner of Baseball 'shall have the authority to specify the applicability' to the major leagues of the more stringent minor league drug testing policy, we should think that the minor league policy would not apply unless and until the Commissioner so specified.

"For another thing, this reading of the Act efficiently resolves what Congress may well have thought were practical problems arising when the Act sought to apply the new registration requirements to pre-Act offenders. The problems arise out of the fact that the Act seeks to make more uniform a patchwork of pre-existing state systems. Doing so could require newly registering or re-registering 'a large number' of pre-Act offenders. That effort could prove expensive. And it might not prove feasible to do so immediately. See 73 Fed. Reg. 38063 (recognizing these problems). Congress' concern about these problems is reflected in the Act's providing the States with three years to bring their systems into compliance with federal standards while permitting the Attorney General to extend that 3-year grace period to five years. 42 U.S.C. § 16924."

"Finally, our reading of the Act takes Congress to have filled potential lacunae (created by related Act provisions) in a manner consistent with basic background principles of criminal law. The Second Statement, for example, says that a sex offender must register before completing his prison term, but the provision says nothing about when a pre-Act offender who completed his prison term pre-Act must register. Although a state pre-Act offender could not be prosecuted until he traveled interstate, there is no interstate requirement for a federal pre-Act offender. And to apply the Act to either of these pre-Act offenders from the date of enactment would require reading into the statute, silent on the point, some kind of unsaid equivalent (e.g., registering or updating within a 'reasonable time' or 'within three days of first post-Act travel in interstate commerce' or 'as preexisting state law requires').

"Pre-Act offenders, aware of such complexities, lacunae, and difficulties, might, on their own, reach different conclusions about whether, or how, the new registration requirements applied to them. A ruling from the Attorney General, however, could diminish or eliminate those uncertainties, thereby helping to eliminate the very kind of vagueness and uncertainty that criminal law must seek to avoid. Cf., e.g., *United States v. Lanier*, 520 U.S. 259, 266 (1997) (noting that 'the canon of strict construction of criminal statutes, or rule of lenity, ensures fair warning by so resolving ambiguity in a criminal statute as to apply it only to conduct clearly covered')."

CASE SIGNIFICANCE: This case involves another issue presented to the Court concerning the pre-SORNA behavior of sex offenders. In this instance, the question is whether people who were identified as sex offenders before the enactment of the federal statute were required to register after its passage. The Act stipulates that pre-enactment offenders are not included in the registration pool until they are designated as such by the Attorney General. Congress foresaw that states would need time to get their systems and current offenders in compliance with the federal law, and that it would be the Attorney General's call to then turn attention to pre-Act sex offenders.

Index